Information Technology for Management

SIXTH EDITION

HENRY C. LUCAS, JR.

Leonard N. Stern School of Business
New York University

The McGraw-Hill Companies, Inc.

New York   St. Louis   San Francisco   Auckland   Bogotá
Caracas   Lisbon   London   Madrid   Mexico City   Milan   Montreal
New Delhi   San Juan   Singapore   Sydney   Tokyo   Toronto

To Scott and Jonathan

McGraw·Hill
A Division of The **McGraw·Hill** Companies

Information Technology for Management, Sixth Edition

1 2 3 4 5 6 7 8 9 0   DOC DOC   9 0 9 8 7

ISBN 0-07-039061-4

Editor: Rhonda Sands
Associate editor: Courtney Attwood
Editorial assistant: Kyle Thomes
Production supervisor: Natalie Durbin
Project manager: Graphics West, Inc.
Copyeditor: Cathy Baehler
Compositor: Graphics West, Inc.
Printer and binder: R. R. Donnelley & Sons Company

Library of Congress Card Catalog No. 96-77621

Credits
Screen capture on page 214. PowerBuilder is a registered trademark of Sybase, Inc. and
its subsidiaries.
Screen capture on page 224 reprinted with permission from Microsoft Corporation.
Screen capture on page 296. Copyright 1995 America Online; Used by Permission.
Screen captures on page 571 provided courtesy of Lotus Development Corporation,
an IBM Subsidiary.

CONTENTS

PART I   The Role of Managers in Information Technology   1

PART II Organization Issues 63

PART III   Information Technology   157

PART IV Systems Analysis and Design 373

PART V   Exciting Directions in Systems   539

PART VI   Issues for Senior Management   615

PREFACE

TO THE STUDENT

Information technology surrounds you—on your campus and in local businesses. When you order merchandise over the telephone, chances are your sales representative is using an information system to check inventory and to trigger the shipment of your goods. Increasingly you will order products using a computer network called the Internet, dispensing with the telephone. When you use an automatic teller machine, make an airline reservation, or rent a car, information technology is working for you again.

Information technology is pervasive in modern organizations—from the largest manufacturing firms to your corner drugstore. The stakes are high as businesses confronted with global competition strive to succeed. Some organizations will flourish; others will fail. Those that succeed in the future will understand how to use and manage information technology to their advantage.

The purpose of *Information Technology for Management, Sixth Edition* is to help you learn enough about the technology to play an active role in the design, use, and management of information technology. You will learn how creative organizations have integrated technology with their corporate strategy, allowing them to surpass the competition to maintain an advantage. You will also see how to use information technology to transform the organization, to create new lines of business and new relationships with other firms. The text also stresses how you as a manager can use information technology-enabled organization design variables to create new organization structures, including the T-Form firm. This new structure takes advantage of electronic communications and linking, technological matrixing, technological leveling, virtual components, electronic workflows, production automation, and electronic customer/supplier relationships to create a flat organization closely linked to other organizations. It uses technology to reduce the number of administrative levels in the firm, to decentralize decision making, and generally to design a highly efficient and effective organization.

You will learn how to exploit the technology to enhance your professional and personal productivity. Information technology is a tool. It enables you to redesign the organization, change the firm's relationship with customers and suppliers, and alter communications patterns in the firm. Technology is a variable that you as a manager will be able to manipulate to effect significant improvements in what the organization and its employees can accomplish.

Once you have completed this course, look through a newspaper or business publication. You will be surprised at your understanding of many of the issues raised in articles dealing with information technology.

In sum, this text is designed to prepare you for the important managerial role of managing information technology, to give you and your company a competitive edge.

To THE INSTRUCTOR

This book is designed for business students with no particular background in information systems. The primary goal is to help prepare students to assume an active and significant role in the design, use, and management of information systems and technology. The approach evolved through extensive efforts to create a required course that would meet this goal for all M.B.A. candidates at the Leonard N. Stern School of Business at New York University. This approach has proven successful with the previous five editions of the text at other schools around the world.

The Objectives of This Text

During the past five years computers and communications technologies have proliferated in offices and homes. Organizations distribute the responsibility for technology to all levels of management and to different geographic locations. As a result, managers from supervisor to CEO encounter information technology on a daily basis. Managers have to take advantage of the technology; they must make decisions about how to use the technology.

Organizations have the opportunity to become more efficient and competitive. Skilled and creative managers are required to accomplish these goals. Today's M.B.A.s need the knowledge and confidence to deal with issues related to technology. They must apply technology aggressively if they are to compete successfully in our global economy. They must take advantage of the ability that IT gives them to change the way work is done, communications patterns, and the very structure of the organization.

One of the most important parts of using the technology is the design of information systems. Much of the distribution of technology to end users results from the rapid diffusion of personal computers or workstations. Applications once considered personal are being shared across networks. Users now are likely to access a number of different applications on different computers through a LAN and probably the Internet as well.

Users may design systems for themselves alone, or they may be one of many users of a system designed by others. The design of multiuser applications is much more complex than the design of a personal computer system for an individual user. Many more people are involved in the process, each with unique and often conflicting needs and expectations.

Recent graduates are likely to find themselves on design teams for multiuser systems. *Thus, it is critical that a course in information systems prepare students to play an active role in the development of new applications that will affect their productivity and their company's competitiveness.*

Based on the discussion above, this book is designed to help students meet these three major objectives:

1. To understand the emerging technological issues facing management so students can effectively manage information systems in organizations
2. To play an active role in applying technology through the analysis, design, and implementation of multiuser systems that will meet the information needs of the organization
3. To learn how to use technology to transform the organization, creating new relationships, structures, and entirely new organizations

ORGANIZATION

The text is organized into six major parts to help students meet these objectives:

Part I The Role of Managers in Information Systems   The purpose of Part One is to emphasize to students the value of information as a corporate asset and illustrate the myriad information systems applications they will face as graduates.

Part II Organizational Issues   Here we deal with the impact of information technology on the organization. The book stresses the use of IT design variables in creating new kinds of organization structures. In particular, I advocate developing T-Form organizations in order to be successful in the highly competitive environment of the twenty-first century. This section also discusses how the firm can use technology as part of its strategy to gain a competitive advantage. This discussion of key managerial issues surrounding the technology and its application help motivate student learning.

Part III Information Technology   Important managerial decisions increasingly require an understanding of the technology. Therefore, graduates need to have knowledge of the hardware and software fundamentals. I have included in Part Three the technical information I consider most important and relevant to future managers.

Part IV Systems Analysis and Design   Poorly designed systems are responsible for many information system problems. When information needs are not met, users are alienated and the value of the system diminishes. Part Four prepares graduates to participate in the development of multiuser systems and make an immediate contribution to their employer.

Part V   Exciting Directions in Systems   Part Five deals with alternatives to traditional transactions processing applications, such as decision support systems, expert systems, groupware, multimedia, and artificial intelligence. An understanding of these emerging applications offers students great potential to enhance their organizations' competitiveness.

Part VI   Senior Management Concerns   At the end of the text, we return to the issues facing management today. Managers need to be concerned with security and control and how to achieve the maximum benefits possible for the firm's investment in technology. Part Six encourages students to evaluate the problems—and opportunities—that changing societal conditions and technological advances will create for their businesses. The table below arrays our three objectives against the six major parts of the text.

Part	Managing Technology	Applying Technology	Transform the Organization
I The role of managers in IT	☑	☐	☑
II Organizational issues	☑	☑	☑
III Information technology	☑	☑	☐
IV Systems analysis and design	☑	☑	☑
V Exciting directions in systems	☑	☑	☑
VI Management control of IS	☑	☐	☐

Note that the first objective—managing information technology—is a theme woven throughout every chapter in the text. In order to manage the technology effectively, students must understand its strategic significance and potential impact on the organization. In addition to these underlying organizational issues, managers must understand the related technical issues.

The second objective—learning to apply technology through a systems analysis and design team—is supported by parts Two, Three, Four, and Five. These parts of the book cover the fundamentals of systems development from a managerial perspective. Using the Simon Marshall case, which is integrated throughout the book, students complete the logical design of a system. This exercise encourages students to confront the myriad decisions and trade-offs that constitute the design of a multi-user system and gain a "real world" understanding of what otherwise would remain abstract.

The third and final objective—transforming the organization—is a theme throughout the text. It is a significant component of parts One, Two, Four, and Five. In one sense, the entire text is devoted to preparing students to use technology to change the way in which organizations are structured and operate.

Learning Tools for Your Students   The text has a number of features designed to facilitate student learning, including the following:

- *Management Problems and Applications Briefs* Most chapters contain Management Problems and Applications Briefs. Management Problems are "minicases" for students to ponder alone or in groups; some instructors use the problems to stimulate class discussion. Applications Briefs illustrate the many different ways information technology is used today. They are intended to help the student become more creative in discovering how to benefit from information systems.

- *Chapter Summary* New to this edition is a summary of each chapter in the form of a numbered list containing the most important points in the chapter.

- *Implications for Management* Another new feature is a paragraph after the Chapter Summary which contains my thoughts on the implications of the material in the chapter for a manager. This personal statement explains the importance of the material the student has just read.

- *Chapter Projects* Most chapters contain a Chapter Project. The projects are designed to help students apply concepts discussed in the chapter. Some projects require the student to conduct research or contact an organization to find out more about its information processing. I usually use one of the systems design projects as a group assignment. Students report that the experience of designing the logic of a system helps pull together much of the material in the course.

- *The Simon Marshall Case* Several of the chapter projects involve the Simon Marshall case. There is a systems analysis and design problem for Simon Marshall that involves PCs, a server, a local area network, a mainframe data source, and a satellite distribution system. This assignment, carried out as a group project, helps students master the technical and design material in the text.

Supporting Materials
- *Instructor's Manual* The *Instructor's Manual* contains a course outline, teaching hints, and answers to selected questions. Also included are a discussion of all the Management Problems and sample course syllabi.

NEW TO THE SIXTH EDITION

In general, the sixth edition of *Information Technology for Management* reflects current thinking about the role of IT in management. The name of the book is new to reflect the fact the information technology is more than computer systems. It includes communications, networks, paging devices, fax, and voice communication among other technologies.

Compared with the previous edition, the sixth edition contains less emphasis on the technical details and more on the managerial issues of IT and state-of-the-art topics. The two chapters on hardware are reorganized in this edition while the software chapter has fewer technical details. I have found that few instructors discuss file systems, so the text now contains a single, expanded chapter on database. The appendix to Chapter 16 still contains a detailed example of structured design. I have added a second example to this appendix using object-oriented design so students can compare and contrast these two approaches.

Over the years, we have seen major changes in the way leading firms use information technology. Transactions processing systems helped improve efficiencies. Strategic systems provide some companies with a competitive advantage. Now, with the addition of workgroup technology, group DSS, and extensive connectivity, we have the ability to use IT to *transform the organization.* This theme of change is now reflected throughout the book. In particular, I have incorporated the concepts discussed in *The T-Form Organization: Using Technology to Design Organizations for the 21st Century* (Jossey-Bass, 1996).

The text has been extensively updated to reflect advances in technology and in its application. There are many more examples of applications and systems in the text to supplement the Applications Briefs that are ruled off in the text.

Chapter 3 presents a new framework for looking at IT in organizations that updates the ideas presented by Gorry, Scott Morton, and others. Chapter 4 has been completely changed to reflect research we are conducting at NYU on the impact of technology on organizations. This chapter discusses how *technology can impact flexibility and how IT can be used in the design of organizations.* This chapter is crucial in making the case that technology can be used to transform the organization.

Chapter 5 on the strategic use of IT stresses the difficulty of sustaining an advantage once it is achieved. This chapter also contains a more lengthy description of a firm that has used the technology over the years to develop a clear competitive advantage.

Globalization is a major trend in business today. Trade barriers are falling and firms are expanding their markets beyond their own borders. Chapter 6 explores the implications of globalization for information technology. What can IT contribute to the international firm? What are the special IT problems created by trying to operate globally? I have always thought that it is important for managers to have knowledge of what they are trying to manage.

Part Three of the text is devoted to information technology; it attempts to provide the student with sufficient familiarity with technology that he or she can make good management decisions.

Chapter 8 attempts to place the different types of computers available today in perspective. It has been expanded to discuss the different generations of Intel chips and the features that are used to increase the speed of these processors. I have attempted to provide a balanced and realistic picture of the role and future of mainframes, both in this chapter and throughout the text. Chapter 9 contains a discussion of the major operating systems choices today: Windows95, OS/2, Unix, and Windows NT.

Chapter 10 presents the fundamentals of database management and describes how the organization uses a DBMS for transactions processing and to extract information to be used in managing the firm. The chapter also stresses how the student can use a DBMS for his or her own personal productivity.

Chapter 11 on communications emphasizes the role of this technology in transforming organizations. The chapter features more material on networks and connectivity along with examples of how firms are using communications technology in creative ways. Chapter 12 on networks is new. It covers topics ranging from EDI to the Internet. Networks are one of the fastest growing phenomena in the field, and this chapter tries to excite the reader about their potential.

There is a great deal of confusion about what kind of architecture is best for a given application or organization. Chapter 13 attempts to clarify any confusion the student may have about people who use the different types of technology described in earlier chapters. This chapter discusses the role of large, medium, and small computers and illustrates them with examples of different systems, ranging from a centralized, mainframe airline reservations system to a highly decentralized, client-server system at Chevron Canada.

A key objective for the text is to prepare students to apply technology through participation in systems analysis and design projects. We have encountered users who developed their own systems on PCs that served as the specifications for the same system to be developed for the entire corporation! The manager who understands how to build systems is at a distinct advantage in business today.

Chapter 15 introduces systems analysis and design. It has been extensively edited and updated. Chapter 16 covers some design details. One of the highlights of this section is the appendix to the chapter. This appendix presents a high-level design for a system for the Hardserve company. There are complete DFDs for the retail store component of the system and for the subsystem in the company's warehouse. This in-depth example should provide students with a good understanding of the output of the design process and the way in which one describes a system. New to this edition is a second example of object-oriented design for a hypothetical community hospital.

Chapter 17 talks about enhancements to the traditional life-cycle approach to developing a system, especially packages and prototyping. Chapter 18 is new and is devoted to the popular topic of business process reengineering. This chapter presents two examples of process reengineering and two examples where IT design variables have been used to reengineer the entire organization.

Implementation is concerned with how you bring about change in the organization. At the level of the individual system you are trying to see that systems provide the maximum return from the firm's investment in IT. In using IT design variable, you are likely to be trying to change the structure of the entire organization, a major challenge. Chapter 19 is devoted to implementation; it is still true that systems are underutilized and that users take advantage of only a fraction of the capabilities of existing, installed technology. Chapter 19 integrates research findings to produce an implementation framework to help the student understand and manage this process. The chapter also suggests how to approach IT-enabled organization change as students prepare to manage in the twenty-first century.

When the first edition of this text was published, there were no hands-on users outside of the IS department. We have moved from no contact to terminals to workstations on the user's desk. Chapter 20 discusses the range of user interaction with technology and suggests ways to encourage it. The evolving model of *client-server computing* means that users on workstations will obtain the data and programs they need to answer their questions from the server.

Chapter 21 describes how IT can be used in non-traditional ways to enhance the effectiveness of individuals and organizations. The DSS part of the chapter contains new examples of how these applications contribute to improving productivity. Material on EIS and group DSS is also new to the chapter. Groupware is one of the most exciting applications for transforming organizations and is discussed in this chapter. A section on multimedia stresses how this technology can be used for business, as opposed to entertainment, purposes.

Chapter 22 on intelligent systems contains an in-depth example of an expert system we developed at the American Stock Exchange. There is also material on neural networks and new coverage of case-based reasoning and genetic algorithms.

Part Six of the text deals with management issues. Chapter 24 includes a discussion of several different models of IT in the firm and an in-depth discussion of the role of the CIO. It also contains guidelines or action steps one might follow to diagnose and improve the IT effort in an organization. Chapter 25 presents framework for categorizing social issues and a discussion of ethics. It also contains predictions on the future of key technologies including multimedia and virtual reality.

CONCLUSION

This sixth edition of the text contains major changes which are intended to help your students appreciate the contribution of information technology and learn how to manage it.

ACKNOWLEDGMENTS

I am indebted to a number of students and colleagues whose comments and recommendations have greatly influenced the original text and its revisions. Ms. Beverly Welch at NYU helped conduct research for the book; I am grateful for her efforts. I benefited greatly from comments and discussions with Ken Marr of Hofstra University.

The following reviewers have helped in making the major changes found in this edition of the text:

Robert Benjes	Pace University
Paul Cheney	University of South Florida
Len Fertuck	University of Toronto
Joey George	Florida State University
Al Lederer	University of Kentucky
Kenneth Marr	Hofstra University
Chris Westland	University of Southern California

Finally, I gratefully acknowledge the invaluable support of my wife, Ellen, and family, who encourage and tolerate the idiosyncrasies of an author.

Henry C. Lucas, Jr.
New York University

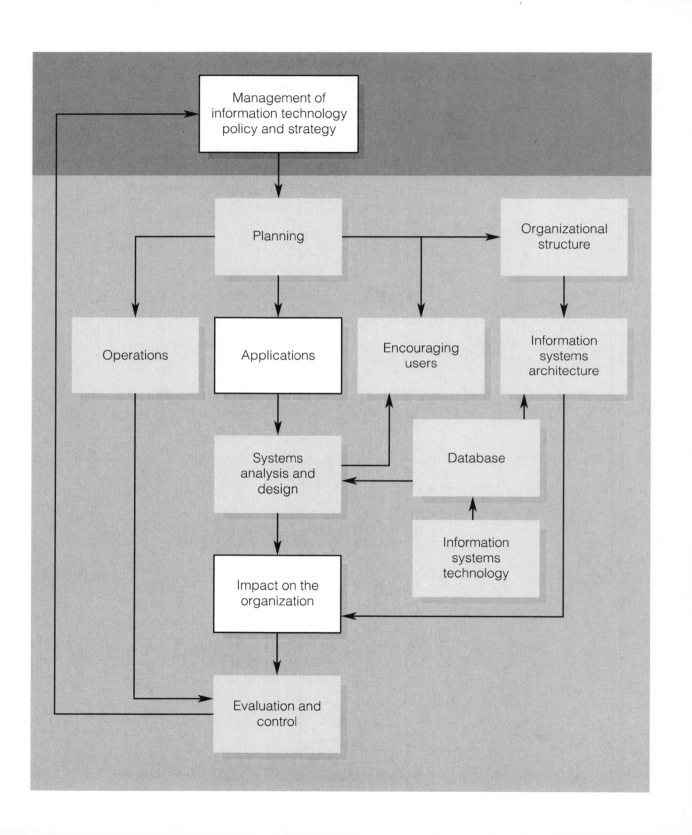

The Role of Managers in Information Technology

In the first part of the text, we define an information system and see how information technology is transforming organizations. Managers have developed creative applications of technology which have altered the way members of the organization work, communications patterns, customer and supplier relations, and the very structure of the firm.

What is the nature of information? How are data interpreted by individuals and organizations to become information? We will examine decision making in some detail because one objective of an information system is to provide information to support decision making. With this background, we can examine frameworks for information systems—frameworks that provide a conceptual model to aid in the design of systems. Part One includes a scenario showing the wide variety of information systems existing today.

Figure 1 depicts the process of managing information technology. This figure will appear in each part of the text to provide an introduction to the topics covered in the corresponding chapters. The figure shows that management must first determine a policy and strategy for information technology.

Managers should develop a plan for systems. The plan is likely to suggest new structures for the organization and it should at least deal with how information services are to be organized. The plan will have an impact on the firm's operations. For example, a plan that includes electronic connections to customers will change the way orders are processed.

The plan will identify new applications areas for technology, meaning it will indicate new opportunities for the use of information technology. The plan may assign a high priority to applications that serve customers or to those that automate a factory. In today's environment, it is likely that the plan will contain ideas on how to encourage users to apply technology to solving their own problems.

The development of an information technology (IT) architecture is closely related to the structure of the organization. Will the firm use a variety of computers from different vendors? Will its computers be networked? Who will manage individual computer installations, and who will authorize expenditures on systems? What kind of communications technology will be used to provide connectivity among different locations and users?

The way the firm develops systems is by conducting systems analysis and design. The design of applications has an impact on users since they will be trying to access data in a new system. The entire area of information technology, computers, communications devices and networks, and databases supports the firm's information systems architecture and systems analysis and design.

The kinds of systems that are created and the architecture developed for them will have a dramatic impact on the organization. Firms that plan well and develop creative applications will find they have transformed all or some significant aspects of their business.

The final management activity is the evaluation and control of information technology in the organization. Does the organization obtain a return from its investment in the technology? Are information systems under management's control, or is the IS effort fragmented and uncoordinated? All of these aspects of the process of managing information technology are discussed in different parts of the text.

In this first part of the text, we discuss the nature of information and different types of applications. Our objective is to develop a common definition of an information system and a shared understanding of the nature of information and types of systems. We should begin to see how technology can lead to major changes in an industry and within an organization. This section of the text sets the stage for the rest of the book.

CHAPTER **1**

Using Technology to Transform the Organization

OBJECTIVES

1. **Learning to manage information technology.**

   There are many different ways information technology can benefit the organization. It can contribute to routine operations and to corporate **strategy**. It can enhance productivity and offer new ways to communicate. The tremendous variety of ways technology is applied presents a major management challenge. You will note in this chapter how a senior executive left his position because he was not adept at managing technology. While reading the description of Kennametal, think about the various management decisions that were necessary for this firm's successful use of the technology.

2. **Preparing to apply technology.**

   This chapter describes several different kinds of systems. When you read about Brun Passot, consider the different ways technology contributes to the company. Each use of technology is an **application** which consists of one or more **systems**. For example, one of Brun Passot's applications is a system to process orders that arrive from customers.

3. Transforming the organization.

Technology is used today to make major changes in organizations, workgroups, and individual jobs. Information technology is altering the relationship among companies and changing the basis of competition in different industries. This chapter introduces the **T-Form organization**, an organization that takes advantage of technology in developing its structure and in all facets of its operation.

INFORMATION TECHNOLOGY IN THE WORKPLACE

We are living in revolutionary times, a revolution brought on by dramatic advances in **information technology (IT)**. If the steam engine, new forms of power, and mechanization created an Industrial Revolution over 150 years ago, computers and communications equipment have produced a Technology Revolution in the last half of the twentieth century. The **computer** has been called "the machine that changed the world." You will encounter many coworkers who have not yet developed a vision for what information technology can create. They may be using rigid, old systems or fail to see the emerging role of IT in communications. We believe that information technology has and will continue to revolutionize management.

To name a few contributions, IT

- Provides new ways to design organizations that can lead to structures like the T-Form organization described later in this chapter.
- Creates new relationships between customers and suppliers who electronically link themselves together.
- Enables tremendous efficiencies in production and service industries through electronic data interchange to facilitate just-in-time production.
- Changes the basis of competition and industry structure, for example, in the airline and securities industries.
- Provides mechanisms through groupware for coordinating work and creating a knowledge base of organizational intelligence.
- Contributes to the productivity and flexibility of knowledge workers.
- Provides the manager with electronic alternatives to face-to-face communications and supervision.

A major objective of this text is to communicate the excitement and opportunities provided by this revolution in information technology.

But, to obtain the benefits described above, you have to be able to manage the technology. In the mid 1990s, two senior managers lost their jobs over information technology. The long-term chairman of Macy's department stores retired because, though a great merchant, he never developed the skills for choosing computer systems or analyzing a balance sheet. The chief executive of the London Stock Exchange, resigned over the failure of the Exchange to complete its Taurus paperless settlements system. The Stock Exchange had spent over $100 million and estimated that it would take three more years and twice the initial investment to finish the project (other financial institutions are thought to have invested even more than this amount in the system).

Fortunately, there are many IT success stories to balance the failures. A good example is Kennametal Inc., a leading producer of metal-working and mining tools. This company quietly spent the 1980s investing heavily in new technology to reverse a market slide and stave off powerful foreign competitors. This strategy "... propelled it into the ranks of the nation's 500 largest companies. ... Kennametal's rebound provides a case study of how even companies in stodgy, slow-growing businesses can use information technology to improve their efficiency and provide new services that turn customers into partners. ... The investment in information technology has allowed it to serve customers more quickly and reduce inventories. The computer systems have also been used to offer customers additional services, like tool management support. Kennametal now stocks and manages the tool storage areas for some customers. (*New York Times,* May 6, 1992)."

A manager must have a number of skills to succeed in the competitive, global economy that characterizes the end of the twentieth and the beginning of the twenty-first century. One of the most important is an understanding of and ability to manage information technology. The purpose of this text is to prepare you for this important managerial role.

A VISIT TO BRUN PASSOT IN FRANCE

Even a relatively small company can use information technology to gain a competitive advantage. Brun Passot is one of four major competitors in the French office supplies industry; however, these companies have a combined market share of only 25 percent. There are some 5000 office products distributors in France! The fall of trade barriers among European Community nations has meant that French suppliers now have to compete with British, German, and even U.S. firms.

Brun Passot was started as a family firm in 1949. By the early 1990s with 160 employees it offered 12,000 products to 6000 customers, delivering to up to 15,000 locations. From 1970 to 1992 its sales rose from 15 million to 254 million French Francs (FF). In 1980 Brun Passot decided that it could distinguish itself from competitors by offering customers the opportunity to purchase items electronically. By 1983 the company developed Bureautel, a system that ran on Minitel, the French national video-text network and allowed customers to place orders electronically. Brun Passot's own employees could also inquire against its inventory and obtain sales and cash flow information from the system.

In 1989 the company enhanced this system by issuing a credit card with a predefined maximum purchase limit per customer department. As the customer placed orders, their value was subtracted from the credit card. The card was not actually used for payment, but as a way to let customer personnel order supplies without generating a purchase order or getting management approval. The system made it easier to order from Brun Passot. The card also helped customers maintain control over their department budgets for office supplies.

By 1985 large customers encouraged Brun Passot to develop a personal computer (PC) based system for them. This system was cheaper for customers than Minitel; they could centralize ordering even though requests were generated from multiple locations. As the capacity of the French telephone system grew, this system was expanded to provide color photos of each of Brun Passot's 12,000 products. In 1989 Brun Passot developed the capability to electronically send product files, delivery status reports, purchase quotes, shipping notices, invoices, payments, and e-mail messages to clients. (Unfortunately, the company had to print paper invoices, too, since the French justice system did not recognize electronic invoices.)

Brun Passot estimates its investment in these applications at FF550,000 with ongoing operating costs of about FF100,000 covered by fees paid by users. By 1992, 40 percent of Brun Passot's orders were electronic. Before the end of the decade, the company expects the number of non-Minitel electronic orders to double. The introduction of these systems simplified procedures and freed 25 people to do more selling and visit customers. Since it is easier to predict customer demand, stock turnover has risen from 9 to 16 times a year; inventory management costs have also dropped 7 percent (Jelassi and Figon, 1994).

Brun Passot presents a successful application of technology. It shows that a company does not have to be in the "Fortune 500" to take advantage of IT. The company realized as it faced increasing competition, technology might help it differentiate its services from others in this crowded industry. *It successfully managed the development of multiple applications of technology.* Management had to do more than just create systems. It changed the way the firm operated to take advantage of the capabilities provided by electronic links to customers. Brun Passot recognized that a computer is more than a computational device; modern information technology provides new opportunities for communications. As technology contributed more and more to the firm, management began to see electronic commerce as a part of Brun Passot's strategy: information technology and strategy became intertwined.

Throughout the text, we shall see examples of firms that have developed creative application of technology to give them an edge on competitors. These cases illustrate the firm's ability to manage technology, and to use IT to transform the very structure of the organization.

WHAT IS INFORMATION TECHNOLOGY?

Information technology refers to all forms of technology applied to **processing**, storing, and transmitting **information** in electronic form. The physical equipment used for this purpose includes computers, communications equipment and networks, fax machines, and even electronic pocket organizers. Information systems execute organized procedures that process and/or communicate information. We define information as a tangible or intangible entity that serves to reduce uncertainty about some state or event.

Data can originate from the internal operations of the firm and from external entities such as suppliers or customers. Data also come from external databases and services; for example, organizations purchase a great deal of marketing and competitive information.

An information system usually processes these data in some way and presents the results to users. With the easy availability of personal computers, **users** often process the output of a formal system themselves in an ad hoc manner. Human **interpretation** of information is extremely important in understanding how an organization reacts to the **output** of a system. Different results may mean different things to two managers. A marketing manager may use statistical programs and graphs to look for trends or problems with sales. A financial manager may see a problem with cash flow given the same sales data. The recipient of a system's output may be an individual, as in the example of the marketing manager, or it may be a workgroup.

Many systems are used routinely for control purposes in the organization and require limited decision making. The accounts receivable application generally runs with little senior management oversight. It is a highly structured application with rules that can be followed by a clerical staff. A department manager handles exceptions. The output of some systems may be used as a part of a **program** or strategy. The system itself could be implementing a corporate strategy, such as simplifying the customer order process. A system might help managers make decisions.

Information technology, however, extends far beyond the computational capabilities of computers. Today, computers are used extensively for **communications** as well as for their traditional roles of data storage and computation. Many computers are connected together using various kinds of communications lines to form **networks**. Through a network, individuals and organizations are linked together and these linkages are changing the way we think about doing business. Boundaries between firms are breaking down from the electronic communications link provided by networks. Firms are now more willing to provide direct access to their systems for suppliers and customers. If the first era of computing was concerned with computation, the second era is about communications.

THE T-FORM ORGANIZATION

How is technology changing organizations? One impact of IT, discussed in depth in Chapter 4, is the use of information technology design variables to develop new organizational structures. The organization that is most likely to result from the use of these variables is the T-Form or Technology-Form organization, an organization that uses IT to become highly efficient and effective (Lucas, 1996). Figure 1-1 presents the characteristics of the T-Form organization.

The firm has a flat structure made possible by using e-mail and groupware (programs that help coordinate people with a common task to perform) to increase the span of control and reduce managerial hierarchy. Employees coordinate their work with the help of electronic communications and linkages. Supervision of employees is based on trust because there are fewer face-to-face encounters with subordinates and colleagues than in today's organization. Managers delegate tasks and **decision making** to lower levels of management and information systems make data available at the level of management where it is needed to make decisions. Some members of the organization primarily work remotely without having a permanent office assigned.

MANAGEMENT PROBLEM 1-1

Marsha Jackson is a recent M.B.A. graduate with a degree in marketing. She has accepted a position with General America, a large firm selling a number of consumer products. Her first assignment is to conduct research on the sale of one of her company's products versus sales of competing products.

This division is responsible for sales of over-the-counter drugs such as headache remedies, indigestion cures, and similar products. In business school, Marsha had worked with a personal computer in her M.B.A. program and was happy to see that General America had a local area network (LAN) for the marketing department. When Marsha looked for data on competing brands, however, she found out that the marketing department subscribed to several different services that provided sales results for over-the-counter drugs. Some of her fellow workers had private databases and a few even keyed data into their PCs from lengthy printouts they had purchased.

Marsha feels that there must be a better way to conduct market research, particularly given the fact that the department has a LAN with a lot of capacity. What solutions to this problem can you recommend?

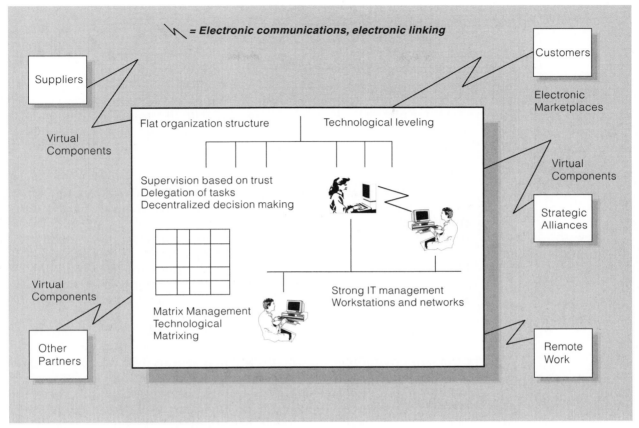

= Electronic communications, electronic linking

Suppliers

Customers

Virtual Components

Electronic Marketplaces

Flat organization structure

Technological leveling

Supervision based on trust
Delegation of tasks
Decentralized decision making

Virtual Components

Strategic Alliances

Matrix Management
Technological
Matrixing

Strong IT management
Workstations and networks

Virtual Components

Other Partners

Remote Work

Figure 1-1 The T-Form Organization.

The T-Form company's technological infrastructure features networks of computers. Individual client workstations connect over a network to larger computers that act as servers. The network has gateways to national and international networks so members of the firm can connect with customers, suppliers, and others with whom they need to interact.

T-Form firms feature highly automated production and electronic information handling to minimize the use of paper and rely extensively on images and optical data storage. Technology is used to give workers jobs that are as complete as possible. In the office, companies will convert assembly line operations for processing documents to a series of tasks that one individual or a small group can perform from a workstation. The firm will also adopt and use electronic agents, a kind of software robot, to perform a variety of tasks over networks.

Most T-Form organizations will use communications technology to form temporary task forces focused on a specific project. Technology like e-mail and groupware facilitate the work of these task forces. These temporary workgroups may include employees of customers, suppliers and/or partner corporations.

The T-Form organization is linked extensively with customers and suppliers. There are numerous electronic customer/supplier relationships. These linkages increase responsiveness, improve accuracy, reduce cycle times, and reduce the amount of overhead when firms do business with each other. Suppliers access customer computers directly to learn of their needs for materials, then deliver raw materials and assemblies to the proper location just as they are needed. Customers pay many suppliers as the customer consumes materials, dispensing with invoices and other documents associated with a purchase transaction.

The close electronic linking of companies doing business together creates virtual components where traditional parts of the organization appear to exist, but in reality exist in a novel or unusual manner. For example, the traditional inventory of raw materials and subassemblies is likely not to be owned or stored by the T-Form manufacturing firm. This virtual inventory actually exists at suppliers' locations. Possibly the subassemblies will not exist at all; suppliers will build them just in time to provide them to the customer. From the customer's standpoint, however, it appears that all needed components are in inventory because suppliers are reliable partners in the production process.

This model of a T-Form firm shows the extent to which managers can apply IT to transforming the organization. The firms that succeed in the turbulent environment of the twenty-first century will take advantage of information technology to create innovative organizational structures. They will use IT to develop highly competitive products and services and will be connected in a network with their customers and suppliers. The purpose of this book is to prepare you to manage in this technologically sophisticated environment of the twenty-first century.

INFORMATION TECHNOLOGY AND THE MANAGER

Managers are involved in a wide range of decisions about technology, decisions that are vital to the success of the organization. Some 52 percent of capital investment in the U.S. is for information technology excluding software (*New York Times,* December 3, 1995); *Business Week* estimates that there are 63 PCs per 100 workers in the U.S. (including machines at home) and others have estimated that one in three U.S. workers uses a computer on the job. A recent survey of 373 senior executives at large U.S. and Japanese companies found that 64 percent of the U.S. managers said they must use computers in their jobs. Other surveys have estimated that as many as 88 percent of managers use computers. Because this technology is so pervasive, managers at all levels and in all functional areas of the firm are involved with IT.

Managers are challenged with decisions about:

- The use of technology to design and structure the organization, as reflected in the discussion of the T-Form organization.

- The creation of alliances and partnerships that include electronic linkages. There is a growing trend for companies to connect with their customers and suppliers, and often with support service providers like law firms.

- The selection of systems to support different kinds of workers. Stock brokers, traders, and others use sophisticated computer-based workstations in performing their jobs. Choosing a vendor, designing the system, and implementing it are major challenges for management.

Virtual Offices at Xerox

By the end of 1995, Xerox expects that all of its 5500 member U.S. sales force will work from "virtual offices." The company will provide each representative with a notebook computer, a modem for communications, an adapter to connect to a local area network, and the Microsoft Office suite of spreadsheet, presentation graphics, and word processing packages. Without a physical office, the sales force spends more time with customers.

One of the major problems Xerox faced in this transition was its aging mainframe computer applications. Some of these systems were over 20 years old, and the entire collection of applications had grown over the years and was unmanageable. The company's products have become more complex with time; Xerox does much more than sell a stand-alone copier. It provides printing systems and network consulting to tie its machines into computer networks. The sales force had to spend a lot of time with clients to learn their needs, but it also had to spend a considerable amount of time tracking down information stored in aging computer systems.

To solve its information problems, Xerox developed a new marketing and customer database containing marketplace information,

customer profiles, order information, and libraries of Xerox solutions to problems. All of these data reside in a relational database (to be discussed in Chapter 10) and can be accessed by the sales staff and others. Xerox hopes to save $250 million each year from the entire effort, including a reduction of 30% in leased office space. The goal is a 20% gain in productivity for a total investment of $100 million.

The project involved several field tests before a commitment was made to go ahead with the system. The company provided extensive training and consulting help for sales representatives; it also helped sales people set up home offices and provided a phone line and printer. The typical physical office is more like an airport frequent flyer lounge; there are cubicles with phones and connections for computers. There are classrooms and a video-conferencing facility. The Waltham, Massachusetts office has 40% less floor space under the new program, but it still supports the same number of people.

If you travel a lot or need to spend time out of the office, it is likely at some point your office will become virtual as it has for the sales representatives of Xerox.

- The adoption of groupware or group decision support systems for workers who share a common task. In many firms, the records of shared materials constitute one type of knowledge base for the corporation.

- Determining a World Wide Web strategy. The Internet and World Wide Web (Chapter 12) offer new ways to provide information, communications, and to engage in commerce. A manager must determine if and how the firm can take advantage of the opportunities provided by the Web.

- Routine transactions processing systems. These applications handle the basic business transactions, for example, the order cycle from receiving a purchase order through shipping goods, invoicing, and receipt of payment. These routine systems must function for the firm to continue in business. More often today managers are eliminating physical documents in transactions processing and substituting electronic transmission over networks.

- Personal support systems. Managers in a variety of positions use personal computers and networks to support their work.

- Reporting and control. Managers have traditionally been concerned with controlling the organization and reporting results to management, shareholders, and the public. The information needed for reporting and control is contained in one or more databases on an internal computer network. Many reports are filed with the government and can be accessed through the Internet and the World Wide Web, including many 10K filings and other SEC required corporate reports.

- Automated production processes. One of the keys to competitive manufacturing is increasing efficiency and quality through automation. Similar improvements can be found in the services sector through technologies like image processing, optical storage, and workflow processing in which paper is replaced by electronic images shared by staff members using networked workstations.

- Embedded products. Increasingly, products contain embedded intelligence. A modern automobile may contain six or more computers on chips, for example, to control the engine, the climate, compute statistics, and manage an antilock brake and traction control system. A colleague remarked a few years ago that his washing machine today contained more logic than the first computer he worked on!

FIVE MAJOR TRENDS

In the past few years, five major trends have drastically altered the way organizations use technology. These trends make it imperative that a manager becomes familiar with both the use of technology and how to control it in the organization. These trends, discussed further in later chapters, are as follows:

1. *The use of technology to transform the organization.* The cumulative effect of what all the technology firms are installing is to transform the organization and allow new types of organizational structures. Sometimes the transformation occurs slowly as one unit in an organization begins to use electronic mail. In other cases, like Kennametal or Oticon, a Danish firm discussed in Chapter 18, the firm is totally different after the application of technology. This ability of information technology to transform organizations, to create the T-Form firm, is one of the most powerful tools available to a manager today.

2. *The use of information processing technology as a part of corporate strategy.* Firms like Brun Passot are implementing information systems that give them an edge on the competition. In Chapter 5 we look at this phenomenon and study some examples. Firms that prosper in the coming years will be managed by individuals who are able to develop creative, strategic applications of the technology.

3. *Technology as a pervasive part of the work environment.* From the largest corporations to the smallest business, we find technology is used to reduce labor, improve quality, provide better customer service, or change the way the firm operates. Factories use technology to design parts and control production. The small auto-repair shop uses a packaged personal computer system to prepare work orders and bills for its customers. The body shop uses a computer-controlled machine with lasers to take measurements so it can check the alignment of automobile suspensions, frames, and bodies. In this text we shall see a large number of examples of how technology is applied to change and improve the way we work.

4. *The use of personal computers as managerial workstations.* The personal computer has tremendous appeal. It is easy to use and has a variety of powerful software programs available that can dramatically increase the user's productivity. When connected to a network within the organization and to external networks like the Internet, it provides a tremendous tool for knowledge workers.

5. *The evolution of the computer from a computational device to a medium for communications.* Computers first replaced punched card equipment and were used for purely computational tasks. From the large, centralized computers, the technology evolved into desktop, personal computers. When users wanted access to information stored in different locations, companies developed networks to link terminals and computers to other computers. These networks have grown and become a medium for internal communications and external with other organizations. For many workers today, the communications aspects of computers are more important than their computational capabilities.

What does all this mean for the management student? Unfortunately, it means that you must become more than just "computer literate." Reading about technology will not be enough for a manager to compete effectively in the future. It is important to have two kinds of knowledge about information technology. The manager must be a competent user of computers and learn to manage information technology. The personal computer connected to a network is as commonplace in the office as the telephone has been for the past seventy-five years. Managers today are expected to make the computer an integral part of their jobs. It is the manager, not the technical staff member, who must come up with the idea for a system, allocate resources, and see that systems are designed well to provide the firm with a competitive edge. You will have to recognize opportunities to apply technology and then manage the **implementation** of the new technology. The success of information processing in the firm lies more with top and middle management than with the information services department.

A PREVIEW OF THE BOOK

With this introduction to the information systems field, we are prepared to explore the nature of information in greater detail. Table 1-1 lists some important IT management issues and indicates where they are discussed in the book. In Chapter 2 we examine the nature of decision making and managerial activities, and Chapter 3 introduces several frameworks for systems. Part Two deals with the interaction of the organization and information systems. Part Three discusses computer technology. You need a basic understanding of computers to make management decisions about information systems.

In Part Four, we present systems analysis and design techniques, topics of vital importance for a user. We advocate that users form a significant part of the design team and that a user be in charge of the design of a new system. Part Five presents some exciting direction in systems. Finally, Part Six discusses issues of senior management concern: the relationship between user departments and the information services department, and the social impacts of information technology.

MANAGEMENT PROBLEM 1-2

Assume you have just been appointed to chair the board of a medium-sized manufacturing firm that makes small consumer appliances. The company has experienced stagnant growth over the past five years, and a new board of directors was recently elected by dissident stockholders.

One of your first tasks is to help top management discover why sales are constant and profits have been declining. Currently, the firm is faced with excessive inventory and problems in acquiring raw materials. Prices for these materials have been fluctuating widely in recent months; the previous management seems to have been unable to cope with this problem.

How will you approach this task? What sources of information will you seek to help understand and solve problems in the company?

Table 1-1
Examples of IT Management Issues

Issue	Chapter	Explanation
Using technology to design efficient and effective organizations	1, 4	IT enables new types of organizations and relationships among suppliers and customers.
Developing a plan for information technology in the organization	5, 24	Planning allows you to anticipate problems and prepare for opportunities. Instead of reacting to problems as they arise, a plan prepares you to make decisions that are integrated with corporate strategy.
Using IT as a part of corporate strategy	5	Firms use IT to gain an advantage over the competition and to sustain that advantage.
Taking advantage of interorganizational systems	4, 5	Using IT to design organizations and as a part of strategy often involves developing applications that connect two organizations, such as links between a manufacturer and a supplier for ordering and delivering materials to a factory.
Deciding on and developing new applications of IT	15–17	Organization design, strategy, and planning will all lead to new applications of technology in the organization. You must design and implement these new applications.
Reengineering business processes	18	Reengineering is a major trend in business; you are seeking order of magnitudes improvements in a business process. This kind of radical change has a major impact on the organization and its employees, making success difficult.
Adopting special applications	21, 22	There are a number of IT applications that can have a real payoff for the organization including Decision Support systems, Expert Systems, and groupware.

Table 1-1 *(continued)*

Issue	Chapter	Explanation
Changing the organization	19	One of the greatest challenges, and a requirement to obtain real value from technology, is to create meaningful change. When you develop new applications, you change some aspect of the business. When you use IT organization design variables, you are transforming the entire organization.
Managing the IT infrastructure in a time of explosive growth and technological change.	13	You must make decisions about:
	13	The migration to client-server computing
	9, 13	Client (desktop) software standards
	11, 12	Networking in general
	12	Presence on and use of the Internet
	12	Electronic commerce
	13	The **integration** of heterogeneous hardware and software across computers and networks
Deciding whether and what to outsource	14, 24	Outsourcing means that you hire some other organization to perform a service. A significant number of firms use outsourcing for some part of their IT function, for example, running a communications network, developing a new application, or even managing the firm's entire IT effort.
Deciding how much to invest in IT	24	All of the decisions above add up to a total sum that you are investing in information technology.

CHAPTER SUMMARY

1. Information technology is responsible for a revolution that will equal or exceed the impact of the Industrial Revolution on business.

2. Managers, no matter what their primary functional interest, marketing, finance, production, or human relations make decisions about technology.

3. Firms that succeed in the twenty-first century will use technology to create their structure, to manage themselves, and to communicate with a variety of external organizations.

4. You will encounter networks of computers within companies connecting a variety of organizations.

5. Managers are responsible for finding creative, strategic uses of information technology, applications that will give them an edge over the competition.

6. You will face a number of challenges managing the technology, and seeing that the firm obtains a return from its investments in IT.

IMPLICATIONS FOR MANAGEMENT

Networking has added a variety of new ways to communicate electronically. *Information technology today provides computational and communications capabilities that were inconceivable a decade ago.* A manager has to know enough about technology to take advantage of the power IT has to offer. We are not talking about building an isolated application, rather the technology exists to affect the fundamental way the organization is structured, its operations, and its relations with other organizations like suppliers and customers. *Companies and managers that succeed in the future will use information technology in all aspects of their business.*

KEY WORDS

Application	Interpretation
Communications	Network
Computer	Output
Data	Processing
Decision making	Program
Implementation	Strategy
Information	System
Information technology (IT)	T-Form organization
Integration	User

RECOMMENDED READING

Cash, J., W. McFarlan, J. McKenney, and L. Applegate. *Corporate Information Systems Management,* 4th ed. Homewood, Ill.: Irwin, 1992. (An excellent discussion of the issues managers face in dealing with the technology.)

Mason, R., and I. Mitroff. "A Program for Research in Management Information Systems," *Management Science,* vol. 19, no. 5 (January 1973), pp. 475–487. (This article describes an information system from the perspective of an individual decision maker. While delving into the philosophical concepts underlying information systems, it presents a very appealing framework for the study of systems.)

Nolan, R., and D. Croson. *Creative Destruction.* Boston: Harvard Business School Press, 1995. (A book devoted to the need for organizational transformation.)

DISCUSSION QUESTIONS

1. What is responsible for the explosion of information technology that has occurred over the past several decades?
2. What role does the manager play in the management of information technology?
3. Why does the introduction of information technology in an organization result in complications?
4. What are the characteristics of the T-Form organization?
5. What is the difference between using technology for computations and for communications?
6. Can you think of definitions of information systems other than the one presented in this chapter? What are the advantages and disadvantages of these definitions compared with the one we adopted?
7. How can there be more than one interpretation of information? Can you think of examples in which the same information is interpreted in different ways by different individuals?
8. What is the value of information? How would you try to assess the value of information to a decision maker?
9. What different types of information exist? Develop categories for describing or classifying information, for example, timeliness and accuracy. Develop an example or two of information that would fall into each category.
10. What kind of management leadership do you suppose was required for Kennametals to turn its business around?
11. How would you define successful implementation? How would you measure it?

12. Can you think of an example in which the failure of an information system led to a major disaster? What can we learn from such a catastrophe?

13. To what extent do organizations now depend on the success of information technology to stay in business?

14. What is the relationship between information systems and marketing?

15. How have the five trends in information technology discussed in this chapter influenced management?

16. How have computers evolved to take on an important role in communications?

17. What advantages does participating in a network provide for a company?

18. What are the most significant aspects of the Brun Passot applications described in this chapter?

19. What factors would you consider if you were placed on a design team developing a new information system? What would be your major concern about the project?

20. What are the pros and cons of not providing workers like the sales force with a physical office, but instead equipping them with information technology for communications purposes?

CHAPTER 1 PROJECT

SIMON MARSHALL ASSOCIATES

Mary Simon and John Marshall were business school students together. They took jobs at different financial firms after graduation. At their five-year class reunion, Mary and John got together to trade notes on their experiences after graduation.

Mary began, "I've had a lot of fun working in the financial business; we've weathered some good and bad times at my company. I had to begin doing financial statement analysis, but in a year I moved into mergers and acquisitions. That's pretty exciting stuff."

John replied, "Sounds like things have been going well for you; there certainly have been a lot of mergers and acquisitions since we left school. I've been into funds management. I manage a pretty big portfolio and also have a chance to come up with new investment products."

"I guess I'm happy, but I sometimes get pretty tired of the bureaucracy of a big company," observed Mary.

"I know what you mean," responded John. "One crazy trader lost $200 million in a week and wiped out our firm's profit for the year and our bonuses along with it. Sometimes I think if I were braver I'd go out on my own."

"Funny you should say that; I've been thinking of doing the same thing ... ."

That chance meeting at the reunion led to further discussions. A year later, the two classmates formed Simon Marshall Associates. They described themselves as a "boutique" for special services.

Mary observed, "We obviously can't offer the same kind of capital that a big investment bank or brokerage firm can. However, we're very good at personal services. Since John is used to managing money, our strategy has been to attract wealthy investors who trust us to take care of their funds."

John added, "I try to find out what they're interested in—growth, steady income, and so on—and then advise them on what to put in their portfolios. We have tried to get clients who are active in business as well as retired people or clients just living on their capital. If I can make a business owner happy, we may have a shot at helping that person with a merger or acquisition."

Mary said, "I knew the merger activity would take a while to get going, and it has. We've helped one firm buy another one, and a couple of our wealthy investors have decided to get back into business, so I found some opportunities for them."

John observed, "I'm pretty satisfied with where we are now. Both Mary and I are making less money than we were before we started the company, but we're having a lot more fun."

Mary went on: "I agree. One thing we have to do, though, is bring in computers. Of course, we have quote machines, but we have been so busy talking with clients that we haven't had much time to keep up-to-date with the technology."

"The computers at my previous firm were fantastic, at least in cost," John observed. "I wouldn't want us to get into that kind of overhead here. I wish we could get something that would be appropriate for our business, not a big system that wouldn't work properly half the time anyway."

Discuss the kind of information you think a firm like Simon Marshall needs. What role do you think technology might have in a firm like this one?

CHAPTER **2**

Interpreting and Understanding Information

⬤ OBJECTIVES

1. **Learning to manage information technology.**

   To manage technology, one has to understand the many ways information is used and communicated in the organization. It is important for you to develop an appreciation for how managers use information in making decisions and managing an organization.

2. **Preparing to apply technology.**

A major problem in systems analysis and design is the creation of systems that provide wrong or inappropriate information. Designers and users need to understand the role of information in decision making and in managing the organization. Most early systems did little to contribute to decision making as they tended to process transactions and highly structured data. New technology and the fact an extremely large number of senior managers now use PCs and workstations mean technology can be used to assist managers at all levels of the organization.

3. **Transforming the organization.**

Frito-Lay has used technology to change the type of decisions made and the location for making decisions in the organization. Its ten thousand drivers use hand-held computers to collect detailed data on sales at each retail outlet. The data are transmitted to a corporate computer center and made available to district managers. The district managers can "micromanage" their territories by retrieving data on exactly what products sold in what package size in a given store.

THE NATURE OF INFORMATION AND DECISION MAKING

Decision making is a key activity for management. Unfortunately, the early information systems developed during the 1960s and 1970s often had few implications for decision making. Today, firms routinely monitor a variety of activities, for example, sales and production. A company is very likely to purchase and store information on its competitors' sales as well. Given the wealth of information kept in corporate databases, there are many opportunities today to use information technology to aid decision making.

At Frito-Lay, the large manufacturer of snack foods, district managers are able to use technology to study sales of individual products at specific stores. The manager can see exactly what products sold in what package sizes at a specific 7-11 in, say, Dallas, Texas! The company built analysis tools to sift through tremendously detailed transactions data that are collected as a routine part of sales to grocery stores and other snack food vendors. Firms have created a tremendous resource by storing transactions in databases. Information technology lets us build systems and provide tools to extract information from these databases to support managerial decisions. In this chapter we look at how individuals interpret information and explore the decision-making process.

What Is Information?

We define information as some tangible or intangible entity that reduces uncertainty about some state or event. As an example, consider a weather forecast predicting clear and sunny skies tomorrow. This information reduces our uncertainty about whether an event such as a baseball game will be held. Information that a bank has just approved a loan for our firm reduces our uncertainty about whether we shall be in a state of solvency or bankruptcy next month. Information derived from processing transactions reduces uncertainty about a firm's order backlog or financial position. Information used primarily for control in the organization reduces uncertainty about whether the firm is performing according to plan and budget.

Another definition of information has been suggested: "Information is data that has been processed into a form that is meaningful to the recipient and is of real perceived value in current or prospective decisions" (Davis and Olson, 1985, p. 6). This definition of information systems stresses the fact that data must be processed in some way to produce information; information is more than raw data. In later chapters we discuss information systems that process data to produce information. In this chapter, however, we focus on information and its interpretation.

An Electronic Hospital

At the LDS Hospital of the University of Utah in Salt Lake City, doctors use a terminal to retrieve patients' records. If a patient enters the emergency room, the staff attaches him or her to microcomputer-based equipment to monitor vital signs. The patient's name is also logged into the hospital's central system. If the patient has been in the hospital within the past fifteen years, a history will be immediately displayed to the staff.

The hospital has 24 computers, 250 terminals, and 70 printers, which support all aspects of health care. Orders for tests are sent to the laboratory; the staff there inputs the results through the laboratory computer to the central hospital system. In the radiology department, the doctor uses the computer to enter findings from X rays. The system suggests possible interpretations to aid the analysis by the physician.

The staff also enters any drug orders into the computer. The drug order is then posted to the patient's data file. The system sets up a drug schedule and is reviewed by an expert system to determine whether an order is safe, given what the system knows about the patient's history and other drug orders.

Technology has been used in hospitals for many years; this system integrates all of the different components of hospital systems into a network supporting the patient's entire interaction with the hospital.

HOW PEOPLE INTERPRET INFORMATION

A classic article on information systems suggested in part that an information system serves an individual with a certain **cognitive style** faced with a particular decision problem in some organizational setting (Mason and Mitroff 1973). In addition to these variables, we suggest the importance of personal and situational factors in the interpretation of information. We shall examine each of these factors to see how they influence the interpretation process. (See Figure 2-1.)

Clearly, the nature of the problem influences the way we interpret information. How serious is the decision? What are the consequences of an incorrect decision, and how do they compare with the benefits of a correct one? An important decision may require more care in analyzing data than would a minor decision. For example, an oil company's decision to enter the information processing field is more important than its decision to lease additional office space. In such a strategic decision as whether to diversify, the consequences and costs involved, plus the impact on the organization, require that information be scrutinized much more closely.

The organization itself affects the interpretation of information. Studies have shown that the individual becomes socialized by the organization. Over time we are influenced by our organizations in the way we approach problems. Thus, in most instances, the attitudes of a new employee will differ substantially from those of the chairman of the board. As the new employee associates over the years with other employees of the firm, he or she is influenced by their attitudes and by the environment of the workplace. Gradually, new employees begin to change their attitudes to be more consistent with those of their associates.

Figure 2-1

Influences on the interpretation and use of information.

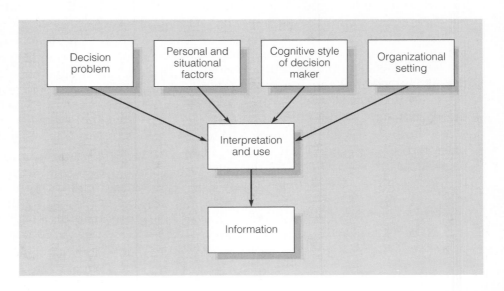

People who have different ideas interpret information differently. Again, many of a person's ideas are influenced by peers and by the socialization process in the particular organization where the individual works. Several individuals trying to influence the government to regulate prices in an industry may use the same information. However, the head of a corporation in the industry, the leader of a consumer group, and a government decision maker in a regulatory agency will probably interpret the same information differently.

Personal and situational factors also influence the interpretation of information. One study done many years ago showed that given comparable information, decision makers interpreted a problem differently depending on their position. In this exercise, finance executives saw financial problems, sales executives recognized sales problems, and so forth. In all the given scenarios, the information was the same—it was just interpreted differently (Dearborn and Simon, 1958). (A more recent study found managers are getting less parochial, though personal experience suggests that many managers are heavily influenced in problem diagnosis by their backgrounds and position.)

Psychologists studying the thought patterns of individuals have developed the concept of cognitive style. Although there is no agreement on exactly how to describe or measure different cognitive styles, the concept is appealing, since people do seem to have different ways of approaching problems. One of the simplest distinctions is between analytic and heuristic decision makers. The **analytic** decision maker looks at quantitative information. Engineering is a profession attractive to an analytic decision maker. The **heuristic** decision maker, on the other hand, is interested in broader concepts and is more intuitive. Most researchers believe that we are not analytic or heuristic in every problem but that we do have preferences and tend to approach the same type of problem with a consistent cognitive style.

A Model for Interpreting Information

We have suggested a number of factors that influence the interpretation of information. How are all these factors combined? What is their net impact on the interpretation of information? Figure 2-2 summarizes all the variables described above. The figure portrays one representation of how a user of information systems develops a model to interpret information and how this model is constantly executed and revised.

In the model, to interpret data a decision maker draws on current data and a history of past decisions and their results. The interpretation turns data into information, and the decision maker takes some action. He or she observes the results and stores them for future reference.

We expect the model to be formed **inductively** by the decision maker and to be heavily influenced by beliefs. For example, a decision maker may observe data on sales and production over time and find that these data seem to predict customers' reactions to a product. The decision maker is

Figure 2-2
Model for interpreting
information.

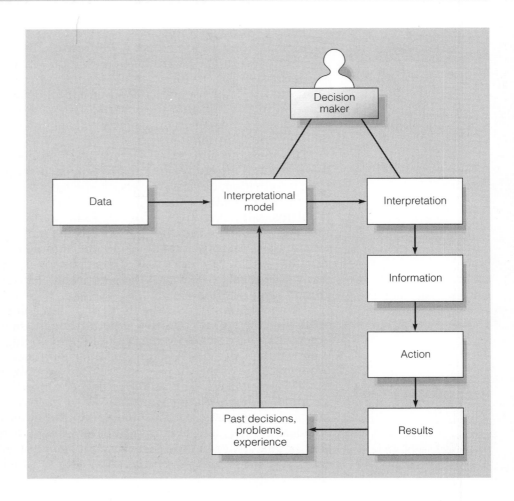

building an interpretational model based on his or her beliefs and analysis of historical data and observations.

After testing the interpretational model and developing confidence in
it, the decision maker uses the model **deductively**. Data are observed, and
the decision maker uses the model to interpret them. Now, the decision
maker perceives data on sales and production as constituting information
on product acceptance; he or she may even ignore other information con-
veyed by these data.

After an interpretational model has been formed, further experiences
are fed back to modify the model. Past decisions, problems, and experiences all influence the future interpretation of information. These experiences are based on actions taken on the basis of information and the
results of those actions. If changes in a new product based on sales and
production data increase sales, the interpretational model described above
will be reinforced.

The Decision-Making Process

We have suggested that one important role of information systems is to support decision making. Before we can continue our discussion of the nature of information, we must examine the decision-making process in more detail to see how information is used.

Problem Finding and Solving

We must be aware of a problem before we can make a decision. A problem exists when the decision maker's ideal situation differs from reality, for example, when sales are below expectations. This example corresponds to something we call **disturbance handling**; the manager discovers a discrepancy between the ideal model and reality and attempts to find some way to eliminate the discrepancy.

After noting the existence of a problem, the decision maker must decide what caused it. Are inventories up? Is the advertising budget too low? After determining the cause or causes, the decision maker tries to solve the problem by developing some program to remedy the situation. There is also another type of problem-finding activity undertaken by the manager who is looking for improvement projects. In this sense, the problem can be defined by asking, "What else could we be doing at the present time?" The manager is trying to anticipate problems and plan for them.

The vast amount of information available in corporate databanks or **data warehouses** combined with the vast information resources of the World Wide Web on the Internet make problem finding an extremely important managerial activity. You must learn how to discover that a problem exists

Shopping on a PC

In the early 1980s, Florsheim Shoe Stores faced a problem: It could not possibly stock all its shoes in all sizes at all stores. Customers were complaining that the shoes they wanted were not available and catalogs were not a satisfactory substitute for seeing the shoes.

The company spent $1 million over a four-year period to develop a custom-designed electronic display of its products. The system runs on a Motorola 68000-based PC controller with a videodisc player, full-color screen, and membrane (touch-sensitive) keyboard.

Customers in the store access the system to browse among shoes; they can try on a different style from the pair they want to order to get size information. The store can then place an order, which is shipped from a million-square-foot central warehouse within a week. There is no charge for shipping. About one-third of the customers in the stores use the system, and business has increased by 22 percent since it was installed.

The Florsheim system is an example of using technology to provide better customer service and to generate revenue. The company has produced an electronic inventory of shoes that are unavailable in the store; within a few days the customer receives his or her order. Shoes can be tricky to purchase by mail-order; Florsheim has combined the benefits of a store with the convenience of direct ordering.

and then use the variety of resources available through computers and networks to locate data. You will use the data to both understand the problem and develop a solution for it.

Types of Decisions

Not all decisions are alike; some involve different levels of the organization and some are more important than others. Anthony (1965) suggests that there are three broad categories of decisions made in organizations, a model still widely used today.

Strategic Planning   In **strategic planning** the decision maker develops objectives and allocates resources to obtain them. Decisions in this category are characterized by long time periods and usually involve a substantial investment and effort. The development and introduction of a new product is an example of a strategic decision.

Managerial Control   Decisions involving **managerial control** concern the use of resources in the organization and often include personnel or financial problems. For example, an accountant may try to determine the reason for a difference between actual and budgeted costs.

Operational Control   An **operational control** decision covers the day-to-day problems that affect the operation of the firm: What should be produced today in the factory? What items should be ordered for inventory?

Who makes the preponderance of each of the three types of decisions? Anthony does not specify who handles each type of decision. However, from the nature of the problems, we suspect that top managers in the organization would spend more time on strategic decision making than supervisors, and supervisors would be more concerned with operational decisions.

HOW DO INDIVIDUALS MAKE DECISIONS?

Stages in the Decision-Making Process

In finding and solving a problem, the decision maker faces myriad decision cycles. What is the problem, what is its cause, what additional data are needed, and how should the solution be implemented? Each of these major steps in solving a problem involves the solution of subproblems.

The Nobel laureate, Herbert Simon (1965), suggests a series of descriptive stages for decision making to help understand the decision process. The first stage is defined as **intelligence**, which determines a problem exists. The decision maker must become aware of a problem and gather data about it. We have described this stage as **problem finding** or identification.

During the **design** stage, the problem solver tries to develop a set of alternative solutions. The problem solver asks what approaches are available to solve the problem and evaluates each one. In the **choice** stage, the decision maker selects one of the solutions. If all the alternatives are evaluated well, the choice stage is usually the simplest one to execute. We should also add a stage to Simon's model called **implementation**, in which we ensure that the solution is carried out.

A more elaborate model of the decision-making process is found in Figure 2-3 (Slade 1992). First, a decision maker must recognize a decision needs to be made. Although this observation probably sounds obvious, there have been many examples of individuals who ignored the need for decisions. Several U.S. presidents have been criticized for a failure to address key problems. It is likely that one of them lost his reelection bid because he failed to recognize that decisions were needed on domestic policies as well as on foreign affairs.

Next the decision maker must identify alternatives, a process similar to the design stage in Simon's model of decision making. For routine or repetitive decisions, the decision maker may be able to simply choose the usual action. When sales of a particular product are up, there may be a standard rule that says to reorder a certain quantity of new products for every increase of one hundred units in sales. Most of the time, however, the decision maker will have to evaluate the alternatives identified in the previous step.

Somehow the decision maker must rate the alternatives on some basis; he or she then chooses the most attractive (or in some cases the least unattractive) alternative. This stage in the Slade model corresponds to Simon's choice stage. As Figure 2-3 suggests, the highest-ranked alternative may still be unacceptable. The decision maker must try to

MANAGEMENT PROBLEM 2-1

Sue Johnson was recently hired by a large bank as manager of the IS user services department. Her first task was to learn what users were doing with their computers and what kind of support they needed. Sue spent a month visiting various PC users around the bank. On completing her survey, she met with her superior, the bank's vice president of operations.

Sue began by saying that she saw a number of areas in which she could provide support to PC users. However, she was very discouraged by the large number of machines receiving little or no apparent use. "The bank has obviously invested a large amount of money in providing its personnel with personal computers, yet many of these computers—in fact, the majority—are used no more than an hour a day or even not at all!"

The vice president of operations shrugged. "What can you expect? People just do things differently. We experimented by providing people with the technology; some will use it and some won't. The computers aren't all that expensive."

Sue was not convinced. What actions can you recommend to encourage the utilization of the personal computer resources the bank has already put in place?

Figure 2-3

Slade's model of the decision-making process.

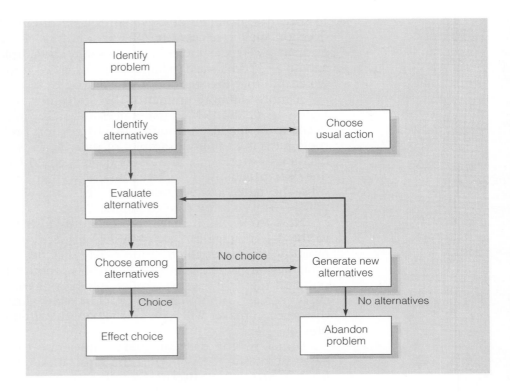

generate new alternatives. If the situation is hopeless, the decision maker may abandon the problem. In most organizational settings, this last course of action is not acceptable, or is certainly not encouraged.

Once the decision maker has made a choice, it is necessary to implement it, that is, to effect the choice. Many managers and leaders have been faulted, not because they made bad decisions, but because they failed to take the action necessary to implement them. Implementation is often difficult for managers because they have to act through others. The individuals charged with implementation may not be committed to the decision, or may have reasons to subvert it.

The discussion so far makes it appear that people are confronted with a clear decision problem and take action within a short period of time. Our recent research suggests that many decisions may actually be made over a long period of time. In one company we studied, the decision to develop a new use of technology took over six months as a group of managers discussed different options. The process of identifying a new option occurred when the managers rejected an earlier option. At least in this instance, the decision makers did not identify all alternatives and then select one at a single point in time. Rather the decision turned into a series of explorations of options and a growing consensus on the best alternative to choose.

Making a decision can be a complex undertaking; however, decisions are what determine the direction of our lives and our organizations. Information systems, among other roles, help provide information for decision making.

THE INFLUENCE OF THE ORGANIZATION

We have been discussing how individuals make decisions. In most organizations, groups of individuals are involved in making decisions. How does this group finally reach a consensus and make a decision that commits the entire firm?

We all have observed different organizations in action and wondered how decisions are made. There are a number of ways to classify organizations. Probably the best known form is the **bureaucracy**. Most universities, government agencies and many large organizations fall into this category. Bureaucracies are characterized by a large number of management layers. There are many rules and procedures to protect individuals; if you follow the procedures, how can you be wrong? Bureaucracies try to survive and to minimize uncertainty; members of these organizations stress job security. We would expect decisions in bureaucracies to be conservative and require modest changes in existing procedures.

The **charismatic** organization is dominated by a strong leader. This individual sets the goals of the firm and tends to make all decisions. His

MANAGEMENT PROBLEM 2-2

The governor of a state is confronted with a series of conflicting recommendations from his staff. All the reports he has read on current welfare problems have indicated that projected payments will rise well beyond budgeted levels for the rest of the year.

The director of the state welfare department suggested in her report that the new payments schedule passed by the legislature was to blame for the problem. The governor's adviser for economic affairs indicated that the recent decline in the state's economy had resulted in a large increase in unemployment. As unemployment benefits ran out, he said, many of the unemployed became eligible for welfare, thus accounting for the increase in expenditures.

A state senate leader felt that most of the increase resulted from people cheating on welfare, which resulted in abnormally high expenditures in the early part of the year. This high rate of expenditures was the basis for the projections for the rest of the year. The obvious solution was to increase the standards for eligibility and investigate applicants and current recipients more closely.

Who is right? What is responsible for so many different positions? How can the governor reconcile these conflicting viewpoints and arrive at the true cause of the problem?

or her decisions are hard to predict because this kind of leader often does not reveal plans to the rest of the organization. It is safe to say that the leader is likely to make the decision that subordinates then execute.

The **adaptive** organization tries to respond quickly to its environment. The organization stresses rapid response times and does not have a large number of layers of management. A small group of decision makers analyze data and come to decisions quickly.

Although there are many other types of organizations, our main point is that individuals usually make decisions in the context of some organization. It is clear that most decisions are not entirely *rational* as advocated by an economist. People are not always able to examine all alternatives and choose a course that maximizes the value of some outcome. The nature of the organization will influence the decision and the kind of information that people making the decision require.

Rental Cars: Competing with Technology

Hertz and Avis are arch rivals in the car rental business. Both companies have introduced hand-held computer terminals so that a service representative can check in a returning car before the customer has had a chance to get out of the vehicle. Each company has taken a slightly different approach to providing this additional customer service.

When a rental return comes into the Avis lot, the service representative approaches the car and enters the Avis registration number on the rear window into a portable terminal that he or she carries on a shoulder strap. The terminal is linked locally to the Avis Wizard mainframe reservation system through the FM radio band. The Wizard system currently handles more than eight thousand terminals around the world. The mainframe system retrieves the information on the rental and displays the customer's name. The service representative obtains the odometer reading and gas tank level and enters the data into the portable terminal; then the mainframe computes the bill and the terminal prints it for the customer. The entire operation takes one to two minutes.

The Hertz system offers the same service, but the portable terminal is entirely self-contained; it is not linked to the central computer. The lack of a mainframe link means that the service representative must perform a number of calculations before printing a receipt. He or she must enter information that is already stored on the mainframe. Later, the data must be manually reentered into the main Hertz computer network.

Has either firm gained a competitive advantage with these systems? The answer is yes, compared to other rental-car firms, but probably no if one only considers competition between Hertz and Avis. Certainly the customer benefits with extremely rapid rental-car returns. Hertz has extended the technology to let members of its special club pick up a car without stopping at a counter (given a prior reservation). In this highly competitive industry, firms may gain a temporary advantage until others catch up, but it is generally easy for the largest companies to copy each other's innovations. In the end, it is likely to be the customer who wins while the rental-car companies continue to seek an elusive competitive edge.

Characteristics of Information

Information can be characterized in a number of ways; some kinds of information are more suitable for decision making than others. The time frame for information can be historical or predictive. **Historical** information can be used to design alternative solutions and to monitor performance. Information may be expected or it may be unanticipated. Some information systems experts feel that information is worthless unless it is a surprise to the recipient. However, information that confirms something also reduces uncertainty. **Surprise** information often alerts us to the existence of a problem; it is also important in developing and evaluating different alternatives. Information may come from sources **internal** to the organization or from external sources, such as government agencies.

Information may be presented in summary form or in **detail** and vary in **accuracy**. **Summary** information is often sufficient for problem finding but summary and detailed information may be needed for other uses. Information can be frequently updated, relatively old, loosely organized, or highly **structured**. An example of highly structured information is a report with clear categories to classify all the information it contains. Loosely organized information might be a report composed of different forms of information from multiple sources.

In general, different types of decisions require different kinds of information and providing inappropriate information is one common failing of information systems. (See Table 2-1.) Operational control decisions are characterized by historical information. Usually the results are expected and the source of the information is the internal operations of the organization. The data—for example, production control data, inventory status,

Table 2-1
Information Characteristics Versus Decision Types

	Decision type		
Characteristics	**Operational control**	**Managerial control**	**Strategic planning**
Time frame	Historical	⟶	Predictive
Expectation	Anticipated	⟶	Surprise
Source	Largely internal	⟶	Largely external
Scope	Detailed	⟶	Summary
Frequency	Real-time	⟶	Periodic
Organization	Highly structured	⟶	Loosely structured
Precision	Highly precise	⟶	Not overly precise

or accounts-receivable balances—must be detailed. Because operational control decisions involve day-to-day operations of the firm, information often must correspond closely to "**real time**." This information is often highly structured and precise.

Information for strategic decisions, on the other hand, is more predictive and long range in nature. Strategic planning may uncover many surprises. Often, **external** data on the economy, the competition, and so forth are involved in strategic decision making. Summary information on a periodic basis is adequate; there is usually no need for highly detailed or extremely precise information. Strategic-planning decisions are usually characterized by loosely structured information. The requirements for managerial control decisions fall between operational control and strategic planning.

Obviously, there are many ways to classify information, and this complicates the decision maker's problem in expressing what output is desired from an information system. The most important thing for the user of an information system to be aware of is the intended use of the information and the type of decision he or she is facing. Then the user should try to decide on the general characteristics of the information needed, using categories such as these as guidelines to develop more detailed information requirements. Consideration of similar characteristics should enable the user to avoid requesting grossly inappropriate information from an information system.

A SCENARIO FOR THE NOT-TOO-DISTANT FUTURE

How will managers in the future solve problems and make decisions? What will the impact of technology be on you as an individual? A scenario, adapted from Jarvenpaa and Ives (1994) suggests how you are likely to work in the future.

The landing gear of the 787 came up as Tara Rodgers in seat 6B linked her personal assistant to an onboard computer built into the armrest of her seat. The display screen on the back of the seat in front of her was larger and had a higher resolution than the screen on Tara's personal assistant. It also provided access to the airline's electronic amenities. Tara tuned into the airline's audio system which gave her capabilities similar to those of her personal assistant including connection to inflight entertainment, the ability to listen to ground control conversations, and special circuitry to eliminate the plane's background noise.

Tara touched an icon on the screen in front of her to view the inflight service menu. She canceled dinner, eliminated nonessential messages from flight personnel (Tara had taken the flight many times before and did not want the captain's sightseeing instructions). She asked for a glass of port to be delivered in two hours. She did not expect her electronic documents to attract the attention of the EUC's customs and immigration systems, but she authorized the system to wake her if an onboard interview with immigration officials was requested. By speaking softly into a microphone plugged into the arm rest, Tara completed her customs declaration. The airline's computers had already entered the flight number, date, and other details of the trip.

Tara barely noticed the soft, classical music that she had chosen as background for her audio system. Her personal profile, stored in her assistant, or possibly the airline's frequent flyer database, had chosen her type of music and preset the volume based on her personal preferences. This profile would also suggest that her morning coffee be served with cream and no sugar.

Tara touched another icon to make arrangements for her brief stay in Oxford. Her trip from New York was sudden and she had not made hotel reservations. The electronic reservation agent her firm subscribed to had booked her into a charming guest house she had liked during her last visit to Oxford. Using the travel agents' virtual reality simulator, she wandered into the rooms with open doors (available this evening) and selected the one with the best view of the college. She also could have looked at a short video segment showing where to meet the car that would take her from Heathrow to Oxford, after booking the car electronically. Had she been closer to London, she could have looked at a prerecorded introduction to her driver.

The airline's computer predicted an on-time arrival with 95 percent certainty and Tara began the work she wanted to complete before trying to get some sleep. First she called her husband and watched her children at play in their family room.

Back at work, Tara touched a key to activate her electronic messaging system and listened again to the message from the senior partner of Worldwide who had sent her off on this sudden trip. "Tara, this morning I received a message from London from Professor Locke at Templeton College, Oxford. Locke has worked closely with our U.K. and European offices on a number of projects; London believes he has the inside track on a promising opportunity, but we have to move quickly."

"The prospective customer is Empire Software, a company that specializes in the production of integrated software systems for the international freight business. Sir Phillip Knight, CEO of Empire, is in residence at Templeton College for a three day forum. Over coffee, Knight expressed a concern to Locke that his firm is not taking advantage of the advances in software engineering and that his management team is poorly prepared to respond to competitive threats. Knight was very interested in some kind of customized educational program for the firm's top 100 employees. Locke has set up a meeting with Knight for tomorrow afternoon at Templeton to talk more. Locke thinks that if we move quickly, we might be able to land this job without Empire going through a competitive bidding process. Locke would like our help in putting together the educational program."

"Tara, you worked with Knight five years ago on a project when he ran development at Dover Software and you were with that awful competitor of ours. When the UK office ran a search, the identifier system came up with your name because of that job and your knowledge of the software industry."

"Empire is a high growth company that has been very profitable. Locke thinks there will be follow-up business if we get the job. Knight feels Empire is in a bad position to operate globally; he thinks software engineering will help Empire compete as well as relying on Eastern European software houses for assistance. Knight likes the kind of wholesale organizational change program Locke has been talking about in the Templeton seminar. I have checked our customer database and find that we have not done much with Empire, though we have a couple of engagements with them in Asia and Europe. We have no U.S. projects with them."

"I checked your availability for the next two days and have started to reassign your responsibilities to other associates. Jerry Wright is your contact from the London office; he has worked with Locke in the past, but doesn't know Empire or Knight. I contacted Mary Ellen Smith who is a doctoral student at UC Irvine to be your special research assistant. She will be at your disposal for the next 48 hours working out of her home. You can ask her to look through our files and external databases to pull together a brief on Empire, their competitors, the industry and so on."

Tara listened to a forwarded message from Professor Locke and Jerry Wright. She checked corporate records for a profile on Wright; his specialty was working on projects that required pulling together diverse resources from the Worldwide Group. He was highly motivated and would perform, though he might be occasionally a bit brusque and overly task-oriented.

Wright had spoken to Locke and forwarded his notes to Tara. Wright had provided the names of several Empire people in the U.S. and Europe that Worldwide was working with. Tara saw that one of these projects pertained to software development productivity. She linked to Worldwide's central databank to review reports on that project. Tara found a presentation prepared and delivered to a technical directions steering committee in Tokyo three months earlier. The findings were similar to Knight's concerns about productivity and global reach. One recommendation was a call for a management education program and an examination of locating a development group in the Pacific Rim.

Tara sent an urgent message to the Tokyo partner who had worked with Empire on this project. He was vacationing on a cruise ship in the Caribbean, but the messaging system located him and forwarded the message in English and Japanese. Tara attached the correspondence relating to her current project and asked for a quick update and one minute summary of the original findings that she could use the next day. Then she downloaded the complete text of the Tokyo presentation to her personal assistant and highlighted the key sections she would use tomorrow if she did not find better information. Finally, she forwarded the results of her work to Wright in London.

By this time, Mary Ellen Smith had forwarded Tara a dossier on Empire. Smith had produced a rich assortment of documents on Empire as well as a strong overview report. Using a global paging service, Tara set up a conference call with Smith and an executive education specialist in Boston. Tara wanted a list of names from the firm, from colleges, and from independent constants of people qualified to participate in a program of this type. She needed data on fees, availability, areas of specialty, and participant evaluations from their past programs. She also wanted to see video clips of each candidate performing in front of an executive audience.

Smith said she would use her electronic agent to search through faculty expertise files in the top tier business schools around the world. Tara asked Smith to identify five to ten top candidates and the education specialist to look for several possible venues for the program. Several of the experts would probably remain at their home base and provide instruction through audio, video, and computer links to the conference site. Checking through uploaded files from other Worldwide personal assistants, she found that Knight had a summer home in Bermuda and suggested that as one possible seminar location.

Before signing off, the education consultant downloaded a multimedia presentation to Tara's personal assistant. Worldwide had recently used this presentation to sell a similar educational project to another client; she could save time by using this "boilerplate" for tomorrow's meeting.

Tara asked the assistant to identify an initial list of individuals who could contribute to the program. Using her firm's database, she checked on their availability over the next six months and watched video clips of several instructors working with executive audiences. She called one presenter in Oregon to ask if she could use his video clip in her presentation tomorrow.

Tara contacted Kolormagic, a firm that provided world-wide graphics work for its clients. Headquartered in Singapore, the company maintained a group of graphics artists around the world who could provide consistent, high quality multimedia presentations for clients. Singapore offered inducements for the company to locate there, including its superior technology infrastructure.

Kolormagic arranged for an artist on Maui to work with Tara. She checked previous work from this artist in the Worldwide database and was satisfied with his work. She forwarded logos from Worldwide and Empire, names, titles, pictures, and links to the previous multimedia demonstration she had reviewed to the artist. She spent the next hour discussing the presentation with the artist. The artist promised a rough presentation by the time Tara reached Oxford. Locke, Wright, and the Japanese partner in the Caribbean would all be able to review the presentation before it was delivered.

Tara completed a summary of her activities and forwarded it to Wright and the Worldwide database. She set a wakeup call for 45 minutes before landing. As the flight attendant arrived with the glass of port, she checked Knight's personal profile from her one previous contact with him; she retrieved the name of his favorite wine and forwarded it to Wright in London. Now it was time for some sleep.

Is this scenario realistic? Much of the technology described here exists today. The advances that are necessary to make the scenario feasible will come from lowering communications costs and increasing capacities for transferring information. Given growing competition in the communications industry, it is likely that you will enjoy the use of the technology described above during your career.

CHAPTER SUMMARY

1. A major role for IT is providing information and frequently this information is used for making decisions in an organization.
2. It is important to understand how individuals interpret information and make decisions using it, as well as how organizations influence each individual's interpretation of information.
3. Different individuals are likely to have differing interpretations of the same data; they may both begin with the same data but come to entirely different conclusions on its meaning and on the appropriate action to take.
4. A variety of interpretations of data raises a major challenge for management in the organization and for those who design information systems.
5. Information has a number of characteristics. The type of information needed for different kinds of decisions differs, for example, strategic planning uses different information than operational control or managerial control.
6. Schools frequently focus on teaching students techniques for solving well-defined problems; it is important to learn how to find problems and understand their cause.

IMPLICATIONS FOR MANAGEMENT

Information is a tricky substance. You can give it away and still keep it for yourself. If someone already knows the information, giving it to them again does not provide any benefits. The same information can have widely differing impacts on different people. Countries with advanced economies more and more use information to add value to products and services. As a manager you will work in an information-rich environment and you will use and communicate information in a variety of ways. Try to keep in mind the unusual characteristics of information, especially the factors that influence how different people come up with radically different interpretations of the same information.

KEY WORDS

Accuracy	Historical
Adaptive	Implementation
Analytic	Inductively
Bureaucracy	Intelligence
Charismatic	Internal
Choice	Managerial control
Cognitive style	Operational control
Data warehouse	Problem finding
Deductively	Real time
Design	Strategic planning
Detail	Structured
Disturbance handling	Summary
External	Surprise
Heuristic	

RECOMMENDED READING

Banker, R., R. Kauffman, and M. Mahmood. *Strategic Information Technology Management.* Harrisburg, Pa.: Idea Group Publishing, 1993. (An interesting and stimulating collection of articles about the strategic use of technology.)

Parker, M. M. *Strategic Transformation and Information Technology.* Englewood Cliffs, N.J.: Prentice Hall, 1996. (An up-to-date look at the way technology changes organizations and the opportunities it provides managers.)

Pounds, W. F. "The Process of Problem Finding," *The Industrial Management Review,* vol. 11, no. 1 (Fall 1969), pp. 1–20. (An insightful article describing the nature of problem finding; the author gives several examples of different kinds of problems that managers in one company faced.)

DISCUSSION QUESTIONS

1. What alternative definitions for information can you propose?
2. What do you think selective perception is? How does it affect the design and use of information systems?
3. Why is information more than just data?
4. How would you measure cognitive style? How does this concept help in the interpretation of information and the design of information systems?
5. Can an organization skew the information it develops and uses?
6. How can different interpretations of information lead to conflict? How can this conflict be resolved?

7. Develop procedures to elicit and define information needs for making a decision. How could you implement your plan? What are the problems?

8. How does the importance of a decision reflect itself in the user's interpretation of information?

9. Would you expect an analytical decision maker to be more favorably disposed toward a spreadsheet model than a heuristic one? Why or why not?

10. Pounds suggests that a problem exists when the decision maker's normative model of what should be conflicts with reality. How does this normative model relate to our information interpretation model? Are the two models completely independent?

11. Can the same information system be used by more than one decision maker?

12. How can we custom-tailor information systems to suit different decision makers at a reasonable cost?

13. Examine for bias one particular indicator with which you are familiar. For example, how valid an indicator of reliability is a grade point average?

14. What other characteristics of information can you define beyond the ones listed in this chapter?

15. Are there information systems that deal with decisions or processes outside Anthony's categories? What types of systems are these?

16. What are the most frequent indicators for evaluating the performance of lower, middle, and top managers?

17. Is there any way to "beat" an indicator like a standardized aptitude test for college admissions? What kind of behavior does this indicator motivate?

18. Of what value are formal theories of information to a decision maker?

CHAPTER 2 PROJECT

THE ADMISSIONS DECISION

One of the most feared decision processes, at least by students, is the *admissions decision* that colleges and universities make. This decision determines whether or not a student will be accepted, and often involves a second decision on the possible award of financial aid. Drawing upon your experiences applying to schools, describe the information that is used in making the decision. What data were you asked to supply? What information came from external sources? What are the characteristics of the information?

Use one of the decision making models in the text, for example Figure 2-3, to describe how the admissions committee processes information and makes a decision. How should this committee interpret information? Should the interpretation be the same for each student, or are there situations in which some information should weigh more heavily for a candidate?

CHAPTER **3**

Information Technology in Perspective

1. **Learning to manage information technology.**

   To manage the technology, you must understand the various ways it can be applied and the management issues that arise from IT. Frameworks help organize your thinking about IT and formulate your approach to solving problems. In this chapter we present some of the original frameworks for IT and update them with modern technology.

2. **Preparing to apply technology.**

   Systems analysis and design is a creative effort. Individuals have developed a number of exciting and imaginative applications, as this chapter suggests. Even if you buy a dedicated application, you must undertake some analysis to determine that the package is appropriate for your needs.

3. **Transforming the organization.**

   In some cases, a major system results in transforming the organization. Other companies transform themselves a little bit at a time by developing one system after another. In particular, this chapter introduces interorganizational systems and workgroup computing. Both technologies have the potential for changing the way an organization relates to other firms and for altering the internal operations of an organization.

A **framework** is a conceptual model that helps us understand and communicate about information systems. The frameworks discussed in this chapter will facilitate future discussions about different types of decisions, their information requirements, and different kinds of information systems.

FRAMEWORKS FOR INFORMATION TECHNOLOGY

A framework provides you with a way to organize your thoughts and analyze a problem. There is no one theory of information systems and technology, though a user or designer of a system needs some conceptual model of an information system. In this text we present several different approaches to frameworks and adopt one for purposes of discussion. It is not essential that everyone adopt the framework we use here. It is important, however, for you to have some conceptual model when making decisions pertaining to these systems.

Decision-Oriented Frameworks

In the previous chapter we discussed the decision-making stages of intelligence, design, and choice proposed by Simon. Anthony is concerned with the purpose of decision-making activities, whereas Simon stresses methods and techniques. In addition to the stages listed above, Simon proposes that there are two types of decisions: programmed and nonprogrammed. Programmed decisions are routine and repetitive and require little time spent in the design stage. Posting journal entries would be an example of a programmed activity. Nonprogrammed decisions are novel and unstructured, for example, deciding on the marketing mix for a set of products. There is no one solution and much time is spent in design since the problem has probably not appeared before. Clearly, few decisions are at one polar extreme or the other and fall along a continuum between programmed and nonprogrammed.

Different types of decision-making technology are suitable for attacking each type of problem. Programmed decisions have traditionally been made through habit, by clerical procedures, or with other accepted tools. More-modern techniques for solving programmed decisions involve operations research, mathematical analysis, modeling, and simulation.

Nonprogrammed decisions tend to be solved through judgment, intuition, and rules of thumb. Over time, we expect to see new technology providing more programming for nonprogrammed decisions; that is, decisions will tend to move toward the more programmed pole of the continuum.

A Synthesized Framework

A framework synthesizing the work of Anthony and Simon (see Chapter 2) is very appealing because it helps us classify a variety of systems (Gorry and Scott Morton, 1971). Table 3-1 classifies Anthony's decision types from operational control to strategic planning, on a scale of structured to unstructured. (Gorry and Scott Morton feel that *structured* and *unstructured* are more appropriate terms than *programmed* and *nonprogrammed*.)

In a structured decision, the three phases, intelligence, design, and choice are fully structured. In an unstructured decision, all three phases are unstructured. Any decision in between the two extremes is semistructured. As in Simon's framework, the line between structured and unstructured

Table 3-1
The Gorry–Scott Morton Framework   DECISION FRAMEWORK

Classification	Operational control	Management control	Strategic planning
Structured	Order processing, accounts payable	Budgets, personnel reports	Warehouse location, transportation mode mix
Semistructured	Inventory control, production planning	Analysis of variance	Introduction of new product
Unstructured	Cash management	Management of personnel	Planning for R&D

decisions shifts over time as new decision techniques are developed and applied to unstructured problems.

From Table 3-1, it appears that many information systems have attacked problems in the structured, operational control cell. These problems are similar in many organizations and are among the most easily understood. It is easier to mechanize these decisions and to predict and achieve cost savings for them than less structured decisions or strategic-planning decisions. Since operational systems are important to the daily functioning of the firm, they are high-priority applications.

Many individuals in the information systems field believe that unstructured decisions have the greatest payoff for the organization. The development of systems for unstructured problems is a major challenge and is undoubtedly more risky than the development of comparable systems for structured problems. The goals and design techniques for unstructured decisions differ from those for structured ones. In the structured case, the goal of an information system is usually to improve the processing of information. In an unstructured situation, the goal of the information system is more likely to improve the organization and presentation of information inputs to the decision maker.

We include a large number of technology applications in this text. Organizations and individuals have been extremely creative in developing new uses for IT. Huge computer complexes support airline reservation systems, for example, managers in a variety of fields use **personal computers** for decision support and analysis. A framework such as the Gorry–Scott

Vanity Fair's Technology

Vanity Fair manufactures a variety of clothing products from Lee and Wrangler jeans to women's undergarments. The company is a leader in computerized market-response systems, systems that restock a retailer's shelves as quickly as possible. Vanity Fair often restocks within three days of an order while Levi's can take a month to supply new product. The company began by connecting its computers to those of retailers like Wal-Mart and J.C. Penney. VF provides hundreds of styles to thousands of outlets; its communications center has some 40 floor-to-ceiling terminals that technicians use to control the network.

Every night Wal-Mart sends data collected on register scanners in 2,100 outlets to Vanity Fair. VF then restocks the stores automatically based on what was sold that day. If VF has the product in stock, it is shipped the next day, so that within three days the new jeans are on the shelf. If the item is not in stock, the VF computer orders a replacement that is manufactured and shipped within a week. Another advantage of this system is that the retailer only replenishes products that are selling. Since the items in stock are what the customer wants, there are fewer clearance sales. The chairman of VF credits the system, which handles half of its jeans orders, with giving the company the largest market share in the jeans business.

Morton model can aid our thinking in studying different kinds of systems. What kind of management support does the system provide? What is the nature of the problem?

Adding Organizations and Decisions to a Framework

An expanded framework in light of new IT applications based on the work of Harold Leavitt provides additional insights (Stohr and Konsynski, 1992). Figure 3-1 shows that an organization develops some internal structure so the people who work in the organization can accomplish their tasks. People perform these tasks so the firm can accomplish its mission or purpose, such as manufacturing and selling a product or providing a service. This framework separates information technology from the other technology in the firm because Stohr and Konsynski believe IT has become central in linking all parts of the organization together and helping it accomplish its tasks.

A significant feature of the framework is the idea that a change in one component is likely to cause changes in others. Chapter 4 explores the use of IT to design new kinds of organizations. A change in the environment may force the company to restructure itself—change its tasks and even the number of people who are associated with it. Many firms in the 1990s have been "restructuring" and "downsizing" or reducing employment to improve profits. Changes in world politics are causing the U.S. government to reallocate defense expenditures. This change in the environment is having a dramatic effect on the defense industry.

Table 3-2 provides more detail on the factors in each component of the framework. For example, there are many ways to structure an organization

Figure 3-1
Modified Leavitt model.

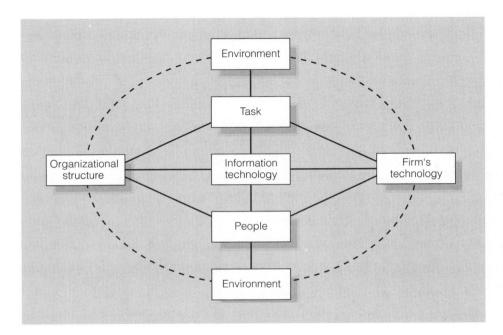

Table 3-2
Elaboration of the Framework

Organizational structure

- Formal organizational structure (hierarchy, teams)
- Corporate roles, responsibilities
- Corporate goals, strategy, policies
- Informal communication structure, culture
- Formal and informal decision processing mechanisms

People

- Intrinsic factors: age, education, knowledge, technical skills, managerial skills, leadership skills, personality types, cognitive styles
- Motivational factors: personal objectives, utilities
- Interpersonal factors: corporate political affiliations, friends, alliances, influence
- Extrinsic factors: roles, responsibilities, position in organization

Tasks

- Management categories: scanning, organizing, motivating, monitoring, controlling
- Repetitive activities, nonrepetitive activities
- Individual level: learning, communicating, deciding, performing

Technology

- Physical asset structure: land, buildings, plant, and equipment
- Financial asset structure
- Geographic distribution of resources

Information technology

- Databases, storage devices
- Computational capabilities, software
- Communication capabilities, networks
- Knowledge bases
- Information architecture

Environment

- National and global economy
- Customers, suppliers, competitors
- Products, substitutes
- Technological innovation

and there are a large number of influences on people. These factors are important to the decision processes in the organization. They impact the way we can use information technology to help the organization achieve its objectives.

A FRAMEWORK BASED ON IT

Changing Technology and Applications

The purpose of employing any technology is to obtain an advantage over old ways of doing business. The frameworks above were developed around early information systems that made use first of computer, and then communications technology. These early frameworks can be improved by taking into account the explosion of world-wide computer networking. Individuals and organizations have shown tremendous initiative in finding ways to apply information technology to improve their operations, gain a competitive advantage, provide personal productivity tools for employees, and even change the very structure of the organization.

Processing Transactions

Today, most transactions processing systems operate on-line, and a number of computer vendors compete for the business of providing hardware and software for **on-line transactions processing (OLTP)** systems. Whenever a customer in a store uses a credit card for a purchase above a certain amount, the merchant places the card in a reader that sends data recorded on the magnetic strip on the back of the credit card to a central transactions processing computer. The merchant enters the amount of the purchase, and the computer looks up the customer's record to determine if a purchase of that amount is authorized. If so, the computer sends back an authorization number to the merchant. No matter what happens between the credit card company and the customer, the merchant is assured of receiving payment from the credit card company after following the authorization process.

Transactions processing systems handle vast amount of data, much of which convey little interesting information to a manager. However, summaries of transactions data are often useful. For example, a summary of sales by product and territory from a sales database could be very valuable for a marketing executive or brand manager. Transactions systems, then, are the backbone of many information systems in firms.

Decision Support, Executive IS, and Expert Systems

Information technology can be used to support decision making in the organization as well as process transactions. Managers running spreadsheet programs on their personal computers to decide whether to launch a new product or make a particular investment use a computer for decision support. There are also special cases of decision support systems (DSS) known as group DSS and executive information systems. DSS designed specifically to support top management are called Executive Information Systems (EIS). Expert systems provide support in another fashion; they capture the knowledge of an expert and encode it in a computer program so the knowledge can be more widely shared. We discuss decision support systems in Chapter 21 and expert systems in Chapter 22.

Personal Support Systems

Large mainframe computers rarely feature applications that enhance the productivity of the typical manager. One of the great appeals of personal computers is the software available for personal productivity. Spreadsheet programs are widely used in business for making decisions and producing reports. The spreadsheet program is a major enhancement to personal productivity compared with the old way of doing mathematical analyses with pencil, paper, and calculator.

For individuals writing documents such as reports or even memos, word processing contributes greatly to productivity. The concept of word processing has been extended to desktop publishing. A desktop system features a powerful program capable of generating text in a variety of fonts and sizes. Hardware is available to scan input images and include them with the text—for example, to add a photograph to a news release. There are also **output** devices to produce high-resolution film that can be used directly in printing.

Personal productivity is also enhanced with packages for presentation graphics. If a manager has to make a presentation, programs exist that enable him or her to generate transparencies or 35mm slides in a variety of type styles, sizes, and colors. Many of these programs have libraries of clip art from which the user can add various illustrations.

Personal productivity has been enhanced by the development of **graphical user interfaces (GUIs)**, such as Microsoft Windows and the operating environment for the Macintosh computer. These systems create a graphical desktop on the computer's monitor and provide many more capabilities than older systems which only allowed character input and output.

Supporting Groups and Cooperative Work-Groupware

One of the most exciting uses of technology is the support of group and cooperative work. When individuals in different locations need to communicate with each other to share information, a distributed network of personal computers with appropriate software can provide a coordination mechanism. Consider a group of accountants working on an audit assignment. The members of the accounting firm need to examine a great deal of information. A computer network with groupware programs keeps various documents in folders that can be accessed by all of the audit team and this software can greatly facilitate the audit task. Groupware programs such as Lotus Notes perform this function. It provides **electronic mail** and communications and automatically **updates** local databases with documents that need to be shared. A development tool lets end users create new applications within Notes.

Interorganizational Systems

Applications that tie two organizations together are known as **interorganizational systems.** Partnerships and strategic alliances are created and enhanced with interorganizational systems. Such systems may be nothing more than e-mail connections, or they can represent full computer-to-computer connections between customers and suppliers as one example. Interorganizational systems make possible **virtual components**, in which a partner substitutes for some component of your company, such as using Federal Express to deliver your products instead of your own fleet of trucks.

Key Technologies: Communications, Networking, and Database

The kinds of applications and systems described above rely heavily on three key technologies: communications, networks, and database. These technologies have developed rapidly during the last decade and are responsible for what you can accomplish with IT. Much of the information and knowledge of organizations is now stored in machine-readable **databases**, huge repositories of all types of corporate information.

A More Contemporary Framework

The Gorry–Scott Morton framework has been a unifying paradigm for the information systems field for three decades. But, we are now confronted with many more types of systems and new technology than when this original framework was developed. The systems we have just discussed may be used by an individual, a workgroup, or the entire organization,

Who Needs a Ticket?

Continental Airlines was the first trunk airline in the industry to offer ticketless flying on a significant number of its domestic flights. It was closely followed by United. Instead of printing the tickets on normal ticket stock and mailing them to travelers, the ticket is a record in a computer database. ValuJet, a small regional airline based in Atlanta, began using "E-tickets" (E for electronic, of course) a few years ago, and Southwest Airlines started offering them on all flights in January of 1995. The airlines hope to save millions of dollars from not issuing and processing paper tickets.

E-tickets are aimed at frequent flyers on business trips. A traveler can make reservations, buy tickets, arrange refunds, and change routes by using the phone and a credit card. You do not have to worry about picking up a paper document or leaving (or losing) your ticket. With an E-ticket, United lets you change your flight up to an hour before departure (of course, there may be penalties, but you can charge them to your credit card). If you request it, you will receive a printed itinerary showing your flights, but no tickets. You can ask for a receipt by mail or fax. At the counter the day of the flight, you must identify yourself with a photo I.D. or a passport. (It is interesting that you don't need a photo to buy a regular ticket!)

It will take time for E-tickets to catch on as only about 50% of travel agencies have reservations systems that are compatible with them. However, the trend is clear; in a few years airline tickets will disappear. What other opportunities are there to replace documents with an electronic record?

or they may be interorganizational systems (IOSs) which connect one or more organizations. A useful framework for information technology for this text appears in Figure 3-2.

As the figure illustrates, information technology supports individuals, workgroups, organizations, and linkages among organizations. Individuals use this technology to help execute managerial tasks like designing the organization, formulating corporate strategy, making decisions, and so on. The changing technology we described in the section above enables the organization to develop applications to support all the tasks involved in managing the firm. The key parts of this framework are:

• A focus on the organization as the most important component of the study of information technology.

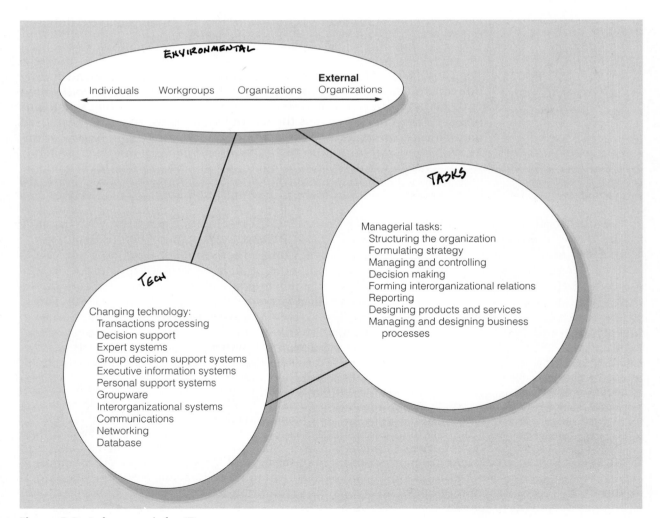

Figure 3-2 A framework for IT.

- The role of technology in supporting managerial tasks.
- The pervasive nature of technology in the organization.

You should keep this framework in mind as we learn about its various components in the rest of the text.

THE BASICS OF INFORMATION SYSTEMS

Some Generic Types of Systems

Figure 3-3 illustrates three different kinds of information systems. A transactions processing system, shown in Figure 3-3(a), processes input provided by a user, such as the fact that a client purchased a certain number of shares of AT&T. The input is first edited for errors and corrected, if necessary. For example, if the person doing the input typed *ATR* and there is no such stock, the system would ask for the data to be typed again. The input then becomes immediate output (a purchase confirmation for the customer) and is used to modify the database of stock records in the system. Input can also be used to request the retrieval of information stored in the system, such as the customer's entire stock portfolio.

Files containing data are a major component of the information system. The files correspond to the information kept in folders, file cabinets,

MANAGEMENT PROBLEM 3-1

Dave Masters is vice president of manufacturing for Siliconix, an electronic components manufacturer. Siliconix runs most of its production control and factory systems on an IBM mainframe computer. The firm has just purchased another company that makes similar components, but the newly purchased division runs its applications on several Alpha workstations made by Digital Equipment Corporation.

Masters has to decide what to do about the different computer applications. The staff of the corporate management department wants to make the new division feel welcome and does not want to upset its employees. Staff members argue that the workstation systems should be left in place. Masters feels that his present IBM mainframe system is superior to the applications at the new division.

To complicate matters further, Masters's assistant, a recent M.B.A. graduate with a lot of personal computer experience, has recommended a third approach. He suggests that Siliconix develop a new production control system in the recently purchased division, using personal computers connected to a local area network, and eliminate the alpha computers. The assistant has even suggested that the firm study downsizing the IBM mainframe and consider one architecture for the firm based on client-server computing.

What do you recommend? How should Masters go about making his decision?

Figure 3-3
Three types of
information systems:
(a) transactions system
(b) decision system
(c) communications
system.

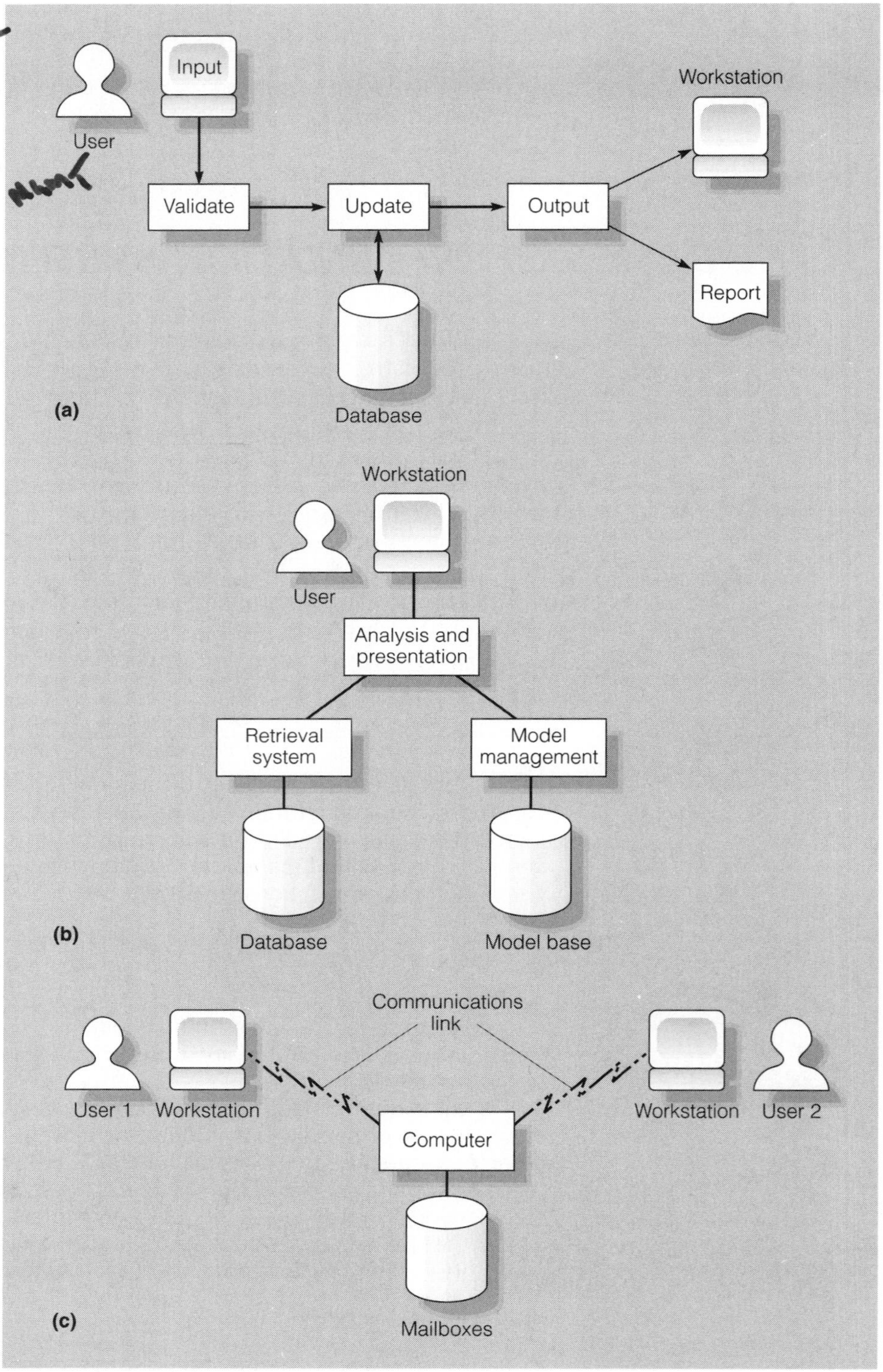

or notebooks in a manual information system. Files are a part of the organization's database. Information may be retrieved from a file, or the file contents may be altered by modifying, adding, or deleting data in the file. We are also interested in some type of output from a system, which may be a short response to a request for information from a file or the result of elaborate computations. Output is produced in any of a number of different formats and modes of presentation, such as a printed report, a display on a screen, or a verbal response.

Figure 3-3(b) portrays a decision-oriented system. The decision maker uses a workstation to run a decision support system. The DSS software allows the user to retrieve data from the database. The same software might contain a model management subsystem allowing the user to apply different kinds of **models** to analyzing the data. The system also provides different modes for presenting the results of analyses to the decision maker.

Figure 3-3(c) illustrates a communications-oriented system. Here there are two users who communicate through a central computer, possibly one that is owned and operated by a common carrier who provides electronic mail services. Each user operates a workstation and sends messages to a file that contains electronic mailboxes for all subscribers on the system. When user 2 connects with the central computer from his or her workstation, there is a message notifying user 2 that there is new e-mail waiting to be read. User 2 can read the mail, forward it to someone else, and/or send a reply to user 1.

Using Different Types of Technology

It is helpful to distinguish among the types of information systems according to the technology employed. In a **batch** system, all input is processed at one time to produce the desired output. The input data are collected and used to update the files periodically—daily, weekly, or monthly. The data are frequently out of date in this type of system because updating is periodic, but batch processing is very economical. A payroll system is an example of an application that is often operated in batch mode, because paychecks are issued periodically. The ratio of batch processing to interactive systems is declining. Almost all new applications today involve interactive processing, even if they have some batch components. All applications in which a user works directly with a computer, virtually everything other than batch processing, is considered to be **interactive**.

An inquiry system lets us process retrieval requests for information on-line. Often inquiry systems accept and **edit** input on-line for later updating in batch mode. This input is saved in a file and is used to update the system later. A production control system could be operated in this manner to accept input from terminals on the factory floor during the day. Then, in the evening, when the computer schedule is less heavy, the files could be updated in a batch processing run.

A fully on-line system actually modifies files as the information is entered from terminals. An example of an on-line system is the American

Airlines' SABRE reservations system which supports tens of thousands of terminals throughout the world.

A **command and control** system or real-time system is one in which information has to be fed back instantaneously to control an operation. For example, sensors on a missile feed information to a computer that must process the data in time to provide guidance control for the missile.

The most popular **architecture** today is **client-server** in which a user's client workstation requests data and programs from a server, a larger computer with a great deal of storage capacity.

Table 3-3 summarizes the types of systems and their characteristics and provides an example of a typical application employing each type of technology. Note that these types of systems may be designed around a number of different kinds of hardware and software. In later chapters we shall discuss different types of architectures ranging from personal computers to massively parallel machines.

THE CASE OF CHRYSLER

Chrysler Corporation illustrates how technology has become a central component of a modern firm. It shows how IT can be used to dramatically improve operations and efficiency, and contribute to saving a company that has been near bankruptcy on two separate occasions.

The dramatic success of Japanese auto manufacturers has created a movement toward **"lean production"** and **just-in-time (JIT)** inventory.

Table 3-3
Characteristics and Applications of Different Technologies

Type of system	Characteristics	Example
Simple batch system	Updating at one point in time	Payroll
Inquiry	Update in batch, retrieve on-line, enter and edit data on-line	Production control with factory-floor input
Fully on-line	All input, output, and updating done on-line through terminals	Reservation system
Command and control	Fully on-line and instantaneous feedback to control some process	Missile launching and guidance
Client-server	Client workstations access corporate data and applications on a server	Analyzing sales data

While these two concepts are often described as synonymous, JIT is only one part of lean production. Lean production begins with a different concept of a factory than typical mass production manufacturing (Womack, Jones, and Roos, 1990). In a lean production facility, space is kept to a minimum to facilitate communications among workers. One sees very few indirect workers like quality control inspectors, people who add little value to the final product. You are likely to find only a few hour's worth of inventory at each production station (yes, this is the just-in-time inventory).

If a worker finds a defective part, he or she might tag it and send the part to a quality control area to receive a replacement part. Each worker is probably able to pull a cord to stop the assembly line if there is a problem, yet the focus is on solving problems in advance.

When developing new products, a lean firm is likely to use matrix management and design teams. The chief designer of the Honda Accord "borrowed" people from appropriate departments for the duration of the project. Key decisions are made early in design and the team is not afraid of conflict. Because manufacturing representatives are on the design team, an effort is made to see that the new product can be manufactured efficiently.

A key aspect of lean production is coordinating the supply chain. A modern automobile contains some 10,000 parts, many of which come from outside suppliers. In a lean auto plant, over 70 percent of the components are likely to be purchased from external vendors. In the Japanese auto industry, the strategy is to establish long-term relationships with suppliers. The manufacturer will help the supplier improve production and quality; savings are split between the auto maker and the suppliers. What one gives up in terms of choosing from competing suppliers has to be made up by dependable and high quality parts from the chosen suppliers.

MANAGEMENT PROBLEM 3-2

Block and Thomas, a regional stockbrokerage firm, hired a chief information officer (CIO), a senior manager who is responsible for all technology in the firm. The brokerage firm uses technology heavily as is typical in the industry. Block and Thomas has a number of systems to process stock trades and support its brokers. It also subscribes to a broker workstation system provided by a market data vendor. Each broker has a personal computer that provides a great deal of data and analytic capabilities in different windows on the screen.

The new CIO surveyed users and potential users at Block and Thomas. He concluded that in the past, users had very negative attitudes toward systems. However, the interviews he conducted convinced him that users' attitudes were now different. The users described problems but also mentioned that they were very optimistic about the potential of technology and wished they could implement the technology faster. The new CIO was surprised by the creative suggestions that came from users during the interviews.

What events do you think are responsible for the new attitudes on the part of users? How can the CIO take advantage of them?

This description of lean production has concentrated on the production process, itself. The most important component of lean production, however, continues to be management and its beliefs about how the firm should operate. The GM-Toyota experiment known as the NUMI plant in Fremont, California shows clearly how management's beliefs and attitudes affect innovation. The idea of the joint venture was that GM would learn lean production techniques from Toyota and Toyota was in overall charge of the plant with various GM managers as a part of the management team.

The plant, using rather limited automation, achieved better production results on a number of measures than plants GM was heavily automating at the time. In spite of the clear benefits of lean production, it was resisted throughout the rest of GM, contributing to the ongoing crisis at the world's largest automaker.

An excellent example of lean production and just-in-time inventory comes from Chrysler who committed itself to lean production. It already was close to Toyota in the number of parts purchased externally—about 70 percent compared to GM's 30 percent–40 percent. Lean production at Chrysler meant working with some 1600 external suppliers who ship materials to 14 car and truck assembly plants in North America. This example shows how information technology, especially communications, enabled Chrysler to achieve its production goals.

Key to lean production and JIT inventory is **Electronic Data Interchange (EDI)** in which electronic messages replace paper documents exchanged with suppliers. EDI is a common format for the electronic exchange of information between companies. In implementing lean production, Chrysler had some 17 million transactions per year with suppliers. These transactions included orders for parts, scheduling and rescheduling of deliveries, and payments upon receipt of the goods. The automaker began lean production in 1984, and by 1990, it reduced on-hand inventory from five days to 48 hours, eliminating more than $1 billion from inventories. Information technology enabled JIT by providing high-speed electronic linking with suppliers and by making it possible to handle the huge volume of transactions in a short period of time.

Chrysler also followed the model for lean production set by the Japanese. It studied components and options and redesigned them to reduce complexity. Engineers worked with suppliers to be sure parts were packaged so that they would not be damaged in transit; there was little buffer inventory to make up for a bad part. The marketing staff developed forecasts to stabilize schedules for the assembly line. A stable build schedule is important for suppliers so they know what goods to deliver and when to send them. Chrysler moved to in-sequence building to provide predictability for parts suppliers. A car begins the production process in a sequence and stays in that position until finished; you do not pull a car off the assembly line for special work.

Pay-as-Built is a program Chrysler has begun with some suppliers to further reduce transactions costs. In this program, Chrysler counts the number of cars built each day and computes the number of a vendor's parts in that car. The computers then wire payment to the vendor for the materials used during the day. If Chrysler built 1000 Jeeps with Firestone tires, it would pay Firestone for 5000 tires (four plus a spare) for that day. The vendor does not have to bill Chrysler and Chrysler has many fewer transactions to process.

Chrysler also took advantage of its JIT capabilities to reduce less-than-truckload (LTL) delivery costs by 15 percent. With a predictable schedule on what is to be built, Chrysler developed scheduled pickup loops. A carrier now follows the same route each day, picking up from multiple locations. As a result, the LTL shipments are "consolidated" and the truck is chartered to Chrysler. Much like a school bus route, the same driver makes the same stops each day. This program has allowed Chrysler to trim some in-plant inventories from two days to four to six hours.

A study of Chrysler's efforts produced an estimate of a $60 per vehicle savings for the typical assembly plant attributed to electronic data interchange. (Mukhopadhyay, Kekre and Kalathur, 1995). These savings come from reduced inventory holding cost and reductions in obsolete inventory, premium freight, and transportation costs. In addition, the researchers estimate that EDI saved $39 per vehicle in information handling costs, for a total savings of $100 per vehicle. At current production levels, the savings total $220 million each year for Chrysler.

The kind of production process described here could not function without information technology. The production automation of manufacturing systems includes forecasting, building plans and materials requirements planning, and creating the kind of stable production and advance notice required for lean production and JIT to work. Because the flow of parts has very little room for error, communications to suppliers must be instantaneous. Electronic linking and communications and electronic customer/supplier relationships are key to making JIT work. These design variables also contribute to efficiency, for example, through the electronic linking of the pay-as-built program.

What has happened to Chrysler's inventory? Where has $1 billion worth of goods gone? Chrysler now has a virtual inventory and this inventory is no longer stockpiled at Chrysler plants. Instead, the inventory exists at suppliers and is linked to Chrysler through an electronic network. This network informs suppliers when goods are needed, and they in turn respond. But wait, what about the suppliers? Do they really have Chrysler's inventory in their warehouses? If Chrysler provides a supplier with predictable demand, then the supplier can practice JIT with its suppliers all the way back through the value chain for a product. Greater connectivity throughout the production system has driven out physical inventory and substituted the electronic flows of information. Certainly IT alone is not enough. The companies involved have to make many other changes in their operations. However, the technology described here is a crucial enabler of lean production and JIT inventory.

CHAPTER SUMMARY

1. A framework helps to conceptualize a diverse field like information systems.

2. Simon and Gorry and Scott Morton provide insights on the different types of systems and decisions that one finds in an organization. The distinction between structured and unstructured decisions is important as we think about applying IT to problems in organizations.

3. An organization is a complex entity with many different components; the environment for applying technology is quite complex. As a result, we find a variety of technologies in place in firms. The prototypes include transactions processing, decision support, and communications-oriented applications.

4. We shall use a framework in the text that stresses the organization and its components: individuals workgroups and links to external organizations. Individuals face a number of managerial tasks and it is possible to support these tasks and the organization through a rich variety of technologies.

5. The Chrysler case illustrates how a variety of information technologies enabled management to implement a lean production system, a system that has probably saved Chrysler from disappearing as a U.S. auto manufacturer.

IMPLICATIONS FOR MANAGEMENT

As a manager, you are interested in results. Why should you care about different kinds of technology? You will be using this technology to produce results, to solve problems and to initiate new strategies. You may restructure the organization around IT. Unless you are fortunate to be starting a new enterprise, you will encounter a collection of hardware and software that has grown in the organization over time. Some of Chrysler's systems were first developed in the 1960s; they have been heavily modified, but they are still in use. You cannot afford to discard all old technology and replace it with new IT overnight, any more than Chrysler can rebuild its manufacturing plants every year. You will have to adapt and use a combination of old and new technologies to accomplish your objectives.

KEY WORDS

Architecture
Batch
Client-server
Command and control
Database
Edit
Electronic Data Interchange
  (EDI)
Electronic mail
Framework
Graphical user interface
  (GUI)

Interactive
Interorganizational system
Just-in-time (JIT)
Lean production
Models
On-line transactions processing
  (OLTP)
Output
Personal computer
Update
Virtual components

RECOMMENDED READING

Gurbaxani, V., and S. Whang. "The Impact of Information Systems on Organizations and Markets," *Communications of the ACM,* vol. 34, no. 1 (January 1991), pp. 59–73. (An interesting article on the impact of IT on the marketplace.)

Mukhopadhyay, T., S. Kekre, and S. Kalathur. "Business Value of Information Technology: A Study of Electronic Data Interchange," *MIS Quarterly,* vol. 19, no. 2 (June 1995), pp. 137–156. (An interesting study of the impact of EDI at Chrysler.)

Stohr, E., and B. Konsynski. *Information Systems and Decision Processes.* Los Alamitos, Calif.: IEEE Computer Society Press, 1992. (An excellent collection of papers on how information technology can support organizations and decisions.)

DISCUSSION QUESTIONS

1. What is the primary appeal of the personal computer?
2. Is there any role for batch processing, given today's technology?
3. Why do you suppose inquiry-only applications were developed instead of fully on-line systems?

4. What are the advantages and disadvantages of fully on-line computer systems?

5. How do backup requirements differ between batch and on-line systems?

6. What applications, if any, exist for command and control systems in business?

7. What is the role of communications in an organization?

8. What are the drawbacks of mathematical models being applied to management problems?

9. What are interorganizational systems?

10. Why has the client-server architecture become popular?

11. What role does information technology have in managing a global business?

12. What are the social issues involved in having massive files of personal data available on-line?

13. What are the major differences among transactions processing and decision support systems?

14. Why are so many personal computer systems developed in users' departments rather than under the control of an internal information systems department?

15. One critic has suggested that management information can never be automated. What is your reaction to this statement?

16. Examine a computer application with which you are familiar. Describe its purpose, input, output, processing, and files.

17. Inventory control is one of the most popular computer applications. Why? What has its impact been on the economy?

18. An entire industry exists for selling information. Make a survey of some of the data for sale and classify them by functional area, such as marketing, finance, or economics.

19. How does electronic data interchange enable lean production at Chrysler?

20. What are the major advantages and disadvantages of inquiry systems in which data are captured on-line but files are updated later—say, at night?

CHAPTER 3 PROJECT

INFORMATION SYSTEMS CRITIQUE

There are information systems all around us. We encounter them at the university, in stores and banks, when making airline, hotel, or rental-car reservations, and in many other aspects of our daily routine. For this project, choose an information system and critique it.

First, describe the system: What are its objectives? Who are the users? Then trace the input of the system to determine who inputs what information. Look at the output of the system. Is it a physical document? Often, systems have to store data on a more or less permanent basis in files or in a database. Can you figure out what is in the database for your system?

Draw a diagram of the input, processing, database, and outputs of your system. What are the major strengths of the system? Do you see any problems with it? What can you suggest to improve the system?

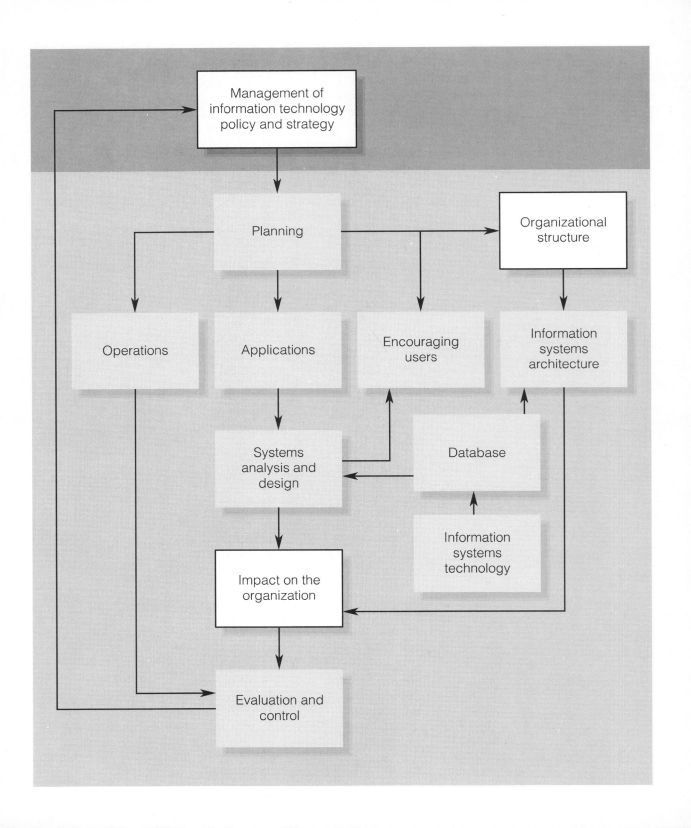

Organizational Issues

In this part we emphasize how technology is used to create flexibility in the organization and how it provides new variables for managers to use in designing organizations. IT offers new ways to accomplish both traditional and more modern requirements for organizing. No longer is a physical location and time as important in constructing organizations. Technology can substitute for physical proximity and contact in a number of situations. *The design of information technology and the design of organizations have become the same task.*

Top management has a key role to play in the management of information processing activities in the organization. There is much emphasis today on using information technology as a part of corporate strategy, a topic that is addressed in depth in Chapter 5. We also see how difficult it is to sustain a competitive advantage when you have achieved it. Once you decide to be competitive with technology you must continue to invest and develop new systems and services.

In this part, we also discuss information systems policy. What are the key areas for the involvement of top management? What policy should top management establish for the information systems effort in the organization? A successful information services function begins with strong and effective leadership at the top levels of the organization.

The last chapter in this section examines IT and international business. Firms are developing their international markets in order to grow and prosper; they are adopting a global strategy. What is the impact of IT on international business? What special problems does operating globally create for managing information technology?

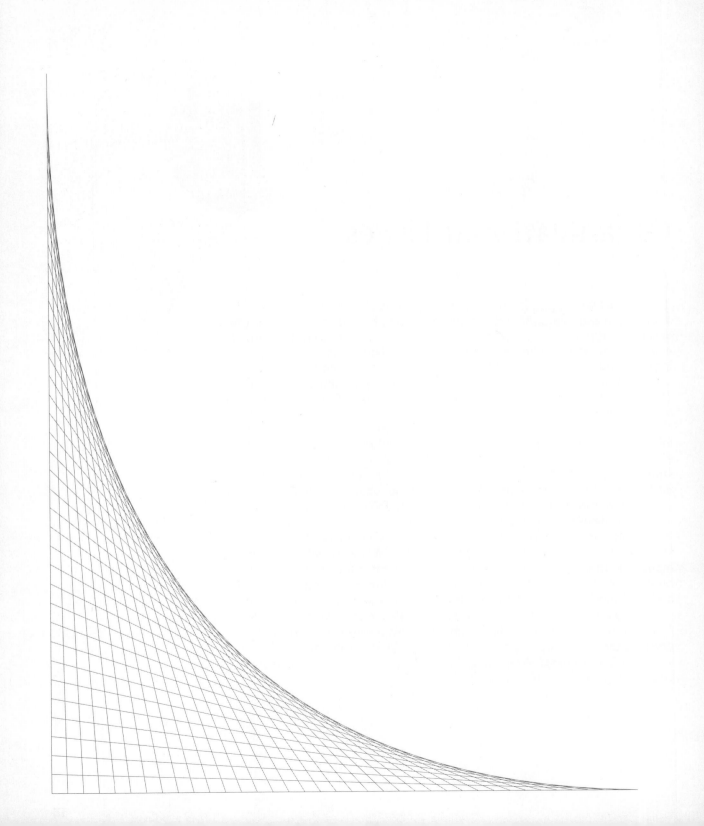

CHAPTER **4**

The Impact of Information Technology on the Organization

OBJECTIVES

1. **Learning to manage information technology.**

   Information technology provides management with the ability to make major changes in organizations. You can design entirely new organization structures or redesign existing ones. We develop systems to have an intended effect, but they may also have unintended consequences, which management needs to consider. As you read this chapter, think about management's expectations when sponsoring the design of individual applications in the securities industry. Do you think these managers expected the second-order effects on the industry? How could they have predicted what this total stock of systems has created?

2. **Preparing to apply technology.**

   The process of designing a system and the results of implementing it dramatically impact organization. Some of the systems described in this chapter are now institutionalized as they become an integral part of the operations of a firm. The first airline reservation systems were developed in the 1960s and it is inconceivable that American or United could operate today without their systems. These systems have not been replaced in their entirety, rather, pieces of them are continually changed and updated. When you participate in designing this type of system, you are creating an application that will influence the firm for years to come.

3. **Transforming the organization.**

   In this chapter we see how technology can be used to dramatically restructure organizations, permanently changing the way we do business. In particular, note how the technology has contributed to **flexibility** when looking at the organization as a whole, even though users may consider individual applications to be inflexible. The information technology variables discussed in this chapter have the greatest potential for transforming the organization, because they provide a way for you to significantly change the structure of an existing organization or design an entirely new, nontraditional one.

BENEFITS FOR THE ORGANIZATION

What benefits can you expect from information technology? IT can affect the structure of the organization, its strategy, its revenues and expenses, and the individuals working within it.

Gaining a Competitive Edge

A number of organizations use technology to gain a **competitive advantage** and design creative applications that allow them to compete more effectively. In Chapter 5 we examine some of these applications. A good example of strategic use of IT comes in the drug supply industry. McKesson Corporation developed a system called Economost that increased and protected its share of the market. The first version of the system featured hand-held terminals used by McKesson customers, generally drugstores. When a product was out of stock or the stock was low, an employee checking store shelves read a product code from the shelf label and keyed it into the terminal. On completion of the inventory, the terminal was used to transmit the order over telephone lines to McKesson's central computer.

Over the next eight years, McKesson enhanced the system and included various terminal types for different needs. There is also a bar-code scanner for picking up a product code directly from a bar code on the shelf label, eliminating the keying operation. Since the system "knows" what products are stored in which aisles, it creates packing lists ordered by shelf location so that items for the same section of the store can be packed in the same container.

McKesson also offers a claims service for programs such as Medicare. Individuals apply for and receive plastic identification cards similar to a credit card. On paying a nominal amount, say $1 for the prescription, they use the credit card to prepare a claims form, which the drugstore uses to obtain the remaining payment from the insurance company. A McKesson subsidiary processes the claims and the entire application tends to keep customers coming back to the same drugstore.

Increasing Revenues

Some firms use technology to generate revenue, for example, by making information products available through computer systems. There is an abundance of financial databases and services to which one can subscribe. It is possible to obtain hundreds of types of data about companies and their financial conditions. Mead Data, a subsidiary of Elsevier, offers a system called Lexis/Nexis that contains citations for various court decisions and an archive of articles from a number of newspapers and periodicals. The system is used extensively in law offices where attorneys and their assistants search for past decisions that may be relevant to the legal problems at hand. Our MBA students and faculty also have access to the system to gather corporate data. The Internet also provides a vast amount of information, though it is hard to find and can seem very disorganized at times.

Reducing Costs

One traditional use of computers in organizations is for cost savings. Companies automate clerical tasks to reduce costs. Insurance companies and banks generate products that are really information; bills, notices, renewals, and so on represent output of products that must be printed and distributed to customers. Some of these systems eliminated existing positions, whereas others reduced the number of additional employees needed in the future.

Manufacturing firms save money by using computers to control their inventory and production. Chrysler used information technology to help it implement just-in-time manufacturing and lean production; we saw in the last chapter that it reduced inventories by over a billion dollars. Systems also control machines in a factory and schedule and monitor production.

Improving Profits

If the use of IT either increases revenues or decreases costs, it should contribute to increased profitability, all other things held constant. In many applications it is very hard to show that IT has an impact on the "bottom line" because so many other factors influence profits. Increasing revenues and/or decreasing costs should certainly contribute to profitability, as long as the amounts involved exceed the operating and capital recovery costs for the IT application.

Improving Quality

One reason to use technology is to improve the quality of output: computer-aided design is a good example. An engineer or draftsperson uses a workstation to create engineering drawings. He or she stores the drawing on a computer file; it can be recalled later for easy modification. A system like this will also plot a drawing copy; changes are redrawn in minutes. The system reduces much of the drudgery of design work and has dramatically reduced the need for draftspeople.

A recent advertisement shows a new Boeing 777 airliner; underneath the plane is a box a little larger than one you might get when you order a take-out pizza. The caption is "This is the plane and the box it came in." The box, of course, is a computer workstation. Boeing claims that the 777 is its first "paperless airliner" and they designed the entire plane using sophisticated computer-aided design programs. Not only could engineers design parts, they could bring them all together on the computer to see that the various designs fit properly. In this instance, the technology has certainly improved quality; it also has reduced the length of time required to develop an airplane and its development costs.

Another good example of using IT to improve quality comes with electronic data interchange (EDI). Firms using EDI connect to each other electronically as we saw with Brun Passot in Chapter 1 and Chrysler in the last chapter. A typical application is order entry and acknowledgment. One company keys an order into its order processing system and that order is transmitted electronically to a supplier. The supplier acknowledges receipt of the order electronically, and the rest of the transaction is completed using electronic communications. The alternative to this procedure is to have each company involved in the transaction key information into a computer at each step from ordering to processing final payment for the merchandise involved. The use of EDI contributes to quality by reducing the opportunity for errors since data are entered only once.

Creating New Opportunities

There may be no other way to do some tasks than to use technology. How else could an airline associate a passenger's name with all the legs of a trip and have the information accessible anyplace in the world in a few seconds? The first American Airlines SABRE reservation system began working only a few months before the airline had estimated that its manual reservation procedure would break down because of overloading. There are many other applications in which, because of the complexity of the procedures, the size of the database, or the necessity to communicate across a wide geographic area, a computer system is the only way to solve a problem.

IMPACT ON ORGANIZATION STRUCTURE

Information systems exist in the context of an organization; they do not operate in isolation. There are a number of definitions of organizations. For our purposes, an **organization** is a rational coordination of activities of a group of people for the purpose of achieving some goal. The activities of the group of people are coordinated; that is, there is a joint effort. In most organizations some division of labor and a hierarchy of authority provide for the rational coordination of activities. The definition also includes the goals of the organization; there are many different types of organizations with different kinds of goals.

Formal Versus Informal Organization

The formal organization is what appears on the organization chart, usually with well-defined reporting relationships among managers and workers that describe its structure. Social organizations, on the other hand, are patterns of coordination that arise spontaneously from the interaction of a group. Social organizations have no rational coordination and generally lack explicit goals.

The informal organization is the pattern of relations and coordination among members of the formal organization that is not specified on a formal chart. It represents social interaction and is a more realistic portrayal of the formal organization, because it reflects how people actually interact. For example, a group of workers may form an informal task force using electronic mail or conferencing systems on a computer network; this task force cuts across traditional organizational boundaries and constitutes a temporary, informal organization.

We must be careful to avoid designing information systems that follow unrealistic standards and procedures. We may find that these prescribed rules are not actually followed and that our system is unworkable because we have adhered too closely to formal organizational considerations. It is hard to observe and describe the informal organization as it depends on the personalities of specific individuals and patterns of behavior that have developed over time.

MODERN ORGANIZATIONS

Unfortunately, we cannot point to one unified picture that has emerged from various approaches to the study of organizations. We still are confronted with many different ideas about organizations and the way they operate.

Organizational Structure and Design

A number of writers studied organizations from the standpoint of their structure to understand how to design better organizations. These approaches help us to understand how information is used in the organization and to appreciate what kinds of changes might be created by the introduction of new information systems.

Uncertainty   One of the major factors influencing organizations is **uncertainty**. Many authors suggest that managers try to eliminate or reduce uncertainty. An organization and its managers confront many different types of uncertainty. There are frequently technical uncertainties about whether a new product can be manufactured or whether or not it will work. Market uncertainties exist when the firm does not know how a product will be received, potential demand, response from competitors, and so on. The internal management of an organization also creates uncertainty. Key personnel may leave or individuals may not adequately perform their assigned tasks. Thus, the organization and its managers face many different types and degrees of uncertainty.

The importance of uncertainty is seen by examining organizations that face differing environments. Consider a chip manufacturer like Intel confronted with the dynamic environment of technological change versus the staid, conservative atmosphere of a regulated utility facing virtually no uncertainty. There is some evidence that uncertainty is most effectively handled by decentralizing decision making to a level in the organization with information to resolve it.

Specialization   Another major consideration in organizational design is specialization. Are specialized skills or conditions required for some tasks? Consider the activity of running a complicated machine tool versus sweeping the building; certainly, the former requires a specialist. From our standpoint, the information services department is highly specialized and requires a level of technological proficiency on the part of its staff.

Coordination   When there is specialization, one task of management is to coordinate the diverse specialties to achieve the goals of the organization. Management must balance differing orientations and resolve disputes between specialized subunits. For example, the marketing department may want to produce a particular item in each style and color for every warehouse. This plan is best for reducing uncertainty and providing good customer service. On the other hand, manufacturing may want to make products of the same color and model, because this procedure reduces the uncertainties in production; that is, there are fewer setups and smoother production runs.

Management must resolve these differences and coordinate the specialists. There are a number of integrating mechanisms to reduce the effects of differentiation or specialization. Sometimes organizations create special liaison positions or even departments to foster coordination. A major advertising agency has a group of expediters who see that all the details of purchasing advertising time and space are organized and that the ads appear in the right place at the right time. We shall see later how information technology can also be used to help managers coordinate groups in the organization.

Interdependence   The last factor we shall consider in organizational structure is interdependence; that is, how do the different departments or subunits within the organization depend on each other? Thompson (1967) has described three types of **mutual dependence**. **Pooled interdependence** occurs when two organizations depend on each other because they are all components of a larger organization; one unit does not depend directly on another. For example, the different divisions of a conglomerate exhibit pooled interdependence.

Sequential interdependence occurs when the output of one unit is the input to another. For example, the painting and finishing department depends on outputs from component assembly. We can view each succeeding station on an assembly line as an example of sequential interdependence.

Reciprocal interdependence occurs when the output of each unit becomes the input for the other. For example, a student depends on the professor to explain concepts in class so that she can do her assignment and the professor depends on students to prepare for class.

Interdependence is an important consideration in organizational design. The type of interdependence affects the amount of power one unit has in the organization. In designing an organization, or modifying the design (for example, through the development of a new information system), various interdependencies must be coordinated. The easiest type of interdependence to handle is pooled, the next hardest is sequential, and the most difficult is reciprocal.

Mintzberg's Model

Mintzberg (1979) has developed an elegant theory of how organizations are structured. First, he conceptualizes the organization as consisting of five major components (see Figure 4-1). The **operating core** carries out the basic work of the organization; in a manufacturing organization it produces the product. It also handles all the support tasks necessary for production.

At the next level in the organization is an administrative component that consists of three groups. At the top is the **strategic apex**, senior-level executives responsible for all the operations of the firm. Below the strategic apex, is the **middle line**, which links the top group to the operating core. At the left of the middle line is the **technostructure**, where analysts standardize the work of others. For example, we would find operations research analysts in the technostructure.

Figure 4-1

The five basic parts of organizations.

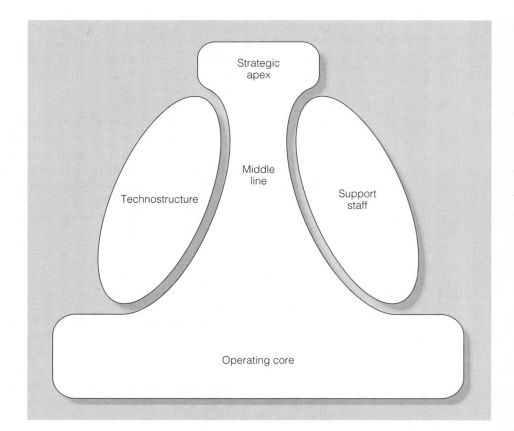

The last group is the **support staff** on the right of the figure. This group supports the functioning of the operating core through indirect activities, for example, the research and development organization, legal counsel, and similar groups.

Using some of the coordination considerations discussed earlier in this chapter and further analysis, Mintzberg modifies the basic model of an organization to describe five typical structures: simple structure, machine bureaucracy, professional bureaucracy, divisionalized form, and adhocracy. In each of these types of organizations, one of the five groups in Figure 4-1 is dominant in importance. His theory is very appealing and provides a convenient framework for thinking about organizations.

It is interesting to note the role of information processing in the Mintzberg scheme (he does not discuss this activity in depth). For many organizations, basic information processing systems really belong in the operating core; the firm needs these systems to function effectively. The systems analysis and design activity, however, probably fits best in the technostructure because this group concentrates on improving the work of others. Systems designers must develop a system, which is a form of research and development, and then in many cases must successfully transfer it to the operating core.

In other instances, a system is designed for middle management, the strategic apex, or even the support staff. The analyst's job then involves a great deal of boundary-spanning activity to integrate activities across a number of organizational boundaries. In fact, many systems are likely to involve information that flows across major organizational subunits.

THE IMPACT OF IT ON THE ORGANIZATION

Can information technology have an impact on organizational structure? Information can be used to reduce uncertainty and to coordinate different individuals and groups. Information helps people function with interdependence. It can also be used to create more flexibility in the organization and design new organizational forms through IT enabled design variables.

How Technology Creates Flexibility

Many individuals think that information technology creates more rigid procedures in firms. Can it also be shown that systems have created flexibility? It is certainly true that individual systems have often been associated with rigidity, particularly **legacy systems**, old systems that generally run on mainframes, that have been around for many years doing critical tasks for the firm. Due to the demand for new systems and the cost of creating replacements, there is often little incentive to change these rigid applications. Changing any computer or communications system is a difficult job. A major system may contain hundreds of thousands or even millions of program statements; and change frequently produces errors. We have a great deal of flexibility in the design of new systems, but many older technologies in place are rigid.

What Is Organizational Flexibility?

Flexibility is the ability to adapt when confronted with new circumstances. A flexible organization defends quickly against threats and moves rapidly to take advantage of opportunities. Flexibility provides the organization with the ability to adapt to change and respond quickly to market forces and uncertainty in its environment.

Technology changes the pace of work. It has speeded up order routing and processing on the stock exchange. Technology has made it much faster to search a library book catalog, to communicate with someone at a remote location, and to perform a number of tasks. Technology can also be used to shorten product development cycles. In general, technology speeds up the pace of work and increases the capacity of the organization to process information.

Information technology also alters the space and time boundaries of work. Using electronic mail and computer conferencing, colleagues working on a project do not have to be in the same physical location. Even people who work together in the same office can communicate easily if traveling. With a portable computer and modem, you can conduct some kinds of business from virtually any location at any time of the day or night.

Thus, we see that technology has the ability to change the pace of work and to alter **time and space boundaries** for work. These impacts of the technology can be viewed as increasing organizational flexibility. With properly designed systems, the organization can increase its ability to respond to customers, competitors, and the environment in general.

Impact on Flexibility

Table 4-1 describes the history and impact of technology in the airline and securities industries.

Information Technology Runs the Airline

In the early days of airline travel, few people ventured forth on the relatively small, propeller aircraft. If you wanted to make a reservation, everything was done manually, and there was no actual record associating your name with your flight. The airline allocated a number of seats to the departure city and to a few other cities. When the number of available seats began to dwindle, a reservations office would have to call a central location to be sure it could sell a seat. One never knew for sure if he or she had a reservation because a name was never associated with a reservations record.

In the late 1950s, American Airlines realized that its manual reservation process could not keep up with the expected growth in travel. At this time almost all civilian information systems ran in batch mode, that is, all data were collected at once, key punched, and used to update computer files at a later point in time.

Table 4-1
Organizational Flexibility in the Airline and Securities Industries

Boundaries	Time	Nature and pace of work	Responsiveness
AIRLINE CRS STAGE 1			
Remove boundary of manual centralized processing; make reservation from anywhere	Make reservation anytime	Confirmed reservation made instantaneously	Alter schedules in response to loads
AIRLINE CRS STAGE 2			
Boundary for making reservation shifts from airline to agent; airport boarding pass moved to travel agency	Extra service by agent, e.g., 24-hour assistance	Travel agent becomes more productive	Yield management programs allow instantaneous adjustment to demand for seats
SECURITIES FIRM BACK OFFICE			
Made data available to brokers on-line	Eliminate need to close exchanges early	Greatly speed processing of trades	Create new products and services
SECURITIES INDUSTRY TRADING AT EXCHANGES AND MEMBER FIRMS			
Able to route orders without intervention of floor broker; floor becomes an extension of brokerage office; may remove need for floor, e.g., NASDAQ, London Stock Exchange	Movement toward 24-hour trading; passing the book around the world for currency; New York City to London to Tokyo; trade anytime	Able to execute trading decisions instantaneously	Enable new investment strategies

Such an approach would not work for an airline reservation system because people throughout the country need to be able to update and inquire against files instantly. Fortunately, IBM had at this time completed a defense system called SAGE, which allows operators to interact with real-time data from radar. The operator could display different information processed by computers from a console.

IBM and American Airlines established a joint project to develop an automated airline reservation system that would be on-line. IBM would develop the control programs that managed on-line processing, while American would write the applications program that provided the logic for making an airline reservations. Surprisingly, the system was completed shortly ahead of schedule, though with a large cost overrun, and provided a basis for the development of others like it by competing airlines.

The computerized airline reservation systems maintain a large database that contains the names of passengers associated with their flights.

In the early days these systems were known as Passenger Name Reservation (PNR) systems because the idea of keeping your name with your flight was so novel. The difference in service is incredible when the computerized reservation systems (CRSs) are compared with their predecessor manual system.

What was the first-order impact of the airline reservation systems? First, they removed the limitation of a manual, centralized reservations group. In terms of time and space, you can make a reservation anytime of the day or night from virtually anyplace in the world.

The features of these systems contributed to their second-order impact: a competitive advantage based on customer service. Airlines with reservation systems could provide better service to their customers. They could also better manage the airline because they had historical data on reservations and boardings. Using their reservation system as a base, airlines have added many functions ranging from meeting special dietary requests to balancing the loading of the aircraft.

A third-order effect is that one would have great difficulty starting up an airline without a reservation system. Donald Burr, chairman of People Express, pointed out the lack of a decent reservation system as one of the factors that contributed to the demise of his airline. People Express had too few reservation lines; it was not unusual for customers to be unable to reach them from early morning until late evening because of the number of callers.

In addition, in recent years the airlines developed yield management systems; these programs look at future flights and dynamically adjust the number of special-fare seats depending on the number of reservations so far. Burr felt that the airlines could use their systems to target People's flights and competitors could selectively lower their fares on competing routes and still keep up their margins on other routes.

Co-opting the Travel Agent

For several years the airline industry waited for an agreement on a common reservation system to be placed in travel agents' offices. Finally, United and American decided not to wait and began placing terminals connected to their systems in travel agencies. This move proved to be a tremendous benefit for both the agent and the airline.

One first-order impact was a dramatic increase in the **productivity** of the travel agent. One of the most tedious and time-consuming tasks in an agency is writing tickets; the agency CRS came with ticket printers. Once the agent made a reservation, he or she could have the ticket printed automatically. Immediately each employee of the agency could write more tickets in a day.

Another major first-order impact is the change in organizational structure and boundaries for reservations. The travel agent has become an extension of the airline's own reservations operation. Enhancements to the systems allowed agents to issue boarding passes with tickets. Thus, part of the boarding process has moved from the airport to the travel agency. Information technology takes care of the first part of boarding the plane well before the day of the flight. Today some airlines are introducing electronic tickets; you do not receive a physical ticket and the airline does not have to process your ticket! What will the impact of E-tickets be on travel agents?

Each airline tried various approaches to using a CRS to increase its own bookings. First, the host carrier (the airline whose system is used by the agent) would list his or her flights first. That is, on American's SABRE system, American's flights between two cities always appeared first. Because over 90 percent of flights are booked from the first reservation screen, the host airline enjoyed a tremendous advantage.

Delta and other airlines complained about this inherent bias in computerized reservation systems. The Department of Transportation investigated and issued a series of rules requiring listings that did not unduly favor the host carrier. The carriers made the changes, grudgingly. By this time, American and United had spent well over $250 million each on their systems and they felt they deserved the rewards from that investment.

A second-order impact of the system is this revenue-generation feature. In addition to this "halo" effect of more bookings from CRS-equipped agencies, the airlines with agency installations gained revenue. When an agent using American books a ticket on Northwest, Northwest must pay American a booking fee of about $2.00 to $2.50 per leg. There is one story of a travel agent in Minneapolis who books most flights on Northwest, but uses the United Apollo system. In one year he generated $1,000,000 in fees for United.

The sale prices show the value of the CRS. When TWA was last sold, one attractive features was its reservation system. Recent suggested prices place the market value of Apollo and SABRE at $1 billion to $1.5 billion. A third-order impact is the tremendous power and revenue potential created by these systems.

The airline CRSs provide flexibility for the airlines, travel agents, and travelers. Technology has impacted the tasks of booking a flight and managing passengers from reservation to flight completion. Service is speeded up and is more convenient. Boundaries from time and space in making a reservation have changed as has the entire process of booking a flight and boarding a plane. Not only does the airline CRS example address flexibility, it also illustrates the first-, second-, and third-order impacts of information technology.

Technology Transforms the Securities Industry

The history of the stock exchanges has been constant increases in volume. From an information processing standpoint, of course, the value of a transaction does not affect back-office functions. If one share or a million shares change hands, the same processing is required. In the 1960s the New York Stock Exchange was closing early because it could not keep up with the paperwork for processing and clearing trades. Yet the volume then was a fraction of today's volume.

As shown in Table 4-1, the securities industry invested in extensive automation of back-office functions, first for handling trades and then to provide information for stockbrokers and traders. Data became available on-line to account representatives, showing them their clients' position so that they could provide better service. These systems eliminated a bottle-neck of time in processing by speeding up the flow of transactions. The New York Stock Exchange developed systems to facilitate routing orders faster to the floor without requiring a floor trader. Brokerage firms also streamline their communications with floor brokers so orders get to the broker quickly. A second-order impact of this technology is its ability to make possible new trading strategies; for example, program trading is greatly facilitated by rapid order execution.

Program trading involves buying or selling a basket of stocks that mir-rors a stock index like the S&P 500. At the same time, the program trader must buy or sell the corresponding futures index on the Chicago exchange. The trader sells the more expensive of the two and uses the proceeds to buy the less expensive. This kind of arbitrage has generated a great deal of trading volume and controversy.

First, program trades are created through computer programs that contain the logic of the program trader. These programs search for an im-balance in the price of the stock index future and the underlying basket of stocks that make up the index then notify the trader who can generate the appropriate buy and sell orders. The orders are probably created by the computer and sent to automated exchange systems for execution. Because the price difference exists for only a short period of time, it is important for execution to be as fast as possible. If an order is too large for an automated exchange system, the trader can generate a large number of

MANAGEMENT PROBLEM 4-1

The Major Life Insurance Company had two committees of senior managers concerned with information technology. The heads of divisions formed an ex-ecutive steering committee; its job was to review budgets and plans and pro-vide guidance to the corporate manager of information services.

The coordinating committee consisted of the top IS staff members in each division; its job was to prevent extensive duplication among applications and systems. All hardware had to be purchased through the office of the corporate manager of information services.

All the personnel involved felt the two committees were not working well. One manager said, "The coordinating committee members just report on what they are doing; they don't want advice on whether their ideas are any good. There are no decisions made."

The executive steering committee did not seem to make any decisions, either. At one meeting they heard about a new technology, and at the next they might be asked to approve the purchase of a new, large computer—a re-quest they could never turn down.

What restructuring can you suggest for these two committees?

trading documents for floor brokers using the computer again. Various studies of program trading do not blame it for increased market volatility or reduced liquidity. In terms of third-order impacts of the technology, it seems logical there is an effect on volatility and liquidity as technology facilitates large-sized holdings and trades.

When the stock market crashed in October 1987, one mutual fund sold more than $1 billion worth of securities. Without information technology, could that firm have managed a multibillion-dollar portfolio? Without technology, could it have generated enough sell orders to liquidate a billion dollars worth of securities? Other firms that day liquidated securities worth hundreds of millions of dollars. The combined impact and demand for liquidity sent prices downward, possibly reinforced by another tool called portfolio insurance. It is possible that program trades and portfolio insurance interacted early during the crash to put pressure on prices. (Later, however, price information was running so far behind that program trading does not seem to have been possible.)

Natural Growth Generates an Impact

Technology dramatically impacted the securities business. At first, the use of technology was for routine transactions processing. Soon the back-office information appeared valuable for brokers so they could know their customers' positions. Traders also adopted technology to facilitate new trading strategies. The confluence of all of these trends has led to a highly automated industry critically dependent on information technology.

Several exchanges are entirely automated or moving in that direction. The "Big Bang" in London, which eliminated fixed brokerage rates and encouraged off-floor trading, has emptied the floor of the exchange. The NASDAQ computer system for over-the-counter stocks in the U.S. has no actual exchange floor; technology has eliminated the need for a physical place to meet to buy or sell stock. By 1995 there were days in which the volume of stocks traded on the NASDAQ exceeded the volume on the New York Stock Exchange.

Today several exchanges offer after-hours trading, even twenty-four-hour trading may become routine. After-hours trading will take place only through computers and communications networks. Within a few years, it should be possible to trade securities from virtually anyplace in the world, anytime of day or night. Technology will completely remove time and space requirements for trading.

Conclusions

These examples show how information technology impacts organizational flexibility in two major industries. It undoubtedly contributes to flexibility in other firms and industries as well. Technology has the ability to change the nature of work, primarily by speeding it up, and to alter the time and place of work. In some instances, flexibility has surprises and unanticipated consequences. The government placed certain requirements on the securities markets and on the ways in which airlines can use their computerized reservation systems. Certainly we want to encourage flexibility, but we have to anticipate the impact of technology on our firm and industry.

CREATING NEW TYPES OF ORGANIZATIONS

In Chapter 1 we introduced the T-Form organization, a new type of organization enabled by information technology. The T-Form firm is created through the use of different design variables. A variable is something that takes on different values, for example, one calculates the interest payment (P) on a simple loan by taking the interest rate (i) times the loan's outstanding balance (B) or $P = i B$. In this equation, P, i, and B are all variables; they can take on different values. The interest rate might vary for different customers or types of loans. Obviously the outstanding balance will differ among loans.

For organizations, we have design variables like the span of control, a number that can take on different values. An organization that has chosen a span of control of 7 subordinates for each manager will be hierarchical while one that chooses a span of 20 will be much flatter.

Trading on the Internet

It is now possible to trade stocks directly on the Internet as shown below. This company is not making a market; it still executes the trade on a stock exchange just as any other broker. However, this and other companies are offering extremely low commissions compared to full service brokerage firms. How do you think these kinds of services will impact the securities industry?

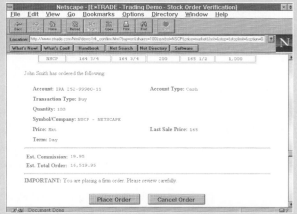

Table 4-2 contains examples of key organization design variables that you can use to build organizations. This table contains two types of variables: those labeled conventional and a set of variables that come from information technology. Information technology is defined to include computers, communications, video conferencing, artificial intelligence, virtual reality, fax, cellular and wireless phones and pagers, etc.

The problem with conventional organization design literature is its failure to recognize the new design variables enabled by information technology. In the case of linking mechanisms, IT such as e-mail or groupware can be used instead of conventional solutions like task forces or liaison agents. The new IT enabled variables may be totally distinct from traditional design variables as we shall see when we examine "virtual corporations." IT enabled variables may also be an extension of traditional variables, as in the case of linking mechanisms.

Table 4-2 arrays the conventional design variables drawn from the literature on organization design with new kinds of IT design variables. The first column of the table groups conventional design variables into four categories: structural, work process, communications, and interorganizational. Column 3 in the table presents new organizational design variables made possible through information technology. These variables are:

Structural

Virtual components: The organization can use IT to create components that do not exist in conventional form. For example, some manufacturers want parts suppliers to substitute for their inventory. The supplier is linked through electronic data interchange with the manufacturer. Using overnight delivery, it provides parts to the manufacturer just as they are needed for production. The manufacturer now has a virtual raw materials inventory owned by the supplier until it arrives for production.

MANAGEMENT PROBLEM 4-2

Boats-R-Us operates a group of 50 discount marine supply houses throughout the U.S., primarily on the East and West Coasts and around the Great Lakes. The company has both walk in and mail-order business. It has been organized traditionally as a retail store and several warehouses. A central order processing site accepts orders over 800 numbers and by mail and fax; this site distributes the order to the warehouse closest to the customer that has the products requested in stock. A large number of purchasing agents are involved in determining what to stock and in negotiating purchases.

The president of the company has read about new organizational forms enabled by information technology. The only technology in place now is the order entry and warehouse inventory system. The president would like to make Boats-R-Us both more efficient and more responsive to its customers. What new kinds of organization forms for Boats-R-Us might be enabled by information technology?

Table 4-2
Conventional and IT Design Variables

Class of Variable	Conventional Design Variables	IT Design Variables
Structural	Definition of organizational subunits	Virtual components
	Determining purpose, output of subunits	
	Reporting mechanisms	
	Linking mechanisms	Electronic linking
	Control mechanisms	
	Staffing	Technological leveling
Work Process	Tasks	Production automation
	Workflows	Electronic workflows
	Dependencies	
	Output of process	
	Buffers	Virtual components
Communications	Formal channels	Electronic Communications
	Informal communications/ collaboration	Technological matrixing
Interorganizational relations	Make versus buy decision	Electronic customer/supplier relationships
	Exchange of materials	Electronic customer/supplier relationships
	Communications mechanisms	Electronic linking

From Lucas and Baroudi, 1994

Electronic linking: Through electronic mail, electronic or video conferencing, and fax, it is possible to form links within and across all organizational boundaries. New work groups form quickly and easily.

Technological leveling: IT can substitute for layers of management and for a number of management tasks. In some bureaucratic organizations, layers of management exist to look at, edit, and approve messages that flow from the layer below them to the level above. Electronic communications can eliminate some of these layers. In addition, a manager's span of control can be increased since electronic communications can be more efficient than phone or personal contact for certain kinds of tasks, particularly those dealing with administrative matters. Technology makes it possible to increase the span of control and possibly eliminate layers in the organization, leveling it in the process.

Work process

Production automation: The use of technology to automate manufacturing processes is well documented in magazines and newspapers. IT is also used extensively for automating information processing and assembly line tasks in the financial industry. In cases where information is the product of a firm, IT is the factory. For white collar workers, intelligent agents that roam networks provide one type of automation.

Electronic workflows: Interest in process reengineering has led to the development of workflow languages and systems. As organizations eliminate paper and perform most of their processing using electronic forms and images, workflow languages will be used to route documents electronically to individuals and work groups that need access to them. Agents that can traverse networks to find information and carry messages will facilitate electronic workflows.

Communications

Electronic Communications: Electronic mail, electronic bulletin boards, and fax all offer alternatives to formal channels of communications.

Technological matrixing: Through the use of e-mail, video and electronic conferencing, and fax, matrix organizations can be created at will. For example, a company could form a temporary task force from Marketing, Sales and Production using e-mail and groupware to prepare for a trade show; participants would report electronically to their departmental supervisors and to the team leader for the show, creating a matrix organization based on technology.

Interorganizational relations

Electronic customer/supplier relationships: Companies and industries are rapidly adopting electronic data exchange (EDI) and other forms of electronic communications to speed the ordering process and improve accuracy.

It is interesting to note that there is no specific IT variable next to the traditional variable "control mechanisms." Firms have used information systems to provide control after the organization has been designed. Examples include budgets, project management applications, and similar monitoring systems. Mrs. Fields Cookies uses a variety of traditional and IT variables in creating an organization with extensive controls. However, even in this case, there is no one IT control variable in the design.

Examples of Designs Using IT Variables

The variables in Table 4-2 can be used to create the T-Form organization described in Chapter 1. In addition to the T-Form, it is possible to characterize four new organization structures that make use of the IT design variables. These prototypes show a mixture of conventional and IT design variables and suggest some of the rich organization forms that will appear in the future.

Table 4-3 shows each organization and how the IT design variables contribute to its development. In some cases the IT variable has a substitution effect for traditional elements; in other cases it is necessary for the very existence of an organization form. In certain instances, the IT variable is optional or not applicable.

Table 4-3
IT Design Variables and Four Prototypical Organizations

Organization Variable	Virtual	Negotiated Organizations	Traditional	Vertically integrated conglomerates
Virtual components	Substitute electronic for physical components	Substitute electronic for physical components	Use to replace isolated components	Force component onto electronic subsidiary
Electronic linking and communications	Essential part	Essential part	Optional	Essential part
Technological matrixing	Participate in matrixed group	Use for coordination	Use for various groups	Use for coordination and task forces
Technological leveling	Use to supervise remote workers and groups	NA	Use to reduce layers of management	Use to reduce layers of management
Electronic workflows	Crucial part of strategy	Crucial part of strategy	Use where applicable to restructure work	Key to coordinating work units
Production automation	NA	Communicate designs	Use where applicable	Coordinate production among work units
Electronic customer/ supplier links	Used extensively	Used extensively	Potentially important	Key to operations

From Lucas and Baroudi, 1994

Conventional organizations historically group workers together to establish communications and coordination. In contrast to physical presence, IT design variables allow for virtual organization structures. The virtual organization started 15 to 20 years ago as people began to see the possibilities of using technology for work at home. With electronic communications a physical organization is not needed for many kinds of tasks For example, many catalog operations use individuals working from their homes using a special phone connected to an 800 number.

The virtual organization creates new management and coordination challenges. The kind of virtual office described above may be necessary to assuage a manager's misgivings about supervision. Perhaps all members of this non-organization will log in to virtual offices each morning to report in and have an electronic discussion with a supervisor. Intel markets a product called Pro-Share which makes it possible to coordinate work on PCs in different locations. CU-SeeMe is a program developed at Cornell. It is available free and lets users on the Internet set up small videoconferences using inexpensive cameras.

At first, only technology companies like IBM and AT&T eliminated employee offices. AT&T found that eliminating commute time with a home office allowed the sales force to spend 15 percent to 20 percent more time with customers. Now, other firms like Chiat-Day, an advertising firm, have eliminated physical offices for a large number of employees. When Compaq Computer Corporation moved its sales force into home offices, sales and administrative expenses went from 22 percent to 12 percent of revenue partially due to this change. Perkin-Elmer, a scientific equipment manufacturer in Connecticut, based 300 sales and customer-service representatives in their homes which allowed it to close 35 branch offices.

A second kind of IT-enabled organization is labeled "negotiated agreement." A flower company in California, Calyx and Corolla, is based on two negotiated agreements. (See Figure 4-2.) The first agreement is with Federal Express to deliver flowers overnight to any destination in the US at a favorable rate. The second agreement is with flower growers. Instead of selling exclusively to wholesalers, the growers agree to put together a number of standard arrangements. The final part of the organization is an 800 number staffed by clerks who take orders. The orders are sent via phone or fax to growers who prepare and address arrangements for pick up and delivery by Federal Express.

Through these negotiated agreements and communications technology, this new company feels it can compete with the neighborhood florist and FTD. Calyx and Corolla is a negotiated organization in that its existence and profitability depend on the agreements it has with others, and the service supplied to its customers by others. Calyx and Corolla is, in effect, a broker using IT to coordinate its negotiated production facility and its negotiated delivery system.

The management challenge for the negotiated organization is to maintain service and quality. The firm depends on its partners to provide a product or service and yet has limited direct supervision of the business.

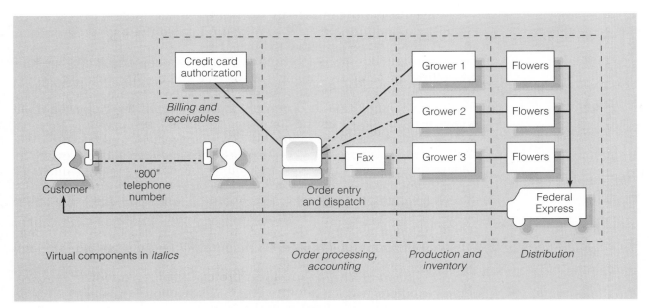

Figure 4-2 A virtual negotiated-agreement organization.

Meeting service targets and deadlines and assuring adequate quality control can be difficult. As an example, the floral firm might place random orders with its growers to have flowers sent to its own management to test delivery time and product quality. Just as department stores have used "shoppers" to test their own personnel and service, and to check on competition, the negotiated organization will need "electronic shoppers." Unlike the purchase of some off-the-shelf product, an alliance that creates virtual components results in ongoing interdependence between the two partners.

The two types of organizations described above are quite different from conventional corporations. Traditional organizations are also using technology to make some changes in structure without making major modifications to the entire organization. An electronics manufacturer has set up a just-in-time Electronic Data Interchange (EDI) link with a parts supplier, changing one component of the organization; the supplier can now be viewed as part of the manufacturer's raw material inventory.

The traditional organization may call its redesign efforts "reengineering." Merrill Lynch, for example, completely redesigned the way it processes physical securities turned over by customers. This effort resulted in the closing of two processing centers and the creation of a new processing site. The firm adopted image processing to dramatically reduce the need to physically handle securities. In this process redesign, 50 percent of the total number of individuals employed in handling securities has been cut.

There are many examples of the use of IT design variables to make changes in parts of traditional organizations. A management challenge in the traditional organization is to transform the organization enough so it can take advantage of the cost savings and competitive opportunities made possible by technology. The objective of process reengineering is to make dramatic improvements in how an organization functions. Today's business environment is characterized by rapid changes and the traditional organization needs to take advantage of technological leveling to reduce layers of management, electronic matrixing to improve coordination, and electronic workflows to reduce paper handling.

The traditional organization today is at risk unless it progresses toward the virtual model and the T-Form to improve responsiveness. IBM, one of the largest and most admired "blue chips" in the 1960s and 1970s, is struggling with declining market share and bureaucracies that resist the kind of sweeping changes necessary to be competitive. IT organization design variables help restructure traditional organizations helping them be more flexible. However, bringing about the kind of changes that are possible given the technology is a formidable management task not well suited for the traditional organization.

The last IT-enabled organization prototype we labeled a "vertically integrated conglomerate," a form viewed with mixed emotions. The movement toward greater exchange of data electronically between customers and suppliers may create vertically integrated conglomerates. The tendency for this form to emerge will be greater if there is a large power imbalance between the customer and the supplier.

As an example, General Motors requires all of its suppliers to use electronic data interchange (EDI.) For some suppliers, GM is such a large proportion of their business that the supplier becomes a component of GM, responding to its orders and demands. GM sends orders to the supplier's production scheduling system and is permitted to modify production

---

MANAGEMENT PROBLEM 4-3

Best Garments investigated the development of its own system for order entry, manufacturing, inventory control, accounts receivable, and other basic business functions. After developing specifications and sending them out for bids, the firm accepted a system offered by a packaged system vendor. This vendor had extensive experience in the garment industry and offered a hardware and software package that did all Best wanted and more.

The implementation plan called for starting the system with accounts receivable. Marilyn Brown, head of the administrative department, spent a lot of time working with the clerical staff to convert data to the new system. However, as an accountant by background, she was appalled by the errors she found in this process. She felt that even though the package was being used in other companies, it must have fundamental flaws. The vendor claimed that start-up problems always happened and that the system would prove to the penny when the data were cleaned up.

Who do you think is right? What can senior management do to resolve the problem?

schedules, priorities, etc. As a result, GM obtains a substantial amount of control and can sever the relationship at any time for little or no investment. Vertically integrated conglomerates may not be desirable for all organizations.

It should be made clear that managers must be careful when establishing electronic links. The efficiency is very appealing but the link may lock a firm into a relationship that reduces its independence. Until the links are standardized, for example using an industry standard or an X.12 EDI protocol, firms involved have more flexibility in switching business relationships. If a link goes beyond simple exchange transactions and actually gives a customer access to one's production planning systems, then the supplier risks becoming a part of a vertically integrated conglomerate for better or for worse.

Adding People to the Design

One reaction to the discussion so far may be that it is a bit sterile; where are people? When do we consider how individuals relate to one another, how they are rewarded, and the nature of the tasks they perform? Where are organization politics? For the most part, concerns about politics and emotions in organizations are not of concern in IT enabled organizations; they are no different here than in conventional organizations! Politics and the beliefs of senior managers are likely to determine the direction of the firm, its strategy, and how resources are allocated. The design remains neutral as its focus is on creating an efficient and competitive organization.

While politics and emotion are not unique to the IT enabled firms, people and tasks are an important component of any organization. The framework in the last chapter shown in Figure 3-1 shows that *in addition to structure and technology, an organization consists of people and tasks.* As

A Town for Telecommuters

Telluride Colorado, a ski resort high in the Rocky Mountains, has become a haven for hardy telecommuters. Community leaders decided that this remote town needed connections to the Internet (See Chapter 12) and with help from the nonprofit Telluride Institute, it has been able to provide Internet accounts for fully one-third of its 1500 residents. A few years ago, the town only had analog, party line phones! Town officials convinced U.S. West to replace these lines with private digital lines and to run a fiber optics trunk line to the town. The closest Internet connection was in Denver which meant high phone bills to use the Net. With grants from the state, the town was able to buy two computers and create an Internet server for the town and a town bulletin board. These two servers are available through a local telephone call. Apple Computer heard about the town's projects, and donated eight Macintosh computers to put in public buildings, creating an overnight sensation as residents took to "cruising the Net." The town is also providing high-speed wireless communications, though this service is much more expensive for users.

some of the examples show, it may be difficult to change an organization if one only attempts to alter its structure. People and tasks may create the greatest challenge for the manager who wants to change the organization.

Table 4-4 adds people and tasks to the structure and technology to provide a more complete picture of organization design. The first three organizations in the table are conventional and show typical assumptions about people and task structuring along with examples.

In a rigidly hierarchical organization, tasks are separated and decision making is done within strict guidelines. Tasks are defined by rules and practice to avoid risk. Bureaucracies assume employees need to be motivated

Table 4-4
Additional Design Variables

Structure and technology (grouping, tasks, jobs, linkages)	People Assumptions about motivation	Tasks Especially decision making	Example
Rigid hierarchy	People need external motivation	No delegation; tasks designed for employee	Military organizations
Bureaucracy	People want direction, procedures, are not good decision makers	Limited delegation and decision authority	Government University (administration)
Adhocracy	Trust, professionalism	Loosely defined; individual decides how to best accomplish tasks	Law firm University (faculty)
Virtual	Trust, self-control	Distributed decision making	Organization of the future?
Negotiated agreement	Trust in partners/ alliances	Basic tasks defined in agreement; details left to individuals	Calyx & Corolla flower company
Traditional with electronic components	Mixed, some suspicion and self-control assumed	Tendency to define tasks for lower-level employees; some discretion for managers	IBM
Vertically integrated conglomerates	Control-orientation; individuals in linked organizations expendable	Tasks tend to be designed for employee, even those in linked organizations	GM

From Lucas and Baroudi, 1994

so they provide elaborate standards and procedures to tell one how to do a job. A professional services firm, on the other hand, is based on trust and professional conduct. For example, members of law and consulting firms tend to define their own tasks.

The virtual organization has to be based on trust and minimal supervision. We expect that this type of organization will be more common in the future as a number of forces, from child-care to clean air, argue for fewer, centralized workplaces to eliminate unnecessary commuting.

In a negotiated organization, one must trust employees who are in allied companies. An agreement may specify the required output or level of service, but it will be up to each member of the alliance to accomplish its tasks as it sees fit.

The traditional firm with electronic components tends to be large and will treat its employees in a variety of ways. Technology can be used to distribute responsibility to lower level managers, or to centralize control over the organization. This structure depends on the firm's assumption about employees and how it defines tasks, especially decision making.

The vertically integrated **electronic conglomerate** is very control-oriented as it drives the systems of a different organization; it avoids the expense, the need for and the risks of traditional vertical integration. As a result, it tends to specify clearly how the firms connected to it electronically must operate.

Telecommuting at AT&T

As a leading technology and communications company, AT&T has been pushing its employees to adopt telecommuting. By the end of 1993, some 21,000 of its 250,000 employees were telecommuting from home while 5000 sales representatives and others who spend time on the road were working from virtual offices with laptop computers and cellular phones. At the end of 1994, the company estimates it had 35,000 employees telecommuting at least one day a week and 12,000 in virtual offices.

AT&T feels there are a number of advantages from eliminating or reducing the use of offices. First, the company estimates that it saved $80 million in 1994 by shutting offices. These moves also help the company respond to Federal requirements for reducing pollution by cutting back on commuting.

The biggest deterrent to the program has been employee attitudes. Many workers are used to the office and fear the unknown of giving it up. They also worry that if they are out of sight, they are out of mind; will anyone remember them when it comes for salary reviews and promotions?

Will you telecommute at some point? It is highly likely. Two research firms estimate that the number of employees who telecommute rose from 2.4 million in 1990 to 6.6 million in 1994 and will reach 11 million by 2000. If you include workers on contract rather than employees, these numbers increase by 20 to 30%.

BUILDING A T-FORM ORGANIZATION

Chapter 1 introduced the T-Form organization. The IT design variables in Table 4-2 can be used to create organizations with the characteristics described in this first chapter. It is likely that you will use these variables to design organizations and their components. An example below shows how to create a new organization using information technology.

People in the T-Form

The pure T-Form organization operates with the assumptions about people found in the virtual and negotiated agreement organizations where managers base supervision on trust in employees and on their self-control. It is not possible to exert close physical supervision. Managers also have to trust partners in business alliances since both partners depend on each other. The details of how people define and execute their tasks is left up to the employee. Decision making is moved to the lowest level of the organization where people have the information and knowledge to make the decision. People and tasks are an extremely important component of the T-Form organization.

Adopting the T-Form: An Example

An example illustrates how IT variables can be applied to the design of an organization. Assume that a traditionally structured manufacturing firm wishes to take advantage of new technology to become a T-Form organization. ABZ is an actual company whose name has been changed to protect the innocent and the guilty. ABZ is a manufacturer of electronic components.

Currently, ABZ has a very traditional organization structure; it has a headquarters with a small staff and a number of manufacturing plants in the U.S. and abroad. The largest of these plants is responsible for most information technology in the company. The firm has generally under invested in technology and is behind its competitors in the industry. Fortunately for ABZ, its products are of high quality and the company has not needed to compete on information technology.

Suppose that management has heard about the T-Form organization and would like to adopt it. What could the company do? Table 4-5 shows how management at ABZ could use the IT design variables discussed in this chapter to restructure the company. ABZ is currently being forced into becoming a **virtual supplier** by its customers who are moving to just-in-time production. ABZ needs to develop the capability to inquire against and monitor its customers' production control and scheduling systems so that it can send products *without the customer even having to order them.*

Electronic linking can be used to link production planning, order entry and marketing. The sales force does not need individual offices. Representatives can use notebook computers and home offices to concentrate

Table 4-5
An Example of Design for ABZ

Class of Variables	Conventional Design Variables	IT Design Variables	Applied to ABZ
Structural	Definition of organizational subunits	Virtual components	Manage virtual inventory for distributors; connect with customer production systems for JIT; use a common order entry system for a single point of contact; contract with overnight carrier for all distribution
	Determining purpose, output of subunits		
	Reporting mechanisms		Use more electronic communications to flatten structure, increase span of control
	Linking mechanisms	Electronic linking	Link production planning, order entry and marketing; notebook computers for sales force; eliminate private offices for sales force
	Control mechanisms		Develop systems to make control information more widely available
	Staffing	Technological leveling	Reduce the number of layers in the organization by substituting electronic communications and groupware
Work Process	Tasks	Production automation	Continue efforts at automation
	Workflows	Electronic workflows	Move toward total electronic tracking of order; use bar codes to coordinate production with an electronic traveler
	Dependencies		Coordinate with e-mail and groupware
	Output of process		
	Buffers	Virtual components	
Communications	Formal channels	Electronic Communications	Use e-mail and groupware, especially to communicate among distributed plants and headquarters

Table 4-5 *(continued)*

Class of Variables	Conventional Design Variables	IT Design Variables	Applied to ABZ
	Informal communications/collaboration	Technological matrixing	Use e-mail and groupware to coordinate on production forecasts and special projects
Interorganizational relations	Make versus buy decision	Electronic customer/supplier relationships	Develop a home page on the Internet containing product information; as soon as feasible, use it or a commercial online service to allow customers to inquire on availability; other options would be EDI and groupware
	Exchange of materials	Electronic customer/supplier relationships	Same as above
	Communications mechanisms	Electronic linking	Establish electronic mail links with customers; consider commercial services, EDI, and/or groupware

on working with customers. Control can be enhanced by developing information systems which make control information available to various levels of management.

Technological leveling is accomplished by reducing layers of management and providing communications tools like electronic mail and groupware to managers. ABZ has a large number of administrative support staff members and others not involved in direct production in the factories. It is this support organization that adds overhead and is an excellent candidate for leveling after analyzing their job functions and determining where the technology makes savings possible.

In the factory, the company has successfully moved toward production automation. Expanded efforts should focus on the creation of an electronic manufacturing environment. Orders arrive electronically from customers and each order generates a bar code to describe the customer and product. When production begins, a worker attaches a bar code to the physical tray that holds the product through the production cycle. At each stage a worker wands the bar code at a workstation to bring up a screen with instructions on what operation to perform. At the end of production after quality testing, the only paper necessary is a label for the shipper.

Electronic mail and groupware can be used for technological matrixing. They address the informal communications vital in managing a company. ABZ can quickly form task forces and other informal groups to address problems. This approach is particularly valuable for communications among plants. For example, one U.S. plant sends "kits" of product to be completed to a plant in Mexico. Various problems between the plants can be resolved quickly using electronic communications rather than physical travel.

Technological matrixing also facilitates a reduction in managerial levels as it encourages employees to take the initiative in solving problems. Suppose that a customer contacts a marketing manager to ask if it would be possible to access ABZ's production scheduling system to schedule products to be built for the customer. The marketing manager using e-mail and groupware can form a task force in a matter of minutes that includes personnel from Production Planning, Marketing, Information Systems, and other interested areas. There is no need to pass this request through layers of management in different departments.

ABZ needs to connect electronically to customers to provide them with a **virtual inventory**. It can also take advantage of more extensive electronic customer-supplier relationships. For example, ABZ can put up a home page on the Web to describe its products. As these services develop, ABZ could include information on the availability of various products as well. Another option is to use groupware to exchange data electronically with its customer and suppliers. Regular electronic data interchange (EDI) and commercial e-mail services are available today to provide this kind of communications.

What is the result of ABZ's adoption of IT design variables? Extensive use of electronic communications and linking results in fewer management layers and flattens the structure of the organization. Fewer layers, combined with the availability of information at all levels in the organization, will push decision making down to lower levels of management. Easy electronic communications encourage employees to contact appropriate colleagues to solve a problem, rather than refer it up the hierarchy through a supervisor. Employees will be able to take on more responsibility and have an IT infrastructure to support them.

Some employees, especially the sales force, at ABZ will no longer have offices. ABZ will move toward complete electronic integration with customers and suppliers. Electronic mail for informal communications, EDI for routine transactions, and in some cases direct links into customer information systems, will increase the firm's responsiveness to customers and suppliers. Electronic workflows in production will eliminate paper, and more importantly, provide better service. Production lots will not get lost if they are tracked electronically and production workers have accurate information on what tasks to perform for each order.

To accomplish this restructuring will take ABZ a long time since it has not kept up-to-date with technology. It will have to invest in a technological infrastructure and people to develop the kind of IT applications described above. ABZ's product quality has helped it attain a commanding market share, and adopting a T-Form organization will help it sustain this position and meet the threats of competitors who currently obtain more from their investment in IT than ABZ.

We should add a note of caution: IT is not the solution for every problem. Competent managers can use the IT design variables in this chapter to improve the organization. They can also use them to create significant problems, for example, a colleague recently reported on a company where a manager only communicates with the staff via e-mail and rarely listens to any of them. It is likely that his strong staff will find other places to work. IT design variables are one approach to improving the organization; outstanding managers will use them with good taste to design efficient and effective organizations.

JIT II-Suppliers in Your Office

Just-in-time manufacturing has become extremely popular in the U.S. given the positive experiences that Japan's factories have shown using this approach. Just-in-time or JIT is a part of "lean production" and is designed to keep inventory at a minimum. Because there is little inventory, the quality of parts and the dependability of the supplier are critical.

An American at Bose Corporation, Lance Dixon, came up with a modification called JIT II; he invited suppliers' sales representatives to sit next to the factory floor and gave them free reign to move about the plant. These representatives can attend production status meetings, visit R&D labs and access Bose's own production planning and forecasting systems on Bose computers. They can write a sales order of their own.

This new approach requires a great deal of trust between the customer and supplier. Not all attempts at establishing JIT II relationships have worked, but where they have, there can be many benefits. A Honeywell plant in Minnesota has 15 representatives from 10 suppliers in cubicles just off the production floor. Some of these representatives work on new product designs, but most oversee purchases. They think like Honeywell employees and look for ways to cut costs. Honeywell runs the factory with inventory levels measured in days rather than weeks; it also has reduced its purchasing agent pool by 25%. Some representatives will order from a competitor if it is best for Honeywell.

In retailing, the same concept is called Efficient Customer Response or ECR; suppliers continuously replenish inventories as the store sells items. Vendors are linked to customer computers which have forecasts and point-of-sale data. The sale of goods "pulls" inventory to the shelves; vendors do not "push" their merchandise on the store. ECR has worked well for some customers and suppliers, but many firms are wary.

JIT II and ECR represent different ways of thinking; they are made possible partially because of information technology. However, to succeed they require management to support the concept and to create an atmosphere in which customers will trust their suppliers to act in the customer's best interests.

*T*HE IMPACT OF TECHNOLOGY ON MARKETS

There is a great deal of interest in the impact of technology on markets and the industry structure. Earlier in this chapter we saw how technology impacted two industries, airlines and securities. In the case of the securities industry, IT helped improve the quality of markets. Technology made it possible to process the large volume of transactions that resulted from market growth. It also enabled new trading strategies that affected the operation of markets. These new strategies led to a linking of the equities and futures markets, creating greater interdependence than existed before.

In the case of the airlines, the reservation systems began to solve operational problems. Soon they evolved into systems to provide a competitive advantage to the CRS vendor. Government regulation tends to reduce the advantage to the point that American Airlines now feels it is providing a market and services but is not getting extra market share from the system. (It does, however, earn substantial revenue in fees from its CRS subsidiary.)

We can look at the impact of IT on the marketplace from the perspective of electronic markets and hierarchies (*Malone et al.,* 1987). An electronic market exists when IT is used to provide information or it actually becomes the market. The airline CRSs have evolved to an electronic market; the

The Big Board's Birthday

The New York Stock Exchange, the "Big Board," is more than two hundred years old. The Big Board has been doing very well; the stock market in the U.S. has been booming, while volume at rival foreign stock exchanges has been falling. From 1989 to 1992, the Tokyo Stock Exchange experienced a 52 percent plunge in share prices.

However, all is not completely well at the Big Board. Growing electronic exchanges and foreign exchanges are taking a considerable amount of business that used to go through the New York Stock Exchange (NYSE). In 1981 the NYSE accounted for 76 percent of the stock trading dollar volume; by 1992 it handled only 59 percent of the dollar trading volume.

Some experts have suggested that the only way for the NYSE to compete in the future will be to eliminate its trading floor. When London deregulated its stock exchange and installed electronic trading systems, its stock exchange floor basically disappeared. These experts argue that trading is moving to a twenty-four-hour-a-day business; physical floors and traders are not able to provide this kind of service.

The Big Board's man-machine system has functioned well in the past; during the 1987 stock market crash it handled 600 million shares on "Black Monday." Brokers at one rival exchange, NASDAQ, stopped answering their phones while the NYSE continued to trade. The Big Board uses a specialist system that creates a lot of human resistance to changing the way it does business. Rival exchanges, however, are posing an increasing threat to its business.

How does the kind of organizational transformation discussed in this chapter affect the NYSE? How do you think it will change in the future?

major systems contain fare and flight information on the majority of scheduled airlines in the world; these systems take complex information on schedules and fares and make it easily available for the travel agent and the public. NASDAQ, the electronic stock exchange for over-the-counter (OTC) stocks, is the market itself.

Firms coordinate their activities through markets because they buy inputs and sell their outputs. Malone, Benjamin, and Yates (1987) draw on the field of transactions cost economics to describe another kind of coordination by hierarchy. When the costs of transactions in the marketplace become very high, the firm may be able to reduce coordination costs by management. For example, if a company needs a very complex machine, it may be easier to contact one supplier whom the firm knows is capable of designing the machine rather than expend the effort in a futile search of the marketplace. The authors show that IT can have different and sometimes conflicting impacts on the use of markets for coordination. Overall they feel that IT will lead away from single-source suppliers to electronic markets. The explosion of interest in the Internet and electronic commerce suggests that a movement toward electronic markets is well underway. As this trend continues, IT will dramatically impact industry structures and the economy itself.

CHAPTER SUMMARY

1. Information technology interacts with organizations and can be used to change the structure of the organization and/or its subunits.

2. Technology, whether intended or not, has an impact on organizations.

3. One desirable impact is when information technology contributes to organizational flexibility.

4. Older, legacy systems often perform critical tasks for the firm. These systems usually run on mainframe computers and are very large and complex. One management problem is deciding if and when to make massive investments to migrate these systems to up-to-date technology.

5. There are a variety of organization structures; some important considerations in studying organizations are uncertainty, specialization, coordination, and interdependence.

6. Mintzberg offers an insightful model of organizations that consists of five components: the strategic apex, the middle line, the operating core, the support staff, and the technostructure.

7. There are a number of IT-enabled variables that you can use to design organizations. They supplement and sometimes replace traditional organization design variables.

8. These variables can be used to create the T-Form structure described in Chapter 1 or applied to produce a range of structures including

virtual organizations, negotiated organizations, and vertically integrated conglomerates. The variables may also be used in subunits of traditional firms.

9.   It is important to remember that organizations and people play an extremely important role in the development and success of technology.

10.   In addition to organizations, IT has had an impact on markets. All things equal, we expect a move toward more electronic markets in the future.

IMPLICATIONS FOR MANAGEMENT

It is amazing that a technology barely capable of computing a payroll and processing orders when introduced in the 1950s can be the basis today for structuring the organization. The evolution of computers and networks has enabled IT design variables for creating new organizational structures. As a manager, you constantly search for ways to improve the organization. IT design variables offer opportunities to make major changes in the organization, changes that can improve both efficiency and effectiveness. *Today, the tasks of designing technology and the organization have become one in the same.*

KEY WORDS

Competitive advantage
Electronic communications
Electronic conglomerate
Electronic customer/supplier
   relationships
Electronic linking
Electronic workflows
Flexibility
Legacy systems
Middle line
Mutual dependence
Operating core
Organization
Pooled interdependence

Production automation
Productivity
Reciprocal interdependence
Sequential interdependence
Strategic apex
Support staff
Technological leveling
Technological matrixing
Technostructure
Time and space boundaries
Uncertainty
Virtual components
Virtual inventory
Virtual supplier

RECOMMENDED READING

Malone, T., R. Benjamin, and J. Yates. "Electronic Markets and Electronic Hierarchies," *Communications of the ACM,* vol. 30, no. 6 (June 1987), pp. 484–497. (A provocative article on the impact of IT on firm coordination.)

Lucas, H. C., Jr., and J. Baroudi. "The Role of Information Technology in Organization Design," *JMIS,* vol. 10, no. 4 (Spring 1994), pp. 9–23. (Presents the IT design variables in detail.)

Lucas, H. C., Jr., and M. Olson. "The Impact of Technology on Organizational Flexibility," *Journal of Organizational Computing,* vol. 4, no. 2 (1994), pp. 155–176. (A paper on which the discussion of organizational flexibility in this chapter is based.)

Lucas, H.C., Jr. *The T-Form Organization: Using Technology to Design Organizations for the 21st Century.* San Francisco: Jossey-Bass, 1996. (The story of the T-Form organization.)

DISCUSSION QUESTIONS

1. What kind of technology is least flexible? Most flexible?

2. The information services department is often considered to provide a support function. Can a support department really be powerful? Are there different kinds of power in an organization?

3. What kinds of management problems result from a lack of organizational flexibility?

4. Are there any organizations that are completely dependent on information technology for their operations?

5. What kinds of employees are most likely to be replaced by information technology? How does your answer depend on the type of system and the decision levels affected?

6. How would you measure the extent of unemployment created by the implementation of IT? What factors tend to mitigate the problem of increased unemployment if it actually occurs?

7. What signs might indicate the need to restructure or redesign an organization?

8. Is information technology creating more centralization in organizations? How do you define centralization? Why should technology have any effect at all on the degree of centralization?

9. How would you recognize a company that is using IT successfully? What signs would you expect to find?

10. How can IT be used to create "virtual" organizations?

11. How should managers introduce organizational changes that employ technology? What are the risks?

12. What alliances were key for the nationwide floral company described in this chapter?

13. Consider a typical manufacturing organization and describe the dependencies that exist among departments.

14. Why should users be involved in the design of systems? How much influence should they have?

15. What are the risks for a small company connecting itself electronically with major customers?

16. What are the problems with legacy systems? What are their implications for management.

17. How can IT be used to help design an organization?

18. What are the IT enabled organization design variables? How do they supplement or replace conventional design variables.

19. What tools does the manager have available to influence IT in the organization?

20. As a user, to whom do you think the information services department should report? Should it be responsible to the finance department?

21. Why are so many users solving their own problems using PCs instead of turning to the information services department?

22. Early forecasts suggested that middle managers would be reduced in number and stature as a result of information technology. Has this prediction been realized? Why or why not?

23. Does technology have an impact beyond the organization, for example, on stockholders or customers? What kinds of effects occur, and what problems are created for these groups?

24. What is the role of the traditional organization given the kind of structures that IT makes possible?

CHAPTER 4 PROJECT

USER SUPPORT

The task of supporting computer users in a university is a difficult one. A large number of schools separate academic and administrative computing because it is hard to give academic users attention when the payroll system for the faculty and staff is not working!

Even with a separate academic computing organization, it is often difficult to support users. Typically, a school has a number of users of its facilities, and management must try to support them all—from the student who has never used a PC before to the faculty member who needs the power of a supercomputer. On top of the problems with a mainframe or minicomputer in a central facility, the academic computing staff may also be responsible for a series of PC laboratories.

Develop an organization chart for academic computing at your university. The chart should show the major entities, such as computer centers, the kind of equipment each offers, its users, and so on. Then describe the kind of user support provided. What are the problems with the school's efforts at support? What recommendations can you make to improve the level of support students receive?

CHAPTER **5**

Strategic Issues of Information Technology

OBJECTIVES

1. Learning to manage information technology.

Today's information systems go well beyond transactions processing and operational control. Leading organizations have figured out how to use these systems for a competitive advantage. The manager who uses the technology strategically will make a major contribution to his or her organization. This chapter shows how technology can be used to gain and sustain a competitive advantage. The last part of the chapter presents an important framework for you to use in managing technology in an organization; it sets the stage for the management issues raised in the rest of the text.

2. Preparing to apply technology.

Strategic applications often involve extending your systems to customers or suppliers, that is, creating **interorganizational systems**. You must be extremely careful when designing systems that involve users external to your organization; the system must be appealing, provide benefits for all users, and it must work properly. As you read about the Merrill Lynch cash management account and the Rosenbluth Travel systems, imagine the magnitude of the disaster if the systems designed for these applications failed to work satisfactorily.

3. Transforming the organization.

Through strategic applications, we first saw the opportunity for IT to transform organizations and industries. Examples in this chapter plus our earlier discussion of transformations in the securities and airline industries demonstrate the power of modern information technology to change the way we do business. One strategy for management is to adopt the T-Form technology-based organization discussed in Chapters 1 and 4. The use of IT design variables to structure the organization creates new levels of efficiency and effectiveness, making the firm a strong competitor.

A recent poll of more than two hundred executives showed they feel information technology is key to a competitive advantage. However, 52 percent of these managers also feel that they are not getting their money's worth from the technology. The survey was conducted by Andersen Consulting and involved chief executives, chief operating officers, and chief financial officers representing companies with annual sales ranging from $250 million to $20 billion. (One positive finding was that 81 percent of these top executives are personally using computers in their daily jobs, nearly double the percentage when the survey was conducted four years earlier.)

This chapter discusses how technology can be used to gain a strategic, competitive advantage. We believe that many of the problems expressed by executives in the survey above come from their failure to actively manage

IT in the firm. After we discuss IT and strategy, we present some ideas on how you should manage technology so that it can contribute to corporate strategy.

INFORMATION TECHNOLOGY AND CORPORATE STRATEGY

A key task of top management is formulating corporate strategy. What does the corporation do well? Can it continue this activity at a high level of performance? What opportunities for new directions are available? What are competitors doing? A firm can continue its present course, maintaining momentum where it is doing well. Alternatively, the corporation can dramatically change its strategy by deciding among competing alternatives for new ventures.

As an example, a single-product, single-market firm might try diversifying to reduce cyclical fluctuations in product demand and to reduce the impact of a major change in consumer buying patterns. A large energy company decided to enter the market for information processing equipment by purchasing a number of high-technology firms and integrating them into a new subsidiary. This new business was expected to grow and help the energy firm cope with uncertainties in its primary petroleum business. A few years later, the firm sold most of its technology businesses after experiencing heavy losses.

Integrating IT and Strategy There are three levels of **integration** of information technology with corporate strategy, as shown in Table 5-1. At the lowest level of integration, we find independent information systems that help the firm implement strategy to improve efficiency. These systems are not directly linked to the strategy formulation process or integrated with a strategic plan. The need for such a system is usually perceived by an operational unit, and its primary

Table 5-1
Levels of Integration of Information Processing Technology

Level of integration with strategy	Primary objective	Secondary effect
Independent	Operational efficiency	Managerial information
Policy formulation	Aid repetitive decision making	Better understanding of problem dynamics
Policy execution	Offer new products, markets, directions	Change the decision-making process, alternatives considered, and evaluation criteria

objective is to improve efficiency. A large number of information systems fall into the independent category. They process routine transactions, produce output that goes to customers, provide exception reporting, and so on.

The second level of integration is characterized by policy formulation systems designed to aid the strategic planning process. In this case, the system helps formulate the plan but is not a part of an end product or service produced by the firm. A planning application is a good example of a policy support system. The data needed for forecasting for a large conglomerate are contained in a common database accessible through the computer. A set of analytic tools in the system includes a bank of models with a large mathematical programming routine that helps select a course of action to maximize corporate performance over a multiyear planning horizon. In addition, econometric and risk analysis models are available. Technology itself becomes a part of the strategy; it expands the range of strategic alternatives considered by the firm.

At the third level, the technology itself becomes a part of policy execution. It expands the range of strategic alternatives considered by the firm. At this level, technology bears an integral relation to a company's strategic thinking by helping to define the range of possibilities. At the same time, it provides a good portion of the means by which the strategy, once chosen, is to be implemented. Several examples follow to help illustrate this level of integration between technology and strategy.

Some Examples

Merrill Lynch is the largest stockbrokerage firm in the United States and plans to become one of the major financial institutions in the world. Several years ago, funds in a customer's brokerage account earned no interest. There could be cash in such an account because of the sale of stock or because of dividends on stock held by Merrill Lynch for the client.

The firm developed a new financial product called the cash management account. At the time the product was conceived, interest rates were extremely high, and a number of small investors were keeping their funds in liquid assets accounts. These funds buy large securities with a value of $100,000 or more then sell shares, usually with a par value of $1 and require a minimum deposit, possibly as low as a few thousand dollars. The funds keep the value of the ownership units at $1 by varying the dividends and buying short-term securities.

Now the small investor, instead of being limited to bank or savings and loan passbook accounts, can take advantage of higher interest rates previously available only to those with a large amount to invest. (Today, banks and S&Ls are able to offer money market accounts, but they were not available at the time Merrill Lynch developed its new account.)

The firm decided an account that automatically invested idle cash in Merrill Lynch's own Ready Assets (liquid assets) Fund would appeal to its customers. In fact, this new CMA (cash management account), is like a bank account and brokerage account combined. The customer can write checks against the account and even receive a bank charge card.

Has it been successful? At first the account was slow to win acceptance, but today Merrill Lynch has more than a million CMA customers. Other brokerage firms have hired Merrill Lynch employees to develop similar products. Merrill patented the account and is asking for licensing fees. In an out-of-court settlement, another brokerage firm agreed to pay $1 million for hiring a Merrill Lynch employee to set up a similar system. Merrill Lynch gained a significant competitive advantage with its cash management account system.

Could this system have developed without confidence in information technology? With a million accounts to update, the magnitude of the catastrophe if computer systems do not work is hard to imagine. In fact, this product could never be offered unless a firm had computer technology and could manage it. The volume of updating and the short time requirements would be just too great for a manual system.

On a smaller scale, information processing technology made it possible for a new market research firm to offer a service it could not obtain from its competitors. The company developed a strategy that is intertwined with information technology. The firm purchased grocery store point-of-sale scanning equipment and, at first, gave it free to fifteen supermarkets in two towns selected on the basis of their demographic makeup. There are two thousand households in each of the two test markets using the scanning equipment and their purchases are recorded on the firm's computer in Chicago. Since each product is marked with the universal product code, researchers can pinpoint a family's purchases by price, brand, and size and then correlate the purchase information with any promotions such as coupons, free samples, price adjustments, advertising, and store displays.

With this technology the company can conduct careful, scientific tests of marketing strategies to determine the most effective approach for its customers. For example, through cooperation with a cable TV network, the firm can target different TV commercials to selected households and analyze the resulting purchases. The imaginative use of the technology has allowed the firm to gain a competitive lead over much larger, better established market research firms. This firm has grown, and recently was able to sell the software it developed for analyzing scanner data for a premium price.

These examples illustrate how the integration of information processing technology with strategy formulation expanded the opportunities for each firm. In the brokerage firm, the technology made it possible to offer a new service that helped expand the firm's market share and increased the size of its liquid assets fund. Technology helped the market research firm gain a competitive edge and set a new standard for service in the industry.

Some Generic Strategies   Michael Porter at Harvard has suggested that firms follow one of three generic strategies:

1. **Low-cost producer.** Here the firm tries to have the lowest costs in the industry so that it can compete on price.

2. **Differentiation.** The firm tries to separate its product image from that of the competition in such a way that the customer wants its product. Luxury automobile manufacturers like BMW are very adept at differentiating their products from other cars. For example, if you are buying a BMW, you are buying "the ultimate driving machine."

3. **Market niche strategy.** A number of firms try to find a market niche and exploit it. A niche is some part of a market that is not being served by others. Hermes has stayed in its niche of producing high-quality, expensive products like women's scarves for a limited clientele.

In today's competitive economy, we have observed firms focusing on more specific strategies that are listed below. Most of the time, the firm adopts only one of these, but it is possible to follow two at the same time:

Customer Driven   Here the firm focuses on its customers. How can we provide better customer service? How can we design products that meet our customers' needs? What technology exists so we can better serve our customers? Customer service is extremely important in commodity businesses, for example, the mail-order sales of personal computers.

Reducing Cycle Times   A firm has a variety of **cycle times**; a typical one is the length of time it takes to design a new product or service. Detroit automobile manufacturers are focusing on reducing cycle times. They now use parallel design and engineering, where tasks are done simultaneously rather than sequentially. In addition to saving time, parallel development results in better coordination among team members working on the design of a new car.

Global Competition   As the unification of Western Europe continues and Asian economies become more open, some firms have decided to follow a strategy of competing in the global marketplace rather than only in

Reducing Design Cycle Time

Chrysler and Dassault Systems of France have developed a computer-aided manufacturing system that Chrysler hopes will allow it to reduce the time it takes to retool factories by 20%. The idea is to use the system to create a "virtual" factory so that engineers can design manufacturing tools needed for a new auto model more easily and quickly. Using the new system Chrysler can retool a factory after approving the design for a new model in about 24 months, down from the 30 months that used to be required. Chrysler has been a low cost leader in designing new cars, but it has been lagging behind Japanese manufacturers and Ford in retoolings its factories. This new system extends the computer-aided design tools to actually design the car to the plant floor where it will be manufactured.

In this example, technology is helping with two strategies, cycle time reduction and low cost production.

local markets. A firm with global presence will need a variety of technologies to help coordinate and control all of its activities. Information technology is a great facilitator for global operations.

Right-Sizing In the U.S., the first part of the 1980s was an economic boom, leading to a number of excesses. The late 1980s and the early 1990s were marked by economic downturns and slow growth. To compete in a difficult economy, firms have attempted to determine their "right size." Usually to right-size meant a serious reduction in the number of workers in the firm, and rather large write-offs for restructuring. Blue-chip companies such as IBM have reduced their levels of employment by tens of thousands of workers.

Quality Japanese manufacturers gained a large market share in a number of industries partially through a fanatical devotion to quality. Many firms around the world are focusing on quality in the hopes of getting ahead of the competition. Quality is an obvious component in the manufacturing sector, but the services firm can also be concerned about the quality of its output.

As we shall see in the rest of the text, there are many ways that technology can be used to support the generic strategies described above.

A Framework for the Strategic Use of IT

Figure 5-1 is a framework for IT strategy which arrays a firm's existing applications against those that are currently under development (Cash, McFarlan, McKenney, and Applegate, 1992).

MANAGEMENT PROBLEM 5-1

Standard International is the subsidiary of a large manufacturing firm; it is responsible for marketing, sales, and distribution outside of the United States. Standard International (SI) does not develop products; all products it sells are created by the parent firm in its factories. SI has operations in thirty countries. In virtually all of these countries the local SI operation is treated legally as a subsidiary of Standard International.

Recently a new president took control of SI. Historically the firm's systems were oriented to finance and accounting because the technology group reports to the vice president of finance. Accounting applications are important because so many different currencies are involved. The new president, however, is impatient and feels that technology should be able to do something for marketing and sales.

She asked you to consult with SI in the hopes of finding a strategic application for information technology: "I want something that will give us a competitive edge," she said. What kind of a process would you follow to try to identify a strategic application? What applications areas look promising? How does a firm like SI develop a strategic system? How does it establish and maintain a competitive advantage?

Figure 5-1
Information systems
strategic grid.

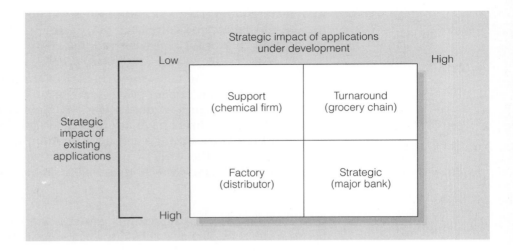

In the strategic cell, companies are critically dependent on the smooth functioning of information systems. These firms need significant amounts of planning. The firm would be at a considerable disadvantage if information processing did not perform properly. The authors found one bank that fit this cell well. Without computers, the bank would be awash in a sea of paper and it could not possibly keep up with the volume. The bank must think of how to use its systems strategically to offer services that will let it capture a greater market share. For instance, banks are offering new services connecting home computers to their computers.

In a turnaround company, there is a need for planning, too. It is likely that corporate performance is inhibited by poor performance in the information processing department. Cash and colleagues found a firm in this cell with adequate operating systems in production but limited new applications critical for keeping up with growth. Without new technology The firm could not maintain control over its rapidly expanding operations.

The authors argue that in the factory setting, there is not much to do but run existing applications. They maintain that strategic goal setting and linkage of information systems to the corporate plan are not too important here.

Finally, in a support environment, information processing is probably not critical to the firm, so strategic integration will not be essential for success. The authors expect to find low levels of senior management involvement in this situation.

The framework in Figure 5-1 is a useful one for diagnosing the state of an organization. We can look at the nature of the business, its plans for the future, and its existing and planned applications. In a turnaround situation, we may want to emphasize to management the importance of leading the information systems effort, whereas in the strategic cell, management may already be aware of the importance of technology to the firm.

However, Cash, McFarlan, McKenney, and Applegate argue that in the support cell, it is quite appropriate for management to be relatively uninvolved in information processing. Although this may be true for certain systems, the advice is bad in general because it encourages management to ignore information technology and the new opportunities it provides. It is quite possible that a firm in the support cell will be able to come up with a strategic application that allows it to gain a competitive edge. In fact, if the support cell position is characteristic of the industry, the firm that first finds a strategic edge through information technology may in fact move far ahead of the competition.

Those authors concerned with the use of information technology as a part of corporate strategy have all taken a slightly different approach to classifying systems. One common thread seems to run throughout the discussions: Technology can contribute to a firm's strategy in a number of ways. It can reduce costs to help an efficient firm compete, or it can tie the firm more closely to suppliers and customers. The technology can also become a product itself, like the Merrill CMA or an airline CRS, allowing a firm to gain a significant competitive edge.

Capitalizing on Information Technology

How does the firm take advantage of information technology and achieve the highest-level integration of technology and strategy? There are four steps to be followed by top management:

1. *Look for ways to incorporate technology in a product or service.* Does information processing provide an opportunity for a new approach to business? Does the technology make it possible to differentiate a product or service from that of the competition? Technology can help open a new market or increase an existing market share.

2. *How can the firm use technology to connect with other firms?* There is great interest in interorganizational systems that link two organizations together. Your firm may be able to connect electronically to its customers so that it is easy for them to order from you. A firm can encourage its suppliers to provide links for placing orders. In these instances, the firms in question are drawn more closely together, making it difficult for the competition. These links are discussed further in Chapter 12 when we describe electronic data interchange (EDI.)

3. *Look for ways to use technology to make dramatic changes in the way the organization functions.* Use information technology organization design variables so management can structure an organization that focuses on one of the strategies described above, for example, providing extraordinary customer service.

4. *Integrate technology with planning.* To do this, the firm needs information about likely future technological developments. To conduct a technology assessment, the organization must invest resources in

research and development. A small group of corporate researchers can collect information from a number of sources to estimate technological trends. The firm can invest selectively in university programs to keep up on research and can sponsor or subscribe to studies conducted by consulting firms.

One of the greatest impediments to using information technology for strategic purposes is an inability on the part of top management to successfully manage the information systems function. If executives do not believe they can control information processing services, they probably will be unwilling to rely on this technology to accomplish strategic goals.

SUSTAINING A COMPETITIVE EDGE

Once a firm gains an advantage, it finds competitors developing similar systems. In fact, the competitors' systems may provide more features or be technologically more sophisticated because the competitor is building on the experience of the first firm to come up with a new approach to business. How does one sustain a competitive edge once having achieved it?

The demands of maintaining an advantage are almost as significant as those of creating the edge in the first place. In the case of airline reservation systems, placing the system in travel agencies represented a major marketing victory for the three or four airlines that gained most of the market. However, to sustain this competitive edge, the leading airlines have invested $1 billion in agency automation via personal computers. The original reservation systems cost about one-quarter of this new investment. In this industry, at least, the cost of staying competitive is significantly greater than the cost of the first strategic use of the technology.

In some instances, a strategic advantage may be lost as other firms imitate the first mover. *Clemons* (1990) offers an analysis of the development of ATM networks beginning in Pennsylvania. The first bank to install automatic teller machines appears to have gained an advantage, but soon installing ATMs became necessary for all banks to compete for retail customers. The leaders and other banks soon turned to shared networks to provide better customer service in different locations. Instead of providing a competitive advantage, shared ATM networks have become a competitive necessity.

Clemons and Weber (1991) suggest four ways to sustain a competitive advantage. One of the most popular ways to sustain an advantage is to be the first mover. The first mover may be able to create an insurmountable lead over the competition. Merrill Lynch has many imitators, in fact the "sweep account" is very common in the investment business. However, no one has been able to overtake Merrill Lynch's lead; it by far has the largest number of cash management accounts of any brokerage firm.

Another way to sustain an advantage is to overwhelm the competition with **technological leadership**. United and American have more than 70 percent of the domestic market for reservation systems in travel agencies. These firms made large investments in technology and in developing skilled staff members who could implement reservation systems. By investing in technology and managing it well, these two airlines provide significant barriers to entry for other airlines and vendors of potential reservation systems. (The original United CRS, APOLLO, is now owned by a consortium of several airlines.)

Closely related to technological leadership is **continuous innovation**. Successful strategic applications such as the classic American Hospital Supply/Baxter Health Care order entry system demonstrate continuous innovation. Today, with this system Baxter offers a service that is the virtual inventory for a "stockless" hospital. IT and a superb logistics system lets Baxter promise just-in-time deliveries to different departments in a hospital.

A final approach to sustaining an advantage is to create high switching costs. By making it very expensive or inconvenient to switch a customer's business to a competitor, you are assured that customers will continue to do business with you. The airline CRS vendors have been very clever at locking in travel agencies. At this point in time, almost all agencies in the U.S. are automated. Increases in the number of customers and market share only come from converting an agency from a competitor's CRS to your own. Each CRS vendor has created very high switching costs for an agency to convert to a competitor's CRS.

Simply finding a strategic application of technology and implementing it successfully is not enough. This approach should provide a short-term competitive advantage, but the innovator must constantly be searching for ways to **sustain an advantage** as the competition tries to imitate its success.

An Example of Technology for Competitive Advantage

Clemons and Row (1991) describe how a small travel agency expanded to a nationwide business through the use of IT. Rosenbluth Travel, headquartered in Philadelphia, has grown from $40 million in sales in 1980 to $1.3 billion in 1990. It is now one of the five largest travel management companies in the United States and has more than four hundred offices.

According to the authors, Rosenbluth was extremely effective in taking advantage of the opportunities offered by deregulation in the travel industry. The firm has used technology to help manage the complexity of modern travel and to obtain economies of scale. Rosenbluth invested in IT over a period of years. While the expenditure in any one year was not inordinate, Rosenbluth created a technology base extremely difficult for a new entrant or even a competitor to match.

Prior to deregulation in 1976, travel agents wrote about 40 percent of all tickets. The role of the agent was only to make a reservation and distribute a ticket. Deregulation changed the role of travel agents, and forced them to manage the increased complexity of travel. Until a recent round of fare simplification, American Airline's SABRE system contained 45 million fares and processed 40 million changes a month. The airline reservation systems used by travel agents were biased toward the airlines, though no more so than one would find calling the airline itself for information. The travel agent, however, could be expected to help the client without a bias toward a particular airline. By 1985 travel agencies were distributing more than 80 percent of air tickets.

Businesses are very interested in managing their travel. It is the third largest expense for most firms after payroll and information technology. Firms began to negotiate rates with airlines, hotels, and rental-car companies. One of Rosenbluth's major business focuses has been the corporate travel market.

The following list of critical technology moves by Rosenbluth illustrates how the firm has used IT for expanding its business:

- About 1981 the firm experimented with processing data from airline computerized reservation systems (CRSs) to provide information for corporate accounts.

- In 1983 Rosenbluth introduced a product called READOUT that listed flights by fare instead of by time of departure. This program made it possible to see the fare implications of taking a particular flight. The normal flight display was by departure time, and the agent had to move to another screen to obtain fare information.

- In 1986 a proprietary back-office system, VISION, created a highly flexible reporting system for clients. The system created a record of transactions made for a client at the time of ticketing no matter the location of

MANAGEMENT PROBLEM 5-2

AgChem is a major chemical firm. Its chairman was once quoted as saying, "I get nothing from our computers." The vice president of finance has the responsibility for information technology in the firm. He has just succeeded in making the department a division, the highest-level organizational entity in the firm. In addition, a new manager of the division has been recruited to try to turn the technology area around.

The new manager and the vice president of finance are trying to develop a strategy for the turnaround, beginning at the top and working through the various levels of the organization.

The vice president is very capable but has no formal experience with technology. He knows, however, that there are many problems. Users constantly complain about information services. The new director of information technology has conferred with his staff. He feels that some of the criticism is justified but that many of the users and top managers just do not realize the extent to which they and the entire firm depend on systems.

The vice president and the new manager of information services would like some help in trying to improve the situation at AgChem. Can you suggest ways they might go about creating both better service and a better image for IT?

the agency or the CRS in use. This system gave Rosenbluth independence from the data provided by the airline CRS. During 1986 Rosenbluth estimated that it invested nearly half of its pre-tax profit in the system. The VISION system was more flexible and produced reports about two months earlier than agencies using only the airline CRS. Rosenbluth used VISION to negotiate special fares with the airlines on heavily traveled routes the system identified.

Instead of competing for corporate clients by offering to rebate part of its commissions, Rosenbluth tried to create a cooperative relationship with clients. It promised clients to reduce overall travel costs through lower fares and used VISION reports to document the savings.

- In 1988 Rosenbluth used a new feature in United's Apollo reservation system to support intelligent workstations. The new Rosenbluth system, PRECISION, made client and individual employee travel profiles, and the READOUT database of flights listed by increasing fares, available to the agent making a reservation. ULTRAVISION is another system that runs with the normal reservation process, monitoring transactions for accuracy and completeness.

- During 1990–91, Rosenbluth began installing USERVISION in its offices. This system lets the user make flexible queries about corporate travel. The data are one day old compared to the forty-five-day lag typical of the airline CRS data.

These initiatives reflect a tremendous growth period as Rosenbluth's sales increased from $400 million in 1987 to $1.3 billion in 1990 while the number of offices increased from 85 to over 400.

The firm has been extremely successful. Business and technology strategy were developed together in an integrated approach to growth. The firm took risks in developing new uses of IT and the in-house expertise to successfully implement systems. Rosenbluth's technology strategy competes through value-added services rather than being the low-cost producer through rebates. It also took advantage of technology to market new services to its clients. The company meets jointly with its clients and service providers to help the client negotiate the lowest possible fares.

INTEGRATING TECHNOLOGY WITH THE BUSINESS ENVIRONMENT

One of the most significant management challenges during the coming decade will be to integrate business and technology. It is no longer adequate to think about technology after other business decisions have been made. Instead, managers must consider how technology affects their decisions and how their decisions affect the technology.

Figure 5-2 describes how a manager can integrate technology with decision making. First, the manager has to search for new technology to learn what is available for new opportunities to employ the technology. These opportunities, combined with the technology itself, lead to new development projects. The development projects are influenced by technological constraints. The firm cannot undertake a new marketing program in which customers inquire about their orders from the Internet, if the firm lacks the skills to set up a home page on the World Wide Web and integrate the page with its existing order-entry system (See Chapter 12).

The box at the bottom of Figure 5-2 represents decision making, planning, and execution of decisions. Technological constraints and opportunities influence these decision-making activities. The firm described above cannot provide customers with inquiry capabilities until it allocates resources to develop a Web site. Management's decisions influence how it manages the existing business and technology. A decision to undertake a major factory automation project will result in a different type of production process to manage.

Figure 5-2

The management challenge of integrating information technology.

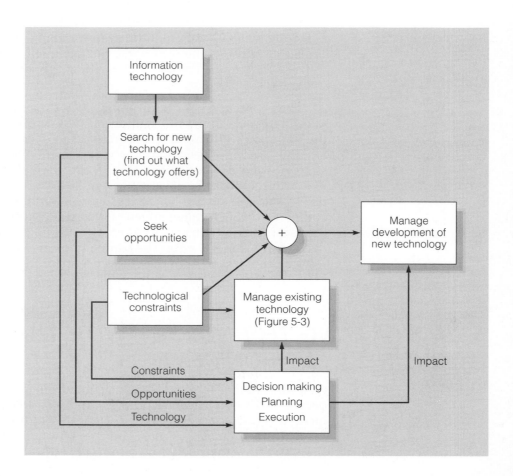

In the future, successful managers will be able to integrate their knowledge of information technology and their business knowledge in making decisions. The manager will be aware of the opportunities provided by the technology and the constraints that already exist for the firm in developing new technologies. This manager will also recognize that as decisions are made, the alternatives chosen will have an impact on technology and its development within the firm. The next section, particularly Figure 5-3, presents a framework for this task of managing information technology.

MANAGING INFORMATION TECHNOLOGY

Figure 5-3 is a framework for managing information technology. The arrows in the figure show the relationship between actions in the boxes for managing and controlling technology. For example, a senior manager first looks at how technology can contribute to the structure of the organization using the IT design variables discussed in the last chapter. The structure of the organization influences and is influenced by corporate strategy. Strategy, structure, and the integration of IT into the firm help generate a **plan** for technology. This plan includes a structure for the IT subunit(s) in the organization along with a hardware/software/network architecture for the firm. The plan describes what new applications and what resources are needed to operate existing technology. It also describes the sources of services, for example, from within the firm or from an outside source. Finally, the plan contains information on how management will control the technology effort.

MANAGEMENT PROBLEM 5-3

Scudder Laboratories is a major manufacturer of prescription drugs. As a part of the manufacturing process, the company has an extensive quality control division. Much of the division's work requires taking and analyzing samples during manufacturing. The quality control division maintains a complete set of laboratories for this testing. Records must be maintained at the company and certain reports sent to the U.S. Food and Drug Administration.

In order to keep better track of the sample and test data and improve laboratory efficiency, Scudder has spent three years and several million dollars developing a laboratory automation system in conjunction with a computer vendor. The system is in the testing stage in one laboratory and seems to be working. It was originally anticipated, however, that all the labs could be run on one midrange. It turns out that a fairly large midrange is needed for each lab, rather than one slightly more powerful computer for all the labs together.

What should management do at this point? Should it consider scrapping the project? How can it make a decision about expanding the application to all of the labs?

Figure 5-3
A framework for managing information technology.

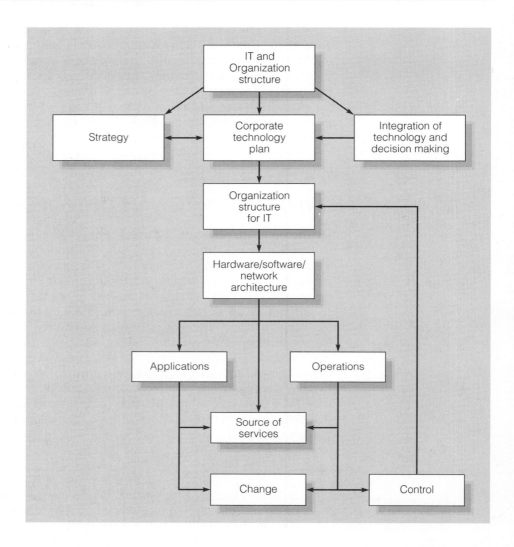

Table 5-2 summarizes the actions for management in each of the areas discussed below. Where possible, we offer recommendations for management policy. When the recommendations depend on circumstances unique to the firm, Table 5-2 lists some of the factors that should be taken into account when developing a policy. We shall discuss some of the issues in Table 5-2 in more depth in Part VI of the text.

Technology for Structuring the Organization

In Chapters 1 and 4 we discussed the use of information technology design variables in structuring the organization. Because a firm's structure is highly interrelated to its strategy, these two aspects of the organization must be considered together. For example, a firm might decide to compete on the basis of extremely efficient operations, to become the low cost,

Table 5-2
Summary of Issues and Recommendations

STRUCTURE	

- Use IT design variable to help structure the organization
- Look for partnership and alliance

Issues	Recommendations
Technology	Having an infrastructure in place
Opportunities	Evaluate alternative structure
Impact	Reaction from employees

STRATEGY	

- Look for opportunities
- Conduct technology assessment

Issues	Recommendation
Technology	Learn about new technologies, e.g., the Internet
Opportunities	Search for new ways to use the technology to gain an edge
Management	Manage the development of new technologies

INTEGRATION OF TECHNOLOGY AN DECISION MAKING	

- Consider the options provided by technology in making decisions
- Use IT to transform operations

Issues	Recommendations
Technology	New technology can create new opportunities to change the way a business functions
Impact	Management decisions may influence or be constrained by the technology.

A CORPORATE PLAN	

- See that a 3-to-5 year information systems plan is developed

Issues	Recommendations
Mechanism	Operational plan of 1 year Longer-term plan of 3 to 5 years Technology assessment

Table 5-2 *(continued)*

Issues	Recommendations
	Link to organization plan
	Separate information technology planning officer
Involvement	User and management input
Contents and format	See Chapter 24
Priorities	Steering committees to choose applications
Reporting	Annual report of information services department tied to plan

ORGANIZATIONAL STRUCTURE FOR IT

- Evaluate various patterns for providing technology to choose the most effective alternative
- Develop a policy that balances coordination costs and local autonomy

Issues	Alternatives
Type	Centralized distributed, decentralized for operations and systems development
Evaluation	Criteria contribution to strategy and service levels, cost responsiveness, flexibility, history of organization
Control	Balance local autonomy with corporate needs

HARDWARE/SOFTWARE STRUCTURAL ARCHITECTURE

- Develop architecture for firm
- Establish information systems policy

Issues	Recommendations
Define architecture	Determine hardware, software, and networking options
Select standards	Select corporate standards for compatibility
Establish policy	Write the standards and promulgate them as policy

NEW APPLICATIONS

- Convene a committee of users and managers to be affected by the system to choose an alternative for design
- Be sure that a realistic number of alternatives are considered, including the status quo or no-new-systems alternative

Table 5-2 *(continued)*

Issues	Recommendations
Generate new ideas	Also form plan, procedures for submission of requests, new applications
Selection	Use of committees; use formal approaches for selection
Development	Extensive user input, management involvement in setting goals, reviewing system
Tools	Acquisition and use of tools-structured approaches

OPERATIONS

- Establish criteria for measuring the performance and service levels of operations
- Measure and evaluate the operations function regularly

Issues	Recommendations
Measurement	Develop user-oriented measures
Evaluation	Administer regular evaluations including a variety of measures
Control	Are there adequate controls?

SOURCE OF SERVICES

- Look for alternatives for more internal staff to outsourcing
- Authorize adequate staffing levels; systems design is labor intensive!

Issues	Recommendations
Evaluation and choice criteria	Develop evaluation methodology
Compatibility among vendors	Establish vendor compatibility policy
Technological assessment	Consider changes in technology in decisions
Staff increases	Examine alternatives such as adding to the staff, contract services, packaged programs, and outsourcing

CHANGE

- The purpose of new technology is to change the organization
- Bringing about change may be management's biggest challenge

Table 5-2   *(continued)*

Issues	Recommendations
Changing structure	See Chapters 1–4, 19
Changing business process	See Chapter 18
Implementing new IT	See Chapter 19

CONTROL	

- Evaluate the contribution of IT to corporate goals and strategy
- Evaluate information services performance with respect to the plan
- Take the needed corrective action to achieve the plan, e.g., add resources, modify schedules, and so on.

Issues	Recommendations
Overall evaluation	Compare results to plan
Frequent feedback	Monitor progress on systems development projects, conduct user surveys as discussed under "Operations"

low overhead producer in its industry. This firm might use production automation to reduce costs and improve quality. It could use electronic customer/supplier relationships to process electronic orders from customers on a just-in-time basis, and to order in a similar manner from its suppliers. The firm could employ technological matrixing to form electronically linked project teams to develop new products and services in parallel. To minimize overhead, it might employ electronic communications and linking with its sales force; providing them with electronic devices like notebook computers with fax modems, wireless communications, and cellular phones in place of a physical office.

Searching for Competitive Advantage

Strategy and structure must be considered together. Beyond the adoption of a generic strategy like becoming the low cost producer, you want to develop technology that will give you a competitive edge. The most difficult part of gaining such an advantage is coming up with an idea. No text can teach creativity or give a formula for it. By reviewing what competitors are doing, staying abreast of the technology, and looking for analogies in other industries, you can develop new ideas for strategic advantage.

It is likely these strategies will include the development of interorganizational systems and alliances with other firms. For a manufacturing firm, IT strategy might involve technology embedded in a product such as the computer chips found in automobiles to control the engine and exhaust. A services firm might look for ways technology can add value to existing services, make it easier to do business with the company, reduce cycle times, lower costs, and make the other contributions discussed in the first part of this chapter. You also need to consider an Internet policy and presence on the World Wide Web. (We defer a discussion of this topic until you have read about the Internet and Web in Chapter 12.)

Integrating Technology and Decision Making

A significant responsibility of management is to integrate technology with all business decisions. Integration means that the manager is aware of how new technology can create opportunities. The technology can literally change the way a firm does business. Concomitantly, the manager has to be aware of the impact of decisions on the firm's technology.

A decision to enter a new line of business has a direct effect on existing information processing systems. For example, the creation of frequent flyer programs had a dramatic impact on computerized reservation systems. At least one major airline required flyers to attach a sticker to tickets to get mileage credit some two years after its frequent flyer program began. The airline finally was able to modify its reservation system to keep track of the miles when the traveler makes the flight!

A Corporate Plan for Information Technology

A plan for information processing should be coordinated with corporate strategy. The plan serves as a road map to show the direction of the systems effort. It also furnishes the basis for later evaluation of the performance of the information processing function.

Many organizations agree that a plan is needed yet do not develop one. A frequent reason is that the three-to-five-year information systems planning horizon is not compatible with the planning horizon of the organization. It is both possible and highly desirable to develop an information processing plan even without a formal corporate plan. The technology is too pervasive and important for planning to occur by default or solely through decisions made by personnel in the information services department. We return to the topic of planning in Chapter 24.

Structuring the Technology Subunit

Existing information technology offers considerable flexibility in developing patterns for the structure of the information services function. (We discuss these issues further in Chapter 13 when we talk about different kinds of IT architectures.) The firm must identify possible **processing patterns**, evaluate them, and choose an alternative for implementation. The processing of alternatives can be divided into three broad groups that represent points on a continuum. At one extreme is completely centralized processing—all systems development is performed by a central group, and all equipment is operated centrally. In today's environment with the proliferation of PCs and client-server computing, it is rare to find total centralization. At the other extreme is complete decentralization; all equipment resides at local sites, and these sites have their own staff for analysis and design work. Distributed processing occurs when local sites are tied together by a communications network or when local users have the ability to create their own local area networks.

Table 5-3 presents some of the evaluation criteria that can be used to select a particular structure for processing. The most important criterion is the contribution of the structure to strategy. Is IT structured and managed to accomplish the firm's objectives? Is there a technological infrastructure that lets the firm achieve its strategy? Other criteria, such as level of service, system responsiveness, and reliability, are oriented toward the interests of the user.

In general, there is no rule as to what kinds of systems are most responsive or provide the highest level of service. It appears that local processing is associated with more favorable user perceptions of service levels and greater responsiveness. The availability of a network of computers or of several computers at a central site provides high reliability. You must look at costs for each alternative. The cost of a particular pattern of processing depends on the configuration, the location of data, and so on. The task of managing either a centralized or a decentralized configuration is complex and will depend on the existing IT organization.

The challenge of a centralized system is to make it responsive. The challenge of decentralized and distributed systems is to make them coordinated. Management must trade off the benefits perceived by users in having and controlling their own technology against the need for overall coordination in the organization. Allowing a proliferation of computers can lead to high costs when the organization connects diverse equipment

Table 5-3
Organizational Structure for Processing

PATTERNS		
	Hardware	**Systems development**
Centralized	X	
Distributed	X	
Decentralized		X

Example: multidivision firm with a central IT group and analysts employed by the divisions

EVALUATION CRITERIA	
• Contribution to strategy	• Reliability
• Flexibility	• Cost
• Level of service	• Management task
• Responsiveness	

through a network. Also, the firm must ask if there are opportunities to develop common systems that can be used in multiple locations to prevent the duplication of development efforts.

Large organizations today often have a federal structure. The firm has networks of computers, many of which are interconnected. There is likely to be some type of corporate IT function that advises and assists local information services departments. The corporate group establishes standards for technology like network, e-mail, and other systems that have implications for the entire organization. Local information services departments develop technology for their subunits and cooperate (in theory) with the central group. We will return to a discussion of the structure of IT efforts and their control in Chapters 23 and 24.

Hardware, Software, and Network Architecture Issues for Management

Closely related to the topic of organizational structure and pattern of processing is the question of a hardware, software, and network architecture. The term **architecture** refers to the basic hardware, software, and network systems in the organization.

There are many options for hardware and software but the firm can afford to support only a few. While in theory it is possible to combine computers from many different vendors in a network, in practice it can be very difficult and expensive to do. Even if the technological problems are solved in developing the network, the problem of different software systems, packages, and user interfaces remains.

$3 Billion to Catch Up at UPS

In 1985 the board of directors at United Parcel Service decided the firm was lagging behind its rivals in technology, especially Federal Express. Even though UPS had the best on-time record in the industry, the board feared that it would not be able to grow and continue its success if it ignored IT. The company launched a five-year, two billion dollar building plan. In 1985 the IS group at UPS comprised 118 people with a budget of $40 million. Today the IS staff has 4,000 people.

The program continues today. In 1993 UPS created the first nationwide mobile data service linking 70 commercial carriers. A program costing $180 million placed handheld data collection computers in UPS' 53,000 trucks. In 1994, UPS was the first to let users order service through CompuServe and Prodigy (See Chapter 12).

It is hard to say that technology is responsible for growth at UPS. However, since 1985 annual sales have gone from $7.6 billion to $19.4 billion with income climbing to $900 million from $568 million. The company is a global force, delivering 3 billion packages a year to 200 countries and has 303,000 employees. The company has budgeted another billion dollars for technology between 1992 and 1997. UPS wants to be able to provide real-time electronic data on each of the 12 million packages it ships daily; it also wants stronger electronic links with its 1.2 million customers.

Software has to be supported and users need someplace to turn for help when problems arise. It can be prohibitively expensive for a firm to have experts available for different software programs on many different vendors' computers. After choosing its architecture, the firm needs to write down its decision as a policy statement. Such a statement might read, "We are able to support the following three computer vendors. ... We currently provide consulting help and services for each of the following operating systems on these machines. ... The firm will support the following two word processors ... and a single spreadsheet package." Management may be willing to let individuals deviate from the policy, but their architecture will not be supported by corporate resources. The individual has to make a case for not needing support or having the resources to provide it.

How does architecture interact with the pattern of processing discussed above? In a centralized company, controlling hardware and software architecture is relatively easy. In a firm that is decentralized with respect to information services, adherence to a corporate policy statement on hardware and software architecture can be hard to enforce. Regardless of the type of structure, the presence of an agreed-upon hardware and software architecture will help executives better manage information services in the firm.

New Applications, New Choices

Rarely today does anyone suggest completely infeasible applications. Instead, a system that will be feasible can usually be undertaken to improve information processing. The question is, what system is both feasible and desirable? A corporate steering committee should choose applications areas as a part of developing a plan for information processing. The task then is to choose what type of system, if any, will be developed. Management must consider the existing portfolio of applications and provide guidance on the amount of investment possible and the balance of the portfolio. Management must also decide what processes, if any, to reengineer and what resources to devote to reengineering projects.

Systems development is an area that requires a great deal of management attention. Managers must demonstrate they are behind the development of a new system and see there is adequate user input in the design process. Frequent group review meetings are important during the design process. Top management must participate in these meetings and make clear that it supports the changes likely to come from the system. Later in the text, we discuss system analysis and design in more detail, along with how the organization can implement successful systems.

Operating Information Services

The major concerns in the operation of existing systems are credibility and service levels. It is very difficult to gain enthusiasm or cooperation in the development of new systems if existing service levels are unsatisfactory. Management must be sure that the information services department is providing effective service as perceived by its customers.

Table 5-4 lists some critical management concerns in operating existing information systems. Efficiency considerations include the utilization of equipment, the quality of scheduling, and smoothness of operations. As hardware becomes less expensive, having a machine that is fully utilized is less important than having adequate capacity for processing.

Efficiency is important, but most managers and users are more interested in effectiveness. Given the rapid pace of technological change, it is hard for management to judge whether its technological infrastructure is adequate. You can benchmark your infrastructure against that of other companies but are you prepared to take advantage of new opportunities? Would the idea for a strategic system be delayed for six months or a year while your infrastructure was brought up to date? The infrastructure may be adequate for current needs, but does it provide the flexibility you need to take advantage of new opportunities?

Another approach to measuring effectiveness is to conduct a detailed user evaluation and survey. For example, one can ask about specific systems. Measures of system "uptime" and availability are also one good indicator of effectiveness. Adherence to schedules is important; so is the error experience of users. There will always be errors, but is their number reasonable, and are there edit and error checks that catch errors? Probably the most important criterion is the overall impact of the IT effort on the firm, as discussed in the previous chapter.

Source of Services

The requirements for operating existing systems and the resources for developing new applications determine staff and equipment needs. One of the by-products of the planning process is the identification of needed resources; requirements are compared with available resources to determine what increments of equipment and staff are necessary. Top management

Table 5-4
Operations of Existing Systems

Efficiency	Effectiveness	Control
Utilization of equipment	Quality of infrastructure	Exposure analysis
	Benchmark other firms	Backup
Scheduling		
	User evaluation and survey	
Smooth operations		
	Uptime	
	Meeting schedules	
	Error experience	
	Impact on firm	

must decide what action to take when there is a discrepancy between the resources needed to accomplish the plan and the resources available.

For the staff, the obvious way to expand resources is to hire more individuals. But there is a limit to the number of people that can be absorbed productively into the organization. Another alternative is to use more packaged programs to improve staff productivity. Outside contractors or **outsourcing** can be employed to develop systems or supply staff members.

All future trends point to the conclusion that hardware costs will continue to decline and there will be an insufficient number of IT professionals to develop systems. These observations suggest that the organization will have to give more responsibility for systems to users. Along with this responsibility, users will need tools to develop their own applications. One of the benefits of client-server computing is to provide users with data that they analyze on their workstations. The organization can prepare to use the technology better by making it widely available and easily understood.

A Network to Process Health Claims

There is a great deal of attention focused on the dramatic increases in the cost of health care in the United States. As a percentage of the Gross Domestic Product, the U.S. spends more on health care than any other industrialized nation. We spend twice as much as Canada as a percentage of GDP.

A group of health insurers has chosen a McKesson Corporation subsidiary to set up a network for the electronic processing of medical claims. Administrative costs are estimated to account for up to 10 percent of all medical costs; they are also a major frustration for all parties involved, from patients to doctors to hospitals. The ultimate objective of the system is to make transactions as easy as buying something with a credit card. In different parts of the country, various organizations are suggesting state- or community-wide electronic networks.

The McKesson subsidiary already has terminals in fifty-two thousand pharmacies in the U.S. It manages prescription drug services for employers and insurance companies. The system lets druggists know how much of a prescription a customer's plan covers and the amount that the customer should pay. The subsidiary pays the pharmacist every two weeks for prescriptions filled under one of its plans.

Plans are for a patient to carry a card like a credit card. Card readers in doctors' offices and hospitals would be used on the network to connect with the patient's insurance company to determine the nature of coverage.

The American National Standards Institute is in the process of developing standardized formats for health insurers, doctors, and hospitals; medicard and Medicaid programs; and other participants in the health-care industry. The use of standards should make it possible to interconnect local networks and create a national health-care network. Such an application of technology will reduce administrative costs and make data more available for instituting other types of program reviews and cost containment efforts.

Making Changes   You develop new technology to change the organization. Most of the time you expect IT to result in some kind of improvement, though all members of the organization may not agree with you. Managing change is one of management's biggest responsibilities and challenges. There are three broad areas for change:

- Changing the structure of the organization using IT design variables.
- Changing business processes through reengineering.
- Implementing new IT systems in the organization.

As shown in Table 5-2, each of these topics is sufficiently important and complex that it is the topic of one or more chapters of this book. Please see the individual chapters for recommendations on how to manage the changes described above.

Control   Management control is concerned with the broad question of whether information technology is contributing to corporate strategy. From our earlier discussions, this contribution could be in the form of independent systems or policy support systems for planning, or it could be through a close linkage between technology and strategy formulation. One reason top management may feel uneasy about information processing is its realization that managers often are not controlling the technology. One way to gain control over information processing is to participate in the decisions mentioned above and be knowledgeable about IT in the organization.

On an operational level, one control mechanism compares actual results with the IT plan. On a more frequent basis, users' reactions to service levels can be measured and reported and progress on individual systems development projects can be monitored. Management should establish performance criteria, and the information services department should report on them.

One major management problem is deciding what action to take when it appears that some part or all of the information processing function is out of control. A common solution, though not necessarily the best, is to replace the Chief Information Officer (CIO) and/or the manager of the information services department. Instead of making that reflex response, top management should take a careful look at how it contributes to controlling information processing. The framework in Figure 5-3 is one starting point for such an examination. Has management helped develop a plan for information technology? Does management get involved in the selection of applications and the determination of priorities? Do top managers set the objectives for new systems and participate in their design? In some instances, changes in personnel may be appropriate when the operation is out of control. In others, however, the best action may be to provide additional resources.

In summary, the first step in exerting control is knowing what to measure. The second step is conducting the evaluation. The third step is determining what action is most likely to improve the situation if part of the operation is not under control.

THE ROLE OF MANAGEMENT COMMITTEES

Because of the size of the investment involved and the importance of key systems to the organization, many firms establish committees to help manage information systems activities. A committee can bring to bear many different points of view on a problem, and it ensures widespread representation of functional areas and management levels in key decisions.

One large multinational firm has organized a series of committees to deal with planning for IT and reviewing proposals for new systems. Offices of the president and chairperson are at the head of this firm. Each major line of business in this firm is organized into a company with its own president and staff. There are also corporate vice presidents for various functional areas, such as a vice president of finance. Service units such as research and development and information technology are corporate divisions reporting to appropriate corporate vice presidents.

This firm has recently established a corporate-level steering committee for information technology. Its objective is to review plans and determine the appropriate size of the firm's investment in IT. The corporate committee reviews division plans, organizes and approves education about systems, and seeks areas for the development of common systems serving two or more suborganizations, such as two different companies with common requirements. The purpose of a common system is to share resources and avoid the cost of developing a tailored application at each site.

Each division also has a local steering committee that is responsible for developing and approving long-range plans for IT in that suborganization. The local committee also reviews and approves short-term plans and the annual budget for information technology activities in the division. This committee serves to review proposals for new systems and to assign priorities to them. Finally, the local committee reviews and approves staffing requirements for information services.

For the multinational firm discussed above, the corporate-level and division-level steering committees deal with policy. In a smaller firm, only a corporate-level committee might be appropriate. Whatever the size of the organization, it should develop a mechanism that involves users and the systems staff to (1) set policy and review plans, (2) select alternatives for a given application, and (3) participate in the actual design of a system.

CHAPTER SUMMARY

1. There are three ways information technology plays a part in corporate strategy; the most exciting is when technology is intertwined with strategy.

2. There are three generic strategies including: being the lowest cost producer, product differentiation, and the marketing of niche products.

3. More specific strategies include being customer driven, reducing cycle times, competing globally, and right-sizing.

4. IT strategy and organization structure are closely related; management can use IT design variables to create an organization structure to accomplish its strategy.

5. Once you have achieved a competitive advantage, the next challenge is to maintain it. A company may be able to sustain its gains by being the first mover, establishing technological leadership, continuous innovation, and/or creating high switching costs.

6. To use IT strategically, you have to be able to manage the technology. The first step in management is to develop a corporate strategy that incorporates information technology and to design the organization using IT.

7. The next step is to develop a corporate plan for IT. This plan will also consider how to structure the IT subunit(s) in the firm.

8. The technological infrastructure, the pattern of hardware, software, and networks in the firm, is an important management consideration; the infrastructure plays an important role in determining the firm's flexibility in undertaking new technology initiatives.

9. Other IT management considerations include choosing applications, routine operation of systems, and overall control over the technology effort.

10. Large firms often use various types of management committees to oversee the IT function. These committees help provide a wide variety of input into decisions about technology.

IMPLICATIONS FOR MANAGEMENT

Applications that generate the most excitement are those that provide the firm with a strategic advantage. I was once asked by a company president to come up with a strategic system for his company. As you might guess, this request was not particularly welcome. An outsider may be able to suggest a process for finding a strategic application, but the actual application will come from within the firm. In fact, it is probably most likely to come from a general manager not working in IT. A number of strategic applications have evolved from rather routine transactions processing systems. Airlines developed their reservations systems to solve the reservations problem. When they put the systems in travel agencies they realized the strategic value of this transactions processing system. American Hospital Supply began its order entry system because it was having trouble providing supplies to a hospital in California. The best place to look for a strategic application may be among the applications you already have in place.

KEY WORDS

Architecture	Market niche strategy
Continuous innovation	Outsourcing
Cycle times	Plan
Customer driven	Processing pattern
Differentiation	Quality
Global competition	Right-sizing
Integration	Strategic applications
Interorganizational systems	Sustain an advantage
Low-cost producer	Technological leadership

RECOMMENDED READING

Baker, R., R. Kauffman, and M. Mahmood. *Strategic Information Technology Management.* Harrisburg, Pa.: Idea Group Publishing, 1993. (An excellent collection of articles about the strategic use of IT.)

Cash, J., W. McFarlan, J. McKenney, and L. Applegate. *Corporate Information Systems Management,* 3rd ed. Homewood, Ill.: Irwin, 1992. (A good book for managing information processing.)

Clemons, E. K., and M. Row. "Information Technology at Rosenbluth Travel," *JMIS,* vol. 8, no. 2 (Fall 1991), pp. 53–79. (An interesting discussion of the growth of a small business analyzing the contribution of information technology.)

Copeland, D., and J. McKenney. "Airline Reservation Systems: Lessons from History," *MIS Quarterly,* vol. 12, no. 3 (September 1988), pp. 353–370. (An excellent history of computerized reservation systems and competition among airlines using information technology.)

Newman, S. *Strategic Information Systems: Competition Through Information Technology.* New York: Macmillan, 1994. (A well-written book that describes how to obtain and sustain a competitive advantage through technology.)

DISCUSSION QUESTIONS

1. Locate an article in the popular business press about the strategy of a corporation. Describe the interrelationship between technology and the strategy of the firm. Compare two firms and note the differences.

2. Why did most firms first develop systems to improve operational efficiency?

3. How can a firm sustain a competitive advantage?

4. What is the first mover advantage? Give an example of a firm that has achieved such an advantage.

5. How can users evaluate the quality of service from an information services department?

6. One bank's information services department developed sixty nine quality indicators for information processing. Do you think this was a good idea? What do you think was the reaction of users?

7. What structural patterns of the organization would influence the structure of information technology?

8. Why has the personal computer proven so popular? What service-related reasons might account for some of its appeal?

9. Why do you think firms might have trouble simultaneously following more than one or two of the generic strategies described in this chapter?

10. How does strategic planning differ between a firm that offers services and one that manufactures a product? Is there a difference in the impact of technology on strategy in the two types of firms?

11. How would management assess the probable information processing technology available over the next five years?

12. What criteria are the most important for an organization in choosing among competing alternatives for a particular application?

13. Why should the decision of what applications to undertake not be left to the manager of the information services department?

14. What do you think the role of top management should be in the design of a specific information system?

15. Some senior executives feel that they do not receive a return on their investments in technology. What factors might account for this feeling? Do you think they are right?

16. It has been said that problems with information technology start at the top of the organization. What does this mean? Do you agree or disagree? Why?

17. Why do priorities have to be set for new uses of IT?

18. Why would managers seem to know more about functional areas other than information technology?

19. What options are open to the organization if equipment and staff needs exceed available resources?

20. What actions can management take if information technology activities seem to be out of control?

21. What is the role of external expertise in the development of a strategy for information technology?

22. Why have information services departments historically been reluctant to develop plans?

CHAPTER 5 PROJECT

STRATEGIC ADVANTAGE

Developing systems for strategic advantage (or calling them strategic) has become very fashionable. As the examples in this chapter suggest, it is unlikely that what is strategic today started out that way. Companies developed systems for one set of reasons. Later, they saw extensions that turned the systems into strategic or competitive applications.

When an organization exists to make a profit and functions in an industry with competitors, it is relatively easy to look at a system and determine that it is strategic. What happens in the case of a different organization, such as a university? Can you identify the "competitors" of your university? How can information technology be used to make your institution more competitive?

CHAPTER 6

International Business and Information Technology

⬤ OBJECTIVES

1. Learning to manage information technology.

Managers are increasingly involved in global business. Information technology is an important part of managing a global enterprise as it plays a major role in coordinating the activities of an international firm. Managing technology in an international environment raises new challenges. As you read this chapter, think about the problems of coordinating twenty or thirty subsidiaries in different countries. How would you convince them of the advantages of using common systems for tasks that do not differ among their operations?

2. Preparing to apply technology.

Designing information systems for a single-location domestic firm can be difficult and the challenge is even greater when designing systems that will be used in several countries. You need to be aware of the special problems encountered when trying to develop systems in foreign countries. Think about local customs and differences that exist in business practices that might make it more efficient to let units in each country design their own systems.

3. Transforming the organization.

Businesses are trying to transform themselves into global concerns. IT is an important tool in making this transformation and in designing the international organization. One researcher who studies international business suggests that information technology is the glue that can hold an international organization together and help coordinate its operations. All of our IT design variables that focus on communications like electronic links, technological matrixing, electronic customer/supplier relationships, and virtual components are available to help manage and coordinate the global firm.

Globalization has been one of the major trends in business in the last decade. It is estimated that 579 global corporations account for about 25 percent of the world's production. These companies range in size from $1 billion to $100 billion. The world's strongest economies have been heavily trade oriented. As the value of the U.S. dollar has fallen, this country has also dramatically increased its exports. Chronic trade surpluses in Japan have focused attention in other countries on world trade and on lowering barriers to trade.

The **European Economic Community (EEC)** has eliminated almost all barriers to trade and is planning to adopt a common currency (though the success of this latter effort is in some doubt). The U.S., Canada, and Mexico have completed the NAFTA free-trade pact that will phase out most tariffs over a fifteen-year period. The consensus among economists is that free trade will eventually benefit all countries that participate. There are also emerging markets in Eastern Europe and the Commonwealth of Soviet States. Globalization can greatly complicate the task of managing IT in a firm. yet, IT can make a greatly improve the management of firms with operations in many parts of the world.

THE IMPACT OF GLOBALIZATION ON BUSINESS

There are a number of impacts of globalization (Ives and Jarvenpaa, 1992):

- *Rationalized manufacturing.* Firms manufacture in locations with a comparative advantage for the type of manufacturing involved.
- *Worldwide purchasing.* Firms can purchase worldwide for their operations giving them a great deal of leverage over suppliers.
- *Integrated customer service.* A multinational firm is likely to have multinational customers and can provide all locations with the same level of customer service.
- *Global economies of scale.* Size, if managed properly, provides for economies in purchasing, manufacturing and distribution.
- *Global products.* Consumer firms have worked especially hard to market global brands such as Kellogg's cereals and beverages like Coke and Pepsi.
- *Worldwide roll-out of products and services.* The firm can test products and services in one market and then roll them out around the world.
- *Subsidizing markets.* The profits from one country can be used to subsidize operations in another.
- *Managing risk across currencies.* With floating exchange rates, doing business in many countries can help reduce risks.

One conclusion from the list above is that global business creates greater uncertainty and complexity. To handle these challenges, the firm will need faster communications and information processing. It will have to rely more on IT to manage the organization.

INTERNATIONAL BUSINESS STRATEGIES

Four major types of international business strategies are portrayed in Figure 6-1 (Bartlett and Ghoshal, 1989).

Multinational

The **multinational** strategy focuses on local responsiveness. Subsidiaries operate autonomously or in a loose federation. The advantage of this type of approach is that the firm can quickly respond to different local needs and opportunities. This strategy reduces the need for communications because local subsidiaries can make many decisions. There are heavy reporting requirements though, as the results from the subsidiaries have to be monitored at a headquarters location.

Figure 6-1
Global business strategies.

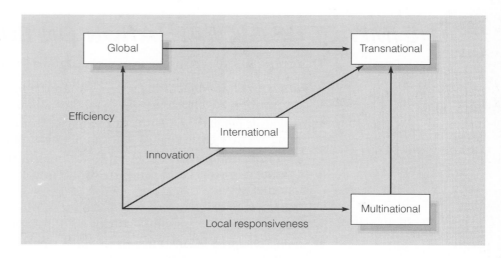

Global
A **global** strategy stresses efficiency because there is strong central control from headquarters. Economies come from standard product designs and global manufacturing. An extensive communications and control system is necessary to centrally manage the global firm.

International
The **international** strategy is much like the multinational as there are autonomous local subsidiaries. However, these subsidiaries are very dependent on headquarters for new processes and products. A good example is a pharmaceuticals company. The research labs in the headquarters company develop products for introduction around the world. Local subsidiaries stress product approval by local governments and local marketing.

Transnational
The **transnational** firm attempts to do everything! It seeks global efficiency while retaining local responsiveness. The firm integrates global activities through cooperation among headquarters and foreign subsidiaries. This difficult strategy tries to achieve local flexibility at the same time that it obtains the advantage of global integration, efficiency, and innovation.

We predict that the various types of firms will tend to strive toward the transnational model over time.

KEY ISSUES IN AN INTERNATIONAL ENVIRONMENT

Information
Needs
An international corporation needs information to coordinate and control its diverse businesses. Reporting and early-warning systems are very important in this environment. Systems that summarize sales data and process accounting information are necessary, but they only reflect what has

happened in the past. These systems represent traditional uses of IT for reporting and control.

Technology offers the international firm many more active tools to help manage the business. Coordination is a major problem for the global firm. IT provides a number of approaches to improving communications and coordination, for example, e-mail and fax. The emergence of group-ware products is very important to international business. These systems let workers in different locations create a shared, electronic environment. As discussed in Chapter 4, the manager can use IT in a variety of ways to design the structure of the global organization. We can see that technology plays a crucial part in the design and operation of international firms.

Implementing International IT

The ultimate objective for the global firm is to process data anyplace in the world without having to worry about the type of platform used for processing. What kinds of problems do you encounter trying to achieve this objective in an international environment? (For a discussion of some of these issues, see *Deans and Kane*, 1992.) The following section outlines some of the typical problems faced by a manager of a global organization.

The first problem is managing local development when the foreign unit does not coordinate with headquarters. The foreign subsidiary may be duplicating development efforts under way in other parts of the world. It also may not have a talented staff, and may end up with poorly conceived and designed systems. The question of headquarters-subsidiary coordination and management is a central one in pursuing an international corporate strategy.

The counter argument from the local company is that it knows the needs in its location. A distant headquarters unit cannot set specifications for foreign countries. This contention leads to the second development issue. How does the firm develop a set of common systems shared across different countries to take advantage of economies of scale? Headquarters does not want each country to develop its own accounting and sales reporting systems. Different countries have different laws and regulations, so it may be impossible to share programs among foreign locations without making special modifications for unique requirements in each country.

The third development problem is that when designing applications, there are real and perceived unique features in each country. Designers, especially those representing headquarters, must recognize what features are required for a system to work in a country and what features are there as an exercise in local independence. For example, Straub (1994) studied the use of e-mail and fax in Japan and the U.S. He found that cultural differences predisposed managers in each country to a choice of communications vehicles. Straub suggests that high uncertainty avoidance in Japan and structural features of the Japanese language explain why Japanese managers have a lower opinion of the social presence and information richness of e-mail and fax, though American and Japanese managers rated traditional communications media like the telephone and face-to-face communications about the same.

Managers must also be aware that more and more firms want to build a worldwide communications network to take advantage of communications and coordination tools to move data freely around the world. This effort can be a major challenge because of different technical standards and regulations. Certain countries regulate the kind of telecommunications equipment that can be used on their network. In a number of foreign countries PTT (postal, telegraph, and telephone) monopolies regulate communications and may restrict the ability to transmit data. Some underdeveloped countries may not have adequate communications capabilities to support private networks. Countries also may prohibit importing certain kinds of computer equipment in order to protect domestic competitors. Different kinds of communications networks and standards can greatly increase the difficulty and cost of building worldwide communications capabilities.

A number of government requirements may impede the development of global information systems (Steinbart and Nath, 1992):

1. A requirement to purchase specific equipment in the foreign country that may not be compatible with the equipment other places the global firm operates.

2. A requirement to do certain kinds of processing in the host country before data can be sent electronically to another country.

3. Restrictions on the use of satellites and special requirements for building private networks.

4. Limited access to flat-rate leased lines or a requirement that all transmission be made on variable cost lines.

A fifth major issue arising from international IS efforts is **transborder data flows**. Moving data across a boundary may be curtailed by government regulation, ostensibly to protect its citizens and their privacy. Another impact of regulation is to reduce the economic power of foreign companies or limit the imposition of foreign culture on the host country. Many of the transborder regulations seem to be motivated by a desire to protect local industry. Countries may have a legitimate concern about the privacy rights of their citizens. This reason is probably cited most often for instituting data controls. To implement control, a country can establish regulations through its telecommunications ministry, levy tariffs, and/or require formal approval of plans to process data in the country.

Examples of barriers to data flows include:

• Restrictive regulations that require processing of data originating in a country in that country only, making it difficult to transmit and share data.

• Exorbitant pricing of communications services by government owned post, telephone, and telegraph (PTT) ministries. However, a wave of "privatization" is sweeping countries and many PTTs are becoming private or quasi-private companies.

- Security. Attacks on computers by various hackers throughout the world have pointed out how difficult it is to secure networked computers.

As with any international venture, language and cultural differences can also present a challenge to developing IT on a global scale. Time differences can make communication difficult for different parts of the world, though fax and e-mail have eased this problem considerably. Some firms stress joint development teams with representatives from different countries to avoid problems stemming from developing a system in any one country or language. Foreign subsidiaries may be more willing to adopt an international system developed by a cross-cultural team.

MANAGING INFORMATION TECHNOLOGY INTERNATIONALLY

What can the manager do to solve the problems raised above? Some of these impediments to IT require political action or deregulation, for example, the policies of foreign PTT utilities. In other instances, management has to take action to solve problems and managers have to be involved in

Designing Around the World

Ford Motor Company has business in the U.S., Europe and Asia. It has design centers in Dearborn, Michigan, Ford's headquarters, Valencia, California and five other centers in Cologne, Germany; Dunton, England; Turin, Italy; Hiroshima, Japan; and Melbourne, Australia. Ford has launched a "Studio 2010 Computer Aided Industrial Design' unit in Dearborn. The objective of this project is to establish interactive video links among the seven design centers to facilitate collaboration among its engineers. Designing a new car today costs in the billions of dollars; Studio 2010 is designed to reduce that cost while encouraging collaboration among Ford designers worldwide. Currently there are high speed data links between Dearborn and Valencia, England and Germany.

The company plans to share multimedia information in videoconferences. A presentation might include videoclips and three-dimensional images developed on the computer-aided design workstations. Ford is a good example of information technology being used to coordinate a global firm; regardless of where an engineer sits or in what time zone he or she works, it is possible to contribute to a design project. Linking the world together was a logical step after Ford's engineers had been equipped with computer-aided design workstations. These workstations contributed to the productivity of the individual engineer; the communications links will contribute to the productivity of the team that is working on a design project.

efforts to develop systems that will be used in multiple countries. It is management that has to sell its vision for the firm's global technological infrastructure and resolve conflicts over IT requirements.

Roche (1992) presents a number of strategies for managing information technology in a global environment. See Table 6-1.

Concentrate on Interorganizational Linkages

In Chapter 5 we discussed the trend toward interorganizational systems— the firm creating linkages with suppliers and customers. This strategy can be extremely effective internationally as well. It can be very difficult to set up these linkages because of differing telecommunications capabilities in different countries. In some regions phone systems do not work well and transmitting data over them is probably not viable. Other countries, like France, have an extremely well-developed infrastructure for business communication, which is discussed later in this section.

Establish Global Systems Development Skills

There are problems managing IT development projects when all participants are from the same country and work in the same location. Coordinating multinational project teams presents an even greater challenge. Language and distance make it difficult to coordinate. A New York bank has a development team with members in New York, Lexington, Massachusetts and Ireland! In some foreign countries, hiring staff with the appropriate skills to work on technology can be difficult. Interviews with IT managers for multinationals in seven countries found dramatic differences in their accomplishments and their capabilities. Lack of personnel skills can be a major impediment to developing international systems; not all countries have educational programs to prepare individuals for systems analysis or programming jobs.

Build an Infrastructure

Justifying expenditures on infrastructure can also be extremely difficult. Infrastructure is the part of technology that does not have an immediate benefit. The easiest example is a worldwide communications network. One money-center bank carefully costed out an international, private network and found that it had a negative net present value. Economic criteria

Table 6-1
Strategies for Managing Global IT

- Concentrate on interorganizational linkages
- Establish global systems development skills
- Build an infrastructure
- Take advantage of liberalized telecommunications
- Strive for uniform data
- Develop guidelines for shared versus local systems

dictate to not undertake the development of the network. However, the bank went ahead and found that the new IT provided a number of benefits that were hard to quantify. Basically, with this network the bank could "plug in" any application to the network and offer it anyplace in the world it did business.

Take Advantage of Liberalized Electronic Communications

The trend toward deregulation in the U.S. is also sweeping foreign countries. France has split France Telecom from the PTT and established it as a quasi-public organization. In the past two decades, France Telecom has replaced an outmoded phone system with a mass market communications network called the Minitel system. It is also a leader in providing packet-switched data communications through Transpac. (Packet switching is discussed in Chapter 12). Changes such as these facilitate the development of the international communications networks essential to managing in a global environment.

Strive for Uniform Data

One of the major problems in sharing data is identifying it. A story is told that a large computer vendor once looked at its logistics systems and found that "ship date" meant six or seven different things depending on the system involved. In one system it might be the promised ship date,

---

MANAGEMENT PROBLEM 6-1

Bill Roberts is the chief information officer for a multinational company. He reports to the company president and has a staff of fifty at headquarters. This group runs systems for the headquarters operation and also tries to provide standards for subsidiaries in foreign countries.

Headquarters has developed a standard library of financial and accounting applications which runs on most of the computers in the subsidiaries. (Bill was successful a few years ago in getting all the subsidiaries except the largest to agree on one model of computer.) Since many of the subsidiaries are not large and have trouble recruiting skilled technology staff members, they are quite happy with the library of programs.

Each country has its own information services department manager, generally reporting to the controller or possibly the president of the subsidiary. Bill and his staff travel extensively to try to help each subsidiary better manage its technology effort.

Bill is facing a major problem in at least two countries; he and his staff think the local person in charge of information systems is not doing a good job. "After several years of working with the people in charge in two countries, I have come to the conclusion that we really should let them go. However, I have no real responsibility; these people report to a manager in the country, not to me."

How can Bill help the company solve this problem? Do you think they need to reorganize the structure of their IT units? Does it make sense to have foreign operations reporting to Bill? If not, how can he influence what goes on in subsidiaries outside the U.S.?

and another the date the item left the loading dock. To obtain economies of scale from sharing data and systems, the firm must have a common vocabulary of terms and definitions.

Develop Guidelines for Shared Versus Local Systems

We can add another important strategy to Roche's list: You need to develop guidelines for when a system should be shared and when a local, autonomous system is more appropriate. The obvious advantage of shared systems are economies of scale and the ability to share data. The problem with shared systems is that they tend to become very large and complex. Also, individual locations and users have special needs which must be incorporated into the system. As the number of exceptions increases, the system becomes more cumbersome and difficult to program.

The advantage of a local system is that it can often be developed quickly in response to a local condition. If it later becomes necessary to coordinate this system with other applications, special interfaces will have to be created. If each location ends up needing a similar system and cannot share this one, the firm has paid for many systems when possibly one would have sufficed.

There are no firm guidelines for making this kind of decision. Firms have had success and failure with both approaches. Systems development in an international environment (or even a domestic one where there are many locations) leads to this problem. Management has to recognize that the problem exists and compare the alternative of local versus global, shared systems.

THREE EXAMPLES

Standard Pharmaceuticals International

Standard Pharmaceuticals International (SPI) is the international division of a multinational drug company headquartered in the United States. The international division consists of thirty foreign subsidiaries located throughout the world. SPI is dependent on the U.S. parent company for all research and new products.

A major challenge for pharmaceuticals firms is to obtain government approval for the sale of new drugs. This process can take many years of testing and the submission of literally a truckload of documents to the Food and Drug Administration. The firm then must wait until the FDA approves or disapproves the sale of the drug.

Some foreign countries will accept U.S. FDA approval as sufficient to market the drug, but many will not. This practice means that the SPI foreign subsidiary must conduct clinical trials in its own country and submit the results to its government for approval. Once approved, the SPI subsidiary markets the drug to physicians and hospitals.

SPI's information services (SPIIS) department has a "federal" organizational structure. The head of the department reports to the SPI controller (based on historical precedent; it has been recommended that this individual report to the SPI president). Each country has its own information services manager who reports to the local controller. (In a similar vein, it has been recommended that the local IS manager report to the SPI local subsidiary president.) The headquarters IS group provides advice to the subsidiaries and tries to set standards. However, the local subsidiary staff does not report to the headquarters IS manager.

Because of the historical reporting relationship, it is not surprising that most of the applications at SPIIS involve finance, accounting, and sales reporting. The headquarters IS group developed a standard library of applications that most of the smaller subsidiaries adopted. Larger subsidiaries do not necessarily have the same equipment, and several of them have significant IS staffs and portfolios of applications.

Recently the parent company appointed a new president of SPI. This individual wants to change the strategy of the IS group with emphasis on supporting the sales and marketing departments. He commented, "I have yet to see how one gets a competitive advantage by closing the books each month two days before the competition."

SPIIS is trying to adjust to this change in strategic focus. One example of the problems they are encountering is the sales representative notebook computer project. The sales and marketing department launched a separate effort from IS to develop applications for a notebook computer for sales representatives. The portable computer should provide information to the sales representative about his or her territory with access to a commercial database of prescription drug sales. These sales reps visit physicians in their offices and at hospitals to explain the company's new products and leave samples for the physician. The system should also keep track of sales calls and keep a record of drug samples left with the physician. (This record is often required by governments in order to limit the number of samples distributed).

The marketing and sales groups tried to keep IS from becoming involved in this project because they felt IS was interested only in financial systems. The IS manager was concerned that the notebook-computer team lacked adequate technological expertise and would waste a large amount of money.

Because of country differences, marketing tried different types of systems in different countries. In one country, marketing bought a package system and invested a reported $1 million before canceling the trial The greatest success has been in France, where the Minitel system made it easy to implement all of the needed functions using existing technology.

SPI is caught in the dilemma of local system versus shared systems development. In addition, the president of the division wants to more than double sales revenues while keeping administrative expenses at current levels. Without providing more resources to the IS staff and investing in a worldwide network, it is unlikely that the president will be able to accomplish his goals.

Asea Brown Boveri

Asea Brown Boveri (ABB) is a Swiss-based electrical company described as one of the most successful transnationals in the world. The company was formed by a merger between Asea, a Swedish engineering firm, and Brown Boveri, a Swiss competitor. The dynamic chairman, Percy Barnevik, has added more than 70 companies in Europe and the U.S. to this pair of firms. ABB is larger than Westinghouse and is competing directly with GE in the United States.

ABB is a transnational firm as depicted in Figure 6-1. Barnevik wants local managers to concentrate on their markets, but he also wants to strive for global efficiencies and take advantage of the purchasing power ABB's size generates. The company is organized as a matrix. Along one axis, the company consists of distributed subsidiaries, each of which makes decisions without regard to national borders or other ABB units. In the second dimension, the firm appears as a group of traditional national companies, each serving its home market. Barnevik and a 12 person executive committee provide the glue that holds the two dimensions of the matrix together. Some 50 or so leaders of business areas report to the executive committee.

The business areas are further grouped into eight segments with a member of the executive committee responsible for each segment. The business leader is responsible for optimizing the business globally. Business leaders know no borders, and are located in many different countries. These leaders allocate export markets to factories, share expertise by job rotation, create temporary multinational task forces to solve problems, and devise global strategies. Within each country, there is a traditional structure with a CEO for ABB operations in that country. The CEO reports to a local board of directors and the business in that country produces its

MANAGEMENT PROBLEM 6-2

SPIIS maintains a library of applications for small subsidiaries. This library is very popular in South and Central America and in other countries that are small from a sales standpoint. The president of the division wants new efforts to focus on the support of marketing and sales. Unfortunately, the library runs on an old minicomputer that is no longer supported by the vendor.

The library will run on the vendor's replacement for the old mini, but it is highly inefficient. Also, the new computer provides opportunities to upgrade the programs in the standard library.

The manager of SPIIS is facing several problems and has asked for your help in solving them. First, there are a lot of users of the library and all of them have suggestions for modification. How can he design a new library and take all of their suggestions into account without having this turn into a ten-year project?

Second, it is clear that SPIIS does not have the staff to convert the library of applications, develop new systems in marketing and sales, and keep present operations running. What are the options for solving the staffing problem? What are the pros and cons of each option?

own financial statements. The CEO may have a number of subsidiaries operating in his or her country. There are approximately 1100 local ABB units around the world (Taylor, 1991).

One significant challenge in this environment is reporting results and finding problems. Shortly after the creation of ABB, the company developed and implemented a new information system called ABACUS. This system collects monthly performance data from 5000 profit centers in 1,300 companies that employ more than 200,000 people in 140 countries. It compares actual performance with budget and forecasts. Local units submit data in their currencies and the system translates all numbers into U.S. dollars for comparison purposes. Barnevik looks at variables like new orders, invoicing, margins, and cash flows around the world to spot trends. As an example, he might see that an industry segment is behind budget; looking for more detail, the problem appears to be in one business area. Further study shows that the problems are in one country and that margins are off. The conclusion is that a price war has broken out. The next problem is to decide on a course of action; the system has alerted management to the problem, but they will have to decide on the appropriate course of action to solve it (Simons and Bartlett, 1992).

The company has only two IT staff members and a part-time manager at headquarters. An IS steering committee serves major geographic and business entities. Each of these groups meets several times a year to approve budgets and ensure that technology plans fit the corporate plans. IS managers work for each of three geographic regions, five business segments, and 45 business areas. Each business chooses its own application. The company is trying to standardize on Lotus Notes as a corporate groupware environment, with some 13,000 users in 1995 (See Chapter 21).

Air Products and Chemicals

Air Products and Chemicals (APC) supplies industrial gases and chemicals around the world. The company wants to increase sales from $2.7 billion to $6 billion in seven years. Because existing markets are saturated, the growth will have to come from new markets overseas (Ives and Jarvenpaa, 1992).

APC has four business areas: industrial gases, chemicals, process systems, and environmental/energy. Its customers often build plants in remote locations to take advantage of raw materials or low-cost labor. They expect APC to supply them wherever the plants are located. APC has had a record of investing in information technology. Senior management within each business group has taken responsibility for its own IT.

In the 1960s and 1970s, APC functioned as a classical multinational. Its European headquarters operated autonomously. APC's chemicals business, however, was more international and centrally controlled because it focused on exports. Ives and Jarvenpaa feel that APC's customers are now demanding a more global approach to business, which will move the firm toward a transnational strategy.

In summary, APC gave its subsidiaries a great deal of independence until the early 1970s, when APC headquarters began to emphasize worldwide applications to increase efficiency. The focus was on minimizing expenditures by avoiding redundant systems. Local subsidiary managers were unenthusiastic about this approach as they had little to gain. During the 1980s the model at APC was to return control to the local subsidiary while headquarters tried to use influence to guide choices made locally. Current pressures are moving the firm toward a global IT strategy to provide consistent customer service around the world.

Business Models and IT Management

Based on this case and their research, Ives and Jarvenpaa (1992) suggest that an international firm goes through the following stages in developing its management of information technology, which are outlined in Table 6-2 on page 148.

Independent Operations   In the 1960s and 1970s many multinationals gave considerable autonomy to foreign subsidiaries, which acquired hardware and software from local vendors. The applications implemented differed considerably across countries. There was little interaction with

MANAGEMENT PROBLEM 6-3

The manager of operations for a major money-center bank, Alexis Montgomery, asked her staff to investigate the possibility of building a private, worldwide communications network to carry all voice and data traffic for the bank. The manager was motivated by a survey which showed that each application running in the bank used its own communications network set up specifically for that application.

As the manager put it, "We have branches with two to four networks in them, one for each application. Every person designing a technology solution to a problem also has to design a network. We need to get to the point that the network will be in the wall like the electricity; all we have to do is plug in a new application."

Of course, not everyone in the bank felt they wanted to use a private network. A manager in the stock-transfer area said, "I've got fifty employees sitting at terminals that are connected directly to one of our mainframes. I get average response times of less than two seconds. Why would I want to go onto a network that will route my transactions over a greater distance that has to slow my staff down."

Alexis was somewhat surprised when her staff came back with an estimate that showed a negative net present value from investing in the network. She commented, "I know this is the right thing to do. Imagine being able to take something we develop in London or Hong Kong and deliver it around the world by just plugging it in. Yet how can I go to the senior management committee for approval with a negative net present value?" She has asked for your help in justifying the worldwide network project.

headquarters or the IT staff there. Headquarters might impose a chart of accounts or financial reporting standards on subsidiaries, however, these data were rarely transmitted electronically.

Headquarters Driven During the 1980s the focus of multinationals turned to efficiency in Information Technology operations. Headquarters based in the U.S. sought to implement worldwide applications on subsidiaries to reduce development and operating costs. The apparent motivation for this approach was efficiency, and local subsidiaries did not see much to be gained.

The Global Reach of the Computer

Less-developed countries, for years on the outside of the computer revolution because of cost and import restrictions, have displayed a ravenous appetite for personal computers. In Brazil where PCs were almost nonexistent three years ago, computers have become a major part of the culture. It is estimated that tens of thousands of Brazilians are banking at home. PCs can be found in Poland, Indonesia, Uganda and Bangladesh. The Latin American personal computer market grew 24% in 1994.

Many of these computers are being used in business, narrowing the competitiveness gap between firms in the less developed countries and developed nations. Because these organizations do not have old technology, they can start with highly cost/effective PCs and a client-server architecture (See Chapters 8 and 13). A bank in Prague with no computer systems moved from paper to a client-server network on Dell computers, allowing it to connect for the first time with world-wide monetary trading networks. Chile's export-promotion agency connected 160 PCs around the world to a group of Compaq servers in Santiago so that prospective buyers could review Chile's export products.

In Latin America, Chile is one of the leaders in applying PC technology. Many small stores use a PC for tracking inventory and preparing invoices. Larger companies like the wine-maker Concha y Toro and the dairy Loncoleche equip their sales force with hand-held terminals or notebook computers. Compania de Petroleos de Chile uses PC-based systems to keep track of diesel fuel sales and monitor the growth of trees. The Chilean government is spending $3 million to put computers in schools. Even still Chile has 3.3 PCs for each 100 people compared to 30 per 100 people in the U.S.

Brazil has relaxed import tariffs on computers and sales have soared. A grocery wholesaler in central Brazil was never able to afford a computer, especially given interest rates of 12 to 14% *per month* on capital. Its major competitor used a mainframe computer to route trucks. However, the wholesaler sent its trucks on the same routes each day whether there were orders or not. With a $3000 PC and a package from a Maryland firm, the wholesaler has been able to deliver 30% more goods with a 35% smaller fleet of trucks. It has reduced warehouse employment from 95 to 80 people, The company also installed bar code scanners to track inventory and a central server to track orders. For the first time, it is ahead of its competitors in applying technology.

Table 6-2
Information Technology Approaches in Globally Competing Firms

IT activities	APPROACHES			
	Independent operations	Headquarters driven	Intellectual synergy	Integrated global
Applications development	Total local autonomy	Modify a working U.S. application for global use	Joint high-level requirements analysis; implementation under local control	Multinational user/IS team designs and oversees implementation of the system
Applications maintenance	Total local autonomy	Centralized maintenance	Total local autonomy	Centralized maintenance on common core modules; localized maintenance on others
Systems software, hardware	Total local autonomy	Headquarters' (HQ) decision	Total local autonomy	Common worldwide architecture
Staffing senior IT positions at subsidiaries	Total local autonomy, a local employee	HQ's decision, often a U.S. expatriate	Advice from HQ's IT group, a local employee	Joint decision, a global search for eligible candidates
Control over IT operations	Total local autonomy	Run from centralized data center	Local autonomy, but incentives from HQ	Local systems run locally; common system run from local/regional data center
Relationship between subsidiary and HQ's IT heads	No formal relationship, little or no informal contact	Subsidiaries' IT heads report to HQ's IT head	Dotted-line relationship; considerable informal exchange	IT heads around the world are peers; considerable informal and formal exchange
Diffusion of IT innovation	Little or no diffusion across country boundaries	One-way, from HQ to subsidiaries	Two-way	Two-way, "centers of excellence" established around the world

Table 6-2 *(continued)*

IT activities	APPROACHES			
	Independent operations	Headquarters driven	Intellectual synergy	Integrated global
Primary basis for common systems	Consolidated financial reporting requirements	Economies of scale in IT activities	Experience accumulated in other parts of a multinational firm	Global business drivers

Intellectual Synergy This approach to IT returns control to the local subsidiary. Headquarters tries to use influence to guide the choices of the subsidiaries. The firm might host worldwide planning conferences. If this model is working, the subsidiaries should request advice from headquarters. Headquarters tries to coordinate the subsidiaries to reduce duplicate development efforts and encourage resource sharing.

Integrated Global IT This approach is often adopted because of pressure from global customers. The firm must provide more consistent customer service internationally. Systems design requires input from around the world. The firm must standardize its data and will probably consolidate data centers. Headquarters will specify certain applications as common systems, such as order entry. There will be limited customization of these systems to fit a subsidiary.

Ives and Jarvenpaa, based on the APC case study, suggest that there is a relationship between approach to IT management and the business models presented earlier. (See Table 6-3).

The multinational firm is expected to favor independent operations. A great deal of autonomy on information technology decisions is given to the local subsidiary. The focus of the strategy is on local response.

Table 6-3
Business and IT Management Approaches

Business model	IT management approach
Multinational	Independent operations
Global	Headquarters driven
International	Intellectual synergy
Transnational	Integrated global IT

The global business model stresses efficiency. We would expect to find a headquarters-driven technology strategy with this approach to business. Headquarters will try to coordinate and centralize to reduce duplication and encourage common systems.

An international business model will probably be combined with an IT strategy of intellectual synergy. Subsidiaries depend on headquarters for guidance and for new knowledge. Headquarters tries to influence subsidiary technology policies through planning and sharing information.

The transnational firm is most likely to follow an integrated, global IT strategy. Headquarters will define core systems that will provide uniform customer service in a global market. Management of the firm realizes that information technology is an important element in its strategy.

TECHNOLOGY FOR THE INTERNATIONAL BUSINESS

One key technology for international business is communications of all types, a topic that is discussed in detail in Chapters 11 and 12. A firm with a significant international presence is likely to need an international network of some kind. The experience of Hong Kong and Shanghai Banking Corp. Ltd. offers an interesting example of networking.

The bank is a principal member of HSBC Holding's, a $265-billion organization that is one of the ten largest financial groups in the world. (see Cureton, 1992). The bank has invested heavily in a telecommunications infrastructure to provide global banking services. The bank has developed

A Global Technology Company

Texas Instruments is a leading manufacturer of semiconductors. Its high-speed telecommuncations chip is the results of a world effort. The chip was conceived with engineers from Ericsson Telephone in Sweden and designed in Nice with TI software tools developed in Houston. Texas instruments makes the chips in Japan and Dallas, tests it in Taiwan, and wires it into Ericsson cards that monitor phone systems in Sweden, the U.S., Mexico and Australia. Through its network, engineers in Dallas can run chip-testing machines at assembly plants in the Philippines. When they find something wrong, they can remotely reprogram the production line by the start of the next shift. Programs distribute orders to whichever plant needs work at the time.

Over 40% of TI's semiconductor group's employees work outside the U.S. generating $6.8 billion in sales. The company feels that a local presence helps it win orders and protects it from currency fluctuations. TI sells 65% of its chips outside the U.S., more than its competitors do. One research firm expects worldwide chip sales to grow from $100 billion in 1995 to $273 billion by 2000, with the majority of the growth outside the U.S.

Figure 6-2
The Hong Kong Bank international communications network.

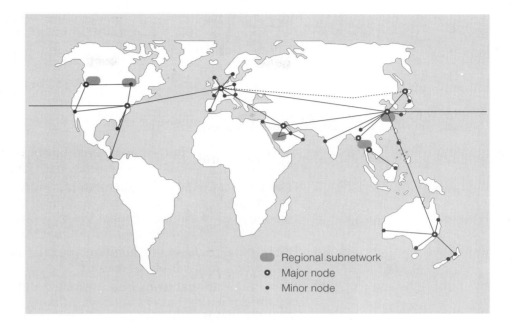

Regional subnetwork
⊙ Major node
• Minor node

an extensive, worldwide network depicted in Figure 6-2. The network is private; the bank leases lines and manages the net itself.

The bank has 45 subsidiaries and 3,300 branches in 50 countries. (HSSC Holding owns Midland Bank, PLC in England.) The Hong Kong Bank International network carries data, compressed-voice, fax, and video traffic. It consists of digital leased lines with speeds of 64 thousand bits per second to 2,048 thousand bits per second. The network spans 73 computer centers. This digital wide-band network handles high-speed and high-volume applications.

The bank also has a private packet-switching network. The leased-line network provides the main links for packet switching (a technology explained in more detail in Chapter 12). The packet-switched network provides communications between any of the bank's computers and some 49,000 terminals. The bank feels that packet switching is well suited to banks where there are large volumes of short transactions. The packet network carries 2 million payments and corporate messages each month to 116 offices in 50 countries.

The problems of developing and managing an international network are reflected in the fact that Hong Kong Bank has to lease lines from PTTs in some thirty eight countries. (The bank has developed its own service index for each carrier and ranks international carriers on their performance.)

Hong Kong Bank spends more than $400 million a year on information technology. About 25 percent of this amount is for the global network. The bank's IT expenditures are about 14 percent of overhead compared to an industry average of 20 percent.

Information technology, particularly telecommunications, is vital for an international company that has significant business in many different countries.

CHAPTER SUMMARY

1. There are at least four international business strategies including the multinational, global, international, and transnational.

2. IT can be used to facilitate international business, especially IT organization design variables that stress communications and coordination. Headquarters-subsidiary coordination is one of the most significant challenges in managing an international business.

3. It can be difficult to implement international applications of the technology for a variety of reasons.

4. Many international firms find they need a global network, a technology infrastructure that ties together far-flung components of the firm.

5. Firms building technology must trade off the advantages of local flexibility and freedom against the benefits and efficiency of common systems.

6. IT challenges in an international environment also encompasses issues like standards, uniform data and dealing with the different quality and regulation of telecommunications in various countries.

What a Node

A recent magazine advertisement features an 855-foot, 70,000-ton node for a Miami network. This gigantic node is usually not in Miami, and in fact it is generally a moving target. What is it? The node is a Carnival Cruise Line passenger ship.

Most local area networks are found in a single location, like within a department in an office building. Of course, many individuals want to connect LANs that might be separated by larger distances. The company placing the magazine ad offers a solution: You dedicate one PC on a LAN to be a remote server. This company provides a program to allow up to sixteen remote users to dial in to the network and become the equivalent of local nodes on the network. The cruise ship simply places a ship-to-shore phone call to the remote server, and PCs on the ship have full access to the services on the LAN.

For companies separated by large distances, this kind of dial-up solution is very attractive, assuming that you do not have to spend a long period of time connected to the LAN.

7. The liberalization of trade and emerging economies in Eastern Europe suggest that international business will continue to be of major importance in the future.

IMPLICATIONS FOR MANAGEMENT

One of the major trends in business is globalization. The IT organization design variables of Chapter 4 are well-suited to helping you manage a global firm. You will want a technological infrastructure that features a world-wide network. Building on this infrastructure you can use groupware, e-mail, conferencing, and other communications technologies to coordinate far-flung operations. With this infrastructure in place it is also easy to create electronic links with customers and suppliers around the world. Technology makes it possible to communicate across time zones and should dramatically reduce the amount of travel required to manage a global enterprise.

KEY WORDS

European Economic Community (EEC)
Global
Headquarters driven
Integrated global IT
Independent operations

Intellectual synergy
International
Multinational
Transborder data flows
Transnational

RECOMMENDED READING

Bradley, S., J. Hausman, and R. Nolan. *Globalization, Technology, and Competition: The Fusion of Computers and Telecommunications in the 1990s.* Boston: Harvard Business School Press, 1993. (A book of articles by experts in technology, strategy and international business.)

Deans, C., and J. Jurison. *Information Technology in a Global Business Environment.* Danvers, Ma.: Boyd & Fraser, 1996. (A book of readings and some cases on the issues in managing international IT efforts.)

Ives, B., and S. Jarvenpaa. "Global Information Technology: Some Lessons from Practice," *International Information Systems,* vol. 1, no. 3 (July 1992), pp. 1–15. (An insightful article that presents several of the models described in this chapter.)

Roche, E. *Managing Information Technology in Multinational Corporations.* New York: Macmillan, 1992. (This book contains a number of interesting case studies of global firms and how they manage IT.)

DISCUSSION QUESTIONS

1. What has motivated the current interest in global business?

2. Why might a country want to regulate the data collected within its borders?

3. One study reported that managers found concerns about regulations on transborder data flows to be unwarranted. Why do you suppose this issue has not surfaced?

4. What are the advantages of providing a subsidiary with a great deal of local autonomy?

5. What are the disadvantages of local autonomy for subsidiaries?

6. How should a manager determine whether a system should be "common" across a number of subsidiaries, or uniquely developed for each subsidiary?

7. Why do you suppose Standard Pharmaceuticals International primarily developed financial and accounting systems?

8. What can the president of SPI do to change the division's strategy toward marketing and sales support?

9. How can information technology support a marketing-oriented strategy in the drug industry?

10. What motivated APC to move toward a more global information technology strategy?

11. What are the risks of a global IT strategy? What are its benefits?

12. What impediments do you see to worldwide networks for coordinating the activities of global firms?

13. How can an international firm see that local staff members have enough expertise to develop and apply IT?

14. What are the problems of establishing common data elements in a global organization?

15. Why does a firm need common data elements and structures?

16. How can IT help coordinate a global firm? Where can it help save money while making the firm more responsive?

17. Roche advocates a number of interorganizational linkages in conducting international business. What problems do you see in connecting a global firm to its many customers in different countries?

18. What kind of business activities do you think are most amenable to common systems in different countries?

19. What are the advantages of making product design information available around the world? How might you use this capability to organize product development?

20. If company management or custom dictates a fairly independent and autonomous IT effort in subsidiaries, what approaches can management take to coordinate these activities?

CHAPTER 6 PROJECT

IMPLICATIONS OF NAFTA

The United States, Canada, and Mexico are working to eliminate trade barriers among these three trading partners. Some South American countries envision a completely free trade zone in the Americas. Using recent articles in the business press, develop a list of the positions, pro and con, taken by various interest groups, such as business, labor, and politicians, on free trade in the western hemisphere. What impact does the Mexican peso crisis of 1995 have on your arguments?

If tariffs are drastically reduced or eliminated, what is the role of information technology in encouraging more trade? In managing firms in the hemisphere?

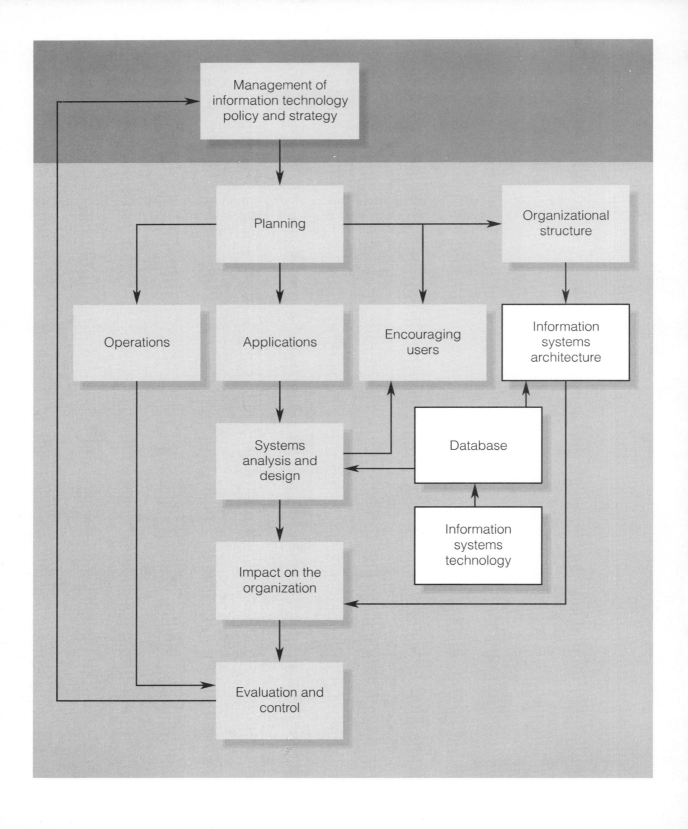

Information Technology

This part contains important material you will need to make decisions about technology, as shown in the accompanying figure. To make decisions intelligently, the decision maker must understand some of the technical issues involved. A basic knowledge of technology is necessary to manage information systems activities effectively.

In Chapters 7 and 8, we discuss computer hardware. Users and managers are often involved in the selection of the appropriate technology for an application. Should the application run on a large or midsized computer, or on PCs connected on a local area network?

The user may be involved in the selection of the entire computer system. Possibilities here range from a personal computer to a large, general-purpose computer system. It is also very likely that the acquisition of specific devices, such as laser printers, networks, optical storage units, and similar equipment will involve the manager. Finally, management must decide where computers will be located and what applications each computer will execute.

There are also many important decisions concerning computer software, a topic discussed in Chapter 9. Should a user buy a particular program for a personal computer?

Many organizations have developed comprehensive databases in order to run basic transactions processing applications. More recently organizations have compiled large amounts of data into "data warehouses" in order to gather information useful for providing better customer service and marketing products and services. Database technology is the topic of Chapter 10.

The topic of communications is of great interest to management. Deregulation by the government, combined with the entry of new carriers, creates many choices for communicating both voice and data. How should computers be configured? What kind of network is desired? What are the opportunities to communicate directly with the computers of suppliers and customers? Chapter 11 introduces communications technology while Chapter 12 discusses the world of networks. Private and industry networks have existed for many years. The mass market networks like Compuserve, America On-line, and Prodigy are a more recent phenomenon. Of course, the most famous network of all is the Internet and we shall explore its potential for business.

Today the manager is faced with a variety of IT architectures. Chapter 13 describes and provides examples of systems that range from large, centralized computers to the more modern client-server architecture.

A manager is always concerned with the various sources available for products and services. In the technology field, there are options on suppliers for both hardware and software. We discuss some of the possibilities and their advantages and disadvantages in Chapter 14. Hundreds of new software products are announced each month for personal computers. Here the problem is not deciding on the source but having enough information to decide what package to buy for a specific application.

The purpose of the material in this part is not to educate technologists. Rather, the objective is for you to gain enough understanding of the technology to make intelligent decisions about it.

CHAPTER **7**

The Fundamentals

OBJECTIVES

1. Learning to manage information technology.

To manage something, the manager needs basic knowledge of how it works. Managers are required to make decisions about what kind of technology to purchase: What processor should we purchase in our new computers? What factors influence how a computer performs? What computers are best suited for what uses? The purpose of this chapter is to help you understand in general how computers work so that you can develop and manage the hardware infrastructure of the firm.

2. Preparing to apply technology.

The systems discussed in this text almost always involve using a computer for processing. Systems designers need to understand the capacities and

159

limitations of the technology available to them. As you develop new applications, you will find that technology has become more powerful and less costly at the same time.

3. Transforming the organization.

The computer is the device that started it all. The machine described in this chapter has been combined with communications technology among others to make dramatic changes in the way organizations are structured and operate.

Why should one be interested in the way computer equipment works? You may already own a computer and find that you do not need to understand much about computers to use it. On the other hand, it is quite likely that you will be involved in purchasing computers, either for yourself, or for other people. The numbers involved are hard to imagine! An Intel executive claimed in 1995 that twice a second, someone bought an Intel-based computer! This manufacturer's chips run in 150 million personal computers.

Today's marketplace is a confusing one. There are a variety of computer vendor chips with different capabilities and prices. What is the bus and how does it influence the speed of a computer? What are RAM and ROM? Does it matter if one computer has a higher clock speed than another? To make intelligent purchasing decisions, you must understand how computers work, and particularly how certain features influence their performance. In this chapter, we discuss the basics of computers. In the next chapter, we trace their evolution to provide background on how the industry reached its present state.

People invented computers and their associated equipment, and one of the most difficult aspects of computers is a consequence of this human design. Of the engineering and design decisions made during computer development, many appear arbitrary. Computer science is unlike a field such as mathematics, in which theorems are developed and proved rigorously. The reasons for a certain design feature may not be obvious even to a computer expert. Designers make decisions by balancing performance estimates of how the computer will be used against costs. Because of the arbitrary nature of design decisions, we discuss general concepts that underlie the operation of most computer systems, although specific machines differ from any general discussion.

The equipment we discuss in this chapter and the next is often referred to as computer **hardware**—the parts of the computer that can be touched physically. Chapter 9 is about computer software—the instructions in the form of programs that command the hardware to perform tasks. Physically, programs are entered in the computer through a keyboard. However, once inside the computer, a program cannot be seen and is represented electronically in computer memory.

THE COMPONENTS OF A PERSONAL COMPUTER

The computer you are most likely to encounter first is a personal computer. There are millions of these devices in schools, homes, and offices. Generally, they feature a keyboard for entering data, a **CRT** or television-like output device for displaying data, and some form of storage. A typical schematic for such a computer is shown in Figure 7-1. In this section, we present an overview of the parts of the computer; in subsequent sections, we discuss the components in more detail.

The heart of the computer is the central processing unit or **CPU**. It contains the logic that controls the calculations done by the computer. In most personal computers, the central processing unit is connected to a bus.

Figure 7-1
Schematic of a personal computer.

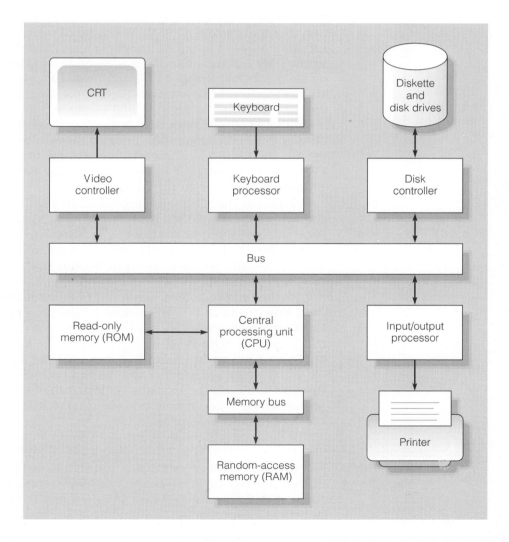

The bus is a communications device, really a connection, among various parts of the computer. The bus carries (1) instructions from programs telling the computer what to do and (2) data. On most modern computers, there is a separate bus between the CPU and **random access memory (RAM)** or what is often called **primary memory**. A separate, high-speed bus is needed here because contemporary CPU and memory chips are so fast, the main bus into which the keyboard and secondary-storage devices are plugged is too slow for the CPU and memory.

Primary memory of the computer holds two kinds of information. The first is data, as one might expect. For example, if we want to add two numbers together, such as 178 and 256, these numbers are stored in computer memory. Once added, their sum, 434, would also be placed in memory.

Instructions in the form of software programs are also stored in primary memory. The instructions or software tell the CPU what to do. Instructions provide the logic of the computer and enable it to perform calculations and manipulate data. One main feature of memory is its passive nature as memory is only a storage place for information. Instructions are executed in the CPU and data are moved between the CPU and memory when a calculation is being performed. Another way to look at memory is to consider that primary memory has no logic capability. It is a repository for data and instructions.

The **diskette** drive or **disk** is another form of storage. This **secondary storage** is usually larger than primary memory and is less costly. In Chapter 10, we discuss secondary storage in much greater detail. Note, however, the disk controller in Figure 7-1. There is logic required to connect or interface the disk to the computer.

Although the CPU contains the most logic in the computer, we can see there are other functions in which a component must display some logic, such as the disk controller. Similarly, there is a keyboard processor to interface the keyboard with the computer, and a video driver to control the CRT. Finally, we have an **input/output (I/O)** processor, which is dedicated to controlling devices such as printers.

The last component in Figure 7-1 is called **read-only memory (ROM)**. Read only memory is used to store instructions to the computer that are in essence, contained in hardware. Your personal computer has something called a ROM BIOS which contains the Basic Input/Output System of the computer and loads when you turn the computer on.

These, then, are the components of a typical personal computer. What the user sees is the keyboard, a systems unit, the monitor or CRT, and the printer. Inside the systems box are all the other components, as well as the diskette and disk drives.

Primary Memory or RAM

Although the central processing unit controls the computer, we need to discuss primary memory before examining the CPU to demonstrate how the computer stores data and instructions. In the next section, we see how the CPU processes the stored program and data to produce results.

The Arithmetic Basis of Computers

A computer can perform computations through an electronic counterpart to the arithmetic operations we perform on a routine basis. However, computer systems at their most fundamental level use a different number **base** from the common base 10 with which we are familiar.

The number 46 in base 10 can be represented as $4 \times 10 + 6 \times 1$. Furthermore, 10 is equal to 10^1, and 1 is equal to 10^0 (anything raised to the 0 power is 1, by definition). In our system of arithmetic, the position of a digit represents the power to which the base is raised before multiplication by the digit. For the number 46 above, 6 is in the 0 position and 4 is in the 1's position. We can represent 46, then, as $6 \times 10^0 + 4 \times 10^1$. This same procedure could be continued for more digits. For example, the number 346 can be represented as $6 \times 10^0 + 4 \times 10^1 + 3 \times 10^2$ Now there is a 3 in the 10^2 position that adds 3×10^2, or 300, to the number.

There is no reason to use the base 10 for arithmetic. It is convenient for human beings, but not for computers. A computer can be designed most easily to function in base 2, or the **binary** system. The two digits of the binary system (0 and 1) can be represented as "on" and "off," for example, through the presence or absence of an electrical voltage.

A binary number is represented in the same positional notation as a base 10 number. The number 101110 in binary, starting with the right-most digit and working left, would be converted to base 10 as follows:

$$
\begin{array}{rclcr}
0 \times 2^0 & = & 0 \times 1 & = & 0 \\
1 \times 2^1 & = & 1 \times 2 & = & 2 \\
1 \times 2^2 & = & 1 \times 4 & = & 4 \\
1 \times 2^3 & = & 1 \times 8 & = & 8 \\
0 \times 2^4 & = & 0 \times 16 & = & 0 \\
1 \times 25 & = & 1 \times 32 & = & \underline{32} \\
& & & & 46
\end{array}
$$

which adds to 46 in base 10.

At the most basic level, computers store and process data in binary form but this is not an easy system for humans to use. Therefore, the binary digits in computer memory are grouped together to form other number bases for performing operations. IBM mainframe computers group four digits to create a hexadecimal, or base 16, machine. Fortunately, even programmers rarely work at the binary level. For many applications, software or design of the hardware makes the machine appear to perform base 10 arithmetic from a programming standpoint.

All types of symbols can be coded and represented as binary numbers. For example, we could develop the following table to encode four alphabetic letters using two binary digits:

A = 00   B = 01   C = 10   D = 11

Thus, a series of binary digits can be coded to represent characters with which we are more familiar.

How Memory Is Organized

Now that we have a convenient way to represent numbers and symbols, we need a way to store them in memory. Different computer designers have adopted different schemes for memory organization. Generally, all computers combine groups of bits (binary digits) to form characters, sometimes called bytes. The number of bits determines the size of the character set. From the example above, we can code 2^n distinct characters with a binary number of n digits. For example, if there are 4 bits, there can be 2^4, or 16, symbols for data. Many modern computers use an 8-bit character, or byte, giving a possible character set of 2^8, or 256, symbols. Symbols are what the computer can display such as uppercase and lowercase letters, numerals, punctuation marks, and so on.

After a character size and set of symbols are developed, the next design issue is to decide how to organize the memory of the machine. One basic use of memory is to store and fetch data so we need a way to reference storage. An everyday example will help to clarify the problem. Suppose we are expecting an important piece of mail. The delivery will be made to the mailbox at our street address. We know that by looking in the mailbox at our address, we shall find the mail if it is there.

Now consider computer memory to be a group of mailboxes. We need an address to define each piece of data stored in memory so it may be placed in a particular location (mailbox) and retrieved from that location. It is possible to have an address for each character in memory, or sometimes groups of characters are combined to form words and the words are given an address. In some computer architectures, four 8-bit bytes are combined to form a word, though each byte also has an address. A word structure is convenient because many numbers will fit within a single word, as do many types of instructions.

Instructions, as well as data, must be stored in memory, and deciding on the instruction format is another design problem. At a minimum, the instruction must contain an operation code that specifies what operation is to be performed, such as add or subtract. The operation code is combined with one or more addresses. Suppose a computer has 8-bit bytes and that four bytes make up a word. Each byte can store either an alphabetic character or two numbers. An instruction on this computer might look like:

```
Byte      1   2   3   4

Contents  A   D   34  56
```

The computer could be designed to interpret this instruction as: Add the contents of storage location 3456 to the contents of a special part of the computer called an arithmetic **register**. (It is unlikely that the computer would treat bytes 3 and 4 the way we have above. It would most probably treat bytes 3 and 4 as a 16-bit binary number to identify a storage location.)

A single-address machine is designed with instructions that have one operation code and one address as in the example above. For most instructions, the single address specifies the memory location for one piece of data to be operated on by the instruction. In the case of an add instruction, the address specifies the memory location whose content is to be added to some data already contained in the central processing unit.

Memory Technology

How does a computer actually store data? Remember, all we need is to distinguish between two states to represent a 0 or a 1. From these binary numbers, we can build an alphabet of symbols and numbers using other number bases. Today's computers all use semiconductor technology for primary or random access memory (RAM). A typical memory cell consists of electronic elements, including the transistor and **capacitor**. The designer of the computer would represent a 1 in memory by the presence of a voltage on the capacitor and a 0 by the absence of such a voltage. An important characteristic of RAM is the fact that it is volatile. When power is turned off, the contents of RAM memory are lost.

How does the computer access a particular memory location? Figure 7-2 is a diagram of primary memory. Note that there are address lines running in both directions through the array of memory cells. By turning on the address line in row 4 on the left and column 5 on the bottom, we select the shaded cell in the figure. A transistor in the cell acts as a switch to connect a storage capacitor to its address line. Using this approach, the computer can access any bit in primary memory.

The IRS Calls

The IRS has added computers to its tax collection force. There are now at least twelve automated collection systems (ACSs) at the twenty-one IRS collection centers. The software running on mainframe computers assists collectors in initiating dunning letters and phone calls to delinquent taxpayers. The system includes an automatic call distributor connected to a large database. If a taxpayer disregards the first four collection notices sent by the IRS regional offices, his or her file is shifted to an automated collection site. Shortly the system will include two thousand operators and terminals.

The IRS has one objective: collect the $27 billion it is owed in back taxes. Forecasts based on test samples suggest that the $100-million computer system will more than pay for itself.

The system updates its accounts weekly. The operator presses a Next Case function key on the terminal, which displays taxpayer name, address, social security number, and tax liability. The display also shows a history of collection steps and their outcome.

If a dunning letter or levy against wages is in order, the operator uses the system to notify the IRS regional office. If a phone call is in order, the operator presses a Dial function key, which tells the system to call the taxpayer using the least expensive routing for the call. If the line is busy, the computer schedules the call for later. The system is designed to take time zones into account and not to call before 8 A.M. or after 8 P.M. local time!

Figure 7-2
Semiconductor memory.

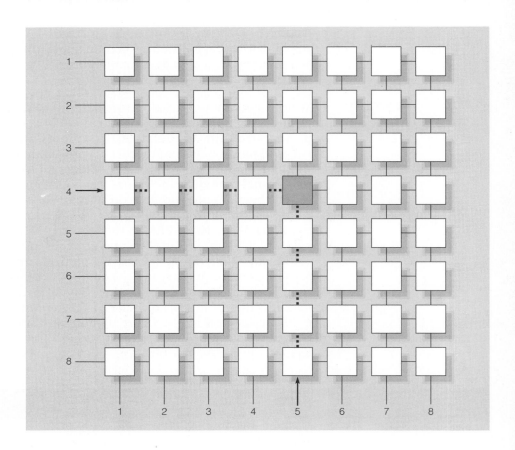

The Central Processing Unit

As stated earlier, the CPU controls the operation of the computer as it contains most of the logic circuitry for the machine. Program instructions are stored in memory along with data. In a basic computer system, the instructions are stored sequentially beginning at some location in memory. By convention, the CPU always fetches the next instruction in sequence and executes it unless the program instructs it to do otherwise.

Doing Arithmetic

Several types of numbers can be processed by computers. A fixed-point number is an integer. The decimal point is fixed and is assumed to be to the right of the right-most digit. Examples of fixed-point numbers are 2,512 and 671.

A floating-point number corresponds to scientific exponential notation. The position of the decimal point is indicated by digits associated with the number. For example, we might have a floating-point format of .1632E03, meaning that the number 0.1632 is to be multiplied by 10^3. The number in conventional form, then, is 163.2. The number 16.32 would be presented by .1632E02. The exponent allows the decimal point to "float." It is also possible to have registers that perform decimal arithmetic.

Are arithmetic registers really necessary? One early computer without registers, performed mathematical operations by looking up information in tables in memory! The presence of arithmetic registers, however, speeds computations. If registers are not used, a program requiring memory and execution time must be written to stimulate desired arithmetic operations. Some early computers had only fixed-point addition and subtraction capabilities. Multiplication was accomplished by successive additions, and division by successive subtractions. In a similar manner, programs simulate floating-point operations on many personal computers. Most contemporary computers feature fixed- and floating-point registers for addition, subtraction, multiplication, and division. Most PCs today have chips with built-in floating-point hardware. The alternative is to use a floating-point coprocessor chip or floating-point arithmetic must be simulated using a program.

How Does the CPU Work?

The central processing unit or CPU on most computers is found on a single chip. Figure 7-3 is a simplified diagram of an advanced CPU chip that contains the following components:

The **control unit** manages the CPU, initiating instruction fetch and execute cycles.

MANAGEMENT PROBLEM 7-1

A business school in a major university recently constructed a new building and installed a state-of-the-art network using fiber-optics connects for the backbone of the system. This complex has twelve servers and a number of specialized processors. For example, there are two time-sharing computers running Unix for student and faculty use, and there are more than nine hundred personal computers on the network, along with a connection to the Internet "network of networks."

As might be expected with a major new installation, the school had a number of start-up problems. The network seemed to have great difficulty printing from standard personal computer software packages. Sometimes the printed output featured different parts printed on top of other parts; other times the printed output vanished without a trace.

The manager of computing services had selected this particular network vendor because it promised a great deal of service. To faculty and student users, it seemed that something was amiss. Shared printing is one of the basic functions of a local area network. Why couldn't the network vendor solve these problems? Had it not experienced them before?

The deans' office suffered through a long semester of complaints from students and faculty. Finally, at the beginning of the second semester, the manager of computing asked for five additional staff members to provide service. He said, "We are in a much more complicated environment now and we need people to keep the network running."

What would you advise the deans to do?

The **bus** interfaces the cache memory on the chip with random access memory chips (RAM). Note that there is a 64 bit wide bus to move data back and forth between the CPU and memory. The address bus is 32 bits wide and it transmits the addresses between RAM and the CPU to fetch instructions and to fetch and store data.

The **code cache** is an 8K byte portion of very fast memory on the CPU chip. The chip copies a series of program instructions here from RAM so that it can reach them faster than it could if they were only on memory chips. (See below.)

The **data cache** is also an 8K byte memory for keeping small amounts of data for faster access than is available from RAM memory chips.

The **instruction location counter** always points to the next instruction in a program to be executed.

The **instruction decoder** determines what each instruction means, for example, it analyzes the ADD instruction and indicates to the control unit that an add operation needs to take place and which registers are required.

Many instructions in the computer reference a location in memory, for example, the ADD instruction might say ADD X, where X is a piece of data in RAM. The **address generator** computes the address in memory for this data. (Note that the code and data caches also have the ability to work with addresses. They have to determine if requested data is in the cache or must be fetched from memory.)

The **integer unit** performs integer arithmetic and the **floating point** unit performs floating point arithmetic. The **arithmetic and logic unit (ALU)** performs logical operations such as comparisons between two numbers.

The CPU typically executes an instruction in two phases. The first is the **fetch phase**. Its objective is to fetch an instruction, pointed to by the instruction location counter, and move it to the instruction decoder for processing. During the **execute phase**, the control unit manages the execution of the instruction, for example, the instruction might say to take data from a certain location in memory and add it to a number already in the integer unit. A clock on the chip determines the speed of operations. For example, a chip with a clock speed of 100 Mhz has a clock that produces 100 million cycles per second. Some instructions can be performed in a single clock cycle, but many require several cycles. Floating point operations usually require the most clock cycles due to their complexity.

Caching   When reading product reviews of computers you may see descriptions of different types of memory caches. The operation of moving data and instructions to and from RAM takes time (several clock cycles). Memory is available that can move data in a single clock cycle, but this faster memory costs much more than regular RAM. Designers build small **caches** or "holding areas" using this high speed memory to hold the data and

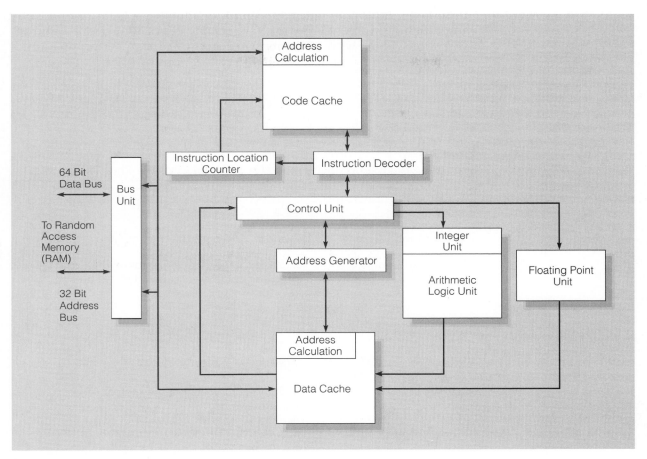

Figure 7-3 Simplified model of an advanced CPU.

instructions currently used by the CPU. This strategy works because most programs need only a small number of actual memory locations at any one time so the cache will usually have the required data or instruction. When the CPU needs data or instructions not in the cache, additional delays are encountered while the slower RAM is accessed for them. CPU designers are responsible for caches within the CPU, which are called L1 caches. Figure 7-3 shows two of these L1 (on the CPU) caches. Computer manufactures frequently add additional caches, called L2 caches, that are outside of the CPU. These are much larger and a little slower than the L1 cache but much faster than RAM. All other things being equal, if you buy a computer with a larger L2 cache, it will be faster than one without this feature.

An Instruction Set What operations can be performed by a typical computer? Table 7-1 contains an outline of instructions for a processor, the CPU chip from Intel which is in "IBM compatible" PCs. Note the different classes of instructions in the table, including data movement, arithmetic, logical comparison, and branching. Large computers have repertoires of well over a hundred instructions, along with ten or more registers capable of performing arithmetic operations or serving as temporary locations for data.

Table 7-1
Examples of Classes of Instructions for the Intel CPU, the Chip Used in PCs

Instruction	Meaning
DATA TRANSFER	
MOV = Move	To move data between memory and registers
XCNG = Exchange	Exchange a register or memory with a register or a register with the accumulator
IN = Input from	Input from a fixed or variable port
OUT = Output	Output to a fixed or variable port
ARITHMETIC	
ADD = Add	Add contents of register or memory to accumulator
ADC = Add with carry	Add contents of register or memory to accumulator with carry
SUB = Subtract	Subtract contents of register or memory with accumulator
SBB = Subtract with borrow	Subtract contents of register or memory with accumulator
CMP = Compare	Compare registers and/or memory
LOGIC	
NOT = Not	Invert
AND = And	Register/memory logical and with register/memory
OR = Or	Register/memory logical or with register/memory
XOR = Exclusive Or	Register/memory logical exclusive or with register/memory

Table 7-1   *(continued)*

Instruction	Meaning
	CONTROL
CALL = Call	Call a routine
JMP = Jump	Jump to a new location to begin execution without conditions
NET = Return	Come back to code from a call
J** = Jump on	**Become a series of letters indicating conditions like jump on less or equal, jump on equal, etc.

CISC VERSUS RISC

The CPU is implemented in electronic circuits. Some instructions are implemented in a single, complex circuit capable of completing the entire calculation in a single clock cycle. Other instructions are implemented on several more general purpose circuits under the control of **microprograms** that are stored in read only memory in the CPU itself. These microprograms, which chip designers create, are not something a programmer ever sees. They are used to implement complex instructions and work by substituting a series of small or "micro" execution steps on several general purpose circuits for an enormously large and complex circuit that would be required to do all the work in a single step.

A **CISC (complex instruction set computer)** processor is one that uses many such complex instructions. For example, one common CISC instruction specifices adding two numbers together in memory. Since memory cannot actually do that, the instruction is implemented by a microprogram that moves the data from the memory to registers, adds the values together, and then stores the sum back in memory. Implementing that many steps in a single electronic circuit requires an extraordinarily large and complex circuit, one that has a very high cost to build and takes a very long time to design and test. Using a microprogram simplifies the design of complex instructions. The many general purpose circuits the microcode uses are easy to design and can be built very inexpensively. However, developing and testing the microcode that implements a complex instruction does take a lot of time.

RISC (reduced instruction set computer) processors are designed with single, simple instructions, such as adding the contents of one register to another. RISC processors contain a large number of identical registers (typically between 64 and 256) that are used for storing intermediate results for immediate use. The objective of the RISC chip designer is to have all instructions execute in a single clock cycle. Compared to CISC, RISC processors are simpler and they execute individual instructions much faster. However, to accomplish the same task, a RISC CPU often must execute more instructions than a CISC CPU. The RISC CPU is likely to be faster and cheaper to build than a CISC CPU, but the two machines might accomplish the same task in the same length of time. Because the RISC processor is simpler, it takes less time to design and requires fewer circuits to implement than a CISC processor. The main disadvantage of RISC architectures is that the language compiler (see Chapter 9) has to be more sophisticated than the CICS language processor.

The debate between advocates of RISC and CISC may not be all that important because it appears that modern chips have components of each type of architecture. For example, one manufacturer is believed to use a RISC architecture to actually implement a CICS CPU in order to be compatible with previous computers. The two architectures may merge in the future so CPU chips have elements of CISC and RISC designs.

WHAT MAKES A CHIP PERFORM?

What factors are responsible for the incredible performance of CPU chips? Table 7-2 contains data on the design characteristics of the popular Intel chip that powers IBM-compatible PCs. Figure 7-4 presents graphs of chip

MANAGEMENT PROBLEM 7-2

A major bank, Eastern National, centralized all its information processing activities when third-generation computers were first installed. The prevailing argument in the industry at the time was that economies of scale justified centralization. Each larger member of a computer manufacturer's family provided more processing power per dollar. That is, moving from one machine to the next more powerful in the line might increase costs by 30 percent while processing power increased by one and a half times. Thus, it made economic sense from the standpoint of hardware rentals to have a few large machines rather than many small machines located in different areas.

What do you think the disadvantages of centralization might be for Eastern National Bank? Are there other considerations beyond hardware cost that might enter into an analysis of centralization?

Currently, Eastern has reversed its trend toward centralization. An information services department spokesman said, "Now, with the availability of cheap PCs and the growth of client-server computing, the arguments for centralization are no longer valid." It is better to have each user develop applications for a dedicated computer on a network. Are there management considerations that should be explored in Eastern's approach? What technical problems might the proliferation of user-developed applications in the bank create?

speed and the number of transistors on successive generations of the chip. The performance characteristics of the PC processor chips form the rows of Table 7-2.

- *Clock speed.* The clock sets the speed of machine cycles. If all else is held constant, increasing the clock speed of a chip will increase its performance.

- *Data path.* The data path or size of the bus refers to how much data is moved between memory and the CPU with each instruction. If all else is constant, having a larger data path speeds the machine because fewer trips to memory are needed to process data.

- *Computation.* If the chip can do computations on more bits at a time, instruction execution will be faster because the instruction will have to be executed fewer times.

- *Memory size.* More memory often lets large programs execute more quickly. It is particularly important when using graphical user interfaces where you have more than one program loaded at a time.

- *Floating-point arithmetic.* If the chip has built-in floating-point arithmetic (or uses a coprocessor with floating-point arithmetic) many numerical calculations will be faster because they can be performed in hardware rather than software.

- *MIPS (million instructions per second).* This figure is an indication of the raw speed of the chip.

A Computerized Production Line

Allen-Bradley produces between one thousand and four thousand controllers for electrical industrial motors each day at its Milwaukee plant. The controllers are competitively priced and are shipped the day after an order is received. This level of production and service is maintained with four people who perform maintenance on twenty-six machines in the 45,000-square-foot plant. The workers also provide the automated facility with raw materials. As many as 180 components are needed to produce 765 different sizes and configurations of controllers.

Allen-Bradley was originally faced with the requirement to adapt to a new electrical standard, which would result in smaller controllers for the same task. It took the company two years of work to install the $15-million line and another year to get it working properly.

Orders come into an IBM mainframe and are downloaded to a microcomputer-based manufacturing cell. One file with order information is downloaded to programmable logic controllers, which control machines. Here it is stored on a hard disk in a four-digit bar code. Along the production line, there are twenty-six machines guided by controllers that use the bar codes to determine what operation to perform.

The new factory allows Allen-Bradley to compete with foreign firms and still make a profit. Its European sales have grown from 3 percent of total revenues to more than 25 percent.

- *Number of transistors per chip.* The more densely packed the transistors, generally, the faster the chip.
- *Parallel processing.* The Intel PENTIUM PRO chip has three instruction registers so it can decode three instructions per clock cycle.
- *Pipelined execution.* A pipeline is a bit like a factory assembly line; instructions move through a series of steps as they are fetched and executed. Instructions start down the pipeline one after another so that more than one instruction is in the process of being executed by the pipeline at once.

So You Want to Buy a Computer

If you ever suggest that you know something about computers, you are bound to be asked a question by a friend (or even a total stranger) about what kind of computer he or she should buy. Here are some of the things you might want to think of when you give advice, or buy your own computer. (Warning, the technology changes so quickly that any computer you buy today is bound to be less capable and more expensive than one purchased six months from now.)

The Box

For convenience, the desktop computer is the easiest for most of us to install and use. However, if you need portable computing, you might give serious consideration to a notebook computer with a "docking station" that lets you plug into a better monitor and keyboard when at your main office. If you plan to get a really big machine, then you probably have to look at a "mini-tower" or floorstanding computer.

The Processor and Memory

Today the processor choice is the Pentium—the faster the MHz the better. For wealthy "power users" the Pentium Pro (P6) is an option. You can probably get by with 16 megabytes of memory, but 32 will make life more pleasant.

EDO DRAM or extend data out will boost overall performance.

A processor cache of 512 K bytes.

Storage

I always recommend buying large hard disks as they seem to fill up with programs, data and documents. One gigabyte (1 billion bytes) is a minimum, and the more, the better.

A floppy drive.

A quad speed CD-ROM drive (or even six times speed).

If you can afford it, a digital audio tape (DAT) backup unit built into the computer can back up from 2 to 8 gigabytes from your hard disk.

Video and Audio

A big color monitor is easy to read if you have the space (and money). A 21 inch screen is a luxury, but aim for at least a 17" monitor if you can. A PCI graphics card with 4 megabytes of video memory will keep your big monitor glowing brightly.

A sound card capable of wavetable synthesis that supports 16 bit, 44.1 khz stereo sampling is the best available.

Two good quality stereo speakers.

Communications

A V-34 compatible modem capable of 28.8 Kbps data rate.

Conclusion: This configuration will let you work with powerful software packages and languages as well as communicate over various networks.

Figure 7-4

(a) Increasing power of successive generations of Intel chips.
(b) Characteristics of PC chips.

*At the time of publication complete specifications for the P7 chip were unavailable; entry is an estimate based on press reports.

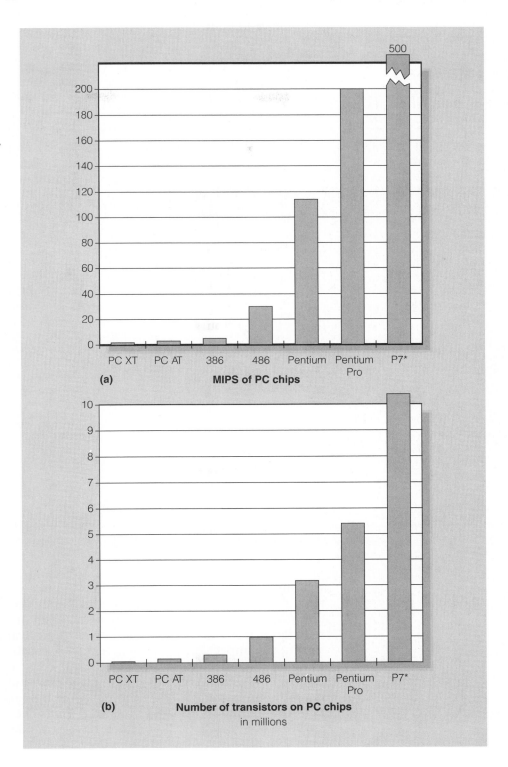

(a) **MIPS of PC chips**

(b) **Number of transistors on PC chips**
in millions

Table 7-2
Characteristics of PC Processor Chips

Performance characteristics of 8088 series chips	PC XT	286 PC AT	386	486	Pentium	Pentium Pro	P7
Clock speed in megahertz	4.77	6–12	16–33	16–50	66–200	120–200	200+*
Data path in bits	8	16	32 16 (SX)	32	64	64	*
Computation size in bits	16	16	32	32	32	32	*
Typical memory-size bytes	640K	2 megs	4–16 megs	4–64 megs	4–64 megs	16–64 megs	16–64+* megs
Floating point	Coprocessor	Coprocessor	Coprocessor	On chip except for SX	On chip	On chip	On chip
MIPS (million instructions per second)	0.33	1.2	2.5–6	20–40	112	250	500
Number of transistors per chip	29,000	130,000	275,000	1.2 million	3.3 million	5.2 million	10+ million

*At the time of publication complete specifications for the P7 chip were unavailable; entry is an estimate based on press reports.

Table 7-2 shows that the first IBM PC is a very slow machine by today's standards! (Few predicted the dramatic success of personal computers, nor did we forecast the huge increases in processing power and reductions in cost.) The 286 chip or AT (for advanced technology) had a significant impact on performance. Clock speed increased and the data path between memory and the CPU doubled in size. The current generation of chips, the Pentium, is extremely powerful, with a speed of more than 100 times the AT. These machines fetch 64 bits of data at a time and perform computations on 32 bits at a time. The newest member of this family is the PENTIUM PRO, which has one model that computes at more than 200 MIPS.

What Techniques Increase Speed?

Although the characteristics above will help you select a computer, they are not enough because the manufacturers have come up with some techniques to make PCs faster. The first option is a **cache memory**—a high-speed memory that is used to speed up slower memory that we first saw in Figure 7-3. Consider a disk drive where it can take 12 milliseconds on the average to access data. Instead of moving that data directly into main memory, it is placed in a cache memory. When the computer reads from the disk, the cache memory is filled with the data requested and extra data nearby. (Often disk accesses occur close to each other.) If the next read is for material in the cache, it can be transferred to primary memory at memory speeds rather than disk access speeds. Of course, if there is no "hit" on the cache it means the data desired are not there and the computer must get them from the disk.

A cache can be used almost anyplace to speed up a computer. Many PCs use a cache with primary memory. An 8-megabyte memory might come with a cache of 128 kilobytes. You can also use a cache or separate memory with the video controller to improve video speeds.

Intel developed a series of chips that featured **clock doubling**. The clock rate of the CPU is twice the rate of processing off the chip. For example, one can buy a clock-doubled 66-megahertz 486 chip in a PC. All operations on the chip take place at 66 megahertz; operations of the

Where Else Would You Use a Chip?

There are many applications in which chips are embedded in a product, for example, your microwave oven probably has an Applications Specific Integrated Chip (ASIC). Europe and Asia have taken to another application of an embedded chip: the "smart card;" some 33 million of them were in circulation at the end of 1994. The technology involves putting a chip in a credit card and it was first developed in the 1970s. Today's chips are much more powerful so that a card can be more versatile. U.S. West is marketing its Telecard in Seattle. The chip in the card is loaded with digital cash for use in pay phones in the city and the company wants to extend the card to retailers.

The idea of the card is to eliminate cash, something that will take a long time, if ever, to accomplish. *Business Week* estimated that in 1994 people spent $1.8 trillion on purchases of under $10, with $560 billion of that in the U.S. Merchants lose 5–7% of cash receipts to the cost of handling the money. Cash cards help speed checkout lines since a transaction takes only one or two seconds compared to making change at a cash register. The issuer of the smart card can keep the float, the money you pay for the card, until it is spent, unlike the credit card where the issuer provides you with float. They also get the "slippage," the cash that is never spent on the card.

A number of companies are looking into offering smart cards. Mondex is testing a system in the U.K. while Visa plans to launch a card at the 1996 U.S. Olympics where 5000 terminals in Atlanta will accept the card. The smart card readers cost from $50 to $800 and the cards, themselves, run $10, much more than the familiar credit card.

chip (for example, memory access) occur at 33 megahertz. Clock doubling is popular because the processor can use existing memory chips that run at up to 33 megahertz. (There were some problems reported with memory chips that a manufacturer tried to run at extremely high clock speeds as they tended to overheat and melt.)

As described above, a **pipelined** computer breaks instructions down into many small steps like an assembly line. Each of these steps or stages is handled by a separate circuit. When an instruction finishes one stage, it goes on to the next one, and the stage it just left begins work on the next instruction.

Also mentioned earlier, the Pentium chip features two integer execution units each fed by its own instruction pipeline, also called **superscalar architecture**. This architecture allows the Pentium chip to execute two instructions per clock cycle. Programs that translate higher-level user languages into machine language (discussed in the next chapter) have to be modified to figure out what user program instructions can be split to operate in parallel. It is not likely that the chip will be able to execute two streams of instructions all the time, as some operations must be done in sequence.

Chips and the U.S. Economy

Manufacturing modern computer chips requires a tremendous investment in equipment and knowledge. A good example is Intel's Rio Rancho, New Mexico plant which produces Pentium and Pentium Pro chips, each containing 3.3 million and 5.2 million transistors respectively. The chips start as eight-inch silicon wafters, nearly 300 to a wafer. There is a 140 step manufacturing process which involves photographically etching patterns on the chips, baking and chemically coating the wafters, and cleaning them.

This process takes place in a five-story factory with more floor space than two dozen football fields. Intel's investment in Rio Rancho so far is $1.8 billion which is expected to rise to $2.5 billion. The plant consists of various laboratory-like spaces whose air is controlled to be thousands of times cleaner than the air in a hospital operating room. Workers look like astronauts in their Gore-Tex suits, hoods, goggles, boots and latex gloves.

Is it worth the investment? The plant has the potential to generate $5 billion a year in revenue, more than all but about the 200 largest companies in the U.S. There are 40 new semiconductor fabrication plants planned around the world, each costing over $1 billion. U.S. firms are building 18 of these plants, followed by Japan with 10. The U.S. will be the home to 13 new plants which is a vote of confidence in the competitiveness of the U.S. and its workforce.

Intel considers its factories, workforce and manufacturing knowledge as competitive weapons. One financial analyst estimates that given current growth rates, Intel could have $11 billion in profits by the year 2000, more than any other U.S. company. "In terms of size, growth and importance to our economic future, information technology is now clearly the basic industry of America," according to Stephen Roach, Morgan Stanley's chief economist.

Since a lot of PC applications today feature graphics, manufacturers have turned their attention to the video controller and its role in the computer. The fastest machines feature **local bus** video. The path from the CPU to the video controller runs at a bus speed more like the bus between memory and the CPU than the bus used for peripherals like a printer or modem. Graphics accelerator cards are video controllers that actually have a processor chip on the computer and a large amount of memory (say, a megabyte or more) to offload the display task from the CPU.

Finally, you can purchase a computer with a wider and faster bus that connects the CPU to peripherals. In the first PCs all components used the same bus—video, memory, printers, and so on. As we have discussed above, 32-bit CPUs have their own data path of 32 bits (in general) to memory. Computers today generally come with a bus to peripherals like printers and disks that carries more data than the standard 16-bit ISA (Industry Standard Architecture) bus. This is the same bus that came on the PC/AT. IBM offers its microchannel architecture which transfers 32 bits at a time. A group of other manufacturers banded together (the "Gang of Seven") to develop their own version of a 32-bit bus called the EISA (Extended Industry Standard Architecture) to compete with IBM. Today the newest bus is the PCI or Peripheral Component Interconnect bus which appears to be replacing the other bus standards.

All of these factors can have a dramatic effect on the performance of a PC. It is not always the case that a computer with a higher clock speed is faster than one with a slower clock speed if the latter machine has a number of the features above to increase its power.

CHAPTER SUMMARY

1. It is important to understand the basic components of a computer and how it works when making decisions about technology.

2. The heart of a computer is the central processing unit or CPU which contains the logic of the computer.

3. Memory is another critical part of the computer. The CPU addresses specific cells in memory using the location's address.

4. A bus which carries data is used to connect the various components of a computer. Modern computers may have several buses to handle the different speeds of computer components.

5. The CPU has registers for performing operations, for example, doing arithmetic computations.

6. Computers calculate using the binary number system because it is easy to represent a 0 and 1 (the binary digits) as "off" and "on." Programs convert binary to the more familiar base 10.

7. All of the instructions that the CPU can execute make up the instruction set of a computer. Generally these instructions encompass moving data, performing arithmetic, logical operations, and control of a program.

8. Reduced instruction set computers (RISC) are designed to implement simple instructions very rapidly. RISC design techniques appear to be merging with processors designed with complex instruction sets (CISC).

IMPLICATIONS FOR MANAGEMENT

The question of how much a manager should know about technology is an emotional one. There are managers who feel they do not need any knowledge of technology; they can leave these issues to staff members. On the other hand, IT is so pervasive in the modern organization and many firms depend on it for critical applications, that a manager needs to be able to make educated decisions about technology. This need suggests that you should have a modicum of knowledge about technology, but how much is that? During your career you are likely to be involved in decisions about what hardware and software to purchase, the hardware and software architecture of the firm, and numerous applications of technology that involve employees, customers, suppliers, and others. Given the demands these decisions will make, it would be difficult for you to know "too much" about IT. One of the objectives of this text is to provide you with a strong base of knowledge about technology. I hope you will be motivated to continue learning about the technology throughout your career.

KEY WORDS

Address generator
Arithmetic-logic unit (ALU)
Base
Binary
Bus
Cache
Cache memory
Capacitor
Clock doubling
Code cache
Complex instruction set computer (CISC)
Control unit
CPU
CRT
Data cache
Disk
Diskette

Execute phase
Fetch phase
Floating point
Hardware
Input/output (I/O)
Instruction decoder
Instruction location counter
Integer unit
Local bus
Microprogram
Pipelined
Primary memory
Random access memory (RAM)
Read only memory (ROM)
Register
Reduced instruction set computer (RISC)
Secondary storage
Superscalar architecture

RECOMMENDED READING

Byte. New York: McGraw-Hill. (A monthly magazine devoted to personal computers; contains feature articles and many ads for different products.)

White, R. *How Computers Work.* Emeryville, Calif.: Ziff Davis Press, 1993. (A clearly illustrated book explaining the fundamentals of computers.)

PC Magazine. New York: Ziff Davis. (A monthly magazine with many articles and comparisons of personal computers.)

DISCUSSION QUESTIONS

1. What is the role of the CPU in a computer?
2. What is the function of primary memory in the computer? How does it interact with the CPU?
3. Why do you think memory chips are easier to build than CPU chips?
4. Why is the binary system suitable for computers?
5. What two major items are stored in primary memory? How can one distinguish between them?
6. What is the advantage of having floating-point arithmetic registers?
7. Why would a designer try to make one computer execute the programs of another computer?
8. What is the role of the different components of the CPU in Figure 7-3?
9. What is the difference between ROM and RAM?
10. How do you store and retrieve data in memory?
11. What is a bus?
12. Why is there a need for a disk controller in Figure 7-1?
13. What are the key factors to consider in purchasing a personal computer?
14. What is the difference between the fetch phase and the execute phase in executing an instruction?
15. Why does a computer need a lot of instructions?
16. Why are there two caches on the CPU chip in Figure 7-3?
17. Explain how a CPU executes an instruction.
18. What changes in technology do you think are responsible for making personal computers possible?
19. What are the minimum features for a home computer? How about for a personal computer to be used in an office?
20. What kind of programs do you think are likely to make the most use of floating point instructions?

21. What are the differences between secondary storage and primary memory?

22. What is the role of microprogramming in a CISC CPU?

23. What are the major differences between CISC and RISC architectures?

24. What is the difference between hardware and software? Where do the lines blur?

25. What are the advantages of using hardware for processing as opposed to software? Where is software advantageous? (*Hint:* Think of speed and then think of ease of making changes to a process.)

CHAPTER 7 PROJECT

SIMON MARSHALL ASSOCIATES

Simon Marshall, the company introduced in the first chapter project, is interested in the possibility of using a computer to help with a number of tasks. John Marshall's brother, Scott, had just finished getting an M.B.A. with a specialization in information systems. When John saw Scott during his summer vacation, he told him about his problems with computers.

Scott advised, "Start with a personal computer and see where things go from there. The power of these machines is phenomenal. Let me give you a suggested configuration, both for hardware and software. You may need a little help with the programs. Why not go to a local college and hire a student part-time to help you learn how to use it? Nothing could be much cheaper."

Scott recommended that Simon Marshall take the plunge and order a Pentium-based computer. He suggested using the copy of Microsoft Windows 95 that comes with the computer. He explained, "The software that runs under Windows offers so much that it is worth the added trouble of learning how to use it." Scott started John with a spreadsheet processor, database management system, and word processor, all written for Windows.

Scott explained his recommendations to John: "The Pentium is a really fast computer. It should serve you for a number of years without requiring much of an upgrade. I've chosen very basic software. After you have begun to use it, I'll be happy to recommend other packages when you need them. This should be enough to get started with."

What is your reaction to Scott's recommendation? What criteria should Simon Marshall use to evaluate personal computers if it decides to acquire one? Why would Scott recommend choosing one of the newest and most expensive personal computers?

CHAPTER **8**

A Proliferation of Computers

● OBJECTIVES

1. Learning to manage information technology.

A critical task in managing technology today is deciding on the organization's architecture for information processing. In this chapter we discuss the types of computers that are available today and present the historical evolution of these devices. You are likely to work in an organization that has used computers for a number of years. The firm's hardware architecture probably includes some older computers. Managing the entire stock of computers requires an understanding of the different types of machines, the way they are used, and the trends in technology that constantly force the evolution of organizations' hardware strategies.

2. **Preparing to apply technology.**

Although we later stress the logical design of a system independent of the computers on which it will operate, at some point designers have to confront computer technology. A system designed for a large, multiuser computer will have different characteristics from one designed for a single-user PC. The end of this chapter also provides an overview of some of the devices available for input and output. These activities help define the user interface with a system, which is vital for its success.

3. **Transforming the organization.**

It has taken many years to reach the point where computers and communications can transform firms and industries. Firms that transform themselves know how to manage a diverse set of computers and other devices. They are successful in responding to trends in technology and to the ongoing changes in the cost/performance ratios of different types of computers.

IMPLICATIONS FOR MANAGERS

This chapter and Chapter 7 contain a great deal of material about computer technology. What are the implications of this technology for management?

- The cost/performance ratio for computers continues to decline as the price is continually dropping for increased levels of computing.
- Logical functions are no longer the most expensive part of the computer. In the first generation, the CPU was the scarce and expensive resource. Today, **very large scale integration (VLSI)** using current technology can put several million transistors onto a small silicon chip. Processing logic is now readily available at a relatively small cost.
- Organizations are spending increasing amounts of money on computers because they are indispensable for many applications. Whereas unit costs may go down, the total expenditure for information technology is increasing in most organizations.
- The ease of use and the appeal of a personal computer help to give many more individuals access to computer technology. To compete in the coming years, a manager will have to be an intelligent user of computers.

It is very difficult to define an appropriate hardware and software architecture for the firm, given the large number of competing demands and alternatives available. Rapid decreases in the cost of making very power-ful chips means that workstations have better cost/performance charac-teristics than mainframes. We discuss architecture further in Chapter 13.

- Companies have a wide variety of computers because it would be very expensive to try and replace old computers and applications all at once.
- In addition to computers themselves, much interest today centers around networks using telecommunications to link computers to-gether. It is no longer sufficient to consider computers alone for most organizations.

A basic understanding of hardware and how it works will help you select and use the appropriate computer equipment. Managers today are faced with a variety of computers of different capabilities. A man-ager may be forced to use existing hardware because it is already in place, or may have the option of acquiring new equipment. In either case, it is important to understand the capabilities of the different types of computers available today.

THE COMPUTERS OF TODAY

How have we achieved our current wealth of computers? In the early days, there were no various types. All computers were known as mainframes (which are described later in this chapter). At one time, eight different companies in the United States manufactured computers. Univac had the early lead in computing but soon lost it to IBM. (Later Univac became a part of Sperry, which merged with another computer vendor, Burroughs, to form the UNISYS Corporation.)

As IBM became the dominant vendor in the United States and abroad, the computer industry was sometimes described as "IBM and the Seven Dwarfs." In the 1950s and early 1960s, companies like Apple, Digital Equipment Corporation (DEC), and Compaq did not exist. RCA and Gen-eral Electric manufactured mainframe computers, eventually taking huge write-offs as they left the business. Today minicomputer and mainframe vendors are reeling from dramatic changes in the cost/performance ratios of "commodity" processor chips versus systems based on proprietary circuit designs.

What trends in the technology have created today's computer indus-try? Why are there so many different types of computers, and what is each one designed to do?

The Rise of the Mainframe

Figure 8-1 presents an overview of the current computer environment. The first computers developed were mainframes, which are large, general-purpose machines. In the early days of the computer industry, one could run only **batch** programs (the staff collects all data into a batch which is processed at one time) on mainframe computers. Many organizations have developed substantial applications on mainframe computers. Today this type of machine is likely to support a number of terminals and personal computers interacting with huge databases containing billions of characters of data. Mainframe computers are used extensively to process transactions and maintain vital data for access by various users. Examples of mainframe systems include order entry and processing at an electronics manufacturer, production planning and scheduling at Chrysler, and airline reservations at all the major air carriers. (We discuss the future of mainframes more in Chapter 13.)

Historically, IBM has dominated the mainframe market, but experienced problems as users have shifted to other kinds of architectures. The challenge for today's mainframe manufacturers is to adopt new technology that will make these machines competitive on cost/performance measures. For example, one crude measure of performance is millions of instructions per second **(MIPS)** that a computer can execute. PCs and workstations cost less per MIP than mainframes.

Mainframe computers feature **proprietary hardware** (instruction sets that in general are unique to and controlled by the vendor). Intel and Motorola make millions of chips a year; the demand for mainframe computers is far less. The proprietary architectures of mainframe computers cannot take advantage of economies of scale in production, and this is why they have a worse cost/performance ratio than smaller computers built around commodity chips. Mainframe vendors are working to reduce the costs of their machines, for example, by designing multiprocessors using chips like the PowerPC.

Today, many mainframe applications are called "legacy systems." These systems represent a heavy investment, they process critical transactions, and they are difficult to change. These mainframe systems are capable of processing a huge volume of transactions given very high speed data channels (defined below). It is difficult to configure smaller systems to handle 1500 or 2000 **on-line** transactions per second, something that

MANAGEMENT PROBLEM 8-1

John Trout is manager of engineering computing for QRX, Inc., a manufacturer of specialized machine tools. Trout is concerned over what he calls the "workstation wars." One of his jobs is to decide what kind of workstations to provide for engineers in the firm. The engineers use the workstations in the design of machine tools and to produce instructions for robots that do some of the actual manufacturing work.

The problem is that each month a different vendor announces a breakthrough in workstations. A new model is announced with more power and at a lower cost than its predecessor.

"No matter what I suggest we buy, my recommendation will look silly in six months. We can't keep replacing our systems every year, and the engineers are crying for more power. What can I do?" What do you recommend to John?

Personal digital assistant (PDA)
A device to support the individual by keeping notes and records and communicating with others. Price: $300 to $1,000.

Personal Computers
General-purpose desktop computers that use 32-bit microprocessors. Price: $500 to $5,000.

Servers The server is a computer used to control a network of personal computers. Price: $3,000 to $30,000.

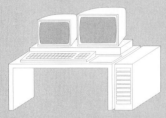

Workstations
High-performance 32-bit computers used by engineers, scientists, and technical professionals who need superior graphics. Workstations, commonly used in computer-aided design, offer the performance of minicomputers but serve one person. The station often sits on or beside a desk and connects to other workstations in a network. Price: $5,000 to $50,000.

Midrange (minicomputers)
Machines in this category can handle the general needs of more than 100 people, who typically work on terminals wired to the computer. Minicomputers are about as big as a two- or four-drawer file cabinet; several often connect to form a company-wide network. Increasingly, such networks are replacing mainframes. Price: $10,000 to $250,000.

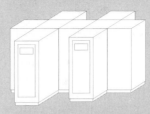

Mainframe computers
Large, general-purpose computers that serve hundreds or thousands of users, all tied to a corporate processing center. A typical mainframe is slightly smaller than a Volkswagen Beetle and requires an atmospherically controlled room. Mainframes generally handle the major processing needs of large corporations. Despite encroachments by networks of minicomputers and PCs, mainframes remain the staple of large processing centers. Price: as much as $5 million.

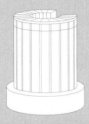

Supercomputers The world's fastest computers, used in science, engineering, and research for the most difficult processing challenges, such as weather forecasting. An average supercomputer is no larger than a mainframe but packs faster processors that are more closely connected to provide greater computing speed. Several companies or organizations often share time on one supercomputer to offset the high cost of these machines. Price: $100,000 to $20 million or more. Most new supercomputers are evolving into parallel computers (below).

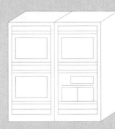

Highly parallel computers
A relatively new type of computer that uses a large number of processors. The processors divide up and independently work on small chunks of a large problem. Parallel computers excel at programs with many independent operations that can be done at the same time; they match the speed of supercomputers at a fraction of the cost. Because supercomputers are inherently limited in how fast they can get data from memory, parallel machines—which put memory in each processor—have become a better-performing alternative. Price: less than $100,000 to $4 million or more.

Figure 8-1 A guide to computers.

a mainframe order entry system does routinely. Even though the firm might be able to buy hardware that has a better cost/performance ratio, it would have to spend a huge amount to develop new applications for this hardware.

Organizations using mainframe computers generally process large amounts of data. The computers may access databases with billions of characters of data and control networks of hundreds or thousands of terminals. As a result, the computers need to be able to handle extensive telecommunications activities and input/output operations.

The mainframe usually has a data channel, which is as powerful as the CPU on some smaller computers. The **data channel** accepts instructions from the CPU, for example, to retrieve data from a **disk file**. The CPU goes on to another job while the data channel is busy. When the data channel finishes, it interrupts the CPU to let it know the data are available. The CPU then restarts the program that was interrupted if its priority is higher than other programs that are waiting to run. Control units on the mainframe serve to interface the computer, in this case the data channel, with different I/O and storage devices. This architecture has created mainframe computers that are extremely fast, which are used in database, transactions processing, and numerous other applications.

Powerful Supercomputers

Mainframe computers are not fast enough for some applications. The mainframe computer was originally developed for business use. It has features to enhance the processing of business data involving character manipulation and decimal arithmetic. Scientists and engineers have computationally intensive problems to solve, often involving numbers with many digits of significance. Examples include the simulation of airflow over an aircraft, weather forecasting simulations, analysis of geological data, and even predictions about the speed of a sailboat designed for the Americas Cup competition.

Companies such as Cray Research manufacture supercomputers. Supercomputers are among the fastest computers today, with speeds measured in hundreds of megaflops (a megaflop is the execution of 1 million floating-point instructions per second) to more than a gigaflop (1 billion floating-point instructions per second). Several companies are trying to achieve a teraflop machine able to execute 1 trillion instructions per second! It is not clear, given the failure of Cray Computer Corporation (not Cray Research) whether or not there will be a continuing market for supercomputers. Some experts argue that the future of high speed computing is in massively parallel machines (described below) or by combining the power of a number of individual workstations connected with a network.

Minis: The Beginning of the Revolution

The next type of computer to develop was the mini. Companies such as DEC found that with integrated circuits they could build a highly cost-effective small computer with an 8- or 16-bit word length. Minis became very popular as stand-alone time-sharing computers and as machines dedicated to a department in a corporation.

Minicomputers evolved as manufacturers increased processing speeds and expanded word sizes to 32 bits. These computers can be classified as "midrange." IBM claims to have sold more than two hundred thousand of its midrange AS/400 system. Companies use this midrange computer for a variety of processing tasks, some of which are similar to what a mainframe did a decade ago. A firm might use this computer for all of its processing. A geographically dispersed company could have AS/400 computers at various geographic locations connected to a larger machine at headquarters. Third parties have developed thousands of applications for the AS/400 as well.

As an example of the trends in medium and larger computers, in 1995 IBM introduced models of the AS/400 built around its PowerPC chip. IBM, Apple, and Motorola developed this RISC chip to compete with Intel. Using a customized version of this chip lets IBM get away from a proprietary architecture and reduce the cost of the computer. However, because there are a huge number of applications for this popular computer, IBM had to maintain compatibility with its original architecture. The computer translates existing applications software the first time it is executed on the new machine without the need to change the original program.

The Personal Computer Has Changed Everything

Next came the PC or personal computer, which was first designed as an 8-bit computer. Apple introduced its famous PC in 1977. The original IBM PC, marketed in 1981, fetched 8 bits at a time from memory but performed computations on 16 bits at a time. Soon IBM introduced the AT, which fetches and processes 16 bits at a time. The next generation is the 32-bit PC or 386 (later the 486 as well) computer, which fetches and processes 32 bits at a time. The newest chips, the Pentium and the Pentium Pro, are capable of fetching and processing 64 bits at a time. The personal computer is used in thousands of ways today and there are many thousands of programs available for it.

Figure 8-1 shows personal computers and workstations as separate categories. Workstations use high-performance 32-bit computers for engineering and scientific work. The workstation features superior **graphics** and is often used for design tasks. Powerful Pentium personal computers running graphical user interfaces (GUIs) fall into the workstation class as well. These PCs have the computational power and software capabilities to become the same kind of personal productivity tool for the manager that the engineering workstation is for the engineer.

The Server

In the client-server model of computing, a user's client PC makes requests of a server computer that has data and possibly programs on it. The server is responsible for the database and is likely to execute transactions to update and manage it. The server also has to extract data and provide it to the client. The user's client does various analyses of the data using its own processing power. At first, the server did not do much but let users download software and print reports in a local area network. However, as PC chips became more powerful, so have servers. They now challenge minicomputers and may soon go after the mainframe market. Intel is so optimistic about the server market that it is marketing complete boards for servers containing four Pentium Pro chips. A vendor can use this board as the major component of a server. Vendors like Sun Microsystems sell powerful servers based on their own chips like Sun's SPARC chip. IBM is even calling its mainframes "enterprise servers."

A large grocery store used to have a $250,000 minicomputer. Now it runs its business on a multiprocessor server that costs $25 to $50,000. One Compaq server containing 4 Pentium processors has been clocked at 600 transactions per second with standard database software compared to 200 transactions per second for some midrange computers. Server makers envision computers with up to 32 Intel Pentium Pro processors achieving the performance of today's high-end mainframes.

Massively Parallel Computers

The highly parallel machine category in Figure 8-1 includes a number of new approaches to computer design. The approaches have in common the idea of trying to avoid the bottleneck in conventional designs where all instructions and data have to be fetched from memory and brought to the CPU for processing. Some of these parallel computers have multiple processors that all execute the same instruction at once on the same data. Others execute multiple instructions on different data. Clearly, coordinating the execution of instructions and programming these machines is a challenge.

IBM has created a parallel supercomputer based on RISC technology in its very successful RS6000 workstation which uses the PowerPC chip. The RISC-based SP1 connects together as many as 64 chips and can run almost all of the software that currently runs on its workstations. A number of experts in the field expect parallel computers to replace mainframes. As the physical limits of computation are reached, one way to gain increased performance is to compute in parallel. The company also offers a parallel machine with 32 S/390 processors tightly coupled together.

A recent strategy followed by some users who need extremely high-speed computing is to connect clusters of high-end workstations with special software that lets them attack the same problem. The software assigns various parts of a complex computation to several workstations, generating considerable increases in processing power. It is possible for some applications that used to require a supercomputer to run on such a connected group of workstations.

A Personal Assistant

The most recent computer is the personal digital assistant or PDA. These machines began as super calculators able to store a user's calendar and phone book. Today these devices often weigh less than a pound and some offer handwriting and voice recognition, fax and modem communications, and even a pager. PDAs are inexpensive enough that firms will develop dedicated applications for them. For example, a sales representative might use a small PDA that has information on contracts. A longshoreman will use a PDA that has a bar-code reader and scanner to record the location of containers. These PDAs will also be consumer products. For example, a rental-car company might have local maps and tour guides available in each city to be downloaded to your PDA. As wireless transmission technology expands and drops in price, PDAs should become more attractive.

In Orange County, California real estate agents now have the opportunity to use a PDA to remotely access, download, and store property information on a Sony Magic Link personal communicator. An agent can use it to communicate via fax, electronic mail and paging, or access a commercial on-line service. The agent can select listings using different parameters such as location and special needs of the client. The PDA will replace printed property listings which were published every two weeks.

We can see why the task of developing the architecture for an organization's computing system is so difficult. If an organization is starting with no computing, one could conceive of buying a large midrange computer, a small mainframe, or a network of personal computers. The question of which option to choose may require a major study and considerable effort. The organization that already has a number of computers in place must decide how to manage and expand its systems as users come up with new needs and ideas for technology.

MANAGEMENT PROBLEM 8-2

Mastercraft Tool Company manufactures a variety of manual and power tools for professional workers and home workshops. The tools are sold through specialty and hardware stores throughout the United States and abroad. For a number of years, the firm has been concerned over production control problems.

Manufacturing a tool involves a sequence of steps requiring different machines. It is a classic "job shop" production situation. There are some ten manufacturing departments at Mastercraft, much work in process, and large finished-goods inventories. The firm manufactures for inventory and fills orders from its stock of tools. There is limited back ordering for popular items.

The top management of Mastercraft has reviewed several proposals to provide better production control information. Because of the rather low skill level of some workers, management is concerned about the impact of a computer system on production employees.

At the present time, the company is trying to decide if it can adapt to bar coding. The president said, "I can see advantages of bar coding; a lot of places use it now. I mean, grocery store clerks have adapted with no problems. But can we use it in our factory?"

As a consultant to Mastercraft, can you help the president with his decision? What factors should he consider in evaluating different input and output alternatives? Which alternatives should he consider?

Why So Many Types of Computers?

The text discusses a variety of different types of computers, but you may be quite happy with a desktop or notebook PC. Why are there so many different kinds of machines, supercomputers, mainframes, minis, and PCs? The discussion above presented the different computers in order of their development. In Chapter 13 we shall see that the most popular architecture today is called a client-server configuration. Why have companies not adopted this configuration and replaced their older configurations?

The major reason for the variety of computers is the applications users have programmed to run on them. There are many applications developed for mainframe computers. It would be very expensive to convert to a new architecture, given that the new system could handle the processing volume of the mainframe. As the industry develops new types of computers, mainframes, minis, and PCs, users write custom applications for these computers. One large financial services firm recently reported having over 75,000 active COBOL programs comprising some 70 million lines of code, a significant investment in one language and system. As a result, there is a great reluctance to throw away existing applications to adopt the latest trend in computing. Instead, companies put new applications on the latest computing platform, create new interfaces for their old mainframe systems, and plan to reprogram applications sometime in the future. You should not be surprised to see a variety of almost all types of computers discussed in this chapter in a company, nor should you think a firm is necessarily behind the times because it still has applications that run on mainframe computers.

Why Not Write Instead of Type?

Detroit Edison is using pen-based PCs to try to reduce the cost of cutting trees near its power lines by $1 million a year. The utility is giving its line-clearance group and private tree trimmers pen-based computers. The goal of the project is to eliminate paper from the trimming operation.

Inspectors from the utility use the pen-top computers while they examine the 1 million utility poles and 3 million trees the company maintains. The inspectors fill out electronic work orders using a pen to complete forms on the computer screen. Input data include the location of the job, the types of lines, and the branches to be trimmed.

This information is stored on a PCMCIA memory card and turned in to form a database.

A separate program compiles work orders for tree-trimming contractors. Each contractor checks out a computer and is given a PCMCIA memory card with its work orders on it. At the end of the job, the contractor completes an electronic invoice showing time and materials. The trimming foreman turns in the invoice, and Detroit Edison processes payments without ever keying any data.

This application is an excellent example of using technology to drastically reduce paperwork. Detroit Edison did not need costly imaging systems and a clever use of relatively inexpensive technology did the job for them.

Input and Output   Computers process data in time measured in billionths of a second. Compared with these internal speeds, getting data in and out of a computer is very slow. Table 8-1 lists some of the most common input/output devices.

Keyboards   Most users interact with systems directly, using a keyboard when providing computer input. A lot of this interaction with mainframes or midrange systems is done through a "dumb" terminal, a terminal that is able to send and receive data from a computer.

PCs for Input   More often, personal computers are being used as terminals. Running a program that emulates a terminal—that is, that makes the PC appear like a terminal—the user works with a remote computer. In a client-server environment, the user interacts directly with a server using the full capabilities of his or her local workstation.

Input-Only Devices   **Bar Coding**   This is an extremely popular way of entering data into a computer. We encounter a form of bar coding in grocery stores equipped with checkout scanners. These devices use a laser to read the **universal product code (UPC)** stamped on grocery items. A laser device reads the bar code and translates it into a product identifier. A computer looks up the price of the item and indicates the charge on a display. Similar types of readers are used in other kinds of stores to mark items. The advantage of such an input device is that a retailer can automatically keep track of inventory and sales.

Other types of bar codes are used extensively in the manufacturing industry. In a highly automated factory, parts are marked with bar codes. The codes direct the flow of the part through the factory and may even indicate to a machine what operations to perform on it. The use of bar coding can dramatically reduce the need for individuals who follow orders

Table 8-1
Popular Input/Output Devices

Both input and output	Input devices	Output devices
PC	Scanning	Printers
	Bar code	Laser
Terminal	Optical character recognition	Inkjet
	Image	
	Pen	Voice
	Voice	Graphics
	Touch-screen	
	Mouse	

through the factory and keep track of where work in process is located, a form of indirect labor.

OCR   **Optical character recognition (OCR)** is an important input technique. Today OCR and image scanning are both sometimes referred to as "scanning." Technically speaking, a **scanner** actually recognizes letters on a document and converts them into computer code like ASCII. You could move the results of the scan directly into a word processing document and make changes to it.

It is very difficult for a scanner to recognize handwritten input as most scanners perform best on printed documents. To recognize letters or characters, a scanner compares the input with a series of stored characters, trying to find the best match. This task is far easier for printed characters which follow some standards. Handwriting defies description in many cases! There are opportunities for great labor and cost savings if scanners can get to the point of recognizing handwriting. Consider the impact on the post office if machines could read 75 percent of the handwritten zip codes on letters.

OCR input saves typing data. One can take information that is not in machine-readable form and avoid retyping it. As one might suspect, recognizing the letters requires far less storage than would an image scan. As an example, the first edition of this book was written before the existence of word processors. To reduce work and speed production of subsequent editions, the publisher scanned the original manuscript and modifications so that the text did not have to be retyped. Only handwritten changes, which could not be scanned, had to be typed manually.

Imaging   Image scanning is used for desktop publishing systems based on personal computers. A user can scan photographs, drawings, and other items and place them on a page. The computer makes no attempt to understand what is being scanned. It simply transfers an image from one medium to another.

An **imaging** device uses a laser to digitize input from a sheet of paper. The image is like a photograph of the page and can be thought of as represented by thousands of dots, say 300 dots per inch (dpi). In the computer, each dot is assigned to a memory location along with associated information. For example, if the scanner is capable of representing shades of gray, it must store information about the intensity of the dot, too. The imaging system does not recognize characters unless it is able to do special processing. You cannot input the image directly into a word processing package to modify the scanned document.

Pen   A number of pen-top personal computers are available on the market. The user works with a pen to print characters or check off boxes on a form. These devices are intended for individuals who do not like to type and for applications where you need portability. To date they are successful for service people such as a delivery person for record-keeping purposes. Pen-top computing has not been applied extensively to managerial applications.

Voice Forecasters predict that **voice input** can change the way we work with computers. Currently available voice input systems are generally quite limited. A system might be used for inputting the addresses of packages on a sorting line or classifying parts. Basically, the systems recognize a few spoken words and allow the user to keep both hands free while working.

Continuous voice recognition is a difficult challenge. The computer has to analyze speech and identify words. The systems described above are discrete word systems. The user has to maintain a period of silence between words. In continuous speech recognition, no pauses are required. Continuous speech systems require a much larger vocabulary than discrete systems, and the ambiguities of spoken language create additional difficulties. What does the expression "time flies like an arrow" mean? The advent of continuous speech recognition may indeed change dramatically the way we interact with computers, but we should not count on having this technology in the immediate future.

Touch Screens This technology provides a great alternative for keyboard entry when the users' choices are somewhat constrained. By putting his or her finger on the screen, the user indicates a choice. A bank can use touch screens for its ATMs. A factory has touch screens for an operator to set up tests on a quality-control machine. The American Stock Exchange uses a touch screen for entering certain kinds of quotations. This type of input is appropriate when there is a small amount of information to be entered, particularly when it is desirable to eliminate a keyboard.

Mouse PC users often work with an input device called a **mouse**. It directs a cursor around the screen and sends commands to programs when you press the mouse buttons. The mouse, or some pointing device, is necessary for machines featuring graphical user interfaces (GUIs) and icons. Placing the cursor on an icon and pressing a button on the mouse selects the item, that is, generates a command signified by the icon. This type of interface is called object-oriented or direct manipulation and is becoming increasingly popular.

Output Devices

Laser Printers The most convenient output device for a personal computer is the **laser printer**. These devices generally print with a resolution of 300 dpi or higher and produce letter-quality output. The laser printing process is similar to photocopy technology. It offers various sizes and types of print, produces high-quality output, and is very fast compared with alternative techniques for obtaining hard copy output. Minis and mainframes also can use laser printers. These higher-speed devices print thirty to forty pages per minute. Much of the output from transactions processing computers is done on laser printers.

Inkjet Printers   Inkjet printers squirt charged droplets of ink onto paper. They are used extensively with personal computers and have a modest cost advantage over laser printers for monochrome output. Inkjets are the clear choice for low-cost, high quality color printing.

Voice   **Voice output** has been available for a number of years. Banks sometimes provide on-line inquiry about account balances. For example, keying in one's account number produces an audio response of the account balance. Voice output is used extensively for telephone information. The information operator indicates which number displayed on a terminal is the correct one, and a computer generates a voice response. The operator is free to answer another call while the first message is playing.

Graphics   Personal computer users often use their machines to prepare for presentations. **Graphics** output devices turn computer displays into presentation output. To produce 35mm slides, output devices are available that copy the screen image onto photographic film.

Reducing a Bottleneck

There are a variety of input/output techniques for computers. Despite the variety, moving information to and from a computer is slow. Most information is typed into computers, yet the world is populated by typists and nontypists. Alternative forms of interfaces such as voice, object-oriented, and touch screen offer ways to encourage the use of computers. One major trend is to reduce the amount of human effort involved in input. Bar coding and the electronic exchange of information both serve to eliminate input labor.

CHAPTER SUMMARY

1. Computer technology is marked by great changes. The early years were the era of the mainframe. They were followed by the development of the minicomputer and then the personal computer.
2. The mainframe computer is often criticized today, but it has a lot of features to recommend it. The most important is the large number of applications that currently only run on mainframes. The cost of redoing all of these systems is staggering! Mainframe technology is also well understood and the machines have achieved a high degree of reliability. However, mainframes feature proprietary architectures which are very costly and they tend to be associated with inflexible applications.

3. The minicomputer has evolved into a "midrange" system. These systems are blurring with file servers that provide data and sometimes programs for PCs in a network.

4. A few manufacturers make supercomputers. It appears that the supercomputer of the future is most likely to be a massively parallel machine or a group of computers on a network all working on the same problem.

5. The personal digital assistant is in its early phases. Improvements in wireless communications and the capabilities of these machines should increase their appeal.

6. The revolution in computer technology came about because of the chip and the ability to put millions of electronic components on a small chip of silicon or other material. An Intel Pentium Pro (P6) CPU on a chip has over five million components and can execute well over a hundred million instructions a second, which is comparable to the speed of many mainframe computers.

7. Many of the features of larger computers are incorporated into PC chips as these devices become more sophisticated.

8. Changes in the technology forces changes in hardware and software architecture. The cost per MIP of a PC is much lower than for a mainframe. PC software is also easier to use and more appealing to the user than mainframe applications. These changes in the technology and the economics of computing have led to the client-server model in which data and some programs reside on servers, midrange computers, and/or mainframes while users work with PCs running programs to access and analyze the data provided by the various servers.

9. Computers are very fast, but secondary storage is not. It takes much longer to access data on a disk than in primary memory. However, it is not practical (or possible) to keep gigabyte (billions of bytes) or larger databases in primary memory.

10. The slowest parts of the computer deal with input and output. For this reason we try to capture data at its source and reduce the amount of data entry and output whenever possible.

IMPLICATIONS FOR MANAGEMENT

While starting your own business is risky and has a lot of challenges, at least you are not likely to be stuck with a twenty-year-old hardware and software architecture. The reason you want to understand something about the variety of computers out there is because you may encounter them. In fact, you may have to help develop an architecture for your employer, figuring out where you want to be and how to get there given the existing stock of equipment.

While you might like to get rid of a particular computer, it is important to remember that there may be some applications that will only run on it. Airline reservations systems will use mainframe computers for processing for sometime in the future. It is also unlikely that you have the resources or patience to throw away all your old applications and develop them again for a different kind of computer. You may save money on hardware, but at a tremendous cost in labor for systems development.

KEY WORDS

Batch
Data channel
Disk file
Graphics
Imaging
Laser printer
Minicomputer
MIPS
Mouse
On-line

Optical character recognition
 (OCR)
Proprietary hardware
Scanner
Universal product code
 (UPC)
Very large scale integration
 (VLSI)
Voice input
Voice output

RECOMMENDED READING

IEEE Spectrum, January issues. (This publication features annual technology reviews and forecasts for a number of technologies. Monthly issues generally have some articles on computer hardware and software and networks.)

Byte and *PC* magazines. (These magazines provide a great deal of information on how PCs work and the latest features of newly released computers.)

DISCUSSION QUESTIONS

1. Distinguish between computer hardware and software. Which most concerns a manager?
2. Why is the cost/performance ratio for a PC much better than for a mainframe?
3. What is the purpose of a control unit? Can the same control unit control more than one type of device?
4. Why can conversion from one computer to another be a problem?

5. Why is it difficult to convert programs from mainframes to client-server platforms?

6. What is the advantage of a data channel? How much logic must it contain?

7. What are the advantages of scanning as an input medium?

8. What are the uses for a supercomputer?

9. Why are CD-ROMs for computers so popular? What is their main advantage?

10. What are the features of mainframe computers?

11. What features should a high-end server have?

12. What are the main characteristics of the client-server model?

13. Why is a computer manufacturer interested in compatibility within its own line of machines? Does a manufacturer want its computers to be compatible with the computers of other manufacturers? What are the advantages and disadvantages of such a strategy?

14. What applications seem best suited to the use of a touch screen?

15. What issues are involved in making a massively parallel computer work?

16. Why does a PC have several different buses?

17. What are the reasons for having secondary storage? Why not just add more primary memory?

18. What are the arguments for having data and servers in a central location?

19. How can networking computers reduce the amount of input and output activity that takes place?

20. Why is there such a mismatch between input/output and internal computer speeds? How can this mismatch be reduced?

21. What is the difference between an image of a page and that same page typed into a word processing program?

22. Can you think of any physical limits on the speed of computer chips?

23. What is the advantage of a workstation over a larger computer?

24. What factors underlie the trend toward networks of personal computers (clients) connected to file servers?

CHAPTER 8 PROJECT

SIMON MARSHALL ASSOCIATES

Simon Marshall has a client who visited its offices and saw the personal computers installed there. The client owns a small manufacturing company that creates custom-machined parts for its customers. The company is able to do very high precision manufacturing and has been quite successful in its niche. The client asked Simon Marshall for advice. He had always avoided using a computer because he thought it would simply add to overhead and not save any money. Increasingly, however, his machines were controlled by computers and his two engineers recommended using some technology in the office.

A representative from a systems integrator (a consulting firm that develops solutions for its customers) visited and suggested a number of possibilities, from a single PC in the office to a network in the firm. The client is confused and asked Simon Marshall for help. Since they are new to computers as well, they have asked for your recommendations. How should their client proceed to evaluate the proposal from the systems integrator? What sounds like the most appropriate technology for him, at least to get started? Why?

CHAPTER **9**

Software Is the Key

◯ OBJECTIVES

1. **Learning to manage information technology.**

   In the early days of computers, the manufacturer sold hardware and gave away software. Today, the future for many vendors is in the sale of software and services as hardware becomes more of a commodity item. Some of the most difficult technology decisions you make will be related to software evaluation and selection. Which of three or four competing spreadsheet **packages** should become a standard in the organization? Should we buy an applications package or use a programming language to develop a custom application?

2. **Preparing to apply technology.**

   The organization designs a system and then must decide how the system will actually be built. Any system that runs on a computer requires software. At some point in the design process you have to deal with issues of implementation, including how the software for the system is to be developed (or acquired). In your own use of a personal computer, you will encounter some of the software described in this chapter.

3. Transforming the organization.

Hardware alone is not enough to bring about major organizational changes. It takes software to do anything useful with a computer. As you read this chapter, think about the examples in previous chapters of companies that dramatically changed the way they do business. Many of the systems in these firms contain millions of lines of software code written by people in a painstaking, labor-intensive process.

MANAGERIAL CONCERNS

Why do managers need to understand software? The choice of software to be used as a standard in the organization for developing applications is an important management decision. As you develop the firm's hardware and software architecture, what operating systems will you choose for the servers? What operating system do you want on user workstations? If you want to develop a new system, is it best suited for programming on the company's existing midrange computer using a higher-level business language, or a fourth-generation language such as those discussed in Chapter 18? (A higher level language has statements that are closer to a natural language like English than to the language the computer executes.) The proliferation of personal computers places the manager in the position of a direct, hands-on user of computers. What software should the manager buy and use? How does one choose?

Because users help design systems, it is important for them to understand which programming tasks are easy and which are difficult. Should a packaged program be used for a particular application? There is considerable difficulty in turning system specifications into working programs, and we have encountered serious problems in writing and managing program development.

To answer the questions above and to make intelligent management decisions about programming and project management, you need to understand the basics of software. How have elaborate programming languages and operating systems been built from the lowest-level languages that look a lot like machine language?

In this chapter, we explore computer programs and languages along with different types of operating systems and packaged programs. Table 9-1 shows that different hardware "generations" can be characterized by differences in computer software. (Remember, we defined software as the instructions that tell a computer what actions to take.) In this chapter, we discuss these different types of software. The software presented here is most often used by an information systems professional (with the exception of a special language like SPSS). Software that is likely to be of interest to a user with a personal computer is presented later in the text, particularly in Chapters 11, 18, and 20.

Table 9-1
Software Generations

Generation		Software
First	1950–1958	Machine language
		Assembly language
Second	1958–1964	Assembly language
		Higher-level languages
		Batch operating systems
		Dedicated on-line systems
		Experimental time-sharing
Third	1964–1970	Preponderance of higher-level languages
		Expansion of packaged systems
		Operating system mandatory
		Mixed on-line and batch applications
		Virtual-memory time-sharing systems
Third-and-one-half	1970–1980	Expanded operating systems
		Virtual-memory batch systems
		Batch, on-line, and time-sharing mixed
		Database and communications packages
Fourth	1980 to present	More application programs
		Higher-higher level or "fourth-generation" languages
		Application generators
		Virtual-memory operating systems for PCs
		Object-oriented languages
		Open systems

We generally divide software into two main types: systems software and applications software. Systems software manages the computer and/or provides a set of standard services to its users. The most well-known piece of systems software is the **operating system**, such as **Windows95**. Database management systems, covered in Chapter 10, are another example of systems software.

Applications software solves an information processing problem in an organization. The programs constituting the systems we have seen so far are classified as applications software. Several computer languages discussed in this chapter are used to create applications software.

It is hard to overemphasize the importance of software. It is the key that unlocks the potential of the computer. Investors think so as well. Microsoft has a market value that is more than 90% of IBM's, yet the latter company has a huge asset base of plants and facilities and sales many times Microsoft's.

Programming Languages

Over the last fifty years, the trend in programming has been to make it easier to give instructions to a computer. The objectives of making programming easier are manyfold:

- To improve the efficiency of developing new applications of technology, especially to reduce the elapsed time required to go from an idea to a finished system.
- To make it easier to develop systems that are appealing to users.
- To encourage non-professional programmers, people like you, to develop applications themselves without having to rely on a programmer.
- To reduce the bottleneck of systems development, the large backlog of suggested applications that exist in most organizations.
- To reduce the number of errors resulting from a systems development effort.
- To take advantage of the tremendous increases in speed and cost reductions of hardware by using hardware less efficiently in order to improve the systems development process.

The first computer languages were **machine language**, the actual zeros and ones the computer executes. Programming in machine language was never particularly enjoyable, and it certainly restricted programming to a small number of dedicated individuals. The first advance in computer software was the introduction of **assembly language**, a language which substituted **mnemonics** like ADD, SUB, MULT for the machine language numbers that perform these instructions. Programmers were also able to use variable names like X, Y, PAY, rather than try to remember exactly what each memory location contained.

Today, assembly language is used only by systems professionals, generally in building systems software or special packages. There is no reason for a user to write assembler code. It is interesting to note that Lotus 1-2-3, a popular electronic spreadsheet program for PCs, was originally written in assembly language for speed of execution. Later versions were written in a higher-level language for ease of maintenance and enhancements.

The kinds of software you will be using are built up from the foundation provided by machine and assembly code. Higher level languages are often translated into machine language to execute a program. As languages become higher in level, they involve more overhead and inefficiencies of computation. Several organizations have experienced embarrassing performance problems using fourth-generation languages for applications they were not designed to process.

THE CONTRIBUTION OF HIGHER-LEVEL LANGUAGES

Higher-level languages make the computer easier to program and extend the use of computers to more individuals. The most significant of these languages appeared around 1957 and is called **FORTRAN** (FORmula TRANslation). This language is designed to facilitate the use of computers by scientists and engineers and is well suited to solving mathematically oriented problems on the computer. With FORTRAN, we can write a complex formula in one statement, for example,

X = (A + B)*(C − D)/E.

An assembly-language program to accomplish this computation is shown in Table 9-2. The assembly-language version requires eight instructions, compared with a single line for the FORTRAN statement. The FORTRAN statement is at a higher level than the eight instructions required in assembly language. For many problem solvers, particularly nonprofessional

MANAGEMENT PROBLEM 9-1

The American Society of Scientists is a large association of men and women who work in biology, chemistry, and physics. The society has a number of services for its members. It holds annual conferences on different topics all over the world. The society publishes six different newsletters and journals. In addition, it has insurance and credit card programs for its members.

For years the society separated its publishing computing from its membership services. The publishing applications run on a **Unix** time-sharing system using proprietary software packages for editing and formatting the publications. Membership services use two in-house VAX computers.

The head of the society wonders if this is the best way to handle technology. Costs have been going up about 10 percent a year across both publications and membership services. The society has asked you to help it evaluate alternatives. Could the publishing function be done better on desktop computers? Should the society try to find an outside organization to handle member services and get out of the information systems business altogether?

programmers, a higher-level language eases the conceptualization of program structure. A number of other higher-level languages have been developed. BASIC is a language very similar to FORTRAN except that it was designed for time-sharing. You can use a variation called Visual Basic to develop applications for Windows95 on a PC.

COBOL (COmmon Business-Oriented Language) was developed to facilitate programming for business applications. An example of a program is found in Table 9-3. For years commercial programs in the U.S. were written primarily in COBOL creating approximately 30 billion plus lines of COBOL code in the world. Organizations are seeking alternatives to this language in order to be more productive. COBOL is associated with unresponsive, mainframe computer systems and a large number of firms are only maintaining or enhancing COBOL programs. They are often doing new development work with newer languages and frequently are using alternatives to mainframes. It is unlikely that either COBOL or mainframes will disappear quickly, but the use of COBOL is expected to steadily decline in the future.

Many organizations, particularly small ones, use a language called Report Program Generator (RPG). This language is suitable for business applications. RPG provides fixed program logic automatically and programmers work from special RPG coding forms. The user defines the file, the output files, extra space for the compiler, input record formats, calculations, output, and any telecommunications interface. Because much of RPG is structured already, the programmer does not spend time with complex control logic. The language also makes it easy to update files, and many versions support direct-access files with indices. The dominant language for development on IBM's popular AS400 midrange computer has been RPG.

Table 9-2

An Assembly-Language Program for the FORTRAN Statement
$X = (A+B)*(C-D)/E$

Program		Comment
LDA	A	Load A into the A register.
ADD	B	Add B to the A register.
STA	T	Store the sum in a temporary location.
LDA	C	Load C into the A register.
SUB	D	Subtract D from the A register.
DIV	E	Divide the results by E.
MLT	T	Multiply the results by T.
STA	X	Store the final result in X.

Table 9-3
A COBOL Payroll Program and Sample Output

```
00001      IDENTIFICATION DIVISION.
00002      PROGRAM-ID. PAYROLL.
00003      AUTHOR, GORDON DAVIS.
00004    *
00005    *THIS PROGRAM READS HOURS-WORKED AND RATE-OF-PAY FOR EACH
00006    *EMPLOYEE AND COMPUTES GROSS-PAY.
00007    *
00008    *
00009      ENVIRONMENT DIVISION.
00010      CONFIGURATION SECTION.
00011      SOURCE-COMPUTER, CYBER-74.
00012      OBJECT COMPUTER, CYBER-74.
00013      INPUT-OUTPUT SECTION.
00014      FILE-CONTROL.
00015         SELECT PAYROLL-FILE ASSIGN TO INPUT.
00016         SELECT PRINT-FILE ASSIGN TO OUTPUT.
00017    *
00018    *
00019      DATA DIVISION.
00020      FILE SELECTION.
00021      FC  PAYROLL-FILE
00022         LABEL RECORD IS OMITTED.
00023      01 INPUT-RECORD           PICTURE X(80).
00024    *
00025      FC PRINT-FILE
00026         LABEL RECORD OMITTED.
00027         01  PRINT-LINE          PICTURE X(132).
00028    *
00029      WORKING-STORAGE SECTION
00030      77  OVERTIME-HOURS        PICTURE 99.
00031      77  REGULAR-HOURS         PICTURE 99.
00032      77  GROSS-PAY             PICTURE 9999V99.
00033      77  REGULAR-PAY           PICTURE 9999V99.
00034      77  OVERTIME-PAY          PICTURE 9999V99.
00035      77  REGULAR-TOTAL         PICTURE 99999V99.
00036      77  OVERTIME-TOTAL        PICTURE 99999V99.
00037      77  GROSS-TOTAL           PICTURE 99999V99.
00038      77  MORE-CARDS            PICTURE XXX.
00039      01  PAYROLL-DATA.
00040         05  NAME               PICTURE X(30)
00041         05  RATE-OF-PAY        PICTURE 99V999.
00042         05  HOUR-WORKED        PICTURE 999.
00043         05  FILLER             PICTURE X(422).
00044      01 DATE-RECORD.
00045         05  DATE-IN            PICTURE X(8).
00046         05  FILLER             PICTURE X(72).
00047      01 COMPANY-HEADER.
00048         05  FILLER             PICTURE X(58)      VALUE SPACES.
00049         05  FILLER             PICTURE X(17)      VALUE
00050                                'THE SMALL COMPANY'.
00051         05  FILLER             PICTURE X(57)      VALUE SPACES.
00052      01 WEEK-HEADER.
```

Table 9-3 *(continued)*

```
00053          05  FILLER              PICTURE X(46)       VALUE SPACES.
00054          05  FILLER              PICTURE X(31)       VALUE
00055                              'REPORT OF WAGES PAID WEEK OF '.
00056          05  DATE-OUT            PICTURE X(8).
00057          05  FILLER              PICTURE X(47)       VALUE SPACES.
00058      01 DETAIL-HEADER 1.
00059          05  FILLER              PICTURE X(56)       VALUE SPACES.
00060          05  FILLER              PICTURE X(14)       VALUE
00061                              'HOURLY HOURS'.
00062          05  FILLER              PICTURE X(13)       VALUE SPACES.
00063          05  FILLER              PICTURE X(27)       VALUE
00064                              'REGULAR OVERTIME       TOTAL'.
00065          05  FILLER              PICTURE X(22)       VALUE SPACES.
00066      01 DETAIL-HEADER-2.
00067          05  FILLER              PICTURE X(20)       VALUE SPACES.
00068          05  FILLER              PICTURE X(13)       VALUE
00069                              'EMPLOYEE NAME'.
00070          05  FILLER              PICTURE X(24)       VALUE SPACES.
00071          05  FILLER              PICTURE X(14)       VALUE
00072                              'RATE WORKED'.
00073          05  FILLER              PICTURE X(15)       VALUE SPACES.
00074          05  FILLER              PICTURE X(24)       VALUE
00075                                  'PAY      PAY         PAY
00076          05  FILLER              PICTURE X(23)       VALUE SPACES.
00077      01 DETAIL-LINE.
00078          05  FILLER              PICTURE X(20)       VALUE SPACES.
00079          05  NAME-PRINT          PICTURE X(30) .
00080          05  FILLER              PICTURE X(6)        VALUE SPACES.
00081          05  RATE-PRINT          PICTURE Z9.999.
00082·         05  FILLER              PICTURE X(5)        VALUE SPACES.
00083          05  HOURS-PRINT         PICTURE ZZ9.
00084          05  FILLER              PICTURE X(13)       VALUE SPACES.
00085          05  REGULAR-PAY-PRINT   PICTURE ZZZ9.99.
00086          05  FILLER              PICTURE X(3)        VALUE SPACES.
00087          05  OVER-PAY-PRINT      PICTURE ZZZ9.99.
00088          05  FILLER              PICTURE X(3)        VALUE SPACES.
00089          05  GROSS-PAY-PRINT     PICTURE ZZZ9.99.
00090          05  FILLER              PICTURE X(22)       VALUE SPACES.
00091      01 TOTAL-LINE.
00092          05  FILLER              PICTURE X(74)       VALUE SPACES.
00093          05  FILLER              PICTURE X(8)        VALUE 'TOTALS '..
00094          05  REGULAR-TOTAL-PRINT PICTURE $ZZZ9.99.
00095          05  FILLER              PICTURE X(2)        VALUE SPACES.
00096          05  OVER-TOTAL-PRINT    PICTURE $ZZZ9.99.
00097          05  FILLER              PICTURE X(2)        VALUE SPACES.
00098          05  GROSS-TOTAL-PRINT   PICTURE $ZZZ9.99.
00099      *
00100      *
00101      PROCEDURE DIVISION.
00102      MAINLINE-CONTROL.
00103          PERFORM INITIALIZATION.
00104          PERFORM READ-AND-CHECK UNTIL MORE-CARDS = 'NO'.
00105          PERFORM CLOSING.
```

Table 9-3 *(continued)*

```
00106        STOP RUN.
00107   *
00108     INITIALIZATION.
00109        OPEN INPUT PAYROLL-FILE.
00110        OPEN OUTPUT PRINT-FILE.
00111        MOVE 'YES' TO MORE-CARDS.
00112        READ PAYROLL-FILE INTO DATE-RECORD AT END STOP RUN.
00113        WRITE PRINT-LINE FROM COMPANY-HEADER AFTER ADVANCING
00114            2 LINES.
00115        MOVE DATE-IN TO DATE-OUT.
00116        WRITE PRINT LINE FROM WEEK-HEADER AFTER ADVANCING 2 LINES.
00117        WRITE PRINT-LINE FROM DETAIL-HEADER-1 AFTER ADVANCING
00118            2 LINES.
00119        WRITE PRINT-LINE FROM DETAIL-HEADER-2 AFTER ADVANCING
00120            1 LINES.
00121        MOVE SPACES TO PRINT-LINE WRITE PRINT-LINE.
00122        MOVE ZEROES TO REGULAR-TOTAL, OVERTIME-TOTAL, GROSS-TOTAL.
00123   *
00124     READ-AND-CHECK.
00125        READ PAYROLL-FILE INTO PAYROLL-DATA AT END
00126                 MOVE 'NO' TO MORE-CARDS.
00127        IF MORE-CARDS = 'YES' PERFORM PROCESS-AND-PRINT.
00128   *
```

The **C language** is now gaining popularity. This powerful language was developed at Bell Laboratories and is used extensively on minicomputers, workstations, and personal computers for developing systems. C is not a language for the casual end user. Systems developers are particularly fond of C because it is very powerful, and probably the most portable language around today. That is, software can be moved from one system to another with minimal effort because there are C compilers for most major computers. Table 9-4 is an example of a C program.

Object-oriented programming is a relatively new approach to developing software. The idea is to create objects that are self-contained modules of code. Designers encapsulate a set of data and all valid operations on that data together in an object. All of the objects in a class inherit the characteristics of that class. A class is an abstract concept for a group of related objects. For example, if a class is automobiles, the members of that class inherit the class properties of having four wheels, an engine, and doors. The programmer can write programs by putting together different modules in different orders. One attraction of object-oriented development is the presence of libraries of objects and procedures. If we could reuse code written in the past for a new application, there would be a dramatic improvement in productivity.

There is an object-oriented version of C called C++. However, the creation of objects in C++ requires a highly skilled programmer. Another popular object-oriented language is Smalltalk, which is at a higher level than C++.

Table 9-4
A C Program to Count Words and Characters

```c
#include ~<stdio.h>

/*
 * Scan standard input and count words and total number
 * of characters in words. A word is defined as any string of
 * non-white space characters. Also print the average word
 * length (to one decimal place).
 *
 * DJB
 */
main()
{
    int n:
    long c_cnt = 0, w_cnt = 0;

    while (n = get. word()) {
        c_cnt +=n;
        w_cnt++;
    }
    printf("word count %d\nnon-white space char count: %d\n",
            w_cnt, c_cnt);
    if (w_cnt) printf("average word length: %.1f\n",
                            (float) c_cnt / w_cnt);
}


/*
 * Get the next word by first scanning leading white space
 * characters and then the non white space characters that
 * make up a word. Return the total number of characters
 * scanned if a word is found, otherwise return 0 (on EOF).
 */
int get word()
{
    int c, c_cnt = 0;

    while (is white space(c = getchar()))
        ; /* ignore white space */

    if (c != EOF) {
        while ((c = getchar())   != EOF && !is white space (c))
            c_cnt++;
        return c_cnt + 1; /* plus 1 for missed first char */
    }
    else return 0;
}
/*
 * Check if character is white space—that includes
 * blanks, tabs, and new line characters. Returns 1
 * if white space, otherwise returns 0.
 */
int is white space(c)
        int c;
{
    if (c = ' ' || c = '\t' || c = '\n')
        return 1;
    else return 0;
}
```

IBM appears to be pursuing a strategy of making Smalltalk available on all the computers it markets. The company is encouraging customers to adopt object-oriented programming and to use Smalltalk as their language. There is great hope for graphical object-oriented languages. In the future it may be possible to develop a program by pointing at objects on the screen to combine them into a program!

A higher level language will often be translated into machine language by a program called a **compiler**. It accepts a program called the source program and translates it into machine language called the **object program**. (See Figure 9-1 for a schematic of the compilation process.)

Another strategy is to create programs to be interpreted. The interpreter is a program that looks at each of your program's statements, decodes it, and performs the instruction. Interpreters make it easier to change a program and rerun it without recompilation, something useful when writing and debugging a program. BASIC is a good example of a language that develops programs using an interpreter. When finished, the user runs the debugged program through a BASIC compiler to produce object code. In general, a compiled program executes more quickly than an interpreted program.

One of the most noted programs today for use on the Internet (see Chapter 12) is a version of C called Java. Java is an interpreted program that programmers use to create "applets" (small programs) to be downloaded to client computers connected to the Internet. (See the sidebar later in this chapter.)

An Example of a Special-Purpose Language

Special-purpose languages are designed with the same philosophy as higher-level languages: to extend the capabilities of the computer to users. Frequently, special-purpose languages are translated into a higher-level language that is compiled to produce machine language.

An excellent example of a special-purpose language is SPSS (Statistical Package for the Social Sciences). This comprehensive statistical system is designed to be used for analyzing data statistically. SPSS makes it possible to name **variables** for a particular study, save the variable names and data in a file, and create new variables from logical relationships among existing variables. The package features extensive data management facilities complemented by a number of statistical tests including: preparing frequency distributions, testing for differences among populations, calculating measures of association, performing analysis of variance, and performing a series of multivariate procedures such as regression analysis and factor analysis.

Figure 9-1
Compilation process.

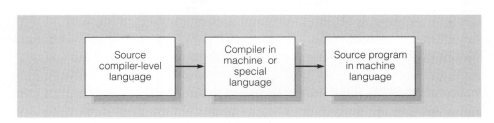

Figure 9-2 shows the interface for the Windows version of SPSS (there are versions of SPSS that run on mainframes, minis, and PCs). The system allows you to input data, for example, by typing it into a spreadsheet program. You can identify each variable or column in the data matrix with a label like Age, Sex, or Marital status. Then you use the variables in various statistical procedures that range from a simple frequency distribution to more complex multivariate analyses like regression. Consider the number of program statements required in a language such as FORTRAN to perform this kind of statistical analysis.

Fourth-Generation Languages Ease Programming

A number of software vendors have developed languages they advertise as belonging to the "fourth generation." Just as compiler-level languages are at a higher level than assembly language, **fourth-generation languages (4GLs)** are at a higher level than compiled languages. The purpose of these languages is to make it easier to access the computer. One does not have to construct as many detailed steps in writing a program. These languages are particularly appealing to users, who can use them to access data on corporate computers.

The following is an example of a simple program written in **FOCUS**, one of the most popular fourth-generation languages:

```
TABLE FILE SALESDAT
PRINT NAME AND AMOUNT AND DATE
BY REGION BY SITE
IF AMOUNT GT 2000
ON REGION SKIP-LINE
END
```

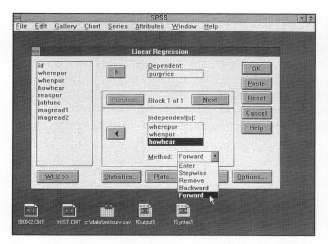 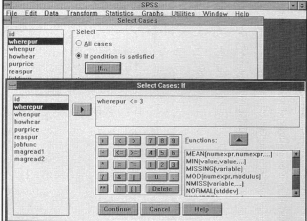

Figure 9-2 The interface for the Windows version of SPSS.

This short program accesses a file named SALESDAT and produces a report that contains the region, site, name, amount, and sales if sales are greater than 2,000. The report is sorted by region and by site, with one blank line between regions. Generating a report like this would require many more statements in a language like COBOL. A fourth-generation language reduces the amount of detail in a program to improve productivity and makes it easier for users to think at a higher level.

PowerBuilder® is a popular 4GL for developing applications on a personal computer and it is well suited to a client-server environment. A major brokerage firm used PowerBuilder to create an elaborate time recording and charge-back program for its internal systems development group. The use of this language made it possible to develop a large application in a relatively short period of time and resulted in a system with an appealing, graphical user interface. Figure 9-3 is an example of PowerBuilder code.

Package Programs Are Another Alternative

Package programs are software written by a vendor to be sold to multiple customers. Packages have been available since the first days of computers, but there has been an explosion in their sale and use.

One of the reasons for this proliferation is that the technology has matured. There are packages around today in the fourth or fifth (or more) version, improving with each version. The other reason packages are gaining in popularity is the standards set by personal computer packages. The

---

MANAGEMENT PROBLEM 9-2

Ted Armstrong is president of Advanced Airlines, a regional carrier in the southwestern United States. Ted and several fellow pilots founded the airline in the early 1990s. Although operations were precarious at first, the firm is now in the position of making a small profit on its freight and passenger operations. In addition, the line has been slowly entering the charter market through contracts for private service with oil and utility companies.

Advanced Airlines has grown to the point where it now needs an automated reservation system for passengers and freight. Since the management of the firm generally consists of pilots with little exposure to computer systems, Ted has explored different possibilities himself.

Two options appear feasible. First, Advanced can obtain a packaged system from a major computer manufacturer. There would be substantial effort involved in initializing the package and installing it. Advanced would also have to lease or purchase its own computer. While the economics are in question, another regional airline has indicated an interest in joining Advanced, so the two lines would be able to share the cost of the system.

The alternative is to purchase reservation services from one of the large trunk carriers that operates its own extensive reservation system. Ted has discussed this possibility with two trunk carriers that sell services on their computerized reservations systems.

Which option do you recommend?

Figure 9-3
A PowerBuilder®
application screen and
some of the code that
produced it.

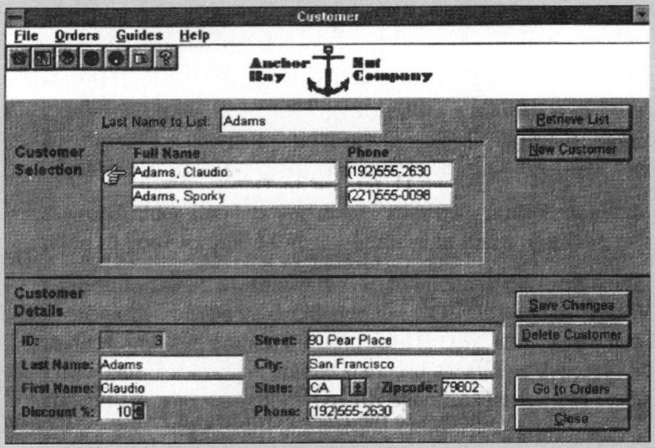

```
// Call the user-defined window-level function wf_delcustorders ( )
// to check whether the customer to be deleted has any orders
// in the database. If so, disallow the customer delete operation.

integer li_returned orders
li_returned orders = wf_delcustorders (li_delid)

CHOOSE CASE li_returned_orders

        CASE IS > 0
                MessageBox("Delete Not Allowed", &
                    "You can't delete a customer who has orders on file. " +&
                    ls_delname + " has " + String(li_returned_orders) +&
                    " orders on file.", stopsign!)
        RETURN

        CASE IS < 0
                MessageBox("Delete Failure", &
                    "Could not determine whether " + ls_delname +&
                    " has any orders on file. " +&
                    "Please call the Anchor Bay support team.", &
                    exclamation!)
        RETURN

END CHOOSE
```

market for personal computers is large, and a vendor knows that it is impossible to provide extensive training to customers who purchase the package. (PCs are often programmed in Visual BASIC, PowerBuilder, or C, but most users work primarily with powerful packages.) Therefore, the PC package has to be user friendly and well documented with an easy-to-use instruction guide. It is hoped that these positive features of packages for PCs will influence packages for all types of computers.

Although packages are certainly a type of software, we defer detailed discussion of them until Chapter 18, where we present packages as an alternative to the traditional way of developing applications.

The Operating System

In the first generation of computers, and for many second-generation installations, the operator of the system had a central role in controlling its use. The operator placed each new program, which had been punched on cards, in the card reader and loaded an assembler on tape. The assembler translated the object program and wrote it on tape, then a loading program loaded it and began execution. For production jobs to be run repeatedly, the object program would be saved on tape or on cards and loaded before execution. It would not be assembled each time it was used.

A skilled operator balanced jobs that needed many tape drives with jobs that needed few or no drives so that the large tape job could be set up while the other job computed. In the case of an inefficient operator, the computer might be idle for a large part of the day while tapes were loaded and unloaded. As this scenario indicates, operations were very inefficient. It became clear that the computer itself could be used to help make operations proceed more smoothly. The first operating systems came into

SPSS at Quaker Oats

Quaker Oats is very interested in the question of whether Americans think Chewy Granola Bars are chewy enough. To determine consumer reactions to its products, Quaker Oats conducts a great deal of market research. To analyze these data, the firm uses SPSS on a UNISYS computer.

The research laboratory receives about eight hundred questionnaires a week on average for three different products. Each instrument consists of about twenty questions. In addition to research, the personnel department uses the system to generate reports on worker productivity and to project personnel requirements.

Researchers also use the package to develop time-series equations to model grocery inventories. The results of this research are used to improve customer service and reduce capital devoted to inventories.

In 1992, SPSS announced a Windows version of its popular statistical analysis package. The package accepts data from a spreadsheet and integrates graphics functions with its statistical processing. The new user interface greatly facilitates the analysis of data, particularly for those of us who remember punching SPSS commands into cards and waiting for batches of jobs to run through a mainframe computer.

widespread use during the late 1950s and early 1960s, with the earliest operating systems written by customers, not computer vendors.

It is important to note that operating systems are **programs** written by programmers. The functions in these programs are different than those in a typical applications program, for example, one that keeps track of inventory items. The operating system programs, as we shall see in this section, manage the resources of the computer. The operating system is concerned with providing your programs with the resources they need to run on the computer.

Early Systems   Batch Monitor   The earliest operating systems were simple **batch monitors** (the terms **monitor**, **executive program**, and *operating system* are synonymous in this discussion) that read special control cards. These cards might include a job card containing information about the programmer and the job, for example, run-time estimate, lines to be printed, and cards to be

Programs Have Bugs

There is an old saying in the computer field that "no program is ever fully debugged." Errors sometimes appear in programs that have been running for a long time due to some untested conditions that caused the error to appear. Typically, the mistake is in some part of the program that was not tested. (It is very difficult and prohibitively expensive to test every possible combination of paths through a program). If you used Windows 3.1, you sometimes encounter a message that some action has caused a general protection fault, and you often terminated the application involved. In this case, the system recognized an error and it tried to let you get around it by closing one application rather than restarting the computer.

A recent software problem in a cellular phone has caused a great deal of trouble for cellular companies and Motorola in Israel. The Alpha cellular phone, manufactured by Motorola, experienced a software problem in a program embedded in a ROM chip. The phone uses time division multiple access (T.D.M.A.) to switch its radio signal from one channel to another at frequent intervals. This strategy makes it possible for a number of phones to

use the same cell at the same time. The software error caused the phone to lock onto one channel and stay there indefinitely, blocking other users in that cell from using it, until the offending phone was shut off or its batteries died. The problem resulted in inaudible voices, poor reception, calls being cut off, and times when the phones did not work.

The problem first appeared in Hong Kong and quickly spread to Israel. Cellular service is very popular in Israel and inexpensive, less than 3 cents a minute compared to figures like 65 cents a minute in the U.S. Many customers in Israel leave their phones on all the time and they use cellular phones eight times more than people in the U.S. Motorola recalled 150,000 of the phones from six countries and fixed the problem within six weeks, at a cost of $10 to $20 million. Several class action suits were filed against Motorola and a cellular phone company in Israel.

Bugs are a major problem; they can be very costly, and even dangerous in applications like air traffic control and medicine.

punched. Some systems also included information for accounting, such as an account or project number. Control cards were provided to tell the operator to set up tapes or to prepare any special paper required for the printer.

The monitor, though simple, sequenced jobs so an entire stack or stream of jobs could be loaded at once. As disks became more common, compilers and work space were assigned to disks so that the operator did not have to mount the compiler, loader, and program object tapes. Operating systems and disk storage have drastically improved the efficiency of computer operations.

Multiprocessing   During the second generation, at least one manufacturer offered a **multiprocessing** system—a computer system featuring more than one central processing unit. In reality, this system consisted of two complete computers. The smaller computer had an operating system and controlled both machines. The larger computer was a "slave" to the smaller machine. The small computer processed all input and scheduled and printed all output, using disks as a temporary storage area. An operating system in the large computer indicated to the control machine that it needed service—for example, when it needed a new program to process—and the control computer answered its request. This approach freed the more powerful slave computer from I/O and allowed it to concentrate on computations.

On-line Systems   During the 1960s, the need became evident for on-line computer access for applications such as inventory control and reservations. The first **on-line systems** featured custom-designed operating system programs to control the computer resources. Applications programs in an on-line system express the logic of the application and are called by systems programs.

The **supervisor** in an on-line system establishes a series of **queues** and schedules service for them. First, the system assembles an incoming message in a communications buffer. This message may have to be converted into a different code and moved to an input queue in memory by an applications program. The operating system notes the addition of this message to the messages-to-be-processed queue.

When the central processing unit is available, the supervisor assigns it to process a queue, say, the one with our input message. An applications program called by the operating system might verify the correctness of the message (correct format, and the like), after which the message is placed in a working queue.

The supervisor calls an applications program to interpret the message, during which time the message may be moved along several different working queues. The supervisor calls different applications programs to process the message further and determine a response. Finally, a program assembles an output message in another queue for transmission to the terminal. The supervisor schedules the CPU to send the output message. This example is considered a **multi-threaded** operation. There are a number of tasks associated with each message, and the operating system assigns a CPU to each task as it is ready for service.

The demands on such an on-line system are extensive. A great deal of bookkeeping is required to enforce and monitor queue disciplines. I/O operations also involve telecommunications activities. There must be adequate fallback and recovery facilities to prevent and handle system failures. For example, messages may be in process in one of a number of queues when the system fails. Recovery programs must try to restore processing and prevent data files from being corrupted.

The Birth of Time-Sharing   As computer systems became more heavily loaded during the 1950s and early 60s, the debugging of programs became

Hot Java!

In Chapter 12 we discuss networks and introduce the World Wide Web which is brought to you by the Internet. The Web provides a tremendous amount of information. It allows requests from client computers to be routed seamlessly to a variety of servers without the user having to be aware of where the data are actually located.

A group of software experts at Sun has developed a language called Java to help bring more interactivity to the Web. The program serves as a kind of universal **translator** enabling programs to move between incompatible operating systems. For example, there are many different kinds of client computers that access the Web including PCs, Macs and Sun workstations to name a few.

Java is a restricted version of C that is interpreted on the client computer. One needs a Java interpreter for each type of client, e.g. a PC, Mac, Sun workstation, etc. Your client's browser (a program that lets you explore the Web) requests Java programs or "applets" and the server sends them over the network to your computer. Then the Java interpreter for your computer interprets the applet. The applet can be the same for all computers because the interpreters hide the unique characteristics of the client PC. The interpreters must all do the same thing given an applet, but their internal construction will differ depending on whether they are for a PC, Mac, etc.

A company named Starwave in Bellevue, Washington, has created a program which can create a real-time simulation of a baseball game while it is being played on your PC. The events at the ball park are reflected on a PC in a lively animation that does credit to the best video games. You see the batter hitting a line drive between the shortstop and third base and watch him run to first base. At the same time, you see his updated batting average displayed on the screen.

One design goal is to have programs operate on any computer. Instead of just downloading data using a Web browser, you interact with it. As an example, suppose that you click on a Web page with a model home. The browser downloads a small program which works on any computer. The browser also downloads a file containing data for the model home. The applet has a program to support multimedia (Chapter 21) which takes you through the model home where you can interact with the environment, for example, by turning on lights.

Java is a new language that has the potential to change the way we think about computing.

a frustrating and time-consuming process. A programmer might be allowed only one test run a day or one run every several days. Programmers found their schedules and lives controlled by machine availability.

There is a clear mismatch between the speed with which humans think (and mechanically enter input or review output) and the internal speeds of computers. Could we make computer users feel as though they have exclusive use of their own machine by rapidly switching the computer from one user to another? One programmer's "think time" would be used by the computer for serving other programmers. Each user would share the time of the computer, especially the CPU and memory. This special case of an on-line system provides the user with computational capability and the ability to write and execute programs.

The operation of early time-sharing systems is illustrated in Figure 9-4. In this representation, only one program is executing at a time because there is only one CPU. A program executes for a short period of time until it is interrupted and "swapped" out of memory onto a secondary-storage device.

Another user's program is swapped into primary memory, and execution begins where it stopped when the program was previously swapped out of primary memory. In a simple round robin scheme, each user is given a maximum time slice in sequence. A program may be swapped out of primary memory even though it has used less than its time slice if it needs to send output or receive input, since these activities are handled by a data channel.

The Next Steps

By the early 1960s, most university and job-shop computer centers used batch monitors, and the commercial time-sharing industry was becoming established. Many business users also used operating systems for their equipment. When the next generation of computers was announced in 1964, manufacturers had clearly embraced the idea of an operating system. The IBM 360 line could not function without the operating system. An operating system manages the resources of the computer, for example, it handles all input/output through **interrupts**. In fact, there are special instructions that can be performed by the computer only when it is in "supervisory state" under the control of the operating system. These privileged instructions are unavailable to programmers, whose jobs run in "problem state." The operating systems also require a certain amount of memory for permanently resident routines. Other parts of the operating systems are stored on disk and brought into memory as needed.

Multiprocessing   In our discussion of hardware, we mentioned the development of data channels to take some of the I/O burden from the central processing unit. There was still an imbalance between CPU and I/O, however, even with channels. Batch operating systems in 1964 introduced the concept of multiprogramming, a process very similar to the program-swapping techniques developed for time-sharing. In **multiprogramming**, we have more than one program in a semiactive state in memory at one time (see

Figure 9-4
Early time-sharing
processing.

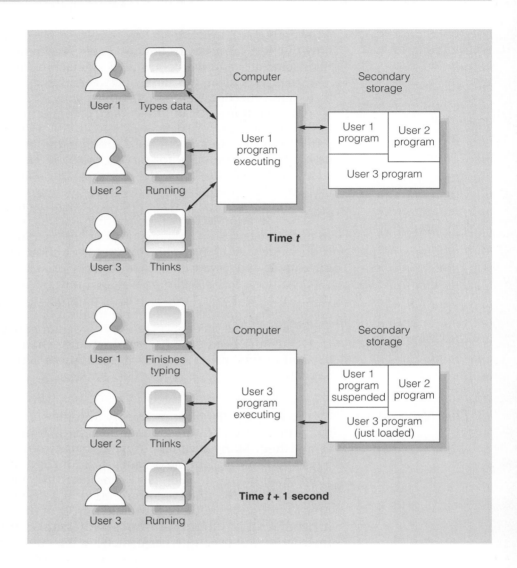

Figure 9-5). Multiprogramming switches the CPU to another program when it can no longer process the one it is working on because the program must wait for something. In the top half of Figure 9-5, we see a multiprogramming scheme with four programs active. Just before time *t*, program 2 was executing, However, it needed to print several lines on a report, and the CPU assigned this activity to a data channel.

The CPU then saved the status of program 2 and looked for another program on which to work. In this instance, the highest-priority task is program 4. The system restores the status of program 4 from its last interruption and execution begins. When the data channel completes the present operation for program 2, it interrupts the CPU, which stops program 4, saves its

Figure 9-5
Multiprogramming.

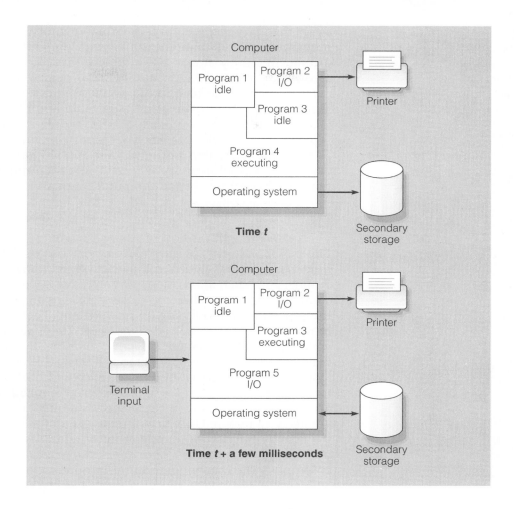

status, notes the completion of I/O for program 2, and checks to see what program to start next, in this example, program 3.

The presence of one or more programs in a semiactive state in memory with the CPU assigned to one after another is a key feature of many modern operating systems. Multiprogramming works because the operating system manages the programs that are running on the computer at one time. The concept behind multiprogramming is similar to what a time-sharing or on-line system does. In fact, if you use Windows95 on your PC, you probably launch multiple programs into memory at one time. When you cycle among these applications, you are assigning the CPU to a different program or application. This technique makes better use of the CPU and other resources of the computer.

Time-Sharing Time-sharing users often run out of memory. Programmers would like to have limitless memory, or a **virtual memory** several times larger than physical memory. In virtual memory, as shown in Figure 9-6, a program and its data are broken into pages. Only those pages needed in primary memory at any one time are loaded. Other pages are kept on secondary-storage devices. In a demand **paging** scheme, a program executes in memory until it needs a page that is not in primary memory. A request for the page generates a page fault, and the supervisor locates and loads the needed page from secondary storage. In loading the page, the supervisor may replace an inactive page belonging to another program in primary memory. This entire process is transparent to the programmer, who sees a virtual memory as large as the total number of pages allowed, not the physical size of the computer's primary memory.

Evolutionary Advances

The 1970s brought improvements and modifications to operating systems. The major advance took virtual memory out of the exclusive domain of time-sharing and included it in batch systems. Today, we have time-sharing, on-line, and batch applications all processing on the same computer system simultaneously. In addition, many packages are available to help reduce the problems of developing on-line systems. There are packages to handle inquiries and telecommunications tasks. These packages can be combined with database management systems, which are discussed in Chapter 11. For mainframes, the dominant operating system is IBM's MVS (Multiple Virtual Systems), and is replaced by a new version called OS/390. This newest mainframe operating system is designed to turn the mainframe into a large server and to promote its role in client-server architectures. Midrange computers are likely to feature Unix or Windows NT, described in the next section.

One useful view of an operating system is as a resource manager. The operating system consists of a series of managers, and each manager must accomplish the following: monitor resources, enforce policies on resource

Figure 9-6
Paging.

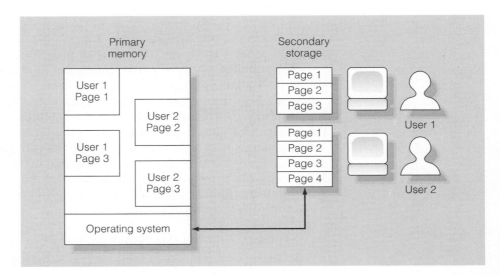

allocation (who, what, and how much), allocate the resource, and reclaim the resource. There are four major resource categories:

1. The **memory manager** keeps track of what parts of memory are in use and by whom and what parts are available. In multiprogramming, this manager decides which process obtains what amount of memory at what point in time.

2. The **process manager** keeps track of the status of processes. It includes a job schedule that chooses among jobs submitted and decides which one will be processed. (It assigns resources as does a CPU).

3. The **device manager** monitors input/output resources—anything connected to the computer through a data channel or bus. It tries to schedule and allocate these resources efficiently.

4. The **information manager** controls the file system and its directories. Information must be protected, and this manager allocates and reclaims resources, for example, by opening and closing files.

Operating Systems for Smaller Computers

The discussion above traced the development of operating systems, and the examples were drawn primarily from large systems. Personal computers also have operating systems, though originally they had fewer features than their mainframe counterparts. The functions of PC operating systems are similar to those of any operating system: to manage the computer's resources.

One of the most popular operating systems for IBM-compatible personal computers is called **MS/DOS**. This operating system is concerned only with a single program executing at one time, so its management tasks are easier than for a time-sharing or multiprogramming operating system.

MS/DOS actually has two layers of interest. The highest level is the command level, seen by users of the system. The lowest level is BIOS, or basic input/output system, part of which is actually in read-only memory. All input and output uses the BIOS routines, so there is no need for each application to write codes to control the lowest level of input and output to the diskettes, printer, or display. Many personal computers run Windows 3.1 as a graphical user interface with DOS. Windows95 represents an advance over the combination of Windows 3.1 and DOS, but it is still based heavily on the original DOS in order to provide compatibility.

The operating system provides a number of commands for the user. The most frequently used commands are concerned with managing secondary storage, the diskette, and hard disk drives. One can obtain a directory of the files on a particular disk, check to see how much room there is on a disk, format a diskette for writing for the first time, and copy individual files or entire diskettes from one diskette to another. It is also possible to list files on the display device or printer and to delete a file that is no longer needed.

Chips with 32-bit processors and 32-bit memory buses are designed with hardware support for virtual memory. Chips like the Intel 80486 and Pentium require an advanced operating system to take advantage of their power. Many of the features of modern mainframe operating systems are found in supervisory programs for the powerful chips of today, including virtual memory and the ability for the user to have several different programs active in memory simultaneously.

There are three major operating systems competing for users of certain minis, PCs, and workstations. Users are rapidly adopting Windows95 as a replacement for the combination of Microsoft Windows 3.1 and DOS. Windows95 offers the user a graphical user interface (GUI) as shown in Figure 9-7. Using a mouse, the user can "click" on a graphical icon on the screen to load a program such as a word processor or spreadsheet, then place this program in a "window" on the screen marked with a border. The user can simultaneously load other programs in other windows and switch among them using the mouse.

It should be pointed out that the windowing interface was first an integral part of the Apple Macintosh system. See Figure 9-8 for an example of the Mac user interface. Newer versions of Windows have finally begun to give the PC some of the same ease-of-use features found in the original Macintosh. (To be completely fair, the whole idea of windows came from Xerox's Palo Alto Research Center (PARC), but Xerox never commercialized its invention.)

IBM's PC operating system **OS/2** is designed to compete with Windows. This operating system has more features than Windows 3.1 and was first

Figure 9-7
Windows95 interface.

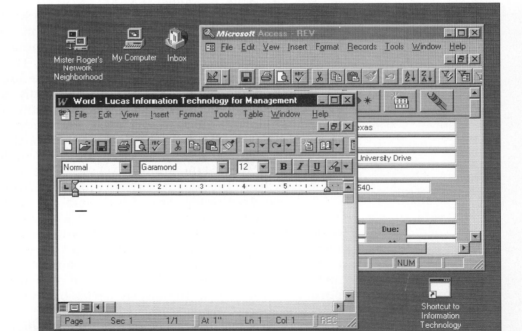

Figure 9-8
Macintosh user interface.

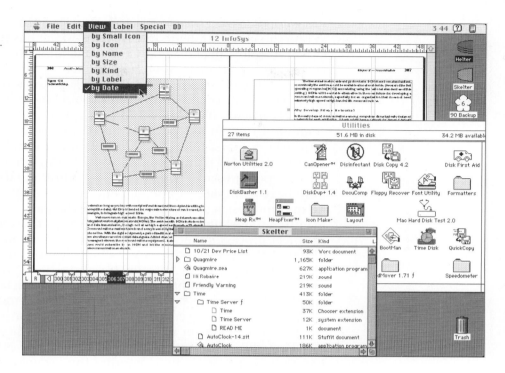

to take advantage of the 32-bit processing capabilities of modern chips. Of course, as an operating system offers more features, it requires more hardware to run, both in terms of primary memory and the amount of disk space required to store operating system modules. To run Windows95 you need at least 16 megabytes of main memory.

The next major contender in the operating systems contest is Unix. Unix has been around for a number of years and has been getting more popular all the time. Unix offers multitasking, a graphical interface (if you add one to it), and high portability. There are versions of Unix that operate on mainframes, minis, and PCs. Unix is written in C, which was originally developed for the purpose of writing an operating system.

Most of the major vendors of engineering workstations, including Hewlett-Packard and Sun, base their systems on Unix. It is also probably the most frequently used time-sharing system on minicomputers. Even IBM, which for years would support only its own, proprietary operating systems, now offers a version of Unix called AIX.

Windows95 and OS/2 are both controlled by single vendors, Microsoft and IBM, respectively. Unix is available from different vendors, each offering versions that differ enough that programs have to be modified to be moved from one vendor's Unix machines to those of another vendor. At first, AT&T was dominant in defining Unix since Bell Labs developed it. However, AT&T spun off Unix forming a company called Unix Systems

Laboratories. Novell bought this company for $320 million in 1993. In 1995, in order to concentrate on its core networking business, new management at Novell sold Unix to Santa Cruise Operation, Inc. (SCO), a major Unix vendor. In addition to SCO, vendors selling Unix include Sun, Hewlett Packard, Silicon Graphics and IBM. It is possible that the presence of so many versions along with the threat posed by Windows, OS/2, and Windows NT discussed below will force these vendors to come together for a common Unix. An independent standards setting body called the X/Open Consortium hopes to create a unified Unix to challenge Microsoft.

Windows NT is an operating system from Microsoft intended for servers and "power users." Windows NT also illustrates the migration of features from larger computers to smaller ones. For example, NT supports symmetric multiprocessing, something that in the past was associated only with mainframe operating systems. Windows NT takes advantage of multiple, identical processors. Remember that processes can be broken down into different threads (see the earlier discussion of on-line processing). Windows NT assigns these threads, based on their priority, to the available processors in a multiprocessor system. Manufacturers of various RISC-based technology, such as DEC, are adapting Windows NT for their machines. Companies spend over $50 billion a year on multiuser software, twice what is spent on PC programs. Much of Microsoft's future depends on being able to capture the server market, and NT is the operating system that is crucial to implementing this strategy. Most observers expect Windows95 to merge with NT so, in the not-too-distant future, Microsoft will only have to support one operating system.

One thing is clear: Users want to have systems that are as portable as possible. **Portability** means that an operating system will run across a number of different computers. We are rapidly approaching the point, at least for minis and workstations, that hardware is like any other commodity. The user will not care, and very likely will not know, what hardware is executing his or her programs. The one thing the user will see is the operating system and program interface. These interfaces need to be as common as possible across all types of hardware.

Who will win? It is very hard to predict what will happen in the operating systems wars. Windows95 sales have been strong. (Windows 3.1 ran on an estimated 100 million computers when Windows95 was introduced in August of 1995). OS/2 started slowly, but the latest version has been selling better, though many feel that OS/2 will not survive. Unix has a solid base of support and is unlikely to disappear. A key question is whether its use will continue to expand. Many experts think that Windows NT will emerge as the winner since Microsoft is such a powerful software vendor. It clearly would like to see Windows NT become the dominant operating system on servers, midrange computers, and on desktops. The major threat to Microsoft is from the Internet and the possibility that users will obtain all processing and services through inexpensive "netsurfing" computers that do not need Microsoft software. We discuss this possibility further along with the Internet in Chapter 12.

CHAPTER SUMMARY

1. Software is the key to the utilization of computers. As hardware becomes less expensive and more powerful, we shall continue to be constrained by the need to develop software programs for new computer applications.

2. Programming can be a time-consuming and tedious task. However, in the span of four decades, software has advanced tremendously and computer languages are becoming easier to use.

3. In a short period of time we moved from machine language to graphical user interfaces and extremely powerful packages for PCs. Each stage depends on the ones that precede it.

4. *A key task of management is to determine what development approach and language are appropriate in a given situation.* If you have modest processing demands and want to develop an application quickly, a fourth-generation language may be appropriate. If you need a high-volume, transactions processing system, then you are likely to need a more efficient language.

5. Because there is so much software in existence, we should expect to find widely varying standards of quality and functionality. You may encounter a mainframe system that was written ten years ago and changed through minor enhancements. It is unfair to compare this system with the newest software for Windows95!

6. No organization can afford to redo all of its software at one time. There may be very good business reasons for continuing to use a ten-year-old system, even though its interface and even its functions are outdated. As a manager, you will have to decide how to allocate scarce resources among maintenance, enhancements, and entirely new systems.

7. Operating systems are extremely important components of a computer. Large mainframes from IBM continue to use the MVS operating system (or OS/390) and run many legacy COBOL applications. Midrange computers tend to run Unix, and Windows95 (or its predecessor) are dominant for PCs. Windows NT is positioned as an operating system for servers, though a number of companies are using NT on clients as well.

8. There is still much to be done to remove the software bottleneck that exists in developing applications. In later chapters we discuss some strategies to reduce the cycle time for developing applications.

IMPLICATIONS FOR MANAGEMENT

Hardware, at least at the level of the PC, is a commodity item. You should be more concerned with the kind of software you can run than the brand of PC you are using to run it. To get something done on a computer, you have to use software. Either you create the application, or you buy it in the form of a software package. For much of what you want to do, it is too costly to use a professional designer or programmer, so you will work with PC software like a spreadsheet and database management system to solve your own problems. Since the beginning of the industry, the trend in software has been to try and make it more accessible and easier to use. Graphical user interfaces have helped a great deal so that a manager can do a lot by "pointing and clicking." One of the hard decisions you will face is whether or not to use some kind of software yourself to solve a problem or whether to turn the problem over to IS professionals.

KEY WORDS

Assembly language
Batch monitor
C language
COBOL
Compiler
Device manager
Executive program
FOCUS
FORTRAN
Fourth-generation language (4GL)
Higher-level language
Information manager
Interrupt
Machine language
Memory manager
Mnemonic
Monitor
Translator
Unix
Variables

MS/DOS
Multiprocessing
Multiprogramming
Multi-threaded
Object program
Object-oriented
On-line system
Operating system
OS/2
Packages
Paging
Portability
Process manager
Programs
Queues
Special-purpose language
Supervisor
Virtual memory
Windows95
Windows NT

RECOMMENDED READING

Bic, L., and A. Shaw. *The Logical Design of Operating Systems*. Englewood Cliffs, N.J.: Prentice-Hall, 1988. (An advanced text on the principles of operating system design.)

Byte. New York: McGraw-Hill. (A popular personal computer magazine including articles on operating systems.)

Fichman, R., and C. Kemerer. "Adoption of Software Engineering Process Innovations: The Case of Object Orientation," *Sloan Management Review,* vol. 32, no. 2 (Winter 1993), pp. 7–22. (A good introduction to object-oriented programming and some thoughts on how likely it is to succeed in becoming the dominant programming methodology.)

DISCUSSION QUESTIONS

1. What motivated the development of assembly language? What trend did this inaugurate?
2. For what purpose is assembly language used today?
3. Why is programming such a time-consuming task?
4. Under what circumstances, if any, should managers write programs?
5. What are the advantages of standardized subsets of languages such as FORTRAN and COBOL, that is, a set of statements that are compatible across all compilers?
6. Develop a checklist of the factors to consider in evaluating a packaged program.
7. What is the major appeal of packaged programs for user departments? What is the major disadvantage of these packages for the information services department?
8. Computer science researchers are working on parallel languages. How would such a language differ from a language like BASIC?
9. What are the advantages to breaking up programs into small pieces or modules?
10. Why does a manager care what operating systems are used on computers in the organization? Why should he or she prefer one system to another?
11. What was the motivation behind the development of operating systems?
12. How have time-sharing techniques influenced the development of operating systems?
13. As PC software is written for 32-bit data paths as opposed to 16, what will the results be?
14. How does virtual memory contribute to the development of programs?
15. Where can problems occur with virtual memory? Under what conditions should we expect performance of a virtual memory system to be best? Worst?
16. What is the advantage of a simple programming language such as BASIC?
17. What factors influence the choice of a programming language for an application? Why should an organization have standards for languages?
18. Why do some programmers prefer to write a program from scratch than modify a program written by someone else?
19. How should programs be tested? What types of data should be used and who should generate the data?

20. What kind of applications will make use of languages like PowerBuilder?

21. Why do users want "open systems?"

22. How is program testing complicated by a client-server environment?

23. How can PCs be used by professional programmers to develop programs for larger computers?

24. What are the major advantages of special-purpose languages? How do they extend computer use to more individuals?

25. Can an entire application be developed with a fourth-generation language?

26. What hardware and software characteristics are responsible for the overall performance of a computer system?

27. How can the quality of software be evaluated? What standards or measures can you suggest?

28. Various goals for programs have been found to influence programmer performance—goals such as minimum number of statements, minimal use of main memory, maximum output clarity, maximum program clarity, minimum number of runs to debug, and minimum execution time. Which of these goals are incompatible? Which ones should be emphasized by management?

29. Why is it so difficult to replace MVS COBOL applications?

30. Does the extensive use of packages make it more difficult or less difficult to change computer manufacturers? On what factors does the answer to this question depend?

31. What are the advantages of massively parallel computers? What are their disadvantages?

32. What advantages does multitasking offer in a PC server?

33. What kind of software does a server for a local area network need to have?

34. What are the differences between a mainframe operating system and a personal computer operating system?

CHAPTER 9 PROJECT

SIMON MARSHALL ASSOCIATES

Simon Marshall is running Windows95 on the PCs in its office. John Marshall has read articles about "operating system wars" and wonders if his firm is keeping up with what is happening. "Windows NT, Unix, OS/2—they're all a bit confusing to me. We've barely begun to get something out of Windows—now at least we can paste spreadsheet graphs into our written reports. I also want to get into groupware, as we do a lot of projects together. I know that I will need a network, but I wonder if I should go to a new operating system before thinking about a network. It's all so confusing."

What advice can you give John about groupware, networks, and a possible switch to a new operating system?

CHAPTER **10**

Database Management

● OBJECTIVES

1. Learning to manage information technology.

The reason for databases is to store and make available data that are important to the organization. Too often we hear managers and others complain they cannot access data they provided to a system in the first place. Managing data and databases is an important part of managing IT. What database management system should we buy? Where should data be stored, and who can access them?

2. **Preparing to apply technology.**

Identifying the data needed for a new system is a major part of systems design. Most of the time, you will want to use a database management system (DBMS) as a part of the design. This chapter also discusses how a DBMS is used as a complete system to design a custom application with minimal programming.

3. **Transforming the organization.**

By giving a supplier access to your production and inventory database, you may be able to eliminate the raw materials inventory. The supplier then becomes part of your corporation, changing the way both of you do business. As you read this chapter, think about the kind of databases necessary to create new relationships with customers and suppliers.

A typical organization has a large number of files, many of which may be stored on a computer device. We call these data machine readable because you can use a computer to process them. Paper files, on the other hand, are much less accessible. Companies frequently refer to related files as a part of a database. This term may be used generically, or it may refer to a specific system or database management software. Examples of database systems for personal computers include Dbase, Paradox, and Access. Databases for midrange systems include Oracle and Sybase, and IBM's mainframe database is called DB2.

FILE ELEMENTS

Computers store data in a **file**, which can be defined simply as a collection of data. A computer file is organized in a particular way with a well-defined structure to the information in the file. A computer file consists of a collection of **records**, each of which are made up of **fields**. The various fields consist of groups of characters, as described below.

Data   The smallest unit of storage of interest is the **character**, for example, the number 9 or the letter A. We generally do not work directly with characters but rather with groups of characters that have some intrinsic meaning, such as Smith or 599. These groupings of characters are called fields, and we identify them with a name. Smith is an employee's surname and 599 is Smith's department number.

Groups of fields are combined to form a logical record, such as the one shown in Figure 10-1. This logical record contains all the data of interest about some entity. In this example, it has all the data in the file about an individual employee.

Example:	Smith, D. J.	599	031875	250	C	G	
Field	Name	Department	Birth date	Salary	Occupation code	Last job code	

Figure 10-1 A logical fixed-length record.

A **key** to a record is a specific field of interest. Many files are organized on a key: Last name is the primary key for a telephone book. That is, the telephone book is arranged in alphabetical order based on telephone subscribers' last names. A secondary key, in the case of the telephone book, is the person's first name or initial. The telephone book, then, is arranged in sequence on the primary key (last name), and within the primary key it is arranged in order by the secondary key (first name). Fields designated as keys are also used as a basis for retrieving information from a file. For example, an inventory part number may be the key for retrieving information from an inventory file about the quantity of the part on hand.

MANAGEMENT PROBLEM 10-1

Marvin Thompson is president of Midwestern Bank and Trust. He has just returned from a bankers' convention at which the major topic was database systems. Midwestern has been studying the problem of central files for several years. The idea of a central file is to consolidate all the information about a customer of the bank. Currently, one system maintains data on loans to commercial customers, another keeps track of demand deposits, a third keeps track of savings and certificates of deposit, and so forth.

The major advantage of central files is that they allow better service. The bank knows the total business picture of any given customer. Thompson feels that a database management system is the best way to set up a central customer file system. His IS staff is conducting research on different DBMSs and have promised a recommendation within a month on what system the bank should purchase.

The vice-president of retail banking has just approached Marvin with the specifications of a package. She argued, "Why should we go to the time and trouble to develop a central file system from scratch when here is just one example of a package that would do the same thing for us."

The head of IS countered, "This is clearly a database application—the tools we are looking at are designed for this kind of a system. We won't just get a database, we'll get a high-level development language and we'll get a query language for users. You haven't really done a thorough evaluation of the package. I'm sure there will be things we need that it does not have."

Marvin is a bit confused by these two arguments. He has asked you to help clarify the issues for him. Who is right?

Direct-Access Files

There are two major types of files: sequential and direct access. Sequential files were the first type of secondary storage. All records are kept in some sequence such as in order by Social Security number. Most of us will encounter sequential access files only in special circumstances. Records in this type of file are located one after another according to a given sequence, for example, the record with payroll number 1 is followed by the record with number 2, etc. With a sequential file, you cannot find a specific record, such as the person with payroll number 127, unless you read the entire file until you locate a record with payroll number 127. On the average, if there are n records in the file, you will read n/2 records to find the one you are seeking.

A direct access file uses a physical medium and programming which facilitate the storage and retrieval of specific records. These files are at the heart of database management systems and of most of today's file storage technology.

Storage Media

The most common device for storing direct-access files is the magnetic disk (see Figure 10-2). One type of disk consists of a series of platters mounted on a spindle. The top and bottom of each platter (except for the very top and bottom ones) are coated with a magnetic material like that on a music cassette tape. Read and write heads are fitted between the platters. They float on a cushion of air created by the rotation of the disk and do not actually touch the surface of the platter. By moving the heads in and out, we can access any spot on the rotating disk. Holding the head in one place traces a track on the disk as the platter rotates under the read/write head. The maximum block size or physical record size for a disk file is limited by the physical capacity of each track. Looking down from the top of the disk, the tracks on each surface form a cylinder. When using a disk file sequentially, we write on a given track of the first platter, then on the same track of the second platter, and so on. This strategy minimizes the access time because the heads do not have to move.

The total access time to read or write is made up of two components: seek time and rotational-delay time. Seek time is the time used in moving the read/write heads from one position to another. Rotational delay occurs because the data we want may not be directly under the read/write heads, even though they are located over the correct track. We have to wait for the disk to revolve to the beginning of the desired data. A PC hard disk might have an average access time of 15 milliseconds.

Each track on the disk has an **address**. Usually, manufacturer-supplied software lets us specify a file and record size and then retrieve a specific record. The records are numbered 1 through n, where n is the number of records in the file. Thus, we can treat a file as consisting of a group of separately numbered records without concern over the physical track address where the record is stored. The software associates the track address with a logical record and finds the desired record for us. The diskette drive

Figure 10-2
Magnetic disk.

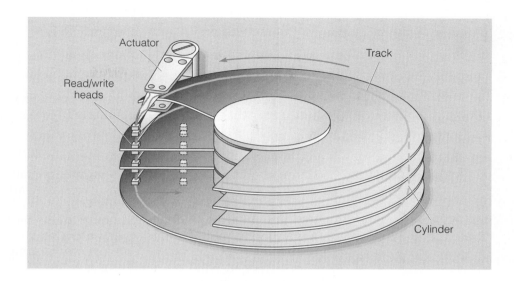

for a personal computer is similar to that for a hard disk except that the diskette is nonrigid (hence the name "floppy disk") and has just two sides. The read/write head actually touches the floppy disk when accessing the file.

Finding Data on the File

In a sequential file, finding the data you want is not too difficult, though it may be time-consuming. Each record is in a sequence, so you simply read the file until you get to the location of the record of interest. (This is the reason that sequential files are associated with batch processing. You update the file at one point in time and make all of the changes, reading the file just once and creating a new version.)

The major advantage of the direct access file is what its name implies. You can locate any record in the file in roughly the same, short (milliseconds) period of time. For example, when you call the airline, they want to access the inventory of seats for the flight you want to take on the date you want to fly without having you or the agent wait on the phone.

If we request a record number, the file management software will supply it for us, then we must associate the logical record number with the information desired. For example, in an inventory application, how do we know where information on inventory part number 1432 is located? What logical record contains data on part 1432? One solution is to begin at the first record on the file and read each record until we find part 1432, but this is simply scanning the file sequentially. One solution to our problem is to create an index like the index to a book. The computer looks up the logical address for part 1432 in the index, and then retrieves that record from the disk.

Key	Index entry	Record address
1432	1432-312	312
4293	4293-137	137

We search the index in primary memory (which is several orders of magnitude faster than searching the disk itself), looking for the key. The index entry tells at what record that key is located. See Figure 10-3.

More-Complex Access

So far in the discussion of direct-access files, we talked about how to locate a unique primary key such as an inventory part number. (This key is unique because there is only one part with a given number.) More-complex structures are also possible with direct-access files. For example, we can ask questions about how many parts are needed for a particular assembly and obtain a response. Consider an inventory example in which it is desired to keep track of what parts belong in what assembly. This situation is depicted in Table 10-1(a). We wish to define a file structure to answer questions such as what parts in inventory are used to build assembly number 103. To find all parts used in assembly 103, it is possible to read each record and see if the assembly field is equal to 103. In Table 10-1(a) we read

Figure 10-3
Index lookup.

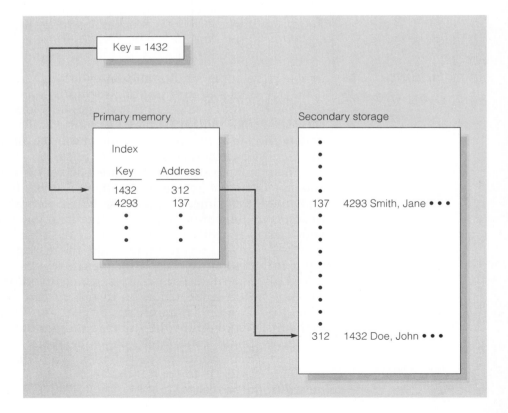

record 1, which is used in assembly 103. Then we read records 2 and 3 without finding assembly 103. We find it again at record 4, and so on. Clearly, this process is not very efficient as there could be a hundred records between each occurrence of assembly 103.

Table 10-1(a)
File Example

Record	Part no.	Assembly	On hand	Vendor
1	4326	103	27	ACME
2	6742	607	51	JOHNSON
3	8137	12	100	DAWES
4	3218	103	13	FRAZIER
5	3762	607	43	ARMOR

Table 10-1(b)
File Example

Record	Part no.	Assembly	On hand	Vendor	Pointer
1	4326	103	27	ACME	4
2	6742	607	51	JOHNSON	5
3	8137	12	100	DAWES	13
4	3218	103	13	FRAZIER	42
5	3762	607	43	ARMOR	106

Table 10-1(c)
Index to Assemblies

Assembly	Record
12	3
25	212
103	1
104	62
607	2

To avoid this reading time we use a **pointer**—a piece of data whose value points to another record. In this case it points to the next record, where assembly 103 is found. The inclusion of pointers in the file is shown in Table 10-1(b). The pointer in record 1 points to the next occurrence of assembly 103 in record 4. Now, when looking for assembly 103, we retrieve record 1 and examine the pointer field. It tells us that the next occurrence of assembly 103 is at record 4. We follow the chain of pointers through the file to answer the retrieval question of what parts belong in assembly 103. This type of file structure is known as a **linked list** or a **chained file**.

How do we find the record of the first part in assembly 103? We could read the file sequentially, but there might be five hundred or six hundred records before the first part in assembly 103 is located. This problem is easily solved using an index like the one in Table 10-1(c). This index simply points to the first part contained in assembly 103. First we retrieve this record, then we follow the chain of pointers in each record through the file.

While you will probably never work with a direct access data file at this level of detail, the discussion of pointers running through a file is very important in Chapter 12 when we discuss hypertext, which is a way of linking text entries in files stored on different computers around the world. In this case, a highlighted word has a pointer to further information about that term, possibly stored on a computer thousands of miles away!

PCs in a Chemical Plant

The Resins Division of Georgia-Pacific uses a database management system and a spreadsheet package on a personal computer to analyze quality-control data. The data are stored on the DBMS in a plant in Painesville, Ohio.

The data are transmitted to a research and development center in Decatur, Georgia, and to the marketing group at headquarters in Atlanta. These locations perform analyses of the data using a spreadsheet package.

It took about ten weeks to write the six thousand lines of code in the DBMS and set up the rather large spreadsheet. In addition, time was required to write a manual and establish telecommunications procedures. The developers estimated that it would have taken them three or four times as long to do the job on a mainframe.

The company has trained more than seventy users in the spreadsheet package. There are other interesting applications as well; for example, chemists in one plant use a spreadsheet to store the recipes for various types of plastics produced at the plant. The calculating power of the spreadsheet package is used to figure what raw ingredients have to be purchased to support production. Other managers track production targets and compare them with goals using the spreadsheet package.

This example illustrates the creative applications users have found for PCs and their powerful software packages.

ENTER DATABASE MANAGEMENT SOFTWARE

Creating complex files using the techniques described above and many others is a tedious and error-prone process. In the 1960s, software vendors developed products called **database management systems (DBMSs)**. These examples of systems software automate many of the tasks associated with using direct access files. As with other types of software originally developed for large computers, today there exist a large number of sophisticated DBMSs for personal computers.

A DBMS has to provide:

- A method for defining the contents of the database.
- A way to describe relationships among data elements and records.
- A mechanism to set up the database in the first place.

Ways to manipulate the data including:

- Updating (adding, modifying, and/or deleting information).
- Retrieval using complex criteria to select data.

Benefits of the Relational Model

The *relational model* is the dominant structure for vendors writing DBMS. The underlying concept of a **relational file** system is very simple: Data are organized in two-dimensional tables such as the one in Figure 10-4. Such tables are easy for a user to develop and understand. One virtue of this type of structure is that it can be described mathematically, a most difficult task for other types of data structures. The name is derived from the fact that each table represents a **relation**.

Because different users see different sets of data and different relationships among them, it is necessary to extract subsets of the table columns for some users and to join tables together to form larger tables for others. The mathematics provides the basis for extracting some columns from the tables and for joining various columns.

Relational database management systems have many advantages. Most DBMSs for personal computers are based on the relational model because it is relatively easy for users to understand. This section presents an example of a relational database and shows how it would be processed by a personal computer DBMS. We also discuss some of the key issues in the design of relational databases.

An Example

Figure 10-5 shows the results of creating two relations using a DBMS called Access, a part of Microsoft Office, and entering data in them. The first relation is Student; the key is student number, and the other fields are name, age, and year in school. The second relation is Class, and its key is also student number; the relation relates student number to class number.

Figure 10-4
A relational database.

Name	Address	Zip code	City	Department number
Smith	16 Main	92116	New York	302
Jones	37 Spencer	07901	Chicago	161
Morris	19 Old Way	83924	New York	302
Able	86 Fulton	10006	Denver	927
Charles	19 Hunter	11126	Chicago	161

Name	Profession	Income
Johnson	Bartender	15,000
Martin	Programmer	14,000
Jones	Systems Analyst	18,000
Carson	Manager	17,000
Smith	Systems Analyst	19,000

Join:

Name	Address	Zip code	Profession	Income
Jones	37 Spencer,	07901,	Systems Analyst,	18,000

Project:

City	Department
New York	302
Chicago	161
Denver	927

Figure 10-6 shows how Access can be used to inquire about all students who are in year 1. The user fills out a table describing the inquiry and indicates each desired field for the answer, then indicates the criteria for selection. In this case, the criterion is that year = 1. The DBMS places the answer on an output screen.

One of the most frequently used relational operations is the **join**, in which two relations are joined on some key. Figure 10-7 shows how the DBMS would be used to join the Student and Class relations. Note the line the user drew between student number in each relation. That line tells Access the common field on which the two relations are to be joined.

The Figure 10-7(a) shows the query form, and the results of the join are shown in Figure 10-7(b). We now have a list of each student assigned to his or her classes. Note that Murray does not appear in the join because there was no record for Murray in the Class relation. Similarly, student 160 is listed as taking two classes, so Berman appears twice in the joined relation.

Normalization

One of the major tasks in designing a relational database is **normalization**. The process of normalization ensures that there will not be problems in updating the database and that operations on the various relations will not lead to inconsistent and incorrect data.

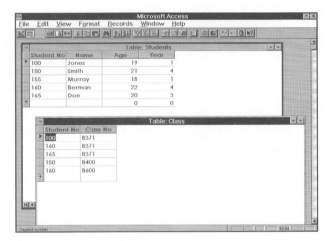

Figure 10-5
Setting up two relations.

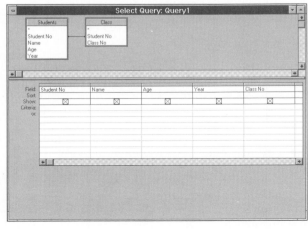

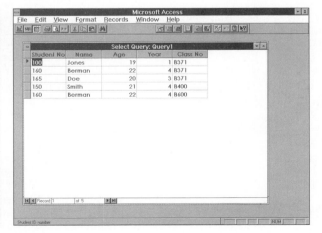

Figure 10-6   Inquiry about students in Year 1.

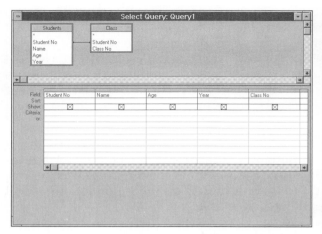

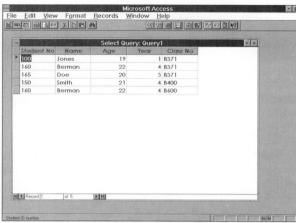

Figure 10-7 (a)   Joining two relations.   **(b)**

Kent (1983) presents a set of guidelines to make normalization more intuitive. His guidelines are easier to understand than the mathematical rules for normalization. During the normalization process, the designer first looks to be sure that the relations are in first normal form. Next, he or she checks for second normal form and finally for third. (There are also fourth and fifth normal forms, but we leave them for more-advanced courses on databases.)

MANAGEMENT PROBLEM 10-2

Marilyn Atkins is vice president of the human resources department for Multinational Manufacturing, Inc. (MM). Her firm employs nearly a hundred thousand people around the world. Filling vacancies when they arise is a constant problem. Preference is given to existing employees, although it is very difficult to know when an existing employee may have the skills needed for an opening so that he or she can be notified to apply.

Marilyn talked to representatives of MM's information services department, and they indicated that a relational database management system might help her. Currently there is a personnel system that is updated once each month. It consists of sequential files kept on a disk. It contains data on the employee including records with name, education, skill, salary, and similar data. Other records reflect job history—the positions the employee has held in the firm.

The new database system extracts data from sequential files like the ones used in the personnel system and then builds relations, which are available for inquiry through a query language that is part of the package.

Can you help Marilyn define relations and formulate a few sample inquiries to extract the kind of information she needs from the existing personnel system using the new database manager?

First normal form requires that all occurrences of a record type contain the same number of fields. As a result, a record cannot contain a repeating group. We could not have one relation that listed facts about a class and have a repeating set of fields for each student in the class. To represent such a problem using the relational data model, we would need more than one relation. The first would be a relation for the class and the second a relation for students.

Second and third normal forms require the designer to examine the relationship between key fields and other fields in the record. To conform to second and third normal forms, each nonkey field must give us information about the entire key and nothing but the key. (Each higher number form assumes that the relations satisfy lower number forms. For example, second normal form assumes that the relation is in first normal form, and so on.)

Suppose that one has a relationship as follows:

Part   Warehouse   Quantity   Address

If Part and Warehouse form a composite key, this relationship is not in second normal form. Note that the warehouse address would be repeated in each record that stores information about a part in the warehouse. If the address changes, every record of a part in that warehouse would have to be updated. The update would require a great deal of processing and could result in an error if one address were overlooked. What would happen if there were no parts in the warehouse? It is possible that the database would lose track of the warehouse because there would be no record having its address.

The relation can be made to conform to second normal form by splitting it into two relations:

Part Warehouse   Quantity   Warehouse   Address

Part Warehouse can be the combined key for the first relation, and Warehouse can be the key for the second. Now the warehouse address appears only once in the database and can easily be changed. We succeeded in normalizing the relation so that it is in second normal form.

Third normal form requires that a nonkey field not be a fact about another nonkey field. Kent offers the following example:

Employee   Department   Location

The key to this relation is Employee. If each department is located in only one place, the location field is a fact about the department in addition to being a fact about the employee. This design leads to the same problems as with the warehouse example: The location is repeated in each record of an employee assigned to that department. Because of this redundancy, the data might become inconsistent and a department with no employees might disappear from the database.

The solution here is similar to the one above: split the relation into two relations:

Employee   Department   Department   Location

where Employee is the key for the first relation and Department is the key for the second.

In general, normalization creates a database in which there is minimum redundancy of data, and risks of damaging the database through updating are minimized. Because the relational model is the dominant data model, it is important to understand the normalization process.

SQL   IBM developed **Structured Query Language (SQL)** a number of years ago. The language was first proposed as a retrieval language for users, but it is difficult to use, so few users are likely to adopt it. It is important to note that SQL is the query language for IBM's mainframe relational database management package, DB2. There is an ANSI standard for SQL, and this language is being adopted by the major DBMS vendors as one way to interact with their systems. SQL also offers a mechanism for universal database access. For example, suppose that the DBMS you are using translates the query language you enter into SQL commands. It could then retrieve data on a different system, so long as they both used the same SQL dialect.

1. The basic structure of an SQL expression has three parts. The **select clause** lists the attributes desired in answer to the query.

What Is 64 Bits Worth?

Oracle sells one of the most popular relational database management systems. The company has developed a 64 bit version of its system, that is, the software will take advantage of processor chips that fetch and perform operations on 64 bits at a time. This DBMS will run on the DEC's alpha chip, one of the fastest chips currently available. The two companies claim that a 64-bit database on an alpha will give serious competition to mainframe databases.

The 64 bit version will allow much more of a database to be processed in main memory at high speeds. With 64 bit processing, it takes fewer operations to move data from secondary storage into main memory.

Of course, not everyone will sell their mainframes and rush to the new system. It is costly and time-consuming to convert applications. There are many applications on the typical mainframe, so all of them would have to be converted before one could eliminate it. Also, the cost savings are debatable. Forrester Research estimates that it costs three times more to support a 5000 user network of computers than it does to support an equal number of users on a mainframe.

Certainly at the level of the processor and DBMS, 64 bit technology has to be a threat to mainframe vendors over the long term.

2. The **from clause** is a list of relations or tables that the query language processor should consult in filling the request.

3. The **where clause** describes the attributes desired in the answer.

As an example, consider the following SQL expressions taken from Korth and Silberschatz (1986):

```
select branch-name
from deposit
```

This is an SQL expression to obtain a list of all branch names from a bank table (branch-name) containing data about branches and customers. One might find all customers having an account in the Midtown branch with the following expression:

```
select customer-name
from deposit
where branch-name="Midtown"
```

SQL expressions can become complicated as we qualify retrieval requests:

```
(select customer-name
from deposit
where branch-name="Midtown")
intersect
(select customer-name
from borrow
where branch-name="Midtown")
```

The above query produces a table of all customers who have both a loan (from the borrow table) and an account in the Midtown branch.

There has been a proliferation of database management systems for all types of computers and SQL appears as the one common thread. Various vendors are designing their DBMS packages to translate queries using the package's interface into SQL commands to query a remote database. Why would a user be interested in such a feature?

Suppose you are working with Paradox, a PC database system, and want to access data located on an IBM mainframe in a DB2 database. You would like to enter Paradox queries and not have to learn about DB2. Using an SQL interface, Paradox could access the data you want on the mainframe. Of course, Paradox must translate your queries into SQL and forward them to the DB2 for processing. You would have to know the names of the fields and the relations in the DB2 database.

The use of SQL as an intermediary and a standard in accessing a large number of different types of database systems should be of great help to users and to systems analysts. Although you may never formulate a query in SQL, you are likely to find it processing queries developed in other languages.

DATABASES IN SYSTEMS DESIGN

It should be apparent at this point that one of the major design tasks in building an information system is determining the contents and structure of a database. The type of retrieval and reporting required by users and the availability of input determine what data to store. However, it is a very complex task to specify these data, group them into records, and establish data structures for a system.

Data Modeling

A data model is useful for a number of reasons. First, it helps us understand the relationships among different components in a systems design. Data models show users more clearly how a system will function. Users are very concerned about data and information. They want to know if there will be adequate data available to perform their jobs.

Billions, Even Trillions of Bytes of Data

Bank of America regularly creates a database that consolidates 35 million records processed by separate computers handling checking, savings and other routine transactions. The consolidated database has 800 billion characters of data. How does the bank use this information? Every day about 100,000 customers call the bank to check a balance, challenge a charge on a credit card or ask about interest rates. The bank decided to try and sell them something when they call.

The way to accomplish this cross selling was to tailor the product to each customer's needs. For example, if you have been accidentally bouncing checks, maybe you would pay for overdraft protection. The consolidated database provides bank employees with incredible insights into customer behavior and preferences. Some companies call these applications "data warehouses" for obvious reasons.

Burlington coat factory depends on a 1.5 trillion byte database that runs on a cluster of eight superminicomputers from sequent computer systems. Company managers use the warehouse to determine a variety of information, for example, what styles are selling best, how are different stores performing, where to open the next store and so on.

These data warehouses are good candidates for parallel computing—multiple processors working in parallel are powerful and cheap enough to perform analyses on billions of bytes of data. John Alden Life Insurance company has a warehouse with four years of detailed medical claims with extensive cross indexing, comprising some 150 billion bytes of data. The company figures that asking a question to compare hospital networks in Illinois and New Jersey on hip replacements would tie up a mainframe all night. A 24 processor Ibm SP2 does this job in the "tens of minutes."

The computer can scan for information users request, or it can look for interesting relationships and patterns, a process called "data mining." This kind of technology provides you with the ability to understand your customers and the nature of your business far better than in the past.

The most common type of data model is the **entity-relationship (ER) diagram**. The ER diagram is easy for a user to follow and serves as an excellent communications vehicle. The ER diagram consists of object types and relationships. In Figure 10-8(a) we see an example of two objects linked by a relationship: A customer purchases a product. The two entities here are "customer" and "product"; the relationship is "purchases." Entities are represented by rectangles and a relationship by a diamond. Some analysts like to use a simple, straight line between entities and label the line with the relationship, (as shown in Figure 10-8b), though certain more-complex relationships cannot be modeled in this manner.

Entities also have attributes, which are the fields we would include in a file record. A product has a product number, size, description, price, cost, and so on. The ER diagram, then, can be used to show relationships while the conventional listing of the file contents contains the attributes of entities.

Figure 10-9 shows another example of an ER diagram. Here the figure shows that a doctor sees a patient. He or she writes a prescription and the receptionist bills the patient. The numbers on the ER diagram describe the nature of the relationship. There is one doctor who writes from 1 to n prescriptions. In this practice, one doctor sees n patients. The receptionist sends one bill at a time to many (n) patients. Many patients buy one or more prescriptions. We can have 1:1, 1:n, n:1, and m:n (many-to-many) relationships.

Another way to show the nature of relationships is to use arrows. A single arrow stands for a 1 relationship, and a double arrow represents a many

Corning Goes Relational

Corning Glass recently installed a relational database management system, called Ingres, to replace an older, homegrown file system. Ingres also provides tools for designing and building new applications. A major application for the relational system is to maintain production information.

The company figures that in the first three months it recovered its investment in the new software. In addition, there have been dramatic time savings. An engineer in Corning's TV-screen manufacturing plant calculated that she can analyze production data in two hours, a task that used to take four to six months.

The system is distributed so that two U.S. and one German plant that make ceramics for auto emission control systems can easily access each other's production data. The system

gathers information from plant-floor controllers, area controllers, and various plant systems during the production process. The data generate reports and can be used for analysis and ad hoc queries.

As an example, at the TV-glass factory as many as four thousand variables are collected from sensors and gauges in a three-story-high glass melting tank. The data go first to local MicroVAXes and then to an Ingres database on larger VAX computers.

Manufacturing firms are concerned about foreign competitors and their ability to compete against low-cost labor. Information technology is one way to improve both efficiency and quality, as this example of using a relational DBMS shows.

Figure 10-8
(a) An entity relationship (ER) diagram.
(b) An alternative ER diagram.

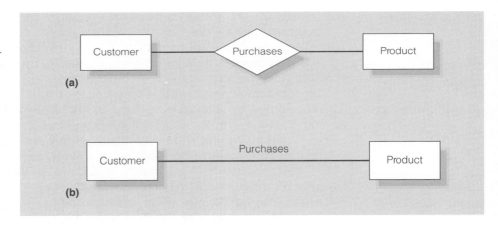

relationship. For users, the added information provided by describing the nature of the relationship is probably not worth the added confusion; these data are primarily useful to the designers of the system.

Figure 10-10 is a data model for a student applying to college. This diagram uses arrows to show the nature of the relationship. A student completes an application and the admissions staff decides about many applications. It notifies candidates by sending out acceptance letters. Figure 10-11 shows what happens when the student works with his or her adviser. The adviser counsels many students and these n students enroll in m different classes—an $n:m$ relationship. Each student has a biography, and there are many different majors from which the student chooses.

Figure 10-11 presents an entire simple database. However, there can be other views for different individuals. A professor might care only about

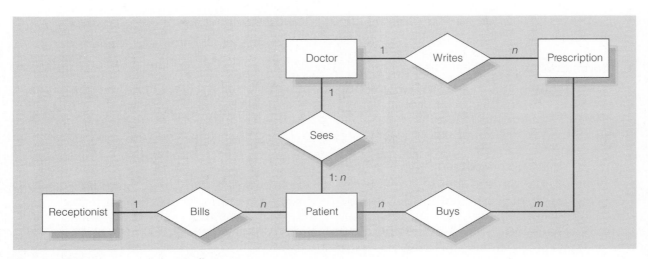

Figure 10-9   Doctor-patient ER diagram.

Figure 10-10
College application
ER diagram.

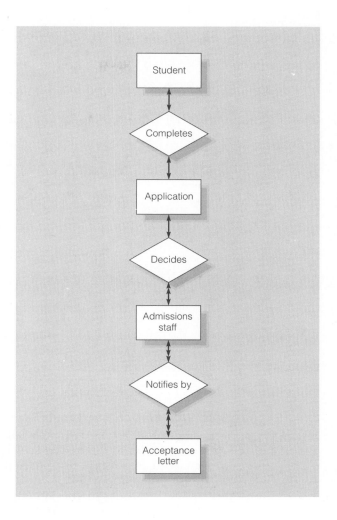

a class list, not about a student's major or adviser. The department chairperson wants to know something about majors in the department.

Sometimes these differences are called **logical views** of the data. It is very likely that different users will have different logical views of data. A key task of design is to integrate these many potential views and create a physical database capable of supporting different logical views with adequate performance.

The Role of the Database Administrator

Many organizations using database software have created a new position known as the **database administrator (DBA)**. This individual is responsible for working with systems analysts and programmers to define the physical and logical views of the data to be manipulated by computers.

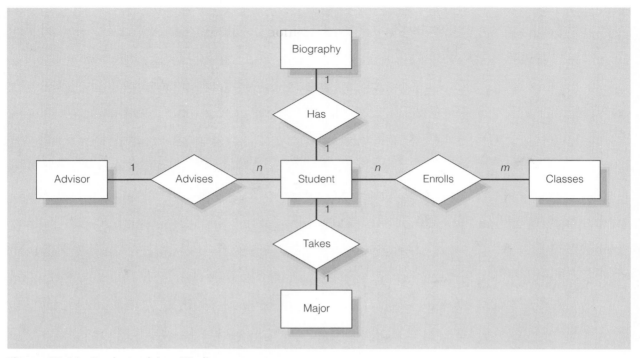

Figure 10-11   Student-adviser ER diagram.

DBMSs in Building Systems

Database management systems are very popular packages for personal computers. These packages feature friendly interfaces that make it easy for users to define the structure of relations and enter data. Using the system, it is possible to update data, process transactions, make queries, and generate reports.

Most of the PC DBMS packages also have development tools or languages, and users have developed many applications using a DBMS. A programmer uses Access to create an order-entry system for a small firm. Using the development language, the programmer can set up a system so that users do not have to know anything at all about the database system. Instead, users see menus from which they choose options. The DBMS processes the menus and manages the application.

There are a number of database management packages for different types of computers from mainframes to PCs. Particularly for smaller systems, a modern DBMS can sometimes serve as the only systems-building tool needed to develop an application.

Distributed Databases

Organizations are building more distributed databases in which different parts of the database are located on different computers in a network. The movement toward client-server computing and the implementation of groupware will accentuate this trend. This type of database raises a number of issues for the organization, including the following:

- Will data be replicated across computers or will there be only one copy?
- If data are replicated, how frequently must different versions be updated to reflect changes (at times there will be different values for the same data if all copies of a file are not updated at once).
- How will updates to the database be coordinated so that its integrity is maintained?
- Who "owns" distributed data and who has access to it?
- Distributed databases offer users easier access to data at the cost of overall higher complexity of the system.

CHAPTER SUMMARY

1. Organizations keep a tremendous amount of material in machine-readable form stored as files on a computer. This trend will continue as firms move away from the use of paper for records.

2. Data in files are stored in records. The most common form is a fixed length record consisting of fields. Each field contains a group of characters that represent a value for the field, for example, a social security number.

UPS Calling

United Parcel Service has a database that consists of 1.1 terabytes (trillion) of data. It is maintained by the IBM mainframe relational database manager, DB2, and is one of the largest DB2 implementations in the U.S. The system is used to confirm delivery of more than 13 million packages each day. Customers can obtain proof of delivery within one hour of an inquiry. The system tracks more than 5 million delivery stops and 4 million customer signatures a day.

The process begins when drivers return from their routes, they plug electronic clipboards into a giant rack which charges the clipboard and transmits to a PC its data about where and when deliveries were made. The PC encodes the data and transfers it to the mainframe system. There are about 6 gigabytes (billions) transmitted each day to the mainframe.

The DB2 database contains 148 relational tables. UPS has 1,800 field centers that can query the database around the clock to find out when a package was delivered. The system can handle up to 188,000 inquiries a day.

This application shows how a combination of database and communications technology can be used to focus on customer service. UPS is trying to succeed in the overnight-delivery business and must offer the same services as the major companies in that field, such as Federal Express.

3. Direct access files are stored on disks with average access times in the range of 10 to 15 milliseconds.

4. A pointer is a number, stored in a field, which directs a program to another record. Pointers are also used to allow a user to follow a logical connection among a variety of computer systems on a network.

5. The database management system automates the tasks of setting up a database. It facilitates defining records and relationships among them, and it handles the updating and retrieval of data from the database.

6. The relational model in which data are stored in tables or relations is the dominant type of DBMS today.

7. Normalization is an important part of the design of a relational database.

8. A key part of the systems analysis and design process is defining data requirements. Entity-relationship models are one way to describe data and relationships.

9. SQL is an intermediate language that may become the bridge among different DBMSs.

10. You can use one of a number of PC DBMS to develop quite sophisticated applications for yourself and others to use.

IMPLICATIONS FOR MANAGEMENT

The ability to store and retrieve vast amounts of data is one of the things that makes a computer so useful in business. While it will probably never happen, one great dream in the industry is to replace paper with data stored in machine readable form on a computer. Database technology is what lets American Airlines keep track of hundreds of thousands of reservations. This same technology lets a credit card firm custom tailor promotions to customers who have a history of purchasing a particular product. A university database keeps track of your progress in school, recording the courses you have taken, the number of credits and your grade. You can also use a DBMS on a PC to develop useful applications in your own work. Database is a key technology. You will encounter it in all the functional areas of business including marketing, accounting, manufacturing, and personnel, to name a few areas. Databases in combination with communications networks are responsible for much of the appeal of the Internet and World Wide Web, discussed in Chapter 12.

KEY WORDS

Address
Attribute

Character
Chained file

Database administrator
   (DBA)
Database management systems
   (DBMS)
Entity-relationship (ER) diagram
Field
File
From clause
Join
Key

Linked list
Logical view
Normalization
Pointer
Record
Relation
Relational file
Select clause
Structured Query Language (SQL)
Where clause

RECOMMENDED READING

Inmon, W., and R. Hackathorn. *Using the Data Warehouse*. New York: John Wiley, 1994. (A short, readable book about data warehousing.)

Kent, W. "A Simple Guide to Five Normal Forms in Relational Database Theory," *Communications of the ACM*, vol. 26, no. 2 (February 1983), pp. 120–125. (A clear article on normalization.)

Kronke, D. *Database Processing*, 4th ed. New York: Macmillan, 1992. (A good introductory text on database.)

Rob, P., and C. Coronel. *Database Systems.* Danvers, Mass.: Boyd and Fraser, 1995. (An excellent introduction to databases with readable chapters on entity-relationship diagrams, the relational model, and SQL.)

DISCUSSION QUESTIONS

1. Why do users have different logical views of their data requirements?
2. Why is direct access so much more flexible than sequential access?
3. How does a DBMS tend to make data and programs more independent? Can programs and data ever be totally independent?
4. What advantages does a query language provide for the IS staff? What disadvantages for users?
5. Why do most organizations use a DBMS for specific applications rather than attempt to define a comprehensive database for all applications?
6. How does a DBMS make it easier to alter the structure of a database?
7. Does a DBMS completely isolate the user from the underlying structure of the data?
8. Do you think users ever need to worry about normalization?
9. Why might you want a DBMS on your PC that could also communicate with a large computer database?

10. What complications are added to a DBMS when distributed processing is involved?

11. What kind of security and controls are needed in a DBMS?

12. In an on-line environment, a common problem is to lock out access to a record while it is updated. Why do you think this is necessary? What scheme can be used to lock the record?

13. Recovery from a computer failure or other interruption of a system is a major consideration for organizations. What problems do you see in recovering from such a failure when using a DBMS?

14. How should one back up a database used for on-line processing?

15. How can accessing data in relational tables be speeded over a straight sequential search?

16. What evaluation criteria would you recommend be applied to a decision of what database management system to acquire?

17. Why is there a need for a database administrator in an organization using a DBMS?

18. How can the systems analyst use the facilities of a DBMS during the design process for a new system?

19. To what extent is performance (in terms of speed of access) a major consideration in database design?

20. In the schema of Figure 10-11, how would an adviser query the system to determine the major for a given student? How would the query language access the database?

21. Under what conditions is it better to program a retrieval option into a system, as opposed to providing a user with a general-purpose query language?

22. Are there any conditions under which it would be desirable to duplicate data in a database? If so, what are they?

23. Think of an application like student registration, and design a relational database for the registrar.

24. Under what conditions might an organization want to have more than one vendor's DBMS? What problems do you foresee if there are multiple database systems?

25. Why has the relational model come to dominate the DBMS market for personal computers?

26. One company markets a special computer that operates as a database "back end." That is, the computer handles only operations relating to the database and interacts with a central computer. What advantages do you see for such an approach?

27. What major trends in the field make database management systems feasible?

28. What does a DBMS mean for users of systems?

29. Does using a DBMS from a particular vendor mean that the organization is tied to that vendor for the foreseeable future?

CHAPTER 10 PROJECT

DATABASE ASSIGNMENT, PART I

In addition to a spreadsheet package, a database management system offers a lot of assistance for a firm like Simon Marshall. The first application Mary thought was appropriate for the database package was one to keep track of the inventory of stock the firm has in safekeeping for customers.

She explained, "A lot of our clients don't want to leave their stocks with a brokerage firm. The brokers sometimes loan the stocks and do other things with them that make our clients nervous. We can't store stocks here, so we have a safekeeping agreement with the bank. Our records aren't too good, and I think putting them on the computer would help us be more disciplined about keeping track of this information."

The problem below involves using a database to solve the inventory problem for Simon Marshall.

INVENTORY

Simon Marshall keeps an inventory of securities for certain customers. Currently, the securities are actually kept by a bank, but Simon Marshall has been concerned about its ability to audit the securities maintained in the bank's vault.

Having just purchased a DBMS Simon Marshall has asked you to develop a simple inventory system to keep track of its holdings with the bank.

The following are the fields in the relation and the data for input:

Name	Stock	No. Shares	Date
John Doe	ATT	100	9/9/95
Mary Roe	GM	200	10/14/89
Karl Anderson	RM	150	11/21/96
Sam Smith	IBM	200	1/1/97
Sally Jones	NAB	150	6/6/90
Howard Cannon	EXX	90	1/19/92
Roger Roberts	BSL	175	7/8/96
Karyn Hanson	ATT	125	9/1/94
Terry Bradley	GM	85	1/15/95
Margaret Smith	NJT	100	9/4/91

You have been asked to:

- Set up a relation in a DBMS to maintain these data. Be sure to enter the date as a date field.

- Input the data above.

- List the relation after you have entered the data.

- Retrieve and list all investors who have more than 125 shares of stock in safe-keeping.

- List all investors who put stock into safekeeping after February 1, 1990.
- List all investors who put more than 100 shares into safekeeping in 1990.

DATABASE ASSIGNMENT, PART II

Over time, John and Mary, principals of Simon Marshall, would like to keep each customer's portfolio on the computer. "We recognize that it will take a long time to get everything on the machine, but once we have done it, we can price out the portfolio in an instant and give really good information to our clients," Mary commented one day.

You are assigned to set up a prototype for the portfolio application. The basic design strategy is to have two relations, one containing information about the security in the Company relation and the other containing the contents of a portfolio in the Portfolio relation.

Using two relations gets around a number of updating and data redundancy problems that are the reasons for normalizing a relational database. Since a portfolio is likely to contain multiple positions in a given stock, it is wasteful to carry all the data about that stock with each position. (Multiple positions exist each time the stock is bought, because it will probably be purchased at a different price. For tax and accounting purposes, each purchase must be recorded separately.) By joining the relation containing stock data with the relation containing the portfolio, we can compute the current value of the portfolio. Such an exercise is part of your assignment.

PORTFOLIO STATUS

Simon Marshall asked you to help design a simple system to keep track of a stock portfolio using a database management system on a PC. You will need two relations, one to hold information about each company and the other to keep data about an individual's holdings. (It would be redundant to keep all of the data about a stock with each position a user might have in that stock.)

The first relation, Company, contains the name of the firm, its location, line of business, and the current price of its stock. The second relation, Portfolio, contains the name of the firm, a lot number to identify each stock purchase, the number of shares bought of that lot, and the total purchase price of the lot. (On many DBMSs for PCs, a relation name must be of eight or fewer characters.)

1. Print all of the records of each relation.
2. Using the Portfolio relation, print a report of only GM shares.
3. Use the Company relation and sort the firms into sequence by location. Display and print the results. Do the same to sort the relation into order by type of business.
4. Join the two relations together.
5. Print a report using the DBMS report-creation option to show net position on each stock and for the entire portfolio.

COMPANY RELATION

Company	State	Business	Share Price
AT&T	New Jersey	Communications	22.78
GM	Detroit	Manufacturing	52.45
IBM	New York	Electronics	178.54
TWA	Kansas	Airline	45.80

PORTFOLIO RELATION

Company	Number	Shares	Purchase Price
AT&T	12345	50	1,200.00
AT&T	54321	100	2,100.00
IBM	88888	60	10,100.00
IBM	44444	100	18,000.00
TWA	11111	50	3,000.00
GM	12121	75	3,750.00
GM	34343	150	8,000.00
GM	56565	100	5,000.00

CHAPTER **11**

Communications

⬤ OBJECTIVES

1. Learning to manage information technology.

Communications is one of the most important activities in organizations. It supports coordination and information sharing, especially in global firms. Information technology includes telecommunications, which allows **connectivity** among computers and between organizations. Many strategic applications involve communications among the computers of different organizations, such as those of a supplier and a customer. Computers and communications are the core components of information technology. As a manager you will be involved in decisions on how to configure communications in the firm and on what sources to use for communications services.

2. Preparing to apply technology.

In this chapter you will see a number of applications of communications, one of the central components of information technology. Many applications developed today make use of communications in one form or another. As you design systems, you have to decide how users will communicate with computers. This chapter describes the basics of communications and networking and illustrates them with a number of examples.

3. Transforming the organization.

Communications technology makes it possible to share data within the company and with external organizations. It facilitates coordination and helps management define new organizational structures as it removes constraints on the time and place for work and makes possible the creation of new structures that cut across traditional lines on the organization chart. As you read about UPS and Ford in this chapter, think about how communications technology is changing the nature of these two companies.

Early computers processed data in batches with intervals of days or months between runs. Devices were soon developed to transmit data on punched cards from one location to another over telephone lines, marking the beginning of the communication of data through an existing telecommunications **network**. The operation took place off-line, and the computers involved were not directly connected to the telephone lines. In addition to card punches that could send and receive, there were devices to send file contents of magnetic tapes from one location to another.

In the early 1960s the first on-line systems were developed. These computers, used for airline reservations, served many **terminals** connected through various types of communications lines. (A few years earlier, the first such on-line systems were developed for defense applications.) At about the same time, terminals were attached to computers used for time-sharing. The major difference between on-line and time-sharing systems is that the former are dedicated to a single application. For example, an airline reservation agent can only make a reservation or inquire about the status of various flights. The agent cannot write a program from the terminal. With time-sharing, the user of the terminal usually does have the ability to write programs.

The use of on-line systems has expanded rapidly. Today a large proportion of new systems have some portion that is on-line, such as data entry, update, and/or inquiry. At the same time, there has been an expansion in the number of alternatives available for establishing communications among computer devices. One has a choice from dial-up phone service to private networks using **satellites** for transmission.

In this chapter we cover the fundamentals of data communications. First we look at a basic model of communications between computing devices. The basics provide the foundation for talking about networks. Organizations are rapidly building and interconnecting networks of computers and other devices. The chapter discusses how a firm can obtain network services from common carriers or from building its own, private network. We also discuss some of the software required for communications-intensive applications. Several applications that depend on telecommunications, such as e-mail and electric data interchange (EDI) illustrate how this technology contributes to the organization.

COMMUNICATIONS BETWEEN COMPUTERS

Figure 11-1 is a high-level diagram of data communications between two computer devices. We shall expand this basic schematic further. The most familiar type of communications is probably the case in which device 1 is a PC and device 2 is a **server** of some type. The transmission line may be nothing more complex than a pair of twisted wires from the terminal leading to a central computer that offers time-sharing services. Figure 11-1 describes the process.

Codes The data sent over the line are represented as some type of **code**. That is, the sending and receiving ends of the communications lines have to agree on how to represent symbols such as the letters *a, b, c,* etc. For telex data, the **Baudot code** is the most common and uses five bits for each letter (a **bit** is a 0 or a 1). The number of symbols that can be represented in binary

Figure 11-1
High-level data communications.

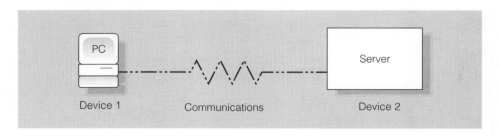

Device 1   Communications   Device 2

by a code is 2 raised to the power of the number of bits. For example, $2^5 = 32$, is a fairly small number of symbols when one considers the length of the alphabet!

The most frequent code for interchanging data is called **ASCII** (American Standard Code for Information Interchange), which is a 7-bit code (there is an eighth bit for error checking) and thus has 128 symbols. A code used with earlier computers was BCD (Binary Coded Decimal), a 6-bit code. Finally, there is a code that is primarily used by IBM known as EBCDIC (Extended Binary Coded Decimal Interchange Code), which is an 8-bit code.

All codes, then, use sequences of 0's and 1's to represent different symbols. As an example, the ASCII code for H is 1001000. On the sending end, an H is translated into 1001000 for transmission. On the receiving end, the string of bits is translated back into an H. (It should be noted that computers are designed to represent data in memory in coded form. However, there is no necessary relationship between the internal coding and the codes used for transmission between computers.)

Codes often feature extra bits or characters that are used to control transmission and to detect errors. A simple transmission scheme that sends one letter at a time might include a start bit and a stop bit to delimit the beginning and end of the character for the receiving station. A basic error-detection scheme is parity checking: The sending device checks to see that there is an odd number of bits in each character and if there is an even number, the sending station makes the parity bit a 1, creating an odd number. Under this odd-parity scheme, the receiving device also counts the bits. If there is an even number, at least one bit has been lost in transmission. The parity scheme is rather simple. There are far more elaborate error-detecting and even error-correcting codes available.

Transmission Modes

There are a number of options for transmitting data over communications lines. The most frequently used approaches are the following:

- *Character mode.* In **character mode**, data are transmitted as single characters as they are typed on a terminal. This technique is very simple and does not require complicated hardware or software.

- *Block mode.* In **block mode**, data are placed temporarily in a hardware memory on the sending device. The block is surrounded by appropriate characters indicating the start and end of transmission. The data are then transmitted as a single block, usually with some type of error-checking sequence at the end of the block. If there are errors, the two **nodes** arrange for a retransmission of the data.

- *Asynchronous mode.* **Asynchronous transmission** is associated with character mode operations, since the characters are sent when entered. A single bit is added to the front of each character, and one or more bits are added at the end. These extra bits alert the receiving device to the existence of the character and delimit it.

- **Synchronous mode.** Block transmission features blocks of equal length, one following another. There is no need for the start and stop bits that are associated with each character in asynchronous transmission, saving considerable overhead using block mode. The beginning of each block is identified, and the sending and receiving devices must be synchronized.

Direction of Transmission

There are several ways to send data over lines. In **simplex transmission**, the data are sent in one direction only, but this approach is rare. Using **half duplex transmission**, data travel in two directions but not at the same time. With **full duplex transmission**, data are transmitted simultaneously in both directions. Note that this approach generally requires two lines, since the same data path cannot carry signals in two directions at the same time.

How Are Signals Represented?

There are two basic ways to represent signals: in analog or digital form. These signals are shown in Figure 11-2.

Analog Signals   **Analog signals** are used because the first data transmission took place over voice telephone lines, originally developed to carry analog signals. Because computer devices communicate in digital form, the digital signal must be converted to an analog signal (**modulated**) for transmission and then changed to digits (**demodulated**) at the receiving end. As shown in Figure 11-3, a device called a **modem** converts the digital code into an analog signal.

Figure 11-2
Analog signals.

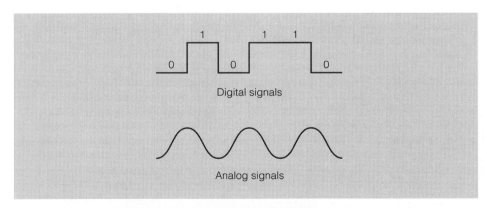

Figure 11-3
Modulation and demodulation.

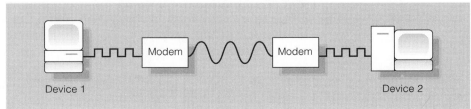

Figure 11-4 shows one approach to this modulation task. In the figure, we see encoding done using amplitude modulation. The analog signal is continuous and has the form of a sine wave. By using different **amplitudes** (heights of the sine wave) to represent a 0 and a 1, the digital data can be encoded for transmission over analog lines. The modem is the device that accomplishes this modulation. It is possible to modulate a signal using the amplitude of the sine wave as described above, varying the **frequency** of the wave or changing the phase of the sine wave to encode a 0 or a 1. Your personal computer probably has a modem that operates at 14.4 K or 28.8K bits per second over a dial-up phone line. Using this modem, you can connect to a variety of computers.

Digital Signals   Due to the explosion in data transmission over the past two decades, telephone companies and private communications carriers have developed digital transmission networks. If the entire circuit from end-to-end is digital, there is no need for a modem. The only requirement is some kind of a line interface device to connect the sending or receiving unit with the transmission line.

With digital transmission, we need a way to send an analog signal! First, there may be a need to interface digital and analog transmission. A communications carrier might provide a digital link between telephone central offices, while the "local loop" to a home or office goes on an analog, copper circuit. Second, there is great interest in digitizing some analog signals so information can be compressed and sent over relatively low-speed lines, such as video-conferencing, multimedia, and home video. The analog signals from a video camera can be digitized and then compressed so the large number of bits required will "fit" on a line. **Compression** involves using some type of algorithm to take out redundant information by coding it. A compression algorithm might look for a pattern in an image that is all dark. It would substitute a code for the number of black elements rather than transmitting all of the black bytes. At the receiving end, equipment would generate the black elements that were not transmitted.

Figure 11-5 shows how it is possible to digitize an *analog wave using* **pulse code modulation (PCM)**. The Y axis on the waveform is divided

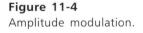

Figure 11-4
Amplitude modulation.

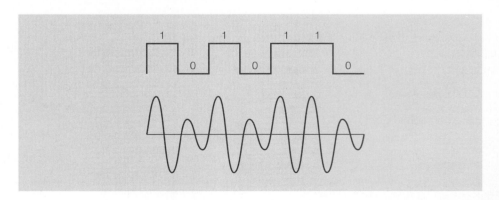

Figure 11-5
Analog-to-digital transformation using pulse code modulation.

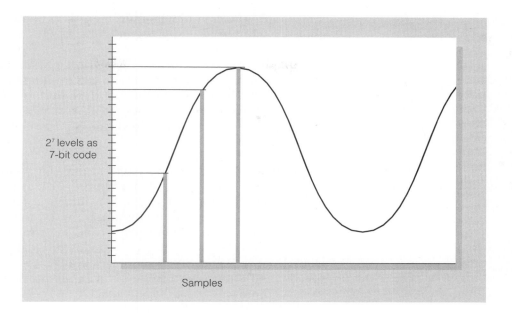

2^7 levels as 7-bit code

Samples

into a series of intervals. If we are using a 7-bit code, we would make 2^7 or 128 intervals. One unique 7-bit pattern is assigned to each interval. If you view the Y axis as a window through which the wave passes over time, at a particular instant or sampling point we would note the interval the wave touches at our window. Then we would send the 7-bit pattern that has been assigned to that interval as a digital representation of the wave.

MANAGEMENT PROBLEM 11-1

Global Manufacturing is considering a new technology application. The company wants to process orders in a central location and then assign production to different plants. Each plant will operate its own production scheduling and control system. Data on work in process and completed assemblies will be transmitted back to the central location that processes orders.

Global now has minicomputers at each plant that perform routine applications like payroll and accounting. The production scheduling and control systems will be a package program running on a new computer dedicated to this application. Global has a high-level systems design for data transmission from the central computer to the plants and for the plant data to be transmitted back to central planning.

The systems staff at Global has retained you as a consultant to help them with further analysis. What kind of computer configuration seems most appropriate? What kind of transmission network do they need? What data should they collect? Prepare a plan showing the information Global must develop in order to establish this telecommunications system.

We would take another measurement when the sampling interval has gone by. Thus, the digital signal consists of a series of 7-bit characters, each of which encodes part of the waveform. To provide an adequate representation of the wave, we might sample 8,000 times per second. With this interval, we generate 7 bits × 8,000 samples/second = 56,000 bits per second as the amount of data sent over the line. It should be clear now why analog data, like full-motion video, require very high capacity lines (the higher the capacity or speed, the higher the **bandwidth** of the line).

Speed of Transmission

Transmission can occur at different speeds. The communications specialist uses a measure of speed called a **baud**, which is the number of times per second that the signal changes. For our purposes, it is easier to think in terms of bits per second or characters (**bytes**) per second. Subvoice-grade lines transmit 45 to 150 bits per second, whereas **voice-grade** lines transmit a maximum of 28K bits per second, with 14,400 being fairly common. Digital transmission is very popular because it is very reliable, offers high speeds, and eliminates the need for modems. A single **T1** circuit, leased from a common carrier, has a capacity of 1.544 million bits per second. A user typically splits this circuit into a number of lower-speed lines. Even faster lines are available if needed. A T3 line has a capacity of nearly 45 million bits per second.

What Is a Protocol?

Transmission involves **protocols**, which are sets of rules and procedures to control the flow of data between points. Both the sending and receiving stations need to follow the same procedures. For example, if blocks are being sent, both stations must agree that the transmission is to be in block mode. A protocol can also increase the efficiency of transmission by reducing the amount of data that must be sent for control purposes.

Paging Goes High Tech

SkyTel Corporation, the leading U.S. paging service provider, is the first company to offer two-way messaging over narrow-band personal communications services (PCS). Subscribers use a paging device named Tango built by Motorola. At first, you cannot write a custom message; instead, when paged, you can send back one of 16 predefined messages like "on my way" and "ok." You can customize these preprogrammed responses, however. If you have an HP 2000LX PDA, you can connect to Tango and send more advanced messages that are free-form. You can buy Tango for $400 or lease it for $15 a month. There is a basic $25 a month service charge.

One early user said that the service was "addictive." Two-way paging contributes to productivity because the person being paged does not have to find a telephone and the person making the page does not have to wait for a response.

We must control the following:

- Setting up a session
- Establishing a path from nodes 1 to *n*
- Linking devices together
- The hardware sending and interpreting the data

Protocols are also used to handle the following:

- Detection and correction of errors
- Formatting
- Line control
- Message sequencing

The International Standards Organization (ISO) has suggested a layered architecture to facilitate communications among different types of equipment. The seven logical layers are as follows (numbering follows the ISO designation of levels):

7. *Application:* The window through which applications gain access to the services provided by the model.

6. *Presentation:* Services here are concerned with data transformation, formatting, and syntax.

5. *Session:* A set of rules to set up and terminate data streams between network nodes.

4. *Transport:* Guarantees that the transfer of information occurs correctly after a route is established throughout the network.

3. *Network:* Arranges a logical connection between a source and destination on the network based on available data paths in the network.

2. *Data link:* Describes how a device accesses the medium in the physical layer and identifies data formats, procedures to correct transmission errors, and so on.

1. *Physical:* The lowest level in the model consists of a set of rules to specify the electrical and physical connection between devices.

The highest levels should remain similar across equipment, whereas lower levels depend more on the devices and manufacturers involved.

Summary

A device sends out a code, such as ASCII letters, to some type of interface, which sends the message over a transmission line. For analog transmission, the interface is a modem, which transmits either characters or blocks of data. At the receiving end, the interface unit must reconvert the code into the appropriate code for processing the transmitted data (see Figure 11-6).

Figure 11-6
Some communications options.

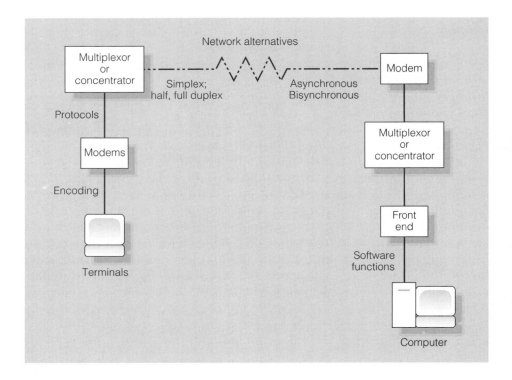

Linking Electronics Stores

Tandy Corporation operates some 5,500 retail stores and has 3,000 more dealer franchise outlets. Retail stores and dealer sites are served from six regional warehouses.

Before a new computer system was installed, order entry, inventory control, and warehouse distribution were handled with a combination of batch and manual procedures. Using printed order forms completed by hand at the stores was slow, particularly because the forms were mailed to the warehouse. At the warehouse, staff members keyed data on the orders and transmitted them to corporate headquarters. The next morning, the warehouse received a printout of the invoices.

A new system uses a personal computer in the store to assist management with information on what and how much to order and when to place the order to maintain optimum inventory levels. The store transmits the order directly to the corporate data center. With communications on-line, the system is much more responsive than in the past.

The Fort Worth warehouse alone distributes 800 shipments daily, requiring some 120,000 lines to be pulled from stock and shipped in 6,000 cartons. Combined regional value totals some 2,100 shipments of 65,000 lines in 28,000 cartons. Data describing 50 million lines and 500,000 shipments flow through the network annually.

NETWORKS

A network connects a variety of computers and other devices. Table 11-1 describes the networks discussed in this chapter.

The largest computer network is the Internet, which we shall discuss in some detail in the next chapter. The largest general-purpose network in the world is the public **switched network** used to carry most voice traffic around the world. Here, one simply dials a number and establishes a point-to-point connection only when it is needed. You probably use this network if you connect to a university computer using a personal computer with a modem. In addition to telephone, there are special private network services also providing switched connections. Such a network covers a huge distance. It would be considered a **wide area network (WAN)**. Some organizations want a network that is local to a given area, and they might configure it using private lines. This kind of network is known as a **metropolitan area network (MAN)**.

Moving from the switched network, one might make a simple connection between a computer and a terminal using twisted-pair cables running directly between the two devices. One can generally wire directly for a mile or two before the loss of signal (**attenuation**) becomes too great and modems are needed.

One way to reduce line costs is to have several terminals connected to a device called a **multiplexer**. The multiplexer combines the signals from various low-speed terminals and sends them over a higher-speed line. In time division multiplexing, the device samples separate incoming signals and combines them on the output line. At the receiving end, the signals must be demultiplexed. With a multiplexer, the speed of the output line must equal the sum of the speeds of the input lines.

A **concentrator** is a hardware device that collects messages from terminals and stores them if necessary. The concentrator sends the messages

Table 11-1
Types of Networks and Examples

Type of network	Example
Network of networks	The Internet
Public switched network	Voice telephony
Wide area network (WAN)	The phone system
Metropolitan area network (MAN)	A campus network
Local area network (LAN)	PC network within a building

over a higher-speed line to the computer. Unlike the multiplexer, however, it can temporarily store the data, so the capacity of the high-speed line does not have to equal the sum of the capacities of the low-speed lines it serves.

Network Configurations

Given the various communications options, one can configure a network of computers and terminal devices in any number of ways. Figure 11-7 presents some popular options. In a hierarchical scheme, one computer controls a series of subordinate computers. An example of this approach might be a central computer controlling local grocery store computers, which in turn control point-of-sale terminals at checkout stands. The star connection is similar, but here a single **host** or **server** can communicate with each remote processor. The local computers communicate with each other through the central system.

In a ring or loop scheme, all processors can communicate with their immediate neighbors. This pattern can be extended to allow communications from any processor to any other processor. The bus typology features a communications bus connecting individual computers. Computers put messages containing the address of their destination on the bus for delivery.

There are a large number of alternatives available in configuring a computer network. In many situations, the help of a communications specialist is called for.

Local Area Networks

The first people to buy personal computers used them as stand-alone devices. These individuals bought freedom and independence from the professional information services staff. Soon, however, users found it advantageous to

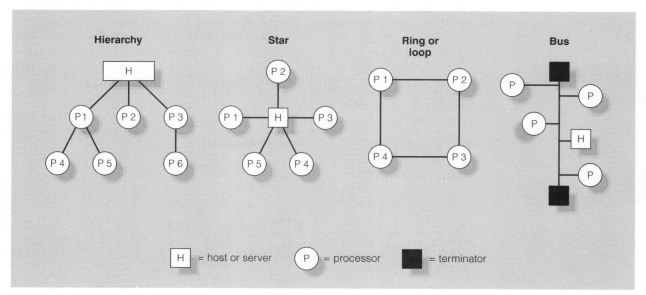

Figure 11-7   Examples of computer-to-computer connections.

share devices like laser printers. The most common way to share devices, data, and programs is through a **local area network (LAN)**. The local area network is an approach to connecting various devices that need to communicate with each other and that are grouped closely together, as in a single building.

There are two major architectures for LANs (see Figure 11-8). The first is a peer-to-peer network in which all PCs are connected to each other. Data on the network are passed from one PC to the next. As a user, you must devote some of the resources of your workstation to accepting and passing data on the network. Each computer on the LAN incurs this type of overhead. Peer-to-peer LANs are relatively inexpensive and represent an attractive alternative for a small network.

The second type of LAN is more popular and employs a file **server**. The **server** is a computer that responds to requests from its clients or user PCs. A client might request that a job be printed on a single laser printer serving a LAN with ten PCs. The **server** puts the client's print job in a queue and prints it when the printer is free. If the client asks for a software program or data, the **server** provides it. The LAN is generally installed for a group of users who need to share something—a database, computer equipment, and/or software. This LAN is more complex than the peer-to-peer

EDI Moves the Shoes

Stride Rite is the maker of such children's footwear as Keds as well as Sperry Topsiders. It is using information technology to improve order processing and customer relations, streamline shipping, and improve the quality of data it collects from retail customers. Stride Rite now has EDI connections with about thirty major trading partners and is aiming to reach fifty.

After beginning its EDI program with major customers, Stride Rite noticed increasing sales to each firm. Because orders come in electronically, Stride Rite can route them to its distribution centers. The shoes are picked and ready for shipping just a few hours after an order is received. Typical turnaround times for an order have gone from three days to a day and a half. The goal is same-day service.

The company is testing electronic invoicing and electronic funds transfer in an effort to get paid faster. Future plans also include using EDI to capture data from retail customers

so that Stride Rite knows what shoes are being sold in which stores.

In a separate project, Stride Rite sales representatives in the kids' shoes and Keds division carry a portable data terminal when they visit stores. The reps use a scanning gun to take an inventory of what is in the store and capture it on the hand-held terminal. The terminal records the universal product codes (UPCs), and the rep plugs it into a phone line to dial a database of UPCs on a value-added network. A small printer then produces a list of the store's inventory. It takes less than two hours to take inventory, instead of eight hours when doing things manually. Future plans include comparing the actual stock with a model stock for the store to help determine what to order.

Stride Rite is using a variety of technologies to focus on the customer and on improving the quality of its services.

network and is usually more expensive. It does free the client workstation from performing any LAN functions for other users.

Two basic technologies were first used to transmit data over LANs: baseband and broadband. The simpler and less costly alternative is baseband, which by definition uses digital signaling. Baseband requires simple cabling and is less complex than broadband. As might be expected, the limitations of baseband include capacity and distance, though for many office applications it is more than adequate. The strength of broadband is the tremendous capacity it offers. This technology can carry a variety of signals on a number of channels. It is based on analog transmission similar to that used for cable TV broadcasting.

More recently, there has been a great deal of interest in fiber-optic connections for LANs. One transmission approach is the Fiber Distributed Data Interface (FDDI) which operates at 100 million bits per second. FDDI uses a "token ring" approach to transmission (discussed below) and is well suited to metropolitan area networks.

Ethernet and Token Ring.   At a low level, the LAN must transmit data over the network. How is transmission coordinated so every workstation does not try to send data at the same time and thus block the data from other PCs? One solution to this contention problem is called carrier sense–multiple access with collision detection (**CSMA/CD**). The transmitting station checks whether a channel is clear by listening for a carrier signal. If the net is busy, the station waits until it is clear and then sends a message while listening for collisions with other stations that might have started to send at the same time. If a collision is detected, the station stops sending and waits a random time interval before starting to send again. **Ethernet** is the best example of a CSMA/CD protocol.

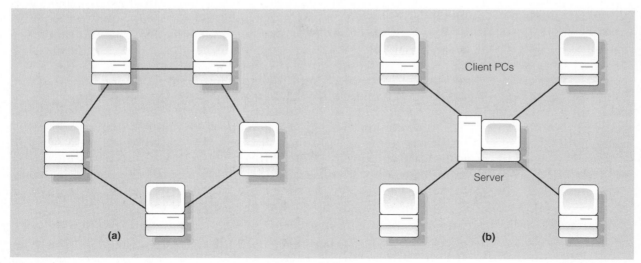

Figure 11-8   (a) Peer-to-peer LAN. (b) Client-server LAN.

An alternative scheme is to use a token that is passed along the network from node to node, an approach adopted by IBM. A station can transmit when it sees a free token come by; this approach is more complicated to implement than CSMA/CD, but it reduces the collision problem. As mentioned above, FDDI uses a **token ring** approach.

As you might expect, LANs grew in organizations without a lot of planning. Different departments and even different floors in buildings have their own LANs. Sometimes these LANs use different standards, one might use Appletalk and serve Macintosh computers while another features IBM PCs and a token ring architecture. Sooner or later, users on these networks want to be connected to each other. The solution is to use a bridge or a router. A **bridge** has very little logic. It connects similar networks. A **router** contains logic and serves to interface two or more networks to each other and possibly to a wide area network. Routers have enough logic to select the best path between two **nodes** on a network. All of the wires for a network come together in some kind of wiring hub. You might use a bridge or a router to connect hubs on different floors of a building or in remote locations. Hubs are continuously becoming "smarter." An organization might route all of the wires from the local wiring hub to an intelligent hub. This smart hub contains bridges and routers and is controlled by software, since the hub itself is a computer.

TCP/IP: A Network Protocol

One of the best-known protocols is **Transmission Control Protocol (TCP)/Internet Protocol (IP)** developed by a Department of Defense research project to connect various kinds of networks, discussed in the next section, to form an Internet. (The Internet, itself, is covered in the next chapter.) The Defense Department was faced with a variety of computers and networks

---

What Does Speed Really Mean?

We frequently talk about various speeds of transmission in numbers that can be a little hard to relate to as users. The following three types of transmission provide a little better sense of the difference transmission speed means in terms of sending a message.

- Using a 28.8 Kbps (bits per second) modem to change a digital signal to analog form and send a 1 megabyte file would require 4.63 minutes if the total transmission occurred at the maximum rate of speed.

- Using ISDN which combines two 64 Kbps channels to give 128 Kbps, this megabyte file would take 62.5 seconds to transmit at peak speed.

- With Asynchronous Transfer Mode (ATM) speeds range from 50 to 622 Mbps (million bits per second). For example, choose 155 Mbps, and the megabyte file takes 0.05 seconds to transmit.

Companies with large amounts of data to send are very interested in ATM networks based on the kind of calculations above. Many of us would like to have ISDN lines to use in limited videoconferencing and to access the Internet.

all produced by different contractors, generally the lowest bidder! It had two objectives: first to create a protocol to allow all of the networks to be interconnected, and second to create a network (of networks) able to carry on if some component or subnetwork could not operate due to failure or destruction.

The IP part of the protocol is responsible for moving packets of data from node to node in a network. IP forwards each packet based on a four byte destination number or IP address. (A computer connected to the Internet must have an IP address.) Gateways and servers move data among departments and around the world. IP operates on these computers. TCP is responsible for verifying the correct delivery of data from a client computer to a **server** and must see that data are not lost someplace on a network. TCP adds support to detect errors or missing data and to generate a retransmission until all the data have been correctly received.

Going Wireless

Setting up a network with cables and wires is not always desirable or feasible. Wireless technology uses some kind of broadcast to eliminate the need for cabling. A retailer might want to use a wireless terminal to keep track of inventory. A trucking firm could use a wireless system to send messages to its trucks and determine where they are at any time. K Mart stores use wireless technology to provide up-to-date information on the sales floor. A clerk carries a terminal that looks like a laser gun. The terminal connects with backroom computers using low-power radio frequencies. When the clerk scans an item on the shelf with the laser gun, he or she can read on a display screen on the gun whether the item is on order and when it is expected to arrive. K Mart claims this system has doubled inventory turns per year.

United Parcel Service began a systems modernization program in 1986 to allow it to compete with Federal Express in the overnight-delivery market. By 1991, UPS invested $1.5 billion to develop its technological infrastructure. The effort included a global data network for $50 million, a $100-million data center in New Jersey, electronic tablets for drivers ($350 million), and $150 million for a cellular network. The company now has nearly 2,000 IS employees, 5 mainframes, 300 minis, and about 33,000 PCs. There are also 1,500 LANs and 69,000 hand-held computers. The company plans to spend another $3 billion on technology between 1991 and 1996.

UPS has equipped its trucks with terminals that send data over the cellular phone system. This approach allows it to track deliveries for all air and some ground parcels during the day. In the past, that information was collected in batch mode and used to update centralized computers at night. The data were not available for inquiry until the next day.

When drivers collect a package, they capture delivery information, including a signature, using a hand-held pen-based computer. This computer fits into an adapter in the truck containing a cellular modem which sends data to a switch in a cellular network. The switch places the data from the truck on the UPS private network known as UPSnet to be sent to the UPS mainframe database in New Jersey.

American Airlines is also joining the ranks of companies using wireless technology for communications. Wireless notebook and subnotebook computers allow passenger agents to roam airports, providing passengers with faster check-in. The system provided by McCaw Cellular Communications, an AT&T subsidiary, provides access to the SABRE database of passenger reservations. The agent is able to offer many of the same services as agents behind counters using fixed terminals. American sees the system expanding to personnel on the tarmac using devices to report maintenance and departure times.

Using one of several wireless networks that offer services in major cities, you can send e-mail messages from your notebook computer without having a phone nearby. A columnist for a computer magazine recently described how she used her notebook computer on an airline flight to compose and store a variety of e-mail messages. On leaving the plane, she had her computer broadcast the messages to a wireless network for delivery.

Finally, Hewlett-Packard developed a wireless mobile unit that lets doctors receive a patient's vital signs for remote diagnosis. The unit is capable of receiving electrocardiograms as well as other vital signs. The system features a $25,000 dispatch system which is linked to medical monitors, and five palmtop computers for doctors. During testing, the system is credited with saving the life of one patient when information about his irregular heartbeat was sent to his doctor in her car. She returned to the hospital while the nurse prepared the patient for treatment, saving a great deal of time.

Voice Considerations

Designing a communications network today usually involves considerations of both voice and data. We measure data transmission in terms of bits per second, whereas voice is usually measured in terms of duration of conversation. The communications systems designer uses statistics on call volumes to determine what capacity the network must have for voice transmission. These calculations are added to the requirements for data transmission to come up with an overall specification for the network.

THE ADVANTAGES OF NETWORKS FOR BUSINESS

There are a large number of sources for communications services. As examples, we have discussed the public switched network, in which telephone lines on the local level connect with AT&T, Sprint, or MCI. We can also pay to lease a line or pay according to the time a line is in use. The actual communications path may be through land lines, microwave links, satellites, or some combination of the three. A firm may develop a private network and/or use services offered by common carriers.

What Are the Alternatives for Wide Area Communications?

A type of network known as **packet switching** is now a standard for transmitting digital data. A circuit-switched network establishes a connection between every pair of points that wants to transmit data, just as the telephone network does. There is considerable overhead in making the connection between the two parties. In packet switching, the network does not make connections for individuals. It routes bunches of data called packets. Network hardware and software break data into packets with each packet having an address. Each node on the network looks at the address and determines the best path to send it on toward its final destination. Network hardware and software reassemble the packets on the receiving end. Packet switching has proven very popular for transmitting data over large distances. There is an international packet-switching standard called **X.25**, and a number of networks use this protocol, including the French Transpac network (see Figure 11-9). You may hear the term **asynchronous transfer mode (ATM)**, which refers to a standard for high-speed packet switching. It includes the packet size, speed, and format. With such a standard, transmission services around the world should be compatible. ATM features high bandwidth (high capacity) and low delay. It is capable of carrying voice, data, image, and video communications.

Frame relay is a promising service offered by some of the common carriers to win data transmission business for wide area networks. The user chooses a data rate and connects to the common carrier's frame relay system through a router. The common carrier maintains a packet-switched

MANAGEMENT PROBLEM 11-2

Mary Levin works in planning for Loadstar, a large trucking company and barge operator in the Midwest. She has looked into a variety of systems to keep track of the location of trucks and barges so that the company can route shipments better and answer customer inquiries. Mary recognizes that barge and truck shipments are quite different.

"My major concern is with the trucks—our barges have commodities and take weeks to move something. It is much harder to keep up with trucking." Mary has collected information on a variety of products that can help track trucks.

"We could do something sophisticated. For example, the Global Position System used for air and marine navigation would allow us to pinpoint the exact location of a truck." This GPS system uses a receiver that tracks up to five satellites that move around the world in relatively low orbit. The clocks on the satellites are synchronized, so the receiver can tell how far it is from each satellite. It computes the length of an imaginary line between the satellite and the GPS unit. For navigation on land or at sea, three lines of position are enough to provide accuracy within a hundred meters or less. Loadstar would need a system that could identify the truck and send the ID and GPS data to headquarters.

Another possibility is to use a cellular phone in each truck and have the driver call in at certain hours. Mary said, "I don't need to know that a truck is at a certain latitude and longitude. If the driver says he or she is at milepost 50 on Interstate 80 in Nebraska, that's good enough."

What solution do you recommend? Why?

Figure 11-9
Packet switching.

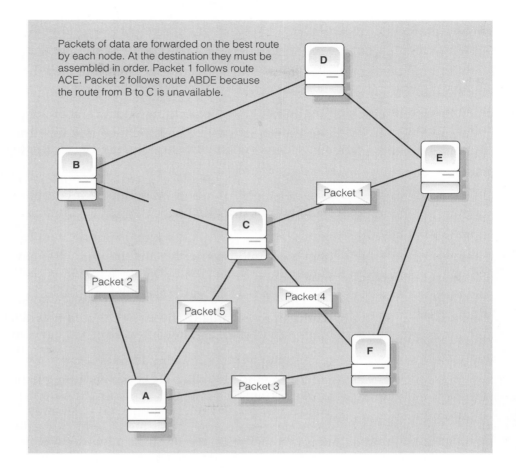

Packets of data are forwarded on the best route by each node. At the destination they must be assembled in order. Packet 1 follows route ACE. Packet 2 follows route ABDE because the route from B to C is unavailable.

"public" frame relay network which offers higher speeds than some private network alternatives. This common carrier network also features extensive backup and rerouting capabilities, making an outage of service less likely. Speeds with frame relay are lower than ATM, ranging from 56,000 to 1,544 million bits per second.

Another service is Switched Multimegabit Data Services, or SMDS. Some regional carriers are now offering this type of service in the U.S. as an alternative to building a private network for high-speed data transmission. SMDS is a high-speed, fast-packet data service with speeds ranging from 1.17 megabits per second to 45 megabits per second. With this service, there are no connections and it is a true packet-switched network. You can send data to any other user on the network if you know the recipient's address (and the recipient is willing to accept the data). SMDS is intended for corporate networks and can be used, for example, to integrate high-speed LANs.

Various common carriers in Europe, the United States, and elsewhere offer **integrated services digital networks (ISDNs)**. The services with ISDNs include voice and data transmission, though not at as high a speed as through a T1 circuit. With the right equipment, a pair of traditional copper wires can carry two simultaneous voice or fast-data signals. A third channel on this line is used for messages between the communications equipment. Each of the two digital data channels operates at a speed of 64kbps while the signaling channel operates at 16kps.

While slow to develop, ISDN offers some real advantages for business and even home use. Using compression algorithms, one can get acceptable video over an ISDN line and use this technology for video conferencing. A business might use ISDN for a wide area connection between LANS, something that takes place on an occasional basis. ISDN has been used to transmit high resolution CAT scans to a consulting physician located remotely from the patient.

As the costs for ISDN drop, it becomes appealing for telecommuters and the home office. An ISDN card in the PC is the only interface needed after a common carrier installs the line. ISDN gives high speed access to corporate computers; and is appealing for accessing the Internet (see the next chapter) and for multimedia applications.

The transmission standards and protocols for ISDNs have been standardized, so eventually the service should be available almost worldwide. ISDN services are a viable alternative for developing a communications network, especially for an organization that does not need extremely high-speed or high bandwidth communications.

The options described above are beginning to blur the definition of networks in Table 11-1. If you use an ATM switch to connect LANs in one building with LANs at a location 1000 miles away, you have formed a seamless wide area network consisting of local area networks. It is quite possible that in a few years, the distances involved will be less important than the number of users connected and the speeds at which they can communicate.

Why Develop Private Networks?

In the early days of communications among computers, firms typically designed a network for each application. A bank might have a network for demand deposit balances, a network for inquiring about loan balances, and so on. The bank branch would be served by a number of separate data networks plus the public telephone system.

More and more companies are building communications networks that carry data, voice, and video signals over the same communications lines. With today's technology and the deregulation of the communications industry, a firm can develop a network that includes common carriers or excludes them completely.

A company might lease lines and use the local telephone company for the local distribution of voice and data at the ends of the leased lines. Alternatively, the firm could bypass the telephone system completely by using satellite distribution. The brokerage firm discussed in Chapter 13 communicates with its branch offices throughout the United States by leasing time on a satellite transponder. It places a satellite dish on its headquarters and one on the roof of each branch office. The firm can now send voice, data, and video signals without using the public telephone network.

The offerings described in the preceding section—frame relay, SMDS (Switched Multimegabit Data Services), and ISDN—represent efforts by the common carriers to offer you an alternative to a private network. Although these same carriers may lease you lines for a network, it is likely that the total amount of service they provide will drop if you install your own network. The decision to use common carrier facilities or develop one's own network is a very difficult one. Even a small firm may lease a line between a corporate headquarters office and a factory some distance away. Large firms often have worldwide private networks. The decision to develop a private network must be based on cost considerations, service levels, planned communications growth, and a forecast of what services will be available from common carriers.

THE CONTRIBUTION OF COMMUNICATIONS

Firms take advantage of the opportunities provided by telecommunications and networks in a number of ways. Two important contributions of this technology are electronic mail (e-mail) and electronic data interchange (EDI). In several industries, information technology is also used to create electronic markets.

A Data Pipeline at Amoco

In today's oil business, an Amoco executive put it simply, "the company that finds the most oil makes the most money." However, drilling for oil is very expensive. A high speed network would let engineers and geologists rapidly access the information they need to identify promising drilling sites. The objective of Amoco's high speed data pipeline project, begun in 1993, is to cut the screening time for drilling data from months to hours.

To accomplish this goal, the company built the Aries network which has nearly a dozen T3 (45 Mbps) circuits and leased lines along with a satellite T1 (1.544 Mbps) link to offshore platforms. The network is based on ATM technology and includes routers, adapters and ATM switches. Actual ATM services are provided by three different common carriers.

At a demonstration in Washington, a participant used the Internet to surf through Web servers in Minneapolis and returned information in minutes instead of the hours required using dial-up links. Geologists at workstations in Houston and Washington worked collaboratively on a huge seismic data set delivered from an offshore oil platform. A site in Chicago broadcast a full motion video segment to Houston, Washington and Tulsa.

Amoco is ahead of most firms in setting up this kind of high-speed network. It is an excellent precursor for the kind of networks that should start appearing in business.

Electronic Mail As a Communications Tool

One of the most beneficial results of the marriage of computers and communications technology is electronic mail. Computer users with appropriate software and communications links can send messages and documents to other computer users. Electronic mail is analogous to physical mail handled by the post office, except it is not stored or handled physically. When someone sends you an e-mail message, it goes into your "mailbox" on the computer. When you check your mail, the message is there for you to read and respond to if you like. It has been estimated that 40 million people in the US use e-mail.

How does e-mail work in industry? Recently some fifty-three engineers at Digital Equipment Corporation in Massachusetts, Arizona, Colorado, Singapore, and Germany collaborated on the design of a new disk drive using e-mail. Most had never met, and the engineers rarely phoned each other. DEC estimates that this diverse group completed their task a year sooner and with 40 percent fewer people than a comparable team assembled in one building.

Most companies with large e-mail systems also have large networks. Hewlett-Packard has a network of 94,000 mailboxes and has a volume of 350 million mail messages a year for its 90,000 employees. (There are more mailboxes than employees because some mailboxes are assigned to workgroups.) DEC's 62,000 employees send 50 million messages a year just between sites. (This total does not include messages within a given site).

In 1991 the faction in the Soviet Union trying to overthrow Gorbachev told the world that he was "sick." They also told the Soviet population that the international community supported their new government. Within hours, computer and fax machines in Russia received information from around the globe that contradicted these assertions. Supporters rallying around Boris Yeltsin at the Russian White House received e-mail messages on a Moscow computer that NATO, the U.S., and other countries were on their side. It was easy for the members of the coup to control domestic newspapers, radio, and television, but it was not nearly so easy (and they probably did not realize it existed) to control communications via e-mail.

Electronic Data Interchange

When we discussed corporate strategy in Chapter 5, we made the point that many strategic systems require the firm to be connected electronically with customers and suppliers. One rapidly growing technique for this type of interconnection is electronic data interchange (EDI). Detroit auto manufacturers were among the first companies to encourage suppliers to accept orders electronically. The idea is simple: A buyer sends an order electronically to the supplier and the supplier acknowledges the order electronically. When the supplier sends the items ordered, the customer electronically acknowledges receipt. Similarly, the firms set up an electronic billing and payment system. The concept is very simple, but the reality of implementing EDI is much more difficult.

Because each firm has its own formats for each of the paper documents used prior to EDI, there are problems of compatibility. Where is the quantity-ordered field on a GM order? The American National Standards Institute (ANSI) has developed a standard known as **ANSI X.12** to specify common document formats for the transactions involved in ordering, receiving, and paying for merchandise. (It can take some seventeen different transactions to complete an order.)

You can purchase packaged software to help implement EDI. Newer generations of this software allow for mapping. A programmer can map the fields from your invoice into the location of fields in a supplier's purchase order system. You can then place your order in its accustomed format, and the software will translate it into an order that the supplier's system can accept. Given all of this overhead, it can take a significant amount of time to develop EDI links with customers and suppliers.

As you might have observed, this type of EDI is basically a batch transmission. At different times during the day, a firm connects its computers with different EDI partners to transmit and receive data. The next step in development will be to have on-line access. Customer and supplier computers will be connected all day so one can obtain up-to-date information in response to queries.

Beyond the Model T

Ford Motor Company has a rich history of technological innovation. After all, Henry Ford developed the first assembly line. Ford is continuing to develop a closer link with its suppliers using EDI. It was a pioneer in the field in the 1970s. Ford began by compressing the time it takes to order and receive goods. Now it is working on eliminating the need to track goods on the way to its plants and to audit supplier invoices.

Most EDI is not real-time. While data are exchanged electronically, the transmission process sends a batch of documents at one time. For many firms there is no need for an order to be processed immediately upon transmission from a customer. However, as manufacturers move toward more just-in-time manufacturing, communications will have to be faster.

Ford established direct links with its suppliers, who can now dial in to Ford's mainframe material system which tracks inventory at the car maker's twenty assembly plants. Ford's sixty-one manufacturing locations and ten of its parts supply sites will soon be on-line. Suppliers send their asynchronous inquiries to a value-added network offered by Tymnet. (A **value-added network (VAN)**, provides a range of services to its customers. The network vendor generally leases lines from a common carrier and adds services or value to the leased lines.) The network converts the traffic to the IBM mainframe data stream needed to access Ford's computers. A typical supplier logs in four or five times a day to check Ford's inventory so it can coordinate production with the automobile manufacturer.

Large suppliers are even establishing dedicated links into Ford systems. Employees at Dana, a major components supplier, will be able to use the terminals already on their desks to toggle between Ford systems and internal

Dana computers. Ford allows suppliers to update its database when they send a shipment of parts.

Ford no longer accepts invoices from suppliers. When parts arrive at a Ford facility, an employee scans a bar code on the crate containing the parts, generating an electronic receipt. The receipt message travels over Ford's network to the accounts-payable department, which matches the order with a price negotiated previously with the supplier. Ford mails a check (maybe someday an electronic payment will be possible) and sends an electronic remittance message to the supplier. All of Ford's suppliers participate in the electronic receipts program while about 150 receive re-mittance information. The advantage to Ford is that the supplier has to audit payment, rather than Ford having to audit invoices.

As you might expect, Ford's EDI program does not end with suppliers. Ford has twelve major railroads with which it exchanges EDI transactions. Ford issues an electronic bill of lading when goods must be moved between sites, using the ANSI X.12 standard. The electronic bill of lading goes to the railroad via a direct link or through IBM's Information Network. The railroad returns an acknowledgment and takes over the responsibility for tracking the shipment.

Ford also wants to encourage its suppliers to communicate with it using e-mail. The firm wants to save on overnight-mail and long-distance charges and improve **response times** over the typical phone call (which ends up on an answering machine). E-mail could also replace a cumber-some paper-based process for cost-saving ideas submitted by suppliers. Ford figures that e-mail will make it so easy to send suggestions, it would get far more ideas from the suppliers than it does today.

Ford also has another network for sending computer-aided design (CAD) diagrams among plants and to suppliers that use Ford's CAD system. This packet-switched network uses a combination of public and private lines. Suppliers can download design plans from Ford to incorporate changes in different parts more quickly.

Building an Electronic Market

As companies use communications for buying and selling products, they are creating electronic markets, as we discussed in Chapter 4. One of the old-est and most successful electronic markets is the NASDAQ, the market for over-the-counter (OTC) securities (securities not listed on the New York, American, or regional stock exchanges in the U.S.). Members of the National Association of Securities Dealers use this system for trading. If you buy or sell OTC shares, your broker uses this system. The NASDAQ is an on-line computer system in which market-making firms post bids and ask prices for individual securities. Other brokers can accept these quotations and transact business for their clients. The system is very successful and was adopted by Japan to create an electronic market.

In the U.S. there are a number of other electronic markets including TELCOT, a market used for trading cotton. In France, the national Minitel system makes it possible for a number of firms to sell their products very inexpensively using computer terminals. To the extent that there are competing firms offering products, a Minitel user can compare prices among the different vendors, creating another type of electronic market.

We could argue from a strategic standpoint that batch-oriented EDI tends to reduce market competition by creating a close link between a supplier and a customer. With a proprietary interface, switching to another vendor is difficult. As industries adopt standards like the ANSI X.12 standard, or use the EDI services of a value-added network, this linkage is weakened because now it is easy to switch to another supplier. In a full electronic market like the NASDAQ, where everyone is on-line at the same time, one can easily switch vendors and there is little strategic advantage to an electronic link between one firm and another. All players tend to be equal in an electronic marketplace.

TRANSFORMING ORGANIZATIONS AND THE ECONOMY

In a mature firm, you are most likely to encounter an infrastructure that features networked computing. There will be computers of varying capacities at different nodes (see Figure 11-10). There are local workstations, terminals with significant logic, and built-in personal computers. Communications networks tie all the various devices together and help to interface dissimilar pieces of equipment. In Figure 11-10 we have a group of interconnected mainframes for transactions processing and access to large data files. The mainframes manage a large database through a specialized database processor. The mainframes also act as large servers for users on the network.

A router links the computer to remote workstations, consisting of personal computers and servers in a local area network. There is a gateway (a connection between two computers on different networks) to other networks as well. All these trends lead to an increasing availability of computation and significant opportunities for inventive information systems.

Figure 11-11 shows how this typical firm is connected with other organizations, including suppliers, customers, and financial institutions. The development of **interorganizational systems (IOSs)** is having a dramatic impact on the way firms operate. In the figure, the company is connected directly with its suppliers and customers, probably through some form of EDI using an industry standard format. For some suppliers, the company may make use of an electronic market for its purchases. The firm is connected to a common carrier e-mail service to communicate with a large number of other entities. Electronic links to banks and other financial institutions eliminate much of the paperwork involved in processing receipts and payments.

The vision of an electronic economy emerges from Figures 11-10 and 11-11. Firms are networked both within the firm and externally to other participants in the economy. They use electronic communications and linking and electronic customer/supplier relationships to design their

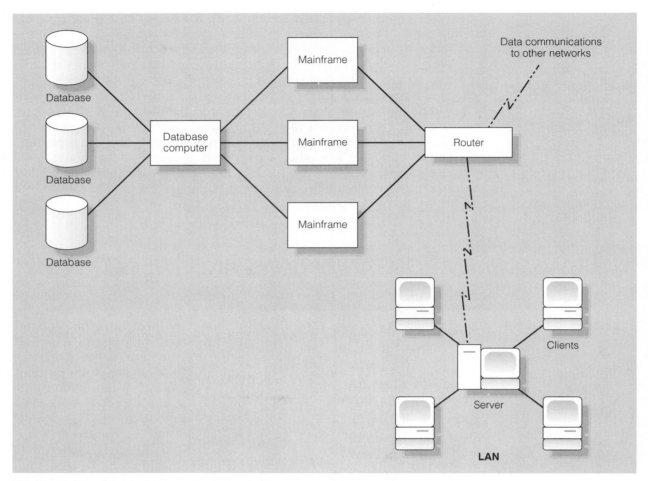

Figure 11-10 A typical computing complex.

organizations. Information technology makes possible the sharing of data and information while facilitating communications and coordination among key components of a postindustrial economy. It is this combination of computer and communications technologies that is transforming not only the organization, but the economy as well.

CHAPTER SUMMARY

1. Communications is the key to developing greater connectivity among individuals within a firm and among different organizations.
2. The simplest communications occur between two computer devices, such as a PC connected to a server.

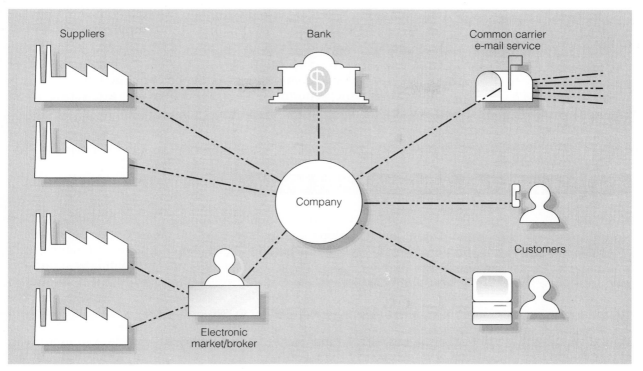

Figure 11-11 The electronic economy.

3. Your PC uses asynchronous transmission and sends characters to the server.

4. If you are using the dial-up phone network, a modem translates the digital signals from your PC to an analog format for transfer over the phone line. At the receiving end, a modem demodulates the signals and produces digital output.

5. Most long-haul communications lines and the lines within many cities are digital. The analog data from the local loop to your phone has to be digitized to use these lines. The phone companies also want to digitize video information (like movies) to send them to your home.

6. A network connects a variety of computers and other devices. The LAN is the smallest such network and may connect only a few computers in a department.

7. Larger networks extend over thousands of miles, and there are a number of global networks.

8. A company may lease lines from a common carrier in order to build a private network. The company can use this network for voice and data transmission.

9. The common carriers are also offering services that companies pay for on a usage basis instead of leasing lines. An example of such a service is frame relay transmission.

10. Greater connectivity through networking has increased the use of EDI which draws customers and suppliers more closely together. It is one way in which communications and networks are transforming the relationship among companies.

IMPLICATIONS FOR MANAGEMENT

The combination of computers and communications has a greater impact than either element alone. Computers alone are great for computation and for maintaining huge databases. Add telecommunications and you create a myriad of new ways to apply information technology. Communications and networks have finally convinced some skeptics who argued that computers are nothing but large, fast calculators. Computers and networks are both computational and communications devices, allowing for an unprecedented level of coordination and communication within and among firms. Communications is one of the fundamental tasks of management. In your career you will have a rich variety of media to help you communicate with colleagues, associates, and a variety of organizations.

KEY WORDS

Amplitude
Analog signal
ANSI X.12
ASCII
Asynchronous transfer mode (ATM)
Asynchronous transmission
Attenuation
Bandwidth
Baud
Baudot code
Bit
Block mode
Bridge
Byte
Character mode
Code
Compression

Concentrator
Connectivity
CSMA/CD
Demodulation
Ethernet
Frame relay
Frequency
Full duplex transmission
Half duplex transmission
Host
Integrated services digital network (ISDN)
Interorganizational system (IOS)
Local area network (LAN)
Metropolitan area network (MAN)
Modem
Modulated
Multiplexer

Network
Node
Packet switching
Pulse code modulation (PCM)
Protocol
Response time
Router
Satellite
Server
Simplex transmission
Switched network

Synchronous mode
Transmission Control Protocol/
    Internet Protocol (TCP/IP)
T1
Terminal
Token ring
Value-added network (VAN)
Voice-grade
Wide area network (WAN)
X.25

RECOMMENDED READING

Black, U. *Computer Networking*. Englewood Cliffs, N.J.: Prentice-Hall, 1989. (A thorough text on all aspects of networking.)

Stallings, W., and Richard VanSlyke. *Business Data Communications* 2e. New York: Macmillan, 1994. (An excellent text on communications.)

DISCUSSION QUESTIONS

1. Why were the first telephone communications over analog circuits?
2. Define batch processing and contrast it with on-line systems.
3. What is the difference between time-sharing and on-line applications?
4. What are the advantages of digital over analog lines?
5. Why are communications between computers digital in nature?
6. Why do we use an 8-bit code for transmission instead of one that is 5 or 6 bits?
7. Draw sine waves of differing amplitude, frequency, and phase.
8. What is a protocol used for in data communications?
9. What is the difference between synchronous and asynchronous transmission?
10. What is the advantage of using voice-grade lines for time-sharing in a university environment?
11. Describe the steps involved in a protocol for communications between an asynchronous terminal and a host time-sharing computer.
12. Describe at least one network configuration. For what applications do you think it is most suited?
13. Why are firms interested in local area networks?
14. What advantages do packet-switching services offer?

15. What are the major differences between a LAN and a WAN?

16. Why would a bank develop its own entirely private communications network using satellites?

17. What function does a multiplexer serve?

18. What is the difference between a multiplexer and a concentrator?

19. What are the implications of workstations replacing terminals, from the standpoint of systems analysis and design?

20. Why might a LAN not have a host computer?

21. Can you think of any disadvantages of satellite communications?

22. What has motivated the common carriers to develop frame relay, ISDN, and ATM communications lines?

23. Why is a communications specialist needed to design a network?

24. Think of a business with which you are familiar. In what ways would a network and data communications aid this firm?

25. Why does the systems designer need to have some knowledge of data communications?

CHAPTER 11 PROJECT

DATABASE ASSIGNMENT, PART III

Mary Simon looked at the portfolio application and said, "This is just what I need for a job I've just taken on. Of course, this job really isn't for Simon Marshall Associates—but then again, one good source of clients would be our alumni." Mary had just agreed to help in fund-raising for her school and realized that the campaign would require some good record keeping.

Your third database assignment is to set up the alumni contributions records system for Mary. The key to this assignment is to remember that relations can be merged through a join operation.

ALUMNI RECORDS

Mary Simon is very active in the alumni affairs of her university. She has been asked to keep track of the alumni contributions flowing to the university, most of which we hope are for the business school. The records she needs to keep are contained in four relations:

Alumni

Contrib

School

Type

Please do the following exercises:

1. Create a list of donors who have given a chair or endowment.
2. Create a list of donors who have given unrestricted funds to the business school.
3. Create a list of cities showing total contributions from each. You will find it helpful to use the sort command and to create a report to do the subtotaling by city.
4. Use the report generator to create a report showing the last name, zip code, and amount of each donation along with a printed message showing the school and type. For example, if someone had a school of 4 and a type of 1, the report should read "Business" and "Endowment." Your report should include the sum of the donations.

Alumni

Last Name	First Name	Street	City	State	Zip
Smith	John	18 Portland Rd	Chicago	IL	12345
Doe	Mary	90 Trinity Place	New York	NY	10006
Carson	John	177 Dover Center	Omaha	NE	68114
Altman	Sam	1600 Pennsylvania Av	Washington	DC	11111
Koch	Ed	City Hall	New York	NY	10101
Smith	Tom	34 Harvard St	Cambridge	MA	02139

Contrib

Last Name	Zip	Type	School	Amount
Smith	12345	2	1	50,000
Smith	12345	1	3	40,000
Doe	10006	4	4	100,000
Carson	68114	3	2	50,000
Carson	68114	4	1	25,000
Koch	10101	3	2	10,000
Smith	02139	3	4	45,000
Smith	12345	3	2	75,000
Smith	12345	4	4	38,000
Doe	10006	3	3	150,000
Koch	10101	4	2	50,000
Koch	10101	2	1	10,000
Smith	02139	4	3	18,000

School

School Code	Name
1	Arts &Sciences
2	Law
3	Medical
4	Business

Type

Type code	Type
1	Endowment
2	Chair
3	Special
4	Unrestrict

CHAPTER 12

Networks and Electronic Commerce

OBJECTIVES

1. **Learning to manage information technology.**

   The time for new technology innovations to diffuse is becoming steadily shorter. IBM brought out its PC in 1981 and it took four to five years for the computer to become commonplace in offices. The Internet became fashionable in less than two years, with thousands of companies trying to figure out how to make effective use of the network.

2. **Preparing to apply technology.**

   The development of commercial networks offers new options for delivering products and services to customers. One can make information available on a commercial service like America Online, Compuserve or Prodigy, or on the Internet. The commercial services have some vendors who allow users to purchase items over their networks, a form of **electronic commerce**. Commerce is also beginning to grow on the Internet.

3. **Transforming the organization.**

Networks facilitate the development of new forms of organization. They are key to building the T-Form organization discussed in earlier chapters. Networks make it possible to connect with partners and customers as they encourage firms to form strategic alliances. Networks facilitate the creation of virtual subunits, when your firm relies on another to provide a component that you would normally manage, like a raw materials inventory.

One of the most important developments in the history of information technology is the evolution of the computer from a calculating engine to a communications tool. As a calculator, computers are extremely valuable. It is hard to imagine businesses operating on the scale they do today without the capabilities of the computer. However, the computer's role as a communications device may dwarf its impact as a calculator. Computers and communications are allowing us to change the structure of organizations and the nature of commerce.

In this chapter we look at the world of networks. The first networks were used by business for electronic linking and communications and for electronic customer/supplier relationships. Most proprietary or private networks were developed for use within a single enterprise. For example, the first bank networks connected tellers in branches with a central computer that had information on customer checking accounts.

Electronic data interchange involves customers and suppliers. Here companies agree to standards for exchanging information. Railroads and their shippers agree on a standard to use for the data that must be exchanged for shipping products by rail. A new customer can begin exchanging data with the railroads by following this message standard.

Mass market networks appeal to consumers. Examples of these networks include **Compuserve**, **Prodigy**, **America Online**, the **Microsoft Network** in the U.S., and the **Minitel** system in France. Minitel has grown to be more than just a mass market consumer network as it provides a number of business services as well. The most significant network in terms of growth is the Internet. The chapter explores the Net and examines the potential all these networks have for electronic commerce.

*T*HE IMPACT OF COMMUNICATIONS TECHNOLOGY

In the last chapter, we discussed the telephone system as an example of a large, international network. This network has a number of important features. First, it is ubiquitous, at least in the U.S. where almost all residences have a telephone. Even though there are different phone companies, they all interoperate. That is, a call from a regional Bell company can be made transparently to a phone in a GT&E company. Through international standards organizations, telephones interoperate at the country level. You can direct dial phones in a large number of foreign countries. This phone network carries voice and data.

One of the nicest attributes of the telephone network is the fact it is there. We have a communications infrastructure that makes it simple to plug a new telephone or fax into the network. We can buy a telephone from a number of different sources and know that it will function on the network because there are published standards and vendors manufacture their equipment to meet these standards.

BUILDING NETWORKS

Developing **computer networks** is not as easy as adding a telephone. There is no single infrastructure comparable to the voice network for data. Of course, one can simply use modems and dial-up voice lines, but for many applications this alternative is either too costly or infeasible because the voice lines are too slow for data transmission.

In the U.S., we typically find that companies have developed two different kinds of networks, electronic data interchange (**EDI**) and/or proprietary data networks. Generally EDI refers to networks in which multiple

More Than a Phone Call

The existing U.S. telephone network is constantly upgraded. Higher speed and capacity links are having a dramatic affect on life in some parts of the country, especially in rural areas. Some 400 rural counties where population dropped during the 1980s are now growing and 900,000 people moved to rural counties during 1990 and 1991. To revive its rural areas, Nebraska state officials pushed local phone companies to install fiber optics lines and digital switches. The carriers laid 6700 miles of fiber-optics lines in the state linking all but five of the state's counties.

The impact of this new network has been dramatic. During the 1980s, Aurora, Nebraska, with a population of 3800, had over twelve empty store fronts and the population was shrinking. Today the unemployment rate is less than 1.5% and all the stores are occupied. An Aurora pet food plant uses the network to link to its headquarters in Ohio and with shippers and customers around the country. The company said that a decade ago communications would not be on its top ten list of reasons to locate a plant someplace. Today it in the top three.

One small high school in a town of 135 people uses the network for interactive television classes in Spanish since the school is not able to justify a language teacher. Students use a fax machine for written work. Ainsworth, Nebraska has a two-way video conferencing unit in the town library. Recently senior citizens used the system to discuss arthritis with nurses in Omaha.

parties have agreed to follow a standard for exchanging data electronically. EDI networks exist in retailing, transportation, and insurance. There is a national standard in the U.S. called ANSI X.12 and a European standard called EDIFACT.

In private industry and government, EDI is extremely popular for lowering costs while increasing accuracy and quality in purchasing goods. One objective of EDI is to reduce manual keying, therefore reduce errors, and speed up the order cycle. By exchanging data electronically, organizations can change their production cycles and the kind of services they offer.

Despite their achievements, EDI networks have less impact than one would expect because they cannot rely upon a common telecommunications infrastructure. As a result, to use EDI effectively takes expertise and resources. The high cost of networking gives larger firms an advantage over smaller competitors in using data networks. The Chrysler JIT-EDI example shows tremendous gains, but Chrysler is a very large company, ranking in the top 15 in sales in the U.S.

Given the lack of a data network infrastructure in the U.S., firms face a bewildering number of choices when considering the development of a network application. These applications are expensive to develop since there is much re-invention with each new network. For companies to exchange data they must completely agree on data formats. A firm sending a purchase order must put data in exactly the right place in the electronic message so the supplier can interpret it.

The **ANSI X.12** standard is intended to facilitate this process, but a number of industry-specific networks do not conform to the standard. Due to incompatibilities, some press reports indicate that up to 50 percent of the data exchanged via EDI needs rekeying. A firm must change its internal computing systems or purchase special software to map the data from existing systems to an accepted EDI standard. While some service companies can help a company get started, and PC EDI packages are available for smaller firms, the start-up and maintenance costs are too high for many companies. It is also hard to get all trading partners to use EDI. Generally large firms are more sophisticated technologically and can afford the development cost.

To alleviate these problems, a group of Northern California companies created a consortium called **CommerceNet**. The objectives of this ambitious project are to allow companies that have never done business before to establish and maintain a relationship electronically. The company plans to use the existing Internet, discussed below, as its underlying network. It must develop agreements on standards for proposals, bids, price lists, and other transactions. The idea is that a company, say in Palo Alto, could put out a request for proposals in the morning and receive bids from respondents all over the world by evening. The next morning it could send an electronic purchase order to the winner. AT&T, Novell, and Lotus are also working together to allow companies to link Notes and NetWare networks more easily to offer another possibility for electronic commerce.

Partially because firms cannot rely on a national data infrastructure, they have developed elaborate private or proprietary networks, sometimes using common carrier facilities, and at other times bypassing them completely. Examples of familiar companies using proprietary networks include: Federal Express and United Parcel for package delivery, United and American Airlines for their reservations systems, Frito-Lay for distribution and decision support, Baxter Laboratories for supplying its customers, and many other firms we encounter on a regular basis. These networks are proprietary because they do not follow any kind of industry standard.

Each of these firms has to bear the expense of designing, implementing, and operating a proprietary data network. Some of these efforts even required inventing new technology. Frito-Lay undertook the development of a hand-held computer for its drivers to use for placing orders and keeping records. If a firm operates in an industry without support for or tradition of EDI, today it has to decide to develop a proprietary data network for an application, use a service company's existing network, or develop its application on the Internet.

Commercial Network Providers

The current generation of U.S. mass market services including Prodigy, Compuserve, Genie, Microsoft Network, and America Online, is doing better than earlier attempts, although they, too, have experienced slow growth. America Online appears to be the most successful at the present time. Several services are thought to be profitable, even though collectively they have relatively small markets. Compuserve caters to computer users. The company does not break out earnings by line of business, but one research firm estimated that the company has a profit of $28 million a year from its consumer-oriented on-line services. See Figure 12-1 for examples of screens from the major services.

Prodigy, a joint venture of IBM and Sears, is family-oriented. It is rumored that IBM and Sears invested over one billion dollars in Prodigy before selling it to a group of investors. America Online has been one of the fastest growing mass market networks in the U.S. In addition to these large, commercial on-line services, hobbyists and small entrepreneurs offer approximately 50,000 private bulletin boards, which offer information and services to users.

While the hope of many network providers was to provide average citizens a national market for goods, information, and other services, these goals have not been fulfilled. Executives at Prodigy expected users to shop heavily and order merchandise on the network. Probably its biggest marketing successes has been PC Flowers which has grown to be one of FTD's top five customers. However PC Flowers had only $10 million in sales in 1993, out of a total U.S. flower market of about $10 billion.

The new Microsoft Network begins with a great advantage. By clicking on an icon on Windows95, the user can register for the network. Subsequently, logging on will only require clicking on an icon as well.

All of these mass market networks are threatened by the Internet, a more open network with a great deal of free information. Each of these networks provides access to the Internet in an attempt to retain their subscribers. They are also threatened by MCI and AT&T, both of which provide easy access by phone lines to the Internet. It remains to be seen how these mass market networks will fare as the Internet expands.

A NATIONAL NETWORK INFRASTRUCTURE: THE MINITEL SYSTEM

There are two examples of national and international networks that resemble the "information superhighway": the Minitel system in France and the Internet based in the U.S. The French Teletel system, popularly called Minitel after the name of its first terminal, was introduced by France

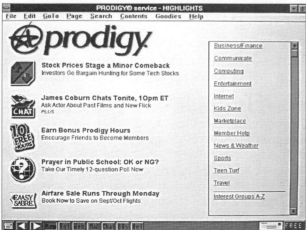

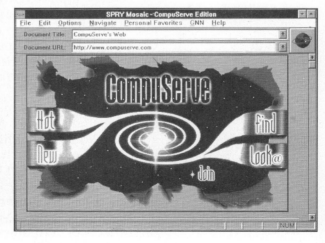

Figure 12-1 Commercial network providers.

Telecom, the French government-sponsored telecommunications company, in 1982. By 1993, Minitel was used in 20 percent of households and 80 percent of businesses in France. Users access a wide array of communication, information, and business transaction services. Approximately 6.5 million Minitel terminals are in service in France, which has a population of 57.5 million. Another 500,000 residents of France use Minitel on their personal computers. Altogether about 40 percent of the non-retired French population had access to Minitel either at work or at home. Some 25,000 services are available on the system, a number growing at the rate of 10 percent a year.

Minitel is considered by many to be a mass market system aimed at the consumer. It is the first and only example of a successful mass market network venture in the world. It is successful in the sense that it reaches a large proportion of French households and businesses; it offers a rich variety of information, communications and services; and it is estimated to be profitable.

In 1989, France Telecom introduced a nationwide electronic mail system for businesses and the general public. Information services include the national, on-line telephone directory, schedules for the French national railroad, as well as want ads, stock market reports, and other information that might be found in a newspaper. There are also short-lived or highly specialized information services for the general public. For example, sports fans can access continuously updated information about the position of boats in around-the-world yacht races and parents sending their children to camp can access daily lunch menus. The Minitel directory, the most frequently accessed Minitel service, is shown in Figure 12-2 in an English version.

Because Minitel is built on a nationwide data network with open standards, businesses also make use of the network for business-to-business services. While Minitel began with a mass market focus, in recent years

MANAGEMENT
PROBLEM 12-1

Pat Washington is chairman of a new company that sells PC software for children, a combination of education and entertainment. The firm experienced rapid growth and two of its products are best sellers. Being a technology company, Pat wants to take advantage of mass market services like America Online, Microsoft Network, Prodigy, and Compuserve. While her products are aimed at children, adults purchase almost all of their software.

Pat is particularly fascinated by the Internet and the World Wide Web. She says, "There must be a way to establish closer rapport with our customers, adults who purchase and the children who use our products, through the Internet." Pat is unsure what to do. Alternatives range from setting up a home page and a product catalog on the World Wide Web to taking orders over the Net.

What should Pat consider in her decision? What are the pros and cons of the different alternatives? How do the commercial services like Compuserve fit into her strategy?

Figure 12-2
The Minitel directory in English.

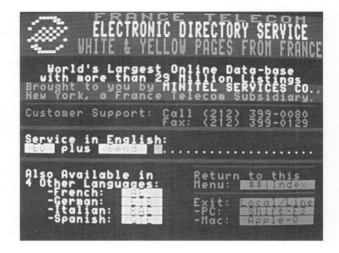

No Branches for 500,000 Customers

First Direct is an example of the future of banking in the world. This bank is located in the industrial city of Leeds, England and its quarters are in a huge building resembling an aircraft hanger next to a nuclear power plant. First Direct is a "telephone only" bank; there are no walk-up branches or windows. It is also the fastest growing bank in England, opening 10,000 accounts a month or the equivalent of two or three physical branches.

Surprisingly, First Direct has used technology to create a more personal relationship with its clients, even though the banker and client do not meet physically. Some 24,000 calls a day come to First Direct's two facilities, staffed at peak times by 150 bankers. Scoreboards on the walls show the number of customers on hold and how long they have been waiting. Posters chart the sales of credit cards and other services for the month.

The bank becomes more personal by using technology to look for opportunities to cross sell new products and services to a customer. When, for example, a customer calls to check her balance and make a transfer to pay a credit card bill at a rival bank, the First Direct representative sees a message on the screen that says "No Adverse Risk" meaning that the bank would be glad to loan this customer money. The representative sees the customer's employment and credit status and a list of prior transactions with First Direct. He asks if the customer has read the information First Direct recently sent on its Visa card, knowing that it carries a lower interest than the bank's rivals. The customer says she will think about it, and the First Direct representative sends her a prepared application for a Visa card.

First Direct is a division of Midland bank and it tends to appeal to professionals with a good income. The average balance is ten times higher at First Direct than Midland while its overall costs are 61 percent less. First Direct makes money on 60 percent of its customers, compared to 40 percent at the average British bank.

Banking with IT will dramatically change the physical structure of the banking industry; First Direct is a model of what is to come.

residential growth has slowed and been replaced by a large growth in business applications. In 1990 about half of the services were business related. Some of these business services are traditional information services, with information—such as stock market listing, economic data, or airline schedules—tailored to the interests of business customers. Other business applications are business-to-business transaction services, very similar to EDI and proprietary network applications in the United States. Brun Passot, the second largest office product supply company in France discussed in Chapter 1, encourages its customers to order electronically via Minitel. For large volume customers, Brun Passot installs a computer with a proprietary connection to its order processing and reporting system.

A number of case studies conducted by Charles Steinfield at Michigan State University illustrate what can be done with a network that connects business to small firms and consumers. A large, multi-national, electrical appliance and consumer electronics manufacturer used Minitel for EDI-like connections to approximately 10,000 separate retailers and independent repair people throughout France. In addition to the major cost savings this manufacturer achieved by better managing inventory and reducing transaction costs, the firm also introduced a revenue producing expert system-based training application that assists the service force in the diagnosis and repair of appliances and electronics products. Repair staff are charged on the basis of connect time for use of this service. In addition, the expert system accumulates data on repair problems and provides feedback to the design and manufacturing divisions of the company in order to help detect and correct potential structural flaws in their products.

Ubiquity enables other innovative business applications as well. In one, a clothing manufacturer was able to use the Minitel terminals already in many boutiques to offer a custom-tailored suit business. A clerk takes a customer's measurements, ships them over Minitel to a computer-controlled cutting machine at the factory, and the factory returns a custom-made suit in several weeks. Another application is the trucking spot market created by Lamy, the French directory publisher. Freight forwarders transmit special shipment requests to a Minitel database that truckers search as they attempt to fill excess capacity or to fill up on a return trip. Upon finding a matching offer, the truckers immediately call the forwarder to make a bid.

Discussions with French firms suggest it is possible to develop a national order entry system using Minitel in several months for well under $50,000, something very difficult to accomplish in the United States if you must build a proprietary network for the application.

The major drawback to Minitel today is its slow speed and lack of interesting graphics. Minitel is well established in France but the question is whether it can be modernized and maintain its dominant position given competition from other mass market services and the Internet. France Telecom, the operator of Minitel, is working to upgrade the speed of the network and to offer more exciting graphics. A "photographic" quality terminal is now available. Customers can arrange to access Minitel through an ISDN line and they can connect to Minitel through a LAN.

INTERNET: A CASE OF PHENOMENAL GROWTH

While Minitel shows one way a national data network can succeed as a result of a centralized governmental telecommunications policy, the Internet provides a decentralized model of a government subsidized network. The Internet is a world-wide, interconnected collection of computer networks. The Internet started in 1969 as the Arpanet, a military-sponsored research project on how to build reliable networks in the face of unreliable components. But over time, as additional research laboratories, universities, and even personal computer networks became connected to it, the Internet became an infrastructure for scientific and educational computing in the United States and in a significant portion of the world.

One of the Internet's main virtues is the fact that it lets a variety of heterogeneous computers connect to the network using a number of different communications options. The network operates on two core protocols, TCP and IP (Transmission Control Protocol and Internet Protocol). These protocols break a data stream into packets and give each packet a sequence number. IP is responsible for getting the packets from the sender to the receiver in the shortest possible time. TCP manages this flow of packets and verifies that the data are correct. There are more than 100 **TCP/IP** protocols based on the core protocols described above. As a result, computers from Sun workstations to personal computers to Macs can connect to the Net from a 2400 baud Radio Shack modem, a gigabit-per-second NSF sponsored line, or even through packet switched radio.

The Internet is not a single network. It is a collection of about 60,000 networks all having at least one server. Networks can be connected directly to one another, but most often they are linked through six official network access points in the U.S. Hundreds of service providers exchange traffic at these access points. A large service provider will have its own communications network. This network will include a number of local access points so customers can minimize their long distance charges. The service provider's backbone network connects all of its local access points to the Internet.

While the National Science Foundation originally subsidized the Net, costs today are shared by the largest users (universities, research and development companies, and government laboratories). In addition, these institutions supply labor in the form of highly paid professionals to maintain and upgrade the network. Institutions pay a flat rate to join the Internet and individuals in these organizations do not pay any fees. External access providers generally charge a flat rate for users to access the network in the range of $15–$20 per month.

While it is not known with any certainty how many users there are, in 1995 estimates were for over 6.6 million computers and over 37 million users in the U.S. and Canada. There are users in at least 150 countries. Recent estimates show the Internet is growing at the rate of a million users a month. Between 1991 and 1994, traffic on the Internet doubled annually. While scientists and engineers were early users, followed by academics, today the

Internet is available to commercial firms and to the general public. Table 12-1 shows the tremendous growth in commercial Internet domain names (service providers) for the Internet in the past few years.

Table 12-1
Internet Domain Names in 1995

Commercial domains .com	101908
Education domains .edu	2030
Network provider .net	5694
Nonprofits .org	8990

(*New York Times* 9/14/95)

The Task Force that manages the Internet is looking at new ways to generate IP addresses, an address that each computer on the net must have so that it can send and receive information. The Chinese would eventually like to have a billion IP addresses! By the year 2000, it will not just be 200 million computers trying to connect to the Internet, it will be *billions* of computers and the current addressing scheme is not adequate for such numbers.

You can connect directly to the Internet through an organization's computers. The domain name identifies the type of organization, for example, our address is first initial followed by last name@stern.nyu.edu. Edu is an educational institution, com a commercial firm, gov the government, and mil the military. With this kind of address your organization has a computer connected directly to the Net. From home, many people use access providers to reach the Net. Mass market services like Compuserve, America Online, and Prodigy all offer access to the Web.

There are also service providers who exist only to connect you with the Web and generally charge $10 to $20 a month for this service. The entry of AT&T into providing dial-up Internet connections has dramatically expanded the appeal of the Net. In November of 1994 the business volume of 800 (toll free) calls exceeded the volume of other business calls for the first time. AT&T wants to see that it captures data as well as voice calls through connections to the Internet on its Worldnet service. These access providers will also have to contend with cable TV companies planning to offer Internet access via cable modems. Since cable has a high bandwidth, it offers the potential for economical high-speed Internet access for home use.

The Arpanet was originally designed so scientists and others could conduct research on computer networking itself and gain access to remote computers and files. The government also wanted to tie together diverse networks developed for the military by various low bidders, each providing different equipment. Within months of the opening of the Arpanet, however, interpersonal communication in the form of electronic mail and computerized bulletin boards became the dominant application. Today there are approximately 8000 bulletin boards distributed across the Internet. On-line, real-time conferences in which users join a group and chat by passing text messages back and forth, are becoming increasingly popular. There are also various multi-user games for recreation.

Today on the Internet one finds a huge variety of applications and information sources. In Philadelphia, PCs provided reading-improvement courses over the Internet to 100 low-income homes in a recent test. No one signed up for classes when offered in the schools, but students and some parents eagerly registered when given the opportunity to use borrowed computers in the safety and privacy of their own homes. The Internet Talk Radio Show provides news and entertainment to users with audio software and speakers on their workstations. A project at NYU helped make the Securities and Exchange Commission EDGAR database of corporate findings available on the Internet. In 1995, one could find current weather maps for any region of the country, an on-line exhibit of items from the Vatican Library, art works from several museums, the complete Grateful Dead lyrics, photos of Cindy Crawford, to name a small set of services.

Government agencies post RFPs to Internet servers and contractors can file their bids electronically. There are a number of job postings available on the network and companies including AT&T list information about themselves on the Internet. Mead Data Central provides Internet access to its Lexis/Nexis database on a subscription basis.

The Internet is also used extensively to share and distribute software. Through anonymous FTP (file transfer protocol), a user can log on to a remote computer as a user with the name "anonymous," use his or her Internet address as a password, and transfer files from the remote computer to a local computer over the network. Dell distributes new versions of its software via the Internet as well as through other channels.

Business Week estimates there are 150 journals published electronically. Some scientists are calling for the elimination of paper journals since the

Checking by E-Mail

More than 20 large banks and IT companies have announced plans to develop an electronic check system for use over the Internet and other mass market services. The proposed system will let you pay bills and order merchandise on-line using electronic checks. You would be required to purchase a PCMCIA card for about $35 and a PC card reader. The PC cards will hold information to allow authorization, digital signatures, and an electronic check register.

It is estimated that banks spend more than $50 billion a year to process some 60 billion paper checks. This bank consortium will face considerable competition from charge cards like Visa International and Master Card, both of whom plan electronic networks. Visa has teamed with Microsoft and will offer a secure transaction standard for electronic payments.

Companies have been using EDI, including funds transfers, for a number of years. However, some electronic funds transfer for individuals will be required for electronic commerce to have an impact on individuals.

lead time for publication is so great. A large number of journals are posting their table of contents on the Internet and some hope to provide information that is not included in the printed version. There are some 50,000 peer-reviewed technical journals, a $4 billion industry. The threat of Internet publishing is very real to these businesses.

The Internet has been criticized for its difficulty of use, **Gopher** servers, the **World Wide Web**, Wide Area Information Services (**WAIS**), and the **browser's** interface are making the network easier to use. Anyone with an Internet address can download free gopher server and client software to set up an information resource. Many universities have created gophers which contain a hierarchical directory to information about various aspects of the school, such as, registration, general information, financial aid, libraries, schools, degrees, etc. Figure 12-3 shows the menu from the NYU IS Department Gopher Server. Anyone on the Internet with a gopher client program can access this information. One publishing firm has placed abstracts of all its products on a gopher server. Gophers can also be accessed by "net browsers" as described below which provide a graphical rather than character-oriented interface.

Wide Area Information Servers (WAIS) provide a distributed text-searching mechanism. Every document in a WAIS database must be indexed

Figure 12-3
A character-oriented Gopher display.

```
                    Internet Gopher Information Client v2.0.15

                        Stern-Wide Information Service

    - - >    1.  About SWIS, The Stern-Wide Information Service
             2.  General Information About the Stern Business School/
             3.  Announcements/
             4.  The Stern WWW Menu <HTML>
             5.  Calendars of Stern Events <HTML>
             6.  Student Information/
             7.  Academic Departments & Research Centers/
             8.  Computing Services/
             9.  Alumni/
            10.  Libraries, Book Centers, Phones Directories & N.Y.
                 Weather/
            11.  Whats New on SWIS/
            12.  NYU Campus Wide Information Services & Other Interesting
                 Gophers/
            13.  Stern WWW Server <HTML>


    Press ? for Help, q to Quit                              Page: 1/1
```

by contents, something done automatically by WAIS software. A user enters search text and WAIS looks for documents containing the words. A public domain version of WAIS can be used with gophers to provide a search capability.

Researchers at CERN in Geneva developed the World Wide Web (WWW) which connects a group of an estimated 30,000 network servers using the **Hypertext Transfer Protocol (HTTP)**. The Web uses hypertext links produced with the **Hypertext Markup Language (HTML)** to link documents and files. Hypertext is created by placing links on words to reference other sections of text or other documents. Clicking on a highlighted piece of text with a computer mouse results in the retrieval of a new file or document, allowing the user to browse through related pieces of information. The retrieved documents may all reside on different computers, but the Web makes all retrieval transparent to the user.

HTTP is a connectionless protocol which means that each client-server connection is limited to a single request for information. This way, the network is not tied up in a permanent connection between the client and server. (The disadvantage is that many connections may be made repeatedly to the same server to request information.) The Web is an excellent example of a client-server architecture—your computer is the client and you visit a variety of Web servers as you search for information. Figure 12-4(a) shows the HTML format of a document and Figure 12-4(b) shows the same document as it appears on the screen to a user running a Web browsing program.

To use the WWW, one needs an appropriate interface program or net browser. Many people feel browsers are responsible for some of the recent growth in net use. These programs work by "pointing and clicking" with a mouse, which is a vast improvement over character-based terminal access to the Internet. A browser connects users to different services, helping them navigate around the confusing and disorganized structure of the Internet. One can also use browsers to create forms and facilitate the publication of data. While not yet close to providing the kind of development environment for service providers one finds on Minitel, Web browsers are moving the Internet in the direction of greater ease-of-use.

Open standards have helped the Internet to grow and enable many people and organizations to become information providers. The World Wide Web, gopher servers, Web browsers, and WAIS clients all operate across many different types of platforms. What is the next likely direction for the Internet?

Two large cable TV operators are considering the use of their coaxial cable networks for providing high-speed access to the Internet while Motorola sells a cable modem for transmission at speeds of 10 megabits, some 700 times faster than over the typical voice-grade lines. About 26 million homes have cable TV and a PC, creating a large potential market for fast Net connections. High speed cable access would make the Net extremely attractive for home use, especially at prices projected to be $25 to $40 a month including modem rental.

Figure 12-4(a)

The hypertext (HTML) version.

```
<!doctype html public "-//IETF//DTD HTML//EN">
<HTML>

<HEAD>

<TITLE>The Department of Information Systems Homepage</TITLE>

</HEAD>

<BODY>
<H2><img align = top src=
"http://is-2.stern.nyu.edu/icons/is-icon.gif" >
The Department of Information Systems</H2>

<! This is a comment>

<P>
<I>Founded in 1973, Stern's Department of Information Systems was one
of the first such departments in a business school. </I><HR>
<P>

<A HREF="http://is-2.stern.nyu.edu/istemp/hcurrent.html" >Current
Events:</A> Affiliates Semin
<P>
<A HREF="http://is-2.stern.nyu.edu/istemp/hresearc.html"
>Research:</A>
The Center for Research in Information Systems, Affiliates
Program, Research Projects and Working Papers
<P>
<A HREF="http://is-2.stern.nyu.edu/istemp/hprogram.html" >Academic
Programs:
</A>The Undergraduate, MBA, PhD and M.S. in Information Systems
Programs
<P>
<A HREF="http://is-2.stern.nyu.edu/istemp/hcourses.html" >Courses:
</A>Undergraduate and Graduate Bulletin Descriptions and Course
Outlines
<P>
<A HREF="http://is-2.stern.nyu.edu/cgi-bin/course-database.pl?request=
teachers" >People:
</A>Faculty, Doctoral Students and Staff Home Pages.

<P>
<A HREF="http://is-2.stern.nyu.edu/istemp/hstudent.html" >Student
Activities:
</A> IS Club, IMA Club, Job Opportunities, Information for Companies
<P>
<A HREF="http://is-2.stern.nyu.edu/istemp/hdept.html" >Department
```

Figure 12-4(a)
(continued)

```
Information:</A> Department
<P>


<A HREF="http://is-2.stern.nyu.edu/istemp/hitcase.html" > IT Case
Abstracts</A>
<P>


<A HREF="http://is-2.stern.nyu.edu/istemp/hisrev.html" >Stern IS
Review:
</A>MBA Student Journal (Electronic)
<P>
<A HREF="http://edgar.stern.nyu.edu" >The EDGAR Project: </A>Access
to SEC filings of over 3,000 companies
<P>


<A HREF="http://edgar.stern.nyu.edu/web95/214.html">
<img src="http://is-2.stern.nyu.edu/icons/icon.new.gif"
align=middle border=0> Our Site Uses En
<P>
<img src="http://is-2.stern.nyu.edu/icons/yellowball.gif">
Portions of this site have been designed using the
<A HREF= "http://irss.njit.edu:5080/papers/isakowitz/isakowitz.html">
Relationship Management Methodology</A> for structured hypermedia
applications
<A HREF="http://is-2.stern.nyu.edu/~tisakowi/ps-files/rmd.ps">
     (Postcript 1,181 K)</A>
<HR>
We hope you find this server interesting;
<A HREF="ftp://is-7.stern.nyu.edu/pub/count.txt">
<img src="http://is-2.stern.nyu.edu/cgi-bin/count.xbm">
</a>have since January 19, 1995.
<P>


<ADDRESS>
Information Systems Department<BR>
Stern School of Business, New York University<BR>
44 W. 4th St., New York, NY 10012-1126, USA<BR>
Tel: +1 (212) 998-0800<BR>
Fax: +1 (212) 995-4228<BR>
Department WWW Home Page: http://is-2.stern.nyu.edu/<BR>


<P>Please direct all correspondence regarding the Stern School
Information Systems WWW Server to
<A HREF="http://is-2.stern.nyu.edu/comment-form.html">
the Webmaster.
bpadmana@stern.nyu.edu</a>


</ADDRESS>
<HR>
```

Figure 12-4(a)
(continued)

```
<h2>
<a href="http://www.stern.nyu.edu/">Stern</a> |
<a href="http://www.nyu.edu">NYU</A>
<p></h2>
</BODY>


</HTML>
```

Figure 12-4(b)
The document as it appears on the first screen.

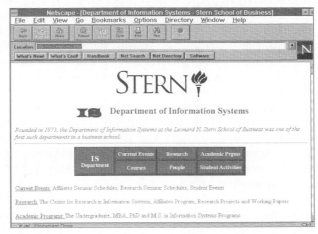

The Origins of the Web

"... A couple of years ago, there was no Web. Suddenly it's ubiquitous. And if ubiquity weren't enough, it's still growing.

Where did the Web come from? ... One day there was nothing; the next day there it was, fully deployed.

My first suspicion of something born so instantaneously perfect is an alien origin. There was probably a meeting somewhere on a distant planet where they debated whether or not it was time for Earth to have the Web. 'They'll only botch it up,' the opponents probably argued. 'They'll put all kinds of garbage on it and ruin our good idea.'

But the alien proponents and supporters of the Web carried the day. 'The Earth has all kinds of talented people eager to get their material out to the public,' they undoubtedly said. 'Wonderful things will happen; just wait and see.'

... Whatever its origin, the Web is here, and it is changing our view of information, society, and business. Perhaps most importantly, it is proving the efficacy of the long believed and hoped-for *Field of Dreams* approach–if we build it, they will come. The people of the earth have been empowered by the Web, and there has been an incredible outpouring of creativity and professionalism by amateurs everywhere. ... When you empower a few amateurs, it's not much competition. But when you empower tens of millions, surprising things happen, some of them breathtakingly good."

—Robert Lucky, e-mail: rlucky@bellcore.com

There is currently a raging debate between visionaries who see the Internet as the next era of computing, and those who see the Net as an important, but not revolutionary advance. The visionaries argue that so much information, software, and multimedia content will be available through the Internet, especially given Java's ability to share programs easily and safely, that no one will need a PC. (For a review of **Java**, a language that lets one distribute programs from servers to client computers on the Internet which clients execute interpretively, see the side bar in Chapter 9.) Sun Microsystems, the developer of Java, and **Netscape**, a company that provides Web servers and browsers, have developed an alliance to market a scripting language called Javascript. A knowledgeable computer user, not a professional programmer, should be able to develop programs in Javascript. If this concept works, then the number applications on the Internet could expand manyfold. Sun Microsystems and Netscape have convinced a group of thirty companies to endorse the technology.

The most extreme view is that the Net will lead to the demise of Intel and Microsoft. There will be cheap, stripped PCs without hard disks or many features at all and users will obtain all software and services over the Internet. Acorn, a UK computer company, is planning to offer a stripped down, "net" computer, possibly a machine using the British ARM chip found in the Apple Newton manufactured by Advanced RISC Machines, Ltd. This chip is supposedly as powerful as a midrange Intel 486, but is smaller, consumes less power, and costs only $20. The chip uses its own operating system, loaded from ROM chips, so a vendor does not have to pay Microsoft a licensing fee for an operating system. Some analysts are skeptical that Acorn can sell the "Netsurfer" computer profitably for $500 and others question whether there is a market for it even at this price.

MANAGEMENT PROBLEM 12-2

California Runner is a mail-order company that sells athletic equipment, primarily for running and jogging. The product line includes clothing and, naturally, a large variety of shoes. The company processes orders that arrive via the mail, fax, or an 800 number. Almost 90% of the orders are by phone. The company uses UPS or Federal Express to deliver its products all over the U.S.

The president of the company, Jim Fleet, observed the Minitel system in France and was impressed by the extent customers used it to order merchandise and do home banking. "The future will be to sell over electronic networks, however I am very concerned about payments mechanisms and security. If customers are worried about the theft or unauthorized use of their credit card numbers, how can we be successful with electronic ordering? I think the Internet is more secure than using your credit card in a restaurant or giving it to us over an 800 number, but customers don't see things that way."

In order to help California Runner, investigate some of the different payments mechanisms available to users of the Internet. What are their pros and cons? What are the risks for the customer and the merchant? What do you recommend to Fleet?

Opposing the view that the WWW will lead to the end of Intel and Microsoft are those who feel the cost of powerful computers is so low that users will not give up local programs and storage on their PCs and rely solely on the Net. As with many arguments, there may be room for both points of view. Dedicated PC users will probably continue to buy ever more powerful machines. For some who have no interest in local computing, there will be "Internet appliances" that provide access to the Net, probably through the cable TV network, with a keyboard attached to a monitor that also serves as a television set.

In summary, the Internet was launched with government subsidies for the network and terminals that helped it become established. For most early users, the network appeared to be a free good. Early use of the network focused on interpersonal communications and the sharing of programs and information. Unlike Minitel, the Internet was first used by academics and scientists. Only in the last few years has use by the general public been growing. Business use on Minitel began immediately while it is a recent phenomenon on the Internet. The Internet's open standards allowed many users and service providers to connect. The network has an open, decentralized and extendible architecture. The Net's open culture and free exchange of software encourages users and providers. Products like gopher servers, Web browsers (e.g. **MOSAIC** and Netscape), and browsers from mass market networks like America Online and Prodigy are making the network

Finding Things on the Web

One of the major problems with the World Wide Web is finding information as there is no central directory. However, there are a half dozen or more organizations on the Web itself that offer **"search engines."** Many of these services are free and they all search based on keywords that you supply. The search engine looks through index pages that a program creates by wandering through the Web. In late 1995, the following search engines were some of the ones available:

Name	Database	Address
Yahoo!	85,000 pages	http://www.yahoo.com
Lycos	8 million pages	http://www.lycos.cs.cmu.edu
Webcrawler	250,000 pages	http://www.webcrawler.com
Open Text	1 million pages	http://opentext.com
InfoSeek Net Search	1 million pages	http://www.infoseek.com

A powerful search engine is also offered by Digital Equipment and is called Altavista. The Altavista server is a parallel machine with several alpha processors. These processors go out in parallel to look for the search target. See http://www.altavista.digital.com/

interface far more pleasant. A spate of articles on the information super-highway, "cyberspace," and the Internet (including a cartoon in the *New Yorker*) have made a network connection highly fashionable. All of these factors have led to the critical mass needed for the network to succeed.

Intranets Internet technology is having a major impact on companies through networks called "intranets" as opposed to Internets. A firm sets up servers and clients following Internet protocols and distributes a web browser to its users. The network is probably not connected to the Internet, rather it is used to publish information internally within the company. This information is likely to be proprietary so the company does not want other Internet users to have access to it. For example, Morgan Stanley, an investment bank, has an extensive Intranet and encourages its employees to publish all of their work on it. That way any member of the firm with a browser can access information like research reports on a company or industry.

It is estimated that 40 percent of the largest U.S. firms are developing or have Intranets. While most of the information on Intranets is textual, one could make some transactions information available as well. If these data become widely available, we can envision an environment in which most employees in a company have access to all of the information they need through one, common browser interface.

THE POTENTIAL OF ELECTRONIC COMMERCE

Starting around 1993, companies became enamored of the Internet. During the next few years, thousands of companies set up **"home pages"** on the Web. A home page is a starting place for someone seeking information. For example, you can create your own personal home page that gives a reader information about you. Prodigy and other services help you create and store your home page.

Similarly, companies create home pages with links to other information. Figure 12-5 shows the home page for General Electric Plastics along with several pages accessed through links on the home page. This particular set of pages is well-designed. The user can quickly access technical information about GE Plastics. A URL or universal resource locator is an address or link to a home page. These links begin with http:// which stands for hypertext transfer protocol. Sometimes the // is followed by www, a period, and then the address of the individual or company. For example, the home page for the Stern School is found at http://www.stern.nyu.edu. Table 12-2 lists home pages that you may want to explore.

What opportunities does the Internet offer for Electronic Commerce—for facilitating trading relationships among companies and between individual

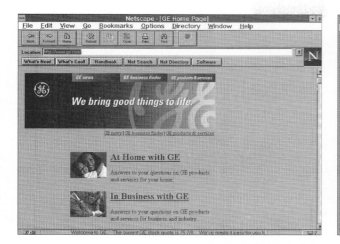

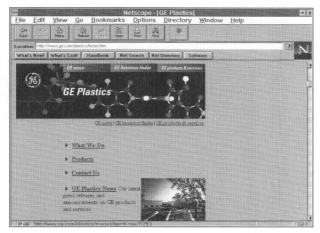

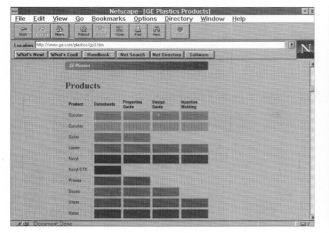

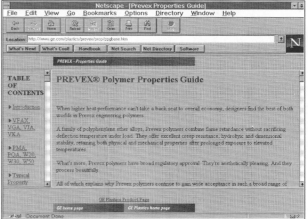

Figure 12-5 Browse through GE's Web server to find characteristics of its Plastics Division products.

Table 12-2
Some Universal Resource Locators for the World Wide Web (URLs).

Category	Information/Service	URL
Investment	Lombard Brokerage on-line trading and research	http://www.lombard.com/
	Dreyfus Capital Management—prospectus	http://www/dreyfus.com/
	Fidelity Investments—graphical performance of funds and links to other information	http://www.fid-inv.com/
Automobiles	Dealer Net—window shopping for cars	http://www.dealernet.com/
	BMW—information on cars and European delivery	http://www.bmwusa.com/
	Mercedes Benz—information on models	http://www.daimler-benz.com/mb/mb_e.html
Venture capital	Accel Partners	http://www.accel.com/
	Olympic Venture Partners	http://product.com/olympic/
Jobs	Online CareerCenter	http://www.occ.com/
Securities information	EDGAR data filed with SEC on NYU server	http://edgar.stern.nyu.edu/
Stern at NYU	Programs and faculty plus other information	http://www.stern.nyu.edu/
	The author's home page	http://is-2.stern.nyu.edu/~hlucas/
Government	The President and Vice President	http://www.whitehouse.gov/

customers and companies? There are a number of ways companies are experimenting with use of the Net including:

- As a universal electronic mail system. Various proprietary systems all have "gateways" to the Internet. If you use America Online and a friend is on the Internet, you can send mail to him or her.
- Posting information on the company and its products as we have seen in Figure 12-5.
- Using the Internet to allow customers to make specific inquiries. Figure 12-6 shows the Federal Express pages for letting customers inquire about the status of a package. Using a "forms" program, Federal Express lets the customer input a package identification number; then the FedEx

Table 12-2   *(continued)*

Category	Information/Service	URL
General Net news	Government, education, and other news	http://www.gnn.com/
Dilbert	Comics	http://www.unitedmedia.com/comics/dilbert/
Companies	IBM	http://www.ibm.com/
	American Stock Exchange	http://www.amex.com/
	AT&T	http://www.att.com/
	Compaq	http://compaq.com/
	DEC	http://www.digital.com/
	Hewlett Packard	http://www.hp.com/
	Intel	http://www.intel.com/
	Jack Daniels Distillery Tour	http://www.infi.net/jack Daniels/
	Kodak	http://www.kodak.com/
	Lotus	http://www.lotus.com/
	MCI	http://www.mci.com/
	Microsoft	http://www.microsoft.com/
	Miller Genuine Draft	http://mgdtaproom.com/
	Novell	http://www.novell.com/
	Oracle	http://www.oracle.com/
	Sony	http://www.sony.com/
	Sun Microsystems	http://www.sun.com/
	Sybase	http://www.sybase.com/
Sailing	Sailing information	http://www.sailnet.com/

Please note that addresses change often on the Web—you can always use a search engine to look for one of these sites if its URL has changed since publication of the book.

Web server looks up the status of the package and displays it for the customer. FedEx also gives large clients software to link to its tracking computers. In May of 1995 customers tracked 90,000 packages through FedEx's Web site. Customers now do 60 percent of package tracking using a software connection to FedEx's tracking computer and/or the Web connection. This approach clearly saves money for FedEx and for UPS, which also has a package tracking application on the Web.

- As a way to distribute software. Hewlett Packard uses a Web site to distribute revisions for its Unix operating system and new software for its printers. Customers download the software using the Web.

- To give customers information about their relationship with the company on the Web. Wells Fargo Bank in San Francisco gives customers Internet

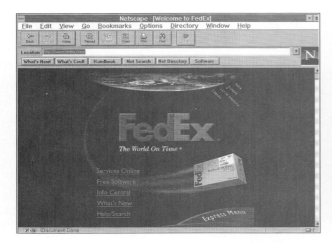

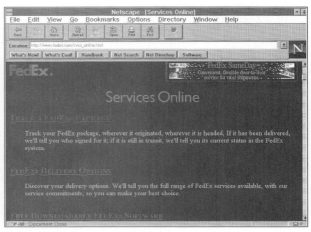

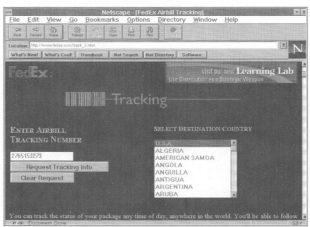

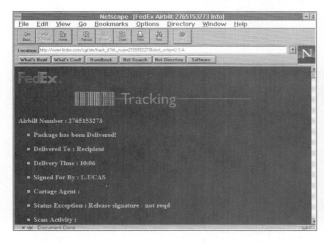

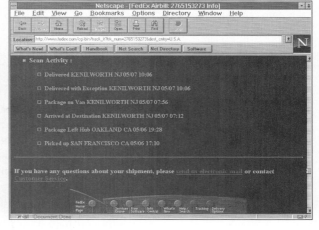

Figure 12-6 Package tracking with FedEx.

access to transactions histories in their checking and savings accounts as well as information on current balances.

- Electronic Data Interchange. The CommerceNet consortium described earlier in the chapter is an example of using the Internet for EDI among companies.

- The purchase and sale of goods and services. This kind of Internet application is starting as several companies offer ways to make "secure" purchases without having to send a credit card number over the Net.

To date, sales of merchandise through the Internet and other mass market networks have been disappointing. One observer speculated that the reason was the failure of companies to offer discounts for products bought electronically. Many retailers maintain a "one price" policy, even though it is much cheaper for them to process an electronic order than other types. The other reason often given for relatively slow sales is the lack of a secure payments mechanism, though companies are developing solutions for this problem.

Many of us expect the Internet to become the "information super-highway" that has been promoted by government officials and others. The range of applications for the Net seems only limited by your imagination and creativity. A relatively high-speed network that spans most of the globe is available at a very reasonable cost. What will you do with it?

The Internet Versus the Government

The Internet has succeeded in confusing a large number of elected and appointed (many self-appointed) political leaders around the world. It is very difficult to regulate the Net since it is a rather amorphous collection of networked computers. U.S. Senators and Congressmen are very concerned about pornography on the Net, yet it is very hard to monitor a stream of digits to know that it is a pornographic image. A provider could simply move a server off shore, out of range of U.S. regulations, in response to any laws trying to regulate the Net.

This same problem applies to countries with regimes that try to control information available to the public, for example, the Peoples Republic of China and Saudi Arabia. In Saudi Arabia, Net users have explored topics like sex, religion and politics—all subjects not often discussed in public. The Saudis are caught in a bind. They want to become technologically sophisticated, but are concerned about the ability of the Net to undermine their strict regime. Business leaders want access to the Net, making it difficult to restrict its use.

Thousands of Saudis dial into the Internet in neighboring countries or through the U.S. They debate taboo topics from atheism to pornography beyond the reach of authorities. Even fundamentalists debate with Western atheists over the Net. The Gulf societies are very closed so the idea of a free exchange of ideas tempts a lot of residents.

The Internet has made possible something that would be very dangerous to do in a group of people, by voice on the phone, or on paper. Its impact on governments will be fascinating to watch over the next decade.

THE IMPACT OF NETWORKS

The existence of networks has the potential to transform the way organizations work. Networks facilitate the development of new kinds of business, business which uses the network to implement the IT-design variables discussed here. Kambil and Short (1994) have studied the impact of electronic filing on the tax preparation industry.

In 1990, the Internal Revenue Service (IRS) began an electronic tax return filing program nationwide. Return preparers or filers authorized by the IRS could transmit an individual return to the IRS electronically. The system returns a receipt and the filer can arrange for a direct deposit of any refund. Eventually this system has the potential to affect 100 million individual taxpayers. Some 75 million of these payers receive an average refund check of $900.

Agents on the Network

An agent is an intelligent piece of software that a user programs to perform some task. As an example, you might instruct your agent to search a network for vendors offering a VCR that has slow motion, four heads, stereo sound, and costs under $400. The agent should report back to you the stores, prices and characteristics of the six lowest priced versions it finds.

Another useful agent would be one that took your order to buy a share of stock and hovered in a broker's network until the stock reached a price you had indicated. Then the agent would execute the transaction. You might also appreciate an agent that could weed out junk messages in your electronic mailbox. **Agents** are a relatively new phenomenon spawned by the emergence of networks. They appear to have a bright future making it easier for users to obtain the resources of a network.

Agents are considered to be an important component of *electronic commerce;* they should facilitate buying and selling over computer networks. In electronic commerce, you will have supply agents that provide information to demand agents, an agent sent out with a request as described above. Sometimes agents are called "softbots" like their mechanical robot counterparts.

An agent will have some or all of the following characteristics:

- Autonomy: the agent takes initiative and follows its instructions without user intervention.

- Goal-oriented: the agent accepts requests and acts on them—it decides how to achieve the user's goal.

- Flexible: the agent does not follow a script, but decides dynamically what actions to take.

- Communications capability: an agent can engage in complex communications to achieve its goals.

- Mobility: the agent can transport itself from one machine to another across a network.

While it may be a while before we have personal robots to clean house and do the laundry, software agents should be making life easier for us in the very near future.

About 40 million people use professional tax preparation services. H&R Block has over a third of this market and is considered a "commodity" preparer. There are also individual or small CPA firms and large accounting firms who do tax preparation work. Finally there are investment services firms who will prepare returns for high-income individuals.

This initiative by the Internal Revenue Service has created new roles in the tax preparation industry. There are now electronic filers, communications network providers, software vendors, consumer credit providers, to name a few. An example of a new initiative promoted by electronic filing is the instant refund. An electronic filer, the tax preparer, and credit provider create a refund anticipation loan. When the electronic return is transmitted, the IRS checks its accuracy. Given this verification, the credit provider issues a loan against the security of the anticipated IRS refund. The return can even mandate that the refund go directly to the credit provider. One New York bank offers a three- to five-day no-interest refund advance along with electronic filing to its customers for a $45 fee.

By stimulating electronic linking, new relationships can be formed in the industry. Information on a tax return gathered by the tax preparer can be communicated to a tax planner. The planner creates customized investment portfolios to reduce future tax liabilities. These portfolio recommendations can be sent electronically to an investment broker.

Another possibility enabled by electronically linking the tax preparer with the IRS is for a retailer to provide consumer credit through an instant refund linked to a store credit card. The retailer, in partnership with a tax preparer, might arrange for a discount on tax preparation or for store discounts if the refund is directed to the customer's store credit card account.

This networking initiative by the IRS, undertaken to try and improve its capabilities for processing returns, creates new opportunities for a variety of businesses. It encourages electronic communications and linking among those involved in tax preparation and electronic customer/supplier relations (the IRS considers us to be its "customers"). This example illustrates some of the benefits that accrue from networks.

Networks and electronic commerce may also have a dramatic impact on a number of industries. What would happen to companies in wholesaling and retailing if manufacturers and customers could establish direct electronic links with each other? What would the impact be of driving transactions costs in markets to almost zero through commerce on the Internet? Will there be a need for publishers in the future, or will we pay a small per page "usage" fee to access books on the Net. The emergence of the Net and WWW offer tremendous opportunties for as well as threats to traditional businesses.

Implications

The development of a national network infrastructure in the U.S. that features high-speed communications of mixed media, openness, published standards, and ubiquitous access should help firms in a number of ways. In particular, it would facilitate the development of the T-Form organization discussed in earlier chapters which relies so heavily on electronic communications for its structure and operations.

What can a company do to achieve the benefits of networking? One solution, of course, is to build your own. You can also explore the Internet as a place to do business, as many firms are today.

Another option is to form an alliance with a provider. EDS has supplied an estimated 50,000 networks to its customers. This services firm takes responsibility for setting up the network and operating it if the customer so wishes. EDS's own network, EDSNet, is the world's largest corporate data network. The company has an estimated $1 billion invested in it. EDSNet links 500,000 workstations and terminals, 95 data centers containing 142 mainframe computers, and 15,000 satellite dishes in 30 countries. The net handles over 50 million transactions a day and has a storage capacity of nearly 50 trillion pieces of data.

EDSNet helped the company reduce the number of layers of management through technological leveling. In 1989 the company reduced the number of levels between the customer and the chief executive from seven to three, in the process forming 38 autonomous business units. EDS uses the network to form virtual task forces for bidding on contracts. The entire resources of the firm can be made available to any business unit. The network can also be used to train employees on new technology. In one class 800 EDS engineers attended a half-day briefing on a new software product in 125 different classrooms linked by the network.

There is no need to wait to obtain the benefits of networking. A firm can use its own resources, form an alliance with an outside contractor, or use the Internet to develop extensive electronic links.

MANAGEMENT PROBLEM 12-3

The IRS electronic filing system is a great success from the standpoint of an innovative use of networking technology. Filing and processing taxes is a labor and paper-intensive process. Electronic commerce offers an opportunity to dramatically improve tax collection, something we all pay for with our taxes!

The first efforts at electronic filing, however, ran into some serious fraud problems. Individuals committed this fraud by using "borrowed" or nonexistent social security numbers and flooding the system with refund requests electronically. From a management and technology standpoint, what steps need to be taken to prevent this kind of fraud which threatens the entire program?

CHAPTER SUMMARY

1. The telephone network offers great ubiquity and connectivity. Computer networks are striving to reach its level of ease of use.

2. A company that wants to develop a network is faced with a variety of choices. In many instances large firms have designed their own, proprietary networks.

3. The common carriers are offering services so using a network looks just like using the phone system. You rely on a common carrier for almost all parts of the communications.

4. Industries have tried to develop standards for EDI. The electronic interchange of information is expanding rapidly in industries such as retailing, transportation, and insurance.

5. There are a number of commercial, mass market services in the U.S. and abroad. The mass market services help business by making its products and services available to the public. However, these networks are not a substitute for an internal, company network for carrying voice and data.

6. There has been much talk of a national network infrastructure or "information superhighway." The French Minitel system was the first example of an information highway, and it offers a number of options for businesses.

7. The Internet, based in the U.S., is a network of networks. The development of the World Wide Web and browsers have contributed to the exponential growth of the Internet.

8. Companies are rushing to put "home pages" and detailed information about themselves and their products on the Internet. They are also investigating electronic commerce using the Net.

9. Networks provide connectivity. They help transform the organization by connecting it to customers, suppliers, and alliance partners. The impact of greater connectivity will be to increase the pace of change in organization structure.

IMPLICATIONS FOR MANAGEMENT

The 1990s will go down in history as the decade of the network. The Internet has exploded during this period, moving from a net primarily of educators and researchers to a network of business applications. The Internet offers companies the ability to provide multimedia information to internal employees, customers, and anyone else interested in the firm. As a manager, networks in general and the Internet in particular offer you another powerful tool for managing and communicating information. This technology reduces the impact of distance and time while dramatically increasing the speed of access for information. The ability for users to input data means they can search information and order products through the Internet. The Internet is rapidly becoming the mechanism for connecting organizations and individuals throughout the world.

KEY WORDS

America Online
ANSI X.12
Browser
CommerceNet
Compuserve
Computer network
Gopher
HTTP (hypertext transfer protocol)
HTML (hypertest markup language)
Home page
EDI
Electronic commerce

Java
Microsoft Network
Minitel
MOSAIC
Network
Netscape
Prodigy
TCP/IP
Ubiquity
WAIS
World Wide Web

RECOMMENDED READING

Lucas, H. C., Jr., H. Levecq, R. Kraut, and L. Streeter. "Minitel: The French National Information Highway," *IEEE Spectrum,* November 1995, pp. 71-77.

Kambil, Ajit, and James Short. "Electronic Integration and Business Network Redesign: A Roles-Linkage Perspective," *JMIS,* Spring 1994.

DISCUSSION QUESTIONS

1. What advantages does the telephone system offer as a model for a network?
2. Why have companies developed so many proprietary networks?
3. Why are EDI standards hard to develop? Why will one standard not serve across industries?
4. What industries are most likely to be able to take advantage of EDI?
5. How do networks contribute to the development of the T-Form organization?

6. What IT organization design variables are affected by networks?

7. What is the appeal of mass market networks?

8. What services to business do mass market networks offer?

9. What are the problems with completing transactions over these networks, i.e. providing your credit card number after ordering merchandise?

10. Why has the French Minitel system been such a success?

11. What was the role of the French Government in developing Minitel?

12. Describe the World Wide Web. How can a word or phrase in something you are reading on the screen result in your being connected to another computer that has more information about that term or phrase?

13. Why are people putting so much information on the Internet, information that they are not likely to ever receive payment for from readers? Is this behavior strange from an economic standpoint?

14. What is a Web browser? How have browsers contributed to the growth of the WWW?

15. Pick a specific company and describe how it might make use of the Internet.

16. Do you think that PCs and the services available from mass market networks and the Internet pose a threat to television?

17. Electronic filing of tax returns was plagued with fraud. How do you think one could defraud the system and what could be done to prevent it?

18. What is the role of the government in stimulating the development of a national network infrastructure?

19. The Internet reaches most countries in Europe and Asia and the Americas. Connections are more spotty in the Middle East and Africa. What are the implications today for a country being "off the net"?

20. There are concerns over pornography on the Internet while authoritarian countries worry about the free flow of ideas on the Net. Is there any way to regulate information content on the Internet? Is it desirable to do so?

CHAPTER **13**

Information Technology Architectures

● OBJECTIVES

1. Learning to manage information technology.

One of the key decisions managers must make is determining what hardware and software architecture the organization should use. Then you must manage this architecture as the equipment is expanded. This chapter describes hardware and software architectures and presents a number of examples to help you in this design and management task. While it is easy to be fascinated with the newest technology, it is important to remember that IT exists to support management's objectives.

2. Preparing to apply technology.

Years ago, it was possible to develop systems without concern about what equipment might be used to execute them. Today, the architecture in place influences the design of a system. A client-server application looks different to the user than a system run exclusively on a mainframe. We discuss the logical design of systems and suggest that, at the highest level, design should be independent of the computer involved. However, at some point in design, you have to decide on the platform for providing the system to users.

3. Transforming the organization.

The basic architecture of the firm will influence the kind of systems that are developed and the types of linkages you develop with other organizations. As you read about airline reservation systems, broker workstations, and the Chevron client-server architecture in this chapter, think about the potential of these three different kinds of architecture to make dramatic changes in organizations.

In the early days, designers were advised to develop systems without consideration of the hardware or software that would be used to run the system. Design, after all, should be independent of hardware and software. Of course, available hardware and software had to influence how a system would operate. For example, a designer could not design an on-line system if the computer running the system was capable only of batch processing.

Beyond gross characteristics like batch or on-line, however, design could be independent of hardware and software. Part of the reason for this independence was designers worked with mainframe computers of differing sizes. In the 1970s, minicomputers became very popular as departmental machines or computers to be used in applications where the power of a mainframe was not needed. Most minicomputers came with time-sharing operating systems, and the natural tendency was to design on-line applications for them.

In the early 1980s the personal computer proliferated and changed the way users thought about information systems. Extremely sophisticated and powerful packages are available for these computers. The packages feature elaborate graphical user interfaces with pop-up windows, mice for input, multiple windows on the screen, and so on. Personal computers made users more familiar with computing and raised their expectations about how information systems should perform. They also created a lot of dissatisfaction with mainframe and minicomputer systems developed in-house by the firm's own staff.

Clearly, the task of developing the architecture for an organization's computing system is difficult. If an organization is starting from scratch, one could conceive of buying a large computer, a midsized machine, or a network of personal computers. The question of which option to choose may require a major study and considerable effort. The organization that already has a number of computers in place must decide how to manage and expand its systems as users come up with new needs and ideas for computing.

WHAT IS HARDWARE AND SOFTWARE ARCHITECTURE?

Architecture is the place where all of the technical topics we discussed so far come together. An organization's architecture includes:

- Computers, often of different sizes from different manufacturers.
- Operating systems, frequently more than one.
- Languages for developing applications.
- Database management programs.
- Packaged applications software.
- Networks ranging from those within a department to an international, private network to the Internet.

Beyond the technology, architecture also includes considerations of the way the organization processes information, particularly at the location processing takes place. We might ask the following questions to characterize a firm's architecture:

- Where is processing done? What computer among a group of computers processes information?
- Where are data stored for access by users?
- Where are data updated?
- What is the user interface? Where do the interface programs run?
- What capabilities for data analysis does the user have? Is there local intelligence?
- What networks are in use including Intranets?
- What is the firm's presence on the Internet?

Just as there are many types of buildings, there are different types of information systems architectures. Table 13-1 provides examples of five architectures that are fairly easy to characterize. There are also many examples of mixed architectures, but generally they include the cases in Table 13-1.

Table 13-1 characterizes architectures according to several criteria:

- *Volume of processing.* The volume of information processed may determine the kind of architecture needed.
- *Database.* The amount of data storage available on each class of computer is increasing, but in general more data still can be stored on larger computers.
- *Interface.* What kind of user interface is generally associated with a given option?
- *Number of users.* How many users can the architecture support?
- *Discretion.* How much processing and ad hoc analysis can the user do on his or her own?

Table 13-1
Typical Architectures

Option	Volume	Database	Interface	Number of users	Discretion
Mainframes	High-volume transactions processing	Large	Simple character-oriented	Large	Limited
Midrange Fault-tolerant	Medium-volume transactions. Designed for OLTP	Medium to large	Simple character-oriented	Moderate number	Limited
PCs and Workstations	Low	Medium to small. User may input and download all data	Elaborate workstation	One at a time	Extensive
LANs	Low to medium	Medium to small. Download capability	Elaborate workstation	Multiple	Extensive
Client-server	Varied	Small to large	Elaborate workstation	Multiple	Extensive

Mainframes for High Volume

The first option in Table 13-1 is the **mainframe**, the traditional machine for developing applications. Today, mainframes are used for very high volume transactions processing. American Express authorizes purchases for holders of the American Express card when a merchant calls to determine if American Express will agree to the charge. This high-volume application to access credit records and decide on approving the charge resides on mainframe computers (see Figure 13-1).

Mainframes are also associated with extremely large databases. It is not unusual for organizations like banks and insurance companies to have data files that contain many billions of characters (gigabytes). These firms have entire rooms filled with disk drives containing important data that are on-line for inquiry and updating.

Mainframe applications typically feature a large number of users of the data. These machines are designed to manage huge communications **networks** in which users using remote terminals access the mainframe and its databases. However, what the user can do is fairly limited. Typically, certain functions are made available to each user. Although it is theoretically possible, most mainframe systems do not provide extensive data manipulation features to users.

Thus, the user's discretion is often limited. However, in transactions processing applications, designers usually do not want the user to have more than limited capabilities. It is not a good idea for a reservation agent to analyze flight data; that job should be done by the marketing or operations department of the airline. The transactions processing system is an operational system, not a system for analysis and reflection.

As discussed in Chapter 8, it appears that manufacturers of mainframes and minis are rushing to develop large computers that consist of multiple versions of popular chips. A good example is NCR, a former subsidiary of AT&T spun off to its stockholders, who is selling mainframes that consist of groups of Intel processors. NCR says that a unit of processing power on its new multiple-chip machines costs about one-eighth of what the same unit costs on one of its conventional, old-line mainframes.

Figure 13-1
The mainframe and midrange architecture.

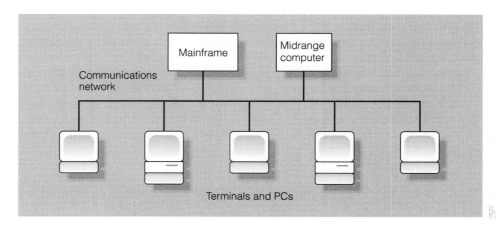

The Midrange Computer Is (Usually) Smaller

Much of the previous discussion also applies to the second option in Table 13-1, except for a **minicomputer** or midrange system generally features lower volumes of data and smaller databases. The demarcation between mainframe and midrange, however, is not always easy. Some midsized computers with extremely high transactions processing speeds are designed specifically for **on-line transaction processing (OLTP)** applications. **Midrange computers** are also used extensively in data communications systems.

To enhance the attractiveness of mid-sized computers in OLTP, several vendors introduced the concept of fault tolerance, or fail-safe operations. Tandem manufactures a line of computers called NonStop—each component is duplicated and all data are written to two different disk drives. Because organizations tend to depend on their OLTP applications, fault-tolerant computers are very attractive. The New York Stock Exchange uses a number of Tandem computers for processing transactions and the American Stock Exchange uses a Stratus computer, another fault-tolerant machine, to update stock quotations.

The PC Is Totally Different

When the personal computer first arrived, users treated it as a computer that belonged to them. Much of the early motivation for using PCs was to get away from the traditional information services (IS) department. The IS department has the reputation of being unresponsive and slow to develop applications. With his or her own computer, the user could become independent of IS (see Figure 13-2).

At first there was hardly any software for PCs. But, entrepreneurs soon saw tremendous opportunities in the eventual market of millions of computers with each owner buying the right package. Of course, the package for the PC had to be a lot different from the package for the mainframe or mini. First, a user not a technology professional, would evaluate and use

MANAGEMENT PROBLEM 13-1

ABZ manufactures electronic components. For many years it relied on a mainframe computer complex. The company has several divisions and a dozen plants. Right now some customers need to know which plant makes the product they want to order. A strategic goal for marketing is having the company appear as a single entity to the customer. Senior management feels that it is necessary to centralize order processing so customers can call one number to place their orders for any product ABZ makes.

The plants are not completely happy with this idea. They would like to have midrange computers or client-server systems of their own. One plant manager said, "We may have to download some production plans from the mainframe at headquarters, but we want to control our own plant systems right here. In addition, our production processes are getting more and more automated. It just makes more sense to do things locally where we know what is going on."

What kind of architecture can you recommend for ABZ? Does your architecture resolve the conflicts between centralized and local computing?

Figure 13-2
A personal computer architecture.

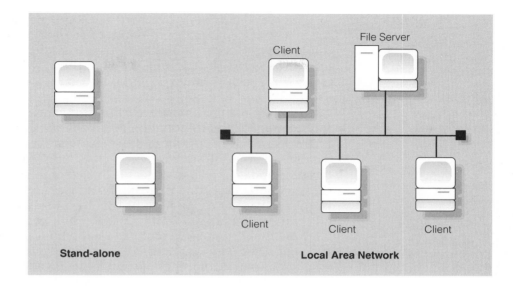

Client

File Server

Client

Client   Client   Client

Stand-alone   **Local Area Network**

the PC package. The program had to be easy to use with a pleasant interface, giving rise to the term user friendly, as opposed to user surly in-house custom systems. The packages had to be easy to use because the vendor could not afford to provide training for a package that cost less than $500.

Users controlled the first PCs and generally entered their own data for analysis. The most popular uses of PCs are word processing, spreadsheet analysis, presentation graphics and database management, though the number of applications packages continues to expand rapidly. User control not only frees the user from dependence on the systems staff, it also provides extensive discretion of what program runs at what time on a computer. Since the computer is not shared, the user can choose when and what to run and has unheard-of freedom.

Of course, the PC seemed too good to be true. The first problem that came up was the user wanted data that was not easily available. The user might have data provided on a mainframe system, but could not get a machine-readable version of the data to the PC. Many organizations found users had to key into a PC data produced by a mainframe program.

This inelegance led to the development of PC-to-mainframe links—combinations of hardware and software used to establish a physical connection between the PC and a mainframe or mini. Just having a connection, however, is not enough. The user must be able to access mainframe data, which are likely to be stored in a way never intended for this type of access. What is the solution? One answer is to have IS consultants who help users obtain the data they want from the mainframe and download it to their PCs.

The user now is once again dependent on the IS staff, at least to obtain data. The user still has the discretion of what programs to use and when to use them once the data are on the PC. Over time, the PC has become more integrated with the rest of the hardware and software in the firm.

How Do You Share?

As users work with their PCs, they develop new ideas for how they can be used. Within departments, the idea of sharing became popular: Why not share common data, expensive devices like laser printers, and so on? The **local area network (LAN)** makes all of this possible. The LAN enables users to share data through a special PC that is a dedicated file server (Figure 13-2).

Consider the pharmaceuticals firm that buys data from an international service that collects information about the sales of prescription drugs. The pharmaceuticals firm is located in New Jersey and the database of market data is in Europe. To reduce access costs, once each quarter when the database is updated, a large extract is loaded onto the file server of a LAN in the marketing department at the pharmaceuticals firm. Whenever a marketing analyst wants data, he or she downloads it from the file server to a PC for further analysis. All of this is made possible by the LAN.

Now the PC can serve multiple users who want to share data. Not only that, but some companies have developed applications we might say look appropriate for a midrange system by using a LAN. Given present technology, there is some overlap at the boundaries for all of the options in Table 13-1. Some OLTP systems on mainframes can run on midrange machines; some midrange applications can run on LANs.

Be Your Own Broker

In the days of mainframe-only computing, if you wanted to buy stocks, you placed a phone call to your broker. He or she completed the order by writing up a ticket that went to the wire clerk in the back office at the brokerage firm. The clerk wired the order to one of the firm's floor brokers on the stock exchange.

Today, you can place an order to buy or sell stock from your own personal computer (or from the Internet as we saw earlier). Fidelity, the large investment company, has developed the Fidelity On-line Xpress (FOX) which is a PC software package that provides everything from direct trading to real-time stock quote plus investment analysis.

The system lets the user access quotes on-line and do on-line trading. You also can prepare an order off-line and submit it for execution when convenient. The system has the ability to provide financial reports from companies like Standard and Poor's and Dow Jones for an additional fee. The system is also tied into Fidelity's databases, so you can check your brokerage or mutual fund portfolio without waiting for a monthly statement. The system has a cash management module and a portfolio function to analyze your assets.

The software has pull-down menus and supports a mouse. All of this is available for less than $120! Of course, you can still trade the traditional way with your broker (who now probably uses a PC and local area network to support his or her work), but architectures made possible by PCs and communications provide the organization with a lot of options.

Power to the Desktop with a Friendly Interface

The major trend we can see in architecture over the past three decades is computational power moving from a central computer facility to the desktop. The days of batch processing, where the user sends data to be keyed for the computer, gave way to on-line systems, where users had terminals for entering transactions. Terminals spread to those who did not necessarily input a lot of data and needed to ask questions and make queries of the system. The personal computer made it possible for users to develop some of their own solutions to problems, but the user soon saw the advantages of being networked. At some point, we will not know or care which computer is working for us. The workstation on our desk will provide an interface to a large network of computers. Some computers will have special purposes, for example, a large machine may be in charge of the database while specialized processors perform the role of file servers. All of this computing power will be delivered to your desktop, completing a movement that began when the first on-line systems were developed in the 1960s.

Moving Toward the Client-Server Model

To further complicate matters, there is no real need to have a pure architecture. In fact, we predict many organizations already have or will move to mixed architectures. Networks of mainframes, minis, and personal computers are likely to appear. The PCs will be on a LAN that has a gateway to a mainframe/midrange network (Figure 13-3).

The connection of PCs to networks of midrange computers and mainframes has resulted in the **client-server architecture**. A client on a personal computer connects to a PC, midrange computer, or mainframe that is the server. The **server** retrieves data and manipulates it in some way for the client. The client may also process the data further after moving it to his or her PC. A network may have more than one server. For example, our network has various servers for different departments, and some servers are dedicated to certain applications, such as running a mathematical problem-solving system. A user can connect to a number of different servers from his or her local PC.

Vendors like Sun Microsystems adopted the client-server model as the basis for their entire product line. Sun encourages customers to purchase client workstations and a larger workstation to act as the server. Sun is working to eliminate the mainframe and minicomputers (not manufactured by Sun) that do its internal processing with its own client-server systems. The company currently runs all of its factories and distribution systems on client-server systems using Unix and uses a client-server system for all order entry and processing. To provide powerful client-server systems in an effort to capture market share from minis and mainframes, Sun has developed a large-scale server expandable to hold up to twenty processors, each with up to a terabyte (10^{12}) of disk capacity and 5 gigabytes (10^9) of RAM. Sun claims that the server supports up to a thousand users initially and up to two thousand in its largest configuration.

IBM has advanced a vision of computing it calls "Network-centric." Its chairman feels that IBM's customers are working to become more efficient

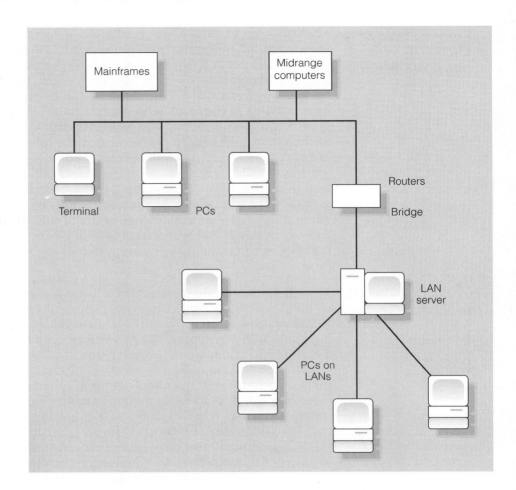

and competitive. They are reducing cycle times and becoming more responsive to customers. All of these efforts require collaboration with customers and suppliers: they all depend on networking. IBM is positioning its computers as servers and/or clients on large networks and providing networking services that charge transactions fees. For example, Walgreen's developed a system that lets doctors send prescriptions to pharmacies electronically over an IBM network and the pharmacy pays a transaction fee to IBM for each prescription. IBM's strategy led it to acquire Lotus in order to obtain Notes, a groupware product discussed in Chapter 21.

Other vendors promote what they call **open systems**—those that enable connections of different sized computers from a variety of vendors. Sun argues this kind of open system is more complex than its client-server architecture running all on Suns because one expects greater complexity when a variety of computers are connected on a network. Of course, many companies have large investments in a variety of midrange and mainframe computers; in the short run their only choice is to move toward an open architecture in which there are likely to be a variety of clients and servers on a network. It is also clear that individual users have developed favorite types of computers. It is almost impossible to dictate to someone what their workstation has to be.

Some users feel that a terminal is fine and they do not need a lot of local processing power. However, they would like to have friendly software that provides windows, something associated with the use of a PC or engineering workstation. Researchers at MIT developed a terminal with these capabilities called the X windows system. A number of vendors offer X windows terminals and software so a simple terminal can provide a graphical user interface.

The vision for the future is client-server computing where the user works with a client workstation to access data from a variety of servers. The size of these servers and their location is of no interest to the user who is accessing the information they provide. The Internet is an excellent example of this kind of architecture. If you add an Intranet and connect it to transactions processing servers in the firm, you may get to the point where the main program the user runs on a client computer is a network browser.

Certainly there are a lot of choices in developing an architecture. Later in this chapter we try to provide some broad guidelines for matching a systems design to hardware and software architectures.

Taking Advantage of the Services of a VAN

Federal Express is using a system developed by GE Information Services, a value-added network, to implement an EDI billing system. FedEx has 60 customers participating in its electronic remittance program, who account for 4,000 payments a day. To put things in perspective, Federal Express has to employ 250 clerks to process the 56,000 checks it receives each day for the daily delivery of 1.6 million packages. The clerks match checks to invoices and then update customer files in a mainframe accounts-receivable application. On occasion a check from a large customer covers a thousand or more bills which greatly complicates the process of tracking and verifying remittances.

FedEx customers use the GEISCO EDI*Express network to send electronic remittances to the company and electronic payments to Federal Express' bank. The bank then credits FedEx with the payment. (Customers who prefer can send a conventional check instead of an electronic payment, but that tends to defeat the purpose of EDI.) GE software automatically processes incoming electronic remittances and updates the FedEx accounts-receivable system.

In this example we see an architecture that relies on a third party to implement inter-organizational systems. Rather than start from scratch or try to develop its own EDI system, FedEx purchased software and a service, and interfaced it with its existing accounts-receivable system.

EXAMPLES OF DIFFERENT ARCHITECTURES

Competitive Reservation Systems

The major airlines have developed complex and sophisticated **computerized reservation systems (CRSs)** (see Figure 13-4). American Airlines developed its SABRE system first to keep track of reservations, as manual reservation systems were predicted to break down in the early 1960s with the expansion of jet travel. Other airlines followed American's lead and developed systems of their own in the 1960s and 1970s.

These CRS applications feature very large mainframe computers. In the case of American, eleven large IBM mainframes (with multiple processors) are specially connected in two groups, one for reservations and one for fare data. One machine is a backup in each group that takes over if something goes wrong with one of the other computers. The SABRE database has contained in one month up to 45 million fares and experienced 40 million changes. The system creates 500,000 PNRs (passenger name records) daily.

Figure 13-4
Airline reservation system.

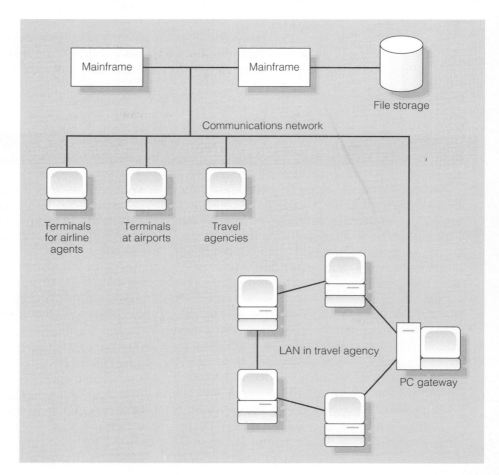

The complex processed a peak of 4,176 messages per second and serves more than 300,000 devices in 74 countries on six continents. SABRE is certainly a high-volume, fast response, mainframe application.

In addition to reservations, CRS applications are expanded to include many other functions. The computers keep track of when flights depart and when they will arrive. (American Airlines jets send radio messages to the computer on take-off to update flight monitors.) The CRS systems also help specialists load aircraft to keep them balanced. A CRS keeps track of special requirements for meals and can connect with other systems to provide rental cars and hotel rooms.

One of the major expansions of reservation systems occurred when American and United decided to place terminals connected to their systems in travel agents' offices. Their systems already showed the flights of competing airlines so reservation agents could answer customer questions. All that was needed was a way to make reservations on other carriers' flights.

Now, the airline industry can be viewed as having a huge network of interconnected computers. The reservation systems are operated by individual airlines, but they all send messages to each other. USAir allocates a certain number of seats on its flights to the SABRE system. When the flight is to be closed, USAir sends a message to SABRE to close that flight segment, and so on. Millions of messages each day flow among the computers.

American and United have about a 70 percent market share in travel agencies, giving them a distinct competitive advantage. The Department of Transportation now regulates reservation systems because of complaints from non-CRS airlines. For example, in the early days of agency applications, each vendor showed its own flights first. Because about 90 percent of flights are booked from the first screen, the CRS vendor had an obvious advantage. That kind of listing is no longer allowed. However, currently the CRS vendor collects a booking fee for each segment of a flight it books on another carrier. SABRE and Apollo (United's CRS) are extremely profitable subsidiaries of their respective airlines. In fact, smaller airlines and start-ups claim that the CRS vendors raise a significant barrier to entry, since it is so hard to operate an airline without a CRS. (It should be noted that United has sold shares in its Apollo subsidiary and that Sabre is a subsidiary of American that is rumored to be for sale.)

A Broker Workstation

Stockbrokers try to assist their clients with investments. The broker is both a consultant and a salesperson and is compensated based on the amount of trading he or she does for customers. The broker needs a great deal of data about the stock market, the securities and other instruments the public can buy, and the client. For many years, brokers have had stock quotation terminals on their desks so that they can get the latest price of a security. Many brokers added their own PCs to keep track of customer portfolios, write letters to customers, and do other information processing tasks.

Several major brokerage firms and independent companies are developing **broker workstation** systems. One of the largest U.S. brokerage firms installed 17,000 personal computers running broker workstation software for its stockbrokers. The objective is to replace all terminals with a single PC-based workstation for each broker. The schematic of one independent's system is shown in Figure 13-5. This firm operates a ticker plant in New York that accepts data feeds from the stock exchanges and companies that sell financial data. The ticker plant relays the data to a satellite, which then broadcasts it throughout the United States.

A customer (generally a brokerage firm office) needs a satellite dish on the roof to pick up the broadcast signal. Within the local office, there are at least two servers and a local area network. One server maintains historical data, which can be accessed by the broker from the workstation. Another server handles communications and accepts the incoming data stream from the satellite.

Because many brokerage firms have their own corporate mainframe systems that maintain customer data, it is possible for the broker to open a window on the workstation and make that window emulate a standard IBM terminal to communicate with the corporate mainframe. The broker workstation provides a number of features controlled by the PC. It provides multiple windows which execute individual applications. The broker can set up monitors to follow a single stock or groups of stocks, for example, set alerts to go off if the stock of XYZ Company hits a certain price. A number of applications packages are also available on the system, including electronic mail, word processing, and presentation graphics.

Chevron Canada Client-Server Model

Chevron Canada used a client-server model to redesign a sales-monitoring application (Sinha, 1992). This application connects Chevron's Canadian distributors to the Vancouver corporate headquarters and replaced a twenty-year-old batch processing, mainframe system. This system is used for order entry, tax, inventory control, and management reporting. Over

Fast Response Jeans

Levi Strauss has developed a fast-response system for mass customization. The company can sew a pair of woman's jeans to fit the size of the customer. The process begins when a clerk measures a customer for jeans in one of the company's Original Levi's stores. The clerk inputs the data into an expert system which sends it to a Notes server at Custom Clothing headquarters in Newton, Mass. Notes sends the data to a fabric-cutting machine at a Levi's plant in Crystal City, Tenn. Factory workers tag the special order with a bar code and send the cut garment out for laundering. It then returns to the factory for stitching. The bar codes match the finished pair of jeans with the customer file. The company sends the finished jeans to the original store or to the customer's home.

Some experts in manufacturing suggest that mass customization or "agile manufacturing" will be the next major trend in industry. It allows companies to focus on customer service and quality, selling something beyond the basic product to the customer.

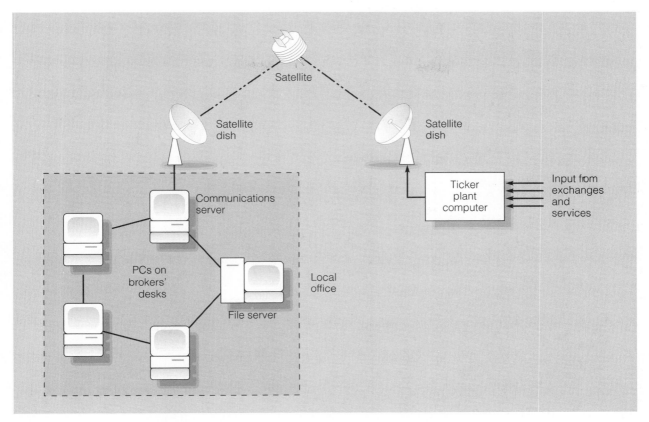

Figure 13-5   Broker workstation system.

the years, it has added on-line transactions processing capabilities and limited decision support functions. As shown in Figure 13-6, the client-server design features a wide area network connected to local area networks. There are multiple servers along with a connection to a mainframe in San Francisco. Eventually the system will handle about 165,000 transactions per month from over thirty-five remote sites; some sixty-five local clients will also make requests. When completed, each client will be connected to a local server containing data relevant to that client. There will be some three hundred relational tables distributed over multiple servers and replicated on a central server in a 3-gigabyte database.

Comparing the Applications

The broker workstation application features a much different architecture from the CRS example. The brokers do either limited or no updating of the database. The data are updated centrally at the ticker plant and copies are kept on each LAN. There is some two-way satellite transmission for broker queries of the database, but higher volume transactions with the broker's own, in-house mainframe computer take place over terrestrial lines.

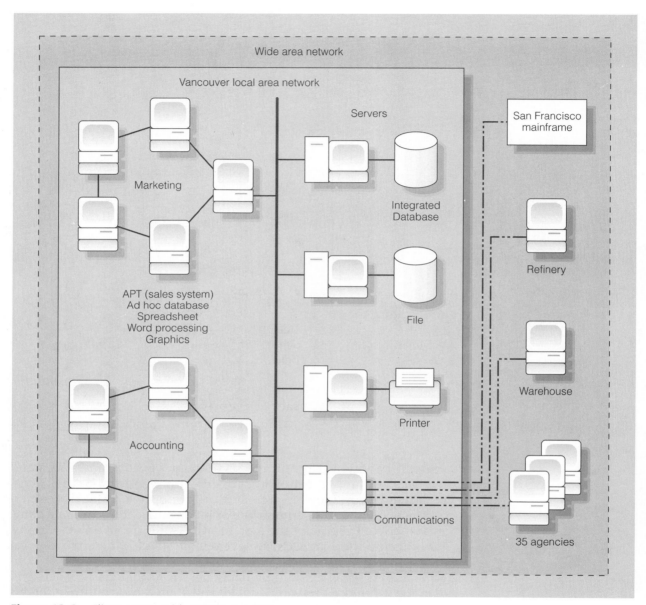

Figure 13-6   Client-server with WANS & LANS.

Users share the price data through the LAN and the personal computer gives them extensive discretion on what they do. One broker may be analyzing a customer portfolio while another provides a customer with a stock quotation. At the same time, a broker's assistant may be using the system to send out a mailing to all of his or her customers interested in a particular stock.

In the Chevron case, the application is similar to the CRS in that both systems process a large number of transactions, but the airline CRS is centralized and Chevron has chosen a client-server architecture. Of course, the Chevron system processes far fewer transactions than an airline CRS, and that is the reason it can adopt an architecture dependent on a number of small computers. It is significant that LANs and client-server systems have developed sufficient power to be used in transactions processing applications at all. With extremely high volumes of transactions updating, you still need a mainframe or large midrange computer. However, client-server architecture is steadily eroding the dominance of mainframes and mid-sized computers in on-line transactions processing applications. In the case of an airline CRS, the need for mainframes is clear. In other applications, the designer will have a choice. Today, cost/performance advantage lies with client-server architectures for many applications.

MATCHING DESIGN TO AN ARCHITECTURE

When the Architecture Is a Given

In many situations, an application will have to run on an existing architecture because that is what the organization is willing or able to provide. In this case, the guidelines below can be used, but they must be modified to fit organizational constraints. Sometimes, however, the architecture can be modified to provide the appearance of a new system. It is very expensive to redesign large transactions processing systems, and some firms have been updating the design of these systems by hiding the old system behind a new PC interface.

One large electronics manufacturer has a major internal transactions processing system that literally controls its entire business. The system was developed in the 1960s and runs on mainframes. Users have complained about the old technology and want a more flexible system. It would cost millions of dollars—possibly hundreds of millions—to redesign the system. The firm is thinking of replacing the present terminals with personal computers and using the PCs to develop a new interface. The existing transactions processing and database system would be left intact.

Suggested Guidelines

In this section we suggest some guidelines for considering the interaction between hardware and software architecture and systems design. The type of architecture will influence design. As systems designers we have radically different choices depending on whether we plan to implement on a LAN or a mainframe with terminals. Some basic guidelines are as follows:

1. Start sizing an architecture at the smallest and least expensive option. Can a suggested application be completed on a PC with packages? If there are multiple users accessing a central database, the answer is probably no. The same is true if there are too many simultaneous users.

A PC will probably run Windows95 or Windows NT and will make use of a popular "suite" of office applications that include a spreadsheet, word processor, presentation graphics program, and database management system.

2. If a stand-alone PC is not adequate, can a system be developed using a LAN? The LAN can accommodate multiple users who can share data files. The same software as above is appropriate but the server will probably run Windows NT. At some point, there may be too many users for the LAN, or more likely there will be too high a volume of activity for the servers. It is also possible that the system must handle a large volume of transactions, in which case the LAN is not currently the best alternative.

3. A client-server architecture featuring workstations or midrange computers as the server is a cost-effective alternative for many applications as long as the system can handle the processing load. The server here may run NT or Unix, while the clients run Windows95. User applications may be developed using the PC database management package, or a midrange DBMS like Oracle or Sybase.

4. Midrange computers have the capacity to handle a large number of transactions and large databases and can control large communications networks. You may program these systems in the language of a DBMS or in a language like C++.

5. Mainframes can handle large volumes of transactions and huge databases. They, too, excel at controlling large communications networks. If the mainframe application exists already, then you will probably

Powerful Servers—An Alliance Between Digital Equipment Corporation and Microsoft

Microsoft is hiring DEC to help customers install and maintain networks that use its Windows NT operating system. Microsoft will pay for training for 1500 DEC service representatives, a cost of $50 to $100 million. Microsoft has also agreed to provide versions of NT for DEC's alpha chip at the same time it provides them for Intel chips.

Also important in this agreement is a cross licensing agreement for patents on cluster technology, something that allows many computers to act like one large machine. Microsoft has a long-term strategy to bring the commodity pricing of the desktop PC to larger servers. New PC-based servers are turning up in offices, displacing much more expensive minicomputers that DEC sells.

Both companies hope that the combination of Windows NT and DEC's speedy Alpha chip will produce extremely powerful servers, especially since Windows NT supports symmetric multiprocessing in which a server has several, identical chips. The operating system has to assign tasks to each processor and coordinate processing. With symmetric multiprocessing and clustering technology, the two companies may be able to offer servers with the power of today's mainframes, but at a much lower cost.

have little choice in the programming language and operating system. However, if the application is new, and you are using a new, large computer, you may be able to use Unix as the operating system and C or a 4GL as an applications development language.

6. If users need local processing power and discretionary use of computers, a mixed network including mainframes and PCs is likely. This configuration is also popular when the organization has a large number of legacy computers and applications; networking them together provides users with the features they need and widespread data access.

7. For providing links with customers, suppliers and others, consider the option of using the Internet and World Wide Web.

Dealing with the Problem of Data

A fundamental aspect of design is where to keep data and where to update it. In the airline CRS, all data are maintained centrally because of the need for instantaneous information and the frequency of update. In the broker workstation system, the users do virtually no updating of the data distributed from the ticker plant. Because fast response is important for brokers, it is a good design decision to duplicate the data locally. The price server in each office has identical information that it accepts from the satellite dish on the roof.

In other systems the trade-offs will differ. The designer has to balance response time, updating frequency, the need for up-to-date information, and the cost of duplicate storage. If there are to be copies of the data, we must also be concerned with the integrity of all copies. Does each copy have to updated whenever the master record changes? In the broker workstation, a constant stream of data updates the local file server. In other applications, it may be adequate to refresh local databases less frequently.

FUTURE TRENDS IN ARCHITECTURE

The discussion in this chapter suggests that the role of the mainframe is changing. Mainframes have been making a small comeback and are likely to be around for a long time. After seven years of decline, vendors sold more mainframes in 1994 than 1993, nearly one million computers. A market forecasting firm predicts 25 percent annual growth for mainframe sales through the end of the century. The old view of the mainframe as the single, central processor for an organization is probably obsolete, but not the mainframe itself.

What is happening to mainframes, or large computers to rekindle their sales? Mainframes are declining in cost because they can take advantage of some of the same technology as PCs. It is anticipated that the cost of mainframe MIPS (million instructions per second) will decline 50 to 75 percent during the last part of the 1990s. Mainframes are undergoing dramatic changes in their architecture as they become more modular or come to feature totally parallel operations. Vendors are producing smaller, more powerful and more affordable mainframes. They are switching from older, more expensively fabricated circuits, to CMOS (complimentary metal oxide semiconductors), a less expensive technology. This technology lets the manufacturer put more logic on fewer chips and circuit boards. IBM is also selling a line of mainframes that feature parallel architectures using RISC-based technology.

A basic requirement of any new design is that the mainframe remain compatible with existing software and meet the timing requirements of on-line systems. Within these requirements, designers are free to try novel approaches to the hardware in an effort to improve the cost/performance characteristic of mainframes.

The role of the mainframe is evolving. Instead of performing all calculations, the mainframe will become an extremely powerful server on networks. It will handle multi-billion-byte databases, providing data to clients on the network. The clients will do much of the processing of these data before returning them to the mainframe server to update the database.

CHAPTER SUMMARY

1. The designer used to be able to remain independent of the hardware and software architecture until fairly late in the design process. Now, architecture interacts with the design because it is central to decisions about the user interface, the volume of processing, and the design of the database.

2. Architecture is the place where all of IT comes together: computers, databases, communications, and networks.

3. Architecture is also concerned with the location of processing and the pattern of computers users access.

4. Mainframe vendors are working to improve their cost/performance characteristics compared to smaller computers. An increase in sales for new mainframes suggests they are succeeding. Mainframes are used for high volume processing tasks and to continue executing critical legacy systems.

5. Midrange computers may be used for on-line transactions processing and as servers in networks.

6. The PC is the workstation of choice for the average user.

7. The most popular architecture today is client-server where client PCs connect to servers which may be other PCs, midrange computers, or large computers.

8. It is difficult to develop guidelines for choosing an architecture. In general you will want to develop an architecture that costs the least while providing the processing power you need.

9. Frequently you will confront an existing architecture because the firm has been using technology for a number of years. You only will be able to make small changes to this architecture because of the applications that currently run on it.

10. While you want a low cost architecture, remember that transforming the organization requires an adequate technological infrastructure. Otherwise you will not be ready to take advantage of opportunities that arise to innovate with technology.

IMPLICATIONS FOR MANAGEMENT

An IT architecture is complex for all but the smallest organizations. The good news is that you will probably not have to decide on one alone. Developing an IT architecture involves both managers and IT professionals. As a manager, you want to see if there is a coherent plan for an architecture and if decisions about the acquisition of new hardware, software, and communications devices are consistent with that plan. A second managerial responsibility is to be sure the firm has an IT infrastructure so you can take advantage of technology when new opportunities arise.

KEY WORDS

Broker workstation
Client-server architecture
Computerized reservations system
  (CRS)
Local area network (LAN)
Mainframe

Midrange computer
Minicomputer
Network
On-line transactions processing (OLTP)
Open system
Server

RECOMMENDED READING

Client-Server Magazine, a publication of *ComputerWorld,* and IDC.

Copeland, D., and J. McKenney. "Airline Reservation Systems: Lessons from History," *MIS Quarterly,* vol. 12, no. 3 (September 1988), pp. 353–370. (An excellent history of the development of CRS applications by the airlines.)

Sinha, A. "Client-Server Computing," *Communications of the ACM,* vol. 35, no. 7 (July 1992), pp. 77–98. (A comprehensive discussion of the technology of client-server computing.)

DISCUSSION QUESTIONS

1. What is hardware architecture?
2. What is software architecture?
3. Why could design be independent of the type of architecture in the 1960s?
4. What kind of applications are best suited to a mainframe?
5. What types of systems are probably best designed for a midrange computer?
6. Why are users so enthusiastic about PCs?
7. What led to the need for PC-to-mainframe links?
8. What is the purpose of a LAN?
9. What does a file server do in a LAN?
10. What are the advantages of mixed architectures?
11. Why might you want to centralize a database and keep only one copy of it?
12. In what situations might it make sense to have more than one copy of a database?
13. Are there applications where it does not matter if multiple databases are simultaneously updated?
14. What problems can exist if data are not updated on identical databases?
15. Why does the broker workstation system store a copy of the data from the ticker plant in the local office?
16. Why would it be difficult to redesign a CRS to run on another type of architecture?
17. What is the motivation behind client-server architectures?
18. Do you think that mainframes will gradually disappear?
19. Where might client-server systems not be applicable?
20. Why might a firm want to connect networks at different locations?

CHAPTETR 13 PROJECT

SIMON MARSHALL ASSOCIATES

In Chapter 9 Simon Marshall asked for your help in thinking about new operating systems. One consultant recommended to Mary that the company stay with Windows95 and that it look at two types of local area networks: a network with a server or a peer-to-peer network. In order to run the groupware that interests John, the consultant said they could use Lotus Notes on the network with a server, or Windows for Workgroups on the peer-to-peer network. What are the pros and cons of each approach? Which do you recommend for Simon Marshall?

CHAPTER **14**

System Alternatives and Acquisition

● OBJECTIVES

1. Learning to manage information technology.

The selection of technology, computers, communications equipment, software, and services is a major, ongoing management concern. Managers need to understand what they are buying and how to evaluate it. Decisions you make today can determine the organization's architecture for the next five to ten years.

2. Preparing to apply technology.

Sometimes a systems design team is forced to develop systems that operate on existing computers. However, you are frequently able to specify the type of computer and communications environment needed by an application and then acquire them. This chapter stresses the alternatives that are available to you.

3. Transforming the organization.

Dramatic applications that change the organization are likely to require the acquisition of new hardware and software. A manager must be prepared to make what are sometimes risky acquisitions to create systems that have a significant impact on the firm. There has been some movement toward outsourcing and toward strategic alliances in order to reduce the time required to develop significant applications.

Managers are frequently involved in the evaluation of hardware and software. In fact, a number of times users try to make these decisions alone. The purchase decision is one that usually warrants advice from systems professionals. This chapter explores the problem of selecting hardware and software and suggests procedures for their acquisition.

After a brief survey of the industry, we discuss how a firm might acquire a major application for a significant system, one that involves a number of individuals in the organization. Then we discuss some of the problems of choosing packages for individual workstations. We close the chapter with an example of poor decision making on the acquisition of a network and discuss the consequences.

THE INDUSTRY

The computer industry today consists of firms that sell hardware, software, and services.

• Hardware firms range from the giant IBM to small companies making their own brands of personal computers from components purchased around the world. IBM, Fujitsu, Amdahl, and Unisys manufacture large computers. DEC, Hewlett Packard, Sun, and similar companies manufacture and sell midrange computers, while a large number of companies like Compaq, Packard Bell, IBM, Dell, Gateway, and similar firms sell personal computers. Apple also manufactures and sells its Macintosh line of small computers, though it has less than a 10 percent market share.

- You can buy software from a large number of companies as well. Manufacturers of large computers often sell proprietary software for them, especially operating systems. (Remember our discussion of IBM and its MVS mainframe operating system.) Companies like Computer Associates sell a great deal of software for large-scale computers. Microsoft sells a wide variety of software for personal computers and servers as do many smaller companies. There are hundreds of small software companies that sell special purpose software, for example, a program for shipboard navigation using a notebook computer.

- The rapid proliferation of technology created a large service industry to help companies integrate technology with their strategy and operations. IBM has a consulting subsidiary which competes with Electronic Data Systems (EDS) and Andersen Consulting, a firm with over 30,000 employees working to implement IT solutions for customers. Services companies will develop a single application of technology or will contract to take over the operations of your entire IT effort, a process called **outsourcing.**

MANAGEMENT PROBLEM 14-1

Dennis Monroe is a plant manager for M&E Electronics. He has just reviewed a proposal for factory management featuring personal computers and is trying to figure out what to do. M&E has a large central computer facility that runs factory management software for the largest plant.

Dennis's plant, however, is relatively small. The amount of information he needs about production is limited compared with that needed for the main plant, which has thirty-two different work centers. Dennis is basically concerned with what goes into the production line and what comes out. He must keep track of yields as well, that is, the number of good units divided by the total number produced.

The proposal is to install a LAN and PCs on different parts of the plant floor. Each PC will be used to report data back to the server which will maintain a database on production.

Dennis is concerned because he has always figured that the plant would need a larger computer than PCs on a network. He wonders if a midrange computer like the IBM AS400 would be a better solution because it already has some programs that might be adapted to his plant. How would you recommend that Dennis proceed? What questions should he ask? What are the important variables in making a decision?

To BUY OR NOT: MAJOR APPLICATIONS

The Decision Context

The first acquisition situation we shall discuss involves a multiuser application such as an order-entry system for the firm, or a production control system. (The design of this type of system is the topic of the following section.) A user makes a request for an information system. Assume a systems analyst responds with a preliminary survey, which is positive. Should one stop at this point and look for a package? Some in the field, particularly package vendors, would say, yes, further analysis is a waste of time.

There are, however, several compelling reasons for further work before examining packages. First, undertake a preliminary analysis of the present system, and create a high-level logical design. This design includes output requirements, database design, and input needed. You should have a good idea of the functions of the system and some of the features it must have in order for users to work with it. This preliminary set of specifications acts as a **benchmark** for evaluating various options.

Now the design team has a plan, a benchmark specification against which to judge various offerings from different vendors. It is far too easy to be swayed by a convincing sales presentation. With a benchmark, the design team determines exactly what is present and what is omitted from various available systems. Different packages can be arrayed against a custom system to estimate the extent to which each alternative meets users' needs and expectations.

Figure 14-1 shows how we might proceed. First, identify the problem and prepare a preliminary design document for a new system. Note that at this point one is not concerned with the acquisition of hardware. Although it is premature to think about acquiring computer hardware, it is important to determine roughly what scale of hardware is necessary for a planned system. Is the system capable of running on personal computers? On a network of PCs? Will it require a midrange or larger computer? These questions can be answered by estimating the size of the system: How many transactions have to be processed? What is the size of the database? What is the volume of file activity? What is the peak volume versus the average? The answers to these questions will help narrow down the hardware alternatives and in turn allow one to think more about the kind of package, since packages are written for certain sizes of operations.

Given a rough design and a feeling for the overall size of a system, alternatives such as those shown in Figure 14-1 can be explored. Alternatives are listed below:

- A custom system programmed to do exactly what is requested in the specifications. Of course, the specifications must be developed in greater detail for programming, but this is the traditional way of developing a system.

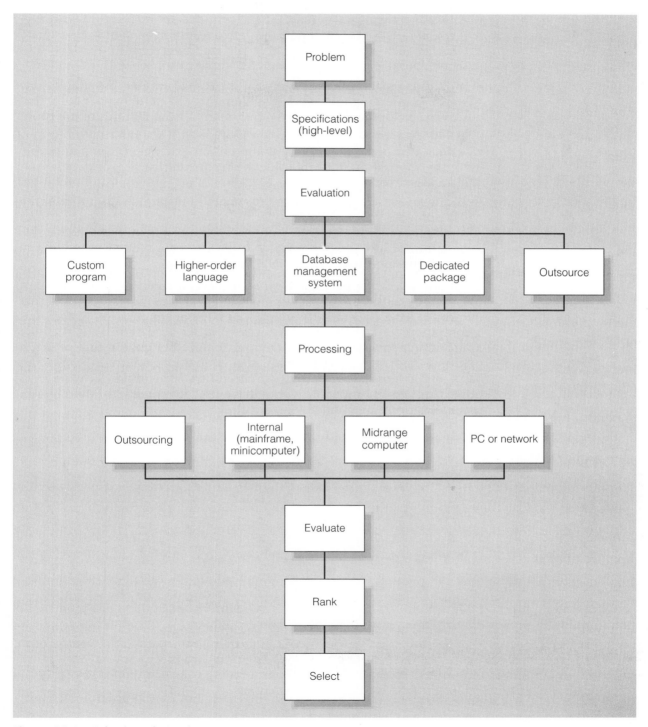

Figure 14-1   Selection alternatives.

- A fourth-generation language. If the firm already uses such a language, it would be a candidate. If not, the design team might want to investigate whether such a language would be a good investment for this and subsequent systems.

- A database management system. This package and the associated software for querying and possibly generating the actual application can speed development while providing many of the features of a custom system.

- A dedicated package—software written by an external vendor particularly for the application under consideration. One difficulty is finding if such a package exists.

- Locate an outside contractor or outsourcer to undertake all or part of the development process. A variety of software consultants provide services in all phases of the life cycle. For example, hire a firm to design the system, and/or hire programmers and staff from an external firm to carry out all the steps following detailed design.

If you select the package alternative, several computer trade journals publish annual surveys of packages. There are also proprietary services that purport to list all major software packages. If the organization already has a computer, contact the vendor representatives to determine if they are aware of any packages for their computers. Another good source of information is industry trade journals, such as banking journals for finding bank applications. The analyst can attend trade meetings to learn from other firms in the industry if they have used or considered packages in the applications area under consideration.

How About Wearing Your Computer?

There are a tremendous number of options for data input; scanning has become extremely popular because you do not have to key in data. The scanner improves accuracy and reduces data entry time.

McKesson Corporation has found a wearable computer incorporating a laser scanning device; the input part of the package fits on the wearer's hand, wrist, and forearm; it is connected to a waist-worn portable computer that uses radio frequency links to download inventory data to a PC from any location in the warehouse. Warehouse workers use the computer to track pharmaceuticals and other goods when they are received and shipped.

The worker can actually scan bar codes from ten to fifteen feet. In one McKesson warehouse productivity has increased 10 percent and the number of incorrect orders filled has been cut by 72 percent

Of course, there is one key to the success of this system: The products coming into the warehouse have to be bar-coded by their manufacturers.

Processing In many instances, the decisions made in the top half of Figure 14-1 determine the hardware that must be used for processing. For example, if you chose a package that runs only on an IBM computer, you will have to find IBM-compatible equipment for processing.

If one is not constrained by the first decisions made in developing a system, what are some of the processing alternatives? First, an outsourcer can be used and these organizations provide all types of processing. The services themselves may have special packages or data available that contribute to solving the problem. Many banks, for example, outsource the processing of their credit card transactions.

For internal processing, the options depend on the architecture the firm adopted, as discussed in the last chapter. The firm may already have a mainframe, midrange computer, or PC network that new systems are expected to utilize. Processing requirements may determine which alternative is recommended for the design of a system, for example, database size or transactions volume.

After exploring the options, you must compare the various possibilities. Each alternative should be examined on a number of criteria, then a decision can be made on the best way to proceed, considering both software and hardware.

THE SERVICES INDUSTRY

We have stressed that custom development is no longer the automatic choice while planning a new application. There are a number of ways to obtain technology support, in both the development and the operation of computing applications. In this section we discuss some of these possibilities.

MANAGEMENT PROBLEM 14-2

Sally Johnson has used a spreadsheet package on her personal computer for five years. The package is supposedly integrated. It contains a database management program and a word processor as well. Sally finds the database part a little too restrictive and, as a part of her upgrade to Windows95, is interested in a package devoted entirely to the management of data.

She investigated three packages, each of which has different capabilities. All three claim to be based on the relational model. Each of them has a forms-definition capability—users describe on the screen the input form, and the system creates it each time they enter data. The systems also have report generators to custom-tailor reports. Finally, they all have the ability to record keystrokes as macros or to use a programming like Visual Basic to develop applications systems. All of the packages are designed for Windows95.

Sally cannot see any major differences among these three candidates. Their prices are almost the same. How can she decide which alternative is best for her? What advice can you give her?

1. *Computing power.* Service organizations have offered computing time and power for a number of years. While some organizations need extra computing power, the steady decrease in already low hardware costs suggests that the market for raw computing power in general will shrink. Service organizations already offer a number of custom programs and proprietary databases so that the customer can obtain a service that is not available in-house. A number of service firms provide value-added networks. A good example of an external service is General Electric Information Services Co. This company offers conversion software, network services, and EDI mailboxes to firms that want to conduct business using EDI without acquiring and setting up their own EDI capability. Another strategy is to use a service like this to get started quickly while you are developing an internal capability.

2. *Proprietary applications.* Software houses, service firms (as discussed above), computer vendors, and others all offer applications dedicated to business functions such as accounts-receivable processing. Many of these systems have been through several major revisions based on feedback from users. The discussion of packages in Chapter 18 points out some crucial considerations in evaluating this type of software. What is the quality of the package? How well does it suit the organization's needs? How willing are the users to change procedures given the cost of modifications?

3. *Proprietary databases.* There is a large body of data that can be used for making various analyses and decisions. By making the data machine readable and easily available, vendors of information create new businesses. One can purchase information on the expected trends in the economy, various statistics about companies and stock prices, and the texts of legal cases, to name a few. These services can be used as an adjunct to an application or may furnish some of the needed input directly.

4. *Communications.* A number of vendors offer communications services and equipment as discussed in Chapter 12. Some of these vendors act as common carriers and provide communications networks. Others offer services like electronic mail or computer bulletin boards, in which individuals communicate about a given topic by sending messages to each other's electronic mailboxes in a computer file.

5. *Consultants.* Software consultants or vendors provide programming and systems design services for custom systems, and some offer special packages as well. The software vendor may contract to manage an entire systems development effort or may furnish programmers to perform work assigned by the client. The staff of the consulting firm writes and tests programs.

Closely related is the systems **integrator**, an organization that pulls together varied hardware and software components to make a system. Because many organizations feature mixed systems with components from different vendors, integrators can be very helpful. Consider a firm that wants to develop a system to send data from a central mainframe to dispersed local area networks around the country. Such a system involves the mainframe and its software, some type of wide area communications network, the local computers, a LAN, and local computer software. A systems integrator would design the architecture of the system, help select the equipment, design and/or purchase software, and get the entire system up and running. Electronic Data Systems (EDS), Andersen Consulting, and IBM's ISSC are three of the largest and most successful systems integrators.

*W*HAT SOURCES SHOULD BE SELECTED?

What are the advantages and disadvantages of different sources for hardware and software? For discussion purposes, we can look at the two extremes in which all activities are undertaken either internally or externally through an outside organization (see Table 14-1).

Hardware   With an internal IS department, an organization must cope with the problem of managing the computer; thus overhead is introduced into the organization. For this price, management gains control over its own computer and communications operations. Data remain exclusively within organizational confines and are accessible only to employees. You establish processing priorities, and no other organization can preempt time from an organization with its own system. Management must provide sufficient resources to accommodate peak loads, so there can be high fixed costs for computer equipment that may not be fully utilized under this alternative. Backup may be limited by the resources that management is able to provide.

Organizations choosing to rely on external services have a contractual agreement with the outsourcing firm. There are few management supervisory responsibilities because these tasks are delegated to an outside company. Control may be less than under the internal alternative because litigation over contracts is costly and time-consuming. Instead, the customer seeks to influence the outsourcer. Many firms worry about having sensitive data in the hands of another organization, particularly when other companies have access to the same computer resources. The priority for applications is also in the hands of the organization providing services. Management influences, but does not control, processing priorities. With an outside organization, the customer incurs a variable cost and pays only for the resources consumed. Frequently, the client has access to more-powerful equipment than would be installed internally, since it is shared among a number of users.

Table 14-1
Comparison of Internal Versus External Services

	Insourced	Outsourced
HARDWARE		
Management	Must manage information services department	Contractual arrangement; no line management responsible except for data preparation
Control	Control potential is high	Only through contract, influence, withholding payment
Security	Under own responsibility; data remains at internal location	Data in hands of external organization; other customers a threat
Priorities	Assigned by own employees	Determined by external management
Resources	Must accommodate peak loads; high fixed cost	Variable cost, pay only for what is used (beyond possible minimum charge)
Capacity	Limited to what is needed	Frequently more powerful equipment than could be justified by clients
Backup	Limited by internal resources	Usually available because of higher capacity
SOFTWARE		
Management	Must manage program development	Contractual arrangements, specifications on cost, time, performance
Staff	May have to hire experts	Expect vendors to have expertise
Implementation	Probably easier in terms of users' reaction to internal staff	May be more difficult for "outsiders"

Software   With internal software development, we must manage the development process. Internal program development often results in duplication. There may be a tendency to start from the beginning with each new system. Because IS staffers can be wary of applications not generated in-house, sometimes they do not adequately investigate package alternatives. Implementation problems, however, should be minimized because internal employees deal directly with the users in the firm.

External software services are handled on a contractual basis, but the customer may still need some individual who is familiar with information technology to work with the contractor and monitor progress. For the most part, however, clients will rely on the vendor's expertise. Implementation can be difficult for "outsiders," although the client may be able to take advantage of an existing package or set of routines whose cost has been amortized over a large group of users.

THE PROS AND CONS OF OUTSOURCING

One recent trend is outsourcing. This involves turning over some or all of your organization's IT effort to an outside firm specializing in operating, developing, and managing various aspects of information technology. Some articles make it sound as if outsourcing is a relatively new invention. In reality it represents more of a name change than a new kind of service. In the 1960s EDS began to offer what it called "facilities management" services.

Today EDS, Computer Sciences Corporation, a subsidiary of IBM called Integrated Systems Solutions, and other firms provide outsourcing services. These firms negotiate a contract with a company that wishes to turn all or part of its technology function over to the outsourcer. What kind of services might you want to outsource?

Obviously, the outsourcing consultant would be delighted to assume all of your IT activities. This firm would operate your existing applications, possibly on the outsourcer's computers or on your existing computers. The consultant would also gladly assume responsibility for running your communications network and for developing new applications.

Some clients chose to retain part of their IT functions and to partially outsource some activities. For example, a large brokerage firm outsourced part of its network management, keeping control of the part it felt was strategic. A major advertising agency outsourced its transactions processing and accounting applications while continuing to develop and manage systems designed to help the creative part of its business. Xerox outsourced its legacy (older IBM transactions processing systems) to EDS so that it could concentrate on developing a new client-server architecture in house.

Outsourcing is controversial: Some managers argue that it makes sense to let a firm that specializes in technology take over and act as an independent contractor. Why should we try to manage something that is not our specialty? On the other hand, others are not comfortable turning over to an external organization technology that may be crucial to corporate strategy. We discuss outsourcing further in Chapter 24.

Strategies for Acquiring Equipment and Services

No matter what alternative is selected, the customer has to acquire computer equipment and/or services. What is the best way to approach this problem? There are several considerations a potential customer should have in mind. First, check the vendor's financial condition. A number of small companies in the computer industry have gone bankrupt. Even major firms have sold or discontinued their computer manufacturing activities. How likely is a vendor to be around in the future to service the product and improve it?

An extremely important research activity for a customer is to contact present users of a product to determine their level of satisfaction. How well does the product or service meet the vendor's claims? What problems did users have? If possible, visit users without a vendor representative to ask these questions. If it is not possible to see a product demonstrated, do

---

McKesson: Adding Value to Transactions Data

McKesson is trying to add value to the drugs it distributes to pharmacies throughout the U.S. through information. The company receives 5000 orders for prescription drugs every day at its computer center in Rancho Cordova, California. In one hour, the company generates almost all of its daily $30 million in revenue. A Tandem computer accepts the orders and routes them to an IBM MVS mainframe for processing; this computer in turn sends orders to AS/400s at 36 distribution centers for next-day delivery. (The pharmacies carry no inventory and depend on McKesson for next-day service.)

The order data is potentially valuable to McKesson's 25,000 customers, so the company is building a "data warehouse." Of course, the information is also valuable to McKesson which is basically in the inventory business. Between McKesson employees and customers, the company expects 5000 users to take advantage of the data to do their own "data mining." McKesson itself will use the data initially for inventory forecasting (the company does 200 million lines of invoices a year.)

Feeling that the mainframe was both too busy and not well suited for this kind of application, McKesson has ended up using a relational database management system from Oracle and symmetric multiprocessing file servers from Pyramid Technology. McKesson's IS staff compared the file servers with two massively parallel processors from other vendors before choosing Pyramid. McKesson asked each vendor to run a series of benchmarks using actual data; a dozen IS employees worked on the comparison of vendors, testing response times and other performance measures. A typical query might include a full table scan of 100 million rows of tables. For a customer to find out its top 10 selling items by geographic region and season could involve a full scan of the invoice table of 181 million rows followed by a four-way join operation.

McKesson's data warehouse project shows the effort involved in building a Decision Support System (See Chapter 21) that will access a large database. It also demonstrates the importance of carefully evaluating potential hardware and software vendors for such a project.

not buy it. Too often, announced products are delivered years late; insist on a demonstration, and attempt to evaluate the performance of the product.

Evaluating Performance

A major activity in acquiring new equipment and software is an evaluation of the performance of the product. We also use evaluation techniques with an existing system to improve its performance through the acquisition of additional equipment. Performance is generally defined as the response time of a system, or the volume of input it can process in a given period of time.

A cruise line presents an interesting example of how performance can be important in the selection of a computer system. The shipping line was investigating a software package for making cruise reservations. On the surface this reservations application sounds like any other, but there are a number of important differences. One is that passengers usually want to book a particular cabin or class of cabins when making a reservation. There can also be different itineraries for the passengers in the same cabin. Thus, a package must be specifically designed for cruising.

The cruise line in this example found such a package, but was concerned about whether it could handle the volume of processing for its ships. Fortunately, the package was in use at another, noncompeting cruise line roughly comparable in size.

The computer vendor offered a **performance evaluation tool**, which monitored data from the actual execution of a job and used these data to develop the parameters of a queuing model of systems performance. The user of the model could ask what-if questions to determine the impact of changing the hardware on system response time. For example, one could estimate the impact of moving to a different CPU, adding memory, and adding disk capacity.

The cruise line obtained monitored data from the firm already using the package and used the vendor's model to analyze the data. The model indicated that performance should be adequate for the cruise line and was helpful in recommending the computer configuration to acquire. In this instance, a combination of evaluation techniques was important in the decision to acquire a new software and hardware package.

ACQUISITION OF A MIDRANGE TO LARGE COMPUTER

Periodically, it is necessary to upgrade a midrange or large computer system, either because more capacity is needed or because technical advancements produce machines with better performance at a lower cost. The acquisition of a new large or midrange computer system can be a complicated decision. In this section, we describe the computer selection process and suggest some criteria to use in making the decision.

Developing a Request for Proposals

After the need for a new system has been identified, the potential buyer will usually develop a request for bids. The request is sent to various vendors, who are asked to propose equipment. The buyer should attempt to have the vendor do most of the work in this process. Table 14-2 shows some of the items that should be included in the request for a **proposal**. All present applications should be described in detail in the proposal. We want the vendor to consider these and recommend the best equipment for the work load. Also, plans for new applications should be included. The vendor should specify what type of support will be provided and present reliability data for the equipment. We are also interested in knowing about backup. Because moving to a new computer system is a major undertaking, the vendor should present a plan for the transition to the proposed system. Are there any special products or services that the vendor offers to ease the transition?

In shopping around for a new system, we should also ask for some descriptive material to get a feeling for the equipment being proposed. This information should include both hardware and software capabilities. What languages, dedicated applications packages, and systems software are available? What general-purpose packages does the vendor offer? Finally, the price for the recommended system should be provided in detail, for both hardware components and software.

Mapping Long Beach

When there is a fire in the city of Long Beach, California, an operator keys in the caller's address and within moments a map appears on a computer screen showing the shortest route from the firehouse to the fire. Each building is coded. For example, if a structure contains hazardous materials, the operator can notify the fire crew responding to the call. In addition, the operator can call up the floor plan of the building, showing where the hazardous material is stored. A second operator can mobilize police evacuation teams. The computer system monitors the likely path of a smoke plume from the building and indicates where an evacuation may be necessary.

While not commonplace, such spatial database systems are in use around the United States in cities like Long Beach. In addition to being a major port, the city has a large number of oil properties and a maze of underground pipeways. The city bought the spatial database software from a firm that designed it to run on VAX computers from Digital Equipment Corporation.

The package features custom-built graphics workstations with digitizing keyboards for inputting traditional, paper-map data into the database. The user digitizes maps into layers, for example, neighborhood, building, and then floor plan. Various attributes can be assigned to the maps in order to develop a complete database.

Spatial databases represent another way computers can be used to manipulate information. In business, one could use spatial representations to examine sales territories graphically. In fact, various PC presentation graphics packages already provide some support for this type of database.

Table 14-2
Items Included in Request for Proposal

1. Present applications
   Database characteristics
   Input-output
   Volume
   Frequency
2. Same as (1) for proposed systems
3. Vendor service
4. Reliability data
5. Backup
6. Demonstration
7. Evaluation arrangements
8. Conversion and transition
9. Descriptive material (hardware and software)
10. Price

Evaluating the Proposal

Meaningful criteria should be established for evaluating each proposal from different vendors. These criteria can include such items as performance, presence of certain software programs, availability of special applications packages, ease of conversion, and feedback from other users currently using a comparable system.

The evaluation team should assign a weight to each criterion. It may be possible to eliminate vendors because of one dominant failing, for example, the lack of an applications package that is critical. If it is not possible to eliminate vendors because of a single major failing, a more formal evaluation procedure will be necessary. One approach is to assign an interval score to each vendor, multiply the scores by the weights of the criteria, then add the weighted scores to form a final weighted total. The results are often quite close, however, and the evaluation team may not have much confidence in a small numeric difference among the vendors. Another alternative is to prepare a brief **scenario** of how the IS department would function with each alternative system and what transitional activities would take place. The decision-making body rank-orders the scenarios and chooses the most desirable one.

Purchasing Other Computers

The purchase of a large or midrange computer is fairly routine, as the preceding section illustrates. Even when one is acquiring a computer that will be dedicated to a single software application, the decision is usually fairly easy once you choose the package because (1) there are usually relatively few computers for which the package is written and (2) the vendor has experience in knowing what kind of computer should be used given the firm's processing demands.

In the category of "other" computers, we must consider PCs, networks, and factory control computers. The large number of vendors for personal computers present a bewildering array of possibilities. The organization is probably well advised to develop a standard (say, to support two or three specific types of personal computers) and to avoid acquiring others because the IS staff can develop expertise to support only so many.

The organization may also be buying a network, following the client-server model example presented in the previous chapter. (See especially Figure 13-6, which shows a network with multiple clients and servers.) In these cases evaluating the capacity and performance of the network is very difficult because it may be hard to find a comparable system running the applications you have in mind.

Decisions for these "other" classes of computers largely depend on the function for which they are being acquired. Many people first bought personal computers just to run spreadsheet analyses. Managers choose factory computers for how well they perform a specific task. One can still apply

MANAGEMENT PROBLEM 14-3

Jack Caradine sat back in his chair and scratched his head as he muttered, "We really opened the floodgates with the ICPC two years ago. Now we can't keep up with all the user requests for packages and systems."

Jack is manager of systems development for Agrequip, a manufacturer of farm implements. Two years ago he helped one plant install a package application called ICPC for inventory control and production control. It was an example of dedicated application: a small computer and the software were acquired specifically for the inventory and production control application.

Since that time, other users found out about the system and requested something similar. These requests presented relatively few problems, since Jack's staff is quite knowledgeable about the package and is now installing it at three other plants. What Jack is concerned about now are the requests for many different types of packages. They start their own research with package vendors and they don't have the slightest idea of what to look for.

Jack's staff is being stretched to respond to these requests and to evaluate the packages. "Users got the idea that a package is a panacea for any problem," Jack complained. "They don't realize what we have to go through to evaluate and then install a package. Every one we put in required some modification. Sure, it can be cheaper than doing it ourselves, but the cost is not just the price of the package; it's the installation, modification, and ongoing expenses of taking care of the thing. Also, we rarely find a package with all the same features we'd have put in a system designed as a custom job inside the company."

What kind of policy does Jack need? What procedures would you recommend for dealing with the explosion of package activities by users?

some of the considerations for larger computers when considering other types, specifically: expandability and compatibility, ability to communicate with other systems, the type of software, the user interface, and vendor support.

Dealing with Obsolescence

An ongoing problem in purchasing both hardware and software is obsolescence. The cost/performance curve for hardware continues to decline while new versions of packages appear about every six months. While cars improve each year, few of us can afford to buy a new automobile every twelve months. Is the same true for computers? Very few applications ever disappear from computers and new ones are always being added. It is fairly obvious, then, that the total amount of computing in the organization is always increasing. Higher powered computers seem to stimulate the creation of more sophisticated and powerful applications. The first spreadsheet programs did calculations. Today's Lotus 123 and Excel offer presentation graphics and even programming languages.

As a result, users apply ongoing pressure for new computers and software upgrades. To some extent, the organization has little choice. While you might still be able to do word processing and run a spreadsheet on a ten-year-old PC, what you do is unlikely to be compatible with other users who have newer models with newer releases of software. The task of managing a large variety of computers and different versions of software is also formidable. Your support staff will try to keep all equipment and software at the same level to make its job possible. Thus, as a manager, you will be forced into continual upgrades. That is one reason why it is estimated over 50 percent of all U.S. capital investment is in information technology.

PACKAGES FOR LARGE AND MIDRANGE COMPUTERS

A dedicated applications package is a program or set of programs written for use by more than one organization. It is designed to be used for a specific application like inventory control as opposed to a general application like word processing. A number of these packages are for sale or rent by computer vendors and software firms.

The major attraction of a package today is the avoidance of developing a custom system. Custom programming is expensive and time-consuming. When a package is available, it should be considered. Another obvious advantage of using a package is cost savings. The package developer expects to sell a number of packages to recover the investment in developing the package. The cost is thus amortized over a number of users. The cost to the developer, though, is usually higher than the development of a single application would be, since the package must be general enough to be used by a number of customers. This increased generality makes the package larger, more complex, and often less efficient to operate than an application specifically developed for a single application. Some of the trade-offs, then, for a package are as follows:

- Package generality versus ease of installation and use.
- Acquisition and modification costs versus the cost of developing the application within the organization.
- The elapsed time to install a package versus the time to develop the application within the organization.
- Operating efficiency of the package versus the alternative of a custom application within the organization.
- Implementation problems of the package versus those of an application developed specifically for the needs of the organization.

The most serious problem with purchasing a package is the need for the organization to customize the programs for its unique situation. (This problem is most severe with dedicated packages such as accounts-receivable programs, which may affect the way the firm has been doing business for years.) Of course, although individual organizations always claim uniqueness, it is often easy to change routine procedures to suit a package. On the other hand, there are also legitimate reasons for maintaining uniqueness in the organization.

We have stressed the importance of meeting users' needs and obtaining their involvement in the design of systems. Many systems developed on a custom-tailored basis fail completely or never reach their potential. It seems that packages are even less likely to succeed because they have a tendency to impose a system on a user. What can be done to lessen the implementation problems of packages?

The package vendors recognize this drawback and generally design packages to allow some custom tailoring. Two ways are often employed for providing flexibility: the use of modules and the use of parameters. The first strategy provides a modular set of programs in the package. The user configures a custom applications package by selecting appropriate modules for a particular set of needs. Little or no programming is required on the part of the user. Packages also make extensive use of parameters or data values to indicate unique features for a particular user.

Often, the customizing features provided by the vendor of the package are insufficient for an organization. The less expensive packages may have to be accepted as is, but for more-elaborate applications, the customer often finds it necessary to write custom code to modify the package. Sometimes the modifications are easy and require only the addition of some reports or the alteration of reports already in the package. Code modification can become quite extensive and may involve rewriting significant portions of the package. One organization uses the rule of thumb that a package will not be considered if modifying it will cost more than 50 percent of the initial package cost. The important thing to remember is that the cost of a package is usually not just the purchase price. We must forecast and consider the costs of transition, modification, and maintenance as well.

Establishing Criteria

The information services department and a project team should agree on screening criteria for packages. Many times packages will be considered as alternatives to developing a system in-house. Table 14-3 lists some possible evaluation criteria for decisions on packages. The major reason for acquiring a package is the function it performs. We want to know how many desired functions are included and what effort is required to modify the package.

It is also important to consider the user interface. That is, how difficult is it to use the package? How much information does a user have to supply? Is it simple to prepare and understand the input? Is the package flexible, and can it be used if the organization's requirements change somewhat?

The evaluation team is also concerned with the package's response time. We are also interested in how much present procedures will have to be changed to use the package. Just as with hardware, it is necessary to evaluate vendor support. Remember that it does not take many resources to program and sell software packages. Updates and improvements for the package should be forthcoming, so we are dependent on the vendor's remaining in business.

With software packages, documentation is vitally important; the IS staff will maintain the package and may modify it. Finally, we must consider the cost. Remember we always underestimate how much it will cost to develop a comparable system ourselves and overestimate the cost required to modify the package!

Table 14-3
Considerations in Evaluating Software Packages

- Functions included
- Modifications required
- Installation effort
- User interface
- Flexibility
- Response time
- Changes required in exiting system to use package
- Vendor support
- Updating of package
- Documentation
- Cost and terms

Making a Final Decision

In this discussion, we are interested in whether or not a package qualifies for consideration. Many of the criteria in Table 14-3 require analysis of package documentation by the systems analysis staff or programmers. We also should contact present users and ask questions about vendor claims and support. Almost all these criteria are subjective, which means several individuals should rank a package on each criterion, for example, on a one-to-seven scale. The responses can then be averaged for each criterion and a score can be developed for the package.

It may be desirable to divide the criteria into essential and nonessential groups. We can insist that a package get a "passing score" (established in advance) on each of the essential criteria to be considered for acquisition. Then we can examine the criteria to see if the package passes enough of them to be considered.

If a package is acceptable and is the only alternative under consideration, we will probably acquire it. However, if several packages are available, the ones that pass the screening test can be compared using ratings or through the scenarios described earlier. If the package under consideration is an alternative to designing an in-house system, use the criteria established by the project team to evaluate the package in comparison with other processing alternatives.

The users, then, help evaluate a package versus a custom-tailored application and decide which would be best. If the user wishes to have the lower costs and faster development associated with the package, he or she will have to agree that all desired features may not be present. If the decision is for a custom application, the user must recognize that costs will probably be higher than the cost of a package and that it will take longer to develop the system.

PACKAGES FOR PCS

Buying software for personal computers shares some of the issues with buying software for larger systems. We are still concerned with the user interface, user documentation, and speed of processing.

For most PC packages, modification is not an issue. These packages are too inexpensive for the vendor to customize for each customer. In order to protect future sales, the vendor rarely sells the source code for the program. The vendor does not encourage modifications because it does not want to support customers who make them.

Research for a PC package is slightly different from that for other types of technology. A number of magazines conduct product evaluations, or the potential buyer can look at package documentation at a retail computer store, see the package running, and sometimes even obtain a demo diskette from the manufacturer.

Some organizations have created internal consulting and support groups to help users with PC hardware and software acquisitions. These groups have packages to recommend and demonstrate for specific types of applications. Fortunately, the cost of much PC software is low enough that one can often afford to buy and use a package for several months or a year and then switch to something else. It is worth research and careful consideration, but there is nothing like trying out the software before buying it to determine the right choice. For generic applications like spreadsheets, word processing, and presentation graphics, the support staff will encourage the adoption of a company-wide standard. This standard makes it easier to share data and easier for the staff to offer you support for the products.

Software for Networks

Most organizations would like to minimize their software expenditures while software vendors would like to maximize sales. Buying a copy of a software package for each personal computer in the organization is expensive, and most companies avoid this approach.

The first solution to reducing package costs is obtaining a site license. Many software vendors will negotiate a fixed price for a license that allows the user to install a package on a certain number of machines. For example, our school has a site license for up to seven hundred copies of all software products offered by one major vendor.

A second solution to reducing software costs is the network. One impetus for networking is to share software among multiple users. Many software vendors offer network versions of their software at a price that is significantly less than purchasing the same number of individual copies. If an organization has a hundred users on a network, it might buy a network license for twenty-five copies of a software package, figuring it unlikely that more than twenty-five people would want to use the package at the same time.

An Example

We have discussed a number of acquisition scenarios in this chapter, ranging from buying a single package for a PC to outsourcing your firm's entire information processing function. A major university recently faced an acquisition decision that involved both hardware and software, which presents an interesting case study of an acquisition decision most people in the school now think was a mistake.

The school was installing a fiber-optic backbone network on its campus. It needed to choose a vendor to provide the networking software for the system. In addition, the choice of network vendor would also determine what file servers to install. The computer center at the school sent proposals to a number of vendors; two returned acceptable proposals.

Vendor A is a computer manufacturer with a strong support organization. Its networking software is proprietary, though it is based on a major PC software vendor's networking system. This network required fairly expensive servers that ran on the Unix operating system. Vendor B provided the networking software that was already in use at the school and is the market leader in networking PCs. The school staff also had experience with this software, because three or four of its networks were operating with it while the decision was made. Vendor B's network used PCs for servers, making hardware costs less than for Vendor A.

The computer center staff liked Vendor A, who it felt would provide extensive services and would better monitor and control their network. The staff convinced the dean responsible for making the decision that Vendor A was the best choice. Faculty with IT experience were in favor of Vendor B for the following reasons:

- The school had experience with the product from Vendor B. It would be throwing away most of that experience and starting from scratch with Vendor A.

- The system from Vendor A was more complex than Vendor B's. It required a great deal of memory on each client computer, which might make it difficult to run certain packages and the networking software simultaneously.

- It would be difficult to get outside help or hire people with experience with Vendor A's products since most professionals knew Vendor B's system.

- The more widely used system from Vendor B was better debugged than the newer product from Vendor A.

What happened? The decision was made to go with Vendor A. As you might expect, the implementation was a disaster. Students could not print in the PC labs, as the network had significant problems handling printing. The entire networking effort has discredited technology in the school. Emotions were so high that an outside review panel was asked to report on the computer center. It concluded the school was in great difficulty from having chosen Vendor A's product. In fact, it turns out that the school had the largest installation of this product! In addition Vendor A has started to "resell" Vendor B's network software, raising the question of whether or not Vendor A would continue to support and enhance its own offering. Three years later, the school is abandoning Vendor A and moving to Vendor B!

How did this disaster happen? The evaluation failed to consider important intangibles, such as the school's experience with Vendor B and the difficulties of finding and training staff for the complex system offered by Vendor A. In addition, it appears the computer center staff did not do an adequate evaluation. They failed to visit sites using the systems from both vendors that would be comparable to the school's environment.

This example should serve as a warning that you must be extremely careful in making major hardware and software acquisition decisions, especially those that affect the entire IT infrastructure of the organization. You must take into account intangibles and management considerations in addition to the technical features of technology products.

CHAPTER SUMMARY

1. Evaluating technology is an ongoing task for most organizations; large numbers of services and packaged programs are available.

2. The computer industry offers a large variety of firms that sell hardware, software, and services.

3. Today, most organizations are interested in reducing the cost, time, and risks associated with custom applications development. The first strategy is to look for a package to accomplish your processing objectives.

4. If you cannot find a package, there may be alternatives like the use of a Fourth Generation Language or DBMS for implementing the application.

5. Outsourcing is becoming increasingly popular for developing applications and for running all or part of a firm's technology.

6. There are a number of tradeoffs between doing the task internally and using an outsourcer. Management has more control over internal operations, but it must take a very active management role in IT under this alternative.

7. Because companies are continually developing new applications, there is increasing demand for hardware and software. This demand means the firm is frequently faced with decisions on acquiring more computer equipment and more software.

8. The acquisition of large and midrange computers is fairly routine. If the firm has an architecture in place, that architecture may dictate what new computers to buy.

9. The IS staff will want to keep up with new technology in hardware and software, both to provide the firm with a powerful IT infrastructure and to make the task of supporting hardware and software manageable.

10. Because packages are such an attractive option, it is important to purchase packaged software with great care. For dedicated applications, you should do a rough systems analysis and design to provide a benchmark for evaluating different packages. For general packages like a word processor, the organization will probably want to adopt a single standard in order to ease support requirements.

IMPLICATIONS FOR MANAGEMENT

The "make or buy" decision is always a difficult one for management. The availability of new technologies in the marketplace and a movement by firms to get back to their core competencies has led many companies to select the "buy" option. Chrysler can get by with making 30 pecent of the parts for its cars because it has EDI links with its vendors to make just-in-time manufacturing work. Because of the high cost and time required to develop software, most managers look first at whether or not they can buy existing software and modify it if necessary to avoid programming an application from scratch. If you decide to buy, it is important to understand the technology and the application so that you can be an intelligent consumer.

KEY WORDS

Benchmark	Performance evaluation tool
Integrator	Proposal
Outsourcing	Scenario

RECOMMENDED READING

Apte, U., and R. Mason. "Global Disaggregation of Information-Intensive Services," *Management Science,* vol. 41, no. 7 (July 1995), pp. 1250–1260. (A paper presenting a framework and discussion about where in the world an organization might choose to obtain processing services and/or outsource them.)

Byte and *PC* magazines have software evaluations and comparisons.

DISCUSSION QUESTIONS

1. Why have established vendors been hurt by "open" architectures?
2. Why evaluate systems performance given today's technology?
3. Describe the trade-offs in considering a dedicated package for a new application.
4. Why would management with an internal IS staff be interested in using a systems integrator?
5. What are the drawbacks of mixing hardware from a large number of vendors?
6. Why should a company consider the use of applications packages? What are their advantages and disadvantages? In what situations would you expect applications packages to be most satisfactory?
7. Is performance evaluation important for purchasing PCs?
8. How would you characterize an existing computer work load for performance evaluation purposes? How would you include consideration for the changes in the work load that might occur in the future?
9. Why might an organization choose to outsource all of its information technology?

10. What are the major differences between outsourcing the development of an application and outsourcing the operation of some part of your information technology activities?

11. What are the advantages and disadvantages of mixed-vendor installations? (For example, there are a mixture of Macintoshes and PCs in the firm.)

12. What factors mitigate against the conversion to a different vendor's computer? How has the development and use of higher-level languages affected this type of conversion? What do you expect the impactof database management systems will be on conversion to a new vendor?

13. Make a list of the types of questions and information desired for a survey of other users of computer equipment under consideration for acquisition.

14. How does the existing IT architecture affect the acquisition of new computer hardware and software?

15. What are the disadvantages of using some weighted scores for ranking competing proposals for computer hardware and software? What advantages are presented by using scenarios for describing how the company would function under each new alternative?

16. Why is it not a good idea to be a pioneer with new hardware or software? That is, why should a company wait before acquiring a newly developed computer system? How can the IS department avoid making frequent requests for additional computer capacity? What are the dangers in your strategy? How does the development of a plan for information technology affect this problem?

17. What applications might the firm want to retain if it is planning to outsource some of its IT activities?

18. Why should applications packages be seriously considered as an alternative to programming and implementing a system? What are the most significant problems with these packages? How can the ease of modifying the package be determined before its acquisition?

19. Compare and contrast the major sources of software. What are the advantages and disadvantages of each?

20. Who should be involved in the decision on new computer hardware? What about software? Does the type of software make a difference?

21. What are the major differences between packages for PCs and for midrange and large computers?

22. Why do some programmers show a great deal of resistance to applications packages?

23. How can the vendor of an applications package make it more appealing to potential customers?

24. How does an "open" architecture provide purchasing flexibility for a firm?

25. There is a great deal of free or low-cost software available for PCs. What are the advantages and disadvantages of "shareware"?

26. Why might a systems integrator be faster in developing a complex application than your internal staff?

CHAPTER 14 PROJECT

BUYING A PC

Several of your friends are thinking about buying a new personal computer. Look through popular magazines like *PC* and *Byte* for the advertisements from different mail-order PC vendors. Then develop a matrix comparing the features of different machines and their costs. Describe what features you would recommend for your friends in each of the following cases:

- The casual user who will mostly do word processing on the computer.
- The "power user" who will spend most of the time running spreadsheets.
- The fan of GUIs and presentation graphics who wants to experiment with desktop publishing.

Be sure to explain the reasoning behind each of your recommendations.

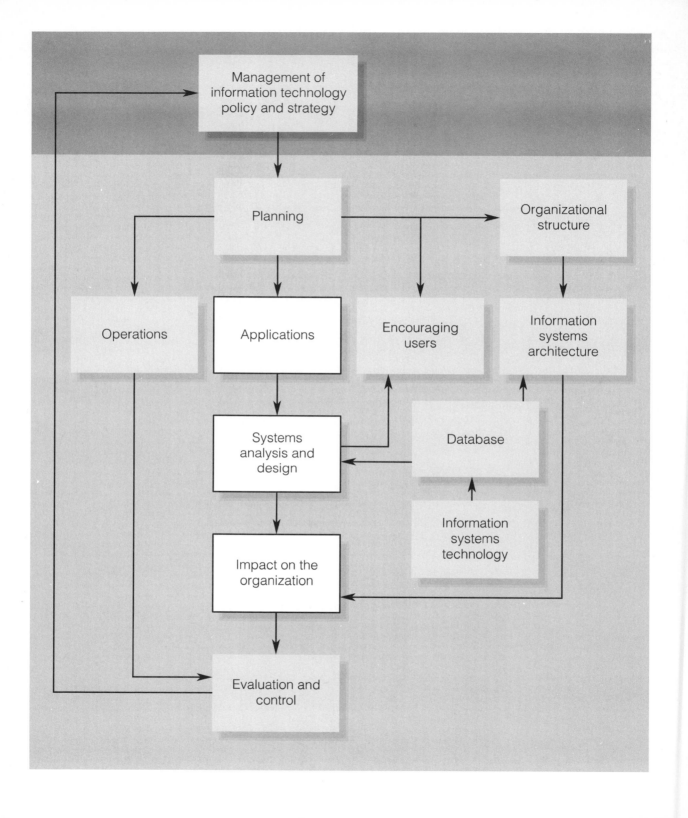

IV

Systems Analysis and Design

In this part of the book, we follow the life cycle of a system from its inception through final installation. From the considerations discussed in Part II, on organizational issues, we recommend an approach to systems analysis and design in which users have control over the design process. The chapters in this part stress the roles of the manager and user in each stage of systems analysis and design. The systems analyst aids the user in making crucial decisions and performs the technical tasks necessary to develop the system. Chapter 16 contains an appendix which provides a great deal of detail about the design of two different systems—one system follows structured design approaches and the other illustrates object-oriented design.

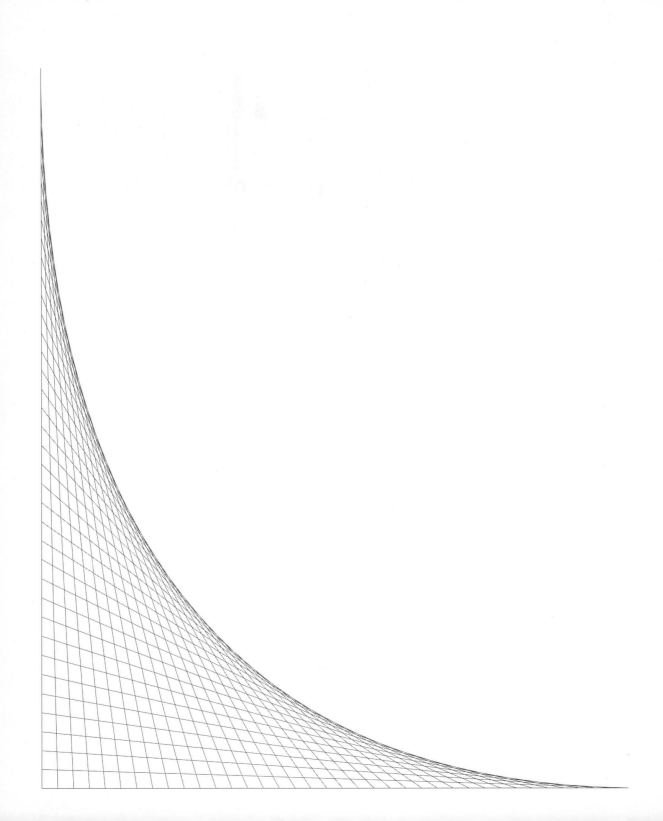

CHAPTER **15**

Building Systems: Creativity with Technology

● OBJECTIVES

1. **Learning to manage information technology.**

   For the manager who wants to bring change to the organization, introducing a new information system is one alternative. What is an applications system, and how is one developed? What is the manager's role in this process?

2. **Preparing to apply technology.**

   Following a simple model, even the systems life cycle model, can help a design team organize its work. In this chapter we introduce the traditional life cycle and describe some of its drawbacks. As you read the chapter, think about the tasks you would actually have to perform as a member of a design team.

3. **Transforming the organization.**

   Applications of technology have the potential to transform the organization. You have to identify and then build them. The manager has many important roles in developing applications that will create dramatic changes in the firm and industry. You will help develop the idea for a system, allocate resources to it, participate in its design, and help monitor progress on the development project. For systems to transform the organization, they must be well designed and they have to work.

THE DESIGN TASK

The design of a new information system is a demanding undertaking. First we become aware of an opportunity to use technology to gain an advantage or solve a problem with existing information processing capabilities. We assess the benefits of using IT to improve these procedures. Then we develop an abstract model of present processing procedures and a systems design team creates a new information system. The team converts the new procedures into system specifications and finally into computer programs. The final stages of development include testing, conversion and operations.

The design of an information system is a creative and labor-intensive task. It is creative because we are building a new set of information processing procedures, just as an architect designs a new building. **Systems analysis** and design is a human, intellectual task. There are some portions of design that can be automated, but most of the creative aspects require human thought. A recent consulting group survey reported that almost one-third of systems development projects were canceled before completion. Another half experienced dramatic cost and time overruns, and reductions in the features originally promised. There is much room for improvement in systems design. One strategy that helps is to have those who will use the system heavily involved in its design.

What are the roles of the user and manager in systems analysis and design? In this chapter, we introduce the systems life cycle and discuss the resources available for developing new systems. We shall see that users and managers have crucial roles in all aspects of systems analysis and design.

What Is a System?

In previous chapters we have seen many examples of information systems. A system consists of a number of interrelated components, only some of which are easily seen. For example, it is difficult to characterize the actions of individuals who are involved in making decisions as a part of an information system. The flow of information and the processing of data by computer programs and/or individuals can also be obscure.

One of the major tasks in systems analysis and design is to describe systems, both existing systems and proposed new systems. Later in this chapter we discuss some of the tools available for preparing descriptions of systems, but first we present an overview of a system.

Information systems can be described by five of their key components:

- Decisions
- Transactions and processing
- Information and its flow
- Individuals or functions involved
- Communications and coordination

It is difficult to observe the decision process, though we can see and review results of a decision. Transactions are usually more visible, though many current systems use computer programs, which are not easy to understand, to process transactions. In principle, an observer can see information and its flows. Individuals can be observed too, but it is not always easy to figure out what information processing functions they perform. Systems also have implications for the way individuals communicate and for coordinating a firm's activities.

Much of systems analysis and design, as mentioned above, consists of developing a sufficient understanding of a system to document it. Consider the following example of a simple inventory system:

Decisions

- What to reorder
- When to reorder it
- How much to reorder

Transactions and Processing

- Place an order

- Receive merchandise
- Withdraw goods from inventory

Information and Its Flow

- Quantity on hand for each item
- Historical usage of each item
- Forecasts of usage
- Cost of each item
- Holding costs
- Reorder costs
- Interest cost (to finance inventory)

Coordination and Communications

- Communication between the warehouse and Purchasing
- Communications between Marketing (forecasts) and Purchasing
- Communications with vendors
- Coordination of inventory replenishment among above departments and with vendors

Individuals or Functions Involved

- Warehouse managers
- Stock clerks
- Receiving clerks
- Purchasing agents
- Vendors

Several other systems are also related to this one, including purchasing and accounts payable. The information above serves only to describe the simple inventory system. We could further document this system by going into more detail, especially concerning the flow of information. We could prepare dataflow diagrams, which are discussed later in this chapter, to help visualize how the system works. We could also document the various decisions in narrative form to provide a better understanding of the inventory system.

Unfortunately, there is no one standard for what constitutes a system or how to document it. A number of different approaches are used, and individuals have to develop descriptive techniques that help them conceptualize a system. Most people find it easiest to start at a very high level and then work toward filling in the details. In our example above, we stated the system is first concerned with inventory. To anyone with experience in working with inventories, this description should bring to mind thoughts of how inventory systems operate in general. By listing decisions, transactions, information flows, and functions, we add details to the inventory system. Further details can be added in top-down fashion as our knowledge about this particular system increases. In the end, everyone involved in trying to learn about this system should share a common concept of it and an understanding of the documents describing it.

Multiuser Versus Single-User Design

It is important to distinguish between multiuser systems and single-user applications when thinking about systems analysis and design. The types of systems discussed in this part of the text are largely multiuser systems used by a number of individuals in the organization. One group usually develops these systems for use by another group of employees. As such, development requires input from a lot of individuals who are likely to be affected by the application.

This kind of multiuser system should be contrasted with a more personal system designed by the eventual user. Individuals frequently develop systems for their personal computers. These applications do not have the same requirements as multiuser systems, because the systems designer is the systems user. He or she does not have to worry about developing a system for others to use, nor does the system have to meet the needs of many different individuals.

Even a personal computer system we use ourselves can benefit from good design practices, but the requirements are not nearly so stringent for a multiuser system. In these larger systems, we must worry about editing, error controls, the careful design of input screens, retrieval capabilities, and file design. We must design for others as well as for ourselves, a much more complicated task!

MANAGEMENT PROBLEM 15-1

The president of Farway Manufacturing Company was pondering the firm's recent disastrous attempt to develop a system for factory-floor data collection. The company wished to improve scheduling and control over work-in-process inventories. A consultant was hired who recommended the development of a new production control system.

The consultant's recommendations were accepted, and he was hired to design the system. It turned out that the consultant designed a similar system for another manufacturing company and proposed to transfer it to Farway. This seemed like a very economical approach, so the president quickly agreed.

The consultant set about his task with zeal. Within six months, the necessary programming changes were made and the system was ready to begin operation. Over one weekend, terminals were installed in all departments. On Monday morning, workers were supposed to begin using the new system to report production. The workers are paid on piece rate and are unionized.

For reasons not completely understood by the president, the system failed completely. No one provided input, and the few data collected were all erroneous. What happened? Why did the systems development effort fail so miserably?

A SYSTEMS DESIGN LIFE CYCLE

A computer-based information system has a life cycle just as a living organism or a new product does. The various stages in the **systems life cycle** are shown in Table 15-1. The idea for a new information system is stimulated by a need to improve existing procedures or take advantage of a new opportunity. This need leads to a **preliminary survey** to determine if a system can be developed to meet the objectives of the individuals suggesting it. If the results of the survey are positive, it is refined to produce a more detailed **feasibility study**. From the outcome of the feasibility study, a decision is made whether to proceed with the design of a system. If a positive decision is made, one of the alternatives sketched in the feasibility study is chosen for development.

In systems analysis, the existing information processing procedures are documented in detail. During requirements analysis, designers attempt to learn what users expect a new system to do. One major task during this phase is to define the boundaries of the system. Does the problem concern only inventory control, or should any new system also consider problems in purchasing when inventory has to be replenished? During analysis, data are also collected on the volume of transactions, decision points, and existing files.

The most challenging and creative part of the life cycle is the **design** of a new system. One approach to this task is to develop an ideal system relatively unconstrained by cost or technology. This ideal system is then refined until it becomes feasible. Designers must prepare detailed specifications

Table 15-1
The Systems Life Cycle

Inception	Specifications
Preliminary survey	Processing logic
Feasibility study	Database design, input/output
Existing procedures	Programming requirements
Alternative systems	Manual procedures
Cost estimates	Building the system
Systems analysis	Programming (or some alternative)
Details of present procedures	Testing
Collection of data on volumes,	Unit tests
input/output, files	Combined module tests
Requirements analysis	Acceptance tests
Design	Training
Ideal system unconstrained	Conversion and installation
Revisions to make ideal	Operations
acceptable	Maintenance
	Enhancements

for the system being designed. They specify the exact logic to be followed in processing and the contents structure of the file. Designers select input and output methods, and develop the formats for input and output. These requirements for processing, inputs, and outputs lead to the specification of programming requirements, which can then be turned over to a programming staff for coding.

In the building stage, we develop the components needed to construct the system. Often this involves writing computer programs to perform the logical operations of processing. In some firms, this task is done by a separate group of programmers. Other organizations use analyst-programmers: The same individuals who perform the systems analysis and design also code the resulting programs. Programs have to be tested carefully, first as units and then in combined modules. Usually a programming task is broken down into a series of smaller subtasks or modules. All the individual modules must operate together if the system is to work properly. During the final stages of **testing**, there will be some type of acceptance test in which users verify that the system works satisfactorily.

Since one purpose of the new information processing system is to change existing procedures, **training** is crucial. All individuals have to understand what is required by the new system. When training has been completed, it is possible to undertake **conversion**; it may be necessary to write special programs to convert existing files into new ones or to create files from manual records. Finally, after all these stages, a team installs the system.

The operational stage begins after the problems of installation are resolved and the organization has adjusted to the changes created by the new system. The system now operates on a routine basis. This does not mean we do not change the system, however; there is a constant need for maintenance and enhancements. **Maintenance** is required because programs inevitably have errors that must be corrected when they appear. Because of the creative nature of design, users and the IS staff may not have communicated accurately, so certain aspects of the system must be modified as operational experience is gained. As users work with the system, they will learn more about it and will develop ideas for changes and **enhancements**. It is unreasonable to consider any information system "finished"; the system continues to evolve throughout its life cycle if, in fact, it is successful.

Figure 15-1 shows the resources required during each stage of the life cycle for a typical system. (The pattern of time required would be much the same.) Few resources are usually required during the inception and feasibility study. Once systems analysis is begun, more expenses are incurred as analysts and users work on the system and its design. These stages culminate in the preparation of specifications for building the system. The building stage is intensive and requires the most resources. Often building involves writing a large number of programs. For a large project, the entire process of design can last two or more years, of which more than a year may be required to build the system. Training will occur in parallel with the later stage of building the system, and finally the system will be converted and installed. After this time, the system reverts to operational status and is run on a routine basis. The resources required at this stage are steady, with some increases as the system becomes older and more changes are requested.

It is important to spend adequate time in analysis and design rather than rushing into development. If a system is well specified, there are fewer changes during programming. These later changes often require major redesign of programs and files, a very time-consuming and costly process. The entire systems life cycle can be compared to constructing a building. Changes are relatively inexpensive in the early, conceptual stages. They become a little more expensive at the blueprint stage and exorbitant once the walls are erected. Systems changes are much the same. In the conceptual stages of analysis and design, they are reasonable. However, while programs are written and some are complete, major design changes have the potential for creating huge time and cost overruns.

THE ROLES OF MANAGERS, USERS, AND DESIGNERS

Users, managers, and the information services staff interact in a number of ways during the analysis, design, and operation of information systems. In this part of the text on systems analysis and design, we often refer to the

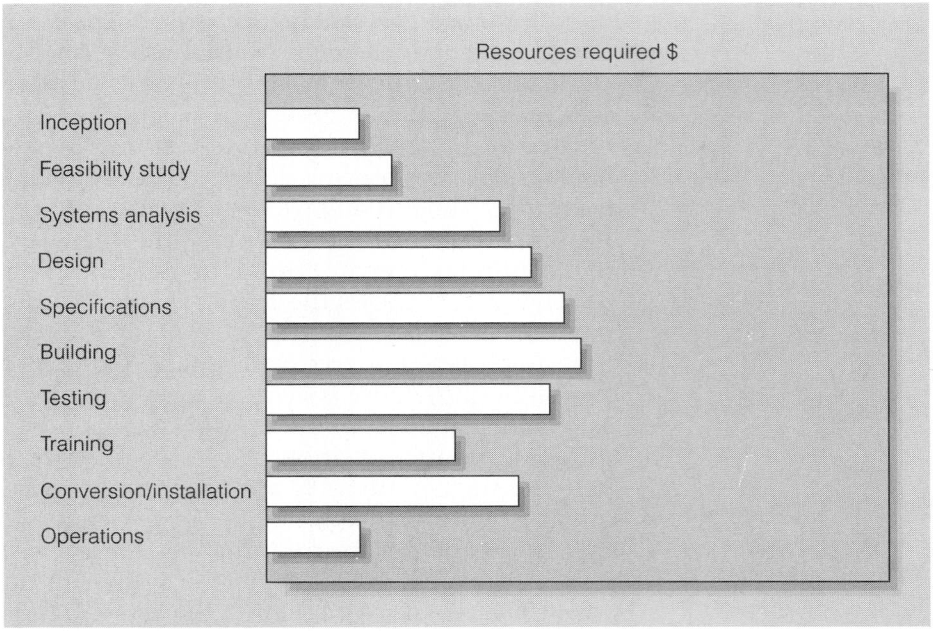

Figure 15-1
Resources required during each stage of the life cycle for a typical system.

Resources required $

- Inception
- Feasibility study
- Systems analysis
- Design
- Specifications
- Building
- Testing
- Training
- Conversion/installation
- Operations

responsibilities of each of these groups in the development of successful systems. Because this task is so complex and demanding, it is essential that all three groups cooperate during the analysis and design process. Table 15-2 restates the stages in the systems life cycle and suggests the appropriate roles of users, managers, and the IS staff.

The user initiates the preliminary survey by suggesting a potential application. The information services department responds with a rough estimate of its desirability and with several alternative systems, such as a package or a custom-developed system, each meeting some percentage of the users' needs. Management must approve of the basic suggestion and the idea of a new application for this area of the firm and participate in setting the objectives for any new system. In fact, it appears that one important role for management is to be a **champion** for a system. We observed a number of cases where systems failed because of the lack of a high-level sponsor and where they succeeded with such a champion.

A preliminary survey evaluates each alternative on criteria developed by a selection committee. The selection committee, with management participation, authorizes a feasibility study, possibly eliminating some alternatives suggested in the preliminary survey.

The IS staff conducts the feasibility study with help and advice from users. Users conduct an analysis of the existing system to evaluate various alternatives on criteria specified by the selection committee. Management reviews the feasibility of the proposed alternatives and develops an understanding of what the system will accomplish. The selection committee chooses the alternative for implementation with participation and review by management. Possibly the committee selects the alternative of no new system, in which case the application may be held in abeyance until changing conditions make it feasible.

If the decision is made to proceed with the development of a new system, users and the IS staff collaborate to analyze the existing system. Users aid by explaining existing processing procedures and providing data. The IS staff uses this information to document the existing system and help establish the boundaries of a new system. Management has a key role to play in this stage. It must provide adequate resources both for the IS staff and for users. It may be necessary to hire additional staff, so users can participate, or hire additional analysts to work on the project.

Next, the design of a new system begins. We advocate that users design their own input and output and basic processing logic. The information services department acts as a catalyst, presenting alternatives for users to consider. Management encourages user design through its own attendance at review meetings. Management may provide special rewards, prizes, or other incentives to encourage user participation in design. At this point, management must also plan for the impact of the system on the organization. Will the structure of the organization be changed? How will work groups be affected? What will specific individuals do as a result of the system? A plan for conversion should be developed, including a forecast of the system's impact on all potential users.

Table 15-2
Responsibilities During the Systems Life Cycle

	RESPONSIBILITIES OF		
Stages	**Users**	**Management**	**Information services staff**
Inception	Initiate study, suggest application, sketch information needs, describe existing processing procedures	Serve as sponsor, approve area for application, set objectives	Listen to requirements, respond to questions, devise alternatives, assess using rough estimates, prepare preliminary survey
Feasibility study	Help evaluate existing system and proposed alternatives, select alternative for design	Review feasibility, understand proposal, choose alternative	Evaluate alternatives using agreed-upon criteria
Systems analysis	Help describe existing system, collect and analyze data	Become system champion, provide resources, attend reviews	Conduct analysis, collect data, and document findings
Design	Design output, input, processing logic; plan for conversion and forecast impact on users; design manual procedures; remain aware of file structures and design	Encourage user design, provide rewards, attend reviews, plan impact	Present alternatives and trade-offs to users for their decisions
Specifications	Review specifications, help develop specifications for manual procedures	Understand high-level logic, key features	Combine users' needs with technical requirements to develop specifications, develop technical conversion plan
Building	Monitor progress	Monitor, provide buffer, extra resources	Organize programming, design modules, code programs, report progress
Testing	Generate test data and evaluate results	Review	Test program modules individually and in entire system
Training	Develop materials, conduct training sessions	Review	Aid in preparation of materials and train operations staff

Table 15-2   *(continued)*

| Stages | RESPONSIBILITIES OF | | |
	Users	Management	Information services staff
Conversion and installation	Phase conversion, provide resources, conduct postimplementation audit	Attend user sessions, demonstrate management commitment	Coordinate conversion, perform conversion processing tasks, help in postimplementation audit
Operations	Provide data and utilize output, monitor system use and quality, suggest modifications and enhancements	Monitor	Process data to produce output reliably, respond to enhancement requests, suggest improvements, monitor service

The IS staff develops detailed specifications based on the logic and requirements specified by users and prepares a technical conversion plan. The users on the design team review the technical plans and work on the development of specifications for manual procedures. It is vitally important at this stage for both users and managers to understand the system. Users must be familiar with the output, input, and processing logic. Management must understand the overall flow of the system and be aware of key decisions. For example, management should be aware if inventory items are to be grouped into classes and different reordering rules applied to each. Management should help set the classification and reorder rules and understand how the logic is to work.

The users' role and management's role during programming is to monitor progress. Is a project schedule maintained, and are resources reallocated as necessary to achieve installation on schedule? The bulk of the responsibility during this design stage rests with the information services department. The IS staff must design program modules, code them, and test them alone and in combination. Managers should realize they need to help when problems arise. The development of an information system is similar to a research and development project; it is very difficult to anticipate every contingency. There will be project slippages, budget overruns, and other problems. The role of management is to provide a buffer for the project and furnish additional resources where they will help.

During testing, users should define data for test programs, and attempt to generate data with errors to be sure the system will catch them. Users should carefully examine test results and evaluate the adequacy of processing. Management should also participate in the reviews of data processed by the system. Some kind of acceptance test should also be conducted by the information services department, and the results should be evaluated by users. A parallel test of old and new procedures or pilot studies may be used for this purpose.

Training is essential for smooth conversion and installation. Users should develop materials and actually conduct the training sessions whenever possible. Managers remain aware of the training program, attend occasional sessions to communicate support for the system, and check that their knowledge of the system is accurate. Training can often be combined with testing. The preparation of test data serves to help train users. The IS staff aids in the preparation of materials and has the responsibility of training the operations staff.

Conversion is a crucial part of the systems life cycle and should be done in phases if possible. For example, can one department or geographic area be converted first? The information services department coordinates conversion and performs conversion procedures such as creating initial files for the new system. Users and the IS staff should jointly conduct a post-implementation audit and report the results to management. How well does the system meet specifications? How good were the specifications. That is, how do users react to the system now? How do the original estimates compare with what was achieved? These data can be helpful in making estimates for future projects.

Finally, during **operations**, users furnish data for input and work with the system. Users and management will probably suggest enhancements and modifications to the system over time. The information services department itself should also look for improvements and respond to modifications suggested by users.

MANAGEMENT PROBLEM 15-2

The information services department at Madison Drugs is trying to stimulate user participation in the design of information systems. A new system for financial management is in the planning stages, but problems with users seem to occupy most of the planning sessions in the department.

One of the key figures in developing the new system is a user named Keith Ryan. Keith has been at Madison for twenty years and is responsible for all financial transactions. The information services department chose him as the most obvious user to head the design effort. Keith is in sympathy with this selection, but says, "I don't have time to spend designing a system; I work sixty hours a week as it is!"

The IS staff recognize the extent of Keith's efforts and devotion to the company, but ask why additional staff cannot be hired to remove some of the load from Keith. Keith says that he has tried to break in new people, but the demands of the job are too rigorous and they all leave.

The president of Madison wants to know why the design of this new system is taking so long. What should the manager of the IS department do? What can he suggest to the president?

Potential Pitfalls in the Life Cycle

The above stages in the systems life cycle are widely recommended. When we have seen them followed rigorously as a checklist, however, the result has usually been systems that fail. What is wrong with the life cycle? Is the concept invalid? There are several major difficulties with rigidly following the stages in Table 15-1 in the development of a system.

First, the stages tend to focus attention on a particular design approach. We shall see several alternatives to conventional design in subsequent chapters. The steps in the life cycle also imply that the analyst is in control of the design process. If a design team works under this impression, there will be too little participation by users.

A very serious shortcoming of the life cycle is many analysts seem to interpret it as requiring the development of only one alternative. Users and managers need to have a series of options from which to choose. They are poorly served by designers who provide a single design for a new system rather than one with alternatives to the status quo. There may be ways to shorten the life cycle and to skip certain stages. Most discussions of the life cycle do not suggest shortcuts in development.

The systems life cycle provides a complete list of tasks, but we need to be flexible in how those tasks are accomplished and in what alternatives are presented to management.

USER-ORIENTED DESIGN

Problems with the Conventional View

In the conventional approach to systems analysis and design described above, the analyst is a skilled leader. The analyst interviews users, collects data, and returns to the information services department to create a new system. Instead of viewing the analyst as the designer of the system, we recommend strongly that users design their own systems. Stressing user input in design has become more popular lately. It is often called **joint applications development (JAD)** and includes both users and analysts. (IBM coined the term JAD and it offers a much more structured series of meetings and steps than described here.)

Does this joint approach mean users actually undertake some of the tasks normally carried out by the analyst? The answer is definitely yes. Our recommended approach raises two questions. First, why should users assume this role? Second, how can they do so? Our experience indicates users are capable of responding to this approach and successful results are possible.

A more user-oriented approach to design may require deviations from the standard systems life cycle. Although the conceptual steps represented in the cycle may be followed, innovations will be included. For example, design is often facilitated by prototyping. A **prototype** is a smaller-scale version of a planned feature for a new system. A good example is sales forecasting. We can code the new forecasting routine on a personal computer and analyze past data for a limited number of products. Users will be intimately involved in this test so they can provide feedback on the prototype and evaluate its output. When they are satisfied, the prototype can be programmed in final form with more error routines, data manipulation features, and so forth, which had been excluded to keep the prototype simple.

As a user, you must be sure you have adequate input in the design process. The professional systems analyst never uses the system—he or she moves on to another system after completing yours. The user often figures out too late that he or she is stuck with an inconvenient or unusable system. If you insist on influencing the design of the system and develop ownership of it, the chances for success are much greater.

Design Team

To coordinate users and the IS department staff, we recommend the formation of a design team with a user as head of the team. Having a user in charge makes the users' role apparent, ensures time will be available from other users, and demonstrates a strong commitment to users on the part of the information services department. Normal job activities should be reduced for the user in charge of the design team.

In cases with too many individuals for all of them to be involved, liaison representatives are suggested. These people interview other users and brief them on the system as it is developed. They are responsible for soliciting participation in phases in which it is meaningful.

The IS department's systems designer guides the design team, teaching the tools and techniques necessary to complete the design and providing

MANAGEMENT PROBLEM 15-3

Eat-Lite is a small chain of health-food stores on the East Coast. The company has grown rapidly and is now investigating the possibility of developing an information system to help control its operations. Wendy Schwartz, the firm's founder, described the reasons. "We need to get better reports back on our sales and we have to replenish the stores faster from our suppliers. We are out of stock too many times."

"I have used e-mail myself and I think it could help us communicate with the local store managers—you know—make the company seem a little more personal. We could also handle sales promotions and new-product introduction using it."

Wendy talked to a number of consultants, each of whom had different recommendations for the kind of system and equipment. The consultant that she liked the best wanted to first decide on the architecture: Should Eat-Lite try PCs in the store and a client-server architecture or think more about a midrange minicomputer at headquarters that would do most of the processing? How should store/headquarters communications be handled?

Wendy was a little confused. The book she read on systems analysis and design made it sound like one should do the logical design of a system without thinking about the hardware on which the system would run. Why is this consultant talking so much about hardware in the first place?

required technical advice and support, for example, by developing detailed file structures after users complete the logical database design. Systems designers monitor the project, describe the different stages, and help to schedule them. The actual analysis and design work is done by the users with the assistance of the analyst, rather than vice versa as in conventional systems design.

DATA COLLECTION FOR ANALYSIS AND DESIGN

What techniques are available to the design team for collecting data? As discussed earlier, the objective is to develop an understanding of key decisions, communications and coordination requirements, and how they are supported with information. The team needs to examine decisions, the flow of information in the organization, communications patterns, and the types of processing undertaken.

Observation One technique for collecting data on a process is to observe that process. Frequently in systems analysis and design we will "walk through" a system, observing crucial information flows and decision points. Then we may use

Changing the Structure of Customer Services

Capitol Holding Company is the fifth largest publicly held insurance company in the U.S. The Direct Response Group (DRG) has 2,500 employees serving 2 million customers and generates premium income of $800 million per year. The company has undertaken a major reengineering effort focusing on customer service. This change is accompanied by a change in business focus. Management wanted to move from mass marketing through direct mail, targeting individual customers with a few products.

The company is reorganizing into ten-person teams. The first team services 40,000 customers by selecting products for those customers, handling premium renewals, processing claims, and answering questions in general. The team concept is a major departure from the typical functional organization of an insurance company in which each activity is handled in a separate department.

Each team member is supported with a workstation connected to a relational database server through a local area network. A gateway and interfacing software allows connection to the traditional mainframe systems supporting other customers. The system was developed through prototyping with a joint applications development team. DRG plans to establish more customer management teams to better serve customers.

In this instance, organizational redesign necessitated the development of new systems to support a new business model. Information technology enabled DRG to implement a new business strategy and a reengineered business process.

one of the graphical techniques described later in this chapter to document our understanding of how the system functions.

Observations can also be quite structured. We may develop a rating form of some type to collect data on the frequency of inquiries, say, in a credit office. The analyst prepares a form showing the possible inquiries and then, during a sample of different days and hours, codes the actual inquiries.

Interviews

The systems analyst spends a great deal of time interacting with others, particularly in interview settings. Interviews have varying degrees of structure. For a first meeting, there may be no structure at all; the analyst may be getting acquainted with the user and gaining a broad understanding of the problem area. Often, as the project progresses, more structured interviews are conducted. The analyst may wish to prepare in advance an interview schedule containing the questions to be asked and the points to be covered. The main thing is to be prepared.

Questionnaires

A questionnaire allows us to obtain data from a relatively large number of people at a reasonable cost. A questionnaire can be thought of as a structured interview form with questions designed so they can be answered without a face-to-face encounter. The design of a good questionnaire is a difficult task. Although the idea is an extension of a structured interview form, the questionnaire is, in principle, capable of being completed by the respondent alone without an interviewer present.

Table 15-3 presents some examples of questionnaire and/or structured interview questions.

Comparing the Alternatives

Both questionnaires and interviews are important for the analyst, though interviewing will probably be used more often. An interview makes it easy to follow a new tangent. The respondent is not constrained by the limitations of the questions but can expand in other directions. If the question is ambiguous, the interviewer explains what is desired. Interviews are the best technique in an unstructured setting and when it is necessary to probe issues in depth.

Questionnaires offer the advantage of being relatively inexpensive to administer to a large group of respondents. They are well suited to expanding data collection beyond the interview. For example, assume a system is developed to be used by a number of sales representatives nationwide. If the firm has five hundred sales representatives, it is impossible to include all of them on a design team. Instead, we would use liaison representatives chosen as typical of the types of salespersons on the force. This group might assist in developing a questionnaire for the rest of the sales force, previously uninvolved in the design process. The questionnaire could explain some of the chosen trade-offs and characteristics of the system to

Table 15-3
Sample Interview/Questionnaire Items

1. Please describe your job.

2. With whom do you interact in your work?

3. What are the key factors in your work unit's success?

4. What factors are critical for your personal success?

5. What type of information and data do you use in your work?

6. Where does it come from? What do you do to change it in some way? Where does it go after you have worked on it?

7. What major bottlenecks exist in your sources and use of information and data?

8. What kind of technology do you use?

9. What do you like about your current technology platform?

10. What are the drawbacks of your current technology platform? What problems do you have? How do you resolve them?

11. If you could have any technology you wanted, what would it look like?

12. If you could redesign the entire work unit here, what would the flow of work look like?

all potential users to obtain their input and feedback. Valuable additional data could also be collected at the same time. Questionnaires are also a good way to obtain feedback in a postimplementation audit.

STRUCTURED VERSUS OBJECT-ORIENTED DESIGN

In response to the high failure rate for new systems, that is, many systems do not meet their original specifications or time and budget targets, we have seen the development of two approaches designed to improve the chances for successful development. Both approaches emphasize logical and structured views of design. The first of these approaches is called **structured design** while the second is known as **object-oriented design**.

The Role of Structured Design

What is structure in design? Basically, we try to take a disciplined, step-by-step approach to reduce complexity. A good example is **top-down design**; this philosophy means that the designer first concentrates on an overview, then moves to successive levels of detail. If at any step the designer becomes confused, he or she backs up one level to a diagram with more of an overview. The major purpose of this approach is to improve understanding and communication.

The process is very similar to the set of plans developed by an architect. When a client asks for a new building to be designed, the architect develops rough sketches and adds detail over time. In presenting drawings to the client or even to construction workers, the architect does not provide a first page with the details of the electrical wiring! Instead, usually we find that the first page is a perspective of the building. The next page might be four side views, followed by a page with a high-level floor plan. As each page is turned, we find more detail.

To Talk to a Computer

For years, voice input has been a dream for computer users. While limited voice recognition systems are available, their use to date has not been extensive in personal computing. (The IBM Aptiva computers for the home have limited voice recognition input.) You can, for example, buy a speech recognition board and software for a PC and issue commands by voice for some popular spreadsheet programs. Common carriers like Sprint do employ voice recognition in an effort to further automate the phone system. However, the phone systems employ a limited vocabulary which greatly simplifies the recognition task.

For example, Sprint might want to recognize several different voice requests to call different people, commands like "Dial Mom." It might also want to recognize the word "bye" so the computer can hang-up immediately on a call. It turns out that the pronunciation of the word "bye" can vary between speakers in the North and the South, and even between men and women. Women have smaller heads than men in general, and this results in higher vocal frequencies. Different people also speak with different intensities.

To recognize single words (identifying continuous speech is much more difficult than recognizing individual words), a computer breaks down sound into 10 millisecond snippets. The computer goes through thousands of snippets looking for matches. The first part of "buy" could be the beginning of bicycle or other words. A system might look at the position of the word in a sentence to further clarify its meaning. For example, "I'll see you tomorrow. Bye." has a structure which suggests the speaker is ending the conversation, especially when compared to: "I'll go by the store for some milk."

Linguists have identified 10 pronunciations of parmesan cheese and 11 of lingerie. If you are thinking about a voice recognition system for ordering pizza or clothing, these kinds of differences present a formidable design challenge. While voice recognition has many attractive features, we may have to settle for graphic user interfaces and a mouse, at least in the short run.

Data Flow Diagrams

One of the most popular structured approaches to design is the use of data flow diagrams (see Figure 15-2). Compared with traditional flowcharts, the **data flow diagram (DFD)** is far less complex, there are only four symbols defined for the highest level of detail.

The DFD approach is more than just the symbols. It is important for the analyst to exercise discipline in preparing the charts. The recommended strategy is top-down: begin with a high-level diagram and place succeeding levels of detail on subsequent pages. In addition, as adding detail makes the drawing cluttered, the analyst should take one process or subsystem and explode its detail on a separate sheet of paper. DFDs can easily be read and prepared by users. One of their most important contributions is to facilitate understanding among all of those involved in a design project.

In later chapters we discuss computer-aided software engineering or CASE. This approach to building systems tries to automate as much of systems design as possible. An analyst uses structured design CASE software on a PC-based workstation to construct DFDs, data dictionaries, and other components of a system.

An Example of Structured Design

Imagine that a group of entrepreneurs decides to open a mail-order business selling software for personal computers. A customer sends in an order form, and employees of the business ship the software to the customer. Figure 15-3 is a high-level DFD for this firm. At this level, we see the basic flow of an order coming to the firm and a shipment going to the customer.

Figure 15-2
Data flow diagram symbols.

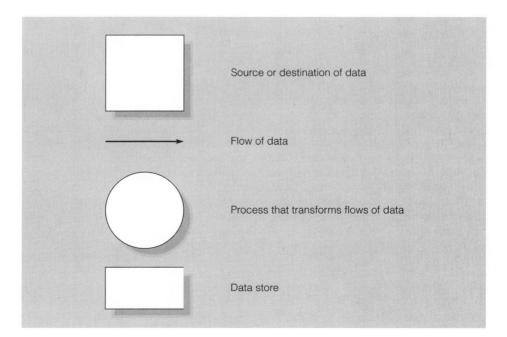

Source or destination of data

Flow of data

Process that transforms flows of data

Data store

Figure 15-3
Overview of mail-order business.

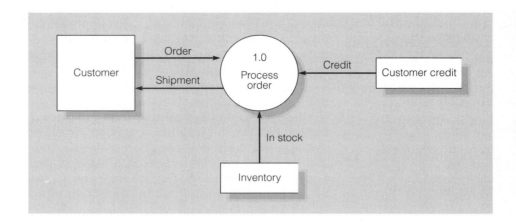

Before shipping an order, an employee must look at an inventory record and check the customer's credit.

Figure 15-4 presents the next level of detail. We see that the first action is to check the inventory to see if the software program ordered is in stock. If so, the employee places the order in a file marked "to be filled." The warehouse staff removes orders from this file, finds them in inventory, packages the programs, and sends the shipment to the customers. If at any point one loses track of the process, it is necessary only to back up one or two diagrams to get an overview.

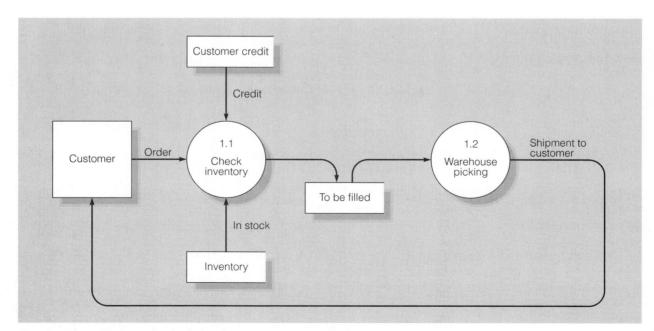

Figure 15-4 The next level of detail.

In Figure 15-5, the designer addresses the question of what to do when the warehouse is out of stock. Management decides that back-ordering is probably not feasible as the customer will look elsewhere for the program rather than wait. However, it is important to reorder when stock is low or entirely gone. If we need more merchandise, an order must be placed with a supplier. There is also a path from warehouse picking to the reorder process if the inventory records do not exactly match the warehouse contents. Here one wants to check the warehouse carefully and then reorder if in fact there is nothing in inventory.

Figure 15-6 adds more detail to the reorder process and includes an accounts-receivable process. We see the firm must check in merchandise when it is received from suppliers and the goods eventually are placed in inventory. Accounts receivable are important if the firm is to stay in business! You must send an invoice to the customer with the shipment of goods, and create a receivables record.

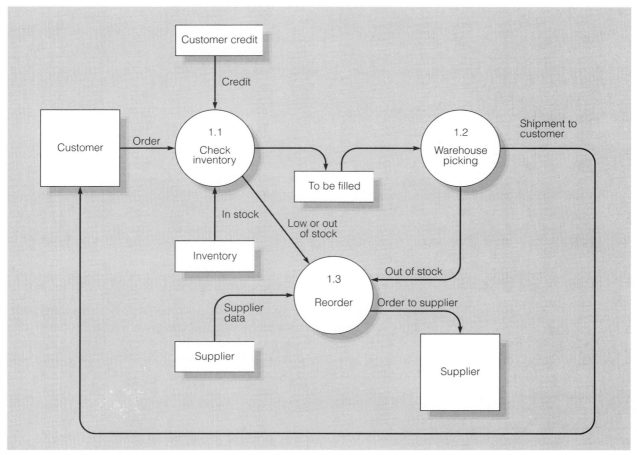

Figure 15-5 Reorder plan.

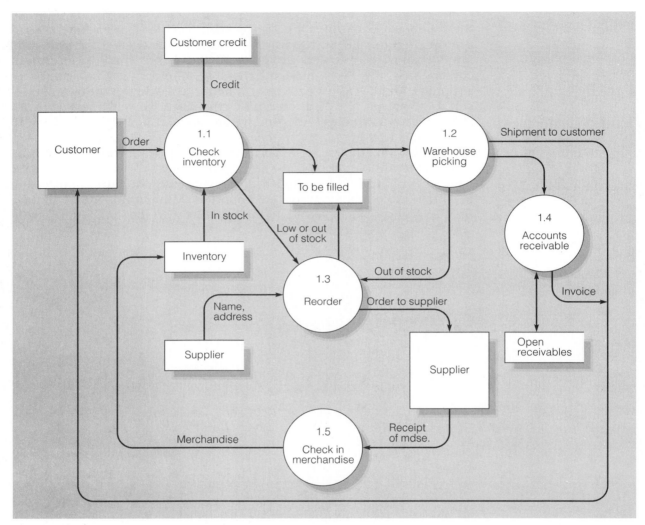

Figure 15-6   Receipt of goods and accounts receivable.

It would be possible to expand Figure 15-6 further, but the diagram is beginning to get cluttered. At this point, the designer would probably take each process and treat it as a subsystem for further explosions. For example, it would be possible to treat the accounts-receivable process as a subsystem and generate several pages of greater detail on how the firm creates and processes receivables.

This example illustrates what we mean by design and logic. The managers of this company are creating the various information flows and processing steps in their new firm. They must design different order-entry procedures and identify the trade-offs among them. For example, they may choose to have customers submit orders on paper, by fax, by telephone with a clerk filling out a paper order, entering the order directly in a computer, use the Internet to order, or any combination of these options. In making this choice, the managers might trade off factors like cost, customer service, and development time.

When the managers decide, for example, to install a toll-free telephone number and have order-entry personnel enter orders directly in the computer, they have designed one part of the system. When the managers specify the questions the clerk is to ask the customer and what he or she is to type in the computer, they are designing the processing logic. They could decide to identify the customer by phone number or by zip code, last name, and first initial. Based on this input the system would retrieve data about the customer (if he had ordered before) such as his complete address. Design is the process of creating this new information processing system.

Object-Oriented Design

There is great interest in a conceptual approach to programming and systems analysis called **object-oriented analysis**. This approach to design is tied very closely to programming: software becomes a collection of discrete **objects** that incorporate data structure and behavior. An object is a representation of some real-world thing and a number of specific instances of that thing. For example, we could define a Ford Explorer as an object. Objects encapsulate attributes and services; this Explorer has four doors and four-wheel drive. All objects have an identity and can be distinguished from one another.

A **class** describes a group of objects with similar properties, common behavior, and common relationships with other objects. The Explorer is a member of the Vehicles class. The grouping of objects into classes makes it easier to work with abstractions. The designer can think about the system at the level of the class without having to bother with individual objects in the class. There are methods or procedures associated with each class. They apply to the objects in the class and change some attribute. The same method may apply to different classes, but it may take on different forms in different classes. This characteristic of a method applying across classes, changing its implementation to match the class, is called **polymorphism**.

A link connects different object instances, for example, Mary Smith (an object) works for (a link) the Widget Company (an object). Links with common characteristics are grouped into an association. Based on what we have seen in past chapters, it may help to know that links and associations are often implemented as pointers between objects and classes. Objects communicate by sending messages. As a result, one object cannot directly access the object in another class, which means that objects are **encapsulated** or protected from damage from other objects. The message generally results in the execution of some method of processing that is stored with the object. Different authors describe this processing as done through methods, procedures, or services.

To build an object-oriented model, you identify the classes and objects in the problem domain. Class diagrams contain classes and show their relationships, while object diagrams show how objects send and receive messages. Over time, one builds class libraries: an objective of this approach is to reuse software. For example, a class and its objects for an inventory system might also be used in a production control system. Reuse is intended to reduce the amount of time spent and the cost of developing applications. Programmers implement object-oriented systems with languages like C++ (C enhanced with features to support object-oriented programming) or Smalltalk, one of the first object-oriented languages.

As an example, assume you are to develop a vehicle registration system. The object of interest is a vehicle. There are many instances of vehicles (cars, trucks), so an object tells us something about a class of real-world things. Instances of vehicles have different attributes (wheels, engines). Figure 15-7 shows a classification structure for vehicles. It shows that cars are one type of vehicle. We are interested in land vehicles with internal combustion engines. (We have eliminated the class of electric-powered vehicles like golf carts and some forklifts.) Within the subclass of cars are vehicles with the following attributes: four wheels, doors, and a body. Cars can be off-road or on-road. An off-road car has four-wheel drive and high ground clearance, and so on.

Figure 15-7
An object classification with inheritance.

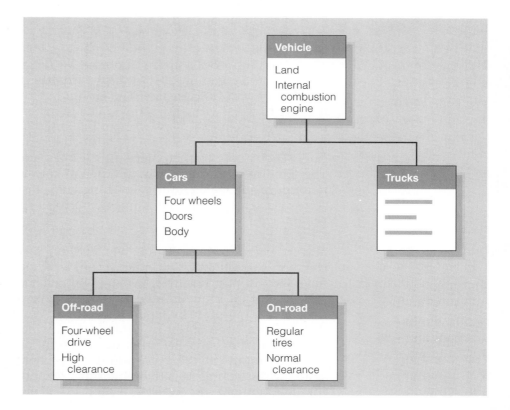

A very significant concept in object-oriented analysis is **inheritance**. Each instance of an object inherits the properties of its class. An instance of an on-road car, a Ford station wagon, inherits all attributes above it in the hierarchy. It is a land vehicle with an internal combustion engine and has four wheels, doors, a body, regular tires, and normal ground clearance.

An important characteristic of object-oriented analysis is communications through messages among different objects. These messages may be in the form of services that are performed for the objects. One example of a service is to register a vehicle and issue license plates. Repairing a vehicle is another kind of service. The message triggers a method or routine stored with the object to change some attribute of the object, for example, a message from a mechanic object might say the Ford wagon attribute "status" should be changed from "broken" to "in service."

Figure 15-8 shows an example of objects communicating through a message. At time t the Ford wagon object is broken. At time t+1 a mechanic object sends a message to the Ford wagon object indicating that the mechanic has repaired the car. This message activates a method or procedure to change an attribute of the Ford wagon object. The results of that change are shown at time t+2. The Ford wagon object now has an attribute that indicates the car is in service again.

Since the routine that makes the change is stored with the Ford wagon object, it is possible to change other parts of the system without changing this object. Other objects also do not have the ability to directly modify the Ford wagon object, reducing the chance for errors. If you change some part of the system, but continue to send messages in the same format as before the changes, there is no need to modify the Ford wagon and other automobile objects in its class. This encapsulation of the object and the methods for changing its attributes makes it easier to change one part of a system without having an unanticipated impact on other components.

Figure 15-8

Message passing and encapsulation in object-oriented systems.

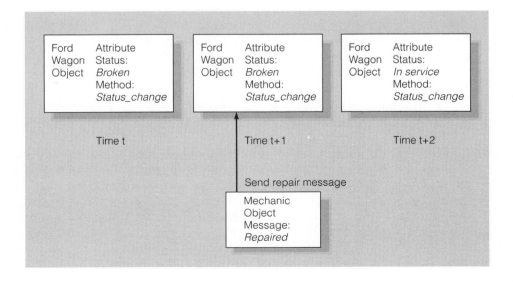

Design incorporates identifying objects, the relationships among objects, and the services that are performed involving the objects. A set of steps for object-oriented analysis adapted from Coad and Yourdon (1990) is:

1. Define classes and objects to form the highest "layer" of the analysis.
2. Proceed to define the detailed structure of classes and objects such as one-to-many relationships (very similar to entity-relationship models) and inheritance.
3. Define the methods to be performed and the messages that will trigger methods.
4. Define the attributes of classes.

Object-oriented analysis is relatively new. It appears very promising and is the appropriate design approach if you plan to use object-oriented programming to implement a system.

A Comparison of Approaches

While it may not be readily apparent, structured methodologies and object-oriented approaches are quite different in underlying philosophies. There is no one standard methodology for each approach. Different authors propose different notations and design steps for both structured and object-oriented design. However, all of these authors agree on certain features for

Airport Objects

The new Denver airport gained fame through extensive delays attributed to an automated luggage system that delivered bags every place but where they were supposed to go. Continental Airlines thinks that its new reservations system interface, in contrast to the baggage system, will be a great success. Continental has outsourced the development of its system to EDS and is planning to deploy it in seven airports and training centers.

Continental's objective was to create a check-in interface that would save money, collect missed revenue, improve productivity for agents and simplify training. It also wanted to accomplish all of this without having to extensively modify its mainframe reservations system. The new system is designed to reduce or eliminate typing. In a typical reservations system, agents type cryptic codes to issue commands to the system. The new Continental system, called ASAP, uses objects to represent business processes. There are about 4300 such objects in the system. One object, for example, knows how to validate credit cards. Customized pictures show what a transaction does, for example, by graphically depicting available seats on a diagram of the airplane. Typing is also in English: instead of entering ORD for Chicago, the agent types "Chicago." Experience to date indicates that a novice agent can do complex transactions and it is hoped that the system will cut training time by 60% to 70%.

The local client is a 486-based PC which is connected to a Novell server running an Oracle database management system. The server, in turn, has a connection to Continental's mainframe reservations system. The system helps both agents and passengers who should get faster service with the new technology.

each approach. Structured methodology is based on the notion of functions; programs consist of modules to meet functional requirements. Function and procedure are the primary focus of this approach, and functions or processes share data. The emphasis is on process modeling rather than data modeling and analysis proceeds in a top-down manner.

In object-oriented approaches, programs consist of interrelated classes of objects; data and procedures are encapsulated within the object. The analysis proceeds from the bottom up. Objects communicate with each other by sending messages to another object, which in turn, responds to the message. One uses object-oriented programming languages designed or extended to support objects, classes, and all of the characteristics of this development approach like inheritance, encapsulation, and polymorphism.

Object-oriented approaches to design are discussed extensively today, though only a small proportion of companies use the methodology. It is not clear if this approach will, in fact, provide substantial benefits until we have more experience with it.

CHAPTER SUMMARY

1. Systems analysis and design is an activity that requires teamwork among managers, the information services staff, and users. It is a creative and exciting process that can bring about substantial change in the organization.

2. It is important to appreciate the difference between designing an application for yourself, say using a spreadsheet on a PC, and designing an application that will be used by a number of individuals in the organization.

3. Traditionally, we have conducted multi-user design following a life cycle model.

4. In designing applications, managers, users, and the professional designers all have important roles to play.

5. The life cycle model, while useful for thinking about design, has problems that can be addressed by extensive user involvement and influence in design and by adaptations like prototyping.

6. There are a variety of ways to collect the information that one needs for design. Interviews are the most popular method.

7. Structured design techniques focus on top-down design. They employ dataflow diagrams and entity-relationship models to describe a system.

8. Object-oriented design is the newest approach. It concentrates on data in the form of objects which communicate by passing messages. Objects, their attributes, and methods or procedures that act on the objects are encapsulated together.

9. The task of learning user requirements and determining the functions for a new system are the most difficult part of design, regardless of whether one uses structured or object-oriented approaches to describe the system.

IMPLICATIONS FOR MANAGEMENT

I am constantly surprised and encouraged by the inventive applications people discover for technology. You can easily find an outlet for your creativity in designing information systems. There are standard kinds of transactions processing systems in most organizations, but even within a routine application like order entry, there are a variety of ways to execute the design. For a multi-user system, you will want to appoint a design team and be sure there are reviews of the system with management and other users. You may also have to act as the chief sponsor for a system you would like to see developed. It is important to remember that professional designers disappear into the sunset after completing a project. Users have to live with the application every day.

KEY WORDS

Champion
Class
Conversion
Data flow diagram (DFD)
Design
Encapsulation
Enhancements
Feasibility study
Inheritance
Joint applications development
  (JAD)
Maintenance
Objects

Object-oriented analysis
Object-oriented design
Operations
Polymorphism
Preliminary survey
Prototype
Structured design
Systems analysis
Systems life cycle
Testing
Top-down design
Training

RECOMMENDED READING

Coad, P., and E. Yourdon. *Object-Oriented Analysis.* Englewood Cliffs, N.J.: Prentice-Hall, 1990. (Presents one often cited approach to object-oriented design.)

De Marco, T. *Structured Analysis and System Specification.* Englewood Cliffs, N.J.: Prentice-Hall, 1979. (An excellent book on structured design.)

Kendall, K., and J. Kendall. *Systems Analysis and Design* 3rd ed. Englewood Cliffs, N.J.: Prentice-Hall, 1995. (A modern systems analysis text including both structured and object-oriented approaches to design.)

Rumbaugh, J., M. Blaha, W. Premerlani, F. Eddy, and W. Lorensen. *Object-Oriented Modeling and Design.* Englewood Cliffs, N.J.: Prentice-Hall, 1991. (A detailed introduction to object-oriented design.)

DISCUSSION QUESTIONS

1. What are the advantages of user-oriented design?
2. What are the disadvantages for the IS staff and users of user-oriented design?
3. Would you expect user-oriented design to be more or less costly than conventional approaches?
4. What is the role of top management in building systems?
5. What type of planning for applications should be undertaken by the IS department?
6. Does a long-range IS department plan make any sense when technology is rapidly changing?
7. How should new systems development projects be charged in the organization? Should overhead, the IS department, or user department budgets absorb the cost?
8. Why have so many existing systems concentrated on information flows and transactions processing rather than decisions?
9. What are the problems of putting a user in charge of a design team for a new system for the IS department?
10. What does a user need to know to contribute to the design of a multi-user system?
11. Develop a questionnaire for obtaining data from potential users of a system on their attitudes, expectations, and thoughts for the goals of a new system.
12. The design of information systems is best accomplished by a team. What possible conflicts might this create for other employees? How should the team structure be presented to reduce these problems?
13. If users design systems, will changes still be necessary after conversion, when the system is in operation? Should as many changes be needed as under conventional design? Why or why not?
14. How can users be sufficiently involved in systems analysis and design in a large organization when there are many potential users who should be included?
15. Can top managers participate in systems analysis and design if they will also be users? Is this activity important enough for their participation?

16. How can management help a user participate in the design of systems? What are the major factors inhibiting full participation?

17. How should the IS department's budget be divided between new applications and enhancements to existing systems?

18. Are there decisions in the operation of existing systems that users should influence?

19. What is the purpose of structured design methodologies?

20. To what extent can personnel resources be reallocated within the IS department to provide more flexibility in meeting demands for service?

21. What are the major characteristics of object-oriented design?

22. Why do many IS staff members resist making changes requested in operational systems?

23. When on a cost-cutting drive, management will sometimes dictate an across-the-board budget reduction of some number, say 10 percent. Does this approach make sense for the IS department? What alternatives are available?

24. What is the most likely reason a proposed system will be infeasible?

25. How do changes in technology, especially advances in hardware, affect the feasibility of new applications of technology?

26. Where are the largest bottlenecks in the systems life cycle? That is, where are the most problems and delays probably encountered in developing a system?

27. Compare and contrast structured and object-oriented approaches to design.

28. Is there one design approach that is best in all situations?

29. What design approach would you choose for a system to process incoming orders for a manufacturing firm?

30. What design approach would you recommend for an interactive decision support system to be used by the treasurer of a firm to manage cash deposits?

31. What are the differences in design for a multiuser system versus a personal system on a personal computer?

CHAPTER 15 PROJECTS

A GROUP DESIGN PROJECT

Please note that this assignment is to be completed in a group. It is very hard to do systems analysis and design alone, particularly if it is the first time you have worked on such a project. An important part of this exercise is learning to work with people on a design team who will have different ideas than yours.

In order to make the assignment a little bit more fun and to create some diversity, your first task is to choose your company and products. The firm you are "designing" manufactures and distributes a product (of your choosing). The company has its headquarters at its one manufacturing plant in Hoboken, New Jersey. There are three warehouses which handle regional distribution throughout the East Coast. (There is some business from other locations, but the firm's major market extends west, from Boston to Cleveland, and south to Washington, D.C.)

Your company obtains sales from three sources:

1. Sales representatives who call on customers; 45 percent of the orders come from this source.

2. A group of three 800 toll-free numbers which customers call directly to place an order; 40 percent of the orders come to the phone desk.

3. Mail; 15 percent of the orders come by mail and fax.

There are a number of problems with the current way orders are processed in your firm. First, there are no computers and no automation. All orders must be written on a standard order form for processing. Sales representatives mail most orders to headquarters and call in urgent orders.

Communications with the warehouses are disorganized. Two or three times a day copies of orders are faxed to the warehouses for picking. The order department phones in emergency orders. Because of all the problems in processing the orders, about 25 percent of the day's orders are urgent enough to be phoned to the warehouse. As a result, the warehouse staff picking orders is not scheduled efficiently.

Second, as the executive vice president said, "We are drowning in paper. Our current system was fine when we were a small company, but our volume has grown 50 percent a year for the last three years. I suspect we are losing orders and I know our delivery time is terrible. Some customers have told us they are going to our competitors because, while our product is superior, we can't get it to them."

Third, your firm does not have the ability to learn anything from its orders. Because they are all on paper and it takes so much effort just to get the goods out, no one can look at the information the orders contain. You don't know what percentage of sales each source of orders represents. Management wonders if it pays to have a direct sales force, but can't get the data to decide. All forecasting for production is done by looking at what was manufactured the previous year. There is no updating from current orders.

Your assignment is to design a new system for order processing for your company. Your report should contain the logical design for a new system including:

1. What data you will collect, where, and how,

2. The way your system will process data,

3. How the system will store the data,

4. How users will retrieve and display data.

You should show the design of at least one input screen and one report.

You are not required to recommend hardware, but you should give some thought to hardware/software architecture. For example, are you designing a system for an airline reservations system mainframe computer or for a pocket Sharp Wizard?

DEFINING A SYSTEM FOR SIMON MARSHALL

In a previous chapter you were asked to develop a simple portfolio system for Simon Marshall Associates. The system you developed was based on a personal computer and used a database management package. Because the problem was relatively well specified, there really was no systems design.

Now, take the problem you completed and think about turning it into a working system for Simon Marshall. First, identify the objectives of a system and its potential users. Then, think about features that might be necessary for different individuals who might work with the system. Is there a need for more data than in the original problem? What kind of output will users want to have, both on the screen and in printed form?

CHAPTER **16**

Building Systems: Further Developments

Other Input
Handling Errors
Backup
Security and Fraud

Computer-Aided Software Engineering
Upper CASE
Lower CASE

● OBJECTIVES

1. Learning to manage information technology.

During the early stages of the design process, input from management can make a major contribution to the success of the system. The manager sets the objectives for the system and reviews its features. Our observation is that systems with more managerial input have greater levels of success.

2. Preparing to apply technology.

The user is most likely to be heavily involved in the stages of the life cycle that precede programming. As you read the chapter, think about the design process and its complexity. There are a large number of tasks that must go well for a project to be successful.

3. Transforming the organization.

It is often the case that applications with the greatest chance of transforming the firm are the most risky and the least likely to demonstrate a clear cost savings in advance. The manager has to decide whether to undertake these risky, potentially high-payoff applications.

In this chapter, we examine the early stages of the systems life cycle, the place where users have the most to contribute. We begin with the preliminary survey and the feasibility study. The output from these two studies is used to determine whether to proceed with the design of an information system and to select a single processing alternative if the system is approved. If a system is feasible, the analysis and design stages are undertaken, and the design team prepares detailed specifications.

SYSTEMS ANALYSIS

Analysis is the study of a problem, generally done before undertaking some action to solve the problem. In the case of systems analysis, the first task is understanding and describing existing information processing procedures in the area of the proposed new system. Many of the techniques recommended in the previous chapter can be used to document our understanding of the present processing system, such as data flow diagrams.

In many instances it will be hard to identify any organized set of procedures that represent the existing information processing system. We need to enumerate problems and determine what motivated the suggestion that technology might help in processing information. Whether there is a well-defined system or not, we should develop the specific information listed in Table 16-1. First, we should identify decisions that have to be made and the decision maker who is to be responsible. What are the inputs and outputs, what is the frequency of the decision, and what are the costs involved?

Next, we should identify crucial information flows including the source, frequency, and volume of information. Information can be characterized according to the decision-making framework discussed in Chapter 3.

Table 16-1
Analyzing the Existing System

Decisions
    Decision maker
    Input
    Output
    Frequency of decision
    Level of costs

Information
    Flow
    Characteristics
    Form
    Source
    Retention

Transactions and processing
    Operations
    By whom performed
    Peak load
    Average load

Individuals/functions

Communications/coordination
    Communication among units, individuals

For example, we can look at the form in which data are gathered and processed, either written or verbal. If documents are involved, how many are there, and what is their information content? What types of decisions are supported?

We also need to identify what processing is done to information as it flows through a system. Who processes the information? What are the peak and average loads? A study should identify the critical communications between organizational subunits and individuals. We try to understand what role the system plays in coordinating work flows and other activities. Finally, we should estimate the current cost of information processing.

For the preliminary survey, we develop very rough estimates and collect samples of documents. We may interview only a few people and use approximations. After we develop a list of objectives for the system, we use the data gathered to make a rough sketch of several alternative new systems. The preliminary survey has a role in helping users develop their vision of a new information system.

The feasibility study goes into much more detail, and instead of making approximations, we actually sample documents and develop more refined estimates. In the feasibility study, we trace the flow of information through the system and spend time with the various individuals who originate and process the data. Thus, the same framework used in the preliminary survey can be used for the feasibility study, though our analysis for the feasibility study will be much more detailed.

SURVEY AND FEASIBILITY STUDY

In this section, we present recommendations for the contents of the preliminary survey and feasibility study. Basically, each of these documents consists of two parts: the present system and an alternative. The latter section actually presents several potential alternatives and evaluates them on technical, economic, and operational criteria. We must estimate technical and operational feasibility and compare costs with benefits.

Costs and Benefits of New Systems

Management usually insists on a cost/benefit justification for a system. You will generally find that the categories for benefits differ considerably depending on the type of system planned. For example, it is likely that strategic systems will have more uncertain benefits and will be justified by improvements in customer service, new sources of revenues, and such. The estimates of costs and benefits for transactions processing systems are usually more certain and detailed. The firm expects to reduce inventory balances by 25 percent, which results in a quantifiable savings in investment and handling.

The tangible and concrete benefits for some systems, particularly strategic applications, are likely not to exceed their costs. Management may decide to develop the system anyway and the cost/benefit analysis helps assess the risks involved.

In examining costs versus benefits, there are a large number of factors to consider. System costs include the following:

Development

- Systems analyst time
- Programmer time
- User time
- Computer time
- Possible hardware purchase costs
- Possible software purchase costs
- Possible outside services costs (e.g., system integrators, consultants)

Operations

- Computer costs
- Communications costs
- Operating staff costs
- Incremental user costs
- Maintenance costs

Development costs are the actual cost of analysis, design, and installation for the system. These costs are highly sensitive to the amount of time necessary to develop the system and are directly proportional to the number of analysts, programmers, and users and the length of their involvement. Computer time for testing tends to be far less expensive than staff time. Historically, the professions' estimates of the time required to design and install a system have been far too low.

When assessing total costs, we should not forget the expenses of operating a new system. A new system may require the use of part of the time available on an existing computer, an upgrade on the present system, or a new computer or network. Many systems involve telecommunications and networks, which can be very expensive. Incremental staff in the IS department and users may be required to operate the system. Finally, there are the costs of routine maintenance and modifications. No system is ever finished; "bugs" will need to be eliminated, and users will request periodic enhancements as they work with a system.

Traditionally, benefits are analyzed from the point of view of tangible cost savings from a system. Often these savings are measured by the reduction of workers currently employed or by an estimate of the number of future employees who must be hired without the system. (Many times, savings projected in personnel prove illusory.) Tangible savings also come from more efficient processing. For example, an inventory control system may reduce inventory balances while maintaining service levels. The firm saves the interest charges on the money previously required to finance the inventory level needed before the computer system. There is great interest in business reengineering or business process redesign, discussed in Chapter 18. Here management is looking for significant paybacks like an order-of-magnitude reduction in costs.

Tangible cost savings can be difficult to estimate in some cases. Emery (1974) has suggested looking at the value of perfect information as providing an upper bound on possible benefits. For example, in a forecasting application, what is the maximum benefit from having a perfect forecast of sales, that is, knowing in advance exactly what sales will be? If the cost of developing the system exceeds the maximum benefit under perfect information, the application will undoubtedly be rejected immediately. If, however, the benefits appear higher than the costs, we can make various assumptions about the impact of less-than-perfect forecasts from the proposed system.

To refine the benefits estimates, a prototype of the forecasting system could be applied using a simple computerized version of the forecast. The model could process historical data to provide an estimate of the improvements the model would produce over the existing forecasting procedures.

Not only should we look at tangible cost savings, we must consider intangibles and unquantifiable savings. This is particularly true as we move from transactions processing systems toward operational managerial control and strategic systems, where intangible benefits are more important. Some of the technologies that we discuss to support work groups in Chapter 21 are also hard to justify on cost savings.

We believe that technology can be used to increase revenue as well as reduce costs. Systems that give the firm a strategic advantage, such as a greater market share, are difficult to cost-justify in advance. The following list of benefits may prove helpful in this analysis:

- The ability to obtain information previously unavailable
- The receipt of information on a more timely basis
- Improvements in operations
- The ability to perform calculations not possible before (for example, the simulation of production schedules)
- Reduction in clerical activity
- Improvements in quality and accuracy
- Improvements in decision making
- Better communications and coordination in the firm
- Improvements in customer service
- Creation of ties with customers and suppliers
- Reductions in cycle time

- Contribution to corporate strategy
- Improvements in competitiveness
- Major redesign and improvements in business processes
- A dramatic restructuring or redesign of the entire organization using IT design variables.

Emery also discusses some of the problems of quantifying the benefits from intangible savings. For example, suppose an automobile manufacturer can increase the probability from 90 to 95 percent that a dealer will have parts in stock. How can the manufacturer quantify (in dollars) the increased customer satisfaction and goodwill that will result from getting his or her car repaired without having to wait for a part? Of course, when a system can be justified on the grounds of tangible savings alone, the quantification of intangible savings will not be necessary.

Although intangible savings data may not be concrete, they can be evaluated. The automobile company can survey a sample of its dealers to determine their estimates of the monetary value of reduced stockouts. Although crude, the estimate is far better than not including this factor in the analysis of the new system. If we develop only systems that show tangible savings, we may ignore many of the benefits of information systems. It is very difficult to justify a planning system or decision support aid on the basis of tangible cost savings.

Many organizations also use subjective techniques to determine whether a project is desirable from a cost/benefit standpoint. They argue that with uncertain intangible benefits, one still has to decide whether a

Cutting the Home-Buying Cycle Time

The Federal Home Loan Mortgage Corporation (Freddie Mac) has installed a system which can check a home buyer's credit in less than four seconds. The objective of the system was to bring more first-time home buyers into the housing market by streamlining a cumbersome, 6–8 week long process with a lot of paper. The new process is designed to require a week only and to use electronics in place of paper to the greatest extent possible. Another benefit: the system should cut closing costs from 20% to 50%. These costs can run as high as $2500 to $3000 and must be paid "up front."

Freddie Mac has automated its underwriting rules in an expert system called the Loan Prospector. It is also offering an EDI value-added network called GoldWorks. Fourteen mortgage firms now use the Loan Prospector to evaluate an applicant's credit worthiness on the spot. The system provides two different ways for lenders to obtain credit information through cooperating credit bureaus, reducing a process that used to take weeks into one that is completed in seconds. Automatic underwriting and a credit network are expected to cut 20 to 30 days from the mortgage application process and save the buyer $1000. It is this savings that Freddie Mac hopes will increase home ownership, which has fallen in recent years from 66% of the population to 64%.

system appears justified. These decision makers use their subjective feelings of what a reasonable figure would be for the benefits provided by the system.

Regardless of the sophistication of the cost/benefit analysis, we need to develop a list of costs and benefits as part of a feasibility study. Then, before proceeding, agreement should be reached by all involved that the system is worth developing.

Another View of the Investment in IT

The discussion above is derived from traditional notions of capital budgeting. Dos Santos (1991) suggests that this view does not do justice to the possible payoffs from an investment in information technology. He argues that we should also try to evaluate the value of the future opportunities today's investment provides. For example, if the firm invests today in a worldwide communications network, the presence of that network in five years may allow the firm to introduce new services worldwide by simply plugging in a PC or terminal. Future applications will not need to be designed with their own communications subsystems.

It is very hard to evaluate this possible future benefit. Dos Santos suggests one approach is to use a classic options valuation model from finance. The difficulty lies in predicting what you might be able to do in the future given today's investment as well as in figuring out what that future application is worth. We should also point out that undertaking any system today can also foreclose opportunities for the future. For example, if we commit a lot of resources to one application, we may not have enough staff or funds to develop a new application that is suggested a year from now. We also can make technological decisions that preclude (or at least make difficult) other options. If we decide to build a private satellite communications network, we may feel that all of our communications must use the

MANAGEMENT PROBLEM 16-1

The order processing department manager at Leisure Clothing has a serious problem. She cannot understand why the information services department is so unresponsive to her requests. The firm has an elaborate on-line order-entry system that serves the entire United States. For the past six months, the order processing manager has logged the requests she has made for changes to the system. The total number of requests now stands at fifteen, and only three of the changes have been implemented!

When the manager of the order-entry system from the IS department stopped in to see her, she indicated displeasure over the lack of progress and suggested two new modifications. The weary systems manager asked, "Do these new changes have priority over the five you suggested last week, or should we try to do those first?"

The conversation grew more heated until finally both parties were shouting. What do you suppose is responsible for this conflict? What steps can each individual take to resolve it? What does the department manager need to appreciate, and what action should the information services department take?

network even if the common carriers come out with an appealing new service that might be a substitute.

The economic evaluation of IT projects is very difficult. It appears that traditional capital-budgeting approaches do not work very well, but no one has found an acceptable substitute yet. We certainly must look at costs and benefits, but we should also be aware of the future consequences of today's decisions and try to include them, if only qualitatively or as an intangible.

Identifying Systems Alternatives

General One of the major activities during the survey or feasibility study is to sketch possible alternatives for a new information processing system. Given the wide range of technology available, it is difficult not to be able to provide some assistance for a problem. The issue is not so much whether a system is feasible as what alternative is desirable.

During a feasibility study, a design team should develop alternatives and criteria for evaluating the alternatives. For a particular situation, a user may take the least expensive and most rapidly implementable system. In another case, a user may opt for a very comprehensive system to be custom programmed. The important point is this: as a user, insist on seeing some alternatives!

Packages For many proposed systems, an applications package offers an alternative. Frequently, large amounts of money and time can be saved by using one of these packages, though there can be a number of drawbacks. An applications package is an over-the-counter program or system of programs purchased as an end product. The package vendor tries to make the product very general. Users supply the data parameters that apply to their situation, and the package does the processing.

Since computer power is becoming cheaper per computation, it makes sense in many instances to acquire a package that may use computer hardware inefficiently, in order to have an application functioning earlier. However, there can be legitimate reasons not to use packages. You should develop a set of criteria for the technical requirements a package must meet to qualify for consideration.

Organizational Impact

You should attempt to estimate the effect of each alternative system on the organization. What departments and individuals will be affected by the system, and what jobs will it change? What will happen to any employees who are replaced by a system? Does the application create new links with customers and/or suppliers? Does technology make it possible to restructure the organization or some part of it? Is part of the intent of this application to support the IT organization design variables in Chapter 4 to move toward a new structure, for example, the T-Form organization?

Technological Feasibility

A proposed system may stretch the capabilities of modern technology, but may be the one that provides the firm with a great advantage. The design team needs to evaluate if a new system is technologically feasible. Burlington Northern railroad developed an extensive prototype of a train scheduling system in one region of the country to provide information on technological feasibility and estimate costs and benefits if the system were installed across its entire service area. This system-wide decision involved a capital expenditure of more than $300 million. Prototyping and testing, however, are appropriate even when smaller investments are involved.

Content Format

The contents of one possible format for a survey or feasibility study are outlined in Table 16-2. The summary presents a brief overview of the reasons for the study and ranks each processing alternative, including the present system, on the criteria established by a steering committee. This summary is the primary input for decision making. Existing systems should be described according to the analysis above. Finally, the report presents each

Table 16-2
Outline of Preliminary Survey and Feasibility Study Contents

I. **Summary**
   A. Goals
   B. For each alternative evaluation on standard criteria

II. **The existing system**
   A. Problems
   B. Goals of new system
   C. Decision considerations
   D. Information flow
   E. Processing
   F. Communications

III. **For each alternative proposed**
   A. Overview—percentage of goals achieved, benefits
   B. Decisions
   C. Information flows
   D. Technical (database, processing logic)
   E. Development effort, schedule, and cost
   F. Operational aspects
   G. Impact on the organization
   H. Total costs and benefits

alternative in detail. Here it is helpful to include a scenario, that is, a reasonable projection of how the system will actually be used, including management, user, and IS department activities under each alternative.

DETERMINING FEASIBILITY AND CHOOSING AN ALTERNATIVE

At one time, the information services department usually decided what applications to undertake. As demands for service increased, problems began to develop because some user requests had to be denied. As more systems of importance to the organization developed, many IS departments felt they were placed in a difficult situation if forced to choose among competing applications. The IS department is not in a position to decide whether a system is feasible or which processing alternative to choose if a system is to be developed.

Selection Committee

One answer to the problem of choosing information systems is to convene a **selection committee** of users and other managers and IS department personnel. When representatives of various functional areas are included, each department is able to see why certain decisions are made. Selection of applications alternatives seems less arbitrary under these conditions. With management guidance, the committee can select applications and **processing alternatives** consistent with functions currently emphasized in the organization.

Problems with Committees

If the ideas expressed above are good, why have a number of organizations become dissatisfied with selection committees? First, the goals of the committees are often not clear, resulting in little direction or continuity during meetings. Frequently, the committees appear to be ratifying decisions already made by the information services department. No alternatives for a given application are suggested. Instead, the IS department presents the option of either developing a complete, elaborate system or doing nothing. Almost no systems are rejected at the feasibility stage.

When decisions are made, there seems to be a failure to apply consistent decision criteria. Finally, in making any decision when costs and benefits are difficult to estimate, it is important to include subjective considerations. Members of committees report the lack of a mechanism for successfully including subjective factors in the decision process.

As mentioned earlier, few applications are really infeasible, though certain alternatives may be impractical or undesirable. The role of the selection committee is to choose an alternative for a given system, even though that alternative may be the status quo, that is, doing nothing.

SELECTING AN APPLICATION

It is desirable to have all new systems suggested and investigated at one point in time so all possibilities can be considered and a subset selected for implementation. Unfortunately, ideas for systems arise almost at random. Some length of time is required to study the suggestions before a decision is made on whether to undertake a suggested application. The decision process recommended below concentrates on the selection of an alternative for a single proposed application. It does not attempt to evaluate

Reengineering Our Taxes

The Internal Revenue Service (IRS) has embarked on a 10-year effort to overhaul its information systems. This government bureau, responsible for collecting income taxes, has 120,000 staff members, 7 regional offices, 10 service centers, 2 computer centers, and 63 district offices. In a typical year it processes 200 million tax returns and 1 billion information documents. It gives 80 million refunds while collecting more than a trillion dollars in taxes. It sends 8 million taxpayer notices, 40 million letters, and makes 36 million phone calls.

The IRS realized in 1989 that it had more than a technology problem; it had a business process problem. Improving quality would require more than new IT, the organization had to rethink the way it does business. Its main objective is to increase the level of voluntary compliance with the tax code, which is now at 85 percent and dropping. (A one percent increase in voluntary compliance generates $7 billion in taxes.) A second objective is to reduce the burden on taxpayers when they deal with the IRS. Finally, the agency wanted to improve its own quality and productivity. The result of the analysis has led to an $8 billion, ten-year effort to re-engineer the IRS.

As an example, the agency is working to get three years of account data and returns on-line for 200 million taxpayers. The IRS has 20,000 terminals in the field to inquire against these data. (The master file of taxpayers is so large that it takes from Friday noon until Sunday night to update it.) Plans are to move toward a client-server architecture with workstations and LANs in regional offices. The agency will use a packet-switched private network to connect offices and service centers.

To provide better service and reduce input, the IRS is conducting several experiments with electronic filing. In 1991, 11 million taxpayers filed electronically; the agency's goal is to receive 90 million electronic returns in the year 2000. The IRS would like to implement EDI for wage reporting. Other initiatives involve the possibility of IRS employees working at home to increase productivity.

The IRS is trying to take a fresh look at its mission and how it accomplishes it. Information technology will play an important part in this effort to redefine the relationship between the taxpayer and the government.

It is interesting to note that in 1996, Congress expressed great dissatisfaction with the management of this project and threatened to withhold funding. No matter how worthy the objectives of a new application, you still have to manage the project well to insure the development effort is successful.

an entire portfolio of projects because we are rarely in a position to compare the entire set of proposed projects at one point in time.

Providing Decision Information

The approach suggested here can be used for decisions at either the preliminary survey stage or the feasibility study stage. The major difference between the two is that the feasibility study contains more data than the preliminary survey and presents more-refined cost estimates.

The first task of the selection committee is to agree with the information services department on the number of alternatives for a single project and how the alternatives should be developed. As an example, suppose one user department has proposed an inventory control system. The alternatives might include (1) doing nothing, (2) purchasing a packaged program from a computer services vendor, and (3) building an on-line system. Each of these alternatives for an inventory control system meets some percentage of user needs at different costs. Probably three to five alternatives for each proposed application are sufficient. However, there should always be more than one alternative for a new system. Selecting the first alternative (doing nothing) is equivalent to deciding that a new system is infeasible.

The next step is for the committee to agree on a set of criteria to be used by the information services department in evaluating each alternative. Table 16-3 contains examples of possible criteria, although criteria will be unique for each organization. The set of criteria should be as complete as possible so that no important evaluation factors will be overlooked. However, the selection committee should avoid enumerating too many criteria, or the data collection and processing requirements for evaluation will become a burden. Each criterion should be measured on a common scale of, say, 1 to 7.

There is no one correct number of criteria to use, but experience indicates that five to ten should be adequate. Criteria can be voted on by the committee and rank-ordered for selection, or a group consensus on important criteria may be possible without voting. It is also desirable to avoid as much overlap in the criteria as possible to avoid overweighting one factor.

Once the criteria are determined, it is necessary to develop weights that indicate the relative importance of each criterion in arriving at the applications selection decision. It is unlikely that all committee members will regard each criterion as equally important. Some method will have to be used to **weight** the criteria for different individuals. Approaches to this process range from simple rank-ordering schemes to partial and paired comparisons. The weights are of paramount importance to applications selection because they reflect the priorities of the selection committee. The committee, of course, cannot expect conditions to remain constant. Shifts in management policies and users' needs necessitate revisions to weights over time.

Table 16-3
Some Potential Criteria for Evaluating Alternatives in Project Selection

Contributions to strategy
Tangible and intangible benefits
    User satisfaction
    Percentage of needs met
    Maximum potential of application
    Costs of development
    Costs of operations
Timing of costs
Timing of benefits
Impact on existing operations
Development time
Time to implement
Resources required
Probability of success
Probability of meeting estimates

Making the Decision

If the recommendations above are followed, the selection committee should be in a position to review a series of alternatives for each application proposed for implementation. Each alternative should be evaluated on the criteria established by the committee. Consider the example in Table 16-4. In this hypothetical decision problem, the selection committee is considering either an applications package or a custom-developed inventory system.

The first column in the table lists the criteria agreed upon by the committee and the information services department. The second column contains the weights assigned to each criterion by the committee. The

Table 16-4
Applications Selection Example

Criterion	Weight	Package	Custom-developed system
Percentage of user needs met	0.35	75%	90%
Cost of development	0.20	$42,000	$90,000
Cost of operations	0.10	$10,000	$7,000
Staff to develop	0.15	1	3
Probability of success	0.20	.95	.75

remainder of the table contains the scores for each alternative as evaluated by the IS department.

There are several ways to arrive at a decision given this information. One approach is to work toward a consensus among committee members. In this example, the applications package would probably emerge as the preferred choice because of its high ratings on the important criteria of percentage of user needs met, development cost, and probability of success.

As conditions change, the committee can modify the weights to reflect new priorities. Also, criteria can be dropped and/or added to reflect new circumstances. The major advantage of the recommended approach is that it forces an objective evaluation of several alternatives for each proposed application and provides a consistent but flexible framework for making decisions on applications.

UNDERTAKING SYSTEMS ANALYSIS

If a system is feasible and one alternative is chosen for development, the next stage is detailed systems analysis. There are few guidelines on the depth of analysis required when the design team examines present information processing procedures. All aspects of the present processing method must be understood and documented, and the analysis should identify key decisions as well as flows of data.

The design team must decide where to place the boundary on its studies. An expansive boundary may be appropriate, but a design team is well advised to take steps slowly in order to outline a manageable task. It is too easy to expand a simple processing problem into a huge system. What initially looks like an order-entry process turns into an accounts-receivable system and a production control system, because eager designers expand the boundaries of the problem into other areas.

The designers should document their understanding of present procedures with reports and memos. Data flow diagrams or object-oriented **documentation** should be constructed and reviewed with users who are not on the design team. When satisfied with its understanding of the present processing procedures, the design team should hold a "walk-through" with all users involved as a final check on the analysis.

UNDERTAKING SYSTEMS DESIGN

The most creative part of the systems life cycle is the design of new alternatives for processing. Although these ideas were sketched in the preliminary survey or feasibility study, the design team has to develop them in far more detail now. For example, in the previous section we chose a packaged program for inventory control (see Table 16-4). Suppose instead that we selected the custom-developed system for development. The information in the feasibility study is general. The details of that system must be designed before programming can begin. What equipment is required? What are the screen formats, the database design and what kind of queries and transactions will users want to process?

Results of the Design Process

The results of this study should be complete specifications for the new system. An example of rough specifications can be found in Appendix A to this chapter. Usually we begin by specifying the desired output. How does the user interact with the system? Then it is necessary to determine what input is required to produce this desired output. A comparison of input and output identifies the data that must be maintained in the database. Next, we consider processing. How are the input data transformed and used to modify the database? How often does data have to be updated? How are the input and the contents of the database processed to produce the desired output? Also, at this point the design team should specify manual procedures for other activities associated with the system.

For input and output, the database, and processing, it is necessary to determine what kinds of errors are likely to occur and then design procedures to locate or prevent them. The final output of the specifications for the system should be a work plan and a schedule for implementation.

GENERAL DESIGN CONSIDERATIONS

Today's design environment is complex. While we would like design to be independent of the underlying technology, that is really not possible. If you are designing a new application for a **client-server platform**, the options available will be different than if you are developing a system that must interact with legacy applications on a mainframe.

Client-Server Design

The newest architecture is client-server. Design for this platform is complex because there are so many components involved including clients, servers, networks, user interfaces, and usually a database management system on the server. Object-oriented design approaches are popular in the client-server environment. The professional designer views this environment as four layers: the application, the server, the client, and the network.

The application is what interests you as a user. It runs on either the client or the server. The application uses the client's user interface to present information, and the database on the server to extract and update information. Typically, about 75 percent of the program code will end up on the client for running the user interface. The professional designer is also concerned with sizing the server. How much capacity will be needed to provide service to all the clients that might simultaneously make requests of the server?

Because so much of the processing takes place on the client, and the client generally sits on a user's desktop, client-server development is well-suited to extensive user input in the design process. The user wants to select what appears on the client's screen to initiate data queries and display. Generally the client will run a windowed, graphical user interface (GUI) like Windows95, and the application should look consistent with this overall interface.

As an example, consider the client-server platform developed by a major investment bank for its brokers. This network features Sun Workstations and servers, all running Unix. The client part of the system provides the user with a number of windows which contain real-time data from the stock and bond markets. The user can also display a client's portfolio in a window, and the sales assistant can access another window which runs the legacy mainframe systems that are necessary to update client information. There are multiple servers for this client—the Sun servers for market data and information, and the mainframe systems that act as servers for transactions processing information—that are important for the broker and sales assistant.

MANAGEMENT PROBLEM 16-2

The top management of Eastern Bank and Trust has an "executive office of the president." The highest four officers of the bank, including the chairman of the board, the president, and two executive vice presidents, meet together to make all major decisions. This committee approves the budget for the information services department and also decides on new applications.

Because of pressing business, decisions related to information systems are often postponed from one meeting until the next. The budget director for the IS department indicated that he waited in the reception area for four meetings before his budget presentation was reached on the agenda.

The budget director's major objective is to have the IS department's budget approved with as few questions as possible. The budget includes the funding for major systems development projects for the coming year. Therefore, approving the budget also involves selecting the major new applications.

The members of the management committee are very dissatisfied with the current approach to selecting information systems projects. They admit that no project has ever reached the feasibility study stage and been rejected. The managers indicate that they are not really making decisions but are just ratifying the proposals of the IS department.

How can the bank solve this problem and develop a more effective project selection procedure? Why is this management committee not working well for decisions about information systems?

Graphical User Interfaces (GUIs)

The graphical user interface, as found in all windowing systems, has become the interface of choice for users. Virtually any system designed for modern hardware and software will feature a GUI. Designers are faced with a number of challenges in developing this kind of interface.

1. The interface must be simple and easy to learn and remember for the infrequent user. The user should not have to go through a lengthy relearning process.

2. The interface should be fast and efficient for the frequent user and should not create awkward transitions or the need to move frequently from keyboard entry to the pointing device.

There are a number of guidelines for developing this kind of interface:

- Try to make the screen look like a familiar physical object, for example, a calculator should look like a physical calculator. When the user clicks on a button, the same thing happens if you pressed the key on a real calculator.

- Try to make the interface consistent across all applications. It also helps to make the interface consistent with the windowing operating system interface and with popular applications that the user already knows how to use.

- Remember that the user is in charge of the windows and the interface should feel natural to the user.

- The mouse (or **pointing device**) is the primary mode for input, not the keyboard. The user will manipulate objects on the screen directly by clicking on them.

- Use modal tools, that is, tools the user can click on to change subsequent mouse actions. An example would be a drawing program where the user clicks on a line tool to draw a line or a circle tool to draw a circle with the mouse.

- The interface should be intuitive enough that, with the assistance of on-line help, the user does not have to revert to documentation on paper about the application (most users will not open the documentation anyway).

The major objective of the designer is to create an interface that feels natural and intuitive to the user, a difficult task. Firms like Microsoft have usability laboratories where subjects unfamiliar with software are observed trying to use it so designers can learn what is intuitive. The same approach makes sense for developing custom applications. Create a prototype and let users work with it before choosing a final design.

Other Input

In the past few years, the trend in information systems has moved toward collecting data as close to its source and as automatically as possible. The objective of this philosophy is to eliminate **data transcription** wherever feasible, to avoid errors and reduce the time required to enter the data into the computer. The ultimate in automatic data collection, of course, is sensors attached to the input of a real-time system, such as a computer monitoring a patient in a hospital. In most commercial computer systems, a popular **source-data collection** technique is to use a terminal and/or scanning technology. EDI also reduces the amount of input required for many business transactions.

OCR scanners are used for direct entry for original documents such as sales order forms. If numbers are printed carefully, the actual order form prepared manually can be used as an input to the computer system through a scanner. By taking a few more minutes to write clearly, the user can enter the order form itself directly into the computer system.

Bar coding is also extremely popular. Parts in production, finished goods, pieces of merchandise, videotapes, and library books can all be tracked by using bar codes and readers. There are also a number of firms who use hand-held terminals or PCs. United Parcel Service drivers use an electronic clipboard to record shipment data. Federal Express drivers use a hand-held device to read bar codes on packages, then upload this information to computers that track shipments. A number of pen-top personal computers are available, and we expect to see more direct entry by marking forms and printing information.

Image processing involves scanning a document and "burning" an image of it on an optical disk. This type of input and storage is well suited to documents that do not change. A large brokerage firm images stock

MANAGEMENT PROBLEM 16-3

John Washington is the manager of sales for Farway Manufacturing Company, a firm specializing in the manufacture of lawn and garden supplies. The firm's products are sold in hardware stores and nurseries throughout the world by a large field force of sales representatives.

Currently, Farway is involved in the design of a new order-entry and sales information system, and John is the user in charge of the project. The design team is in the process of choosing a method for data input and is divided over which alternative would be most desirable.

One group in the firm favors the use of a Personal Digital Assistant (PDA) or notebook computer. Each sales representative would use a radio or cellular modem to communicate orders directly back to the factory. The representatives would have to key in orders instead of checking off the items ordered on a form.

A second group that is uneasy about the technology has proposed continuing with the same familiar order form. All changes would take place at the factory and would not be noticed by the sales force. When the orders arrive at the factory, operators would group them into batches of fifty and enter them on-line to the computer. This alternative features the advantage of batch error control combined with immediate feedback as the data are entered.

John is trying to determine what criteria to use in deciding between these alternatives for input. Which alternative sounds best to you? How should John resolve this deadlock on the design team?

certificates that customers send in for transfer to another name or other processing, as described in detail in Chapter 18. The firm must keep a record of these certificates and wants to handle them as little as possible. By imaging the certificate and its accompanying documentation, various departments in the firm can retrieve all the necessary information about the certificate and the transaction from a terminal while the certificate remains safely in the vault. The image is represented as a series of dots (called pixels) and is not stored as characters as you would find in a word processing program. If you want a computer to process the data on an image, you must convert the thousands of pixels that represent each character to a standard character code like ASCII.

Handling Errors

A well-designed system handles errors. That is, it corrects the errors or notifies someone of them and continues producing valid output. It is not unusual to find more than half the instructions in a program devoted to error detection and handling. Users on the design team should be aware of input-error possibilities, and design procedures to minimize their occurrence and any adverse effect on the organization.

As an example, consider an order-entry application in which the sales force sends a completed order form to the factory. In the factory, clerks place a day's receipts of orders in a batch and add the number of pieces ordered to provide a total. Then an operator at a workstation enters the information from each order. First, the operator types in the customer number and the computer retrieves and displays the customer's name and address; the operator checks the computer-retrieved data against the order. If there is an error, the operator corrects the account number and continues. Each item on the order is keyed in, and the computer checks to see if the item numbers are legitimate. For example, is style 3245 made in blue? Various totals are computed on the order as a further check. For example, all the items entered from the CRT can be added and the total compared with the total manually computed on the order. A listing of the day's orders with a batch total should correspond to the manual batch total computed for the orders before they are entered into the system.

If the company gave notebook computers to the sales force to prepare their orders and then transmit them electronically, you would still need to perform error checks. Designers would create an editing program on the notebook computer to catch some errors at input, and would look for others when accepting the electronic orders in the order entry system. What errors would you try to catch at each stage?

Backup

In addition to error controls during processing, we must consider the availability of backup. An **audit trail** is necessary; that is, there must be some way to trace transactions through a system from input to output. In an on-line system, one reason for keeping a file of transactions is to make sure there is an audit trail. Special audit transactions may be created as a legitimate type of input for use by auditors in checking the system.

Fault tolerance means the critical features of a computer are duplicated, both in hardware and software, so the failure of any part does not cause the computer to fail. Tandem and Stratus both make fault-tolerant computers. These machines have found a market for high-volume transactions processing applications such as those at the major stock exchanges.

Security and
Fraud

There has been a great deal of publicity about the problems of fraud and security with computer systems. In designing a system, we have to take reasonable precautions to avoid the possibility of fraud. Independent programmers should be used for critical parts of the system, and multiple users should be involved. Procedurally, we should avoid giving authorization for sensitive changes to only one person. Security is enhanced not only by having backup files but by storing them in separate physical locations.

Recently, a great deal of attention has been generated by computer viruses. A **virus** is a program that damages a computer. It is run unknowingly on a system and wreaks various kinds of havoc in the computer. Some virus programs have plagued personal computer users. Perhaps the PC owner has copied a public-domain program from a bulletin board. The program contains some code that is activated by an event, often a date. The code might be as innocent as displaying a message on the screen or as pernicious as destroying files on a disk. Other viruses have been introduced into computer networks and have propagated throughout, slowing and sometimes stopping computers on the network.

Preventing computer viruses is very difficult. The techniques for detecting and preventing a virus so far are not equal to the cleverness of programmers who create them. You can buy virus-detection programs that will scan your hard disk for infected programs. Generally, you must delete these programs and install them again.

COMPUTER-AIDED SOFTWARE ENGINEERING

You may have drawn the conclusion after reading this far that systems analysis and design is a very labor-intensive process. The people who bring automation to the organization have almost no automation to help in their work. **Computer-aided software engineering (CASE)** is an attempt to automate as much of the design process as possible (see Figure 16-1).

There are two areas CASE has been applied, sometimes called "upper" and "lower" CASE. Upper CASE applies to the early stages of the design process, tasks like undertaking systems analysis and drawing data flow diagrams (DFD)s. Lower CASE focuses on the later stages in the design cycle, such as automatically turning system specifications into working computer programs. The basic idea is that the power of PC-based workstations, can be used to facilitate systems analysis and design. Today, few

Figure 16-1
A CASE approach.

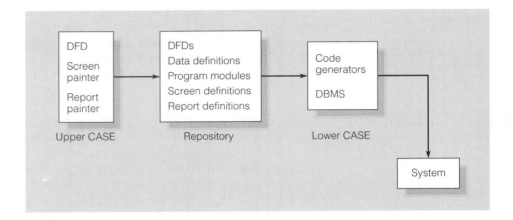

examples of CASE tools are fully integrated, which means they offer all the features imaginable in such a tool and cover both upper and lower ends of the design cycle.

Upper CASE   There are a number of tools found in different CASE products to help in the early stages of analysis and design, including the following:

Diagramming tools.   These tools, which help build DFDs, are the most frequent components of CASE products. Structured design has a variety of rules about how DFDs are to be constructed, and some of these products strictly enforce the rules.

PCs for a Hilton Reservation

Hilton Hotels has adopted the philosophy that local PCs in hotels can perform a number of local functions in addition to serving as reservations processors. Hilton has developed a system called EAST that uses personal computers at hotels' front desks for check-in and local functions. The PCs are connected to a large IBM mainframe in Dallas, which keeps central reservations information.

Locally, the PCs handle tasks like check-in and checkout, guest look-up, registration information display, cashier functions, auditing, group arrivals and departures, and housekeeping.

The mainframe system, called NORTH, communicates with a personal computer in each hotel; the local PC routes the data from NORTH to a personal computer that is a file server for the local area network at the hotel. Another personal computer functions as the report processor, while a third handles updating. The entire NORTH system and the EAST systems in each hotel must be able to handle four hundred thousand transactions per day.

A hotel downloads a day's reservations to the file server the night before. A desk clerk can then display all information about a guest on arrival.

Screen and report generators. These products can be used to quickly prototype a report by entering columns or fields on a screen. They are similar to the report-generating features of some PC database management systems. Sometimes they provide the ability to generate computer code to produce the report or input screen.

Repository. This is a huge database for storing everything about a system, including database design, DFDs, and more.

Lower CASE

Lower CASE analysis and design tools include:

Code generators. These are programs that produce other programs based on specifications created earlier in the design process.

Code restructurers. There is much poor code in existence. These products take, for example, COBOL programs and convert them to structured programs to facilitate maintenance.

More recently, CASE tools facilitate object-oriented analysis and design. Sometimes these features are added to an existing CASE system that is already based on structured design concepts. Since object-oriented design is often associated with client-server technology, some of the tools generate code for client-server platforms. For example, one product generates PowerBuilder code, a client-server development language from PowerSoft Corporation.

We have seen the tremendous amount of manual labor involved in designing technology-based information systems. What will CASE do to design? Will it eliminate the designer? It is unlikely that designers will become obsolete. CASE tools aid the designer just as PC spreadsheet packages aided a large number of individuals who perform calculations on paper spreadsheets.

CASE tools should make it easier to develop examples of screens and reports and show them to users; feedback during development can come more quickly. To the extent that CASE tools reduce programming time and facilitate changes to a system, they should reduce the total time required for the systems life cycle. The task of developing programs in the future may require less skill. In fact, it is very likely that for a large number of systems, the analyst will be able to generate program code using a CASE tool, bypassing the programmer altogether.

The crucial bottleneck in developing new applications is systems analysis and design. Any tools like CASE that support the designer will help to improve productivity in building systems. It is the lack of productivity, the lengthy time required to develop systems, and the budget overruns that make many users and managers dissatisfied with information services. Designers need to experiment with and adopt whatever tools help solve these problems. It is unlikely that you will use a CASE tool, but you may be involved in acquiring and implementing such a tool in your firm.

CHAPTER SUMMARY

1. Systems design is one of the most creative activities in modern organizations. Information technology offers the opportunity to radically reshape work processes and even the organization itself.

2. Unfortunately, design is a labor-intensive task that requires a great deal of tedious effort.

3. Remember that professional systems designers never use the systems they design. You use the systems that are designed by analysts, whether they work for your company or for an external consultant. It is important, therefore, that you understand the objectives and functions of any new IT application that affects your responsibilities.

4. It is important to have more than one alternative to consider when making the decision to invest in a new application of technology.

5. We recommend the use of a selection committee to evaluate proposed applications. The committee should develop a series of criteria for evaluating proposed alternatives and a procedure for making a choice.

6. Systems analysis involves understanding present processing procedures while design involves creating new ways to apply technology to improve information processing.

7. Users are likely to be most heavily involved in the first part of the systems life-cycle, in defining the system prior to actual programming.

8. Client-server is the most popular platform for design today; a design team must determine what tasks will be assigned to the client and to the server, and must develop the user interface for the client.

9. Interfaces for users today are mostly graphical. The design of these GUIs requires great care and experimentation.

10. The user needs to be concerned with reliability and backup for critical applications.

IMPLICATIONS FOR MANAGEMENT

One of the worst-kept secrets in systems development is how labor intensive and time-consuming the process is. Almost anyone who has worked on a development project will tell you that the project took more work and more time than anticipated. While there are CASE tools and structured approaches to design, no one has figured out how to automate the process of requirements definition—figuring out what the system is supposed to do. There is a saying that "The Devil is in the details" which applies nicely to systems development. If you want technology to assist you in improving some business process, you have to identify exactly, in excruciating detail, the logical steps in the process. Even if you plan to purchase a package, you have to know what the system is supposed to do so you can see if the package meets your needs.

KEY WORDS

Audit trail
Client-server platform
Computer-aided software
  engineering (CASE)
Data transcription
Documentation
Fault tolerance

Pointing device
Processing alternatives
Selection committee
Source-data collection
Virus
Weight

RECOMMENDED READING

Deng, P., and C. Fuhr. "Using an Object-Oriented Approach to the Development of a Relational Database Application System," *Information and Management,* vol. 29, no. 2 (August 1995), pp. 107–121. (The basis for the example in Appendix B of this chapter.)

Dos Santos, B. "Justifying Investments in New Information Technologies," *JMIS,* vol. 7, no. 4 (Spring 1991), pp. 71–90. (An interesting discussion of the future consequences of investing in IT today and a suggestion for how to compute the value of this "option.")

Wu, S., and M. Wu. *Systems Analysis and Design.* St. Paul, Minn.: West Publishing Co., 1994. (A straightforward book on systems development.)

DISCUSSION QUESTIONS

1. Why is the selection of an information systems project so important to an organization?
2. What are the major sources of frustration in selecting applications?
3. What problems arise if the information services department is in charge of the design and makes unilateral decisions?
4. Why collect data where it originates?
5. How would you expect an IS department to react to the idea of evaluating several different alternatives for a single system?
6. In your opinion, what kind of technology has the most pleasing user interface?

7. Can systems design be described as a science? What is scientific about it? What characteristics make it appear to be an art?

8. What are the major components of a client-server application?

9. What is the drawback for users in serving on a selection committee and/or a design team?

10. What other approaches to selection of information systems projects can you suggest?

11. Who should be on a selection committee for applications selection decisions?

12. Suggest a mechanism for deciding which enhancements to existing systems should be undertaken. How does this problem differ from selecting new applications? How are the two decisions similar?

13. Why present multiple alternatives in preliminary surveys and feasibility studies?

14. How do projects already under way influence decisions on undertaking a proposed application?

15. How can one find out what applications packages might be available as a possible source of processing in a proposed system?

16. How should risk be considered in evaluating proposed applications? What are the risks in systems analysis and design? Should an organization have a portfolio of projects balanced on risk?

17. What is an audit trail in an information system? Why is such a trail of transactions necessary?

18. What is the role of the server in a client-server system? The client?

19. How can you determine what size the server should be for an application?

20. Is it possible for technology to eliminate paper reports?

21. What contribution can the user make to a preliminary survey and feasibility study? How can the use of this information lead to biased recommendations?

22. Describe guidelines for designing a graphical user interface.

23. What other creative tasks are there in the organization in addition to the design of new information systems? How do they differ from this activity?

24. What are the prospects for automating systems design tasks? Where could automation be fruitfully applied in the systems life cycle?

25. Design a procedure for developing criteria and assigning them for project selection.

26. Does a system have to use the most modern technology to be successful? Why or why not? Are there disadvantages to utilizing the most up-to-date technology?

27. What is CASE? What is its role in systems design?

CHAPTER 16 PROJECT

SYSTEMS DESIGN PROBLEMS

1. One of the most common applications is payroll. Many organizations have custom-designed payroll systems, and a large number of service bureaus offer packages to compute an organization's payroll. The logic of the payroll process is common across many organizations.

   Usually a file contains data about each individual who is on the payroll. An example of the data to be included in setting up this database for employees would be as follows:

Name	Medical plan
Number of dependents	Pension
Marital status	Employee number
Deductions	Wage rate
Union dues	Social Security number
Hospital plan	

   On a periodic basis, such as weekly or monthly, input is necessary to trigger computation of the payroll and production of a check for each employee. At minimum, this weekly input would have to include the following:

   Employee number

   Regular hours worked

   Overtime hours worked

   Sick leave

   Special deductions

   Once the system is run on a periodic basis, checks should be produced along with various accumulations for different year-to-date categories. The computer program would subtract all deductions and withhold funds for tax purposes. Also included in the output would normally be a payroll register. On an annual basis, the computer system would produce W2 forms, the summaries of earnings and taxes withheld from wages for tax purposes.

   a. Design (1) the input screens to be used to place a new employee on the payroll file and (2) the screens to be completed for each employee for a payroll.

   b. List the file contents and approximate field sizes for the payroll file. Do not forget to include year-to-date totals.

   c. Draw at least two levels of data flow diagrams for the payroll system.

   d. Describe the modifications necessary for the system to wire a check to the employee's bank automatically if the employee so elects, and to include a notice to the employee.

   e. Design the file maintenance and change screens necessary to alter information about employees.

2. Most organizations, whether manufacturing firms or service organizations, have some kind of accounts receivable. Accounts receivable was one of the first applications undertaken by many firms when computer systems were acquired. Service bureaus also offer accounts-receivable packages for sale or rent. Originally, most accounts-receivable packages were typically batch applications. Today, we would expect to find on-line input and payment processing.

    Consider an on-line accounts-receivable system. An accounts-receivable transaction is generated by a shipment of a product to a customer. An operator at a PC enters the following information:

Order number

Shipment number

For each shipment:

> Product code
>
> Quantity
>
> Date
>
> Shipping costs
>
> Special shipping mode
>
> Special discounts
>
> Comments

The program accepting this input responds with the customer's name and address when the order number is entered. It also prints the product descriptions, the price extension, and the total invoice cost.

    The customer receives the statement and sends in payment for one or more invoices. The next task is for an operator to enter the payments and to match them against outstanding invoices. The operator enters the invoice number, the total payment, and exceptions to indicate partial payments for items on an invoice that are not paid.

    In addition to the printed invoices, invoice register, and monthly statements, the system provides an accounts-receivable listing, a daily cash balance, and exception reports for invoices that were partially paid or not paid at all. There would also be a function to allow inquiry concerning payment history.

    Of course, as with any system, it is necessary to establish new customers. The new customer information has to include the following:

Account number

Name and address

Credit payment terms

Normal shipping mode

    a. Design the database including customer, shipment, and invoice tables.
    b. Describe the overall flow of data for the system.
    c. Design the screens for data input and inquiry.
    d. List the edits and controls necessary in this system.

3. Sales reporting can be a very important application. Often, data for sales reports come directly from shipping and/or invoicing systems in the organization. At minimum, this application requires a customer file including customer number, geographic code, shipment date, order number, item number, quantity shipped, and price.

   From these data it is possible to generate an output sales report. This report might be summarized by product, product type, region, or salesperson.

   a. Design an inquiry system for a client-server platform that would answer questions interactively concerning customers or products.
   b. Assume that historical data are available on sales for the past ten years. What kind of forecasting system would you design for this organization? What would be your considerations in choosing a forecasting system?

4. The manufacturing or production function in an organization includes many activities, such as materials acquisition, production scheduling and control, work-in-process inventory control, and finished-goods inventory control.

   One way to start the manufacturing process is with the preparation of a bill of materials. A bill of materials lists all the components necessary to manufacture a product. Usually the input that is provided is the number of new products identified by product number and quantity. The output from this system is a list of subassemblies and the quantity required. That list contains all the parts needed to manufacture the particular product.

   a. Design the database for a bill-of-materials processor.
   b. Describe the logic of the explosion program.
   c. Assume that the input to the bill-of-materials processor contains both the product and the date it is to be shipped to the customer. Design a system to produce a report on products that must be manufactured by a given due date.

5. A budget is a fundamental managerial control tool in an organization. In setting up budgets, minimal input includes an account number, the type of account, a description, and where a control break is to be taken to add up the totals for a subaccount. Then, for each budget cycle, input is provided on the account number, the budgeted amount of money, and the actual money spent. The output from such a system is the budget report. It shows the account, the description, the budgeted amount, the actual amount, variance amounts, and usually percentage totals as well. Design a database for a budget application, and describe the format of a budget report.

6. Technology is used extensively in the retail industry, particularly to supermarket checkout operations. In these systems, some type of OCR scanner reads the universal product code (UPC) on items sold in the store. A midrange computer in the store contains a file with the UPC numbers and the current prices. As items are scanned, their prices are read from the file and the entire cost of the grocery order is computed.

   All during the day, the computer in the store maintains a record of items sold. In the evening, the data can be transferred to a central computer to update master records, which represent sales and, more important, inventory balances. These inventory data can then be used to restock the supermarket so that it is not necessary for store personnel to place formal orders with the warehouse.

Such systems were designed to speed the checkout process and to ensure more rapid response for the resupply of grocery products.

a. Design the database for the local grocery store and the database for the central host computer.

b. Develop a backup plan that will become operative if the computer in the supermarket fails.

c. What reports could be generated from the system for use by store management? What kind of queries will managers make?

Designing a Distributed Client-Server System

*T*HE HARDSERVE CASE STUDY

This case study describes the design of a distributed system for Hardserve, a company that specializes in the wholesale distribution of merchandise to retail hardware stores. Hardserve buys goods from manufacturers and stocks them in a warehouse. Retail hardware stores order merchandise from Hardserve, which then ships it from inventory. If Hardserve does not have the goods requested by the retail store, the store will go elsewhere. Hardserve has usually been the first choice for retail stores trying to find an item. The company's objective is to design a new system for its stores and the central warehouse. The case presents a preliminary survey and then sketches specifications for the Hardserve system.

Goals We have identified the following goals for a system.

1. Reduce inventory levels while maintaining a desired level of customer service.
2. Reduce the reorder cycle time for the local stores: Get replenishment stock to local stores two days faster.
3. Improve management for seasonal and slow-moving items.
4. Capture sales data so purchasing can analyze trends and stock the proper merchandise.
5. Smooth the operations of the local stores by improving customer service and reducing paperwork.

THE EXISTING SYSTEM

Problems   The existing system is illustrated in the flowchart of Figure A-1. At the present time we have manual processing of papers and an old inventory control package running on our warehouse computer. For some items we tend to overstock from fear of running out, and in others we miss a reorder point and incur a stockout. Purchasing hears from the warehouse when a particular item has reached a reorder point on the computer file. This reorder point is set by the warehouse manager, based on experience. We also have no real sales forecasting because we don't track which items are moving. Accounting analyzes the physical inventory, and at the end of the year purchasing looks at what items have sold. By that time it's too late for the data to do any good.

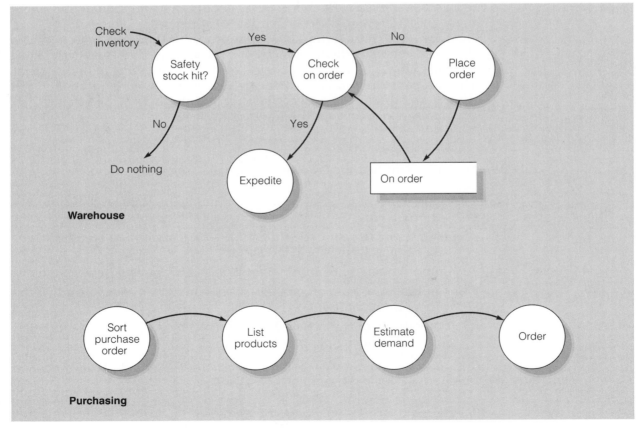

Figure A-1 Flowchart of the existing system.

**Decision
Considerations**

1. We have identified the following crucial decisions in our business.
2. What should be ordered for each new season?
3. What should be reordered during the season and when?
4. How much should be reordered each time?
5. What items should be dropped from inventory?
6. What and when should the local store reorder?

**Information
Flows**

Current information processing is shown in Figure A-1. The warehouse computer indicates when physical stock has dropped below the reorder point and sends a report at the end of the day to purchasing. The purchasing agent either reorders the item, if it is not on order, or expedites it if an order has already been placed. At the end of the season, the purchasing department analyzes purchase orders and estimates what will be needed for the next season. Decisions on the reorder amount are based on the purchasing agent's negotiations with the supplier. Approximate volumes of orders and other related data are given in Table A-1.

Table A-1
Approximate Monthly Values

Average number of orders	
January	4,100
February	6,700
March	7,800
April	8,400
May	5,400
June	4,600
July	5,000
August	5,100
September	6,200
October	9,500
November	10,100
December	8,200
	81,100

- Average orders per month: 6,758
- Maximum orders per day: 500
- Average orders per day: 311
- Average number of items per order: 5.1

A DISTRIBUTED SYSTEM

Systems Design   A local-store client PC, probably using bar coding and a wand for reading data into the computer, automates as much of the store's interaction with customers as possible and reduces store paperwork. The local-store computer orders from a warehouse server through a communications link, dramatically reducing local-store inventory replenishment. At the warehouse, we streamline processing.

With orders coming electronically, the warehouse system can consult inventory records and prepare picking lists almost instantaneously. The system also uses an economic-order quantity to suggest reorders to purchasing. We try to reduce the amount of paper involved in cutting a purchase order and in warehouse receiving when the purchased goods arrive.

The rest of this discussion presents some preliminary design specifications for this system. For this design, to provide a little variety, we are using a modification of the data flow diagrams introduced in Chapter 15. The rounded rectangle for processing in the DFD is replaced with a circle to produce the "bubble charts" found in this example.

Figure A-2 is labeled a level 0 diagram, though in structured design that designation officially belongs to something called the context diagram. Figure A-2 is a pseudo-context diagram since it has two "bubbles"—one for the store and one for the warehouse. In this example, using the two process symbols makes it clear that we are designing two systems that must interface closely with each other.

As the diagram shows, the hardware-store system involves several roles: a manager and sales, payables, and inventory clerks. In fact, these roles may actually all be played by one or two people. The sales clerk uses the system to check merchandise out at the "cash register," which is a personal computer with a bar-code scanner. The inventory clerk uses the PC to scan the bar codes on new inventory items as they are received from the Hardserve warehouse. The store system also accumulates a summary of payables for the payables clerk. Since the store purchases its goods from the warehouse, there is only one major payable.

The store PC, then, keeps track of the inventory in the store. It subtracts sales at the cash register from inventory and adds the receipt of new items and customer returns to the inventory. The store system checks its files each day at the close of business to determine what items need to be reordered from the warehouse. It sends these reorders to the warehouse, as shown in Figure A-2.

The warehouse system is very similar to the store system in that it maintains an inventory, too. The warehouse system interfaces to several systems. It sends a record to the existing Hardserve accounts-payable financial system, because the warehouse buys from a number of vendors and has a significant payables function. The warehouse system also includes the purchasing function, since the warehouse must purchase all of its supplies

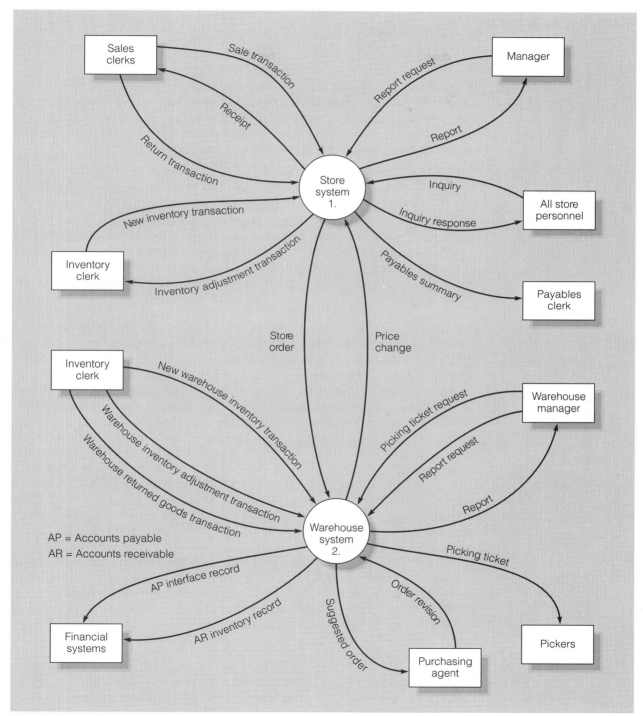

Figure A-2 Hardserve Diagram 0—pseudo-context diagram.

from different vendors. Finally, the warehouse system helps run the warehouse by creating picking slips for workers to use in filling the orders to be sent to the local hardware stores.

System Specifications

What kind of hardware is needed to support this system? The systems designer will generally seek advice from hardware and software experts in the organization building a system. For Hardserve, the general architecture is fairly simple. Each store will need a minimum of one PC and the warehouse will need a larger server to keep track of inventory.

Systems Overview: The Local Store

Figure A-3 shows the local-store system. The most important processes are sales (1.1), inventory control (1.3), and connect to the warehouse (1.4). For the sales function, the design team is looking to various optical reading devices, such as wands, that read the universal product codes (UPCs) on merchandise. The designers have to survey the warehouse and check stores to see how many products have bar codes. If too few are coded, Hardserve might print codes and apply them as it receives merchandise to be placed in the warehouse.

The inventory control process must keep an accurate "book" or file of the items in local-store inventory. As inventory is received from the warehouse, this process adds it to the store file: "Store item prices and inventory." The same logic is followed if a customer returns merchandise to go into inventory. There may be inventory adjustments. It is likely the store will take a physical inventory at least once a year and adjust the "book" inventory to conform to the physical. When there is a return transaction, the inventory process also should update the store sales file. As merchandise is received from the warehouse, the inventory control process updates open orders to reflect the receipt and posts data to the store payables file.

The local store may wish to view various reports about its sales on a daily, monthly, and year-to-date basis. Designers will also have to consider the level of detail desired by store owners. For example, some users may want to see sales by product class while others want sales of individual products. The designers also have to determine if the reports need to show last year's sales to date as well.

Process 1.4 directs the store's PC to dial the warehouse so the local store can transmit reorders to the warehouse. This process consults the store item price and inventory file to determine what items have reached their reorder point; it then places an order for the item. Process 1.4 posts each day's order to the open orders file so the merchandise can be checked off when it arrives.

Sales

Figure A-4 is a level 1.1 diagram for the sales process. During the day when customers are in the store, the sales screen will probably be "up" most of the day. The user will scan purchases and the scanner converts the UPC to a product number and the local-store computer looks up the price of the

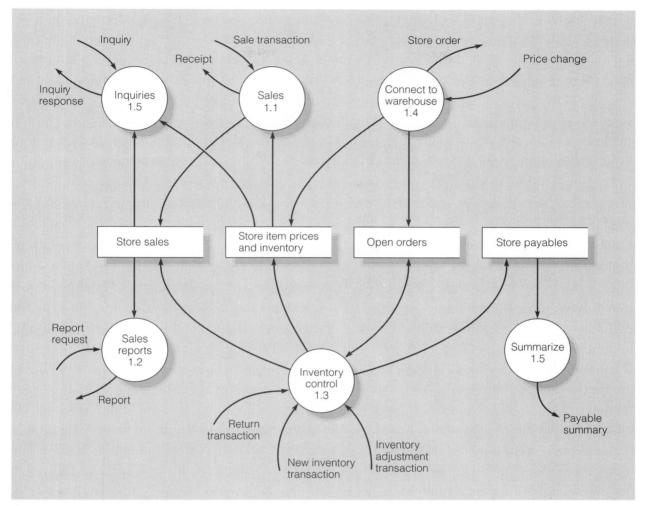

Figure A-3 Diagram1—local-store system.

item in an item price file. The computer calculates any extension (the clerk can type a number to indicate multiple purchases). If there is no UPC on the item, the clerk keys in the item number and the price and quantity. For example, it is unlikely that individual fasteners like nuts and bolts will have UPC numbers on them.

The computer must reduce inventory in the store (process 1.1.1) by the amount of the sale, and post sales to the sales file (process 1.1.5). If it is the last item, the computer calculates sales tax and prints a receipt for the customer. The designers are also looking into the possibility of having the local-store computer automatically dial a credit authorization number for customers who are using credit cards. The computer could then print the sales receipt to be signed by the customer for the credit card charge as well.

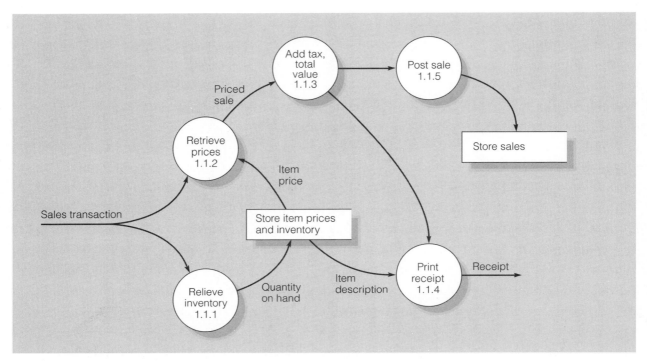

Figure A-4 Diagram 1.1—sales.

Inventory Control   Inventory control is one of the major functions of the system. Figure A-5 shows the next level of detail for inventory control. Returns of merchandise must update the store sales file and the store item prices and inventory file. An inventory adjustment transaction updates the latter file.

Process 1.3.1 shows what happens when inventory is received from the warehouse. Three files are affected. The system displays a screen to be used in scanning input items. The Hardserve warehouse prints shipment labels corresponding to orders so that the local store can scan items as they are received. The computer must update a file of store open orders and the store item prices and inventory file to reflect the receipt of goods. The user must enter any discrepancies between what was ordered and what was received (for example, the warehouse may only be able to send six of an item when the store ordered twelve). Finally the process updates the store payables file. The inventory receipt process is shown in another level of detail in Figure A-6. Similar DFDs are needed to provide additional detail on an inventory returns and adjustments.

Although not shown on Figure A-6, the check-in procedure for receiving merchandise will also probably require the ability to key in a receipt, as the warehouse may not be able to print scannable labels for each item sent.

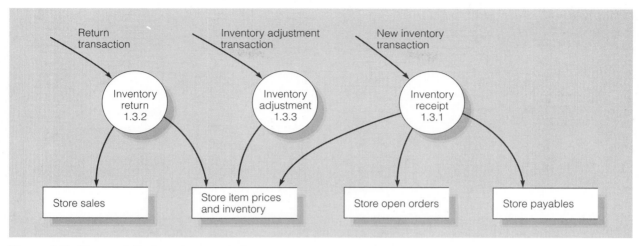

Figure A-5 Diagram1.3—inventory control.

Connecting to the Warehouse

Figure A-7 shows the process for connecting to the warehouse. In this case, the external event of closing the store results in the connection. Process 1.4.2 accepts price changes from the warehouse and updates prices in the store item prices and inventory file. Process 1.4.1 scans this file and sends the orders to the warehouse while updating the store open orders file.

Figure A-6
Diagram 1.3.1—
inventory receipt.

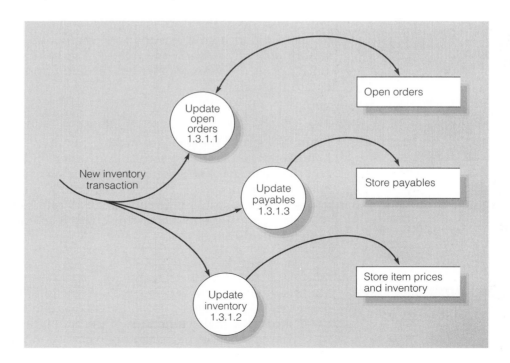

Figure A-7
Diagram 1.4—connect
to warehouse.

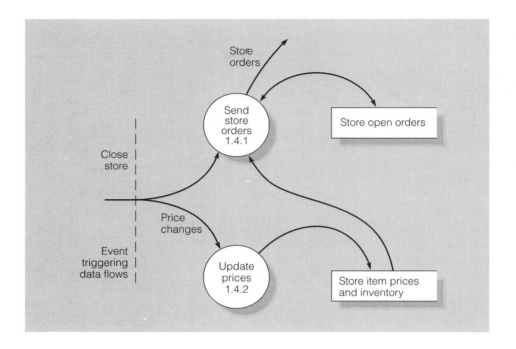

The process of transmitting orders is shown in more detail in Figure A-8. Process 1.4.1.1 looks at inventory balances and reorder points and the reorder quantity in the store item prices and inventory file. If the quantity on hand for an item is less than the reorder point, the process generates a store order by posting the item to the store open orders file. Process 1.4.1.2 reads the store open orders file and transmits the order created today to the warehouse.

Inquiries   Figure A-9 shows the logic for making inquiries. The user can display any field from the inventory record on the screen and inquire about prices and the quantity of an item on hand. The user may want to inquire about items that are on order. The response to this query shows both on-hand and on-order quantities. Finally, the user can inquire about sales. (There is a sales reporting screen, but this query is intended for a short response for a few items rather than a comprehensive report.)

Systems Overview: The Warehouse   The warehouse system is very similar to the local store system. Figure A-10 (on page 448) contains a second-level diagram for this system. This diagram shows the major functions of the warehouse system including picking stock, sales reporting, inventory control connecting to the local stores, and purchasing goods.

Figure A-8
Diagram 1.4.1—send store orders.

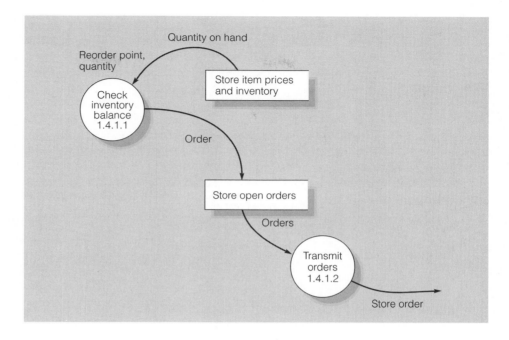

Figure A-9
Diagram 1.5—inquiries.

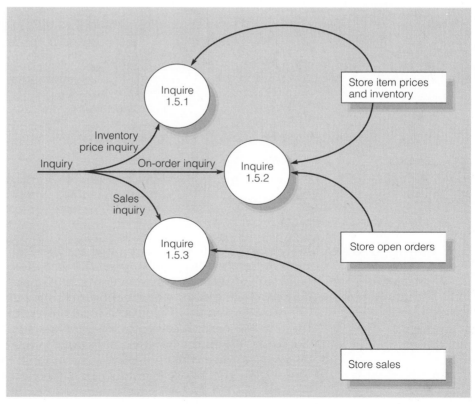

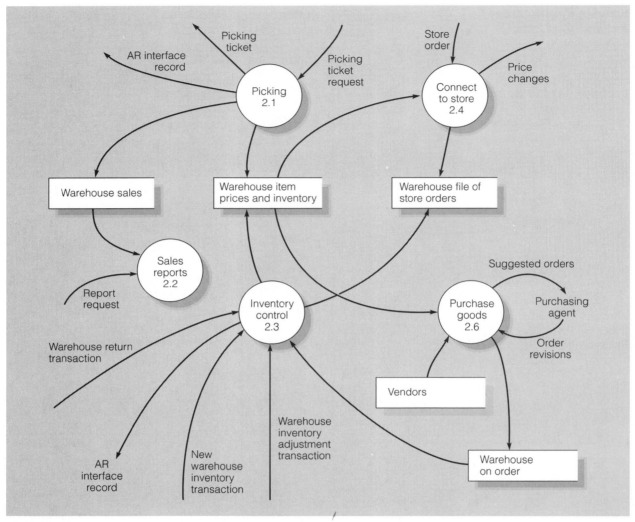

Figure A-10 Diagram 2—warehouse system.

Filling Orders   An important role of the computer for the warehouse is to see that local-store orders are filled and shipped the day after they are received. (During busy seasons sometimes an evening shift picks orders and the merchandise arrives at the store in the morning following entry the night before.)

As orders come in from the local stores, the warehouse server posts them in the order received to a warehouse file of local-store orders (Figure A-11). When the warehouse manager is ready for another batch of orders to be picked, she enters the number of orders she wants to generate. The system chooses that number of eligible orders from the picking file, and process 2.1.2 checks each item ordered against the warehouse item

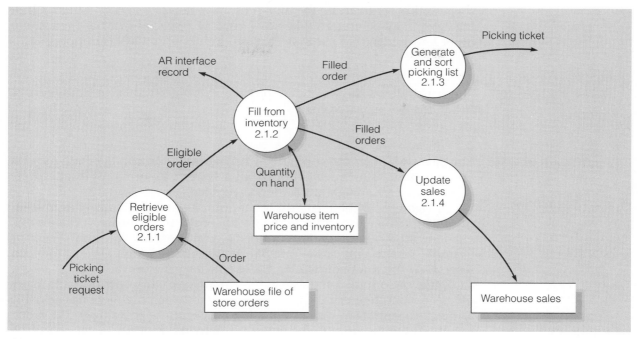

Figure A-11   Diagram 2.1—warehouse picking.

price and inventory file. If the item is out of stock, the system prints a notice on the order-filling form. The system does not need a backorder capability because the local-store system will reorder again, since its quantity on hand will be below the reorder point if no merchandise is shipped from the warehouse to replenish the inventory.

Process 2.1.2 reduces the inventory to reflect the planned shipment of the item and creates a filled-order form, which is sent to process 2.1.3. This process generates a picking list and sorts it into the sequence in which merchandise is stored in the warehouse. As a result, the stock picker does not have to retrace his or her steps, but can move down a row in the warehouse in one direction and fill the order.

Process 2.1.4 updates warehouse sales while the order-filling process creates an accounts-receivable interface record. Sales to the local hardware stores represent a receivable account for the warehouse.

Purchasing   Figure A-12 shows Diagram 2.6 with more details on purchasing. Process 2.6.1 is triggered by a purchase agent who wants to review inventory. It scans the warehouse item prices and inventory file to determine items for reorder. The logic is similar to the processing of the store file. Instead of actually making the order, process 2.6.2 creates a suggested purchase order that is reviewed by the purchasing agent. Process 2.6.3 modifies the suggested order to create the final order that goes to a vendor. The purchasing agent may be able to take advantage of a special offer or have some other knowledge that the system lacks, so human review is important.

Other Processes

The remainder of the warehouse processing is quite similar to store processing and is not repeated here.

The Database

The data flow diagrams combined with a description of a database provide an important set of specifications for a system. Figure A-13 is an entity-relationship (ER) diagram for the store system.

In Figure A-13 the relationships appear on the lines connecting the entities. The arrows also indicate the nature of the relationship. A one-to-one relationship occurs when one entity is associated exactly with one other. For example, one receipt causes one payable and there is one payable for each receipt, so the lines connecting these entities have one arrow.

There can also be 1-to-m (many) relationships. One order contains many different order items, so the line connecting order to order item has a double arrow pointing to the order item and a single arrow pointing to the order. Finally, there are m-to-m, or many-to-many, relationships. There can be many items on a sale and many sales of an item; double arrows point to each entity.

Figure A-14 (on page 452) is a rough-draft ER diagram of the warehouse system. Here we use the convention of single and double arrows to

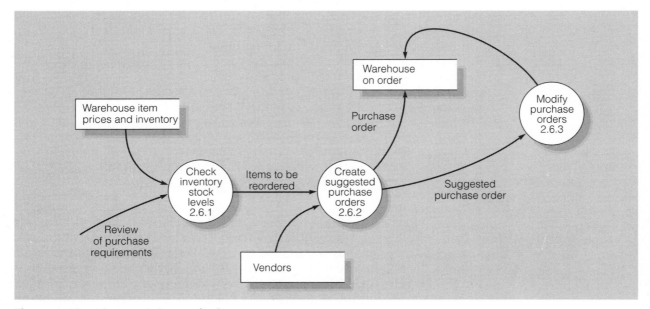

Figure A-12 Diagram 2.6—purchasing.

Figure A-13
Entity-relationship diagram of store system.

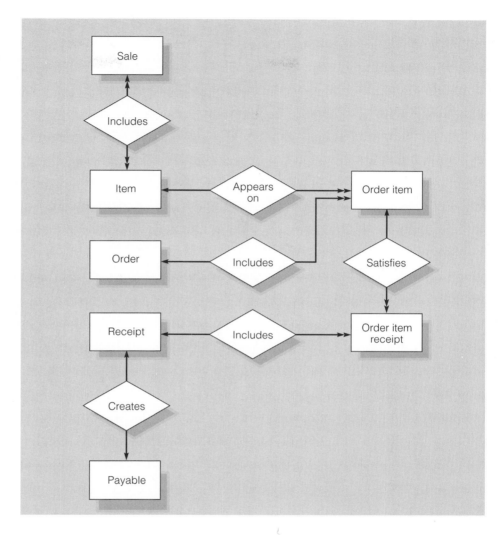

represent 1:1, 1:*n*, et cetera, relationships. Can you refine this diagram until it resembles Figure A-13?

Table A-2 (on page 453) contains the preliminary contents of the data items for the files in the local-store system. At this point, no particular data structure or database model is specified. Later, as the design team refines the specifications, they will address the question of data models. If the team decides to use a packaged database management system for a PC, they will have to adopt its structure for these files. Note that a number of the files imply repeating groups. For example, an on-order file contains an order that is likely to contain a number of individual items. In Table A-2 we do not list repeating groups, as that is a function of the type of data structure chosen. If we use a relational database, the order number might be repeated with each item number on the order.

Figure A-14
First-draft entity-relationship diagram of warehouse system.

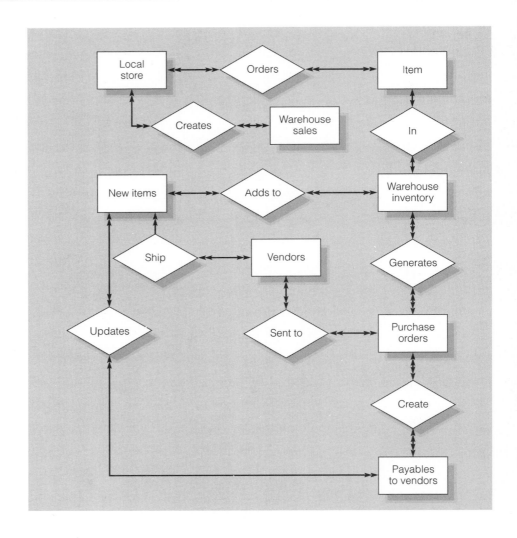

Input and Output   The design of the PC menu for the local store, input screens, query forms, and printed reports are left as an exercise for the reader.

Summary   In this case we have seen the results of a tremendous amount of work on the part of a Hardserve design team. They have developed a conceptual model of a client-server system that has two parts: the local store and the Hardserve warehouse. The team has specified the major functions that each system has to perform and the interfaces among the two systems. There is a preliminary database specification and ideas on the menus the user will see in the local store. There is more work to be done, but this would certainly be a good place to have an all-day review session with users to be sure they understand and approve of the major choices reflected in the design to date.

Table A-2
Preliminary File Contents

File	Field	Size	Type	File	Field	Size	Type
Store sales	Item number	8	A	Warehouse sales (cont.)	Sales last year		
	Sales this year				January	12	N
	January	12	N		.		
	.				December	12	N
	.						
	December	12	N				
	Sales last year			Warehouse	Item number	8	A
	January	12	N	item price	Description	50	A
	.			and inventory	Units	5	A
	.				Unit price	10	N
	December	12	N		Quantity on hand	10	N
					Reorder quantity	10	N
Store item	Item number	8	A		Reorder point	10	N
price and	Description	50	A		Warehouse location	15	A
inventory	Units	5	A				
	Unit price	10	N	Warehouse	Store number	8	A
	Quantity on hand	10	N	file of	Order number	8	A
	Reorder quantity	10	N	store orders	Order date	6	A
	Reorder point	10	N		Item number	8	A
	Store location	15	A		Quantity on order	10	N
Store open	Order number	8	A	Warehouse	Item number	8	A
orders	Order date	6	A	vendor file	Vendor number	8	A
	Item number	8	A		Vendor address 1	30	A
	Quantity on order	10	N		Vendor address 2	30	A
					Vendor address 3	30	A
Store	Order number	8	A		Vendor city-state	30	A
payables	Order date	6	N		Vendor zip code	10	A
	Payable amount	12	N		Vendor rating	30	A
Warehouse	Store number	8	A	Warehouse	Order number	8	A
sales	Item number	8	A	on-order file	Order date	6	A
	Sales this year				Item number	8	A
	January	12	N		Item cost	10	N
	.				Quantity on order	10	N
	.				Shipping instruct.	30	A
	December	12	N				

A = Alphanumeric field   N = Numeric field

APPENDIX B

An Object-Oriented Example

This appendix presents an example of a systems design following an object-oriented methodology, due to Deng and Fuhr (1995). The application is for a hypothetical hospital that the authors describe as a medium-sized, non-profit organization. The hospital's objective is to provide high quality health care while minimizing cost to patients. The hospital wants to replace its batch processing system with an on-line system that will handle tasks such as patient registration, billing, inquiries, the tracking of medical staff, laboratory results, and patient treatments. After a lengthy study, the hospital identified ten basic functions for the hospital containing 22 total processes. A model resulting from this effort is shown in Figure B-1.

Figure B-1
Enterprise model of the patient care administrative system.

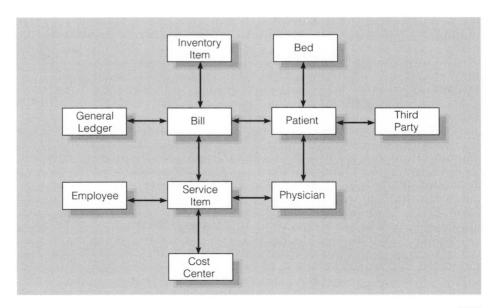

455

OBJECTS AND CLASSES

A key activity in object-oriented analysis is to identify objects and group them into classes, and then into superclasses. The designers fully define classes by indicating the purpose, its tasks when called upon, and any collaboration with other objects to perform a task. Table B-1 shows a list of candidate classes after the elimination of redundancies. Table B-2 shows related classes grouped into superclasses. A class must have a purpose, that is, a definition of what it is as shown in Table B-3.

Table B-1
Candidate Classes After Elimination of Redundant Classes

Patient Name	Physician Name	Room (Location)
Treatment	Patient Record (Patient)	Physician Identification
Patient Bill	Insurer	Patient Balance
Patient Service	Service Charge	Date Admitted
Expected Date Discharged	Date Discharged	Physician Specialty
Room Accommodations	Patient Address (Contact Info)	Patient Identification
Patient SSN	Room Identification (Location)	Room Phone Ext.
Main Menu	Physician Phone Ext.	Third Party (Insurer)
Patient Information Display	Patient Bill Display	Patient Treat. Display
Room Utilization Display	Services Display	Physician Info Display
Phone (Contact Info)	Patient Procedure (Treatment)	Service Identification
Patient Home Phone	Patient Charge	Patient Contact Info
Room Location		

Table B-2
Superclasses Identified During the Exploratory Phase

Super Class	Classes	Super Class	Classes
Display	Main Menu	Identification	Patient Identification
	Patient		Patient SSN
	Information		Physician Identification
	Patient Billing		Service Identification
	Patient Treatment		Location Identification
	Physician Information		
	Service Information		
	Room Information		
Phone	Room Phone Ext	Name	Patient Name
	Physician Phone		Physician Name
	Ext		Insurer
	Patient Home		
	Phone		
Charge	Patient Charge	Date	Date Admitted
	Service Charge		Expected Discharge Date
			Discharge Date

Table B-3

Purpose of Each Class

Class	Description and Purpose of Class
Patient Name	First, Middle Initial, Last Name identifying patient
Physician Name	First, Middle Initial, Last Name identifying physician
Treatment	Procedure physician performed on patient
Patient Bill	Patient charges for services rendered at the hospital
Insurer	Third Party agency for cost coverage
Patient Balance	Amount Patient owes for a particular service
Patient Service	Service/item a patient has received at the hospital
Service Charge	Default amount that is charged a patient for a service
Date Admitted	Date patient was admitted into the hospital
Expected Date Discharged	Expected date patient will leave the hospital
Date Discharged	Date patient was discharged or released to coroner
Physician Specialty	Specialization or title of physician
Room Accommodations	General/specific room characteristics
Patient Identification	Unique number identifying patient (SSN can change)
Patient SSN	Patient social security number
Physician Identification	Unique number identifying physician (SSN can change)
Room Phone Ext.	4 digit extension for rooms that have a phone
Main Menu	Entry menu of patient care administration system
Patient Treatment Display	Entry/Query screen for patient treatment (from main/info)
Physician Phone Ext.	4 digit extension for physicians that have a phone
Room Utilization Display	Entry/Query screen for room information (from main/info)
Services Display	Entry/Query screen for services information (from main menu)
Physician Info Display	Entry/Query screen for physician information (from main menu)
Service Identification	Unique code identifying type of service
Patient Home Phone	Home phone number to reach patient/immediate family
Patient Charge	Amount patient charged for service (may be different than default service charged)
Patient Contact Information	Mailing Address, city, state and zip code of patient
Room Location	Unique room number identifying a particular room
Patient Information Display	Entry/Query screen for patient information (from main menu)
Patient Bill Display	Entry/Query screen for patient billing (from main menu/info)

Remember that in object-oriented design, objects pass messages back and forth to initiate processing. The next step is to identify the role of each class and show the operations an object in the class must perform upon receipt of a message. Table B-4 shows the roles for each class. Then, the designers identify interactions between classes, or their collaborations. You might view this activity as defining the first part of a message by identifying the receiving object, without defining yet the detailed flow of control and data involved in a message.

At this point, the designers develop detailed messages for each class. They document this work with graphs of each class hierarchy, a graph of class interactions, and the messages supported by each class. It is also necessary to identify what inputs are needed from other classes for a given class to perform its tasks. Note how this design is similar to a client-server environment where one class (a client) requests some kind of action from another class (server). This demand and supply relationship is shown in

Table B-4
Roles of Each Class

Class	Roles of Class
Patient Name	Identify patient
Physician Name	Identify physician
Treatment	Provide medical/surgical care to patients
Patient Bill	Inform patient of charges incurred and balance due
Insurer	Identify agency for partial/full payment of patient bill
Patient Balance	Accept/Display balance due for service rendered
Patient Service	Accept/Display service rendered
	Provide service/item to patient
Service Charge	Accept/Display default service charge for service
	Display default charge when adding patient billing record
Date Admitted	Accept/Display date
Expected Date Discharged	Accept/Display date
Dale Discharged	Accept/Display date
Physician Specialty	Accept/Display specialization
	Query doctors for particular specialization needed for a patient
Room Accommodations	Accept/Display accommodations
	Provide specific options for patient care bedding
Patient Identification	Accept/Display/Validate unique identification
Patient SSN	Accept/Display/Validate unique SSN
	Inform third party agencies of SSN for identification
Physician Identification	Accept/Display/Validate unique identification
Room Phone Ext.	Accept/Display phone extension
Main Menu	Present user with choices
	Determine when and what user responded to
Physician Phone Ext.	Accept/Display phone extension
Patient Information Display	Present user with choices:
	(add/edit/delete/view/query/search/help)
	(treatment/billing/room)
	Determine when and what user responded to
	View/maintain Patient Information records
	Validate/Update corresponding room information if patient assigned to a location
	Validate patient not assigned to multiple rooms or occupied rooms
Patient Bill Display	User choices: (add/edit/delete/view/query/search/help)
	Determine when and what user responded to
	View/maintain Patient Billing records
	Return to main menu if selected from main menu
	Return to patient information if selected from there
Patient Treatment Display	User choice: (add/edit/delete/view/query/search/help)
	Determine when and what user responded to
	View/maintain Patient Treatment records
	Return to main menu if selected from main menu
	Return to patient information if selected from there
Room Utilization Display	User choices: (add/edit/delete/view/query/search/help)
	Determine when and what user responded to
	View/maintain Room Information records
	Validate patient not assigned to multiple rooms
	Return to main menu if selected from main menu
	Return to patient information if selected from there
Service Display	User choices: (add/edit/delete/view/query/search/help)
	Determine when and what user responded to
	View/maintain Service Information records

Table B-4 *(continued)*

Class	Roles of Class
Physician Info Display	User choices: (add/edit/delete/view/query/search/help)
	Determine when and what user responded to
	View/maintain Physician Information records

Table B-5 where numbers in parentheses indicate what the client requests from the server. As an example, the class Patient Name is required for the classes Patient Information Display, Patient Bill Display, Patient Treatment Display, and Room Utilization Display and Patient Bill. The Patient SSN will send a message to the Patient Name class.

Table B-5
Message Request and Provision Between Client and Server Objects

Class (Client/Server)		Message
Patient Name	1.	Identify patient (35,36,37,38,41)
Physician Name	2.	Identify physician (40)
Treatment	3.	Provide medical/surgical care to patients (37)
Patient Bill	41.	Inform patient of charges incurred and balance due (36)
Insurer	4.	Identify agency for partial/full payment of patient bill (35,41)
Patient Balance	5.	Accept/Display balance due for service rendered (36,41)
Patient Service	6.	Accept/Display service rendered (36,39,41)
	7.	Provide service/item to patient
Service Charge	8.	Accept/display default service charge for service (36,39)
	9.	Display default charge in patient charge when adding patient billing record (36)
Date Admitted	10.	Accept/Display Date (35)
Expected Date Discharged	11.	Accept/Display date (35)
Date Discharged	12.	Accept/Display date (31,35)
Physician Specialty	13.	Accept/Display specialization (40)
	14.	Inform, through query, those doctors for particular specialization that is needed for a patient (37)
Room Accommodations	15.	Accept/Display accommodations (38)
	16.	Provide specific options for patient care bedding
Patient Identification	17.	Accept/Display identification (1,3,5–7,10–12,19,26,28,30,41)
	18.	Validate that patient identification is unique (35)
Patient SSN	19.	Accept/Display SSN (1,4–7,10–12,41)
		Validate that patient SSN is unique
	20.	Inform third party agencies of SSN for identification (41)
Physician Identification	21.	Accept/Display identification
		Validate that physician identification is unique (37)
Room Phone Ext.	22.	Accept/Display phone extension (38)
Main Menu	23.	Present user with choices
		Determine when and what user responded to
Physician Phone Ext.	24.	Accept/Display phone extension (40)
Patient Information Display	35.	Present user with choices:
		Determine when and what user responded to
		View/maintain Patient Information records
		Validate/Update corresponding room information if patient assigned to a location
		Validate patient not assigned to multiple rooms or occupied rooms (23,36,37,38)

Table B-5   *(continued)*

Class (Client/Server)	Message	
Patient Bill Display	36.	Present user with choices:
		Determine when and what user responded to
		View/maintain Patient Billing records
		Return to main menu if selected from main menu
		Return to patient information if selected from there (23,35)
Patient Treatment Display	37.	Present user with choices:
		Determine when and what user responded to
		View/maintain Patient Treatment records
		Return to main menu if selected from main menu
		Return to patient information if selected from there (23,35)
Room Utilization Display	38.	Present user with choices:
		Determine when and what user responded to
		View/maintain Room Information records
		Validate patient not assigned to multiple rooms
		Return to main menu if selected from main menu
		Return to patient information if selected from there (23,35)
Services Display	39.	Present user with choices:
		Determine when and what user responded to
		View/maintain Service Information records (23)
Physician Info Display	40.	Present user with choices:
		Determine when and what user responded to
		View/maintain Physician Information records (23)
Service Identification	25.	Accept/Display identification
		Validate that service identification is unique (41,8, 9,39)
Patient Home Phone	26.	Accept/Display phone number (35)
	27.	Reach patient/immediate family if emergency
Patient Charge	28.	Accept/Display charge (41,36)
	29.	Display default service charge when adding record (36)
Patient Contact Info	30.	Accept/Display contact information (41,35)
Room Location	31.	Accept/Display Room Number (38)
		Validate that number is unique

Table B-6 contains the "signatures" for the patient care system. Message passing among clients objects and server objects is controlled by the signature. It specifies the type of parameters and objects that the class can receive and send.

Creating Subsystems

A subsystem combines classes and superclasses into an efficient grouping for implementation purposes. The main menu structure is shown in Figure B-2. It has six choices or subsystems for patient care information. (Dotted lines show data flow relationships between two subsystems in the figure.) Figure B-3 (on page 463) shows the main menu screen. Physicians treat patients, so the treatment subsystem is accessible through the physician subsystem. Similarly, patients receive service charges in the form of a bill, so the billing subsystem is accessible through the service and patient subsystems. (These two subsystems appear on a pull-down menu of the Patient command on the main menu bar in Figure B-3.) In Figure B-4 the structure

Table B-6
Signatures of Each Class

Class	Signatures
Patient Name	Get_PatientName(Text)
Physician Name	Get_PhysicianName(Text)
Treatment	Get_Treatment(Text)
Patient Bill	PrintBill(Text) returns (Boolean)
Insurer	Get_Insurer(Text)
Patient Balance	Get_PatientBalance(Currency)
Patient Service	Get_PatientService(Text)
Service Charge	Get_ServiceCharge(Currency)
Date Admitted	Get_Admitted(Date)
Expected Date Discharged	Get_ExpDischarge(Date)
Date Discharged	Get_Discharge(Date)
Physician Specialty	Get_PhysicianSpecialty(Text)
	Query_Physician(Text) returns Physician Info Display
Room Accommodations	Get_RoomAccommodations(Text)
Patient Identification	Get_Patient(Integer)
	Validate_Patient(Integer) returns (Boolean)
Patient SSN	Get_PatientSSN(Integer)
	Validate_PatientSSN(Integer) returns (Boolean)
Physician Identification	Get_PhysicianId(Integer)
	Validate_PhysicianId(Integer) returns (Boolean)
Room Phone Ext.	Get_RoomPhone(Integer)
Main Menu	Display_MainForm(Text)
Physician Phone Ext.	Get_PhysicianPhone(Integer)
Patient Information Display	Display_PatientInformation(Text)
	AddPatientRecord(Boolean)
	EditPatientRecord(Boolean)
	DeletePatientRecord(Boolean)
	ViewPatientRecord(Boolean)
	QueryPatientRecord(Boolean)
	SearchPatientRecord(Boolean)
	HelpPatientRecord(Boolean)
	Validate_RoomNumber(Integer) returns (Boolean)
Patient Bill Display	Display_PatientBilling(Text)
	AddPatientBillRecord(Boolean)
	EditPatientBillRecord(Boolean)
	DeletePatientBillRecord(Boolean)
	ViewPatientBillRecord(Boolean)
	QueryPatientBillRecord(Boolean)
	SearchPatientBillRecord(Boolean)
	HelpPatientBillRecord(Boolean)
Patient Treatment Display	Display_Treatment(Text)
	AddTreatmentRecord(Boolean)
	EditTreatmentRecord(Boolean)
	DeleteTreatmentRecord(Boolean)
	ViewTreatmentrecord(Boolean)
	QueryTreatmentRecord(Boolean)
	SearchTreamentRecord(Boolean)
	HelpTreatmentRecord(Boolean)
Room Utilization Display	Display_Room(Text)
	AddRoomRecord(Boolean)
	EditRoomRecord(Boolean)

Table B-6 *(continued)*

Class	Signatures
	DeleteRoomRecord(Boolean)
	ViewRoomRecord(Boolean)
	QueryRoomRecord(Boolean)
	SearchRoomRecord(Boolean)
	HelpRoomRecord(Boolean)
Services Display	Display_Service(Text)
	AddServiceRecord(Boolean)
	EditServiceRecord(Boolean)
	DeleteServiceRecord(Boolean)
	ViewServiceRecord(Boolean)
	QueryServiceRecord(Boolean)
	SearchServiceRecord(Boolean)
	HelpServiceRecord(Boolean)
Physician Info Display	Display_PhysicianInformation(Text)
	AddPhysicianRecord(Boolean)
	EditPhysicianRecord(Boolean)
	DeletePhysicianRecord(Boolean)
	ViewPhysicianRecord(Boolean)
	QueryPhysicianRecord(Boolean)
	SearchPhysicianRecord(Boolean)
	HelpPhysicianRecord(Boolean)
Service Identification	Get_ServiceId(Text)
	Validate_ServiceId(Text) returns (Boolean)
Patient Home Phone	Get_PatientPhone(Integer)
Patient Charge	Get_PatientCharge(Currency)
	Display_ServiceCharge (Currency)
Patient Contact Info	Get_PatientContactInfo(Text)
Room Location	Get_RoomNumber(Integer)
	Validate_RoomNumber(Integer) returns (Boolean)

Figure B-2
Structure of the main menu.

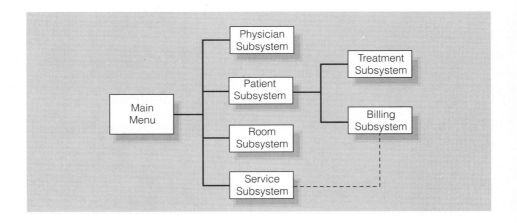

of the patient subsystem which displays the information is shown on the right side of the figure. Figure B-5 is a sample screen from the patient subsystem.

Other subsystems include one for the physician which shows his or her specialization for patient treatment. The room subsystem shows room location within the hospital, phone extension, and the type of accommodations. The purpose of the service subsystem is to keep track of services performed by the hospital staff. The billing system shows what each patient owes, the original amount and the remaining balance. A treatment subsystem records services performed by physicians.

Figure B-3
The main menu screen.

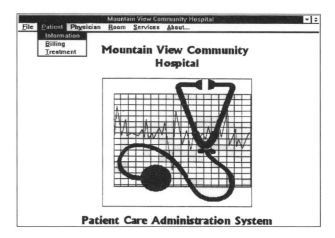

Figure B-4
Structure of the patient subsystem.

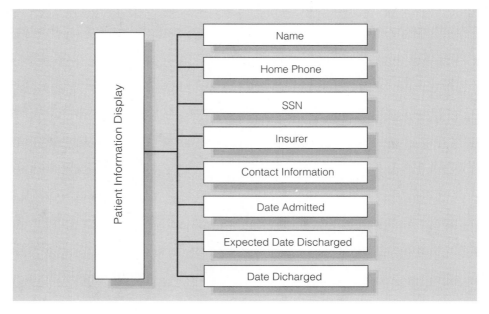

Figure B-5
A sample screen of the
patient subsystem.

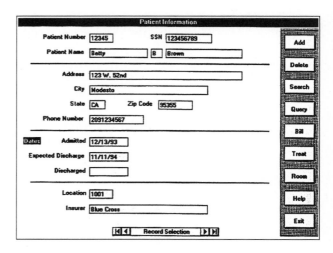

Observations   Object-oriented design is an approach that uses objects, classes and messages to model processes in the real world. Objects can be both clients and servers in performing their roles. This approach to design is well-suited to a client-server hardware and software platform, an increasingly popular architecture.

CHAPTER 17

Enhancing the Life Cycle

OBJECTIVES

1. Learning to manage information technology.

The traditional approach to systems analysis and design is associated with cost and time overruns and systems that do not meet specifications. Management needs to understand its options for developing systems in nontraditional ways and managers must decide what technique to use in a given situation.

2. Preparing to apply technology.

The design team has a lot of influence on how a system is developed. For example, it can begin to develop a prototype early in the design stage and can suggest that the final system be developed using a fourth-generation language.

3. Transforming the organization.

Applications that change the organization carry a lot of risk. Through nontraditional techniques the manager can reduce some of these development risks.

There are a number of problems with developing custom applications by following the systems life cycle. First, a great deal of time usually elapses before the user comprehends all the features of a system. It is very difficult to understand specifications. Usually it takes a significant period of time to progress from specifications to the first tests seen by the user. If the user did not understand the specifications or did not conceptualize all the features of the system, it might be more than a year from the time the application is first discussed until its characteristics become known through test results. In addition, the development of custom systems is associated with cost and budget overruns, particularly during the programming and testing phases.

In this chapter, we discuss a number of enhancements to the life cycle and explore the options of fourth-generation languages and prototyping to shorten development time for custom systems. We also look at purchasing a packaged program as an alternative to custom development.

The topics in this chapter are discussed in independent sections, however, you should not conclude that they are in some way exclusive. It is quite likely that you will develop a prototype using a fourth-generation language. The prototype itself might turn out to provide a set of specifications for evaluating different packaged programs. All of these approaches are potentially interrelated and likely preferred to following the traditional steps in the systems life cycle.

FOR WHOM ARE THESE APPROACHES INTENDED?

It is easy to read the material in this chapter and think that it is relevant only to an information services professional. Why might you take an interest in the topics discussed here? First, it is highly likely you will end up developing some of your own solutions to information processing problems. Depending on the IS staff to meet all your processing needs often takes too long, and there are sometimes not enough IS staff members to answer all of your requests.

Throughout the text we stress that companies are moving toward client-server architectures. You and other managers will be the clients using PC-based workstations to access data located on servers. Who will write programs for the client to use once it accesses the data? You may be very fortunate to have someone in the organization to create these programs. It is more probable that you will develop your own programs using packages and fourth-generation languages.

Second, as a manager and user of systems, you want systems development to proceed quickly and successfully. The approaches described here can help reduce uncertainty in development and can increase productivity. You may want to insist on seeing a prototype of a proposed system. In fact, you may want to develop that prototype yourself to illustrate your vision for a new system.

Does anyone follow the systems life cycle anymore? Did anyone ever follow it? The systems life cycle has always illustrated the general approach designers take to developing systems. A working designer would not draw a lot of the distinctions in the model, but would think about design while doing an analysis of an existing system. At some point, a team decides that a system was well-enough specified for programming to begin. The alternatives to a traditional approach of analysis, design, and programming discussed in this chapter alter or replace this series of steps. They are adopted to take advantage of advances in technology and to overcome some of the time and cost problems of the traditional life cycle.

FOURTH-GENERATION LANGUAGES

The need to improve productivity in developing systems has led to the development of new languages for building applications.

Fourth-generation languages are often called **nonprocedural** because the programmer does not have to specify procedures in detail as with a third-generation language. Nonprocedural languages have commands at a higher level than languages like COBOL or C. A nonprocedural language may simply interpret a series of commands entered by the programmer and do what they indicate, such as sort records, summarize them on a field, and print a report.

Two popular fourth-generation languages are FOCUS and PowerBuilder. These languages are able to create and manipulate databases. FOCUS is available on a variety of systems from PCs to mainframes. Its developer has created software routines so that it can serve as a central access point for data stored in a number of different **database management systems (DBMS)**. PowerBuilder is a high-level language designed for the client-server environment and is very popular for developing applications for this platform.

Users of these very **high-level languages** report impressive benefits. An electronics firm programmed a new order-entry system using the fourth-generation language NATURAL in less than half the time it predicted would be necessary had COBOL been used instead. In addition, users are pleased because working at a high level makes it easy to make changes to the system. Users feel that the programmers working on order entry are the most responsive group in information services because they respond so quickly to change requests.

The major drawback associated with 4GLs is performance. Some firms found these languages are enough less efficient than compiler-level languages to not be useful in a heavy transactions processing environment. However, Morgan Stanley, a major investment bank, rewrote its entire back-office system using NATURAL for processing all of its routine transactions. On balance, a fourth-generation language appears to be a good approach for increasing responsiveness in development.

GENERAL PACKAGES

We introduced packages in Chapter 14. In this chapter, we want to explore their use to speed development. There are a number of general packages in common use today such as spreadsheets and database management systems which offer an alternative for developing an application, especially for a small number of users working with PCs. Spreadsheet packages include the ability to record **macros**, a sequence of keystrokes which can be played back automatically. In addition to actually recording keyboard

MANAGEMENT PROBLEM 17-1

Jane Rollins runs a small investment firm that manages securities for a number of corporate entities and individuals. For example, Jane has her own stocks in two entities, one as an individual investor and the other in a trust established for her by a relative.

Each of the entities may own any number of different shares of stock. As shares are bought and sold, an exact record of the lot of stock, the number of shares, and the price at purchase and sale must be maintained. In addition, the bookkeepers at the firm must post all cash and stock dividends to each entity's records each time dividends are received.

All this processing is currently done on a manual basis. The staff is able to keep up, though it can take four to six weeks after quarterly dividends to finish posting. Closing the books at the end of the fiscal year and producing reports for the firm's accountants takes a great deal of time and work. Also, it is not easy to answer Jane's questions when she asks about various entities' stock holdings, for example, how much AT&T stock is managed in total across all accounts.

Jane is thinking about a computer system. However, she feels that the firm is unique, and she is not optimistic about finding a ready-made package. What advice can you give her? How should she proceed?

input and replaying it, elaborate macro languages exist for several spreadsheet packages. Microsoft has adopted a strategy of interfacing its office products to Visual Basic, a quite powerful programming language. Thus, from within an Excel spreadsheet, a user can execute macros written in Visual Basic.

Because Visual Basic and other macro languages are so powerful, you can develop extremely sophisticated applications using these general packages. One of my faculty colleagues uses an Excel spreadsheet to contain pictures of the students in his class, and Excel macros to retrieve a picture and biographical information about each student. The disadvantage of these packages and their macro languages is that they are at a much lower level of detail than the commands typically used to build a spreadsheet. As a result, developing an application with these tools is a lot like programming, something that most users try to avoid.

Another general package that makes a great development tool is a database management system. Vendors of packages like Access and Paradox designed them for a range of uses and users. You can develop a simple application working directly with relational tables, doing each operation and updating information yourself. You can also use the languages with these packages to create input forms, update tables and generate output automatically for a user who knows little or nothing about relational databases. The further you get into custom development, however, the more the tasks involved look like conventional programming.

DEDICATED PACKAGES

A package is one solution to the problems of custom systems design. We usually think of packages as software, but an increasing number of vendors sell both software and the hardware on which the software is run. Thus, a package can be thought of as a problem solution that is partially or completely ready to implement. The use of a package can dramatically reduce the time required to install a system by saving both design time and the effort devoted to programming. We can expect to spend far more than the cost of the package by the time it is installed, and it is unlikely that the package can be purchased one day and fully utilized the next!

It is important to realize that we are talking about dedicated packages in this section. The **dedicated package** is designed for a specific problem and is far less general than say a spreadsheet package. For example, a dedicated package for accounts receivable can be used for a variety of accounts-receivable operations, but that is all. It is useless for accounts payable or general ledger. With a dedicated package, you are buying much more of a custom solution to your problem; it is much less general and flexible than a package like a spreadsheet processor.

Advantages of Packages

There are a number of advantages to packages:

1. A package should require less total development time, since detailed programming specifications are not needed, nor is as much programming usually required as with a custom system.

2. In total, a package should result in lower costs, though it is not always clear that costs are lower by the time one learns how to use the package and makes modifications to it.

3. We often find that a package has functions or extra features that we might not have bothered with in a custom design.

4. If the package has been used in other locations, many of the programs included in the system have been debugged or at least run successfully in an operational environment.

5. From the standpoint of user understanding of a system, a package usually provides the opportunity to see in operation what one is purchasing before being committed to its acquisition.

A Competitive Advantage Through Micromarketing

The Target store on the eastern edge of Phoenix sells prayer candles, but no child carrier bicycle trailers. The Target store 15 minutes away in the affluent town of Scottsdale sells trailers, but no portable heaters. Heaters are located in the store in Mesa, 20 minutes away. If all of this sounds confusing, it makes sense to Target, a 623-store discount chain owned by Dayton Hudson Corporation.

Target is a master at "micromarketing," a high technology approach to customer service. The idea is to tailor merchandise in each store to its customers. Target has experienced rapid growth following this strategy. The average store has increased sales by 7% and Target has had an 11% increase in operating profits. It plans to open 65 new stores in 1995, well ahead of its rivals KMart and Wal-Mart.

Buyers no longer believe that the best purchase is a large purchase. They may have to buy smaller quantities of tailored products. Buyers were convinced that they needed different merchandise in different stores as Target's sales of team logos in the stores near where each team plays reached $100 million in 1994. Some suppliers have to provide specialized products.

Micromarketing requires a large investment in information technology and takes sophisticated systems to stock thousands of different items in each store. The process starts with a computer-driven planning process in which buyers create merchandise assortments to fit the racial, ethnic and age features of different groups of customers. Planners match the merchandise to the community profile and local store managers refine the model based on their knowledge of local tastes. Target feeds actual sales data into the system to generate sales and profit tallies for each square foot of space. These results are used to allocate space to different products.

Information technology allows companies to deal with incredible levels of detail and complexity; it enables a store like Target to practice micromarketing.

Disadvantages of Packages

While there are a lot of advantages to packages, there are some counter-arguments that raise questions about this approach:

1. A package may not include all the functions we would like to have.

2. As a result, many packages have to be modified before they are acceptable to users. **Modification** is difficult; it requires changes to existing code and may be possible only through the vendor. Changing existing code can be expensive and is likely to introduce errors in the system. As with any programming endeavor, modifications also take time, reducing some of the benefits expected with a package from reduced development time.

3. To avoid making major changes in a package, we may elect to change procedures in the organization. Such changes are not always easy to accomplish and can be disruptive to the firm.

4. We become critically dependent on **vendor support** for the software. If the vendor is not viable, we may be left with software and no way to support it, that is, to have errors corrected, receive new versions, training, and so forth.

5. The package may not run on the kind of computer we would like to have. The package may necessitate the purchase of hardware, and that system may not be compatible with our existing hardware or our overall plan for information processing in the organization.

MANAGEMENT PROBLEM 17-2

Jack Robinson manages the information services department for Sports World Manufacturing Company, a full-line manufacturer of sports equipment. He has just finished reading a proposal from one of the smaller plants for a complete inventory control and production scheduling package that runs on a local area network. The network would have to be acquired, as the plant has no in-house production system at present. (There are some non-networked PCs in various offices.)

Robinson is concerned because his department operates a large mainframe computer that is not fully utilized. He wonders: How can I be sure that the new system will work? Is the package proven? What about the money we have invested in the mainframe? Is it wise to buy another computer given the fact that we have an underutilized system now?

Jack feels that he must respond to the request from the plant, and he is not sure what to do. He has asked for your help in defining the issues. Should his staff undertake a study to evaluate the package? He could compare the package with the use of a custom system on the mainframe, or he could look for a package with the same features that would run on the larger computer.

In addition to this request, Jack feels this is an important issue that will come up again in the future. Jack is concerned that the mainframe is "losing business" to midrange and to networked personal computers. He would like to develop a way to handle the problem when it recurs. What is your advice?

Package Design

The vendor wants to produce a program that can be used in a large number of organizations. How can one build this generality into a system? There are four strategies:

1. Design the software with a lot of input parameters or tables. For example, an airline reservation package must have tables for city pairs between operating flights. The input tables and parameters allow each user to tailor the system to his or her environment.

2. Provide different **modules** for different situations. Assume that a company is selling a registration package for universities. There must be a module to handle grades. The vendor might have separate modules depending on the type of grades used—A through F, 100 to 0, and so on. It is unlikely that the same institution would use more than one grading scheme, so the appropriate module is included for each customer.

3. The vendor may expect the organization to change its procedures to use the package. Often it is pointed out that a small **procedural** change to use the package is cheaper than the alternative of program changes. For packages that address very similar applications across companies or industries, the organization will seriously want to consider making some of these changes.

4. Plan for custom tailoring and modifications for each customer. With this in mind, the package might be offered with a very flexible report writer so the desired reporting formats of each customer can be developed when the package is installed.

Some combination or even all of these approaches may be followed for any given package. Whenever a package is to be installed, the more dedicated it is to a given application, the more input will be required by users to describe their organization and environment.

Modifications may turn out to be the largest expense of the package, depending on how much programming is required. Some package vendors will not sell their source code; only the machine language is provided. Under these circumstances, we are totally dependent on the vendor to make any needed modifications. Are modifications that run 20 to 50 percent of the cost of a package justified? In one situation, the manager of a warehouse could not fill orders with the procedures included in a package. The package had to be modified. Otherwise, he could not use a procedure followed for a number of years of allocating products to preferred customers while shipping only orders completely filled by available stock.

Regardless if the vendor, an in-house programming staff, or some third party makes package modifications, there are precautions that should be taken to try to minimize future problems. One good strategy is confining modifications to certain modules. All changes should be carefully documented, with comments on the modified programs and external documents detailing the changes. Most packages go through continual revisions and improvements. If changes are made and not noted, the organization will be unable to install new versions because the staff will not know what modifications to make to keep the new version compatible with custom changes in the prior version.

A CLASSIFICATION FRAMEWORK FOR PACKAGES

The dedicated packages described above are generally easy to identify. They are devoted to solving a particular problem and cannot be generalized to another domain. A large variety of packages have been designed for different purposes and types of computers (see Figure 17-1). There is some debate as to what is a package and what is a language. We shall take a broad view and include a variety of candidates for classification as a package. Packages are often developed for certain types of computers, large, midrange, or personal computers. Some experts refer to the first three categories listed below as "tools," because the user works with them to develop an application. These tools are used to develop an application in-house, as opposed to the previous alternative of a dedicated package. It is often the case, however, that the buyer has to modify a dedicated package, so it would be misleading to suggest that the dedicated package involves no in-house development.

Fourth-Generation Languages   4GLs have statements that are at a considerably higher level than a third-generation language. These packages are languages. They are not dedicated to a particular application but instead require the user to apply them to a problem. Some of the languages are designed for specific problem areas such as financial modeling, but a number exist that are basically general-purpose.

Figure 17-1

Examples of packages.

Package type	Computer		
	Large ─────→	Midrange ─────→	PC
Fourth-generation	FOCUS	Oracle	PowerBuilder FOCUS (version for PC)
Systems software	DBMS	Ingres	Paradox, Access
Problem-oriented languages	SPSS, SAS	SPSS, SAS	Lotus 1-2-3, Excel, Quattro Pro
Dedicated	Accounts receivable	Garment system R/3 from SAP	Accounting

Systems Software   Software packages also exist that are designed for a specific purpose, such as a set of programs to provide database management or to control the interaction of a computer with terminals. These are **systems software** packages and can be quite general. DBMS may follow the relational model, but that places few limitations on the kind of problem that this package can solve. These programs may also be designed for just one computer or a small number of computers. Many would classify database management systems as systems software. Vendors of these packages often provide sophisticated development languages to create packages that are a lot like fourth-generation languages.

Problem-Oriented Languages   Packages in this category are like higher-order languages in many respects but are aimed at a specific problem. A good example of this type of package is SPSS (Statistical Package for the Social Sciences), which is used by nonprogrammers to analyze data. An example of this package for Windows may be found in Chapter 9. Although a language, these statements are not difficult to learn, and many nonprofessional programmers use this package.

The popular spreadsheet packages in this category include Excel, Quattro Pro, and Lotus 1-2-3. These packages make it possible to construct elaborate models and test their sensitivity to changes. Users reference cells in the spreadsheet through numbered rows and columns designated by capital letters. This ability to relate rows and columns using formulas gives spreadsheet programs their power. A few data items can be changed and the results for the entire spreadsheet are updated automatically. Spreadsheets

---

MANAGEMENT PROBLEM 17-3

Bob Harris is manager of systems development for Atlantic Manufacturing Company. This firm makes a variety of tools for home craftsmen and professional carpenters, mechanics, and other tradespeople.

Bob is reviewing a request from one of the plants for an integrated production scheduling and control system for shop-floor control. This particular plant manufactures hand tools. The tools are relatively simple, ranging from four or five parts to fifty parts in a completed tool. Although the number of parts is relatively small, the volume at the plant is quite high, and scheduling is a problem because a tool can be made in a number of different ways. The plant is the classic "job shop," as opposed to an assembly line.

Harris has just returned from a two-day professional seminar on prototyping, and he is eager to try this new approach to systems development. The request in front of him has raised the possibility of trying prototyping for the first time at Atlantic. Harris has discussed the idea with two other analysts. They, however, were quite skeptical. "The system would be so large that we would need conventional specifications and design," one advised. The other asked, "How can we build a prototype of a system this complex?"

Where do you think prototyping could be used for this suggested application?

are the most popular tool for building decision support systems, a type of system discussed in Chapter 21.

Dedicated Packages   The last category in Figure 17-1 contains dedicated packages, systems devoted to a particular application. This group is experiencing explosive growth as more and more installations look first to buy before programming a custom system. This kind of package presents the greatest **implementation** challenge. There are dedicated packages for making airline reservations and managing production. Other examples include general ledger, accounts payable, accounts receivable, bank demand-deposit accounting, bank trust management, and so on.

These packages are most likely to require modifications or changes in the buyer's procedures or both. They are not intended to be used as a language but are designed as an off-the-shelf substitute for a custom-designed and custom-programmed system. The fundamental trade-off is to what extent one should (1) take the package as is, (2) pay to have the package changed, or (3) change company procedures.

Packages have been around for a number of years, but three factors account for the increasing interest in this option for developing a system:

1. The cost of programming is rising, as are the risks of not completing a project on time and within budget. We now realize that specifications and features are often compromised in a custom design, so the user ends up not getting everything that was desired in the specifications.

2. The packages themselves are getting better, as many have passed through several generations of improvements.

3. The declining cost of hardware means that we can afford to run a package that operates inefficiently on the computer in order to save development time and cost.

An Example of a Package   Accounts receivable is a common business computer application. Almost all firms that sell a product or provide a service need to send bills to their customers. The shipment of a product or provision of a service creates a receivable, that is, an asset that represents money due from customers. It is important to keep track of receivables, as this item appears on the balance sheet and because receivables must be managed. As payments are received, they must be credited against open receivables. If payments are overdue, it is important to work on collecting them.

One services and consulting firm offers a complete package for garment manufacturers. If the manufacturer is small, it can rent terminals and run the package on the vendor's computer. A larger customer buys the package and a computer on which to run it. Although the package is quite comprehensive, we concentrate here on the accounts-receivable portion of this dedicated application.

The package has the following functions, all of which operate on-line:

1. Initialization of files, file creation, and maintenance
2. Daily entry of summary invoices and product returns
3. Daily posting of cash receipts
4. Daily sales and cash journal processing
5. End-of-month aged accounts-receivable reports, customer statements, and commission reports for sales representatives
6. Information reports for credit and sales analysis

The system has files containing details about the company and the division, various codes and terms, sales representatives, the buying office, and customers. These files of semi-permanent data that change infrequently are supplemented by files of daily transactions. The first of these is accounts-receivable items—a file of all transactions and open receivables. An item record includes garments shipped, quantity, and cost. A transactions

Going Paperless

The paperless office has long been an unobtainable dream. While it is unlikely that any office will completely eliminate paper, Princor, a mutual funds firm in Iowa, installed a packaged imaging and workflow system to reduce the amount of paper it processes. The company manages $2 billion in mutual funds for 150,000 customers with a staff of 125 people. Customers send transactions by mail, phone, fax and electronically. Until 1992 all customer transactions were based on paper. (The company even printed electronic orders before processing them.) Princorp kept a paper file on each customer containing all of their paper transactions recorded on microfiche. For every transaction, an employee removed the file and sent it to an outside vendor for processing.

A system from Sungard Data Systems called PowerImage allowed Princor to eliminate a great deal of paper and processing time. There was no need to customize the software; rather Princor reengineered its processing using the features provided by the package.

The system uses an IBM RS/6000 RISC processor which connects to a mainframe. Connected to the server are IBM 486 compatible computers from AST Research; these machines run Windows and are connected on a Novell network. The company purchased two IBM scanners and an optical storage "jukebox" with 144 optical platters capable of holding 1.2 gigabytes of data each. The company scans about 1000 documents a day.

Princor scans every incoming piece of mail, though it does generate paper and forms that it sends back to customers. A customer services representative creates an electronic form when taking information from someone over the phone. The system, of course, eliminated all the filing of paper folders and documents. It has also eliminated the need to look up signatures to verify checks; the system stores signatures on an optical disk and retrieves them electronically. The workflow software allows employees to route documents electronically. A representative having trouble with a transaction can route it to a supervisor for help. In the future the company is considering letting people work from home since the system, rather than human beings, routes documents for processing.

file of cash receipts is also maintained with all customer checks and pointers to the invoices paid by the checks.

The last major category of files are those for posting totals. Here we find cash receipts control—a file of pointers to all open items for each customer. The customer credit file has totals owed, which appear on the customer credit inquiry screen on a CRT. There is also a file of customer sales, which has various totals of sales for each customer.

This package is dedicated, and all transactions are processed on-line from terminals. The software runs on a midrange computer under the control of a proprietary time-sharing operating system and a database manager. If the other modules of the system are purchased, they create the open receivable in the accounts-receivable file when merchandise is shipped from the warehouse. Basic information for the entire package begins at order entry, when the customer's order is entered using a CRT.

When cash is received in the form of checks, a clerk working from a CRT enters the total amount and then applies the payment to open items. The clerk looks for invoices paid entirely by the check. If these are not obvious, he or she must figure out what items are being paid by the check.

Acquiring Packages

Choosing a package is not an easy task. First, we have an information processing problem. If it looks as though the application is dedicated, we should perform a systems analysis and design tudy. The study should be carried through to a high-level design for a new system containing outputs, the contents of the database and inputs. This design becomes a benchmark against which to evaluate various packages.

In today's environment, we should not begin to look for hardware yet. Instead, it is time for research on possible packages. There are trade journals in the computer field that rank packages, and certain proprietary information firms keep listings of packages. Another good source of information is trade journals in the industry. The garment firm above found out about the system in a garment industry trade journal. Finally, for software for personal computers, one can visit various computer stores and look at their documentation on packages.

Evaluation of a package is difficult. It is important for users and the information services staff to understand the package in detail. We should be sure to see the package work and ensure that users understand what it will and will not do. Then we should estimate the extent of modifications and determine whether the package will really work in our environment.

Implementing Packages

Package implementation is not a trivial task. In certain respects it may be even more difficult than the development of a custom system. Refer to Figure 17-2, which is a framework for package implementation. The environment of the organization, users' needs, and users' **expectations** about what the system should do all combine to create **processing requirements**.

The package vendor offers a solution to these requirements. It is unlikely that the package will exactly match the customer's requirements,

Figure 17-2
Packages implementation.

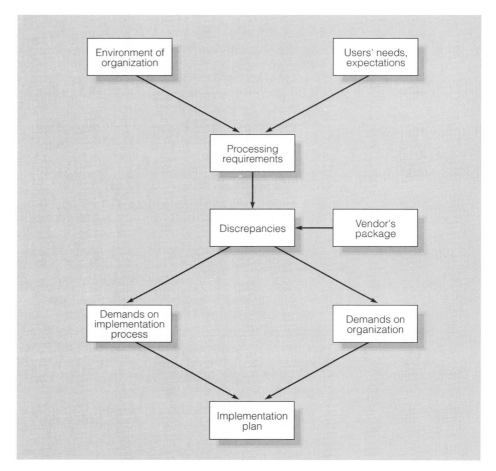

giving rise to **discrepancies** between the two. As an example, the customer may use eight-digit part numbers, whereas the package has provided for only six digits. During implementation, we must resolve these discrepancies, either through making changes in the organization or through special considerations in the implementation process. Finally, an implementation plan should be the result of the effort.

The vendor can help in package modification by providing flexibility in the design of the system. Database management systems to support the package, good query languages, and report generators to custom-tailor the output all help. Thorough documentation is very important, as is consulting help in implementation. A number of vendors also offer telephone hot lines to answer calls from users who have problems.

SAP is a company that offers a client-server integrated package called R/3 that is extremely popular. The package handles a wide variety of business functions and has had particular success in manufacturing companies. SAP suggests that customers reengineer their processes to fit R/3 rather than undertake modifications of the package. Clients often agree to this strategy because they have read about reengineering successes and they are eager to obtain improvements in their business processes. Even still it is reported that implementation is difficult because so much change is required.

It may appear to users that they do not have to become involved, since we are purchasing a package already developed. In all likelihood, users will be more involved in the acquisition of a package, or at least more intensely involved over a shorter period of time, than with custom development. We must be sure that the requirements analysis is complete, that users in fact define processing requirements. The users also must understand in detail how the package works and think about it in their present job environment. They must provide help in outlining the discrepancies and in deciding how they are to be resolved through package changes or changes in company procedures. There have been just as many examples of package implementation disasters as disasters with custom systems!

Conclusions   Packages are increasingly important in systems development. It is too costly to develop systems with custom programming if a package exists that will work for a given task. Remember to develop specifications on requirements at least at a high level before talking to a package vendor. It is very important to have a basis for comparing all the different packages and to avoid being swayed by features that one really does not need or want.

PROTOTYPING

The objective of prototyping is to reduce the time needed to develop requirements for a system. The traditional design approach features an analyst who spends time with users to elicit requirements. The analyst prepares specifications, which are given to the user to approve. Most users seem to have difficulty comprehending the specifications. As a result, it may not be until the testing stage that the user first gains an understanding of how the system will or will not work.

A **prototype** is a model of a system that will eventually be developed. Its purpose is to do the following:

1. Reduce the time before the user sees something concrete from the systems design effort.
2. Provide rapid feedback from the user to the designer.
3. Help delineate requirements with fewer errors.
4. Enhance designer and user understanding of what systems should accomplish.
5. Bring about meaningful user involvement in systems analysis and design.

A prototype does not have to be real. For example, an architect's model of a building made from card stock is a representation of the building. Part of a system can be "dummied" using sample data, and output can be incomplete. The prototype may become a living specification that is constantly changed as the prototype is refined. In fact, the prototype may grow into the final system without even the development of detailed specifications!

The external appearance of the prototype must be very clear. As an example, the prototype for a transactions processing system is likely to provide a fixed set of screens that accept input from the user, process it, and possibly return output. The full logic of the system has not yet been developed, so there will be restrictions. However, there should be enough of a system present that users can understand how the final version will operate.

How to Develop a Prototype

It is important that the prototype be developed quickly and feedback occur in a timely manner. The actual development process is likely to be a sequence of activities (see Figure 17-3).

Figure 17-3
The prototyping process.

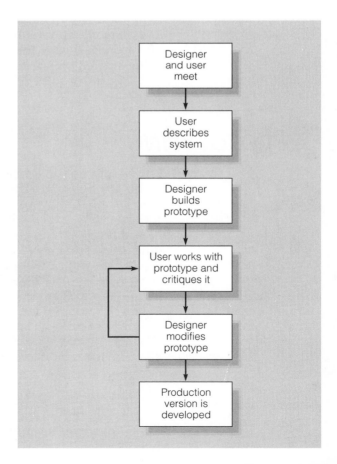

1. The designer meets with the user.
2. The user describes the system.
3. The designer builds a prototype.
4. The user works with the prototype and critiques it.
5. The designer modifies the prototype or starts again.
6. The process then returns to step 1 or 4.

Changes here should be encouraged, not discouraged! We choose the prototyping approach because a set of system specifications is usually very abstract to the user. The prototype makes the system come alive. We want users to interact with the system and make it into what they would like to have. To accomplish the objective of rapid development, the designer will need to use one or more tools to develop the prototype.

Software   The designer can use any one of a variety of tools for developing a prototype. A fourth-generation language like PowerBuilder, a conventional programming language enhanced to make developing graphical user interfaces easier like Visual Basic, or a database management system. Good candidates here include Paradox for Windows, and Microsoft's Access. These systems make the task of developing and modifying data structures much easier than is possible with most programming languages. High-level programming languages and the ability to record your keystrokes and replay them (macros) make it possible to develop prototypes quickly.

Effective programming and development tools are a requirement for prototyping. Remember that the prototype begins as a model. It does not have to include any of the editing and error-checking of a finished system. The purpose of the exercise is to show what can be accomplished, not to demonstrate that a system is complete.

An Example   The firm that developed the following system offers services throughout the world. The firm was investigating a change in its ownership. It is owned by its employees, but new U.S. legislation made some alterations potentially attractive in ownership structure. The vice chairman of the board asked the manager of the information services department to develop a small system to project the financial position of the firm several years in the future if the new form of ownership were adopted.

At first, the IS department manager simply wrote a small program in BASIC to model the plan. The output of the model formed one part of the recommendations made to the board of directors. After that meeting, at which the new plan was adopted, several managers noted the ability of the computer to forecast. One of them asked the IS department manager if it would be possible to forecast the benefits an employee would have several years in the future.

The industry is competitive, and firms frequently hire staff from each other. Because there are a variety of stock and benefit plans, it was difficult to show an employee the total value of remaining with the company. The information services staff began to work on this problem with help from different personnel and financial managers. Various formulas were programmed and the results checked by different groups until the rules were regarded as satisfactory.

The manager of the IS department had a feeling that the system would grow, so he had the staff develop it using database management software. The treasurer kept most of the data needed on benefits available to each individual, and he became very interested in the system. Computing bonuses took a long time and required heavy overtime, In general, records for each employee were scattered over several files, and reports were often inaccurate. The treasurer asked that the system be made capable of maintaining all employee records and benefits. Because of the database approach and good development tools, it was fairly easy to meet his requirements. The system has evolved into a comprehensive personnel records and benefits application.

This system succeeded because it was able to grow and change over time. As users saw new features, they developed ideas for extending the application. The primary user changed to the treasurer from the president, who had originally requested the projection system. The application had high visibility, and senior management provided extensive input.

The use of tools was also very important in the success of this effort. High-level languages, screen development aids, and a database management system made it possible for the system to evolve. In addition to intensive user involvement, the analyst working on the application listened carefully and followed the logic defined by the users. She brought the results back to them, and the managers actually debugged their own rules. By not trying to be in charge of everything, the analyst was able to develop a system with which users felt comfortable because they understood the details of how it worked.

Not every system could be developed in this manner. In other circumstances, there might be a need for concrete specifications. However, the use of prototyping to show users what the system will do should be applicable across a wide range of settings.

Prototyping is a very effective way to improve the requirements definition phase for a system. The approach appears to be good for attracting users to the design process and obtaining their involvement and input. Done properly, it should result in systems that more closely fit user needs and that are completed more quickly with fewer operational changes required.

CHAPTER SUMMARY

1. In many cases, management and the design team may adopt an alternative to custom development of a system following the traditional life cycle model of the last chapter.

2. The objective of alternative techniques is to reduce the length of time required to follow the systems life cycle and to provide early feedback to users.

3. Table 17-1 describes the pros and cons of the different alternatives and suggests the advantages from these techniques do not come for free.

4. Fourth-generation languages have been available for a number of years. They make more efficient use of human time at the cost of some inefficiencies in execution.

5. The general package program, like a spreadsheet, offers a number of tools for developing custom applications. These tools, when explored in detail, look a lot like conventional programming languages.

6. A dedicated package is designed to let the user eliminate custom programming.

7. The selection and implementation of a dedicated package is a challenge. Often the organization or the package must change in order to work successfully.

8. Prototyping is an excellent way to generate user input in the design process. We recommend that, where feasible, the designer develop a prototype for different parts of any system under development.

Table 17-1
Comparison of the Alternatives

Pros	Cons
FOURTH-GENERATION LANGUAGES	
Very high level statements, claims for high productivity, ease of use, speed of development and modification	Can be inefficient in processing OLTP applications, expensive, proprietary, depend on single vendor
PACKAGE PROGRAM (GENERAL)	
User often develops solutions	Can be a lot like programming
PACKAGE PROGRAMS (DEDICATED)	
Avoid custom programming, faster implementation, debugged programs, more features than custom system	May have to change package or procedures
PROTOTYPING	
Users see immediate results, good for motivating involvement and feedback, reduce risk of misdesign	Time to develop, cost, may be seen as slowing progress.

9. The prototype may serve as a model and partial specifications for the final system, or it may evolve into the final system itself.

10. These techniques will improve the systems development process. However, they will not produce the order of magnitude improvement in development efficiency that the profession so badly needs.

IMPLICATIONS FOR MANAGEMENT

Personal computers and their associated software packages make it relatively easy to prototype all or parts of a system. A prototype is probably the best way to focus users on what a system will do. It is much more riveting than a set of specifications on paper. One of the real problems in design is communications between designers and the users and managers specifying the system. A prototype helps users think about how they will do their jobs with the new system. If you are evaluating packages, you will also want to see the package at work in some other company to see if it is a good fit with your environment.

KEY WORDS

Database management system
  (DBMS)
Dedicated package
Discrepancies
Expectations
Fourth-generation language
High-level languages
Implementation
Macros

Modification
Modules
Nonprocedural
Problem-oriented languages
Procedural
Processing requirements
Prototype
Systems software
Vendor support

RECOMMENDED READING

Kleper, R., and D. Bock. "Third and Fourth Generation Language Productivity," *Communications of the ACM,* vol. 38, no. 9 (September 1995), pp. 69–79. (An interesting study of productivity and language use in a number of projects at McDonnell Douglas; there appear to be productivity advantages for 4GLs.)

Lucas, H. C., Jr., and E. Walton. "Implementing Packaged Software," *MIS Quarterly,* vol. 12, no. 4 (December 1989), pp. 537–549. (The report of a study of package implementation offering insights into the key variables for success.)

Mason, R. E. A., and T. T. Carey. "Prototyping Interactive Information Systems," *Communications of the ACM,* vol. 26, no. 5 (May 1983), pp. 347–354. (A helpful article with recommendations on prototyping.)

Martin, E. W., D. DeHayes, J. Hoffer, and W. Perkins. *Managing Information Technology: What Managers Need to Know.* New York: Macmillan, 1991. (See especially Chapter 10 for a discussion of prototyping.)

To compare different packages for PCs, look at *PC Magazine* and *Byte.*

DISCUSSION QUESTIONS

1. What is the primary motivation behind the use of fourth-generation Languages?
2. How does a query language such as the ones found in DBMS reduce programming?
3. What are the advantages of a PC DBMS in prototyping?
4. Should we be concerned if 4GLs use the computer inefficiently? Why or why not?
5. Why are some very high-level languages called nonprocedural?
6. What are the advantages and disadvantages of using a spreadsheet package for applications development?
7. How can it be faster for a user to write a program using a 4GL than to have a professional programmer prepare the report?
8. Why must a user understand the structure of databases to use a 4GL?
9. Will the tools in this chapter eliminate the need for professional programmers?
10. How would you locate candidate dedicated applications packages for evaluation and selection?
11. Is there still a place for writing custom programs in applications development?
12. Why has the progress in developing faster and cheaper hardware been so dramatic, while productivity in systems development is so low?
13. To what extent should users develop applications using tools like spreadsheets and DBMS. What are the pros and cons of this approach to development?
14. What are the special implementation problems of a dedicated package?
15. Under what conditions should an organization change its procedures to use a package?
16. Why are more companies looking first at dedicated packages rather than custom-development for new applications?
17. How do packages reduce development time for a system? How can packages lower costs?

18. What are all the costs associated with a package beyond the purchase price?

19. In buying a package, does one always get debugged programs?

20. Why should one insist on a demonstration of a package?

21. Why might a package not include some of the functions we want?

22. Why is a vendor reluctant to change a dedicated package for one customer?

23. Why is it important to control changes to a package carefully?

24. Why should you still develop a set of high-level specifications even if you are thinking about acquiring a dedicated package for a new application?

25. Is a large organization likely to change procedures or change a package? Why might a large firm have more need to modify a package than a small one?

26. How can a package vendor design a package to be flexible?

27. Why might the programming staff be opposed to the use of packages?

28. Is accounts receivable likely to be the same type of application no matter what the firm? What characteristics might differ among companies?

29. What is the user's role in determining whether to acquire a package?

30. Develop an implementation strategy for the accounts-receivable example in this chapter.

31. Why is a package a more viable alternative to a custom system today than it was ten years ago?

32. What are the advantages of prototyping? The disadvantages?

33. How does a prototype for a computer system differ from an architect's model? How are they similar?

34. Why does a prototype need to be developed quickly?

CHAPTER 17 PROJECT

FOURTH-GENERATION LANGUAGES

There is a great deal of interest in fourth-generation languages, as they offer one way to reduce the time required to program and install new systems. The languages can also help users answer some of their questions faster, as we shall see in Chapter 20.

Find a language manual for a 4GL such as FOCUS or PowerBuilder and compare the structure of that language with that of a third-generation language you know, like Visual BASIC, FORTRAN, or C. What are your conclusions? Does the 4GL appear to accomplish its objectives? Could you code faster using the 4GL?

CHAPTER **18**

Reengineering: Changing Businesses and Business Processes

OBJECTIVES

1. **Learning to manage information technology.**

   Reengineering has captured management attention as a way to reduce costs and increase effectiveness. It has focused attention on business processes and on the importance of obtaining significant improvements from investments in technology.

2. **Preparing to apply technology.**

   Many organizations do not design systems any longer; they reengineer them. In this chapter we try to place reengineering in perspective and explain where it is an appropriate solution to a problem.

3. Transforming the organization.

The discussions early in the book, especially Chapter 4, suggest that you can use IT to change structure, moving toward the T-Form organization. In this chapter we see examples of two firms that have reengineered the entire organization rather than a single business process.

*W*HAT IS REENGINEERING?

One of the most popular management topics today is business process redesign, or **reengineering**. Unfortunately, definitions of reengineering sometimes are circular. It seems that the experts in this field define reengineering as the redesign of some process that creates at least an order of magnitude improvement or cost savings over existing procedures. An approach like this means that every reengineering process is a success by definition! A definition not tied completely to an outcome is:

> "Reengineering is the fundamental rethinking and radical redesign of business processes to achieve dramatic improvements in critical, contemporary measures of performance, such as cost, quality, service, and speed (Hammer and Champy, 1993)."

This framework has four key words:

1. Fundamental: Why does the firm do things a certain way?
2. Radical: Get to the root of a process. Look for reinvention as opposed to making superficial changes or minor enhancements to what is already in place.
3. Dramatic: Reengineering is not about marginal or **incremental improvements**, but rather it focuses on achieving quantum leaps in performance. Results like a 10 percent improvement are not reengineering.
4. Processes: Traditional design often is centered on tasks, jobs, people and structures. Reengineering looks at a business process which is a collection of activities that takes one or more kinds of inputs and produces some output of value.

In an earlier article, Hammer described the spirit of reengineering as "obliterating" rather than automating. He argues that systems developers too often simply automate existing processes without thinking about the need for **radical change**. What does **"obliterating a process"** mean? Does one have to achieve an order of magnitude gain to claim a reengineering success? What are the likely impacts of a successful business process redesign effort on the organization?

The discussion above centers on reengineering versus incremental improvements to business processes. Figure 18-1 suggests these characterizations of business process redesign are really endpoints on a continuum.

Figure 18-1
Avoid the middle ground.

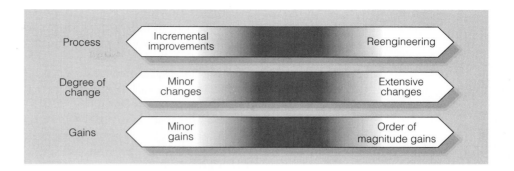

Reengineering and radical change are on the right-hand side of the continuum, small enhancements to a process fall to the left. (Possibly obliteration is off the scale on the right!)

It is very likely that the middle of the continuum represents an area of maximum work for minimum payoff. This middle ground is a place designers should avoid. One contribution of reengineering is to call management's attention to the fact designers should concentrate on incremental improvements or the radical redesign of processes. Working in the middle ground often results in high expenditures to automate an existing, inefficient process.

If reengineering creates such dramatic gains why would the organization ever be satisfied with incremental improvements? First, managers should always be looking at ways to improve work processes. Second, reengineering often results in dramatic reductions in the workforce, and demands more work from those remaining. Management has to balance its obligation to improve processes against the firm's responsibility to its employees.

Working on the reengineering side of the continuum is risky. Changes of great magnitude may even appear to some as doing violence to the organization. When management selects reengineering over incremental improvement, it is taking greater risks in the hope of obtaining greater benefits. In fact, if one takes a more historical view, the evolution of applications systems can be characterized by on-going incremental improvements punctuated by major reengineering efforts.

WHAT IS A PROCESS?

Most of our discussion to this point has focused on the structure of the organization and how IT design variables can be used to change structures. The main contribution of reengineering for us is to focus attention on **processes** as opposed to structures. What is a process and how is it related to structure?

One of the fundamental processes for a firm that sells a product is order fulfillment. Picture a mail-order firm in which operators take orders when customers call on an 800, toll-free number. The order entry department is responsible for talking to customers and entering their orders into a computer system. The system checks a "book" inventory to determine if the goods requested are available. If so, it produces a picking list for the warehouse staff to use in completing the order. If the requested merchandise is out of stock, the system notifies the Purchasing Department that it is time to reorder, and it creates a backorder on the system so that it can fill the order when a new shipment arrives.

This brief scenario describes the order fulfillment process, a process that cuts across at least three departments in the structure of the organization: Order Entry, Warehousing, and Purchasing. Business process redesign is likely to employ four or five of our IT design variables from Chapter 4. The radical reorganization of a process is likely to result in **technological leveling** as technology is used to reduce the need for multiple layers of management related to a process. Reengineering is often associated with **production automation** and **electronic workflows** as well as virtual components. It may also introduce **technological matrixing** in the redesign of business processes.

REENGINEERING A PROCESS AT MUTUAL BENEFIT LIFE

One of the early examples of reengineering was at Mutual Benefit Life Insurance Company. Before business process redesign, Mutual Benefit Life (MBL) processed life insurance applications in a long, multistep process which included credit checking, quoting, rating, underwriting, etc. An application might go through 30 steps across five departments with up to 19 people involved. Typical turnarounds ranged from 5 to 25 days. Another firm estimated that a life insurance application spent 22 days in process for 17 minutes of actual work.

To redesign this process, MBL used computer networks, databases, and an **expert system** to make information and decision support available to employees. It created a new position called a case manager who is a *process owner*. This person acts as a case manager and has total responsibility for an application from the time it is received until a policy is issued. Files are no longer handed from one person in a chain to another across departmental boundaries. Case managers are able to perform all of the tasks required to process an insurance application because they have technology to help them. An expert system provides advice while their PC-based workstation connects to a variety of databases and applications on a mainframe computer.

What were the results? MBL can now complete an application in as little as four hours and the average time to turn around an application and issue a policy is two to five days. The company was able to eliminate 100 field office positions while its case managers can handle nearly twice the volume of applications MBL could previously process. It is a sad footnote that MBL's investment performance was not as good as its reengineering; the company was taken over by the state of New Jersey. One has to be able to manage all aspects of the business to be successful!

This example shows the use of *production automation* in which workstations provide the information needed for an individual to make a decision. The workstation, mainframe computers and network create a *virtual applications processing workflow* for each case worker. He or she has access to credit checks, quotations, ratings, and underwriting electronically rather than physically.

REENGINEERING A PROCESS AT MERRILL LYNCH

Merrill Lynch is the largest brokerage and financial services firm in the United States with over 500 branch offices. The objective of the securities processing operation is to receive certificates from customers, perform the proper processing of the certificates, and post data to customer accounts. See Lucas, Berndt, and Truman (1996).

A very high-level process flow consists of the following steps:

1. The customer brings documents to a branch office.
2. The branch does preliminary processing.
3. Certificates are sent to a processing center.

MANAGEMENT PROBLEM 18-1

Betty Adams read several books and articles about reengineering. She is wondering how to apply it to her own areas of responsibility. Betty is executive vice president of Preferred Life Insurance, a medium-sized company that offers a range of life and health insurance policies. She, like others in the company, has been concerned for some time about the rising costs of health care and the company's processing costs.

A recent study showed that a typical health claim took three weeks to process. Preferred was thinking of going to managed care where it would organize doctors into a health maintenance type organization. A client's primary care physician would receive a capitation fee monthly, a kind of retainer. Clients would pay a flat fee for health coverage. Betty thought about the plans for this kind of service and the kind of processing that would be required. She wondered if something radical was necessary to take advantage of this kind of system where the insurance company had contracts with doctors and hospitals.

Sketch the plans for a reengineered information system for a managed care network. Can you scale your plans up to a national health program?

4. The center verifies and checks the certificates.

5. The center processes certificates.

6. The center posts data to the customer's account.

On a typical day, Merrill Lynch offices around the U.S. receive some 3500 securities which need processing of some kind. What are some of the reasons for customers bringing securities to a branch office?

1. The customer has sold the stock and must surrender it so shares can be issued to the buyer.

2. A person has inherited stock and must have the shares registered in his or her name.

3. A company has reorganized and has called its old stock to issue new shares.

4. A bond has been called by the issuer.

5. A customer wants Merrill to hold his or her securities.

The Old System

The customer brings the security plus other supporting documents to the branch office cashier. The cashier provides a receipt and batches all of the securities together to be sent for processing. Before the development of a new process, the branch would send these documents to one of two securities processing centers, either Philadelphia or Chicago. (See Figure 18-2 for a high level DFD.)

The objective of securities processing at the centers was to credit the customer's account as soon as possible, certainly within the 24 hours suggested by the Securities and Exchange Commission. Because of exceptions and the possible need to contact the customer again, sometimes it was not possible to achieve this goal. A good example of problems is in the area of legal transfers when someone inherits stock. There are requirements for supporting documents like a death certificate. If the customer does not bring the documents and the branch does not catch the fact that a necessary piece of paper is missing, the securities processing center must contact the branch and ask them to contact the customer.

Because many of the securities are negotiable, the security processing centers (SPCs) must be extremely careful in processing. Merrill Lynch is required to keep an accurate audit trail whenever it moves a security. This requirement led to frequent, repeated microfilming of securities as they moved around a center.

To the Merrill Lynch Financial Consultant (FC) or broker, the securities processing task seemed to require an inordinate amount of time and lead to numerous problems. (There are some 15,000 FCs at Merrill.) The branch operations staff had to continually monitor accounts to see if securities were credited properly. FCs were forced to contact clients to obtain additional documents. There was a great deal of friction between the sales side of the business and securities processing department.

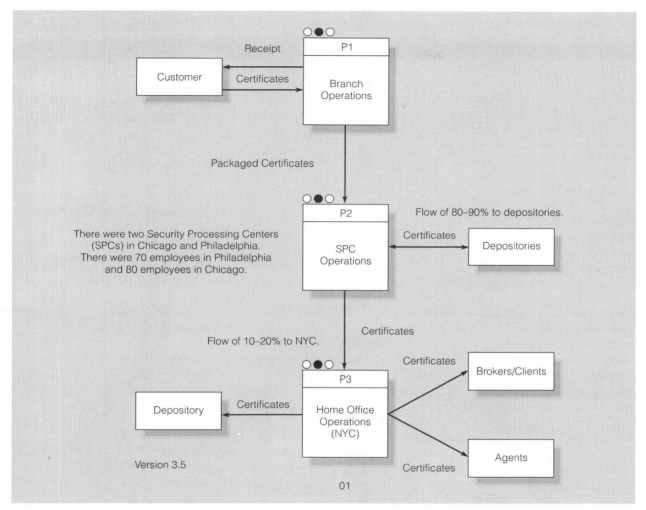

Figure 18-2 SPC overview.

All of these reasons plus the labor intensive nature of processing led to a desire to improve securities processing. The most radical approach would be to "obliterate" the process entirely. Unfortunately, this option is out of the control of Merrill Lynch. While there has been much publicity about "book entry" shares of stocks, there still are a large number of physical shares of stocks and bonds in circulation. Obliterating the process would require industry-level and government cooperation to eliminate all physical certificates, replacing them with an electronic record. This solution would also require consumer acceptance and a massive effort to record electronically and eliminate all existing paper certificates.

After suggestions by the operations staff and extensive research, the systems group at Merrill proposed a new process using image technology to capture an image of the security certificate and related documents that accompany a transaction. The focus of the project was on workflow redesign, not just the use of image processing. Workflow redesign involved the closing of the two processing centers described above and the development of a securities processing department at a single site in New York (now New Jersey).

In this old process, customers brought securities and supporting documents to a branch office or sent them to Merrill through the mail. This set of documents will be referred to as a "certificate," the terminology used at Merrill. After receiving the certificates, the branch conducted a manual review for negotiability. If this preliminary review verified that the security was negotiable, a clerk typed a receipt for the customer. If the certificates appeared not to be negotiable, the clerk told the customer what additional information was necessary to complete the transaction. (See Figure 18-3.)

During the day, several branch clerks accepted certificates and accumulated them. At the end of the day a courier took all certificates to one of two securities processing centers (SPCs) in Philadelphia or Chicago. The

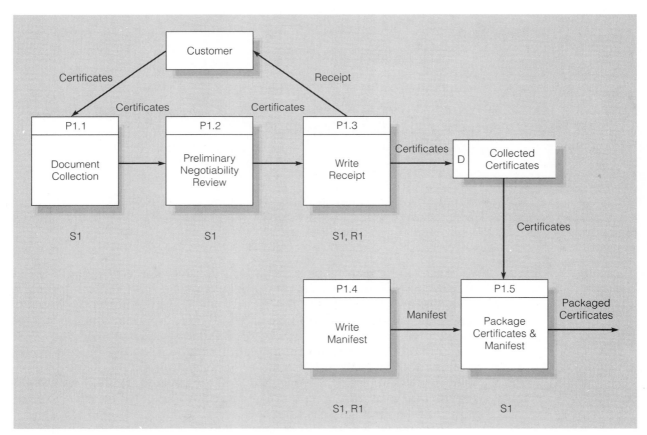

Figure 18-3   Branch operations.

clerks attached a manually prepared manifest to the package summarizing its contents.

Normally the package arrived at the SPC the next day. Upon arrival, an SPC clerk inspected the package and checked that its contents balanced to the manifest. The clerk contacted the branch office to resolve any discrepancies. All certificates that matched the manifest continued to the next stage in processing. (See Figure 18-4.)

The first step after bursting packages was to microfilm all certificates. Next, clerks conducted a second negotiability review which is contingent on the type of transaction: legal or non-legal. An example of a legal transaction is a stock transfer because the customer inherited the security. Regulations require that certain documents accompany the security, for example, a death certificate for the person in whose name the security is currently registered.

If further review showed the certificate was not negotiable, it was segregated. A clerk logged this status into a Merrill Lynch securities control

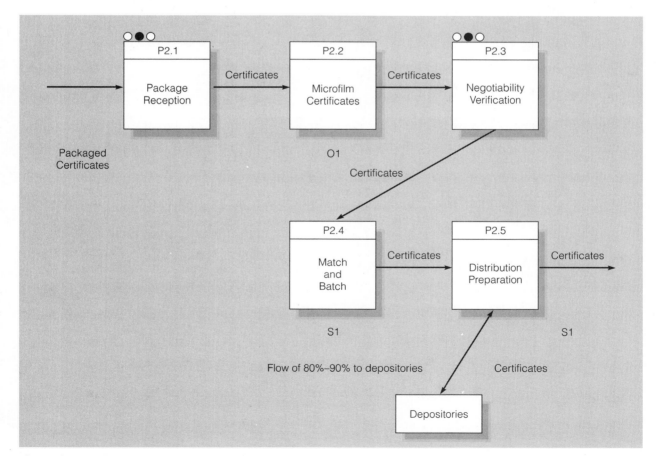

Figure 18-4 SPC operations.

system. Once classified as negotiable, the certificate moved to a final holding area for distribution.

The SPCs sent 80 to 90 percent of the certificates directly to depositories. The remaining certificates were distributed to specialty departments in New York for further processing, for example, a department handles exchanges of stock necessitated by a stock split. Upon arrival at a depository or at a Merrill specialty department, the certificates were again microfilmed and staff members updated their status in the control computer system. Certificates were microfilmed yet again before consignment to their final holding area.

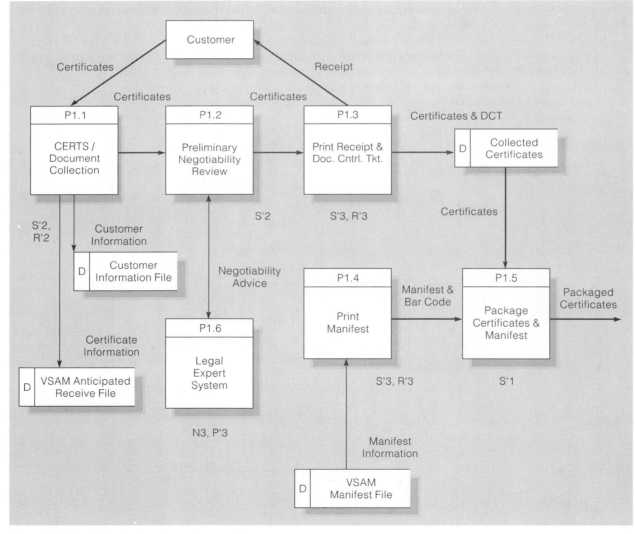

Figure 18-5   New system branch operations.

Why did this process entail so much microfilming? Merrill must carefully control securities and credit them to a customer's account as soon as possible. Given the volumes of paper involved, microfilming became an integral part of the control process. Merrill must also pass audits by the SEC which checks controls on securities processing.

A New System

Merrill completely redesigned the SPC process. As in the old process, customers bring securities to a branch office or mail them to Merrill. The branch cashier conducts a preliminary negotiability review supported by an expert system (see Chapter 22). This system helps the cashier determine negotiability status. It also prints a customer receipt and generates a document control ticket that travels with the certificates. The expert posts a record of the certificate to a computer file, including a unique identifier number for the transaction.

At the end of the day, clerks package all certificates to be taken by courier to the single securities processing center in New Jersey. The system generates a manifest sheet for the package and updates a manifest file so that it contains information on the shipment.

At the SPC, the staff first wands a bar code on the package to verify receipt. Clerks check the package against the manifest; if there is a discrepancy they update computer files and the system notifies the branch of the problem. Branch personnel have access to these files so they can check the status of processing of any security at any time. (See Figure 18-5.)

Negotiability must be verified in the new process, both for legal and non-legal documents. However, the presence of the expert system in the branches reduced the number of certificates arriving without the documents needed for negotiability by 50 percent for legals and 75 percent for non-legals.

A major technological innovation in the process was the introduction of image scanning and **character recognition** for certain key fields on the stock certificate. The scanning system recognizes a reference number via the bar code on the control sheet accompanying the certificates. The system uses the reference number to access the computer record which shows the scanner operator the certificates included in the transaction. The operator scans the certificates and any legal documents. At this point the images and physical certificates diverge. (See Figure 18-6.)

The scanned certificate image undergoes a character recognition procedure to turn three areas of the image into characters that can be processed by a computer. (See Figure 18-7.) From a technical standpoint, this recognition employs a proprietary algorithm embedded in "firmware" in the **imaging** computer. This recognition process converts three important fields from image to character format: the CUSIP number (a unique number for each security assigned by the securities industry), denomination of the security, and the security number. These three numbers are already recorded in the computer; recognition of the imaged fields is to establish rigorous control and provide assurance that the right documents have been scanned.

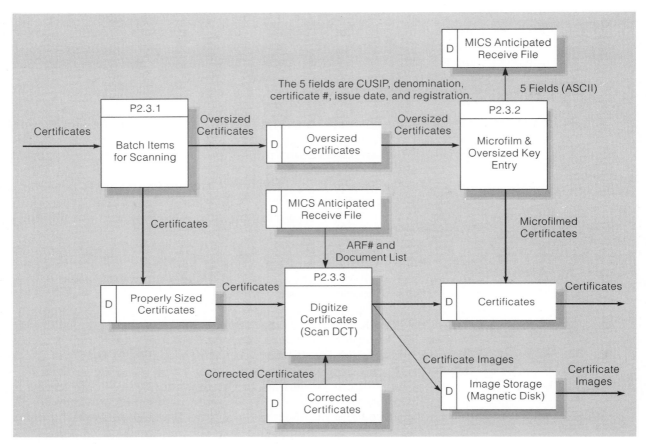

Figure 18-6   Image capture.

The recognition task is complicated by the fact there are no standard formats for securities. The three fields may exist any place on the security. The recognition algorithm needs to know where to look for the fields it is trying to convert. This information comes from a template database which indicates where the three fields are located on the security. Merrill has developed a template for each CUSIP and date of issue combination. The scanning computer routes any certificate whose template is not yet in the database to a workstation operator. The operator uses a mouse to draw a box around each field and the system records this location information in a new template for the security.

The system performs the image-to-character conversion by referencing the image, overlaying the template, and executing the algorithm. If the converted character fields match the same fields from the computer, the system updates the computer files to show scanning is complete and stores the images for this transaction permanently to optical disk. If there is a mismatch between the converted characters and the computer record,

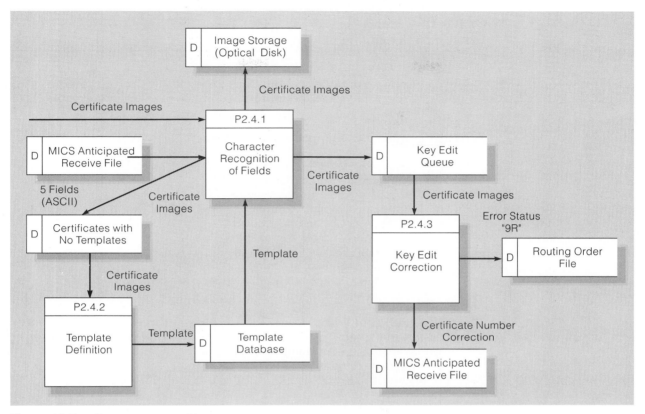

Figure 18-7 Character recognition.

or other non-recognition, the system refers the transaction to key edit. There, operators examine the image and input data to unrecognized fields.

The staff takes the physical certificates for distribution to their final location. The system executes a procedure to provide routing orders for each certificate and it specifies a destination box for the certificate.

When a user needs access to security information, he or she can retrieve the image of the security on a graphics workstation. There is no need to access the physical security, or to hunt through microfilm records, a process that could take as long as three days in the old process.

Evaluation Table 18-1 lists the major changes from the Merrill Lynch SPC process. The reengineering effort resulted in the elimination of two process centers and the creation of a securities processing department at a central site. The process supports major changes in tasks and workflow, beginning with the receipt of securities at a branch office. The interface to the process for all groups having contact with it has also been changed.

Technology changes include: the expert system for the branch office input, scanners, a template library, character recognition from images,

Table 18-1
Evaluation of Certificate Processing

Changes in organization structure

> The major organizational change was the elimination of two securities processing centers and the consolidation of all securities processing in a central site.

Changes in workflows and functions performed

There are many such changes:

> Branch office input changes
> Branch office customer receipt
> Anticipated receipt information
> Package receipt and bar coding
> Elimination of most microfilming
> Legal negotiability workflow changes
> Imaging operation; scanning and key edit
> Retrieval of image rather than physical security

Interface changes

> Branch office interface
> Customer interface
> Worker interface with scanning equipment
> User interface retrieving images

Major changes in technology

> Expert system to assist branch cashier receiving certificates
> Incorporation of scanning to replace most microfilm and provide better control, including:
>
> > Scanners
> > Template definition
> > Key Edit
> > Computer facility with optical disk jukebox
> > Retrieval of scanned documents
> > Modifications to existing control system

Impact

> Improvements in customer service
>
> > Better customer receipt
> > More information captured at point of contact
> > Broker can query system for status of processing
> > Better control

Certificate level control
High quality images compared to spotty microfilm
Reduction in up to 3 day searches for microfilm to instantaneous retrieval
Significant cost reduction as detailed in the next section
Reduction in research time

and optical disk storage. There have been significant increases in the level of customer service and the quality of support securities processing provides to the branches. There is much less handling of physical securities and retrieval time for a certificate image is nearly instantaneous. The time to research a security has been dramatically reduced; from up to three days in the old process to virtually instantaneously in the new.

The new securities processing system has had a dramatic impact on resources:

1. Reduction of occupancy from two locations to one
2. Reduction in depository fees
3. Interest savings on receivables
4. Reduction of microfilm costs
5. Savings in security services
6. Reduction in staff of 168 positions leaving a current total of 165 including temporary staff

The new process required an investment of approximately $3 million. The return on the investment was calculated as a payback period of less than two years which translates to a savings of around $1.5 million a year.

This example shows how one can execute a major redesign of a business process. Merrill used technology along with process redesign for *technological leveling* and reducing the number of processing centers and the number of managers needed to staff them. It applied information technology to automating the flow of certificates through the SPC, a form of *production automation*. The image system captures the certificates electronically and employees in different departments can retrieve the image of a certificate in seconds without the need to visit a vault. The certificate image can be routed to any terminal capable of displaying it within Merrill illustrating *electronic workflows*. (As of this writing we have learned that Merrill is in the process of outsourcing all securities handling to a third party; the simplification of securities processing has made it possible to turn over all handling of securities to a separate firm that will use electronic linking and communications to work as a partner with Merrill Lynch.)

Merrill Lynch's SPC illustrates how one can use business process redesign to make substantial changes in one part of an organization. The SPC is one area in a very large firm. Are there examples where process redesign has affected the fundamental structure of an organization?

REENGINEERING THE ENTIRE FIRM AT OTICON

Bjorn-Anderson and Turner (1994) have written about the Danish company, Oticon. This firm is one of the five largest hearing aid manufacturers in the world, with approximately 1200 employees and sales of $80 million.

Oticon exports more than 90 percent of its production to over 100 countries. The firm has its own research department and production facilities.

Oticon positioned itself to be the preferred partner for leading hearing aid clinics around the world. Company headquarters are in the Tuborg industrial park to the North of Copenhagen. There are three manufacturing facilities in Denmark and other countries.

The company began producing its own hearing aids during World War II. It was family owned until 1956 when new management took over and began mass production. By the end of the 1970s Oticon had reached the number one position in the world market with a 15 percent share and sales in over 100 countries. It was a leader in miniaturization for hearing aids worn behind the ear.

From 1979 through 1985, Oticon's market share dropped from 15 percent to 7 percent as competitors developed hearing aids that fit inside the ear. The company had losses in 1986 and 1987, leading the board to bring in new management. A new president, Lars Kolind, came to Oticon in 1988. His first action was to start a cost-cutting program in an attempt to regain profitability. Kolind also changed the firm's marketing strategy. For years, Oticon stressed high quality hearing aids, but now competitors were also building quality units. Kolind decided that the most appropriate strategy for Oticon was quality *and* customer satisfaction. Oticon focused its business on dispensers or retailers of hearing aids who were most interested in producing satisfied customers.

After two years, Kolind realized that cost cutting and a new marketing strategy had accomplished about all they could.

> "I sat down on New Year's Day ... and tried to think the unthinkable; a vision for the company of tomorrow. It would be a company where jobs were shaped to fit the person instead of the other way around. Each person would be given more functions and a job would emerge by the individual accumulating a portfolio of functions."

Kolind wanted to transform Oticon from an industrial organization producing a standardized product to a "high quality service organization with

MANAGEMENT PROBLEM 18-2

You have spent a significant amount of time involved with the "education industry." In the U.S., a child is likely to start a nursery school program by age 3 or 4, and may continue to college and graduate school until age 25 or greater. Roughly one-third of a typical life span for this individual is spent getting a formal education, and most graduates must continue to learn throughout their lives to keep up with the pace of change.

Just as one can think of reengineering a business process, you could conceivably reengineer an educational process. Think about the processes involved in education, from learning to administration, and develop a plan for reengineering some aspect of education. You may want to use some of the IT design variables and concepts of the T-Form organization from Chapter 4 as a basis for your reengineering effort.

a physical product." He envisioned an organization in which various functional units worked together in an integrated manner to develop innovative products. Kolind realized that he would have to create a new, **flexible organization**.

Kolind wrote a memo describing Oticon as one team of 150 employees at headquarters, all continuously developing and learning new skills. Each employee should be able to do several tasks—those he or she already did well and those where the employee would be challenged to learn new tasks. The idea was not to focus on functional expertise, but for each person to be able to do several jobs. Kolind also felt that paper hindered efficiency, as paper hides information instead of sharing it. He imagined computer systems that would eliminate paper and allow all employees to share information.

Kolind called his new plan a "**spaghetti organization**" since he envisioned people playing multiple, intertwined roles in the firm. To begin, he combined two separate offices into a new building designed for his new organization. Unlike many business process redesign projects, Kolind invited the participation of his employees in designing the new organization. It should be noted that, at first, there was a great deal of resistance to Kolind's proposals. When Kolind backed off a plan to move headquarters to Jutland, a remote part of Denmark, and chose instead to locate in the Tuborg industrial park, resistance faded. It is clear that the changes described below would not have happened without Kolind's strong and forceful leadership.

The first step was to eliminate traditional departments. The head office became one large department and work was organized as projects. Oticon views projects as temporary. Employees with different skills work together on different projects. This team-oriented arrangement works very well when the workload is uneven. In a more rigid structure, the marketing department would have to be staffed to handle its heavy load in the fall for exhibitions and trade shows. In the new structure, the marketing task becomes a project and enough resources are assigned to complete it. Normally about five people work consistently on marketing tasks. When the busy season arrives, this core group recruits other employees with different backgrounds, like R&D, to help out.

The second major innovation was to organize work in the form of projects. There is a project manager and a number of other employees who work on the project. The project manager is responsible for staffing the team and for carrying out the task. A project manager advertises the project on an electronic bulletin board on the Oticon system and employees at their workstations sign up for a project.

Employees occupy several positions at Oticon depending on the number and variety of projects for which they volunteer. This approach to organizing takes maximum advantage of diversity. An employee in accounting might sign up for a project involving marketing, bringing a whole new perspective to the marketing project.

To be successful, Oticon had to adopt a new philosophy of control. Management must trust employees to sign up for projects. This voluntarism should result in greater commitment to the firm and to more worker responsibility. Managers spend less time monitoring workers while managers must be innovators and motivators.

To bring about this new structure, Oticon had to rearrange its physical and technology domains. First, Kolind eliminated all private offices, including his own. All employees have identical desks and chairs in a large open space. There is a workstation and a mobile phone charger on the desks. Desks are not assigned. A worker moves his or her small, lockable caddie to a desk. The caddie has a drawer for personal items and shelves for storing up to ten files. Access to information is gained through the workstation.

Kolind also wanted to banish paper and Oticon's technology eliminates 95 percent of the paper in the office. The company scans all documents as they are received and workers are prohibited from keeping paper files. Original documents are shredded. All of this information is stored in electronic form and users can retrieve it from their workstations, given they have access rights.

When an employee enters his or her ID into the workstation, the system is configured with that individual's electronic desktop. The system has tools for creating, transmitting, and storing documents containing text, drawings, and graphics. This combination of physical and electronic flexibility makes it possible to create task forces almost immediately to solve a problem.

Oticon has enjoyed a return to profitability; 1992 profits were nine times better than those of '89 and '90. Sales are increasing and the company has reduced its cycle time to market new products. A new hearing aid that adjusts itself to the level of ambient sound was brought to market six months earlier than it could have been without the new organization.

Oticon demonstrates *technological leveling,* using the technology to reduce layers of management and substitute work groups. This approach also changes the role of the manager, making this person much more of a leader than a person who monitors employees. The company also illustrates *technological matrixing* since employees work on many different projects. Information technology helps form the **project teams**, facilitates communications, and provides tools to team members to help accomplish their task. Oticon has created a highly flexible and virtual organization through process redesign combined with the use of several IT design variables. Oticon is a good example of a firm making progress toward becoming a T-Form organization. It also shows how reengineering can be applied at the level of the firm rather than a business process.

REENGINEERING THE ENTIRE FIRM AT LITHONIA LIGHTING

Our last example of reengineering also involves an entire organization, though we are not sure others would call it reengineering. Lithonia Lighting was founded in 1946 in Lithonia, Georgia. The current senior management team arrived in the early 1960s to a strong, regional company. There were few national firms in the industry and Lithonia was no exception with sales of $18 million primarily in the southeast.

Management embarked on a strategy of becoming the number one lighting supplier in the U.S. Most of Lithonia's growth was internal, though they did buy a few other companies. By 1990, an industry of over 1300 companies coalesced into nine major manufacturers of lighting fixtures which accounted for 75 percent of industry sales. In 1990, Lithonia had sales of over $700 million.

The lighting industry has complex distribution channels. Lighting can consume 50 percent of the electricity in a commercial building and architects work with contractors to manage this kind of energy consumption. Most of Lithonia's products are aimed at the commercial lighting industry which means the customers are industrial builders, not end users. Architects, contractors, electrical engineers, distributors, and agents all are involved in Lithonia's sales.

The industry has found it must sell through lighting agencies rather than sales people. Lithonia deals with about 85 independent lighting agencies.

Where Have All the Middle Managers Gone?

A *Wall Street Journal* study in 1995 suggests that reports of the demise of the middle manager are somewhat exaggerated. Between 1990 and 1994 the number of managers per 100 employees reported to the Equal Employment Opportunity Commission (EEOC) dropped from 11.83 to 11.17. The managerial ranks of the Fortune 500 and other companies have remained almost the same at five million.

These aggregate data, however, hide some trends. The following are changes in managers per 100 employees from 1989 to 1994 for selected industries: services, -12.54%; agriculture/ forestry/fishing, -10.92%; transportation/ communications/utilities, -10.91%; retailing, -9.74%; manufacturing, -5.06%; finance/ insurance/ real estate, -4.79% and construction, -2.18%.

At least one expert thinks that there may be "title inflation;" after workers spend a certain amount of time in the workforce, they expect to have a managerial title. This line of reasoning suggests that some of these managers may not really be doing much management, but they do have a nice title. Another view is that the nature of work is changing; knowledge work can be expected to require more managerial personnel. AT&T has gone from a third management jobs in 1985 to about half in 1995 (before its split into three companies); the reason is that the company now has more marketing needs in a competitive environment.

The combined payrolls of the largest employers (over 50,000 employees) show fewer management jobs in 1994 compared to 1989. However, companies with less than 20,000 employees have *added* 180,000 management jobs since 1989, with the largest growth coming in companies with 10,000 to 20,000 employees.

Executive search firms report strong demand for information technology managers in systems planning, technical services, new technologies, communications and health care. Knowing something about information technology could be beneficial to your employment prospects!

An agent sells to distributors who in turn sell fixtures off the shelf. However, the majority of agency sales come from efforts to influence the buyers for large construction projects, such as a new office building. The agents do not stock products, nor do they carry inventory. The electrical contractor who bid successfully on a project makes the ultimate decisions on what fixtures to buy. Agents tend not to handle competing products.

In 1979, the IS manager at Lithonia was asked to find a way to tie together all of the major players in Lithonia's business including agents, distributors, contractors, warehouses, and so on. The IS manager's team soon found that it had to take Lithonia out of the center of its diagrams. The only picture that made any sense was to put the agent at the center of the diagram.

This exercise convinced Lithonia to change the way it looked at its business: the agent became the key to sales. Lithonia developed a series of innovative computer and communications applications called Light*Link to coordinate sales and distribution. In fact, the high level of cooperation between the CEO and IS manager at Lithonia won an award from the Society for Information Management, SIM.

The general assessment of the Light*Link system is that it generated considerably more sales volume without a concomitant increase in staff. In fact, one agent changed its ratio of sales representatives to administrative staff from 1:1 to 3:1. Lithonia credited the system with dramatic gains in sales. Of course, we should be cautious about such claims because sales are primarily determined by the health of the construction industry.

Lithonia developed its new concept of business before anyone invented reengineering or business process redesign. In retrospect, it seems to be a clear case of a firm redesigning itself and its processes with a fresh view of the environment. The Light*Link system provided a number of *electronic workflows* and the ability to communicate easily with Lithonia. To some extent, the systems also provided *production automation* as computers were able to generate some quotations and specifications for customers.

IMPLICATIONS

In summary, Mutual Benefit Life and Merrill Lynch represent classic cases of business process redesign. Each firm first looked at its own business in detail. Reengineering's major contribution to management is its focus on process and on asking whether or not a process, itself, is necessary. The questions that one should ask include:

1. What are our key business processes?
2. Do we have to execute this process at all?
3. What totally new ways, taking advantage of information technology, exist to perform this process?

4. What does redesigning a process imply for the structure of the organization?

5. How can we use IT design variables in conjunction with process redesign to change the structure of the organization?

Oticon and Lithonia practiced a different kind of reengineering. They focused on the entire organization instead of isolated business processes. In their reengineering efforts, these firms used technological leveling to reduce the number of layers of management and supervision. They substituted electronic workflows for the physical movement of documents and applied production automation where possible. Technological matrixing helped solve problems and encourage employees to make decisions themselves rather than refer problems up a managerial hierarchy. All of these changes combined produced organizations with virtual components.

CHAPTER SUMMARY

1. Reengineering focuses attention on business processes. These processes are related to tasks and they cut across functional departments in an organization.

2. Reengineering seeks to make radical changes in the organization, ten times improvement in outcome variables is an example.

3. It may be possible to eliminate some process entirely, or to turn it over to an external organization so that it becomes a virtual component of your organization.

4. There may be a limit to the number of reengineering efforts an organization can mount at one time. They require capital and human investment, and they can be traumatic for the people involved.

5. Incremental improvement is a reasonable strategy for a number of systems in the organization.

6. It is wise to stay out of the middle ground in Figure 18-1 where you end up investing a great deal for modest improvements.

7. Reengineering applies to the structure of the entire organization as well as to individual business processes.

8. A company like Oticon offers an example of applying the IT organization design variables from Chapter 4 to restructuring a company that was losing market share and money.

9. A manager needs to stay alert to the opportunities for reengineering processes or the entire organization.

10. Reengineering serves to focus attention on business processes and the difference between radical and incremental change.

IMPLICATIONS FOR MANAGEMENT

It seems that no one is designing systems any more, they are reengineering them! In fact, many reengineering projects are actually conventional, old systems analysis and design. It also appears that a large number of reengineering projects fail. It is difficult to create the significant improvements in a process demanded by reengineering. You may want to limit your efforts to a reasonable number of reengineering projects because of the problems creating massive changes in the organization that go with each project. Reengineering the entire firm, as attempted by Oticon, is also a major challenge. However, if organizations want to remain competitive in the twenty-first century, they will have to take advantage of IT in structuring themselves.

KEY WORDS

Character recognition
Electronic workflows
Expert system
Flexible organization
Imaging
Incremental improvement
Obliterating a process
Process

Production automation
Project teams
Radical change
Reengineering
Spaghetti organization
Technological leveling
Technological matrixing

RECOMMENDED READING

Davenport, Thomas. *Process Innovation: Reengineering Work Through Information Technology*. Boston: Harvard Business School Press, 1993. (A readable account of reengineering.)

Lucas, H. C., Jr., D. Berndt, and G. Truman. "A Reengineering Framework for Evaluating a Financial Imaging System," *Communications of the ACM,* vol. 39, no. 5 (May 1996), pp. 86–96. (A discussion of the Merrill Lynch system.)

Bjorn-Anderson, N., and J. Turner. "Creating the 21 Century Organization: The Metamorphosis of Oticon," IFIP Working Group 8.2 Conference, August 1994. (A good description of changes at Oticon.)

Berkley, James. *Lithonia Lighting.* Boston: Harvard Business School Press, 1992. (A case study of Lithonia.)

Gould, R. Morgan, and Michael Stanford. *Revolution at Oticon A/S (A&B).* Lausanne, Switzerland: IMD, 1994. (Two cases about Oticon.)

Hammer, M., and J. Champy. *Reengineering the Corporation.* New York: HarperCollins, 1993. (An expansion of Hammer's first paper with a number of examples of reengineering.)

DISCUSSION QUESTIONS

1. What is a business process? How does it relate to a function?

2. What is your definition of radical change?

3. What is incremental change? Where is it appropriate?

4. What is "the middle ground" and how can it lead to problems?

5. What is the difference between an image and a character representation of, say, this page of text?

6. What is a spaghetti organization?

7. What problems do you see in an organization that does not seem to have a formal organization chart?

8. How does Oticon staff projects?

9. What is the role of the expert system for receiving securities in the Merrill Lynch Branch office?

10. If the Merrill Lynch control computer has information from the expert system, why is it necessary to recognize three fields on the documents scanned in the SPC?

11. Why did Lithonia Lighting find it necessary to put its agents at the center of its business processes?

12. How did Mutual Benefit Life use technology to change the way its staff processed information? What other kinds of assembly line processing of information might make use of this kind of reengineering?

13. What is the major contribution of reengineering?

14. Why has reengineering been so popular with senior management? What kind of business strategy does it promote?

15. Is reengineering fundamentally driven by technology?

16. Look at a firm or at your university and outline the major business processes. Then examine what functional departments play a role in each process.

17. What role does comparing your operations with those of similar companies play in reengineering?

18. How did reengineering make it possible for Merrill Lynch to outsource some of its securities processing operation?

19. Do you think Oticon's success has been influenced by the fact that it is located in Denmark with a different tradition of worker-management relationship than the U.S.? Do you think Oticon's structure would work in another country?

20. The U.S. healthcare system is often described as a candidate for major change. Do you see a way to reengineer it?

CHAPTER **19**

Implementing Change

⬤ OBJECTIVES

1. Learning to manage information technology.

Management is interested in the **successful implementation** of **change** in the organization. How can we increase the probability that a system will be used and will make a positive contribution to the organization? What strategies can you follow to demonstrate support for a systems effort? What strategies can you employ to implement extensive organization change, for example, using **IT design variables** to restructure the firm?

2. Preparing to apply technology.

To a large extent, the implementation process for a system begins the day the system is suggested. The way the design team approaches its job has a great influence on the ultimate success of an application. As you read about implementation, think about the consulting model in this chapter and how the factors found to be related to success might influence your behavior on the design team. Then consider what is involved in making massive changes to the entire organization, changes that go far beyond a new application.

3. Transforming the organization.

For IT to transform the organization, you must be successful in implementing change. First, you have to adopt the required technology and develop applications successfully. Then you must take advantage of what the technology offers to restructure the organization. As suggested in earlier chapters, we think that IT will naturally lead toward the T-Form organization structure.

Managers frequently complain about the low return they receive on their organization's large investment in information systems. Many of these systems are not used to their potential or are not used at all.

- A mining company spent several years designing a complex inventory system at its largest division. The system was finally installed and showed definite cost savings. Several years later, some managers in the company were still successfully resisting the installation of the new system in their divisions.

- A major computer vendor and a brokerage firm formed an alliance to develop the "next generation" broker workstation. After several years and a large investment of time and money, the firms abandoned their efforts.

Managers and other users of systems want to be certain that the systems work. In this chapter, we explore some of the problems associated with implementation, which is basically a behavioral and organizational process. Our goal is to develop an implementation strategy that maximizes the benefits from applying information technology.

POTENTIAL PITFALLS

The problems described above have several sources:

- The original design of the system
- The interface of the system with the users
- The **process of design** and implementation
- The operation of the system

Table 19-1
Some Potential System Problems

The original design of the system
The system will make substantial changes in the organization
All needed functions are not included
The database is incomplete
Procedures for processing information have errors
There are design errors, e.g., incorrect specifications
There are programming errors
The system has communications network problems

The interface of the system with users
Input or output is difficult for the user to understand
Input screens are complex
The user has no incentive to provide input
Input devices do not work well, e.g., a defective wand cannot read a bar code
The work force has been inadequately trained to provide input
The system permits a large number of input errors

The process of design and implementation
Users are not consulted on crucial design decisions
Users are not motivated to participate in design or use the system
The system attacks an uninteresting problem, one that is not crucial
Designers make arbitrary decisions that turn out not to work in practice
Users do not take time to participate when invited to do so
The design and programming process drags on for an inordinate amount of
    time
There are significant conversion problems due to poor planning

The operation of the system
The system has bugs
Response time is inadequate
The system is unavailable for long periods of time on a frequent basis
The system is not backed up
The IS staff is not responsive when there are problems

Table 19-1 lists some of the things that can go wrong in developing a system.

The system may be very unpopular in the organization. Employees may object to a substantial reengineering project because they do not like the changes the effort is likely to make in their jobs and in the organization. The original design of the system may be faulty and not provide the functions the firm needs. Specifications may be incorrect or incomplete, so an important action is not included in the system. Systems may not work technically, for example, there may be so many errors that no one trusts the output from the system.

The interface of the system with the users refers to the way in which we come in contact with the system, for example, through printed forms, terminals, or printed reports. In one system, terminal input was so complicated that no one submitted data and the system had to be discontinued. Users may also be unhappy about the way designers went about developing the system: the process of design. For example, designers sometimes make arbitrary design decisions and fail to consult relevant users.

Finally, the operation of a system involves longer-term issues after a system is designed and installed. If the **operations** section of the information services department does not provide good service (for example, having excessive response time or downtime), systems will not achieve their potential.

IMPLEMENTATION

What Is Implementation?

Implementation is part of the process of designing a system, and is a component of organizational change. We develop a new information system to change existing information processing procedures and often to change the organization itself. Implementation refers to the design team's strategy and actions for seeing that a system is successful and makes a contribution to the organization.

Our definition stresses the long-term nature of implementation. It is part of a process that begins with the very first idea for a system and the changes it will bring. Implementation terminates when the system is successfully integrated with the operations of the organization. We expect most of implementation to be concerned with behavioral phenomena,

MANAGEMENT PROBLEM 19-1

A major stock brokerage firm developed a sophisticated operations-research model to help customers decide what stocks to buy and when to enter and leave the market. The model is solved each week by a large computer system and reports are distributed regularly to brokers across the country.

In a study, each broker was found to have a slightly different way of using the recommendations. Some of the brokers call their clients who are interested in the model to give them the results. Other brokers assimilate the results and then call clients with recommendations based on the reports but do not reveal the source of their recommendations.

Some brokers do not use the system at all, while other brokers use it primarily as a sales tool. That is, they show a brochure on the model to prospective customers to demonstrate the advantage of opening an account with their firm. One broker became an expert in the use of the model. However, instead of working with customers, this broker spent too much time studying the model.

How do you explain the different reactions of brokers to this model? Base your assessment on the discussion in this chapter. As a manager in the brokerage firm, what steps would you undertake to obtain the best results from the modeling effort?

since people are expected to change their information processing activities. Implementation becomes more important and difficult as systems design becomes more radical. If a firm undertakes a major reengineering project, it wants to make major changes in tasks to reduce costs and improve productivity in the organization.

Success or Failure

How do we know that we have successfully implemented a system? Researchers do not agree on an absolute indicator for successful implementation. One appealing approach is a cost/benefit study. In this evaluation, one totals the costs of developing a system and compares them with the dollar benefits resulting from the system.

In theory, this sounds like a good indicator of success, but in practice it is difficult to provide meaningful estimates. Obtaining the cost side of the ratio is not too much of a problem if adequate records are kept during the development stages of the system. However, an evaluation of the benefits of an information system has eluded most analysts. How do we value the benefits of improved information processing? With transactions processing and some operational control systems, we can usually show tangible savings. For example, many transactions systems have resulted in increased productivity in processing paperwork without a proportional increase in cost. Operational control systems, such as those used to control inventories, may reduce inventory balances, saving storage and investment costs while maintaining existing service levels. For systems that aid a decision maker or provide customer service, it is much more difficult to estimate the benefits. Most strategic applications have defied cost/benefit analysis even after they have been installed and working for some time.

In lieu of the more preferable cost/benefit analysis, we can choose among several indicators of successful implementation, depending on the type of system involved. In many instances, use of a system is voluntary. A manager or other user receives a report but does not have to use the information on it or even read the report. Systems that provide interactive retrieval of information from a database also can often be classified as voluntary. The use of such a system is frequently at the discretion of the user. A manager with a personal computer in his or her office is not required to use it. For the type of system in which use is voluntary, we shall adopt high levels of use as a sign of successful implementation. We can measure use by interviews with users, through questionnaires, or in some instances, by building a monitor into the system to record actual use.

For systems whose use is mandatory, such as a production control system or a computer that provides stock market quotations for a broker, we shall employ the user's evaluation of the system as a measure of success. For example, one can examine user **satisfaction**, although it will probably be necessary to measure several facets of satisfaction, such as quality of service, timeliness and accuracy of information, and quality of the schedule for operations. An evaluation might also involve a panel of information processing experts reviewing the design and operation of the system. We should also note that managers might well consider a system to be successful if it accomplishes its objectives. However, to accomplish its objectives, a system must be used. We would also hope that one objective of a system would be extensive use and a high degree of user satisfaction.

Finally, though it is difficult to do, we can try to estimate the **impact of a system** on individuals and the organization. How has a system affected personal productivity and output quality? Can the organization point to added sales or increased revenues from a competitive application? Can we show that IT has had an impact on performance, either for individuals or the organization?

RESEARCH ON IMPLEMENTATION

Most research on implementation is an attempt to discover factors associated with success. What independent variables are related to successful implementation as defined by the researchers? If there is any basis for believing a causal connection exists between independent and dependent variables, we can develop an implementation strategy around the independent variables. For example, suppose we found in several studies using different research methodologies that top management's requesting a new system and following through with **participation** in its design is associated with successful implementation. If there were sufficient evidence to support this finding, we would develop an implementation strategy that emphasized top-management action.

Although individual studies of implementation address a number of independent variables, there is no real consensus in the field on an explanation of successful implementation or on a single implementation strategy. Table 19-2 contains a list of some of the variables employed in past implementation studies. Dependent variables used to measure implementation success generally can be classified as measures of use, intended use, and/or satisfaction with a system. The independent variables fall into several classes, as shown in the table.

A Model of Implementation

There have been a number of different studies of systems implementation, many of which are reviewed in Lucas, Ginzberg, and Schultz (1991). In this study, the authors propose and test a model of implementation for system users. Figure 19-1 is a model based on the most significant findings from the research in the study above. The model suggests that the user's personal stake in the problems addressed by the system will be an important determinant of use. Personal stake refers to how important the domain of the system is for the individual. A marketing manager is expected to have a high personal stake in a market research system that addresses the brands she manages. Personal stake is hypothesized to be influenced by the level of **management support** for a system. The most consistent finding across

Table 19-2
Variables Associated with Implementation Studies

INDEPENDENT VARIABLES

Information services department
    Policies
    Systems design practices
    Operations policies

Involvement
    User origination of systems
    Involvement and influence
    Appreciation

User demographics
    Personality type
    Business history
    Social history
    Past experience

User's personal stake
    Problem urgency

User attitudes
    Expectations
    Interpersonal relations

System characteristics
    Quality
    Ease of use

Decision style
    Cognitive style

Management
    Actions
    Support
    Managerial style

Organization support
    Ease of access

User performance

DEPENDENT VARIABLES

Implementation
    Frequency of inquiries
    Reported use
    Monitored frequency of use
    User satisfaction

---

implementation studies is the importance of management support and leadership in successful implementation. **Problem urgency** is likely to influence personal stake. The more urgent the problem, the higher the personal stake.

We expect personal stake to influence use directly, when use is voluntary. **System characteristics** will also influence use. A poorly designed system may be virtually unusable. User **demographics** like age and past computer experience are also likely to impact system use. **Organizational support** refers to actions that make a system easy to use. For example, we found that use of a system increases with the ease of accessing the system. If a user must leave his or her office to find a PC, usage levels are lower

Figure 19-1
An implementation
model.

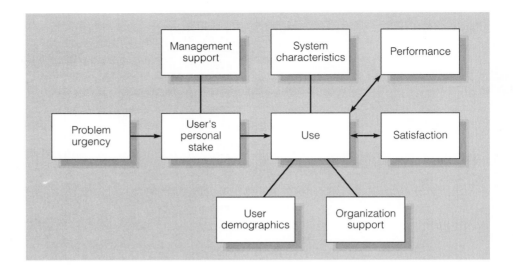

than when a PC is located in the office. The model suggests that high levels of use should lead to high levels of satisfaction and high satisfaction is likely to increase levels of use.

Although the evidence is not strong, it does appear that use of technology is related to either individual or firm performance in certain instances. This relationship is likely to be complex. For example, one study found that high-performing sales representatives used the output of a system to work with buyers in a store to figure out what to order. Low-performing sales representatives also used the output of the system, but they focused on information that might indicate what was wrong in their territories. There are also a number of technology efforts where it appears a firm has reduced costs or increased revenues. However, it is hard to demonstrate causality in such situations because so many variables are changing at one time.

The Implementation Process

The research described above deals with variables or factors associated with successful implementation. There is also a school of thought that stresses the process of implementation as the most significant determinant of implementation success. The implementation process refers to the ongoing relationship among individuals involved in developing a system. A process model might look at various stages during implementation and describe how different parties work together during these stages.

Our process model includes the stages outlined in Table 19-3. This model emphasizes tasks that take place in design. In reading between the lines, however, we can see the need to concentrate on the relationship between designers and users. During the early stages, the individuals involved with the system must develop trust in each other's objectives and competence. The designers should want to help users, and users must be willing to spend time working with designers and on their part of the design. If those involved do not develop a cooperative relationship and become adversarial, the system is doomed.

A major objective during the design process is for users to accept ownership of the system. Professional designers, ironically, almost never use the systems they design! The user is left with a system at the end of a project. If the user does not "own" the system from a psychological point of view, the system is unlikely to be successful. There has been some research to show that the termination stage in the model above is the most important. Here is where we learn if users have developed feelings of ownership and commitment to the system.

Table 19-3
A Process Implementation Model

Stage	Activity
Initiation	The first contact between the users and designers
Exploration	Getting a feel for the problem
Commitment	Making a decision to proceed with a system
Design	Developing the logical design and specifications for the system
Testing	Verifying that the system works
Installation	Converting to the new system
Termination	Design team finished; users must now own the system
Operations	Routine operation plus enhancements and maintenance

MANAGEMENT PROBLEM 19-2

The Major Mining Company hired a consulting firm to design a new system for inventory control. The consultant was supposed to coordinate his efforts with the company's IS staff located in two parts of the United States. The consultant was retained because the existing work load at the company prevented staff members from developing the system and the consulting firm had extensive technical expertise.

The IS group designated to work most closely with the consultant was extremely hostile. The standard reaction of the personnel to the consultant was: It's your system; you design it. The consultant had a rather low opinion of the IS staff, but knew that the staff would have to program any system designed. Therefore, the consultant tried to obtain systems analysis and programming personnel from the IS group. Much time was spent on this rather unproductive activity, and progress on the new system was very slow.

The consultant described these problems to Major's vice president, who had retained him. Although the vice president could order the IS staff to cooperate, he knew that it would be impossible to force cooperation. What can the vice president do to solve this problem? Is the problem solely with the IS group? What can the consultant do?

An Implementation Strategy

We need an implementation strategy that takes into account the crucial process issues in designing an information system as well as the factors that appear to influence success. We also view systems design as a **planned change** in activity in the organization. We stated earlier that the reason for developing a new information system is to create change. Dissatisfaction with a present situation stimulates the development of a new information system. Alternatively, a user sees how the technology can be used in a new way to improve the firm's competitive position.

For many years, articles and books on design stressed user participation in the design process based on research in psychology which maintains that a change approach based on user participation is most likely to succeed. The first part of our strategy, then, is encouraging users to participate in and influence design. Some of the reasons for a participation strategy are:

- Participation builds self-esteem, which results in more favorable attitudes.
- Participation can be challenging and intrinsically satisfying, leading to positive attitudes.
- Participation usually results in more commitment to change. In this case, commitment means that a system will be used more.
- Participating users learn more about the change, and therefore get to control more of the technical qualities of the system and become better trained to use it.
- Technical quality will be better because participants know more about the problem domain than does the IS staff.
- Users retain much of the control over their activities and should therefore have more favorable attitudes.

How should users participate in the design of a system? Participation requires the efforts of both the IS staff and the users. The IS department has to encourage participation, while users have to be willing to participate and devote considerable effort to design work. In the past, although most information services departments attempt to involve users, the effort frequently produced what would have to be classified as "pseudo involvement." To bring about the necessary participation, it has been suggested that users actually design their own systems.

THE ROLE OF DESIGN TEAMS

Most information systems today are designed by teams consisting of managers, end users, and systems professionals. How do users and professional systems analysts work together on a team?

The first task delineated by the analyst might be a discussion of the functions the system is to perform. Working together, the team might develop high-level data flow diagrams for the system. The analyst, from knowledge of the capabilities of technology, presents alternatives for the user to consider.

Users help conduct interviews to determine the requirements for a new system. They also contribute to and review the design of the system as it unfolds. Users should have the final say in how the system will function. In this way, users become knowledgeable about the system and develop ownership, one of the major objectives of the process model.

An Implementation Framework

A team approach that stresses cooperation and participation addresses the issues raised in the process model of implementation, but what about the factors discussed earlier in the chapter? Our complete implementation strategy comes from merging the most important factors with the steps of the process model (see Table 19-4).

The combined model in Table 19-4 arrays the steps of our process model with the variables from the factor model of Figure 19-1. During **initiation**, one key to success is having a sponsor or champion for the system. Without the active support of a senior-level person in the organization, the chances for success are greatly reduced. Similarly, the factor model suggests that attacking urgent problems is a good strategy. It is hard to develop enthusiasm for boring systems that are unlikely to have an impact on the firm. We want to locate users with a stake in the problem and start to think about who users will be when the system is done. User demographics are not under our control in the short run.

Tracking Signatures at FedEx

Before 1995, the recipient of a FedEx package signed for each package delivered. The FedEx driver wrote delivery addresses by hand, and it took a week to respond to proof of delivery requests. About 2500 customers a day request proof of delivery. Today a scanning system captures each signature and matches it with related records of delivery information. After scanning, 27 Sun workstations index and build a database of signatures for retrieval purposes. Thirty customer service representatives in Memphis access the system and fax documents with a signature image to customers. In the near future the system will be rolled out to 4000 agents throughout the U.S. Users also have on-line access to signature information via FedEx's home page on the World Wide Web (http:www.fedex.com) and through package tracking software at customer sites.

FedEx is an excellent example of a company that has used technology actively as a part of its strategy to offer the best customer service in the overnight delivery business. It is unlikely that the firm had a comprehensive vision twenty years ago of what technology could do. However, it has continued to innovate with systems to provide better service to customers through the tracking and control of customer packages, adding value by providing customers with information about the status of their package at any time.

Table 19-4
An Implementation Model

Phase	Management support	Problem urgency	User's personal stake	System characteristics	Use	User demographics	Organization support	Satisfaction	Performance
INITIATION	Having a sponsor is key	Attack the most important problems	Find users for whom the stake is high	Determine requirements and architecture	Who will use the system?	Not under the control of designers	Find the champions	One objective is satisfied users	Determine any performance objectives
EXPLORATION	Sponsor commits resources	Urgent problems help provide motivation	Show how system is important to user	Choose among alternatives	Who pays the costs of use?	In longer term may be able to choose team members	Be sure someone will provide the resources you need	Design for satisfaction	Is there likely to be an impact on performance?
COMMITMENT	Sponsor provides time for users to work on system	Dealing with key problems helps obtain cooperation	Involve the important stakeholders	Develop prototypes to aid in design	Who gains from use?	Look for users with successful history of working on IS projects	Get a commitment before starting	Consider user surveys	Be honest about what to expect
DESIGN	Sponsor helps make key policy decisions	Urgent problems demand quality designs	High stakes should lead to a lot of design input	Build the highest-quality system possible!	Design to encourage use, e.g., good interfaces	Provide education where needed—prototypes help	Make the system as easy to use as possible	Design for satisfaction	Try to understand what leads to performance, and design for it
TESTING	Sponsor reviews results	Test carefully	Let the stake-holder verify the results	Test exhaustively	Make sure system is usable	Let the worst critics help test	Get resources for testing	Let users plan tests, too	Test carefully if system impacts performance

Table 19-4 (continued)

Management support	Problem urgency	User's personal stake	System characteristics	Use	User demographics	Organization support	Satisfaction	Performance
INSTALLATION								
Sponsor provides added resources	Plan installation to minimize disruptions	Users with a high stake should plan installation	Use extensively	Expect and prepare for use problems	Everyone will have to help	Be sure there is enough support	Try to plan a smooth installation	Install carefully if performance is an issue
TERMINATION								
Sponsor rewards team	Is the problem solved?	Stakeholders should own the system	Tranfer ownership to users	If successful, expect high use	With luck, there will be new supporters	Support users with help desks, etc.	High satisfaction should lead to user ownership	If successful, user will use system to enhance performance
OPERATIONS								
Sponsor continues to provide resources	Continue to work on problem	High-stake users should continue their interest	A high-quality system is easy to use	Continue to refine to encourage use	Even the skeptics will use a good system	Provide ongoing organizational support	Obtain ongoing feedback from users	Monitor performance changes

When we are exploring possible solutions, we need management support to provide resources. It is also useful to think in cost/benefit terms. Who pays the costs to use the system and who gains? If users are expected to provide complex input but receive no benefits from the system because the data are used only by senior management, there may be resistance to the system. During **exploration** we begin to see the architecture for the system and can determine what kind of organizational support we need to encourage use. During the **commitment** stage, the sponsor has to prepare the organization for the design effort, often by providing release time and resources for the design team. One good way to enlist support and to show how the systems design effort will solve problems is to develop a prototype of some or all parts of the system. We might also employ user surveys to gain information for design.

During **design**, we need the sponsor to help make key policy decisions. For example, if we are planning an EDI application, what is the target audience? How do we approach suppliers and customers? Will senior management negotiate with potential EDI partners? Remember that we want to attack urgent and important problems. These problems demand a high-quality design that will encourage use.

Testing is extremely important in preparing for installation. Management and as many users as possible should be involved in designing and verifying tests. **Installation** is difficult because any system is designed to change existing procedures. Because we want to tackle important problems, the risks are very high. A failed installation threatens some key component of the organization. We need careful testing, a good cutover plan, and a lot of help from users to succeed in installation.

Termination marks the departure of the professional analysts and probably the completion of the design team's responsibilities. If the design team is successful, users will develop a sense of ownership of the system. The installed system will help solve an urgent problem for user stakeholders, and the organization will provide adequate resources to support the system. Users will be satisfied with the resulting system.

When the system is in *operational* status, it is not finished. As users work with the system, they will see ways to improve it. Business conditions are also likely to change, necessitating ongoing maintenance and enhancements. The organization must continue to support the system by expanding it as conditions warrant. The operations staff of the IS department must provide maintenance and should obtain periodic feedback from users.

This combined implementation model is based on implementation research and experience. It can help develop systems that are successful and that will be used. The threats to a successful system are many and varied, as portrayed in Table 19-1. Following a conscious implementation strategy is the best way to maximize the probability of a successful design project.

Some Examples

The procedures for systems design recommended above have been used for the development of several successful information systems. In one instance, a feasibility study and systems design were carried out for a grass-roots labor organization. The design team consisted of union members, and faculty and students from a university. The union members in general had a low level of formal education, and the design team was concerned about the effect of computer technology on the union and its individual members. Because of hectic union organizing activities, the union staff could not devote the time needed to develop a system, although eventually several full-time union staff members began to work on the project.

To begin the analysis, the university design team interviewed members of the union staff and gathered data on existing procedures and requirements. After jointly determining a system was feasible, the design team developed a rough design. To turn ownership of the system over to the union and to be sure the union staff was in control of the system, a day-long review session was held to present the draft of the system. At this meeting, the union president explained to the members that there were many tasks to be done and that no one would be replaced by a computer. He stated that instead workers probably would have more interesting jobs, and he asked members to think about how the system could help the union.

The design team began its part of the meeting by stressing that the session would be successful only if at least half of the system presented was changed: The team offered ideas, not a finished product. They did not use elaborate flowcharts and visual aids. Instead, a very simple tutorial on computer systems began the presentation. The designers spoke from rough notes and listed report contents, files, and inputs on a blackboard. The highly motivated union staff quickly grasped the relationships among reports, files, and input documents. Substantial changes to the rough system were made in front of the audience during the meeting.

Several weeks later, a follow-up meeting was held with union leaders, who suggested management-oriented reports. The design team helped the union develop specifications for bids and worked on a consulting basis with the union staff, which finally developed a system. The designers intentionally reduced their role as the union became more capable in the systems area. The system was successfully implemented. The level of use was high, and users, from the union president to clerical personnel, appeared pleased with the system.

In another situation, a system was developed to support the decisions of a group of three managers. These managers were responsible for setting production schedules in the commercial laundry products division of a major manufacturing company. The production manager wanted to minimize setups and have long production runs. The marketing manager wanted to have wide product availability at warehouses throughout the country to provide high levels of customer service. The market planning manager had to resolve differences in objectives so the three managers could develop a feasible production plan. Because future production depended on the decision for the next month, a twelve-month planning horizon was used.

In the original manual system, managers generated possible solutions analyzed by clerical personnel who performed a large number of manual calculations. On evaluation, it was usually found that a solution had to be modified because some part of it was infeasible. More meetings and more clerical computations were required. Sometimes almost the entire month elapsed before the next month's schedule was ready.

The research group trying to improve this decision process observed the managers at work for some six months. After three months, a rough system featuring an interactive graphics display terminal was developed. The first prototype system was shown to the market planning manager, who learned how to operate it. This manager made many suggestions for changes, which the designers incorporated into the system. Then the market planning manager trained the production and marketing managers in the use of the system. They too had numerous suggestions for modifications, which were incorporated into the system. Over time, the researchers modified the system for the managers in this particular decision situation. The managers were very satisfied with the system and resisted attempts by the information services department to discontinue it after the research project was officially completed.

MANAGEMENT PROBLEM 19-3

The Airflow Manufacturing Company has retained a consultant to help design an order-entry and accounts-receivable information system. Airflow manufactures precision parts for the aerospace and automotive industries.

The consultant believes in the design techniques discussed in this chapter. As a result, she stresses the importance of extensive user involvement in the design of the system. The president of the company agrees intellectually with the consultant's advice but recognizes there could be problems in trying to obtain the needed cooperation.

The most serious bottleneck appears to be one key employee in the office. Most of the work on processing orders and receivables is under the supervision of this one individual. There is no real second-in-command, even though the president has tried unsuccessfully for a number of years to have an assistant trained. Several were hired but left during the training period because of unknown problems.

Because of the lack of an assistant and the increased information processing load created by a good business year, the president knows that obtaining help from this key supervisor will be difficult. However, the consultant, after a few days of working in the firm, indicates that this individual is probably the most logical person to place in charge of the design effort.

What can the president do? Can he afford to have this key supervisor in charge of the system? If there is no alternative, what steps can the president take to be sure that the system is designed well and that normal information processing tasks are completed?

IMPLEMENTING IT-BASED CHANGES IN THE ORGANIZATION

The discussion above focused on the changes caused by an individual system or a reengineering effort. How do you implement the massive changes required to use information technology to transform the organization and create new structures and relationships within the firm and with external organizations? Earlier we argued that the IT design variables of Chapter 4 could be used to create a new kind of structure: the T-Form organization. The advantages of this structure include:

1. A **lean organization** with the minimal number of employees necessary for the business to function.
2. A **responsive organization** that reacts quickly to threats from competitors and changes in the environment.
3. A minimum overhead organization.
4. A structure with low fixed costs due to more virtual components, partnerships, and subcontracting.
5. An organization that is responsive to customers and suppliers.
6. An organization that is more competitive than firms with traditional structures.
7. An organization that allows its employees to develop their capabilities and maximize their contribution to the firm.

One of the major advantages of this kind of organization is its lack of a large number of hierarchical levels. The firm is flat with few levels of management. This organization is *responsive* because decisions are made quickly; large numbers of levels of managers do not slow decision making. All of these features add up to lower overhead than the traditional bureaucratic organization. The end result should be a firm that is more competitive than traditional, hierarchical organizations due to its responsiveness and lower operating costs.

There are costs that go along with these benefits including:

1. The organization has to invest in information technology.
2. The firm has to be able to manage IT.
3. Employees have to learn new technologies and constantly update their knowledge.
4. Managers have a large **span of control**.
5. Managers have to supervise remote workers.
6. Firms have to manage close relationships with partners and companies in various alliances.

Another cost of using technology to transform the organization is learning new technology. Products and systems are constantly changing. New releases of PC software, like spreadsheet packages, seem to average more than one per year. If you do not upgrade and learn new systems, eventually it becomes difficult to share with others. And, of course, you forego the improvements in the new version of the packages.

The T-Form organization features a large span of control for most managers. The idea is to substitute electronic for face-to-face communications. Implicit in a large span of control is a degree of trust in subordinates. Electronics will not substitute for the close control one can exercise over subordinates when a manager has only five or six direct reports. A recent news story on Japanese management showed a large number of workers arranged in two rows of desks, each row facing the other. At the end of the row sat the workers' supervisor, with his desk perpendicular to the workers where he had them under constant view. Evidently a common feature of Japanese organizations, this physical structure is probably the ultimate in close supervision. The T-Form organization is at the opposite end of the spectrum. It requires managers to place more responsibility with subordinates to do their jobs.

Closely related to the need to adopt a management philosophy stressing subordinate responsibility is the problem of managing remote work. Companies are likely to eliminate physical offices for employees who spend a great deal of time traveling or who work from a satellite office or home. Work-at-home experiments have shown that some managers feel uncomfortable trying to supervise subordinates they rarely see. Remote work also requires the manager to trust subordinates, and of course, requires subordinates to act responsibly. Some subordinates have reacted negatively to losing their offices and to using part of their homes as offices. They feel the company is forcing its overhead costs onto them. Virtual offices will undoubtedly call for new managerial skills and relationships between managers and the people reporting to them.

The final management cost of a technology-based organization is handling relationships with external firms. These firms might be suppliers or customers, partners in a strategic alliance, or governmental agencies. These partners are a vital part of your business, but they do not report to you. Managers have to manage a cooperative arrangement without having the usual "tools" given a manager such as reporting relationships and control over subordinates' salaries.

Balancing Costs and Benefits

When trying to implement something new, it is helpful to compare the costs and benefits as we have done above. Figure 19-2 contains a vertical line that represents an equilibrium in which costs and benefits balance each other. Moving the line to the right is progress toward the T-Form organization and moving it left is toward traditional, hierarchical firms. The benefits of the T-Form organization are on the left pushing toward the right with the costs on the top of the right pushing left. When managers see the benefits exceeding the costs, they will move toward the T-Form.

Figure 19-2
Forces for changing organization structure.

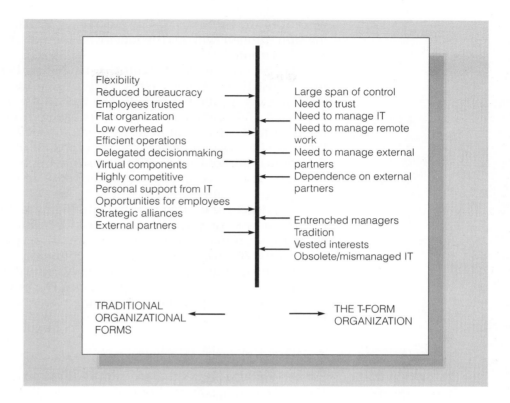

Flexibility
Reduced bureaucracy
Employees trusted
Flat organization
Low overhead
Efficient operations
Delegated decisionmaking
Virtual components
Highly competitive
Personal support from IT
Opportunities for employees
Strategic alliances
External partners

Large span of control
Need to trust
Need to manage IT
Need to manage remote work
Need to manage external partners
Dependence on external partners

Entrenched managers
Tradition
Vested interests
Obsolete/mismanaged IT

TRADITIONAL ORGANIZATIONAL FORMS   THE T-FORM ORGANIZATION

We would expect the advantages of the T-Form for new organizations would far outweigh its costs as the T-Form fits start-ups very well. A number of Silicon Valley companies employ virtual components and electronic linking and are well along the way in using IT design variables. One startup, Visioneer, makes a scanning system and software that is aimed at eliminating paper in the office. The corporate office in Palo Alto is responsible for design, marketing, and sales. The product is manufactured by subcontractors: the circuit board comes from Singapore, and a Boston firm makes the case, tests the product, and ships it to customers. Other partners help write the software. Six sales representatives in the field do not have physical offices. They are linked by mail, voice mail, and cellular phones.

What are the possibilities of moving more traditional firms toward the T-Form? In addition to the costs and benefits of Figure 19-2, there are additional forces acting against the T-Form in hierarchical firms. These forces are "costs" to the current employees of the firm as the technology-based organization clearly threatens many vested interests. A minor restructuring of a department or workgroup will not let the firm enjoy the benefits of a new structure for the organization. We are suggesting a massive change which includes all employees and units of the firm. You might start in one department or division, but as with other technologies we have seen, you need a critical mass. E-mail does not achieve its potential if only 50 percent of the firm uses it. Customers may be happy to use EDI with one division, though they may wonder why the rest of the company does not offer electronic linkages.

Massive changes are difficult to carry out as there are many forces acting against them. Major change programs create a number of threats to those already in the firm. The first of the threats is to the entrenched bureaucracy. Middle managers and others have proven very adept at protecting their jobs. As a result of many IT-stimulated restructurings, it is likely there will be fewer employees. The new organization structure will require the company to downsize. Clearly downsizing is a threat to existing employees and it is natural for them to oppose an organizational form that encourages a smaller firm.

A manager committed to using IT design variables will also ask fundamental questions about all of the tasks performed in the organization. Should we continue to operate a transportation system, or should we contract with outside carriers? Should we eliminate all forms of payment except credit cards and do away with the Accounts Receivable Department? Should we contract out our IS operations? The threat of any of these partnerships or alliances is certain to arouse resistance on the part of current employees.

Motivating Organizational Change

Figure 19-2 also shows the addition of these "costs" helping to maintain the status quo, traditional organization. It will be very difficult in many traditional firms to create movement toward the T-Form organization. What might motivate such a firm to change structures?

1. A merger or acquisition,
2. A major crisis, e.g. substantial losses,
3. Bankruptcy,
4. Rebellion by the Board of Directors,
5. Legal or regulatory reversal.

Mergers and acquisitions often result in new management teams. New managers might look at the firm and realize that integrating two companies is a good time to develop a new overall structure. Unfortunately, sometimes it takes a major crisis to motivate managers. We might include a rebellion by the board of directors here as well. The chairmen of companies with significant problems have been asked to resign in record numbers in the last few years. Powerful chairmen at IBM, DEC, Westinghouse, and GM among others have suffered this fate. Being a new manager in a crisis situation provides a certain amount of leverage for changing the organization.

Bankruptcy is a traumatic event that may well provide the opportunity for a dramatic restructuring of a firm. Unfortunately, the bankrupt firm is at a bit of a disadvantage with efforts to partner and form alliances given the history that put it into bankruptcy in the first place. It may also lack the funds necessary to develop a technological infrastructure. Finally, a legal or regulatory reversal may also provide the motivation for a firm to use IT design variables to come up with a new structure.

It appears that a crisis may be the strongest motivation for reorganization. Possibly the second reason is the competition. If a firm sees the competition performing significantly better after adopting a new structure, it may imitate the competitor.

A Change Program
How should a manager go about trying to create a T-Form organization? You are trying to move the organization from one state, say a traditional, hierarchical organization, to another, the T-Form. Change is one of the most difficult things to bring about; our discussion earlier in the chapter has pointed out a number of forces acting against the manager who wishes to change a firm's structure. Figure 19-2 can be thought of as a **force field** as it shows the forces acting for and against change. To bring about change, the manager can either increase the forces for change and/or decrease the forces opposing change.

We suggest some approaches to strengthening the forces for change, but each organization is different and a change program must be custom tailored. Table 19-5 describes the key steps and some recommended actions. It is based on some of the ideas of Nadler and Tushman (1988).

The first step is to motivate the change. We have suggested some crises that may provide enough motivation for action. There may be some less dramatic events that convince everyone change is needed. It is helpful here to have broad support from the Board of Directors and others with influence in the firm.

Having a plan for the transition to a new organization form is very important. It provides a roadmap for action and keeps employees aware of what is happening. Task forces for developing the plan are a good way to bring employees into this process and tap their knowledge for building the new organization. The results of the task force should be widely disseminated. Be sure to take maximum advantage of the IT design variables discussed in Chapter 4.

Employees will experience much anxiety with just the suggestion of a change in the status quo that could alter their jobs or eliminate them. Nadler and Tushman suggest that one job for management is to manage anxiety in the change process. Involving workers is one way to reduce, but not eliminate anxiety. Individuals will be aware of the company's plans, but they may also see changes that look very threatening to them.

On balance, it is a good idea to stress open communications rather than keep plans secret. In today's business environment, a responsible firm will also provide counseling and outplacement services for employees who are no longer needed.

Making the transition to a technology-based organization requires that the firm have adequate technology in place. You may develop the

Table 19-5

Moving Toward the T-Form Organization

Step	Action
Motivate the change	Explain reasons such as competition, falling sales; look for broad support from places like the Board; communicate with everyone in the organization
Develop a transition plan	Use a task force to develop the vision for the new organization; describe steps that must be taken to reach a new organization structure; take full advantage of IT design variables
Accumulate power and resources	Obtain support from key individuals and groups in the organization; be sure you have the influence and resources to bring about change
Manage anxiety	Communicate with employees; consider a groupware rumor mill application; provide outplacement and counseling; involve employees in designing the new organization
Build IT capabilities	Technology must be in place to enable the T-Form; there is often a lead time for implementing IT before you can make changes in the organization

capabilities needed in house, or you may turn to outside vendors. At a minimum you need a communications network and e-mail. Depending on your business, you need electronic connections to buyers and suppliers. Some of these links can be "purchased" through value added carriers and other service companies. Workstations in offices and networks connecting them are important. Increasingly, it appears that groupware like Lotus Notes (discussed in Chapter 21) and the Internet will become important ways of managing within the organization and a mechanism for linking to external partners.

The task here is to design the firm's technology so it will enable, not constrain, its ability to move toward a T-Form organization. Once the technology is in place, one can use the IT design variables to develop the structure of the organization. Below are some questions to assist in using IT variables in the design. It is important to recognize that each organization will develop its own, unique structure.

1. What are the most significant processes in the organization, e.g. order fulfillment, manufacturing, etc.

    a. To what extent should these processes be redesigned?

    b. What opportunities do new technologies and IT design variables offer for improving these business processes?

2. Who are our major partners including customers, suppliers, and others (banks, accountants, and law firms among others)?

    a. What opportunities are there for electronic linking and communications with these organizations?

    b. Where should we try to establish electronic customer/supplier relationships?

    c. What additional services can these partners provide? What opportunities are there to create virtual components?

3. How should we structure our strategic organization—by product, region, or a combination of factors?

4. What is our competitive strategy? How do IT design variables help us implement this strategy?

5. Given the major processes in our business, how do we assign personnel to be sure these processes are accomplished?

    a. Can we use technological leveling to minimize the number of layers in the organization?

    b. Do production automation and electronic workflows have something to contribute to our business processes?

6. What kind of managerial hierarchy is necessary?

    a. Can we use technological leveling to reduce layers and broaden the span of control for managers?

    b. Can we use *technological matrixing* to form temporary task forces and work groups instead of establishing permanent departments and reporting relationships?

The overall objective is to create an organization with a flat structure, flexibility, responsiveness, decentralized decision making, effective communications, links to business partners, and the other characteristics of the T-Form structure.

Significant organizational change is a challenge. Machiavelli summed it up over 400 years ago in *The Prince:*

> There is nothing more difficult to take in hand, more perilous to conduct, or more uncertain in its success than to take the lead in the introduction of a new order of things.

We think that the major challenge facing managers in the twenty-first century will be to design organizations that take advantage of the IT design variables discussed here. Moving toward the T-Form organization requires new ways of thinking for the start-up organizations and massive changes for traditional organizations. Senior managers must decide if the benefits we claim for this kind of organization are sufficiently compelling to confront the perils of changing the organization.

Chapter Summary

1. Implementation is a change process that is designed to alter existing practice. With information technology we make changes through individual applications and by using IT variables to redesign the organization.

2. The ability to use IT to change procedures and organizations, themselves, is one of the most exciting parts of technology. *With IT, a manager can make a difference in how an organization functions and in its chances for success.*

3. There has been a great deal of research on the implementation of individual systems, but it is still too often the case that new applications fail completely or fail to achieve their potential.

4. The chapter reviews factors thought to be related to successful implementation and a process model for the stages of systems development and implementation.

5. Table 19-4 combines the factor and process models to provide guidelines for improving the chance of successful implementation for an individual application of the technology.

6. The chapter recommends a high level of user involvement and influence in the design of a system for a number of reasons, including the psychological commitment that involvement helps create and the knowledge that a user brings to the design project.

7. It is important to transfer psychological ownership of a system to the users of the application.

8. The problems of implementing change are multiplied when the change target is the entire organization.

9. IT organization design variables are some of the most exciting contributions of the technology; however, using these variables to adopt a new design like the T-Form organization is a formidable challenge.

10. A force field analysis of the forces encouraging and inhibiting change can help to plan for a new organization structure.

11. It will in general be easier to use IT design variables when creating a new firm than when trying to change the structure of an existing one.

12. The motivation for a traditional organization to adopt a technology-based structure is likely to come from a crisis, or from seeing competitors become T-Form converts.

13. Change is one of the most difficult assignments, but it is through change that management assures organizations will survive and flourish in the future.

IMPLICATIONS FOR MANAGEMENT

Implementation of change is clearly a management responsibility. Managers should constantly be looking for improvement projects, ways to operate more efficiently and effectively. The hardest part of this assignment is implementation—seeing that changes occur in the organization. If you look at stories about successful managers, they usually have brought significant change to their organizations. This is particularly true for "turn around" situations in which the manager rescued a sinking company. As a manager, you will find change one of your most challenging and frustrating tasks.

KEY WORDS

Change
Commitment
Demographics
Design
Exploration
Force field
Impact of a system
Implementation
Initiation
Installation
IT design variables
Lean organization
Management support

Operations
Organizational support
Participation
Planned change
Problem urgency
Process of design
Responsive organization
Satisfaction
Span of control
Successful implementation
System characteristics
Termination
Testing

RECOMMENDED READING

Lucas, H.C., Jr. *The T-Form Organization: Using Technology to Design Organizations for the 21st Century.* San Francisco: Jossey-Bass, 1996. (A book devoted to the design of technology-based organizations.)

Lucas, H. C., Jr., M. Ginzberg, and R. Schultz. *Implementing Information Systems: Testing a Structural Model.* Norwood, N.J.: Ablex, 1991. (Presents a review of implementation literature and a new framework for approaching implementation.)

Nadler, D., and M. Tushman. *Strategic Organization Design.* New York: HarperCollins, 1988. (An excellent book on traditional approaches to organization design.)

DISCUSSION QUESTIONS

1. Why is implementation more than just the last few weeks of the systems life cycle?

2. What other definitions and measures of successful implementation can you suggest other than the ones in this chapter?

3. What are the responsibilities of users in the systems design process?

4. How do the responsibilities of managers and, say, the clerical staff differ during systems design?

5. What are the crucial differences between an internal information system and an interorganizational one from the standpoint of implementation? What are the key similarities?

6. What is the role of a consultant in helping to design information systems? How does this role change under the systems design policies suggested in this chapter?

7. What approaches are there to evaluating the benefits of information systems?

8. How would you measure the impact of an information system on decision making?

9. What factors mitigate against massive change in the organization?

10. What might motivate a firm to use IT design variables to make a radical change in its structure?

11. What problems does user-oriented design create for users, their management, and the IS department?

12. Can user-oriented design work for a system encompassing large numbers of people, for example, a reservation system involving hundreds or thousands of agents? What strategy could be adopted in this situation?

13. What are the advantages of an organization with a large span of control? What are the disadvantages?

14. Why do some IS departments resist heavy user input in design?

15. What implementation strategy does the process model suggest?

16. Why do some authors think the hierarchical organization is doomed in the twenty-first century? What are the advantages of a flat organization structure?

17. What is the role of the IS department analyst in the design techniques discussed in this chapter?

18. As a potential or present user of information systems, how do you respond to the idea of being in charge of the design of such a system?

19. Why are we interested in the relationships among system use, user satisfaction, and performance?

20. Are the techniques suggested here applicable in other contexts? What situations can you suggest in which user control might be more successful than control by a group of technological experts?

21. How can you transform a huge firm like General Motors with the help of information technology?

22. When does planning for successful implementation begin in designing an information system?

23. What is the role of the technological infrastructure in moving toward the T-Form organization?

24. What challenges do you see trying to manage in a T-Form organization?

CHAPTER 19 PROJECT

A SYSTEMS SURVEY

In any organization, you will observe large differences in the extent to which individuals use information systems. Find an organization that will allow you to conduct research, for example, a place you once worked, a university, or some public agency. Develop a series of interview questions about the kind of systems available to members of the organization, ranging from administrative systems to the personal support provided by PCs.

When you have interviewed ten to fifteen members of the organization, see if you can diagnose why there are wide-scale differences in system use. What points do your findings suggest for systems designers? For management? What kind of implementation strategy can you recommend?

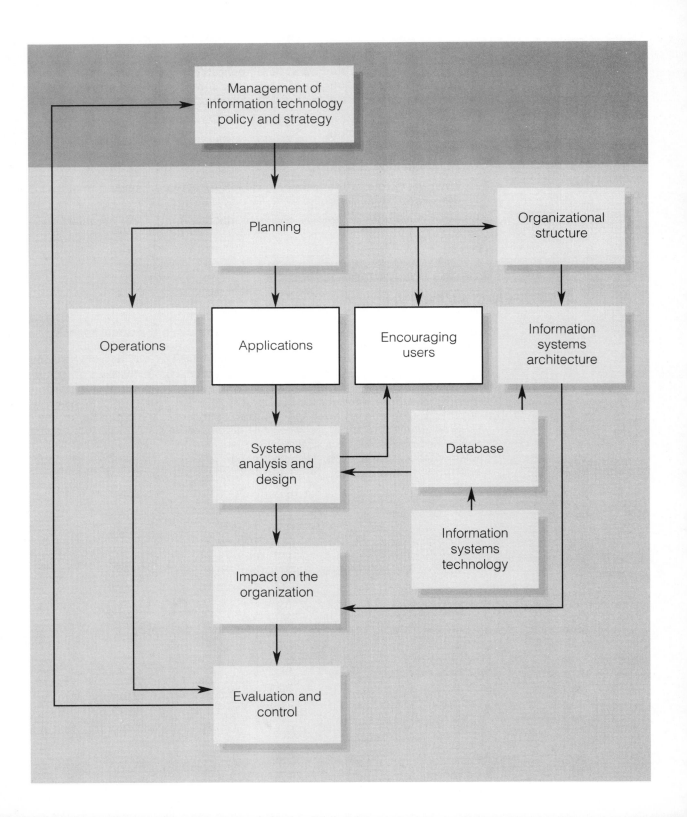

Exciting Directions
in Systems

This section of the text explores recent trends in information technology. Of particular interest is supporting users who work with technology. Most professionals today, and practically all in the future, will have a workstation on their desk. You will be connected to a network and will access various computers and databases over the net.

Decision support systems are an exciting way to use information technology. These applications help managers make decisions. A decision support system does far more than just process transactions.

Technology is increasingly used to support individuals and work groups in their tasks. Groupware has the potential to dramatically change the way firms are structured and the way co-workers interact.

In this section we also explore multimedia and look at the various purposes for this technology.

Intelligent systems represent an applied area within artificial intelligence. These systems capture the expertise of an individual or group of individuals and make it widely available throughout an organization. Intelligent systems have a great deal of potential for applying the technology in a way that is quite different from traditional data manipulation.

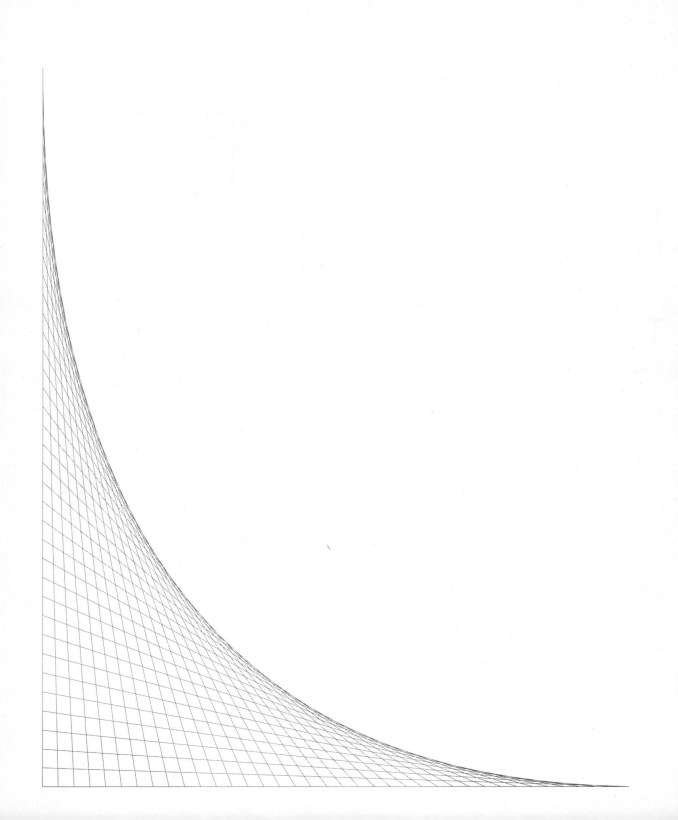

CHAPTER **20**

Supporting Users

OBJECTIVES

1. Learning to manage information technology.

Management needs to understand the pros and cons of users doing more with technology. Should managers and staff members spend time developing applications? What are the support requirements? What is the impact on their normal responsibilities?

2. Preparing to apply technology.

The tools of end-user computing offer an alternative for developing an application. Possibly a custom system is not really needed. Instead, the user can be taught how to work with a PC package or a 4GL to solve his or her own problem. This chapter identifies the trade-offs of encouraging users to do more to develop their own systems.

3. Transforming the organization.

Users with their workstations are changing the nature of the organization. Individuals within and external to the firm are connected to each other, making it possible to restructure workgroups and form alliances with outside organizations. To some extent, users are going to do their own computing. How much encouragement should you provide?

In the 1980s a phenomenon known as end-user computing grew out of frustration. Users found that it took an inordinate amount of time for the information services department to process requests for changes to existing applications, such as the creation of a new report. Why does it take so long for a simple request to be completed?

The IS department has limited resources. Analysts and programmers can work on new applications or they can be assigned to maintenance. It is the maintenance staff that generally handles requests for enhancements like new reports. Since most IS managers feel they are understaffed, and because management's focus is often on new applications, maintenance and enhancements sometimes get a low priority.

IBM of Canada conducted an experiment to see if it could satisfy more of its internal users. This company set up something called an **information center**, a room staffed with terminals and consultants to help users become familiar with technology. The center helped end users work with high-level languages so they could retrieve data from the company's computers and prepare their own reports with the data. This effort was the beginning of attempts to support end-user computing.

Who, then, was the user? This individual is generally considered a nonprofessional in the systems field. He or she is in a different function from information systems, for example, a user may be a professional in finance, accounting, or production.

Today, with the movement toward desktop computing and a client-server architecture, the term end-user in somewhat outdated. It is clear that most of us are users of the technology in some way. The question is what do we want to encourage users to do with IT and how do we support their efforts?

THE RANGE OF USER ACTIVITIES

Table 20-1 shows the different ways users are involved in computing. For the most part, users work with personal computers and networks, often accessing data on file servers and/or mainframe computers. The user might begin working with a system like a spreadsheet package. The vast majority of **spreadsheets** are created by users, rather than some intermediary. Users also tend to develop their own graphics for presentations. Finally, a user may define his or her own database using a program like Paradox or Microsoft Access. However, the user may also let a professional set up the application and only perform queries on the database.

Queries on a PC can be done in at least two ways. The first is to use the query processor that comes as a part of the **database management systems** described above. A second way is to use a **fourth-generation language** (4GL). These languages were first developed for midrange and large computers, but vendors offer products like FOCUS that run on a variety of platforms. Performing queries can become quite complex, particularly when accessing large and intricate databases on midrange and large computers through a network.

The third row in Table 20-1 describes systems-building tools. There are varying levels of sophistication among users. Some want to build complete systems and others do not. As we have seen in earlier chapters, defining and constructing an application of information technology is a time-consuming, labor-intensive task. However, there are probably small applications you may want to develop yourself. There are many tools for building PC-based systems, including languages like Visual Basic. This language facilitates the construction of an application that will run under Windows. However, you are getting heavily into programming if you select this alternative.

Table 20-1
User-Computing Alternatives

PCs	Midrange and large systems
PACKAGED LANGUAGES	
Spreadsheets	
Database management systems	Special-purpose languages, e.g., SAS, SPSS
Presentation graphics	
QUERY LANGUAGES	
Fourth-generation languages	Fourth-generation languages
Database query facilities	Database query facilities
DEVELOPMENT TOOLS	
Visual Basic	Fourth-generation languages
PowerBuilder	DBMS development languages, e.g., Oracle
Forms-based packages	
DBMS development languages	
Object-oriented languages	

Other options for developing custom applications include a PC database management system. These systems make it possible to define input screens and output reports, and to link together different relations in the database. Although they are not as difficult to use as a general-purpose programming language, it would still take considerable effort for you to develop a system using one of them. In the future, we hope that object-oriented programming will develop so you simply have to point to various icons on a screen with a cursor, click a mouse key, and assemble the icons into a program. We are not quite at this point yet, however.

The proliferation of PCs and networking reduce the amount of work that users are doing on midrange and large computers. Special-purpose languages like SPSS and SAS are heavily used on mid to large computers. However, there are PC versions of these packages and many users prefer to use them locally. As PC CPUs become more powerful and PC disk storage capacities increase dramatically, there are fewer and fewer reasons to run these packages on larger computers.

Fourth-generation languages and database management systems are available on midrange and large computers. If a database resides on one of these computers, it may be easiest to use the query facilities directly on the machine with the database. It is unlikely that too many of you will ever develop applications for midrange or large computers. If you do, a 4GL is probably the vehicle that will be available for this task. Some DBMS packages have rapid development tools to help in setting up applications.

As firms move more and more toward networks and client-server computing, users will find themselves spending more time interacting with the technology. Table 20-1 presents some alternatives for this interaction.

MANAGEMENT PROBLEM 20-1

A major East Coast business school has a computer center staffed by more than forty individuals. It operates a modern network with twelve servers, five Unix time-sharing computers, and more than a thousand PCs. Because faculty and students found the staff unresponsive, the director of the center established a new department called user services, which consists of five people, each of whom is assigned to help one or more academic departments with its problems.

In general the representatives from user services have been very well received by the faculty. They have limited student contact at this point. The problem is that user services reports directly to the director and has no group reporting to it. As a result, when it finds out that something is wrong, user services personnel have to negotiate with other departments in the computer center to have the problem fixed. For example, if there are problems in the PC labs, the head of user services must ask the head of the PC labs to fix them.

Although the user services representatives would like to help their users, their hands are tied because they can only ask others in the center to solve problems. Needless to say, the members of user services are very frustrated.

What actions can you suggest to solve this problem? How might the organization be restructured to improve the services provided to users?

Will Users Design the Entire System?

The unanswered question about computing is exactly how much responsibility do users want. Will they want to do more than use a fourth-generation retrieval language? Will we find that in ten years, there will be no more systems analysts and programmers, only users who work on computers?

It is unlikely users will want to develop large, multiuser systems because the time required is considerable. Also, when one moves from defining reports to database design, communications networks, and so on, the average user does not have the expertise required to develop a major application.

You may, however, want to develop a simple application for colleagues in your department to use. The tools described above offer some alternative approaches to this task. You will probably need some kind of consulting help in order to complete such an application. One approach to providing this consulting is to recruit "power users" from within the organization.

At General Electric, personal computer consultants volunteer from the ranks of the heavy PC users. These people may spend more than 60 percent of their time helping others with PCs rather than on their primary job. If users are to develop significant systems, they will have to devote a considerable amount of time to computing. As development tools improve, you will be able to accomplish a great deal in a "part-time" systems-building effort.

Supporting Users

Computing cannot be the sole responsibility of the user; there must be support. The information services staff should help select whatever tools are provided for the user. The department should see that there is adequate training available in the use of the systems acquired. Finally, IS staff members should provide ongoing consulting on the use of these tools. There will be a need for consultants to help answer questions about the systems and languages with which users are working. The IS staff should help the user locate data and they may need to write programs to collect data from different files or to process these data in some way before the end user can access it.

The term *information center* has become popular for describing a support group for users. Typically, the center is located in a suite of rooms in a user area. The information center contains terminals, personal computers, reference manuals, and most important, consultants to work with users. The center makes available different computers and peripherals along with different software packages. The user can try different computers and programs in a relaxed atmosphere.

Consultants in the information center have a number of duties:

- Teaching courses about the computers and software packages available
- Consulting on the use of packages and languages
- Providing assistance in deciding on the acquisition of computers and peripherals

Some Advice on Spreadsheets

Spreadsheets are one of the most popular and frequently used PC packages. Users often develop their own spreadsheets, and this practice creates a great deal of risk for the organization. Professional systems designers worry about error detection and correction, especially the input of incorrect data. There is nothing inherent in a spreadsheet package that forces or even helps the user to enter correct data. No routine checks the accuracy of formulae that you construct. You may file away a spreadsheet for six months, and then retrieve it again for further use. However, it is quite likely that you have forgotten what assumptions are in the model, and it is easy to make a mistake when you try to modify the spreadsheet for further use. Based on experience and reported errors, the following suggestions are intended to improve the quality and reliability of spreadsheets you build:

- Use a block structure for your spreadsheet model. The upper left hand block should contain:

  The name of the developer

  The date the spreadsheet was created

  The date it was last revised

  The name of the spreadsheet stored on disk

- The second block, well away from the actual model and formulae, should contain any macros developed to automate the spreadsheet. The rows and columns of the macros should not overlap with any of the rows and columns of the spreadsheet itself. Otherwise, a change in the spreadsheet could alter the execution of a macro, creating an error.

- The third block should be a table of parameters and values used in the model. Each of these "variables" should be labeled clearly. For example, I is the interest rate, expressed as a percent, for the prime rate.

- The final block is the actual model. This model should:

  Be obvious to anyone who sees it, which means that all rows and columns are identified with labels.

  Describe in text the calculations being performed in formulae since formulae cannot easily be seen on a printed version of the spreadsheet.

  Have *no* numbers embedded in formulae. All values should be referenced through the parameters block. If you include a formula and enter a prime rate of .07, when you look at the spreadsheet six months later, you may think it is easy to rerun it with a new prime rate by changing the value in the parameter section for I. However, your formula did not reference the cell for the interest rate. The interest rate is in the formula. What are the chances you will see the hidden interest rate?

  Be tested with test data and a calculator, hopefully by someone other than the person who developed the spreadsheet.

- Finally, you want to be alert for the following kinds of errors reported from actual spreadsheets: mistakes in logic, incorrect ranges in formulae, incorrect cell references, confused range names, incorrectly copied formulae, incorrect use of formats and column widths, overwriting of formulae, and errors in the use of built-in functions.

- Spreadsheets are very powerful and represent one of the most frequently used management applications of technology. It is important to be sure that you use this powerful tool carefully and that you produce dependable and correct results.

- Helping users by extracting, merging, and reformatting data on company databases and making the data available in a file for easy access by users

The consultant aids the user, answers questions, and provides help in accessing data. The user determines the data needed and creates the program to process the data.

Information centers are transforming themselves to focus more on departmental needs and solving business problems as opposed to teaching people how to use computers or specific packages. The information center needs to be a consultant for the user who wants to develop applications and solve problems.

The Data Warehouse

One strategy adopted by companies in which many users primarily want to access data on corporate files is to create a user data bank. The **data warehouse** contains data of interest to users in a format that is easily accessible to them. For example, professional programmers access data stored on a large computer DBMS and format it for processing on a personal computer database manager.

Users working on their own PCs access these relational-file structures to answer their questions. In a client-server environment the user will access corporate data by making requests of the server for information to be transmitted to his or her local workstation. The success of the data utility depends on choosing the right information from the main corporate database and making it available on the user's computer. A data warehouse is very appealing for users as they can finally access data they know is available!

PCs Can Help You Get a Job

Good news for job seekers! Companies are trying to reduce the fees they pay agencies when hiring staff members. Instead of filing your résumé in some remote file cabinet, more companies are scanning them into databases so that they can search for employees with particular skills at will.

If you don't want to bother sending your résumé to hundreds of companies, you can instead submit it to an independent résumé databank. You pay a small fee to have your résumé on-line for a specified period of time, say, six months to a year. You can also note where you do not want your résumé to go,

such as your current employer. Some job banks are free to college students.

University Pro-Net serves the alumni of nine universities including Carnegie Mellon, Stanford, and M. I. T. For a lifetime fee of $25, alums complete a résumé using a program and diskette supplied by Pro-Net. (This approach ensures that information appears in a common format for searching purposes.) For an extra fee, you can indicate that you are actively searching for a new job. Otherwise, you can pay the $25 and sit back waiting for that perfect job to come along.

Policy Issues for Management

Support   One policy question for the information services department is how many resources to devote to supporting users. A more difficult problem is to **control** the proliferation of hardware and software. Users conducting their own research may come up with a number of different approaches. Each new system, be it hardware or software, requires the IS staff to learn how to support it. Such an effort is costly and time-consuming. Thus, information services, with support from senior management, may establish a policy that all software and hardware be purchased through and with the approval of the IS department. Then the IS staff can evaluate the systems recommended and allocate staff members to become familiar with them. The IS department can keep control so that a reasonable number of different systems are acquired.

Making Mistakes   There are many examples of users making costly mistakes doing their own computing. Users are not systems professionals and they may not develop adequate test programs. One construction firm actually sued Lotus (the suit was dismissed) because a user included a new item in a bid but failed to include the new item in the final summation of all costs. As a result, the bid was too low and the contractor lost money.

   If management gives users the freedom to develop applications, it needs to provide some guidelines and training on how to do it. Management should also expect mistakes and react accordingly. For example, you might want to have crucial numbers checked by another user, or even a separate system. It never hurts to use a calculator to check a spreadsheet, or to try a new database application to see if you can make it fail!

Standards   As users acquire local computers, the information services department will have to coordinate acquisitions. Various pieces of hardware will probably be linked in some kind of network. **Compatibility** among the different devices is of concern here. Again, multiple hardware vendors and different types of software place a heavy support burden on the computer staff.

   On the other hand, users often develop their own applications to avoid the controls and perceived unresponsiveness of a central IS group. Senior management may well see the need for hardware and software standards, but it should also realize that users need some freedom if they are to do some of their own computing.

Data Access   The user is, by definition, not a systems professional. For most applications, the IS staff allows access to data under its control but will not allow users to change these data. The systems professional must be concerned about error checking, editing, data validation, and protection of the integrity of the database. There is no reason to suspect that the user is necessarily aware of this aspect of systems operation. The consulting staff can raise some of these issues, particularly when local, self-contained systems are being developed by users. For corporate data entrusted to the information services department, however, the staff will have to establish controls on data access and updating.

Is Computing the Right Use of Time?

How much should users do? One senior manager does not want executives writing programs. He insists they be written by a professional programmer, whose cost is far less than that of a senior executive. But what is most productive? What is a program? If a manager constructs a balance sheet using a spreadsheet package on a personal computer, is that programming? Is the use of a DBMS to define a personal application considered programming?

One answer is for you to become very facile in the use of these tools so that you will not spend an excessive amount of time using them. If it is possible to do so, developing one's own personal application can be fast and should result in a system that meets user requirements. We mentioned an Andersen Consulting survey earlier that indicated 81 percent of the senior managers queried were using personal computers. It is unlikely that these managers will discourage others from doing the same thing!

BENEFITS FROM ENCOURAGING USERS

Users have already discovered the benefits of user computing. They are purchasing personal computers and packages with great enthusiasm. Other users are demanding tools they can use to solve their own problems. To some extent, the information services department has lost the initiative. To regain it and see that the systems effort is coordinated and to avoid duplication and waste, the IS staff needs to establish a hardware and software architecture and a support mechanism for users.

Encouraging users to solve some of their own problems is another way to reduce the time required to develop an application. This approach provides immediate feedback. The user becomes the designer of the system. This strategy also adds to the total number of persons working to solve systems problems. By increasing the number of individuals brought to bear on the problem, the backlog of systems work should be reduced. Users can reduce the length of time they have to wait for an application.

CHAPTER SUMMARY

1. You are a likely candidate to solve problems using information technology, probably using a personal computer.

2. A key management issue is how much time users should take from their normal activities to devote to systems development.

3. Management also has to worry about supporting users. Information centers, data utilities, and user training are not free.

4. The benefits from encouraging users to solve problems can be substantial if users are supported. Users can cut the waiting time for information, and they can develop simple systems and reports without involving a systems professional.

5. The user can accomplish a great deal from his or her workstation, given tools and support. The user, rather than the systems professional, is in control of computing.

6. As a manager, you have to decide how much and how to use a personal computer yourself, and you must provide guidelines for those working for you.

7. It is clear that users are constantly doing more of their own development.

8. It is also clear that, despite the attractive interfaces of personal computers and windowing software, information technology is getting increasingly complex. We expect there will continue to be a need for professionals to develop the IT infrastucture and multiuser applications critical to the organization.

IMPLICATIONS FOR MANAGEMENT

Different managers have quite different views on how much time they want their subordinates to spend developing applications for their own use. How do you know when the user has exceeded his or her knowledge? When do you call in the professional? It is safe to say over time that users have and will be doing more development as the number of computers expands and software becomes more powerful. You will have to make the difficult decision on how the people working for you should spend their time. If you feel they should have to develop their own applications, then think of ways to support them with educational programs and consulting help when needed.

KEY WORDS

Compatibility
Control
Data warehouse
Database management system
  (DBMS)

Fourth-generation language
Information center
Spreadsheets

RECOMMENDED READING

Mirani, R., and W. King. "The Development of a Measure for End-User Computing Support," *Decision Sciences,* vol. 25, no. 4 (1995), pp. 481–497. (This paper describes the development of an instrument to measure support for users; the categories into which various items group are very interesting for a manager interested in encouraging users to work with IT.)

Sprague, R., and B. McNurlin. *Information Systems Management in Practice,* 3rd ed. Englewood Cliffs, N.J.: Prentice-Hall, 1993. (An excellent book with much material on supporting users and a new view for information centers.)

DISCUSSION QUESTIONS

1. Why is everyone computing today?
2. What are the advantages of users solving their own problems? Should management encourage it?
3. What is an information center?
4. What kind of support is needed for users?
5. What is a data warehouse?
6. How much programming should users actually do?
7. How do modern tools make it difficult to define what is programming and what is using a package?
8. Why has the use of IT by individuals accelerated in the past few years?
9. Why is a query language alone not sufficient to allow users to access their data?
10. How does having users solve some of their own problems affect the traditional role of the systems analyst and programmer?
11. Will more user development eventually eliminate the need for professional systems analysts and programmers?
12. What is the impact of client-server architectures on users?
13. What guidelines would you give your subordinates about the extent to which they should develop applications for their own use?
14. What kind of errors do users make with spreadsheets? How can the chance of these errors be reduced or eliminated?
15. How can a manager encourage users to become more involved in systems design?
16. With what kind of project or at what point in time should a user call in a systems professional rather than undertake a project himself or herself?

CHAPTER 20 PROJECT

CHOOSING A 4GL

One problem for an organization planning to encourage users to solve their own problems is deciding what language to acquire. There are fourth-generation languages that run across several families of computers, for example, PCs, Digital Equipment Corporation computers, and IBM mainframe computers. Other 4GLs work on one or a small number of different hardware types. Some 4GLs are closely tied to a proprietary database, whereas others have their own database routines built into the language.

You have been retained as a consultant to a medium-sized firm that is trying to determine how to go about choosing a 4GL. Develop a set of evaluation criteria. What factors should the company consider? Describe how the firm should use your criteria to conduct research about the different 4GLs and decide which to acquire.

CHAPTER **21**

Organization Support Systems: DSSs, GDSSs, EISs, Groupware, and Multimedia

⬤ OBJECTIVES

1. **Learning to manage information technology.**

   What is the difference between a decision support system and other systems? Can you as a manager gain anything from the use of an executive information system? What do GDSSs and groupware offer the organization? In Chapter 2 we discussed managerial decision making. In this chapter you have a chance to see how technology can support managerial decisions.

2. Preparing to apply technology.

The design team should consider whether the system it is developing has implications for decision making. Should a DSS or EIS be part of the system? If so, you have the additional challenges of designing a system around a managerial decision, perhaps one that is not particularly well structured.

3. Transforming the organization.

The technologies described in this chapter can play a major role in transforming the way you do business and manage the firm. EISs, DSSs, and groupware offer support to the manager and ways to coordinate the organization that would not be possible without IT. Think about the potential for these systems to make dramatic changes in the organization as you read the chapter.

This chapter discusses a wide range of systems intended to support the way people work. These systems by and large *do not* process transactions. Instead they provide information for decision making or they support groups of people working together on some task. They may use data collected and processed by a transactions system, but they analyze these data far differently than the system that maintains the database.

Decision Support Systems

A **decision support system (DSS)** is a computer-based system that helps the decision maker utilize data and models to solve unstructured problems (Sprague and Carlson, 1982). One of the most frequently used DSSs is a spreadsheet package. The user builds a model and looks at the impact of changing certain variables or assumptions. A user might look at the impact of a change in interest rates on a possible investment in a new manufacturing plant.

Alter (1980) offers a framework for classifying different types of DSSs. His original framework has a number of categories that can be summarized into two main types: data-oriented and model-based DSSs. A data-oriented system provides tools for the manipulation and analysis of data. Various kinds of statistical tests can be run, and data can be combined in different ways for display. A model-based system generally has some kind of mathematical model of the decision being supported. For example, the model might be an operations research optimizing model or a simple model represented by a balance sheet and an income statement for a firm.

Decision support systems offer tremendous power for managers who can generate and try many different **alternatives**, asking what-if questions and seeing the results. One manager said, "I'm not being forced to take the first solution that works, just because it takes so long to generate an answer; using a model and a spreadsheet program on a PC, now I can try different alternatives and choose the one that looks best."

Some Examples

The following examples illustrate the characteristics of decision support systems.

A major airline developed a model to help reduce fuel costs. The airline system stores data on fuel prices and availability along with storage costs and fuel capacity at each of the cities it serves. Performance parameters and the monthly itinerary are included for each of its aircraft. The system produces a list of the best fueling stations and vendors for each flight.

The system requires about fifteen minutes to produce a schedule that required a month of time to prepare manually. As a result, the airline can compute the best fueling strategy anytime conditions change, several times a week if necessary. The airline calculates that it saves 2 cents a gallon on fuel in a month. Since the planes consume 25 million gallons of jet fuel, the savings are in the neighborhood of $500,000 per month.

A manufacturing firm planned to install a $50 million production system at one of its plants in the Pacific Northwest. Using an ad hoc DSS, the firm investigated thirty-two alternative locations and decided instead to locate the new system in a southeastern plant, saving some $7 million annually in distribution costs.

A California producer of food supplements, cosmetics, and household cleaners was growing rapidly, and management was making decisions based on entirely subjective criteria. The firm built a database that includes plant location, products manufactured, unit costs, production capacity, and details on 500 line items, 360 customers, and 100 distribution centers. A model in the computer calculates the effects of various delivery requirements on transportation costs, distribution costs, and the cost of carrying inventory. For the first time, management is able to understand the financial effects of various service-level decisions. The firm expects to reduce operating costs by $850,000 a year and, more important, to cut delivery time to customers by one-third.

DSS Design

How does the development of a DSS differ from traditional design?

- The focus is on decisions, not data flows.
- The construction of a DSS tends to follow an iterative or prototyping approach.
- Building one of these systems forces the user to become involved in the design process.

- The system may be designed with the help of a systems analyst or by the user alone. Many DSSs built on PCs are constructed by the decision maker alone.

With a DSS, the user wants to be able to interact with the system and change parameters, doing "what if" analyses and trying different scenarios. Even in a DSS in which the system is used primarily to supply data and statistical analysis, it is helpful for the user to be able to generate the statistics interactively from a PC. The systems professional working to develop a DSS faces a problem for which the conventional systems life cycle may not be well suited. The DSS often involves an unstructured decision problem, making it difficult to develop detailed logic specifications. If a group of users is involved, there may be no consensus on the identification of the problem or on the definition of a system.

Under these conditions, an evolutionary, prototyping approach is likely to be the most successful. The developer begins by building a small model of the system. As users are exposed to the model over time, the specifications evolve. An evolutionary approach has the advantage of providing rapid feedback to users, both to obtain feedback on design and to maintain the users' interest in the project.

Today, users develop the preponderance of DSSs on their own PCs. The user will not follow a formal design process, but will build and test different versions of the DSS until satisfied with it. This ability for you to develop decision models quickly and easily on your own PC has had a major impact on the way decisions are made in the firm. Instead of arriving at

MANAGEMENT PROBLEM 21-1

Jim Gilmore is executive vice president of Precious Metals, a firm that buys and processes rare metals such as gold and silver. Recent price fluctuations in the world market have created many problems for Precious Metals, and Jim has tried to find some way to predict price changes.

He knew that some firms were successful in building computer models of various economic markets. With this in mind, he hired Management Models, a consulting firm, to investigate the possibility of building models for each of the commodities purchased by Precious Metals. The company and the industry have very good data on historical prices and other economic indicators.

The modeling effort proceeded very smoothly. The resulting model produced valid results when confronted with the rapid price fluctuations of recent years. Management Models indicated that short-range forecasts should be very good but that the model should not be trusted for extrapolations past one year.

Jim now wonders how to integrate the model into purchasing decisions. For a long time, the brokers at Precious Metals based their decisions on intuition and experience with the market in making purchases. The new model is available on personal computers on the company LAN, and Jim wants the brokers to use it. He feels sure, however, that none of them will take advantage of it if they are merely told that it exists. Jim wonders how to gain acceptance of this new tool. What is your advice?

a solution that works, you will try many different scenarios and pick the best one. Information Technology is clearly doing more than processing transactions. Through a DSS it addresses key operational and managerial decisions in the firm.

FURTHER EXAMPLES OF DSSs

In this section, we look at three decision support systems in more detail than those described earlier in the chapter.

Yield Management: How to Overbook Gracefully

American Airlines faces a problem common to the industry: how to maximize the revenue or yield from each flight. Yield management for an airline is like inventory control for a food manufacturer. If food items are left in inventory past a certain date, they must be discarded as spoiled. American estimates that without controls to allow for overbooking, 15 percent of its seats would be "spoiled" on sold out flights.

American estimated that solving the yield management problem using a nonlinear, stochastic, mixed-integer mathematical program would

Let's Go Sailing

The French marine research company CRAIN has developed a routing system for sailors who make long passages. Generally the packages are used by racers who participate in some of the around-the-world races like the BOC Challenge or the Whitbread Race.

The program uses a sailboat's polar performance data. These data are based on the size and shape of the sailboat and generally are created through velocity prediction programs. They show for a given windspeed what the boat's maximum speed should be at any angle to the wind. A sailor who "goes by the numbers" then adjusts his sails and angle to the wind to try to achieve the predicted speed.

The data from the weather map can be difficult to provide to a sailboat at sea. Most racers have a PC. If they have a built-in fax modem, they can receive weather faxes and display them on the screen of the PC. The

user then copies the chart into a Jason file and the program has to digitize the isobar lines of constant pressure.

The Jason routing program uses weather map data to develop a series of isochrones, which are places the boat can reach in a given period of time. From these data the program calculates the optimum course. Jason takes data about the boat's latitude, the pressure gradient, variations of pressure gradients over time, isobaric curvature over time, and a database on air and water friction to calculate a wind field.

Finally the sailor enters the starting point and time, and the next waypoint or destination, and the program produces a route in the form of a graphic map of isochrones and options. All of these data show the sailor the best way to get to his or her destination in the least time.

require approximately 250 million decision variables for its entire route system. Instead of developing a single model, American's operations research group developed a series of models to attack three more manageable subproblems (Smith et al., 1992).

Overbooking   The first of the models controls overbooking, the practice of intentionally selling more reservations for a flight than there are seats on the aircraft. An airline overbooks because it knows that a certain number of passengers will cancel and others will be no-shows at the gate. The second model helps American decide how many discount seats to offer on a flight. Finally, traffic management controls reservations by passenger origin and destination to maximize revenue. Because of the current hub-and-spoke system, the flights are interdependent; a passenger flying into the Dallas/Fort Worth hub may leave on any number of other flights to reach his or her final destination.

Figure 21-1 illustrates the overbooking problem. Overbooking allows the airline to accommodate more passengers, but there are penalties associated with denying passengers boarding if they have a confirmed reservation. The airline must compensate "bumped" passengers and it must provide an alternative flight for them. This cost of overbooking actually increases with the number of passengers denied seats. For example, the airline may have to offer more hotel and meal vouchers and may have to transport the bumped passenger on another airline's flights.

Figure 21-1
Overbooking allows more reservations to be accepted.

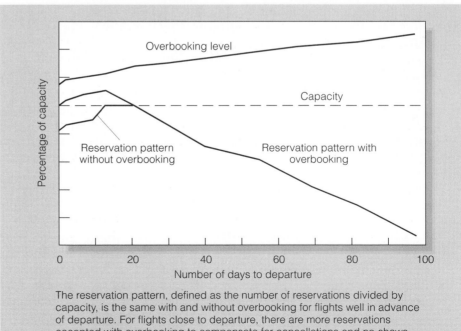

The reservation pattern, defined as the number of reservations divided by capacity, is the same with and without overbooking for flights well in advance of departure. For flights close to departure, there are more reservations accepted with overbooking to compensate for cancellations and no-shows.

American developed an **optimization** model shown in Figure 21-2. As the overbooking level increases, net revenue, which is passenger revenue minus overbooking costs, rises to a maximum value and then decreases as the cost of an additional oversale exceeds the value of an additional reservation. The overbooking model draws on data from the SABRE reservation system. The overbooking level has a constraint to prevent degrading passenger service too much. It relies on four forecasts: the probability a passenger will cancel, the probability of a no-show, the probability that a bumped passenger will take another American flight, and the oversale cost.

Discount Seats The large number of special fares and discounts greatly complicates the problem of maximizing revenue from a flight. Because there is a fixed number of seats on a plane, selling a seat at a discount that could be sold for a full fare reduces overall revenue. American cannot control fare classes independently, otherwise it could sell a low-fare seat while turning away a passenger willing to pay full fare. American uses a marginal revenue approach to determining how many seats to sell in a given fare class. The approach uses a heuristic that finds an acceptable, but not necessarily optimal, solution.

Traffic Management With the hub-and-spoke traffic system, American's percentage of passengers flying into a hub to connect with another flight has gone from 10 percent to more than 60 percent. Consider the example

Figure 21-2
An optimization model.

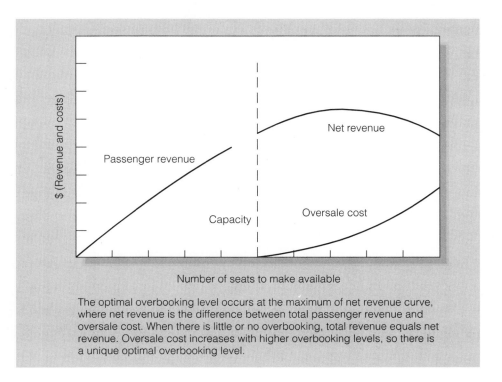

The optimal overbooking level occurs at the maximum of net revenue curve, where net revenue is the difference between total passenger revenue and oversale cost. When there is little or no overbooking, total revenue equals net revenue. Oversale cost increases with higher overbooking levels, so there is a unique optimal overbooking level.

in Figure 21-3, which shows a number of alternatives for arriving at and departing from a hub. Flights that used to serve a single market now may serve thirty or more markets. In the example, one might expect that the Portland to Dallas/Fort Worth full fare is less than the Portland to Miami discount fare (connecting through Dallas/Fort Worth), which should be less than the Portland to Miami full fare. American cannot just look at a fare class, it must also consider likely routes. If the airline controlled by just full fare and discount fares, it might accept a full-fare Portland to Dallas/Fort Worth passenger while turning away a discount seat from Portland to Miami, a decision that would lower total revenue.

Ideally, the airline would control on a market and fare class basis. However, the large number of markets and fares makes this computationally infeasible. American developed a method of clustering similar market/ fare classes into groupings it calls "buckets" to make the problem more manageable. All the market/fare classes on each flight are clustered into eight buckets. First and business class go into separate buckets while coach market/fare classes are in the remaining buckets (see Figure 21-4). As sales increase, the availability of seats is restricted first to low-value reservations regardless of market/fare class. Although this problem may seem simple, American currently has 150,000 market/fare classes.

Figure 21-3
The hub-and-spoke traffic system.

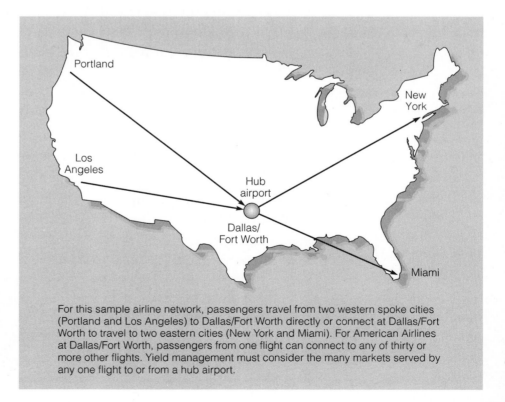

For this sample airline network, passengers travel from two western spoke cities (Portland and Los Angeles) to Dallas/Fort Worth directly or connect at Dallas/Fort Worth to travel to two eastern cities (New York and Miami). For American Airlines at Dallas/Fort Worth, passengers from one flight can connect to any of thirty or more other flights. Yield management must consider the many markets served by any one flight to or from a hub airport.

Figure 21-4

To control market/fare classes, American clusters them into "buckets."

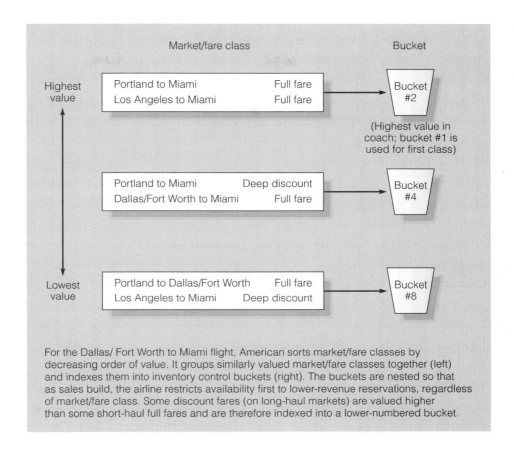

For the Dallas/ Fort Worth to Miami flight, American sorts market/fare classes by decreasing order of value. It groups similarly valued market/fare classes together (left) and indexes them into inventory control buckets (right). The buckets are nested so that as sales build, the airline restricts availability first to lower-revenue reservations, regardless of market/fare class. Some discount fares (on long-haul markets) are valued higher than some short-haul full fares and are therefore indexed into a lower-numbered bucket.

American uses a dynamic programming algorithm to index the market/ fare classes into buckets. The idea is to maximize the variability of market/ fare class values between buckets while minimizing the variability within a given bucket. Every time a passenger requests a flight, the SABRE system accesses a condensed table containing bucket information. The system scans the bucket information until it finds the appropriate category for the reservation request, and then makes a decision on whether or not to offer the seat at that fare.

Results   American has developed models to estimate the benefits of the DSS described above. The overbooking DSS has been in use since 1990 and it is estimated to have increased revenue by more than $200 million each year. The discount-seat allocation model is estimated to have obtained from 30 to 49 percent of the revenue opportunity from discount sales resulting in additional revenue of $200 to $300 million. In three years, the total yield management program has produced quantifiable benefits of more than $1.4 billion for American. For that same three-year period, American had a net profit of $892 million.

This example shows that sophisticated operations research models within decision support systems can have substantial returns for the organization.

Distributing the Gas at APC

Air Products and Chemicals produces industrial gases like oxygen, nitrogen, hydrogen, argon, and carbon monoxide. The company sales exceed $1.5 billion per year with nearly 19,000 employees in 13 countries. The industrial gas division uses highly automated equipment to manufacture and distribute liquid gases. However, scheduling and delivery of the gases used to be a manual process. Liquid oxygen and nitrogen are produced in APC's automated plants, which also serve as supply depots. The supplier maintains and monitors storage tanks at customer locations. Because the production costs for all manufacturers are about the same, competition is based on service, marketing, pricing, and lower costs from more-efficient distribution.

The nature of the relationship with customers provides the gas supplier a great deal of freedom in planning operations. The supplier decides when to send a shipment based on the inventory in the customer's tank. The supplier also decides how much to deliver, how to combine different loads on a truck, and how to route the vehicle. This large amount of freedom makes APC's scheduling much more complex compared with other scheduling problems. Typical APC problems involve several hundred customers and twenty trucks per scheduler.

The Vehicle Scheduling System   APC formed a team to improve the operational efficiency of delivery scheduling. The completed system, developed

---

Another Way to Fill Perishable Airline Seats

American Airlines has begun to auction seats for flights on the World Wide Web. One bidder won two first-class round-trip tickets from Ontario, California to Hartford, Connecticut with a bid of $375, saving $3,701 off the full price. By providing information on-line the airlines can reduce calls to their toll free numbers and possibly the staff required to make reservations. If passengers book by computers via the Internet, the airlines save 10% or more on travel agent commissions.

Cathay Pacific Airline generated $325,000 in revenue from its first three auctions at its Web site. Because the seats auctioned are unlikely to be sold, the auction is all incremental revenue for the airline. It is also inexpensive to run on the Web; there is no need for a physical location or an auctioneer! American not only has an auction, it will send out e-mail offers of deep discounts for weekend travel on the Wednesday before to anyone requesting the information. (http://www2.amrcorp.com/cgi-bin/auction/user.cgi)

A few experts believe the World Wide Web will have the same revolutionary impact on the airlines as computerized reservations systems.

and tested carefully before being widely implemented, makes use of six data files:

1. Customer file, including capacity of tanks, safety stock levels, and historical product usage
2. Resource file, containing a description of each truck in the system, capacity by state, and list of customers feasibly served by the truck
3. Cost file, including a per-mile rate for vehicle fuel and maintenance and driver pay regulations
4. Mileage file, a network representation of the road system of the United States
5. Time and distance file, containing the distance, travel time, and toll cost between any pair of customers computed from the mileage file
6. Schedule file, containing the schedules developed by the system

The scheduling system produces a list of trips to be taken over the next several days, including start time, scheduled vehicle, quantity of product for each customer, time at which delivery should be completed, and length and cost of the trip. A scheduler can examine this output and make changes due to contingencies not reflected in the system.

The scheduling system solves a very large mixed-integer program to near optimality using a special algorithm developed for this project. The model

---

MANAGEMENT PROBLEM 21-2

Nancy Swanson is vice president of planning for Beauty Aid, a major manufacturer of cosmetics. The top management at Beauty Aid recently heard a presentation on planning and felt that the firm should be looking into this area. Beauty Aid has grown rapidly through its own efforts and by acquiring several smaller companies. Because of its highly profitable business and good cash position, it has been able to make acquisitions easily.

Top management realizes business is becoming more complicated and the next round of acquisitions will involve far larger companies than in the past. Therefore, the computational burdens of evaluating potential acquisitions and projecting conditions after the acquisition will become even more severe.

Nancy is investigating the use of computer models to help in the planning process. After conducting research on the possibilities, she has narrowed her consideration to the following alternatives:

1. Hire a group of consultants to build a model of the firm.
2. Have the internal staff in the planning department construct a model using a general-purpose computer language.
3. Design a model with the present planning staff using a higher-level planning language.
4. Get started on planning by using a spreadsheet package on a personal computer.

What are the advantages and disadvantages of each alternative? What course of action do you recommend to Beauty Aid?

can contain up to 800,000 variables and 200,000 constants. The authors believe that this is one of the largest **integer programs** regularly solved to a state of near optimality.

This DSS contains one of the largest operations research models reported in routine use in the literature. It is an example of how the power of the computer can be used not only to compute a solution but to present it to a user through a decision support system.

THE PROMISE OF DSSs

The systems described in this section provide information to support decisions. A number of decisions are programmed into the systems. They also evaluate different alternatives and process information that is presented to and acted on by the decision maker. The American and APC systems showed costs savings, something that is more difficult for other types of DSSs. What is the value of better planning? How do we know that the decision makers using these systems perform better than they did under the previous manual systems? For many DSSs, justification is not done or is based on the faith of the managers involved that the model is helping to solve a problem.

EXECUTIVE INFORMATION SYSTEMS

A number of consulting and software companies suggest that firms need an **executive information system (EIS)**. What is an EIS? Companies build an EIS to bring to senior management information that needs its attention. For example, the executive vice president of Phillips Petroleum uses an EIS to check the state of the firm's oil and chemicals business. The system also provides a summary of world news. The vice president feels that the system saves him an hour a day because it pulls together previously less accessible information in one place.

An EIS often involves a mainframe, where much of the data of interest to senior executives reside. However, the data are not easily accessible, and the EIS software must summarize data and make them available for downloading to a personal computer in the executive's office. Since many managers do not like to type and are not comfortable with computers, EIS designers focus on providing an appealing interface and a system that is easy to use.

One characteristic of these systems is a "drill down" feature. The user first sees figures at a high, summary level. If these numbers look all right, the user continues. However, if some total looks unusual, for example, sales in the western region are lower than expected, the user puts the cursor on the suspicious figure, clicks the mouse button, and sees a display that contains more detail on just the western region. Depending on how the system is designed, the user might be able to drill down several levels to get to quite detailed data.

Senior managers who use these systems praise them highly. A power company president reports that he can view a series of corporate indicators with one keystroke. He can create a personal menu to look at the indicators he needs to review on a daily basis. This executive feels that the system has improved communications throughout the organization.

Another executive uses the system to look for trouble spots and find out why a division's expenses are higher than anticipated. He gets a quick snapshot of his competitor's financial position through the system as well. Another manager uses the firm's EIS to check for exceptions, such as shipments to customers that are taking too long. Setting up the system forced his company to think about its business and what indicators it wanted to monitor.

There are a number of ways to develop an EIS. Several vendors offer software designed to access mainframe databases and provide a graphical user interface (GUI) for executives. At least two of these products are windows applications. See Figure 21-5 for an example of one of these products. With the wide-scale availability of GUIs on Macintosh computers and on PCs through Windows, it is also possible to develop one's own EIS within the company.

Is an EIS any different from a DSS? An EIS is a type of DSS, but in general it will tend to be data rather than model oriented. The systems created to date allow executives to view data and summarize it in different ways. Of course designers have to be very careful and resourceful when designing an application to be used personally by the highest levels of management in the organization!

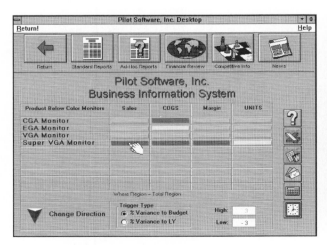
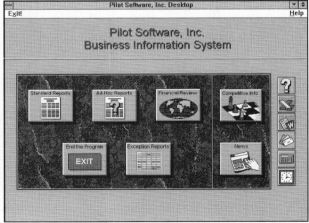

Figure 21-5 An example of an EIS GUI.

GROUP DECISION SUPPORT SYSTEMS

There is much interest in using information technology to support work-groups. A workgroup consists of individuals who have some need to work together. Theoretically, any number could be involved, but typically we find two to twenty people who must work on a problem forming a group. How can IT support such a workgroup?

One way is with a **group decision support system (GDSS)**. A GDSS consists of special software and physical facilities, such as a conference room containing PCs for each person in the room. The software helps identify issues and evaluate alternative decisions and actions. A GDSS might also contain a model whose solution provides participants in the group with insights into their problem.

Workgroup decision making may also be supported using technology when the workgroup is dispersed. Electronic mail allows members of a group to exchange messages at any time of the day or night and is insensitive to time zones. An extension of e-mail is the electronic conference. Individuals can all be on-line to a computer at the same time for a

An EIS at Quaker Oats

The president of Quaker Oats is known to turn on his PC after dinner at night. He logs on to the firm's mainframe and runs Quaker's executive information system. The president is particularly interested in sales figures; he reviews them and generates a printout for a breakfast meeting with the head of a business unit, all in an elapsed time of fifteen or twenty minutes.

Quaker's chairman was the instigator of the EIS developed by this $4.4 billion multinational company. The system is used by twenty-three top Quaker executives, many of whom have PCs at home for off-hours access. The system retrieves and displays key financial data as well as sales information. The chairman likes to see key financial statistics broken down by the firm's strategic business units (SBUs), such as hot cereals, ready-to-eat cereals, and so on.

The data he wants always existed on the mainframe, but it might have taken several hours or even days to produce them in a suitable format. The first EIS was command driven and clumsy to use. The second generation featured menus, what-if capabilities, color screens, and other options. The system has proven so easy to use that executives need only a thirty-minute training session.

In-house staff members bought packages for some parts of the EIS and developed the rest themselves. Managers can obtain internal financial data on brands and SBUs and consolidated information on fifty variables, such as sales and gross margin. Quaker designed a front end to the Dow Jones Retrieval System to make it easy for users to search for data using English commands. Lotus is available, along with certain custom spreadsheets for managers who do not know how to use Lotus. Users feel the system is successful because of the information it provides and because it is so user friendly.

conference, or they can join the conference whenever they like, reading and responding to the comments of others at their leisure.

Existing computer packages can be used in a group setting. A network of personal computers might be used to share data on a problem or to share a spreadsheet. A database management package on the network server could provide common data for each participant in a group at his or her own personal computer connected to the LAN.

Technology-Assisted Meetings

A number of companies use specially equipped meeting rooms with GDSS software to conduct meetings. IBM installed a number of electronic meeting rooms based on a room developed at the University of Arizona. A typical meeting room has participants seated at a horseshoe-shaped table, each with a personal computer connected to a network and file server. A projection screen is placed at the open end of the horseshoe to show what is on the discussion leader's (facilitator's) PC.

The role of the leader is very important in setting the pace of the meeting and in helping to form a consensus. A typical meeting might begin by stating the problem to be addressed. Participants brainstorm at their PCs for some period of time, say, fifteen minutes to an hour. Each comment appears on all workstations, but without attribution. That is, no one knows who typed a particular entry. This anonymity is one of the features that makes an electronic meeting very different from a conventional one. It is felt that participants will be less reticent, particularly around superiors, if their comments are anonymous.

Next, another piece of software can be used to group alternatives into categories generated in the first stages of the meeting. Each participant could then numerically rank suggested alternatives. The meeting room software would average the ranks and sort the suggestions according to their average. Different software packages offer a variety of features designed to facilitate achieving a consensus about some issue or problem.

Do the electronic meeting rooms work? Participants in meetings generally seem enthusiastic about their experiences. Some claim that the use of these facilities and software reduce meetings by a factor of 10. It has also been argued that solutions are better because no one will be intimidated by a superior, as contributions are anonymous.

We should view these claims carefully. Could similar results be achieved without a special room and elaborate software system? Certainly what the computer system does could be done manually by a facilitator and an assistant. The computer helps to automate this process, but one could also simply write ideas on a blackboard for all to see. The use of the computer and a high-tech meeting room may make participants feel better about the results of the meeting. Certainly the act of using such a room says that the topic being discussed is important.

What are the drawbacks of electronic meeting rooms? In one case, participants generated about a thousand alternatives in half an hour. It is not clear how a group can deal with this number of suggestions! It seems likely that the appropriateness of this type of meeting depends on the subject matter. If we are looking for a number of creative suggestions to a problem or are trying to generate a lot of alternatives, the room could be very useful.

GROUPWARE AND ORGANIZATIONAL INTELLIGENCE

One of the most difficult questions to answer is, "What do managers do?" For the first three or four decades of information technology, IT did little to help managers in their day-to-day tasks, often because IT staff did not understand managers. There were not very many management information systems, though many companies claimed to have them. The last five years witnessed the development of groupware, designed to support both the daily tasks of management and coordination, and to provide a repository of organizational intelligence.

Over twenty years ago, Henry Mintzberg (1973) conducted a classic study of managers. He observed their behavior by living with them for a week. Based on his observations, Mintzberg identified a number of roles that a senior manager plays in an organization. One role of management that seems to be universally agreed upon is leadership: the manager is, and should be, a leader for the organization. In this role, the manager sets direction, acts as a public spokesperson, and tries to see that the resources of the organization are employed to achieve the objectives he or she has set forth.

Looking at the Data

Many people find it difficult to understand data that appear in the form of a table. However, a graph makes trends clear. Even better for certain kinds of information is a map produced by a Geographic Information System (GIS).

As an example, the points on the map might be customers, and a firm can calculate distances and driving times from a warehouse. Pointing to a customer, a system can access data about an account at that address.

Johanna Dairies in Union, New Jersey uses a GIS to plan its distribution network. The company uses digital street maps and a computer-aided routing and scheduling program developed by a third party. Customer orders are downloaded from a midrange computer to a PC. The package tries to eliminate overlaps between routes and minimize travel distances.

A router can draw a circle around a group of customers, and the computer will generate a route and display the number of cases to be delivered, their value, and suggested delivery days. The package has helped improve customer service. Because it costs the dairy about $100,000 per route, saving a single route paid for the $40,000 cost of the software and another $40,000 of consulting time. The dairy has sixty routes that can make use of the GIS.

It appears a picture here is worth a lot of words.

Management researchers have emphasized the decision-making nature of management since the 1950s. Certainly, we expect managers to make decisions in many different domains. Important decisions include funding R&D, product development, and the decision to introduce a new product. Many managerial decisions revolve around issues of resource allocation. Almost every organization is confronted with limited resources and competing demands for them.

A role that managers often face is as a disturbance handler. Dispute and problems in the organization find their way to a manager who is in a position to resolve them. These disturbances may come from inside the firm, or they may be prompted by problems with suppliers or customers.

Managers also deal with information in their jobs and function as the spokesperson for the firm. A good manager scans the environment for competitive actions, threats, and new opportunities. Today, companies are very dependent on government regulations and actions. Trade treaties can make a major difference to a firm's strategy and operations.

The discussion so far has been about managerial roles, but what actually does a manager do during the day? Mintzberg divided his observations into five categories. The first of these was scheduled meetings, which consumed over half of the day for the CEOs he studied. Next came unspecified desk work. Unscheduled meetings took 10 percent of the day while phone calls consumed 6 percent of the managers' time. Finally, managers spent a small amount of time on "tours," or "management by walking around."

This distribution of time begins to get at the tasks managers perform. Two activities cut across all of the roles and tasks: communications and information processing. As a leader, spokesperson, decision maker, disturbance handler, and in most other roles, the manager is communicating with others. He or she disseminates the strategy and goals of the firm. The manager receives communications from subordinates, customers, suppliers, the financial community and many others. Meetings, both scheduled and unscheduled, involve communications as do phone calls and tours. Much of desk work involves letters and memos, another form of communications.

Many communications and much purposeful managerial work revolve around information processing. We frequently communicate to obtain new information. When making a decision, the manager must process information to determine the appropriate course of action to take. Suppliers and customers want information. The securities industry seeks information about company plans and performance.

The technology described below is designed to support people in the organization in the tasks they are expected to perform. This technology lets managers and other workers redesign their tasks. It provides a great deal of flexibility and a number of alternatives for the flow of work, communications, and coordination.

Most information systems prior to the development of **groupware** are oriented toward solving problems in the organization, such as how much of a good to produce, how to process orders, and so on. Groupware is aimed at what a manager does—*it supports members of the organization who have a common task and who operate in a shared environment.*

Groupware is sometimes called coordination software because it helps managers coordinate the work of others in the firm. By coordinate, we mean to assure that the resources of the firm are applied to achieving its objectives. Coordination means managing dependencies, that is, seeing that individuals or groups that depend on each other or on common resources function effectively.

With groupware, it is difficult not to focus on Lotus Notes, a product with about a three-year head start on the competition. At the beginning of 1996, **Notes** had an installed base of nearly 5000 companies and more than 1 million users around the world.

What is Lotus Notes? (See Figure 21-6.) Groupware and Notes are hard to define. Even the vendors have difficulty describing the nature of the products. First, Notes is based on client-server computing; the product assumes that users or clients are connected on a local area network with a server. Databases to be shared are kept on the server, though you may have a local database on your own PC. One of Notes' major features is its ability to replicate databases across departments and organizations. You can tell Notes how often to synchronize databases and it will be sure that all information is consistent.

For example, suppose that you worked for an advertising company and that the New York and Rome offices are preparing a campaign for a global client. If teams in New York and Rome use Notes, the system could be set up to automatically update databases at, say, 9:00 P.M. U.S. time. Notes will update both databases to add new information without losing existing data. Thus, team members in New York and Rome can make changes during the day with impunity. The software replicates those changes on both copies of the database. (If two individuals change the same information, Notes flags the changes and leaves it to the people involved to resolve the conflict.)

This database replication feature is one of Notes' coordination features. The software coordinates diverse workgroups and allows them to share information without worrying about updating anomalies. Just having the same database easily available to multiple individuals working on a project, regardless of replication, promotes coordination as well. Notes also has its own e-mail system so Notes users can communicate with each other.

The second feature of Notes that makes it suitable for supporting individuals with a common task is its applications development tools. It is fairly easy to design quite powerful applications and share them on the system. For example, it took about fifteen minutes to design a shared database of the common materials (videotapes, computer demonstrations, etc.) available for each class session of one of our MBA courses in information systems.

Notes has aggressively integrated its products with the Internet and World Wide Web. Lotus has modified its original Notes software so that a

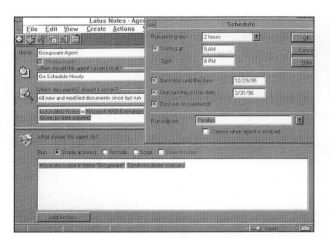

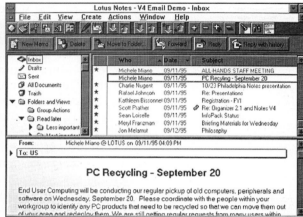

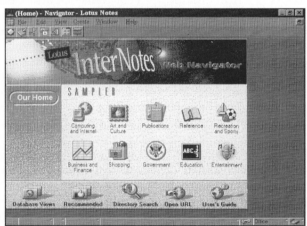

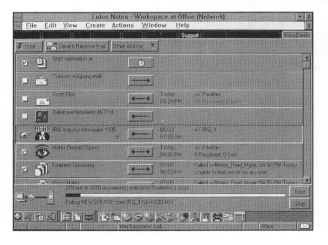

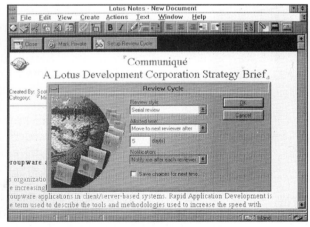

Figure 21-6 Notes software by Lotus.

Notes server is also a Web server. The software automatically translates information on the server into HTML format if a Web browser requests it, or in Notes format for a Notes client. Lotus believes that Notes is a natural authoring environment for Web information. More than that, Notes is positioned for easy applications development on the Web. Companies want to conduct transactions over the Web and need software that does more than retrieve static information. You must interact with the person using the client. For example, a magazine publisher wants to have a button on its Web site that a person visiting the site clicks on to get a form for subscribing to the magazine. The publisher wants to accept that person's credit card, search its database to see if this is a new subscriber and send a message welcoming a new reader or welcoming back an old subscriber. For more information on Lotus's Internet strategy, see the sidebar.

How are firms using Notes? Significant adopters of the system include General Motors Europe, major consulting firms and several Big Six accounting firms including Peat Marwick and Coopers & Lybrand. We studied how one consulting firm used the technology. Interestingly enough, Notes was not used extensively to manage customer engagements. Rather, the firm was using Notes internally to improve administration.

Just as with any other company, a consulting firm has to administer itself. This consultant, with revenues in excess of two billion dollars a year, has to administer personnel, manage billings and collections, administer contracts and perform a wide variety of administrative tasks. The practice manager for the Northeast described how Notes improved his operations. The firm had developed a number of administrative applications. His group of direct-reports from around the region was able to dramatically reduce the number of meetings through the use of groupware.

Compaq Computer found that its sales staff uses Notes to communicate with customers and rarely comes into the office, preferring to work at home. Boston Market is growing at 100 percent a year. It uses Notes to keep track of expansion plans, market research, advertising, cooking procedures, and recipes. Essentially Notes (and groupware) is becoming the leading dispenser of knowledge in the corporation.

Chase Manhattan Bank is another major Notes site with over 2700 users across a highly distributed network. One of Chase's major applications is a service that follows investment reports from providers like Dow Jones. The system is designed to help the analyst spot differences between the bank's evaluation of a company and the evaluation from these other services. Explanations about the differences are posted to a database where they are widely available.

The CIO at Chase feels that Notes is unique because it lets you develop applications not previously undertaken. That is, the applications are easy enough to construct that ideas for systems that were infeasible using older technologies, suddenly become easy to justify. Chase is using Notes in its systems development division on a variety of different kinds of projects. It is particularly useful in coordinating employees who work in London, Brooklyn, and Lexington, Massachusetts.

Lynda Applegate and Donna Stoddard (1993) reported on the use of Notes at Chemical Bank prior to its merger with Chase. At Chemical, it was the Corporate Systems Division (CSD) that first became interested in groupware. The senior VP of corporate systems was launching a productivity

Notes on the Net

Comments at a Press Conference by Notes President Michael Zisman announcing Notes strategy for the Internet: "… it's our view that essentially all infrastructure components, … servers, database servers, transaction servers, all the servers you can imagine, are going to become Web servers. Virtually all client applications (will be) Web-enabled so that applications go out to the Web directly.

The Web today is a distributed file system …. access to that file system will be implemented in all sorts of applications. The Web is unbelievably ubiquitous. … All sorts of servers plug into the Web … At Lotus, we have over 8,000 (Web) pages and 83 different Notes databases that roll up into our Web site … Suddenly I need tools for searching the site and viewing indexes of data. I need to be able to get forms out. I need to be able to accept that data back. I need to be able to search back in databases (and to) … interface to transaction processing systems. I may want to implement workflow. I may want to have data … coming back, bringing it together with database data and then moving this among a number of people …

… the Notes document database can contain either HTML pages or Notes documents in Notes formats. … We do dynamic translation between HTML and Notes structures … If I author a document in Notes and store it in a Notes database and someone accesses it from a Web browser, we on the fly translate it to HTML. Likewise if a document is authored in HTML, stored in a Notes database using … Word … and someone accesses it from a Notes client, we translate it to Notes format …

We bring to the Web server market a database approach as opposed to a file system approach. We have in Notes … a richly-structured document database we think gives us a great advantage in Web sites as they get larger … Lotus's Web site has 8,500 pages … a year from now it will have 20,000 pages. IBM's Web site today has 40,000 pages.

… All the development facilities that exist in Notes are now available to build Web applications. … Most of the applications built by our 11,000 partners that run on Notes servers can now be accessed from Web browsers. A Notes application consists of defining databases, defining forms, defining scripts that the client and server use to manipulate the data and in many applications providing the linkage to relational database systems to transactions systems, etc.

… We will deliver … four specific application frameworks, one for publishing which includes full subscription management, one for electronic commerce, … one for customer service and one for marketing … All of these are built on top of the Notes server. … The most compelling part of … Notes … on the Web is (this) … piece. It's the ability to rapidly build the kinds of applications we think people are going to demand on the Web. … People can use Notes clients to build these applications, deploy them on Notes servers and have them fully accessible on the Web … Notes is optimized for symmetric multiprocessing systems to support upwards of a thousand simultaneous sessions per server."

program to generate more output from the design and programming staff at the bank. He felt that the division's work was communications intensive and that it was breaking down using conventional forms of communicating. His estimate was that Notes would allow a 15 percent productivity improvement for a staff whose salaries totaled $15 million a year. The VP also viewed a test in CSD as a good preview for rolling Notes out in the rest of the bank.

The bank brought in a groupware consultant and offered training in the use of Notes in anticipation of its implementation. The VP hired a full-time Notes specialist and formed a Notes support group to assist users. Roll out began with 20 senior managers and their secretaries. In a period of less than two years, 300 CSD employees were using Notes and the bank had developed more than 90 applications with Notes.

In the middle of this effort, Chemical decided to centralize IT resources then initiate a 40 percent reduction in IT staff. Shortly thereafter, Chemical Bank announced its merger with Manufacturer's Hanover Bank. During this period, turmoil ruled the systems division. One major application the VP initiated was the "rumor mill." Concerned employees could post rumors to the rumor mill database, and senior managers would respond. The VP felt that this simple technique helped create a feeling of trust and openness in the group.

One manager remarked that Notes let developers create applications quickly to respond to a business need. It also helps create geographic independence. In one application a group in New York worked with developers

Notes Versus the Web

Companies are using the World Wide Web to set up internal web sites. These sites may be isolated from the Internet and only available within the firm, or outsiders may be given access. Much of the information on an internal web server could also be put on Notes. Which platform is best suited for each different type of information?

Companies are taking a mixed approach. Andersen Consulting is one of the largest Notes customers with over 23,000 users worldwide. The company is using Web servers for a training program in its object-oriented development methodology. The Web's hypertext environment made it easy for students to use the system. The developers praised the Web as a teaching environment.

Notes has a real advantage in terms of document control, security and workflow features. Notes is also appropriate for coordinating groups who must work on the same documents. Notes makes it easy to route documents electronically and it has automatic database replication across different servers. Notes has developed its own links to the Internet in order to satisfy customer interest in the Web.

It appears that the Web is the biggest threat to the success of Notes at this point. Will companies move exclusively to one of these approaches, or in fact will your organization have to maintain Web site and a groupware system?

at a Texas bank owned by Chemical. Notes also helps make work independent of time since it reduces the need for face-to-face communications.

In late 1993, the *Wall Street Journal* had an article about groupware and its impact on the organization. The staff writer found that it tended to erode the hierarchical nature of organizations. In some cases, however, groupware created problems for management. The Chemical VP discussed above resigned after the Manufacturer's Hanover merger and his successor eliminated the rumor mill. It seemed that the forum became "unruly" and began to receive a number of cutting criticisms of management.

The thrust of the report, however, was more positive. The reporter talked to various managers who felt that groupware helped dissolve corporate hierarchy by making it easy to share information. The rank and file can join discussions with senior management if given access to groupware.

One major contribution of groupware is providing organizational intelligence where it is needed. A worldwide consulting firm like Andersen Consulting, with thousands of employees, has a great deal of expertise. A consultant in Japan needs a way to find out if the company solved a problem similar to the one she is facing in some other country; Andersen uses groupware to provide this base of intelligence.

A side benefit of groupware is the way shared information can be used to enhance decision making. This technology may make it easier to create Decision Support Systems and Expert Systems since data and expertise are now widely available in an organization.

A number of companies are using Notes to connect with clients and suppliers. Officials at Notes present this system as the "defining element of the Information Superhighway," feeling that electronic commerce is far more important than video on demand or games. Compuserve and Notes offer a service called "Enterprise Connect" on Compuserve. It provides wide area connectivity for Notes users who do not want to establish their own networks.

Notes also enhanced its system with the capability of storing images. One could use its applications development language for workflow processing, for example, the Merrill Lynch system described in Chapter 17. Notes also entered into a partnership with Intel to use ProShare personal conferencing software with Notes. One can have real-time collaboration using these two products together. You and a colleague can edit a document together while having a conversation about it, even though you are located thousands of miles apart.

Of course, there are a few cautions needed. Like the phone or any other network, the system works only if everyone who needs to be involved has access. Networks only become useful to service providers and consumers when they reach a critical mass. Another major threat to Notes is the World Wide Web (see the sidebar above). A number of companies are posting information to the WWW. Morgan Stanley is using internal Web servers, called an Intranet, (protected from access by unauthorized users) to present information like telephone directories, equity analysis reports, and

SEC filings. These applications could also be implemented with Notes. Lotus has added Internet extensions to Notes and it will be interesting to see if Lotus and IBM are able to turn the threat of the Internet into an alliance.

MULTIMEDIA FOR BUSINESS, EDUCATION, AND ENTERTAINMENT

Multimedia is generally defined as a combination of different presentation media which are coordinated through a personal computer workstation. Media that might be included are:

- Artwork or still pictures
- Full or partial motion video
- Sound
- Text
- Graphics
- Animation

Multimedia is used with a windowing user interface. A few examples will help to illustrate the concept (unfortunately a printed book cannot present all of the media above!).

We have created a multimedia presentation of the Merrill Lynch system reengineering project in Chapter 18. The student begins reading one of two narratives about the system. By using the mouse to select a highlighted part of the new system description, the student can choose to see a data flow diagram of that part of the system in a window on-screen. (The DFDs were created with a CASE package for the PC.) The student can move around the DFD and use the mouse to go from a higher-level to a lower-level diagram. He or she can click on a process in the DFD, and a window appears with a video scene showing that processing. Using the systems design narrative, the user clicks on highlighted phrases, and an individual appears in a window discussing that part of the design process.

There is a series of CD-ROMS that read to children. In "Arthur's Birthday Party" the computer reads a story to a student while highlighting the text being read. The program reads and displays text in English or Spanish. The student using the program can move the cursor to objects on the screen and click on them after the program finishes reading that page. Each object does something, for example, a baby in a highchair cries and throws food, a teapot does a dance and whistles a tune, etc. The program fascinates children, and motivates them to improve their reading skills.

At Dartmouth, students studying Italian use a Macintosh to play vignettes from Italian television. The student can select synchronized text and ask the computer to define difficult words, provide a translation in

English, or provide a commentary on the culture. At Yale New Haven Hospital, medical residents are learning to identify heart problems using a multimedia computer system. The system displays an animated heart in one window and video clips of real, diseased hearts taken by an ultrasound machine on another monitor. By clicking on a stethoscope icon, the student hears a recording of how the diseased heart sounds. This system saves time for the teaching physicians as the residents learn from the multimedia system how to interpret ultrasound images of hearts with different types of problems.

The World Wide Web is becoming a significant source of multimedia for education, entertainment, and product promotion. We mentioned the Java programming language in a sidebar in Chapter 9. This language makes it possible for an Internet browsing program to download and execute programs from servers on the network. The downloaded programs are interactive and can feature graphics, video, and audio segments. Macromedia, a San Francisco company that sells multimedia software, distributes a program that plays movies on Netscape's Navigator 2.0, a Windows browser. This program, called Shockwave, displays interactive content on the Web, similar to Macromedia's CD-ROM development programs. The program makes it possible to have automation, sound, and features like rotating billboards for advertisers. The Web is a natural distribution channel for multimedia, especially as bandwidths become larger, for example, through ISDN or cable TV access to the Internet.

How is multimedia used? From the discussion above, it offers a great deal of potential for education. It allows the instructor to bring together

A New Videodisk

Two warring camps agreed on a new standard for high-capacity digital disks. The importance of this agreement comes from the fact that this new standard is expected to apply to video players, audio players and computer CD-ROMS. For the first time, all forms of digital disks will be compatible.

The good news is that the disks will be about the same size as current CD's and players will be able to play current disks. You do not have to replace your CD collection yet. It is expected that pictures and sound will be of higher quality than with current disks because new players will retrieve about ten times as much data per second as current players. More bits means a sharper picture and better sound.

The disks will have the capacity to store a two hour movie. First, four bits of data are recorded in the space occupied by a single bit on current disks. In addition, much of the data will be compressed using a new compression method, MPEG2 (Motion Pictures Expert Group 2)

The developers expect that it will be possible to laminate two thin disks together so that either one side can be read underneath the other, or the user will have to turn over the disk to get to the other side. If double siding works, a disk could hold four hours of movies.

The new disk is one small step for digital convergence!

a diverse set of teaching materials and to guide access to them. The user can often choose the path through the system to select the parts of a presentation to view. The coordination provided by the computer plus this element of choice makes multimedia much more powerful than the use of any single medium alone. There are a number of CD-ROM products for education, some from traditional print publishers and others from companies dedicated to educational software. Corporate training departments create their own CD-ROMS when they need to train a large number of workers and want to avoid the expense of courses. Sun Microsystems offers a server designed for presenting video information to various clients. This system is aimed at corporate traning centers who want to use multimedia presentations.

There are applications besides education and training. Vendors of goods and services would like to extend their sales outlets without dramatically increasing overhead. One possibility is to use more automated sales outlets in places where a large number of individuals are present such as airports, train stations, and shopping centers. These automated outlets can make use of multimedia to lead customers through a transaction. Firms have provided their sales forces with notebook computers having CD-ROM drives in order to make multimedia presentations to clients. A second use for multimedia, then, is in business for applications that interactively present information to customers.

The third area for multimedia, and probably the application with the greatest investment, is entertainment. Many promoters and companies feel that interactive multimedia will be at the center of the next generation of electronic entertainment. Entertainment and technology companies are forming alliances at a rapid pace. US West, a regional phone company, has invested in Time-Warner, a cable and entertainment firm that is merging with Turner Broadcasting. Microsoft would like to have Windows adopted for managing home entertainment. The converter box that sits on top of your TV is expected to be a PC with at least the power of a modern Intel chip.

What factors inhibit the spread of multimedia? First, the lack of standards and the need to add expensive hardware to a system presents a problem for educational institutions with budgetary restrictions. It is also very labor-intensive to develop multimedia applications. Will multimedia significantly improve learning? Preliminary evidence suggests that multimedia helps to motivate students, which is an important part of education. As we have seen with other innovations, we have very powerful technology; the challenge is in understanding how to apply it successfully.

What Is Digital Convergence?

What is digital convergence and who are the players? **Digital convergence** is the concept that all of the information coming into your home will be digital and multimedia. There will be one or more "digital" pipes bringing strings of binary digits to you. By 1995, it was estimated that consumers were spending more on home computers than on television sets. By the year 2000 it is estimated that one-third of U.S. homes will have a computer. The converging digits entering your computer (or television) will include phone calls (voice and video), television, movies on demand, and information from mass market services and the Internet, at a minimum. Often interactive television is presented as one objective of these firms, including the ability to interact with programs, order products on the screen and generally treat the TV as you might a PC capable of retrieving and presenting all types of media. The least you would be able to do is choose from about 500 channels of television.

The players in digital convergence include:

- Content providers: television and movie studios which create entertainment programs, home shopping networks.
- Broadcast television and cable television: these companies distribute entertainment to the home.
- Long distance and local common carriers: these firms want to supply the pipeline that carries information to the home.
- Hardware and software manufacturers: companies that want to make set-top boxes and the software to control them.

A Dissenting Opinion on Multimedia

David Gelernter, a prominent Yale University computer scientist, has questioned some of the enthusiasm about multimedia. Gelernter is enthusiastic about computers, as many educators are. However, most educators would have to admit that so far the technology has had a rather modest impact on primary and secondary education in the U.S. In the 1960s visionaries argued that computer-aided instruction would revolutionize education. It has not. Today's visionaries seem to be making the same claims, only about multimedia.

Gelernter fears that "new computing trends combined with our laziness about education could lead to disaster." He worries that the use of computers will undermine the teaching of basic skills. Is it a better idea to have a student draw on a computer or with crayons on paper? Which helps the student learn more? Will multimedia and hypertext turn education into entertainment? Do video clips to illustrate a book help a child develop an imagination? Hypermedia appeals to the Sesame Street generation. In a few milliseconds you can click on a button and move on to the next topic you highlight. The reader never has to develop the discipline or skill to learn what material to study and what material to skim.

Gelernter suggests that these new media are praised because children love them. He argues that as a child he enjoyed seeing a movie in class because he did not have to think. Are we substituting technology for thought? Gelernter does suggest using the computer for simulations to involve students in, say, labor negotiations or designing a new city.

Let us not be overwhelmed by slick presentations. We must ask what it is we want students to learn and how best it can be taught. Parents, students, and, hopefully, educators will revolutionize our schools, not information technology.

All of these firms have been buying companies in allied businesses. For example, in 1995 Walt Disney Studios bought ABC television and Time-Warner merged with Turner Broadcasting. None of these players wants to be left out, or lack content and the ability to deliver it. The local phone companies have a problem because their twisted pair wires into the house have very low bandwidth. While engineers figured out how to send a movie to the home through **compression** algorithms, their scheme is not yet practical over long distances. The cost of bringing fiber optic cable to the home (curbside) is very high. Local phone companies want to purchase cable systems and use their cable as a pipeline for digital information entering the home.

Cable reaches more than 95 percent of all TV-equipped households and 90 percent of all suburban business campuses in the U.S. Some local cable companies are now competing with phone companies by offering high speed data communications lines over their cable networks. Unfortunately, cable companies are not terribly popular. Their reputation for providing good service gave pause to some companies thinking about using their equipment for crucial data. Many cable operators offer companies bypass facilities to avoid using a local phone company. Some plan to connect to the Internet and provide high-speed switching services like ATM and frame relay.

How to Get a TV Signal

If you ask most people how they get a show to appear on their television sets, they might mention that it comes through the air or over a cable. In fact, there are six possibilities for a TV signal to reach your set:

- The tower—This is the traditional and first approach to TV. Signals are broadcast from the TV tower to an antenna on your house or your set.

- Cable—The transmission is carried overhead or underground into homes by coaxial (bundles of copper wire) or fiber optic cables. Fiber optics has the capability to send more channels than copper wire.

- Microwave—A transmitter on a building sends a signal to individual dishes on homes or apartment buildings. In a city, a building has a receiving antenna on the roof and signals are sent from it to wires running throughout the building.

- Satellite—A satellite in geosynchronous orbit at 22,300 miles from the earth beams a signal to a receiving dish on a home from which it goes to a TV set. Satellite TV has been extremely successful as it allows a broadcaster to transmit signals to an extremely large area at one time.

- Digital satellite—Using digital rather than analog signals only requires an 18-inch dish as a receiver. You buy a dish from an electronics dealer and purchase a package of digital channels for a price comparable to cable.

- Video dial tone—This term has been used for phone companies that want to get into the interactive TV business. The idea is for TV transmissions to use telephone lines. The video dial tone allows you to dial the movie or program you want to see whenever you would like to view it.

Are there less expensive alternatives? A satellite TV service called DirecTV had reached the level of a million customers by 1995. The company offers up to 150 program channels, including as many as 50 channels of current movies that can be ordered every half hour (soon to be every 15 minutes). With this capability, will users want to pay for 500 channels of TV coming into their homes by wire?

The entertainment companies see the television set in your home as the end of the digital pipeline. One contemporary PC comes with a cable-ready TV receiver, an answering machine, fax, stereo radio, and a CD-ROM drive capable of playing audio or software CDs. Some experts in the technology field challenge that assumption: they think that the end point will be the personal computer and that the home PC will be able to provide interactive television faster than the companies described above. In this view, the Internet and the World Wide Web already offer what the multimedia companies are trying to create, or at least the Net comes close. Currently the Net can bring buyers and sellers together as one can purchase products on the Web. You can access photos and video, though the latter takes a great deal of computer power. As high speed communications like ISDN lines come down in price, the Web will become even more attractive.

By the year 2000, expect a ten-fold improvement in the home multimedia computer you can buy for $2000 and the ability to connect it to a network at, say, 100 million bps. With this kind of equipment, it will be feasible for you to download a movie from the Net and show it on your high resolution monitor! If you do not want to spend $2000 on a computer, possibly you will be able to buy one of the "netsurfing" $500 computers to get your multimedia and TV from the Internet.

The debate continues about digital convergence. The local Bell phone companies have slowed their trials and are trying to figure out what services customers really want. Two "Baby Bells" dropped applications to the FCC to erect interactive networks after the Agency had been considering them for two years. Estimates are that it will cost from $1000 to $2000 to wire a home for interactive multimedia. (Running fiber optic cable to each home in the U.S. could cost $120 billion.) Meanwhile, AT&T is offering dial-up service for customers to connect with the Internet, and at least one cable TV company is planning to offer telephone service. Other cable systems offer high-speed Internet connections over special cable modems. Some experts argue that the home PC and the Internet are the only technology capable of providing multimedia services (except **interactive TV**) in the next few years. It will be several years until the digital convergence scene becomes clear.

Hypertext: The Engine for Multimedia?

Most text that we read, including this book, is sequential and flat. You might be able to use the index to look for a particular term that is not clear, but in general you are constrained by the sequential nature of the medium. **Hypertext** is nonsequential. If you are reading about a soccer game and come to a passage where it mentions an off-sides penalty, and that term is highlighted, you could click the mouse on it and open up a window that would explain the off-side rules. You might be able to click on a word in the rules to call up a diagram of a soccer field showing typical off-sides violations.

In hypertext, sections of text have links to other pieces of text. The **links** are **pointers**, just as we saw with direct-access files. Now, instead of pointing to a particular record in a file, the pointer must reference a piece of text that is also stored in the system. (See Figure 21-7 for an example of a hypertext session.)

Hypertext is used for documentation, user manuals, advertisements, and customer guides. The Soft-Ad Group produced a number of hypertext ads for automobile manufacturers such as Ford, Buick, and BMW. These ads use hypertext so the viewer can move around and select different parts of the presentation. For example, you might first be asked to choose which

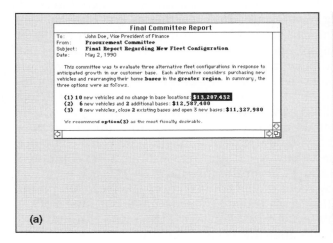
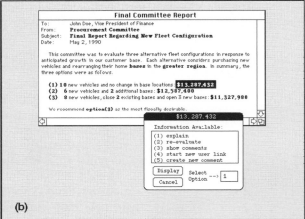
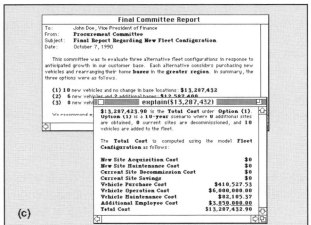

Figure 21-7   (a) User highlights vehicle cost and clicks mouse button. (b) Menu appears and user chooses "explain." (c) The cost figures are shown in detail.

model of car you want to explore, and then be given a choice of statistics, engine and drive train, performance, and so on. Each choice brings up a display and the option to choose another display that provides more information on part of what is currently viewed. The price list of various options is followed by a spreadsheet in which you choose the options you want and come up with a total price for the car. The London Design Museum has a hypertext information system for its visitors. The user can access information about various design movements or they can see information organized by country or manufacturer. You can also access information about individual designers or products.

Hypertext provides the user with the ability to navigate through a variety of material. If this navigation includes different media, hypertext offers a natural vehicle for constructing multimedia applications. Hypertext, then, is one possible model for the overall control of multimedia applications. It may be used in its own right on text alone, but it can also be expanded to become **hypermedia**.

CHAPTER SUMMARY

1. The systems in this chapter offer a stark contrast to transactions processing applications as they directly support the efforts of the knowledge worker.

2. Decision Support Systems have existed the longest among the group discussed here. They help a decision maker solve a problem.

3. A DSS may supply its users with statistics and analysis, or it may be based on some kind of operations research model as we saw in the examples from American Airlines and Air Products.

4. An EIS is designed for a top level manager. Its objective is to provide the information this executive finds personally relevant.

5. A good EIS has a graphical user interface and allows the user to "drill down" to lower levels of detail to understand the results displayed.

6. A group DSS provides support for a group of decision makers working together on a problem. The GDSS may be used remotely or at a specially constructed meeting room featuring a facilitator and technology to support the meeting.

7. Groupware is a product that epitomizes the transformation of the computer from a purely calculating device to a communications medium. Groupware assists individuals faced with a common task in a shared environment.

8. Communications are important for coordination and for assuring that individuals are working for the objectives of the organization and for resolving dependencies. Groupware fulfills an important coordinating role in the organization.

9. Lotus Notes, the most successful groupware product, also features an applications development facility. Many users are developing quite sophisticated applications with it.

10. Groupware is also a repository of organizational intelligence, as we saw with a consulting firm that uses it to keep track of its past engagements and the skills of its staff.

11. Multimedia refers to the combination of various media like audio and video. It is used for education and entertainment as well as by corporations to help present their products.

12. Multimedia has generated tremendous interest, but it is not trivial to develop multimedia presentations.

13. Digital convergence refers to the pipeline carrying information into the home. Various content providers and communications companies are all trying to figure out how to control the pipeline and what comes through it.

14. The consumer demand for digital convergence, especially in the form of interactive TV or the ability to choose among 500 channels, is not clear at this point.

15. As a manager, you may find multimedia most valuable for training employees, video conferencing and meeting support, providing information to employees and customers, and similar tasks.

IMPLICATIONS FOR MANAGEMENT

Groupware is one of those exciting applications that seems to happen about once every ten years. It has the potential to fundamentally change the way we do business. There are two aspects of this class of software which really stand out. The first is the most obvious, allowing people to work together on a shared task while located in a wide variety of places. The second, and potentially the more important, is the use of groupware to collect and disseminate organizational intelligence. You might think of the Notes database developed by the world-wide consulting firm as an intelligent system, making the experience of the firm available to others. What other kinds of organizations could benefit from this kind of database of organizational intelligence?

KEY WORDS

Alternatives	Group decision support system (GDSS)
Compression	Groupware
Decision support system (DSS)	Hypertext
Digital convergence	Hypermedia
Executive information system (EIS)	Integer programs

Interactive TV   Notes
Links   Optimization
Multimedia   Pointers

RECOMMENDED READING

Coleman, D., and R. Khanna. *Groupware: Technologies and Applications.* Upper Saddle River, N.J.: Prentice-Hall, 1995. (A very good book of readings about groupware.)

Nielsen, J. *Hypertext and Hypermedia.* New York: Academic Press, 1990. (An excellent introduction to hypertext by one of the leaders in the field.)

Smith, B. C., J. Leimkuhler, and R. Darrow. "Yield Management at American Airlines," *Interfaces,* vol. 22, no. 1 (January-February 1992), pp. 8–31. (A detailed description of the DSS discussed in this chapter.)

Stohr, E., and B. Konsynski (eds.). *Information Systems and Decision Processes.* Los Alamitos, Calif.: IEEE Computer Society Press, 1992. (An excellent collection of articles on organizational support systems by some of the leaders in the field.)

DISCUSSION QUESTIONS

1. What is a decision support system?
2. How does a DSS differ from a traditional system?
3. How does a DSS involve users in its design?
4. For what types of systems might the user need assistance in building a DSS? (Hint: Consider Alter's framework.)
5. How are electronic spreadsheet packages used on a PC for building a DSS?
6. What kind of DSS is a manager most likely to build, a model-based or data-based system? Why?
7. Why is an EIS likely to be data as opposed to model based?
8. What are the objectives of group decision support systems? How do they differ from an individual DSS?
9. What do graphics capabilities contribute to a DSS?
10. Should users actually write programs? Is building a DSS programming?
11. How does prototyping contribute to a DSS?
12. What are the pros and cons of electronic meeting rooms as a DSS?
13. What is the role of a model in a model-based DSS?
14. Why do managers want to be able to change values and run a DSS again?
15. What features distinguish an executive information system from a DSS?

16. What is a "drill down" facility and why is it important for an EIS?

17. How has technology changed the cost/benefit ratio for these decision support systems since the early ones developed in the late 1960s?

18. Why have information services departments generally not developed decision support systems? Why do they seem to concern themselves with transactions processing applications?

19. What are the major applications for multimedia presentations?

20. What is digital convergence?

21. Who are the major players in digital convergence?

22. What is the promise (and the mythology) of digital convergence?

23. How can a company use multimedia today?

24. What is hypertext and what is it used for?

25. What is groupware? To what kind of problems is it addressed?

26. What is Lotus Notes? What features does it provide?

27. How does groupware contribute to coordination within the organization?

28. How does groupware provide a base for organizational intelligence?

29. How would you align the incentive (pay) system for an organization to encourage the use of groupware?

30. Compare and contrast groupware, the Internet and WWW.

CHAPTER 21 PROJECT

A DECISION SUPPORT SYSTEM

Mary Simon is looking for help in a recurring decision she faces. When helping a client evaluate a business for purchase or merger, she analyzes a great deal of information from the balance sheet of the firm. In addition, she does a competitive analysis by looking at other firms in the industry to see how the potential acquisition is performing. Sometimes she is looking for a leader. In other cases she wants a firm that is not doing well but has a lot of potential.

Describe the overall design of a system for Mary. How do you think it should be developed? What kind of computer and what language or package would you recommend? How much will Mary have to know to use the DSS? What role will she have in building it? Can you use any of the PC tools you have learned to build a rough prototype for Mary?

CHAPTER **22**

Intelligent Systems

OBJECTIVES

1. **Learning to manage information technology.**

   There has been much excitement about intelligent systems. How can they contribute to the organization, and what are the issues in developing one of these applications? Think about whether or not these systems represent a high risk to the organization, because they may not always be successful. What is the potential payoff?

2. **Preparing to apply technology.**

   Intelligent-systems development is called **knowledge engineering**. Is this approach different from conventional systems analysis and design? Are special skills and tools needed for knowledge engineering? How does the development of an expert system differ from a transactions processing system, and what are the implications for the design process?

3. **Transforming the organization.**

The systems described in this chapter have the potential to transform the organization by capturing and applying human knowledge. To date, they have not lived up to this potential. What are the reasons for this shortfall? How can intelligent systems lead to competitive advantage and organizational transformation?

ARTIFICIAL INTELLIGENCE

Expert systems, case-based reasoning, neural networks, and **genetic algorithms** represent an applied branch of the computer science field of **artificial intelligence (AI)**. Workers in AI try to develop machines and programs, the behavior of which might be considered intelligent if viewed by humans. At what activities are humans very good? Men and women are able to learn from experience, they can make sense out of contradictions, and they can reason to come to a conclusion. People are also able to reason inductively—to look at evidence and generate a hypothesis about the process that generated the evidence.

Can a machine do any of these things? Certainly, there is no one machine that can do them all. In looking at AI systems, we must consider their domain—the area in which the system functions. A program to diagnose tumors may work very well with tumor information, but it would be hopelessly lost if asked about viral infections.

How can we agree that a program or device exhibits intelligent behavior? Alan Turing, a British mathematician, proposed a test named after him. Turing's test is to place a computer and a human in two separate rooms. An interviewer in a third room, who cannot see the human or the computer user, asks questions that are passed to the computer and to the human. If the interviewer cannot tell the difference between the answers from the computer and the human, the machine is said to exhibit intelligent behavior.

AI *Versus Traditional Programs*

Just as the goals of AI programming differ from those of a conventional information processing system, so do the characteristics of these programs. First and most important, in AI one is manipulating symbols rather than numbers. A program to diagnose diseases does not need to compute arithmetic expressions. Instead it has to manipulate logical symbols, just as someone solving a geometry problem would manipulate symbols rather than numbers.

It is also claimed that AI programs are non-algorithmic. An algorithm is defined as an effective procedure for solving a problem. If the algorithm is followed, one is usually guaranteed of finding a solution to the problem. As opposed to algorithmic programming, AI programs often employ **heuristics** or rules of thumb for finding problem solutions.

Many AI programs are concerned with pattern recognition. In fact, some of the early work in AI is responsible for successful optical-scanning devices, since these devices must read input symbols and match them with patterns already in the scanning device to identify the input. Pattern matching is an important human capability. We are able to make sense out of many varied patterns.

EXPERT SYSTEMS: APPLIED AI

Currently, there are few applications in business that a computer scientist would call AI. Instead, organizations take advantage of an applied branch of artificial intelligence called **expert system**s—advisory programs that attempt to imitate the reasoning process of human experts (Turban, 1995).

Why build such systems? One purpose is to make the expertise of an individual available to others in the field. One company built an expert system to help diagnose and solve the problem of oil exploration rig drills getting stuck. The knowledge of the firm's best drilling expert became available on all rigs through the expert system.

Another motivation for creating an expert system is to capture knowledge from an expert who is likely to be unavailable in the future, perhaps because of an impending retirement. An expert system also provides for some consistency in decision making. Imagine a brokerage house in which the compliance department must see that brokers follow the firm's and the SEC's rules. If the firm uses an expert system to help advise its analysts, each case of suspected rule violations will be evaluated consistently.

MANAGEMENT PROBLEM 22-1

The head of information services at Chemway has just finished reading an article about a competitor in the chemical industry who claims to have implemented more than two hundred expert systems. The competitor provided expert-system shells on PCs to various scientists and engineers and encouraged them to build systems. Most of the systems involved 100 to 250 rules and were run on a routine basis.

The Chemway official worries that his firm might be losing out to the competition. "I never realized there were so many possible applications of expert systems in this industry," he remarks. His question is how to get started.

I could offer courses, provide consultants, or even start my own expert-systems development group. I wonder what would be the most effective way to take advantage of this technology.

What do you recommend?

Components of Expert Systems

An expert system (ES) consists of the following components:

- The user interface
- The knowledge base
- The inference engine

In our research, we found the **user interface** to be an extremely important component of an expert system. Possibly because users are not accustomed to systems that provide advice, they are more demanding. Also, if the advisory system is used frequently, it becomes an important part of the user's daily activities. A good interface makes the system much more pleasant to use and helps promote its acceptance.

What is a **knowledge base**? How does it differ from a database? One important way to represent an expert's knowledge is through the use of rules. An example of a rule might be as follows:

IF the broker sold stock in an account on one day

AND bought the same stock for the same account the next day,

THEN investigate the transaction p=10

This hypothetical rule indicates that the probability of an investigation is to be increased if the broker sold stock one day and bought it back the next. The broker might be trying to generate commissions when there was no valid investment reason for the transactions.

A database stores numbers and symbols. It might show a simple relationship among the data because they are stored together or defined as connected in some way. A rule in a knowledge base, however, contains some of the logic of an application. The rule above implies something about when an investigation should be undertaken. An ordinary database makes it very difficult to figure out the logic of the application. A knowledge base contains more information about logic than a conventional database.

Knowledge Representation

The production rule above is an example of one type of knowledge representation. It is one of the most popular for building expert systems in business. Another representation technique is known as a **frame**. The frame provides a way to gather a lot of information about an object into one place. For an expert system to advise us on what personal computer to buy, a frame might contain the characteristics of each PC, including its memory size, the type of chip, the speed of the chip, the type of video board, the monitor, and so on.

Finally, an expert system can use a **semantic network**. In a network, information is connected through a series of nodes. The program traverses the nodes along the paths of the network when it is seeking information for its computations.

The Inference Engine

The **inference engine** is the reasoning part of the expert system. It is one of the major components of an expert system's **shell**, a program that is designed to facilitate the development of an expert system. Many of these shells are designed for personal computers, and typically they work through production rules. The inference engine examines the rules and tries to find rules with true IF conditions. A true rule then "fires" and performs the action indicated in the THEN clause. The inference engine may employ forward or backward chaining.

An example will help illustrate how the inference engine might work (Luconi, Malone, and Scott Morton, 1986). Figure 22-1 contains several production rules for personal financial planning. Suppose the client's tax bracket is 33 percent and her liquidity is more than $100,000 and our client has a high tolerance for risk. **Forward chaining** involves going through the rules one at a time to infer that exploratory oil and gas investments are the best recommendation.

If we are interested only in whether exploratory oil and gas investments are the best recommendations and we are not interested in other possible investments, backward chaining is more efficient. In **backward chaining**, the system begins with a goal. In this case, the goal is to show that the client needs exploratory oil and gas investments. At each stage, the inference engine establishes subgoals that, if achieved, would indicate the client needs exploratory oil and gas investments.

Looking at Figure 22-1, assume we know the THEN condition of the third rule is our goal. To conclude that the exploratory shelter is recommended, we need to know risk tolerance is high (which is already known), and we need a rule to show a shelter is recommended. By checking other rules, the inference engine finds if rule 1 is true, it can achieve its subgoal of having a shelter recommended. The IF conditions of rule 1 are true, so the subgoal is attained and rule 3 is true.

Systems Development

The development of an ES follows much the same process as recommended for a DSS in the previous chapter. Expert-system development lends itself naturally to prototyping and learning through test cases. Sometimes the individual designing the system is called a "knowledge engineer" to distinguish him or her from a traditional systems analyst. The development process is different because advice is far more tentative than the numeric solution of a problem or the processing of transactions.

We should point out, however, how difficult it can be to conduct knowledge engineering. In the AESOP example presented below, many hours were spent in meetings with the expert and many meetings were canceled due to his schedule. It was not until the meetings moved to the floor of the American Stock Exchange just after the close of trading that we managed to make progress on the system. The expert is extremely knowledgeable and it was difficult for him to explain his logic because he was not conscious of his decision-making steps.

Figure 22-1
Expert system example.

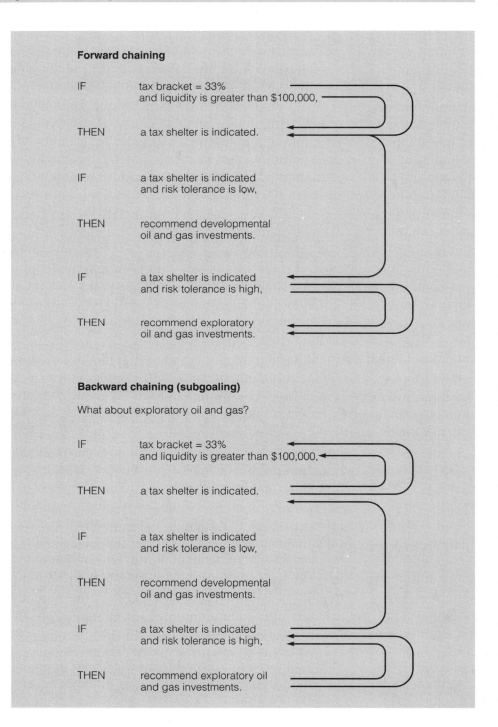

In some instances, experts are reluctant to reveal their expertise to systems developers. In many cases, systems are developed as an experiment and never fully implemented. The kind of systems described in this chapter may be some of the most difficult to implement successfully.

Three Examples

Internist-1   One of the earliest and best-known expert systems was developed to provide physicians with a consultant on internal medicine. See Figure 22-2 for a dialog with this system, which is called **Internist-1**. Professor Harry Pople and Dr. Jack Meyers at the University of Pittsburgh developed the program and built the knowledge base. The system now covers about 80 percent of internal medicine and has knowledge of some 500 diseases and 3500 manifestations of the diseases.

The Authorizer's Assistant   American Express developed an expert system called the Authorizer's Assistant. Between two hundred and three hundred authorizers work for American Express at four U.S. centers. They have the responsibility of authorizing transactions charged to American Express cards while the customer is in the store waiting for the sales transaction to be completed.

The cost of making a wrong decision is high. A refusal might alienate a customer or cause him or her to use a different card. American Express would also lose the discount it charges the merchant for processing the transaction. If credit is approved and American Express cannot collect the funds from its cardholder, it has lost the money. Losses from unpaid bills are estimated to be in the hundreds of millions of dollars per year at American Express.

Some 95 percent of the authorizations are approved automatically by a computerized system following set statistical algorithms. Remaining requests are routed to authorizers. Before the Authorizer's Assistant was developed, the human authorizer would receive a screen of data and then access more than a dozen separate database records to synthesize the information needed for a decision.

The Authorizer's Assistant expert system contains about eight hundred rules, some for combining data and others for making recommendations. The authorizers see a single screen with an accept/reject recommendation and the data on which the recommendation is based. The human still makes the final decision.

The company claims a 20 percent increase in the productivity of its authorizers as a result of the system and expects the system to pay for itself in less than two years. We should note that the user interface provided by the expert system greatly simplified the presentation of information to the human authorizer, demonstrating the importance of the interface in ES design.

Figure 22-2
An example of a session
with Internist-1.

Manifestations are expressed by means of precise sequences of terms in a controlled vocabulary; there are presently approximately 3500 vocabulary items that can be used to describe positive and negative findings.

```
   DISREGARDING: EXPOSURE TO RABBITS OR OTHER SMALL MAMMALS. LEG<S>
WEAKNESS BILATERAL. LEG<S> WEAKNESS PROXIMAL ONLY. PRESSURE ARTERIAL
ORTHOSTATIC HYPOTENSION. CREATININE BLOOD INCREASED. UREA NITROGEN
BLOOD 60 TO 100
```

```
   CONSIDERING: AGE 26 TO 55. SEX MALE. ANOREXIA. MYALGIA. VOMITING
RECENT. FECES LIGHT COLORED. FEVER. JAUNDICE. LIVER ENLARGED SLIGHT.
SKIN PALMAR ERYTHEMA. SKIN SPIDER ANGIOMATA. WBC 14000 TO 30000.
PLATELETS LESS THAN 50000
```

```
   RULEOUT. HEPATITIS CHRONIC ACTIVE. ALCOHOLIC HEPATITIS. HEPATIC
MILIARY TUBERCULOSIS. MICRONODAL CIRRHOSIS <LAENNECS>. HEPATITIS
ACUTE VIRAL
```

At this point, Internist-1 reports concerning the initial differential diagnosis that will be the focus of problem-solving attention. Three lists are displayed, labeled, respectively, DISREGARDING, CONSIDERING and RULEOUT. The CONSIDERING list identifies those positive findings whose differential diagnostic tasks were combined in coming to the differential diagnostic focus, which is described by the RULEOUT list. The DISREGARDING list tells what positive findings are not consistent with the differential diagnosis as formulated and are therefore being disregarded for the moment; they will, however, be attended to in due course. The key word RULEOUT indicates what strategy Internist-1 is going to pursue relative to this task definition; in this case, as in any case when the differential list contains five or more alternatives, the program will try to find questions to ask that, if the response is negative, will serve to downgrade the score of one or more diagnoses on the list. While pursuing a RULEOUT strategy, the program limits the questions to be asked to items of information obtainable via history or physical exam.

```
   Please Enter Findings of JAUNDICE HX
   *GO
```

There are two formats used for asking questions. In the preceding line, the user is asked to provide any data that might be available within the specified category of findings. Actually, the respondent is free to enter whatever positive or negative data are desired and is not constrained to the category mentioned in the query. In this case, the user chose to respond GO; this passes the initiative back to the program, which then typically follows up on the general question by asking about the specific finding of that category for which it particularly wants a YES or NO answer.

Figure 22-2
(continued)

```
    JAUNDICE INTERMITTENT HX?
    NO
```

If the respondent did not have any information concerning this direct question, he could have answered N/A—meaning not available.

```
    Please Enter Findings of APPETITE/WEIGHT
    *GO
```

```
    WEIGHT LOSS GTR THAN 10 PERCENT?
    NO
```

The program asks a series of questions that have been selected in accordance with its problem-solving strategy, then repeats the scoring and partitioning of the task definition procedure.

```
    DISREGARDING: EXPOSURE TO RABBITS OR OTHER SMALL MAMMALS. LEG<S>
WEAKNESS BILATERAL. LEG<S> WEAKNESS PROXIMAL ONLY. PRESSURE ARTERIAL
ORTHOSTATIC HYPOTENSION. CREATININE BLOOD INCREASED. UREA NITROGEN
BLOOD 60 TO 100.
```

```
    CONSIDERING: AGE 26 TO 55. SEX MALE. ANOREXIA. MYALGIA. VOMITING
RECENT. FECES LIGHT COLORED. FEVER. JAUNDICE. LIVER ENLARGED SLIGHT.
SKIN PALMAR ERYTHEMA. SKIN SPIDER ANGIOMATA. WBC 14000 TO 30000.
PLATELETS LESS THAN 50000
```

```
    RULEOUT: HEPATITIS CHRONIC ACTIVE. ALCOHOLIC HEPATITIS. HEPATIC
MILIARY TUBERCULOSIS. HEPATITIS ACUTE VIRAL. INFECTIOUS MONONUCLEOSIS
```

Except for the substitution of an acute process (infectious mononucleosis) for a chronic one (micronodal cirrhosis), this differential diagnosis is not significantly changed from the initial formulation. Note that the possibility of cirrhosis has not actually been ruled out; it has merely dropped out of sight because its score has fallen below the threshold used by the task definition procedure.

```
    Please Enter Findings of PAIN ABDOMEN
    *GO
```

```
    ABDOMEN PAIN GENERALIZED?
    NO
```

```
    ABDOMEN PAIN EPIGASTRIUM?
    NO
```

```
    ABDOMEN PAIN NON COLICKY?
    NO
```

Figure 22-2
(continued)

```
    ABDOMEN PAIN RIGHT UPPER QUADRANT?
    NO


    DISREGARDING: JAUNDICE. SKIN SPIDER ANGIOMATA. CREATININE BLOOD
INCREASED. UREA NITROGEN BLOOD 60 TO 100


    CONSIDERING: AGE 26 to 55. EXPOSURE TO RABBITS OR OTHER SMALL
MAMMALS. SEX MALE. ANOREXIA. DIARRHEA ACUTE. MYALGIA. VOMITING RECENT.
FEVER. LEG<S> WEAKNESS BILATERAL. LEG<S> WEAKNESS PROXIMAL ONLY.
PRESSURE ARTERIAL ORTHOSTATIC HYPOTENSION. PRESSURE ARTERIAL SYSTOLIC
90 TO 110. TACHYCARDIA. WBC 14000 TO 30000. PLATELETS LESS THAN 50000


    DISCRIMINATE: LEPTOSPIROSIS SYSTEMIC. SARCOIDOSIS CHRONIC SYSTEMIC
```

The effect of the negative responses concerning abdominal pain has been to lower the scores of all of the hepatic disorders considered in the previous differential diagnosis. This time, when the partitioning algorithm is invoked, the highest-ranking alternative is systemic leptospirosis; the only other diagnosis on the list capable of explaining substantially the same set of findings is systemic sarcoidosis. The key word DISCRIMINATE indicates that the list of alternatives contains between two and four elements, the leading two of which are selected for comparative analysis. When engaged in a DISCRIMINATE mode of analysis, the program will attempt to ask questions serving to support one diagnosis at the expense of the other; more costly procedures may be called for in order to achieve this objective.

```
    Please Enter Findings of VOMITING/REGURGITATION
    *GO


    HEMATEMESIS?
    NO


    HEMOPTYSIS GROSS?
    NO


    Please Enter Findings of TEMPERATURE
    *GO


    RIGOR<S>?
    YES


    Please Enter Findings of NEUROLOGIC EXAM CRANIAL NERVE<S>
    *GO


    NERVE PARALYSIS SEVENTH CRANIAL BILATERAL?
    NO
```

Figure 22-2
(continued)

```
    SPLENECTOMY HX?
    NO
```

The program is not actually interested in the answer to this question; what it wants to know is whether the spleen is enlarged. Because of the possibility of being misled by a negative answer, appropriate blocks have been created to prevent the program from asking about an increased spleen size in a patient whose spleen had been removed.

```
    Please Enter Findings of PALPATION ABDOMEN
    *GO


    SPLENOMEGALY MODERATE?
    NO


    Please Enter Findings of XRAY LUNG FIELD<S>


    CHEST XRAY HILAR ADENOPATHY BILATERAL?
    NO


    DISREGARDING: JAUNDICE. SKIN SPIDER ANGIOMATA. CREATININE BLOOD
INCREASED. UREA NITROGEN BLOOD 60 TO 100


    CONSIDERING: AGE 26 to 55. EXPOSURE TO RABBITS OR OTHER SMALL MAMMALS.
SEX MALE. ANOREXIA. DIARRHEA ACUTE. MYALGIA. VOMITING RECENT. FEVER.
LEG<S> WEAKNESS BILATERAL. LEG<S> WEAKNESS PROXIMAL ONLY. PRESSURE
ARTERIAL ORTHOSTATIC HYPOTENSION. PRESSURE ARTERIAL SYSTOLIC 90 TO 110.
RIGOR<S>TACHYCARDIA. WBC 14000 TO 30000. PLATELETS LESS THAN 50000


    PURSUING: LEPTOSPIROSIS SYSTEMIC
```

The questions about rigors (shaking chills) is enough to separate the scores of these items so that now there is only one alternative left in the differential diagnosis. Before concluding that this diagnosis is actually correct, however, the program will now attempt to achieve a degree of separation between this diagnosis and its nearest competitor (now below the threshold and not printed out) that is twice the threshold value. The program invokes a PURSUING strategy, which calls for the identification and acquisition of clinching data; at this stage, the level of questioning is unconstrained so the program can ask about biopsies, if useful, or other specialized procedures capable of providing pathognomonic data.

```
    LEPTOSPIRA AGGLUTINATION POSITIVE?
    YES
```

This finding is enough to clinch the diagnosis. However, the program proceeds to ask additional questions that are automatically included in each consultation.

AESOP: A System for Stock Options Pricing

Background   A **stock option** is a security giving the holder the right to buy or sell an asset at a specified time. A stock option call is the right to buy a share of stock at a certain price at a future date, a put is the right to sell a share of stock. The price at which one may purchase or sell the stock is called the strike price. On the American Stock Exchange (AMEX), options have an expiration date at which time they may be exercised. A position in an option may be closed out by purchasing an offsetting contract. All options expire on the third Saturday of the month of exercise.

Table 22-1 is an example of a call option for XYZ stock. The price of a May option to buy a share of XYZ at $40 (the "ask" price) is $3 and seven-eighths. (Options below $3 are priced in one-sixteenths, and above $3 are priced in one-eighths.) The "bid" price for the May 40 is $3 and five-eighths. The quote for the May 50 call option is "no bid," one-eighth asked. The price is given for an option to buy or sell one share of the stock, however, contracts on the AMEX are for one hundred shares. An option for a stock at a certain strike price is called an options series.

Assume that the current price of a share of XYZ is $42. A May 40 call is said to be "in the money" because, if the stock price holds until expiration, an option owner has the right to buy a share for $40 and can sell it immediately for $42. The May 45 and 50 calls are "out of the money."

An Expert Consultant for Your Doctor

A group of physicians realized that the database for an internal medicine expert system named Internist contained a wealth of information and that a retrieval program and relatively modest expert system could make this program invaluable to the physician. This group markets QMR or Quick Medical Reference, which is a PC-based diagnostic system for general internal medicine.

The program acts as a front-end to the Internist knowledge base. The system is a cost-efficient way to combine all of today's overwhelming volume of medical information. It is almost impossible for any one person to maintain a current knowledge of all medical literature, something that is important for the internist who is first and foremost a diagnostician.

On the first level, the system is an electronic textbook that displays disease descriptions and differential diagnoses for patient findings and diseases in the database. The second level of the system lets the user explore relationships among findings and disease. The third level is an expert consultant which analyzes the data and suggests diagnoses.

The system contains information on more than 4,300 symptoms and 600 internal disorders. The developers are committed to adding new diseases and the results of research findings. The program is particularly useful for diagnoses of unusual diseases or diseases where similar symptoms make diagnosis difficult.

Systems like this one turn research expert systems into decision support systems that can improve the quality of medical care and drive down costs from misdiagnosis.

Table 22-1

An Example of a Call Option

	XYZ Calls Stock Price $42					
	40		45		50	
	Bid	Ask	Bid	Ask	Bid	Ask
May	$3\frac{5}{8}$	$3\frac{7}{8}$	$0\frac{5}{16}$	$0\frac{4}{8}$	$0\frac{0}{8}$	$0\frac{1}{8}$
June	$4\frac{1}{8}$	$4\frac{3}{8}$	$0\frac{13}{16}$	$1\frac{0}{8}$	$0\frac{0}{8}$	$0\frac{1}{8}$

For puts, the opposite logic holds. A May 40 put is out of the money because, if the $42 stock price holds until the option expires, there is no gain from having the right to sell a share of stock at $40 when the market price is $42. The May 45 and May 50 puts are in the money.

The Specialist   The options specialist is a market maker in an option. He or she is responsible for posting the bid and ask quotes for the stock option at the options post on the floor of the exchange. There is only one specialist on the exchange for each stock option. The specialist maintains an inventory of options and can trade from his or her own account. Specialists also maintain a position in the underlying stock as a hedge on their inventory of options. The role of the specialist is to ensure a fair and orderly market. The specialist buys and sells from his own account to prevent price changes from being unduly erratic.

If the specialist posts an incorrect price, he or she does not obtain the maximum return on invested capital and runs the risk of incurring a large loss. Investors, noting a discrepancy between the price of the option and the underlying stock, will arbitrage against the specialist. Errors in pricing provide the investor with an opportunity for nearly risk-free profits. (The specialist's exposure is limited because a public quote is good for only a limited number of contracts.)

An important role of the specialist is to represent limit orders. The limit order is a bid to buy or sell an option at a particular price. The specialist is responsible for executing a trade for the limit order when the option price reaches the price on the limit order, assuming that he has a customer who will take the other side of the trade or that he will handle the trade from inventory.

For example, assume the specialist has a customer who puts in a limit order to buy at 4 and two-eighths and the current bid price for the option is 4 and three-eighths. The specialist can lower his quotation so that the public bid price is 4 and two-eighths. However, he cannot lower it to 4 and one-eighth because he holds a limit order from a buyer willing to pay

4 and two-eighths. Representing limit orders is currently a manual process relying on slips of paper and a good memory on the part of stock options specialists at the AMEX.

The specialist involved in this project used the Black-Scholes options-pricing model for a number of years and was reluctant to change models. The specialist provides the parameters for the model. His most frequent change is in the underlying stock price. The stock for his options is traded on the New York Stock Exchange, and the monitor at his posts displays the bid and ask prices as well as the last sale price of the underlying stock at the NYSE. The specialist also changes the interest rate for the model and inputs new volatilities for the stock.

The output of the Black-Scholes model is of invaluable assistance to the specialist. Due to the assumptions of the model and the unique situation of the specialist, however, he must modify the theoretical prices. The problem domain of the specialist requires that he take the following constraints into consideration when pricing:

1. The model outputs point estimates and the specialist must put a bid/ask spread around the theoretical price. (The specialist has a desired spread which is one of his decision variables. The stock exchange also has guidelines for spreads which are a constraint on the decision process.)

2. The specialist cannot price through limit orders. He must constantly check his book of limit orders.

3. There are a number of exchange rules which apply to pricing. For example, on the maximum spread allowed between bid and ask prices, the requirement to price is one-sixteenths below $3 and one-eighths above.

4. The specialist's own inventory position in a series.

5. The possibility that certain quotations when combined provide an opportunity for someone to arbitrage against the specialist. (The theoretical price prevents arbitrage, but some of the constraints cited in this section force the specialist to post prices that differ from the theoretical price and therefore create opportunities for arbitrage.)

6. The level of current trading activity in the option.

The Expert System   AESOP integrates the Black-Scholes mathematical model with an expert system and attempts to provide recommended quotations for the specialist that are closer to what he can post than the theoretical prices produced by the mathematical model alone. The AMEX sponsored the development of the system with a research grant. Its objective was to assess the use of expert-systems technology at the exchange. A major goal of this project was to show such a model could succeed in a challenging environment like the floor of a stock exchange.

Many expert systems are advisory and operate with loose time constraints. The options-pricing specialist must function in close to real-time as the market changes. The existing Black-Scholes model was used in batch mode. Typically the specialist worked with a printed report showing theoretical options prices for different underlying stock prices. AESOP would have to function on the floor of the exchange and provide recommendations whenever the specialist changed input parameters. The recommended prices would have to appear quickly enough to be posted to the public quote board before a trader could take advantage of an "old" price.

The expert system was developed over a two-year period with a senior options specialist at the AMEX as the human expert. The ES uses rules to represent the knowledge of the specialist. This particular approach to knowledge representation seemed natural given the environment. The American Stock Exchange has a series of rules that apply to options prices. The heuristics used by the expert specialist also seemed to follow an if-then structure: "If I am long on contracts, then reduce the asking price by one increment."

Figure 22-3 presents an overview of the AESOP system. The specialist interacts with the system through the user interface managed by AESOP's control module. When the user changes any parameter, the control module invokes the Black-Scholes mathematical model to generate theoretical prices for each series. If the specialist has four different strike prices for each month for four months for both puts and calls, there are thirty-two theoretical values to be computed (four strikes × four months for puts and calls). The expert always considers the specialist's desired spreads (the difference between bid and ask prices) and always applies the specialist's rounding rules. (Public quotations must be stated in sixteenths and eighths of a dollar.)

If the specialist's position in any series exceeds a threshold level, the expert model adjusts the price of that option to encourage (specialist is long) or discourage (specialist is short) trading. The symbolic model also

Figure 22-3
The AESOP model.

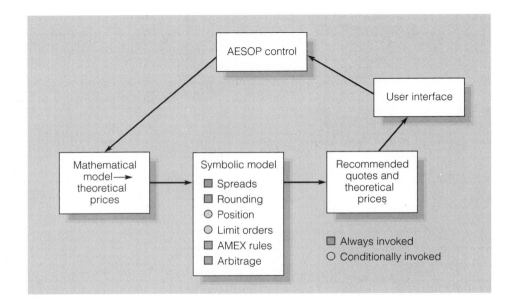

looks for limit orders and adjusts the bid/ask prices based on the presence of these orders. Limit order adjustments are the most complicated and potentially the most valuable feature of the symbolic model.

The expert system always checks the AMEX rules to be sure exchange regulations are not violated. The model also scans for arbitrage possibilities. In almost all cases, arbitrage arises because bid/ask prices are adjusted away from the theoretical price for some reason, most often because of the presence of a limit order.

The user interface presents the recommended quotations of the symbolic model along with the theoretical prices generated by the mathematical model. The user is free to override any recommendations, ask for an explanation or trace of the symbolic model, and/or change parameters, and rerun the entire system.

Figure 22-4 is a print of the main AESOP screen, but the figure in no way does justice to the color coding and pop-up windows that characterize the interface. The menu within the user interface is activated by function keys shown at the bottom of Figure 22-4. Submenus appear on the second and third line of the screen and follow Lotus conventions.

The user interface provides the following functions:

- Entering and processing limit orders

```
AESOP - AN EXPERT SYSTEM FOR OPTIONS PRICING          ACCT: RIC OPTION: TANCALLS

                                                                 2:05 PM

     MONTH  STRIKE  TH.VA    LIMIT.BOOK     RECCO.QUOTE     CURR.BOARD
                             BID    ASK     BID    ASK      BID    ASK   STOCK
     MAY    40.00   3.72                    3^5    3^7      3^6    4^0    43.500
            45 00   0 35                    0^05   0^4      0^3    0^09   XDIV
            50.00   0.00            0^1     0^0    0^1      0^0    0^1    06/25/09
     JUNE   40.00   4.15                    4^1    4^3      4^2    4^4    INT.RATE
            45.00   0.89                    0^13   1^0      0^7    1^1    10.25
            50.00   0.06            0^2     0^0    0^1      0^01   0^03   V1
     JUL    35.00   9.15                    9^0    9^3      9^1    9^5    22
            40.00   4.52                    4^3    4^6      4^4    4^7    V2
            45.00   1.34    0^09            1^1    1^3      1^2    1^4    21
            50.00   0.21    0^2    0^5      0^2    0^05     0^2    0^3    V3
     OCT    40.00   5.65    2^1             5^4    5^7      5^4    6^0    20
            45.00   2.54           4^0      2^05   2^09     2^3    2^5    V4
            50.00   0.88           1^3      0^13   1^0      0^7    1^01   20

                                                                 FN.KEYS
                                                                 AF1 DEL.LO
                                                                 AF3 CHG.PR
                                                                 AF5 DL.OVR

     F1-LimO F2-OVS F3-Parms F4-Expln F5-Ovrd F6-Send F7-Posn F8-Log F9-Calc F10-End
```

Figure 22-4   The main AESOP screen.

- Invoking a system for updating contracts, positions, etc.
- Changing parameters in the Black-Scholes model or bid/ask spreads
- Explaining the reasoning behind each recommended quotation and alerting the user to arbitrage possibilities
- Manually overriding any recommended price
- Posting recommended quotations to the "Current Board" columns on the screen
- Displaying the position or changing the threshold position for position rules to apply
- Turning a log on or off
- Running the Black-Scholes model

AESOP was used on an experimental basis for two months by a specialist who works with one of the system designers. Figure 22-5 compares AESOP's recommendations with the actual quotes posted by the specialist for calls with an ask price in eighths. The graph presents the number of times the specialist posted what AESOP recommended (the "=" column in Figure 22-5) and a distribution for the number of increments by which the specialist's and AESOP's quotes differed. As an example, Figure 22-5 shows that 269 times the specialist posted the ask price in eighths recommended by AESOP; 151 times the specialist raised the recommended bid by one-eighth, and 256 times he lowered it by one-eighth.

Further analysis of puts and calls showed that AESOP performs best on calls. There is more trading activity in calls than in puts. AESOP also performs better on eighths than sixteenths, which seems reasonable as it is more difficult to select the "right price" out of sixteen increments than out

Figure 22-5
Calls ask price in eighths.

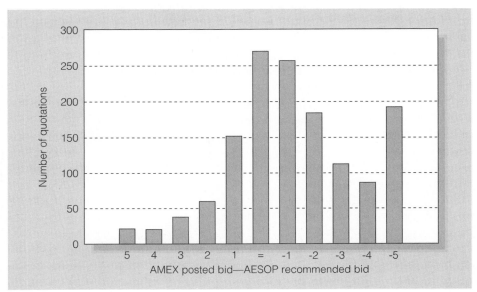

of eight. It appears AESOP is successful in demonstrating an expert system can improve the ease of use of a mathematical model and it can do so in a demanding, semi-real-time environment.

NEURAL NETWORKS

The field of **neural networks** has recently received a great deal of attention. This approach to AI was first suggested many years ago but only recently became fashionable. The first neural networks were loosely based on how the brain functions. The brain consists of **neurons** which can be thought of as small processing units. Outside stimuli or other neurons provide input for a given neuron. The neurons are connected in a large, complex network.

The network has **dendrites** which transmit messages across various paths. The dendrites are like highways connecting the network. A **synapse** exists where the network connects with a particular neuron. There can be many dendrites (thousands) leading to a single neuron. In the brain the neurons function through a chemical or electrical impulse. These impulses can either excite the neuron and it can "fire," sending a message across the network, or the impulses can inhibit a neuron to keep it from firing. This output goes across a single axon that transmits the neuron's signal to the network. It is estimated that there are trillions of neurons (possibly 10^{12}) in the human brain (Zahedi, 1993).

How does the analogy of the human brain help create an AI program? The most popular type of neural network is used to classify input into different categories. Figure 22-6 shows the basic building blocks for a neural network: neuron i connected to neuron j. The weight w_{ij} represents the strength of the connection between the two neurons. In a neural network, there are at least two layers of neurons. The input layer receives input from the external environment. The output layer consists of neurons that communicate the output of the system to the user. Figure 22-7 shows a neural network consisting of three layers.

Figure 22-6
Neural nodes.

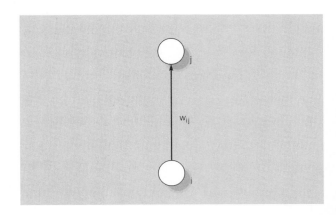

Figure 22-7
A three-layer neural network.

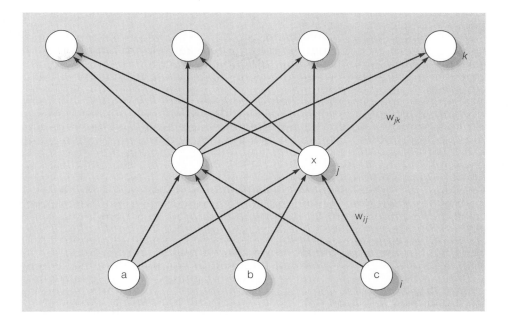

The input to a neuron consists of a weighted sum of all the neurons connected to it which fired. For example, in Figure 22-7 the input to neuron x consists of the output from neurons a, b, and c (assuming that they fired) multiplied by their respective weights. If the sum of this output exceeds some threshold value, neuron x will fire and send its output to the next layer according to the weights connecting it to layer k. The network has to be trained to establish the weights for the connections.

In the simplest network, neurons in one layer are connected only to neurons in the next layer. More-complex networks feature neurons that are connected within a layer. Probably the most common business uses of neural nets feature **feed-forward networks**; the neurons in one layer receive inputs from the layer below and send outputs to the layer above. In a feed-forward network the flow of inputs is in one direction, from the input layer, through intermediate layers, and finally to the output layer.

Neural networks have proven to be quite robust in classification problems. For example, suppose that your firm wants to classify new customers into four types: those who are likely to pay their bills on time, those who may take between two and three months to pay, those taking three to six months, and those who are not likely to pay at all. You might design a neural network to try to classify potential customers. The input to the network would be information about the customer, and the output would be a classification into one of four groups corresponding to the likely payment categories.

First you must design the network and then train it. Typically you would choose a feed-forward network with at least three layers. There is an input layer and an output layer plus one or more hidden layers in between. The layers have connections from the input to the hidden to the output layers. There are also backward connections which are only used for training the network.

To train the network, you present it with past cases, data on customer attributes, and how these former customers paid their bills. Learning is through **back propagation**, because the learning program looks at the output and then works backward to adjust the **weights** for the connections between neurons. There are various learning rules which are used to adjust the weights during training. For example, the delta training rule attempts to minimize the sum of squared errors between the actual output of the system and the correct output. If, during the training, your network misclassified a former customer, the delta rule would adjust the weights to try to minimize the error. After training with a large number of cases, the weights should stabilize and the network is ready for use. At this point, you begin to use the network to classify new customers based on the same kind of input information you used to train the network.

There are PC shell programs available to help develop neural net applications. This AI approach is used to predict bankruptcies and help identify thoroughbred horses based on blood samples. A neural network is one way to think about some classification and prediction problems. There are also other ways to classify and predict based on classical statistical procedures such as discriminant analysis, linear regression, and exponential smoothing, to name a few. One challenge is to find the most appropriate technique to use for a given problem.

Neural Net After Credit Card Thieves

Large criminal cases make the news, but credit card and other types of banking fraud have hit all-time highs. Mellon Bank of Pittsburgh has installed a fraud detection system on a mainframe computer, designed to catch credit crooks using neural net technology. The software automatically changes the way it weights different variables and learns to recognize patterns in credit card transactions.

The system creates and manages its own database of credit card customer accounts. It examines more than a million transactions per hour on the mainframe and assigns each card a score based on the likelihood that it is fraudulent. The bank specifies what score it wants to use to take an action like checking identification at the point of sale or denying purchases.

Visa and MasterCard report fraud losses of more than $500 million per year, and in the last year, Mellon's losses increased 50 percent. The neural network learns customer spending patterns and detects subtle changes that may indicate fraud. It replaces a rule-based system that flagged entries only if card activity was very high or purchases began to exceed a preset amount.

Case-Based Reasoning

Case-based reasoning (CBR) captures lessons from past experience and uses them to find solutions to a new problem. CBR is both a problem-solving approach and a model of how some experts think individuals learn, remember, and think about problems. A case-based model is particularly appropriate when rules cannot express the richness of the knowledge domain. CBR is described as most useful when there is rich experience, but little knowledge.

A case-based system needs cases, a similarity index, a case retrieval mechanism, and an explanation module. A case is similar to the cases you study in school: it has a set of features, attributes and relations, and an associated outcome. A case is specific to a given situation, unlike a general rule in a rule-based expert system. The PERSUADER is a case-based system for mediating management and labor disputes. For this CBR, a case is a past labor dispute similar to the one it now faces. A repository of past cases is crucial. The more cases and the greater the variety of experiences they represent, the better the recommendations from the system.

A set of indices is the mechanism through which cases similar to the one under consideration are located. The indexing process stores cases and generates similarity indices to be used in retrieving cases similar to the one at hand. The task of developing robust indices is one of the biggest challenges facing developers of case-based systems. Another component, the retrieval mechanism, must retrieve cases with the closest match between attributes of past cases and the current case on which advice is sought. The explanation module allows the system to explain its analysis of the current problem and a proposed solution. It should describe why and how the present problem is similar to past cases.

A user presents the system with a problem and the system indexes its attributes, features, and relations based on standards built into the system. The system uses these indices to retrieve a set of similar past cases and their solutions based on the indices created when the cases were originally added to the knowledge base. The system examines the cases retrieved from "memory" to find the best fit with the current problem. It also examines the solution to past cases until it can generate a proposed solution to the problem at hand. If the system's proposed solution is accepted, it incorporates the current case into its knowledge base to be used again in the future.

Genetic Algorithms

The traditional approach to solving problems in artificial intelligence involves looking at a single candidate for a solution and iteratively manipulating it using various heuristics or "rules of thumb." Genetic algorithms work on a population of candidates at the same time. This population of candidate solutions may be as few as ten to several thousands. Figure 22-8 describes these **evolutionary computations**. In general the approach involves generating a population of possible problem solutions (the unrated population in the figure) and rating them based on some **fitness function**. The next step is to apply a selection function to the unrated population to select "parents" for the next generation of solutions. A reproduction function generates copies of the parents. These copies go through **mutation** operations to create the next generation of solutions for evaluation, closing the loop in the figure at the "unrated population" in the upper left-hand corner.

To start, a genetic algorithm rates how good each solution is for the problem under consideration using a fitness function. This function is similar to a cost function used in other search techniques. The function returns a number denoting the worth of the solution just evaluated. The objective of the genetic algorithm is to minimize (or maximize, depending on the problem) the value returned by the fitness function.

Once the fitness function evaluates all candidates, the genetic algorithm selects a subset of the population to form "parents" for a new population. The algorithm chooses parents based on the relative worth of the candidates in the population as determined by the fitness function. Genetic algorithms feature a variety of selection methods to designate the parents. As an example, a simple strategy would be to take the best half of the current population to be the parents for the next generation. Most of the time, the selection of the better part of the population is augmented with lesser fitness scores to promote diversity.

Are the Markets Efficient?

Most business school finance and economics faculty members have an abiding faith in the efficient capital markets hypothesis. This hypothesis states that the market reflects all information and that securities prices are therefore random. Having past prices and new information does not let you predict future stock prices. Markets are considered to be very efficient processors of information so that people in the market react instantaneously to information; the market has discounted information and relected it in the price of a security before you can move.

One economist argues that it might be possible to get an edge because the efficient capital markets hypotheses was developed during the days when there was ample time for information about a stock to be absorbed by traders and reflected in the price. Today, networks deluge traders with huge amounts of information, more than a person can digest. It is hard to believe that all this information is reflected in the price at every instant.

Two physicists who have done research on complex systems have started a company that is trying to find hidden patterns to predict stock prices. Prediction Company uses AI software to analyze market and financial data; it sends trading signals to its partner, the Swiss Bank Corporation, which places bets on the movements of foreign exchange rates, interest rates, stock and commodity prices. Some of the company's programs use neural nets while others use genetic algorithms.

If the company is doing well, according to the efficient markets hypotheses, it could be a matter of luck; if the markets are random you will guess right some of the time. How much success would Prediction need to convince you that an expert system is better at predicting the market than other techniques, or that the market is not a random walk?

Figure 22-8
General procedure
for all evolutionary
computations. A
complete cycle from
unrated population to
unrated population
represents one
generation of the search.

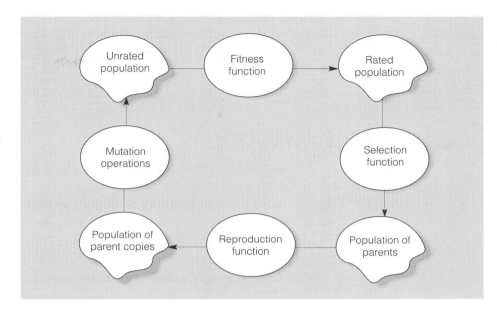

To create a new generation of possible solutions, the genetic algorithm applies operators known as mutations to copies of the parents it has selected. These mutations alter the content of the parents. As shown in Figure 22-9 genetic algorithms represent problem solutions as fixed length vectors containing features of the solution. Genetic algorithms mimic the manipulation of DNA and gene sequences. The mutations include **inversion**, point mutation, and **crossover** as shown in the figure. The inversion operation reverses the order of randomly selected, contiguous portions of the vector. A point mutation alters a single feature, replacing it with a randomly chosen value. The crossover operator randomly selects a sequence of features and swaps them between two parents. This later mutation is the most popular and most frequently used. The creation of populations stops after a set number of generations or after the fitness function reaches a predetermined value.

A rule-based expert system will show the rules that "fired" and allow the user to trace through the solution. Like neural networks, genetic algorithms

Figure 22-9
Inversion (a),
point mutations (b),
and crossover (c)
operations used in
genetic algorithms.

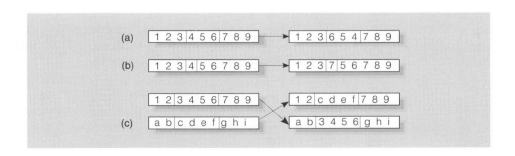

do not provide the user with an understanding of how they reached a solution. Both of these techniques provide good solutions to a variety of problems despite the drawback that their solution mechanism is not obvious.

CHAPTER SUMMARY

1. Intelligent systems exhibit behavior that would be called intelligent if viewed by a person.
2. Intelligent systems process symbols as well as numbers.
3. The first widespread applications of artificial intelligence to business was through expert systems.
4. An expert system has a knowledge base and inference engine.
5. An expert system may represent knowledge through the use of rules or frames.
6. An ES is developed through prototyping and it is important to test it carefully.
7. Expert systems perform well in the domain for which they were designed, but have no knowledge of other domains, while most humans are capable of reasonably intelligent behavior over a variety of domains.
8. Neural networks are an intelligent system loosely based on how the brain functions.
9. The user trains a neural network with a number of cases so the network can solve future problems with similar characteristics.
10. Case-based reasoning uses past experience as a guide to offering a solution to a current problem.
11. Genetic algorithms are based on evolution. They evaluate a large population of potential solutions to a problem, select parents for the next generation of solutions, and apply mutation operators to produce the next generation of solutions for evaluation.
12. Intelligent systems may provide the firm with a number of advantages. For example, they can make expertise widely available in the organization.
13. These systems can also perform more mundane tasks, such as the expert system for accepting securities in the brokerage office in the Merrill Lynch example in Chapter 18.
14. The technology discussed in this and the previous chapter extends the power of the computer to the direct support of decision making and management action. The manager does not have to scan a report and interpret data. He or she interacts with a system designed to support decisions.

IMPLICATIONS FOR MANAGEMENT

When expert systems first became popular, some forecasters suggested that they would forever alter the nature of information processing. Initial enthusiasm waned as the difficulties of developing intelligent systems became more apparent. There is certainly a role for this technology as the examples show. However, you have to regard the development of an ES as an R&D project. It is certainly more risky than a conventional application.

KEY WORDS

Artificial intelligence (AI)
Back propagation
Backward chaining
Case-based reasoning (CBR)
Crossover
Dendrite
Evolutionary computations
Expert system
Feed-forward network
Fitness function
Forward chaining
Frame
Genetic algorithm
Heuristic

Inference engine
Internist-1
Inversion
Knowledge base
Knowledge engineering
Mutation
Neural network
Neuron
Semantic network
Shell
Stock option
Synapse
User interface
Weight

RECOMMENDED READING

Clifford, J., H. C. Lucas, Jr., and R. Srikanth. "Integrating Symbolic and Mathematical Models Through AESOP: A System for Stock Options Pricing," *Information Systems Research* (December 1992). (A paper describing the AESOP system presented in this chapter.)

Gill, T. G. "Early Expert Systems: Where Are They Now?," *MIS Quarterly,* vol. 19, no. 1 (March 1995), pp. 51-70. (The author presents a survey of users of expert systems and reports that only about a third of the systems continue to be used; he offers some conclusions about the difficulty of implementing ES.)

Gupta, U. "How Case-Based Reasoning Solves New Problems," *Interfaces* (November-December 1994), pp. 110-119. (A good introduction to CBR.)

Luconi, F. L., T. Malone, and M. S. Scott Morton. "Expert Systems: The Next Challenge for Managers," *Sloan Management Review* (Summer 1986), pp. 3–14. (An excellent introductory article on expert systems.)

DISCUSSION QUESTIONS

1. What are the reasons for developing an expert system?
2. What are the differences between an expert system and conventional system?
3. In what ways does an expert system resemble a decision support system?
4. What is backward chaining? Forward chaining?
5. Why are production rule systems popular for advisory systems in business?
6. What is the attraction of using an ES shell on a PC for developing a system?
7. What is the difference between knowledge engineering and systems analysis?
8. How could a system like Internist-1 be used?
9. Why is a mistake costly for American Express in authorizing credit card purchases?
10. Why is prototyping a good approach for the development of an ES?
11. What is the purpose of the inference engine in an expert system?
12. How is symbolic processing different from numeric processing? (*Hint:* Review the example of forward and backward chaining in the chapter.)
13. Why is the user interface an important component of an expert system?
14. What are the differences in managing an expert-systems development project and designing a transactions processing system?
15. How does one go about identifying the expert to be used in developing an expert system?
16. What techniques can you suggest to help the designer extract and document the expert's knowledge?
17. How does a knowledge base differ from a conventional database?
18. What kinds of problems are best suited to the use of a neural network?
19. What steps are involved in creating a neural net?
20. Explain the way a genetic algorithm functions. What is the underlying model for this approach to intelligent systems?

CHAPTER 22 PROJECT

EXPERT SYSTEMS

The admissions department in your school has asked for your help in developing an expert system for rating candidates. The system should take three input conditions into account:

- Graduate Management Aptitude Test (GMAT) score

- Grade point average (GPA)
- Experience (good, average, poor)

The user will evaluate experience directly from the application. The expert system should come up with a value for overall academic performance as good, average, or poor by combining the results of the GMAT and GPA. The rules are as follows:

GMAT and	GPA	Performance
>= 575	>= 3.3	Good
> 525	<= 2.8 GPA < 3.3	Average
< 525		Poor
	< 2.8	Poor
525=< GMAT< 575	> 2.8	Average

The rules for acceptance are as follows:

Academics	Experience	Action
Good	Good	Accept
Good	Average	Accept
Good	Poor	Waiting list
Average	Good	Waiting list
Any other combination		Reject

Use an expert system shell on a PC to develop this expert system and run several examples to demonstrate how it works.

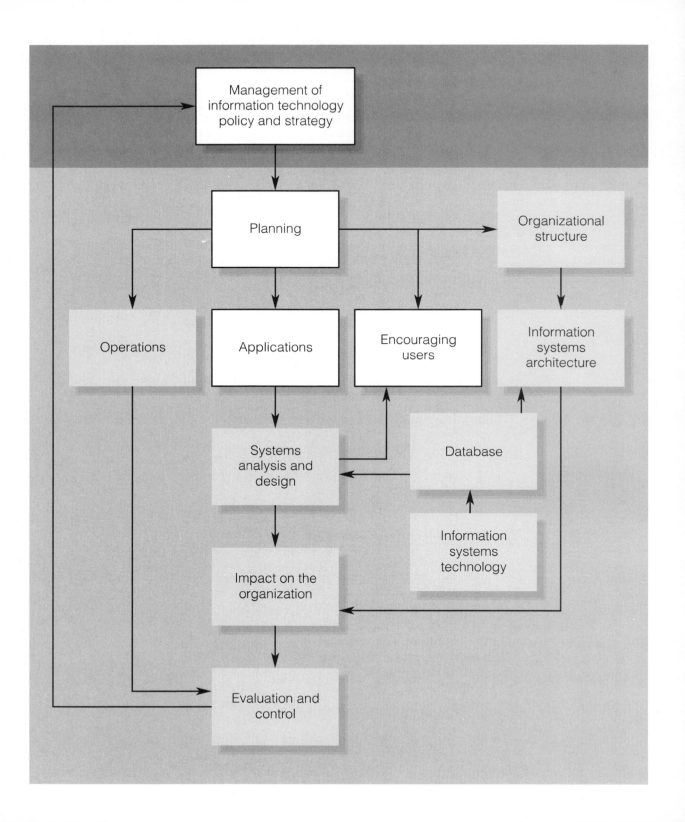

Issues for Senior Management

VI

We conclude the book with an examination of special management concerns about information technology. What are the special problems of managing IT? What do future trends in management and technology mean for the organization? How will new technologies affect the firm? To enjoy all of the benefits from IT we have discussed to this point, you have to be able to manage the technology.

The last chapter expands the boundaries of information systems beyond the organization to include society at large. What social implications should the manager consider when making decisions about information technology? What is the future of this technology? Will IT continue to transform the organization and the way we work?

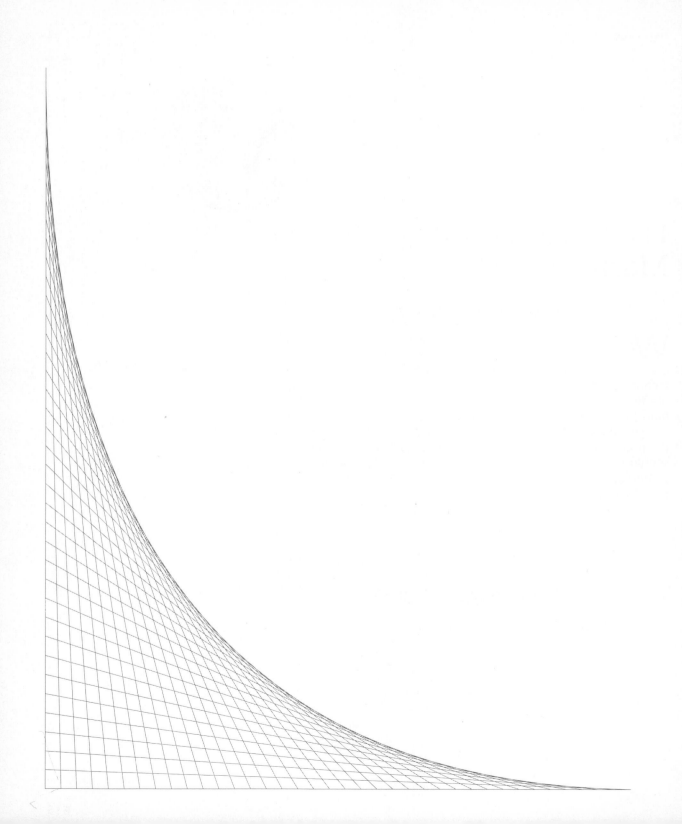

CHAPTER **23**

Management Control of Information Technology

OBJECTIVES

1. **Learning to manage information technology.**

   Control is one of management's major responsibilities in the organization. Information systems offer one tool for controlling the organization, for example, through budget systems or applications to monitor risk. Management must also control information processing, as the firm's investment in technology becomes significant in terms of both capital investment and operating expenses. You also need to control technology because most organizations depend on it to continue functioning!

2. **Preparing to apply technology.**

    A design team must carefully consider control issues in developing a system. Think about how you can apply the control model presented in this chapter to the design of a new information system.

3. **Transforming the organization.**

    Information technology can provide novel ways to control the organization making possible new organizational structures and alliances with external firms. Managerial control and coordination are closely related. New organizational forms must address the issue of how management can control the organization.

MANAGEMENT CONTROL

One of the fundamental roles of management in an organization is control. What is control? How do managers control the organization? This chapter seeks to answer these questions, particularly with respect to information systems.

Control Theory

Process control offers a useful model for thinking about control in general. Consider Figure 23-1, which shows a typical control system. In this system, an adjustable standard sets desired performance. A sensor determines actual conditions, and a comparison device compares the standard with what actually exists. If the difference between reality and the standard is too great, the comparison device sends a signal to take action. The action

Figure 23-1
A control system.

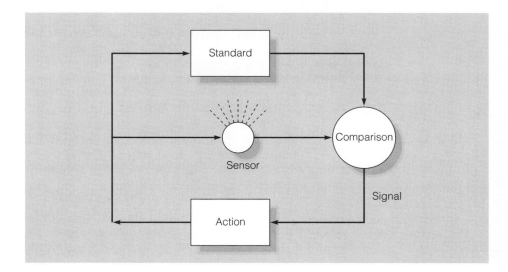

taken in turn affects the sensor and standard, and the cycle continues until the comparison device finds agreement between sensor and standard and stops signaling for action.

A real example of this model may be found in an automobile's cruise control system. We set the adjustable standard—the speed we desire—using the cruise control button. A sensor determines the car's speed, and a control unit compares the desired setting and the current speed. If the difference between the two is too great, the cruise control system increases or decreases the throttle appropriately.

This example shows how a basic control system functions. In an organization, we can apply the same concepts. Managers have a notion of a standard, and they must become aware of deviations from the standard. Given that some indicator deviates from the standard, management must take action to bring the organization back into control.

Control in the Organization

Figure 23-2 shows some of the tools available to managers at different levels for controlling the organization. Top management can create control through the structure of the organization. For example, management can decide to decentralize and to have local managers responsible for comparing their performance with the goals the managers set for the year. As an alternative, top management can opt for a high degree of centralization so it can set policy and review all decisions.

Our discussions of the T-Form organization suggest that in the future, management will have a more difficult time using traditional methods such as structure for control. Hierarchical structures are in retreat and managers will have to trust subordinates and come up with new ways to exercise their

Figure 23-2
Tools of management control.

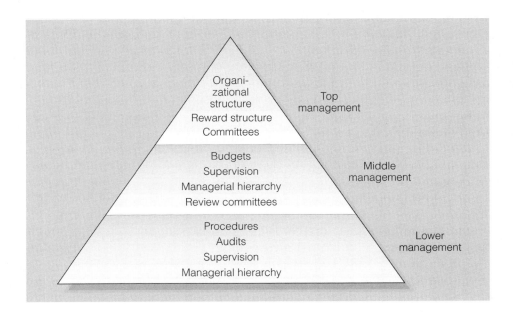

responsibility for control. An example later in the chapter shows how Mrs. Fields Cookies uses technology and IT to develop a unique control system.

Top management also exerts control through the reward structure. Several brokerage firms suffered control breakdowns, partially, we suspect, because of a reward structure encouraging heavy risk taking in bond trading. The firms paid bond traders very large bonuses based on performance as bond trading is highly competitive among firms. More than one firm found it lost well over $100 million in a few weeks when the market turned against its traders. There was a highly motivating reward system and almost no managerial control over the traders. Two banks recently found losses of over one billion dollars in unauthorized trading, forcing one bank into a merger.

One form of managerial control that is used frequently and probably could have helped ameliorate the bond trader problem is the management committee. For many years banks have employed loan review committees. The lending officer has a certain limit he or she can approve on a loan. Any loan larger than the limit must be discussed and ultimately approved by the committee. The committee serves a review and control role in the firm.

The most frequent middle-management control device is the budget. Many managers in the organization receive periodic budget reports that inform them of actual versus targeted performance. Budgets are extremely important tools for controlling expenditures.

Taurus—The Project That Couldn't

In 1989 the Bank of England started a working group to design a new, paperless system for processing settlements on the London Stock Exchange. The Exchange had become electronic after the Big Bang in 1986. The cost of a centralized clearing system was estimated at 60 million pounds, so the committee came up with a design based on distributed databases at hundreds of sites, with many different kinds of hardware and software linked to the Stock Exchange through a network. Work started on the system in 1990 with an estimated budget of 50 million pounds. A package from a New York firm was to be the base of the system (it was the market leader); the design would use a structured methodology.

The date for completing the system gradually slipped and its costs rose, first to 75 million pounds. By the fall of 1992 it was clear that the basic architecture of the system had not been completed. A full review in January of 1993 determined that its underlying problems were so serious that it would take another three years to complete and that its cost would double. In March of 1993, the Stock Exchange announced that work on Taurus was to be abandoned. By this time costs had reached 400 million pounds! The failure of Taurus was significant enough that the head of the London Stock Exchange resigned because of its failure.

Management has to control the organization, but it also needs to control individual projects, especially when they are critical to the organization. Taurus cost a huge amount of money and cost a senior executive his job.

Middle managers are also expected to exert direct supervision over their subordinates, though more remote work makes this difficult. When in doubt they can refer problems up through a managerial hierarchy. The entire structure of management serves to control the organization and keep it on course. Middle managers can also establish review committees to foster greater control.

At the lowest levels of management, we find procedures describing how operations should be done. Procedures were particularly evident in paperwork transactions processing departments. If one visited an accounts-payable operation, it was possible to see clerks who carefully looked up each bill the firm receives to find the purchase order that authorized the purchase. The clerk saw that the goods or services purchased actually arrived and delivery was satisfactory. Then the clerk authorized the payable and put all the documents relating to the payment into a voucher, which was filed for a number of years.

This kind of manual accounts payable operation is rapidly vanishing, which creates new control problems for the organization. Consider Chrysler's Pay as Built program where it calculates what it owes suppliers based on each day's production and sends an electronic payment. How does Chrysler know and how do its suppliers know the calculations and payment are correct? At some point in time, the number of components shipped to Chrysler should match the payments, but verifying these transactions could be a formidable task.

Regular, routine audits help to establish control by showing control is important and by sending the message there is a form of quality control over all the firm's procedures, or at least those that affect the financial statements. Lower-level managers also have direct supervision responsibilities. They too can make use of the managerial hierarchy to obtain approvals or additional guidance.

Failure of Control

What happens when management control fails? Very often, a firm fails as a result of a control breakdown. In the computer industry, there are notable examples of firms with very few controls. While the single product the firm sold was in demand, it was possible for high sales to mask the lack of budgets and the absence of controls over expenditures. However, when demand for the product dropped, the failure to have a budget or to control expenditures pushed the computer firm into bankruptcy.

Information and Control

One contribution of information systems is to strengthen control systems. A manager needs information about the deviation of actual from standard, or targeted performance. Computerized budget systems help managers identify exceptions and take action. Executive information systems, discussed in Chapter 21, monitor critical indicators for management. Senior management may be able to take immediate action if sales are falling below projections. Managers may alter production schedules, emphasize different products, and/or begin to reduce expenditures.

Although information systems can help to improve managerial control, they create a tremendous control problem themselves. Information systems are very complex. For example, it is likely no one person understands everything about a large system like SABRE. Managers who do not necessarily understand the technology are responsible for seeing information systems are under control.

Control Through IT at Mrs. Fields

Mrs. Fields Cookies is an oft-cited example of a firm that has used information technology as a part of its organization structure. Mrs. Fields Cookies is a chain of small retail outlets, typically found in shopping malls, which sell several varieties of cookies and a few other selected food items. In 1988 there were approximately 500 retail stores world-wide. Stores follow a formula of consistent, uniform quality and price regardless of location. However, Mrs. Fields Cookies has a unique structure. It has two parallel organizations, one of which has a traditional span of control and another which has a very high span of control.

The traditional hierarchy is formed by 500 store managers, 105 district sales managers, 17 regional directors, four senior regional directors, a VP of operations and finally Debbie Fields. The span of control of this hierarchy is about 1:5.

The second organization is a formal reporting relationship for control purposes; here 500 store managers report to six store controllers, who report to the VP of operations. The span of control between store managers and controllers is 35 to 75: 1, which represents a very flat organization structure. The "human" side of management at Mrs. Fields is through a traditional hierarchy. The "numbers" side is a flat organization made possible through information technology.

Until recently, every shop was wholly-owned by the company rather than franchised, and the company was under the strong centralized control of Mrs. Fields and her husband. The unique organization of Mrs. Fields Cookies allowed the owners maximum flexibility in adapting its offerings to the changing tastes of customers in a "fad" business.

IT is an integral part of the structure of Mrs. Fields Cookies. Each store is connected on-line to a central database, and there is extensive automation of production quotas, sales volumes, etc. based on recent daily sales records for each store. In fact, each store is given hourly sales projections and reports hourly sales results. All ordering of supplies (e.g., chocolate chips) is done automatically from the central database with direct delivery to the store.

Each store's product mix, sales quotas, and special promotions, is customized by an expert system that adapts to hourly sales. The company also uses IT for coordination, through voice mail and electronic mail so each store manager has direct personal interaction with Mrs. Fields herself. Company-wide announcements are frequently broadcast to each store by voice mail, significantly personalizing the announcement compared to memos and reports. (Debbie Fields was a cheerleader in high school and voice mail seems a natural way to rally the troops.) Each manager may send Mrs. Fields electronic messages for particular problems and expect a personal response within forty-eight hours.

CONTROL OF SYSTEMS DEVELOPMENT

An important area in which organizations face loss of control is in the development of new information systems. As discussed in Part Four, each new system has a research flavor. It is hard to predict how long it will take and how much it will cost to develop something new. Since most systems have components that are new, there is a great deal of uncertainty in development.

There have been management problems at Mrs. Fields. The firm expanded rapidly, possibly encouraged by the success of its technology, and ran into difficulty integrating its acquisition, La Petite Boulangerie, with its traditional cookie stores. While Mrs. Fields can change its mix of cookies easily, the original cookie operation is basically a one-product business. The firm is also reported to have had difficulties with its product and market mix when it entered international markets.

Unfortunately, Mrs. Fields' high debt created problems in 1991. Trading of its stock was suspended pending restructuring of its $70 million debt. Undeterred by debt, in 1992, Mrs. Fields Cookies and Pastereleria el Molino announced a leasing agreement to open 50 stores in Mexico over a five-year period. In May of 1992, Mrs. Fields launched Fields Ice Cream. The company also started Mrs. Fields Mini Cookie Store, a cart equipped with a cookie baking oven designed to be set up in grocery stores.

The March 1, 1993 Business Week reported that Mrs. Fields "is throwing in her apron." On February 17, Debbie Fields, who started her cookie-making empire in Palo Alto, Calif., back in 1977, stepped down as president and chief executive officer. Fields, who retains her position as chairwoman, turned over nearly 80% of the company to four lenders led by Prudential Insurance Co."

Mrs. Fields' problems probably did not stem from its control system. Rather, it appears that Mrs. Fields as an organization became overconfident of its abilities to manage businesses that were not a part of its core. A bakery chain like La Petite Boulangerie is different from a cookie store. Did the technology lead management into a false sense of confidence and invulnerability?

The example shows that you can use technology to personalize and control the business. All Mrs. Fields stores look alike and suffer from high labor turnover. Mrs. Fields was very concerned about control and about quality. The technology helped her manage these two aspects of the business. First, store controllers are a control mechanism. Second, the control of quality is an important issue for Mrs. Fields. The combination of in-store computers, uniform recipes and cooking instructions, and uniform ingredients help provide quality control. Voice mail and e-mail helped motivate, and to some extent, control employees. At Mrs. Fields, control comes from a combination of structure and technology; there is no single IT variable for control. A group of design variables and the structure of the organization together provide control.

The technology allowed Debbie and Randy Fields to create different types of organization structures within the same firm. They could also "micromanage" what was happening at individual stores through the controllers at headquarters. The unanswered question is whether or not the technology helped lead top management away from their core business into ventures they did not understand well.

It is quite possible that the majority of information systems developed to date have suffered from being over budget, from being beyond targeted completion time, and/or from not meeting their specifications. How can general management control systems development?

Some of the development techniques discussed earlier, especially the alternatives to traditional design examined in Chapter 17, help provide control. The use of a package, if carefully selected, should reduce uncertainty because we can see the package and we know code exists that has been executed before installation. Prototyping should help in forecasting what effort is required to develop a system. The use of fourth-generation languages can reduce programming time, given that the language meets performance requirements.

Managers also help control development projects by attending review sessions and providing input. Projects slip for a number of reasons, including lack of user input, too few resources, too few individuals working on the project, and lack of management support. Managers who stay in close contact with the progress of a project are in a position to allocate new resources or to influence development priorities.

It is also important to be sure that the information services staff is concerned about project management. There are many programmers and analysts who view their profession as a craft-like trade. They feel that time spent managing a project is wasted and could be better spent in doing analysis or programming. Management must demonstrate that it wants projects to be controlled. One approach is to insist on the use of project management tools like CPM. Another is to consider the use of tools like designers' workbenches and CASE tools to help manage and control projects.

CONTROL OF OPERATIONS

In addition to controlling systems development, management must be concerned about controls over the operations of systems.

- At least twice before the collapse of the Soviet Union, air defense alarms signaled the launching of Soviet missiles aimed at the United States from both land bases and submarines. The first time, officers in charge of the system suspected something was wrong with the data. In flight, the missiles supposedly appeared on only one sensor and not on others. However, the defense command remained on alert status for more than five minutes, and fighter planes were sent aloft while the data were checked.

The monitors were wrong. Through a human error, a connection was made between an off-line computer running a simulation exercise of the firing of land- and submarine-based missiles and the on-line computer monitoring air defense at the time. Because the test tape did not simulate data from all sensors, the officers in command were suspicious. What would have happened if the simulation were complete? (No details were released on the second incident.)

- Near the end of 1985, a computer problem at the Bank of New York nearly halted the treasury bond market for twenty-eight hours. The computer program had a counter for the number of transactions that could reach as high as 32,000 items. On the day of the failure, the number of transactions exceeded 32,000 for the first time. The computer then stored each record on top of the last one, losing data and corrupting the database.

Control in the Air

We have seen that elaborate computer networks help you make a reservation on an airplane and help the airlines manage all aspects of their business. What happens when you get on the plane and the Air Traffic Control (ACT) system takes over? What is supposed to happen is that the airport tower assumes control for takeoff and hands the plane off to a Terminal Radar Approach Control (TRACON) facility which directs planes at low altitude and around airports. The TRACON passes the plane to a Control Center which directs aircraft after they are at high altitudes.

For a variety of reasons from government procurement policies to poor project management, plans to upgrade the air traffic control (ATC) system have left us with an antique system. The good news is that it seems to work most of the time. However, at least 11 times in 1994-5, air traffic control centers have had problems or broken down completely. Some of the computers that help track planes are 25 years old. Unfortunately, much of the original software was written in assembly language or a special language called JOVIAL. This code must be updated before the computers can be replaced.

When the main computers fail, a backup system from the 1980s takes over to provide radar data to the controllers. However, they do not have the full information provided by the first-line system. For example, in backup mode, the system can no longer project a plane's route, warn when planes are too close or might collide, or provide a minimum safe altitude warning. When the backup system fails, the amount of information provided the controller is even less.

Right now, the system causes frustration for controllers and pilots and results in expensive delays. The FAA claims that safety is never compromised, but the combination of failure-prone equipment, reductions in the maintenance staff, shrinking ATC budgets and an increasing number of flights seems like a disaster waiting to happen. A multibillion dollar effort began years ago to upgrade the system, but progress was so slow that the Clinton administration stopped the program and asked for a redesign. Technology had changed so much during the project that its original design no longer made sense. For example, the airlines have installed Global Position Systems (GPS) in most of their aircraft providing location data within 100 meters. With this kind of information along with onboard collision avoidance alarms available to pilots, it was necessary to rethink the entire system.

It is interesting to compare the airlines' huge investment in technology with an Air Traffic Control System running on computers that may be older than the reader!

This control failure rippled through the financial system. Because the Bank of New York did not know its position, it could not demand payment from customers to settle trades. The bank had to borrow the cost of carrying the securities from the Federal Reserve and asked for $20 billion overnight. The interest on this loan was $4 million per day!

Since other banks were expecting to pay for the bonds, they had an extra $20 billion on hand overnight, causing the federal funds' rate to plummet from $8\frac{3}{8}$ percent to $5\frac{1}{2}$ percent. When there are rumors of problems in the bond market, traders buy platinum. The price for January platinum delivery rose $12.40 per ounce on a volume of nearly 12,000 contracts, a twenty-nine-year record at the New York Mercantile Exchange.

- Programmers in a financial institution computed interest calculations on savings accounts as if there were thirty-one days in every month. In the five months it took to discover the error, the institution paid more than $100,000 in excess interest.

- Programmers and analysts in a large mail-order house designed a "perfect" system. It would operate only if all errors were eliminated. After installation, auditors discovered that errors were occurring at the rate of almost 50 percent. The system collapsed and had to be abandoned after an investment of approximately a quarter of a million dollars.

- A group of Milwaukee teenagers used a network to illegally gain access to a number of computers around the United States. They were able to find passwords and log onto the systems, in some cases damaging files.

- A student at a major university introduced a virus, or, more correctly, a worm, into one of the major networks connecting various computers. He is thought to have exploited a little-known opening in systems software to send a program to other computers. The program replicated itself and slowed the computers to a near standstill.

These examples all represent failure of control in the organization. For a control system to work, the organization must have a model of its desired states. Often, this model is in the form of routine procedures or generally accepted accounting practices. For problems like controlling a sales representative, standards are less clear, as is our ability to influence behavior.

All levels of control in the organization are the responsibility of management. The Foreign Corrupt Practices Act makes operational control a legal as well as a normal management task. This act requires that publicly held companies devise and maintain a system of internal accounting controls sufficient to provide reasonable assurances of the following:

- Transactions are executed according to management authorization.

- Transactions are recorded as necessary to permit the preparation of financial statements according to generally accepted accounting principles.

- Records of assets are compared with existing assets at reasonable intervals, and action is taken when there are differences.

Information technology gives organizations the ability to process large numbers of transactions in an efficient manner. These same systems create significant control problems and challenges, however. With thousands of transactions processed in a short period of time, an error can spread through an immense number of transactions in minutes. Control failures can become costly and firms have been forced out of business because of their inability to control information processing activities.

There are many opportunities for errors to occur in computer-based processing. Figure 23-3 is a diagram of the most difficult case: a client-server system with widespread connections outside the organization. The figure highlights eight areas where the system is vulnerable.

1. The operating systems for the client and server control the operations of the computers and allocates computer resources. Operating systems can and have been penetrated. They also have errors in coding, as does any other program. Someone who is unauthorized could gain access to the network through the operating system of the server, or possibly through a client machine. An intruder would masquerade as a legitimate client in order to gain access to the server's operating system.

2. Applications programs contain the logic of individual systems operated in the organization. These programs may have errors or may be incomplete in their editing and error checking for input and processing. The programs may execute entirely on the client computer, or on some combination of the client and the server. The server might manage to replicate an error across all the clients using a certain program.

Figure 23-3

Components of a client-server system.

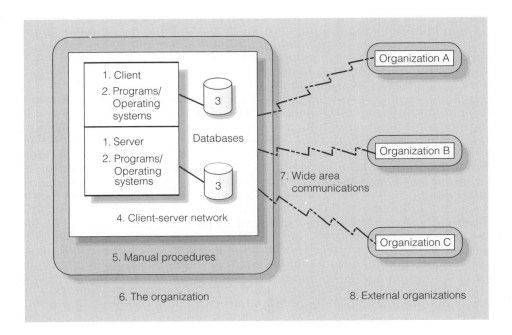

Controlling Financial Risk

Financial institutions and their customers have to be concerned with the control of risks. Individuals trading financial instruments can create significant exposure for their employers. The following is a list of traders and some problems they created:

Name	Loss	Employer	Explanation
Toshihide Iguchi	$1.1 billion	Daiwa Bank (1995)	For 11 years hid bond trading losses trying to make up an original $200,000 loss.
Nicholas Leeson	$1.4 billion	Barings P.L.C. (1995)	Had control of trading records as well as doing trades; used futures contracts to bet on a rise in Japanese stocks. Barings forced to merge, Leeson sentenced to 6.5 years in Singapore.
Joseph Jett	$350 million	Kidder, Peabody (1994)	Fooled the accounting system into crediting him with $350 million in profits from fictitious trades, while real trading lost $100 million—he denies wrongdoing
Victor Gomez	$70 million	Chemical Bank (1994)	Trader over-reached authority in trading Mexican pesos; loss occurred after devaluation of the peso
Howard Rubin	$377 million	Merrill Lynch (1987)	Ignored instructions and took a risky position of $500 million in mortgage-backed securities.
Paul Mozer	$290 million	Salomon Brothers (1991)	Ignored new rules limiting the amount of securities a single dealer could buy at Treasury auctions by submitting false orders in the names of clients; served four months in jail and chairman of firm resigned

The combined total of all these "problems" is over $3.5 billion in losses for the companies involved! Barings Bank had to merge with a Dutch company, which dismissed the senior management of the bank. General Electric sold Kidder Peabody, partially because of the trading losses above, and the head of Daiwa Bank resigned after its loss became public.

In addition a number of client companies are suing banks for losses they incurred trading derivatives. A derivative is a complex financial instrument whose value is linked to, or derived from, an underlying asset. This asset might be a stock or bond, a foreign currency, or a commodity to name a few.

Banks and brokerage firms are working to install systems to value complex derivatives, both to help them determine the prices of these instruments and to help control risk. Management wants to know the extent to which the firm is vulnerable if certain events happen, for example, an increase in the prime rate or the devaluation of a foreign currency.

3. Databases exist on the server and there may be local user data on the clients. Data are often proprietary or confidential within the organization. Are the data safe from accidents? Are crucial data files on the server backed up?

4. The entire network must operate reliably if transactions are to be processed effectively. Is the network operating system reliable and secure?

5. Many applications have a number of associated manual procedures for the submission of input and the processing of output after it has been produced by the system. These procedures must be developed with adequate controls to ensure the accuracy and integrity of processing.

6. At a higher level than the individual user, the organization itself must be structured with control in mind. Management must take its responsibilities seriously and emphasize control.

7. Networks provide connectivity. Wide area communications links are subject to failure, penetration, and sabotage.

8. Many systems are also available to external users from other organizations. These individuals may make mistakes or intentionally try to misuse a system. Controls must protect the system from these users and the users from themselves.

Robbing Citicorp

One day a trader at a company in Buenos Aires was startled by information on his computer screen showing company funds were being transferred from Argentina through Citicorp computers to an account in San Francisco. The trader knew the transfers were unauthorized. He was witnessing an international plot designed to loot Citicorp's customers around the world.

Citicorp had known something was wrong and had called in the FBI. The trader in Argentina notified the bank, and this lead gave the investigators the break they needed to track down the suspects. With the help of Russian police, the trail led to a computer operator in St. Petersburgh, Russia.

Citicorp was extremely concerned; it transfers $500 billion a day. Fast action by governments and banks limited the scheme to accessing $12 million in customer accounts and to actual losses of only $400,000. The investigation has led to arrests in the Netherlands, Tel Aviv, San Francisco, New York, and Britain in addition to Russia.

Citicorp maintains this is the first time its systems have been breached; it has upgraded security even further after the suspects broke into the system 40 times over five months. The Russian suspect managed to break into Citicorp's computers masquerading as a customer, and then transfer money to accounts opened by confederates who began to withdraw the funds. Citicorp does not know or will not reveal how the suspect managed to gain access.

This example, though rare, illustrates the problem of securing systems which process high volumes of payments or perform other critical tasks.

AUDITING INFORMATION SYSTEMS

Accounting firms developed procedures for conducting an audit of information systems because so many of their typical clients' transactions are processed by computer. The auditors are most concerned about systems that affect financial statements, the balance sheet, and income statements. Auditors also render an opinion about the viability of the firm. If "mission critical" information systems are not well controlled, the future of the firm is in doubt.

The auditor examines a system as a whole, focusing on controls and their effectiveness. Typically the auditor runs programs to examine databases and transactions. These programs verify the logic used in processing. Many large organizations have internal auditors who continually examine information systems. Based on the discussion above of the places where an organization is vulnerable, it can be seen that auditing a technologically complex system is not a trivial task. Many managers are concerned about the threats posed by a system that has a major breakdown but continues processing and producing erroneous results.

MANAGEMENT ISSUES

Many of you will eventually be responsible for systems in your functional areas of business. What are the issues you will confront in this role?

MANAGEMENT PROBLEM 23-1

The T-Form organization stresses electronic communications and linking, electronic customer-supplier relationships and strategic alliances with other organizations. Firms in the future will increasingly be interconnected, not just to send messages, but to actually provide input to each other's computers. For example, a supplier might update a customer's production control system to indicate when parts are to arrive. The supplier might even be entrusted to check the customer's system and send reorders automatically without involving a purchasing agent.

This kind of connectivity has a number of ramifications for security. Clearly you have to be able to trust the organizations with whom you establish links. A number of transactions will have their own controls. For example, if you end up with a lot of left over parts or in process inventory, then a supplier is not performing as expected. However, there will undoubtedly be opportunities for employees of partner firms, or even your own firm, to put you at risk of a major loss. Not only can this happen from partners, it is possible for outsiders to penetrate the network you are using for links to other organizations.

What kinds of control need to be considered by the manager who is using IT design variables to develop a T-Form organization?

- *Backup.* It is extremely important to have **backup** for systems, including off-site data storage. When terrorists bombed the World Trade Center in 1992, firms with backup data quickly set up systems in other parts of the East Coast and were back in business. Firms without backup had a much more difficult time recovering from this disaster.

- *Security.* Personal computers have created a host of **security** problems because they are so accessible. Users routinely leave diskettes containing important data lying around, and few users physically lock their computers or use start-up password-protection programs. As a manager, you will have to decide how much security is necessary to safeguard the data and systems for which you are responsible.

- *Keeping to the budget.* The appetite users have for technology seems to be insatiable. Computer sales consistently exceed manufacturers' projections. Yet, the organization cannot afford to buy all of the technology users want, at least in any one year. How will you exert budgetary control and set priorities for acquiring hardware and software and developing new systems?

- *Project management.* As mentioned earlier, IT projects frequently get out of control. If you have the ultimate responsibility for a development project, you will need to be sure the project is under control. Consider using a project management system to track and monitor progress so there will not be unpleasant surprises in place of a finished system.

- *Control over data.* The accuracy of data used in making decisions is always an important management consideration. As we develop more distributed databases, accuracy and consistency among different copies of the same data will become a critical issue for control.

SECURITY ISSUES: VIRUSES, WORMS, AND OTHER CREATURES

The proliferation of personal computers and the development of communications networks gave rise to a category of programs that can only be called malicious (see Figure 23-4 for a classification of these programs). It is difficult to develop controls to thwart these programs.

On March 6, 1992, the 517th anniversary of Michelangelo's birth, a virus bearing his name damaged software on 2000 PCs. The virus randomly overwrote the computers' hard disks. It was estimated that some 65,000 computers were infected with the virus. It is not clear how many viruses there are, but a test center in Germany has identified more than three hundred types that attack PCs.

As shown in Figure 23-4, not all of these malicious programs are viruses. A **Trojan horse** is hidden in a useful piece of code. Once this bit of hidden code is inside a user's computer, it becomes active in some way and executes

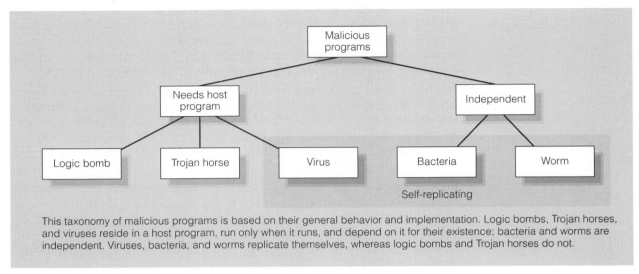

This taxonomy of malicious programs is based on their general behavior and implementation. Logic bombs, Trojan horses, and viruses reside in a host program, run only when it runs, and depend on it for their existence; bacteria and worms are independent. Viruses, bacteria, and worms replicate themselves, whereas logic bombs and Trojan horses do not.

Figure 23-4 Taxonomy of bad code.

malicious acts or subverts the system. One Trojan horse application is to subvert security in a computer so an unauthorized user can gain access to it.

A **virus** is usually a small program, say, 2 or 3 kilobytes of code. This program attaches itself to other programs and executes as the first few instructions of the host program. During replication the virus makes copies of itself, but does not harm the system. In its active phase it changes character and generally damages the computer in some way.

Most viruses leave a string of characters to show that a program is infected. Usually the virus replicates by randomly selecting an executable file. It looks to see if the character string is present. If it is, the file is already infected. If not, the virus infects this file by inserting itself into the program contained in the executable file. The virus wants to infect as many program files as possible, since it can cause damage only when an infected program is run. Usually the virus has a triggering condition, like the date or the number of times the program has been run. If not triggered, the virus remains in the program. When triggered, of course, it does its damage to the system. A number of programs are available to detect viruses and to disinfect systems.

In 1995, a new type of virus appeared, one attached as a macro (piece of executable code) to documents in Microsoft Word. Prior viruses were always found in executable code. This new Concept virus exists in documents as well as code. In addition, most present security systems will not be able to detect this virus as it travels on documents and through e-mail. (You can download a Concept virus checking program from Microsoft's Web site at http://www.microsoft.com/.)

A program with a **logic bomb** "explodes" when some event triggers it. This explosion usually destroys the host computer's files. The logic bomb gets into the computer through a Trojan horse or by a virus. Logic bombs are the favorite tool of disgruntled employees who want to get back at their employers. Logic bombs can also be used for ransom. The person planting the bomb will reveal its location if the organization meets his or her demands.

A **worm** travels through a network from one computer to another. If the computer containing a worm is on a network, the worm searches for other computers that are connected. Finding a victim, the worm establishes a communications link and downloads itself to the new computer. Although the worm may do no overt damage, it can quickly overload a network. The only known remedy is to shut down the network, expunge the worms, and restart the network.

Some people consider **bacteria** to be a virus, but bacteria do not require a host program to infect a system. A bacterium program replicates itself. It acquires as much computer time as possible and in doing so, slows down the host system. The bacterium program may also try to fill up disk space. The Christmas bacteria got into a university network called Bitnet a few years ago. It displayed a Christmas tree on the infected machine and used the mail distribution system to send a copy of itself to every user currently connected to the network. The bacterium program grew geometrically and quickly slowed the network to a crawl. Again the solution was to shut down the network and find and purge each copy of the program.

Our defenses against malicious programs are weak, particularly in a university environment where we want systems to be easy-to-use and available to all members of the community. Passwords on systems are the major defense against unauthorized access. There are also programs that can be run on Unix systems to check for places where the system is vulnerable to penetration. As mentioned above, there are virus-detection programs which can be run periodically to check for system intruders.

On a stand-alone computer, you have a better chance of avoiding infection. If you are very careful about the source of programs or data you add to your system (known as practicing "safe computing"), you can probably avoid contracting a virus. On a network, we are all more vulnerable. The best insurance is to maintain a backup copy of crucial programs and data that is not accessible during normal computer operations.

CHAPTER SUMMARY

1. At the highest level, management control over technology deals with planning, organizing, and monitoring information processing.
2. At this highest level, management establishes plans and policies, assesses the technology, and looks for ways to apply information processing creatively.
3. Coordination across the corporation is one major control problem for senior management.

4. Middle-level managers in various divisions and locations share many of the same problems as top management. These local managers need to devise organizational structures and management policy for information processing in the areas for which they are responsible.

5. Both groups of managers also must relate to information processing managers. In some corporations, there will be a chief information officer to provide coordination and help local management obtain more from its investment in computing.

6. All levels of management are responsible for operational controls, though usually the details will be left to middle and lower management in the firm.

7. Information processing systems process vital transactions for the firm. They must have adequate controls built-in. There are many places where things can go wrong in processing.

8. The information services department must have control over the ongoing operation of systems.

9. Management issues for controlling IT include backup, security, keeping within the budget, and project management.

10. As an individual and as a manager, you are concerned about malicious programs that can damage computers, networks, and, ultimately, the organization.

IMPLICATIONS FOR MANAGEMENT

Control is not a very exciting subject, yet it is important for managers to see that the organization is well-controlled. You have a tradeoff here between excessive control and the risk that some disaster will befall the firm. You can use technology to help control the company as Mrs. Fields did. However, at some point you have to trust your employees. As your company becomes more dependent on technology, and more networked, you have an exposure to various kinds of electronic threats. In addition to managerial control, you now have to worry about control of the technology.

KEY WORDS

Backup	Trojan horse
Bacteria	Virus
Logic bomb	Worm
Security	

RECOMMENDED READING

Lederer, A., and J. Prasad. "Nine Management Guidelines for Better Cost Estimating," *Communications of the ACM,* vol. 35, no. 2 (February 1992), pp. 50-59. (This paper discusses cost estimating, an important part of controlling projects.)

Smithson, C. W. *Managing Financial Risk, 1995 Yearbook.* New York: Chase Manhattan Bank, 1995. (A review of financial risks with much data and stories of significant risk problems, especially a disaster at Metallgesellschaft.)

Weber, R. *EDP Auditing: Conceptual Foundations and Practice,* 2nd ed. New York: McGraw-Hill, 1988. (An excellent text on computer audit.)

IEEE Transactions, August 1992. (A special issue devoted to the problems of data security.)

DISCUSSION QUESTIONS

1. What are senior management's problems in controlling information processing?
2. Why should users worry about a virus?
3. How can users avoid getting a virus on their PCs?
4. What is the difference between a virus and a worm?
5. Why is control over systems important for users?
6. What are the issues in managing and controlling data given today's trends in technology?
7. Will controls ever completely protect systems?
8. What are the major control systems that exist in most organizations?
9. What are a manager's concerns with respect to a budget for IT activities in his or her department?
10. What kind of backup plan would you recommend for fellow students?
11. What are the threats to an interorganizational system?
12. Can we expect to catch fraud with computer systems?
13. Have computer systems made fraud easier? Do you think more or less can be embezzled from a computer system than from a manual system?
14. Is there any way to detect fraud if there is widespread collusion among IS personnel and management?
15. Why do you think viruses are created and spread?
16. What problems can viruses cause a PC user?
17. What kind of file backup procedures are needed in the average organization?
18. Can a worm hurt a LAN that only operates within a company?

19. Why audit a system?

20. Why do companies create "firewalls" between their systems and the Internet?

21. Can an information system be overcontrolled? What might happen under such conditions?

22. Describe how a virus actually works. What kind of files does it want to infect?

23. What do you think of computer "break-ins"? Are they harmless pranks or do they cause serious damage?

24. What devices does management have to control the organization?

25. How does organizational structure influence control?

26. How do budgets exert control?

CHAPTER 23 PROJECT

ORGANIZATIONAL CONTROL

In 1995, Barings Bank in London went out of business due to a trader in Singapore who made a large number of risky, unauthorized trades. That is, the individual lost money and then continued to trade beyond the trading limits set by the firm. The trader was evidently convinced he could "make up" the losses by more trading. Unfortunately, more trading led to more losses until someone finally noticed the problem. Barings, a venerable British bank, was purchased by a Dutch financial institution which replaced all of its senior officers. See the sidebar in this chapter.

Since these events, "risk exposure" systems have become popular. First, describe the organizational control problem faced by a securities firm. Then consider to what risks the firm is exposed. Finally, develop a high-level design for a system to monitor those risks and report to management. What kind of control does your plan represent? How can information technology help management reduce risk?

CHAPTER **24**

Information Technology Issues for Management

OBJECTIVES

1. Learning to manage information technology.

The success of the IT effort begins at the top of the organization. As a manager you must deal with the complex issues that surround information technology. Managing technology is not something that can be ignored or delegated to others.

2. Preparing to apply technology.

A design team needs the involvement and support of senior management. The team has to obtain input from management and assistance in gaining cooperation throughout the organization for developing an application. The leadership role of management is apparent in every development project.

3. Transforming the organization.

We have discussed how various firms use IT to transform themselves and their industries. The key to making all of this happen is management. Management must lead the IT effort and see that technology is used to make the kind of transformations that will keep the firm competitive in the future.

Information technology has become an integral part of the way organizations function. Success in the future may well depend on how well the organization manages information technology.

MANAGEMENT IN A TECHNOLOGICAL ENVIRONMENT

No matter what their functional area, managers today and in the future will face a highly technological environment. The cost of processing logic and communications **networks** are so low, and the potential of this technology so high, that the proliferation of technologies will continue to accelerate. How will we manage under this increased level of technology? What are the management challenges?

What Do CEOs Think?

A recent survey of CEOs showed they want their IS departments to produce fast and flexible systems that would impress customers and increase markets (ComputerWorld CE/CFO Survey, 1995). Some 88 percent of these CEOs report using a PC. Almost half of the companies did some outsourcing for IT services, the major reason being cost savings. Unfortunately, about half of the CEOs and CFOs surveyed said they are not getting an adequate return from their investments in IT. This level of dissatisfaction is a serious one given the huge amounts of capital invested in technology. What can management do to improve the effectiveness of the technology effort?

A Political Model of Information Technology

We have discussed IT as a major, pervasive part of the organization. Yet there are those who argue that the information-based firm is a fantasy (Davenport et al., 1992). These authors present a political model of IT in the firm and argue that information politics is what determines how successfully you apply information technology. Table 24-1 describes the political model.

Firms that practice **technocratic utopianism** are fascinated with the technology. There is an assumption in the firm that technology will solve all problems. The firm will develop databases, desktop workstations, and networks, and purchase large amounts of software. This organization lacks a vision of how all of this technology will be used to further its objectives.

Table 24-1
Information Politics

Technocratic utopianism	Reliance on technology; model the firm's IT structure and rely on new technologies
Anarchy	No overall information management policy
Feudalism	Management of IT by individual business units; limited reporting to the corporation
Monarchy	Strong control by senior management; information may not be shared with lower levels of the firm
Federalism	Management through consensus and negotiation about key IT decisions and structures

Anarchy results when technology is not managed. Management abrogates its responsibilities to control IT and lets a thousand flowers bloom. This strategy may encourage the bold to acquire computers and connect them, but as the firm matures, the lack of overall planning and standards will create tremendous problems. Many firms practiced this style of management in the early days of PCs, letting users purchase whatever equipment they pleased. As a result, these firms found it very difficult and expensive to connect all of their diverse computers to a network.

In the *feudal* model, powerful executives control technology within their divisions and departments. These executives determine what information to collect and choose the technology for their fiefdoms. They also make the decision on what information to forward to higher levels of management. This model is most often found when the firm stresses divisional autonomy. Because it is unlikely two chiefs will follow the same model, it again can be very difficult to coordinate different feudal systems if senior management decides that is a more appropriate technology strategy.

In a **monarchy**, the CIO becomes the CIC, the chief information czar. Instead of playing the consultant role, the CIO establishes and enforces standards that will be followed throughout the corporation. The monarchy often emerges when the firm finds that it has suffered too long from the feudal model. A possible halfway point between **feudalism** and a monarchy is a *constitutional monarchy,* in which a document sets out the powers reserved to senior management and those that fall to the divisions.

In today's environment, the **federal model** may be the most appropriate. The firm tries to reach a consensus on what IT decisions belong at each level and how information should be shared. The emphasis is on what policies make the most sense for the corporation as a whole, not just for a specific department or division. Senior management recognizes that local divisions need some autonomy, and local managers recognize that information belongs to the company and may often be of great strategic value.

The Chief Information Officer

The increased importance of IT to the firm has led to the creation of a **chief information officer (CIO)** position. This individual is, of course, in charge of information technology in the firm. However, the chief information officer is also an influential member of senior management and is usually a vice president or senior vice president in the firm. In addition to traditional information processing, this individual is responsible for voice and data communications and office technology. The job demands someone who can assume a role in planning, influencing other senior managers, and organizing information activities in the organization.

The issues discussed in this text are the concerns of the CIO. He or she must worry about strategic planning for the corporation and how information technology can provide a competitive edge. The executive in this role must provide **leadership** and control over processing. It is important that planning, systems development, and operations are all undertaken successfully.

The CIO is a relatively new position in organizations, but we expect that more and more firms will create such a post. It is not unusual for a large firm to spend more than $100 million a year on information technology. A manager, not a technician, is needed to obtain a return from this kind of investment.

Earl and Feeny (1994) describe ways in which CIOs should try to add value to their organizations. They found two types of CEOs, those who see IT as a strategic resource and those who see it as a cost. Table 24-2 presents various issues in managing IT as seen by CEOs in these different positions.

MANAGEMENT PROBLEM 24-1

Roberta Hobart is president of *Fashion News,* a monthly magazine for the fashion industry and consumers. The company has an information services department that operates a number of systems in the areas of accounting, advertiser billing, and subscription processing. Recently, the manager of the department left to accept a position with another firm.

Two good candidates for manager of the IS department are Bill McDonald and Lyn Phister. Bill is not really an IS professional. He began his career in finance but has been very involved with technology. Roberta feels that he is probably quite knowledgeable except in the most technical areas. Lyn, on the other hand, is a true IS professional. His past jobs have included working for a computer manufacturer, designing software, and programming for several firms. At *Fashion News,* he has been manager of systems and programming. In this task, he performs very competently, especially in solving technical problems.

Roberta feels that both men could do an adequate job. She is worried about Bill's lack of technical experience but gives him high marks on management. The opposite evaluation applies to Lyn. He should be superb at solving technical problems, but Roberta is worried about his lack of experience as a manager, particularly in working with users.

What are the essential components of the job? Can you help Roberta make her decision? What additional information would you like to have about each candidate?

Table 24-2
Perceptions of IT

Issue	IT a Cost/Liability	IT an Asset
Are we getting value for money invested in IT?	ROI on IT is difficult to measure; the organization as a whole is unhappy with IT.	ROI is difficult to measure, the organization believes IT makes an important contribution.
How important is IT?	Stories of strategic IT use are dismissed as irrelevant to this business.	Stories of strategic IT use are instructive.
How do we plan for IT?	IT plans are made by specialists or missionary zealots.	IT thinking is subsumed within business thinking.
Is the IS function doing a good job?	There is general cynicism about the track record of IS.	The performance of IS is no longer an agenda item.
What is the IT strategy?	Many IT applications are under development.	IS efforts are focused on a few key initiatives.
What is the CEO's vision for the role of IT?	The CEO sees a limited role for IT within the business.	The CEO sees IT as having a role in the transformation of the business.
What do we expect of the CIO?	The CIO is positioned as a specialist functional manager.	The CIO is valued as a contributor to business thinking and business operations.

From Earl and Feeny 1994

If you are the CIO of a firm whose CEO holds the views in the middle, liability column, then the job will indeed be challenging. Earl and Feeny argue that the CIO must find a way to add value to the corporation from its use of IT so the CEO will view IT as an asset.

One role of the CIO is to determine if success stories from other industries or from competitors are relevant to the company. In one chemical company, managers dismissed stories of competitive advantage from IT saying they were not applicable in their industry. Unfortunately, at the same time a competitor was developing technology that gave it a competitive advantage.

It appears the most successful approach to obtaining benefits from IT is not to identify *separate* IT and business strategies; rather business strategy subsumes IT strategy. The job of the CIO is to build relationships with other functional managers so IT requirements become a part of business strategy. This approach means the CIO has to be involved in planning and strategy meetings across the company.

To provide confidence in technology, the CIO must build a track record of delivering IT as promised, on time and within budget. Users quickly become cynical when delivery dates, cost estimates, and functional specifications do not meet expectations.

Rather than scattering the development effort, a well-run company focuses its IT efforts on opportunities and areas where the firm is weak. The task of the CIO here is to determine not how to use IT, but rather where it should be used to most benefit the organization.

The CIO has to be a promoter, marketing the potential of IT to transform the organization. A track record of delivering what has been promised will increase this manager's credibility as will good examples of organizations that have undergone technology-driven transformations.

Table 24-3 summarizes the characteristics Earl and Feeny found among CIOs for firms that considered IT to be an asset rather than a liability. This table shows how the CIO can add value to the organization.

The CIO of Time Warner spoke at a recent NYU class about his role in the company and his comments provide further insights on adding value. According to this CIO, he adds value by finding new business opportunities for the company and using technology to conduct business in new ways. The company manages IT in a federal structure, so he takes responsibility for infrastructure like a world-wide network. IT managers in each division develop systems for their divisions and worry about the day-to-day operation of their systems. The role of the CIO will differ among companies, but first and foremost this person has to be a manager concerned with the business as well as someone who understands information technology.

Table 24-3
The Added Value of the CIO

---

1. Obsessive and continuous focus on business imperatives.

2. Interpretation of external IT success stories as potential models for the firm.

3. Establishment and maintenance of IS executive relationships.

4. Establishment and communication of IS performance record.

5. Concentration of the IS development effort.

6. Achievement of a shared and challenging vision of the role of IT.

From Earl and Feeny 1994

A Vision and Plan for IT

One task of a CIO is to be sure there is a vision in the firm for what IT can accomplish and a plan to provide a guideline for management decisions about technology. A vision is a general statement of what the organization is trying to become. For example, a vision might include a statement about the kind of technology architecture the firm hopes to provide, say, a client-server environment and a global network for communications. A vision might go on to describe, possibly in scenario form, the environment seen by a user. "We will use information technology to support our strategies of providing the best customer service in the industry and becoming a global firm. Our first priority is to develop electronic links with customers and suppliers. Next, product brand managers will be furnished with a client workstation that can access the sales database. They will be provided with decision support tools to conduct their own analyses of global data. Product development engineers will have workstations capable of running the CAD/CAM software. ... " The vision needs to be sufficiently compelling so it creates enthusiasm for the plan to achieve it.

In Chapter 5, we suggested that it was important for IT strategy to be subsumed as a part of overall business strategy. Corporate and IT strategic planning should be part of one planning effort. The IT plan expands the IT component of the strategic business plan and describes how to execute the agreed upon strategy. This plan must combine the vision of IT with strategy to produce a document that guides IT decision making. Suppose the overall strategy of the company is to become the low cost producer in its industry. This strategy is to be achieved by reengineering existing processes and installing automated production equipment in manufacturing plants. The vision of the firm in five years is to have process owners in charge of business processes that have extensive technology support. The overall architecture is client-server, with a network connecting all plants and office locations. In addition, to pursue its low-cost producer strategy, the company will establish electronic links with key customers and suppliers.

Thus, the vision and strategy provide the goals for an IT plan which will describe how to achieve them. This more operational plan will depend on the company and its strategy, but in general it will discuss hardware and software, communications, and individual applications. Continuing the example above, the plan would detail the equipment needed to move toward the client-server model and a schedule for implementation. This section would also discuss networking including the hardware and services required to provide communications.

A key role of the plan is to identify the most important new applications of technology and prioritize them. It is important to focus efforts on applications which contribute to achieving the vision and strategy of the company. For the example above, do not be too concerned about routine applications. Management will probably decide resources should be applied to one or two reengineering projects and an effort to develop EDI with customers and suppliers. The plan would describe each of these projects in some detail including cost, time, and staff requirements for completion. If management decides it wants to undertake more applications than there is staff available, some of the development will have to be outsourced.

Having a plan makes managing IT requests easier for the CIO and for management in general. The rapid diffusion of technology has led to a flood of ideas and requests for how to use IT. The typical organization cannot afford to undertake every application suggested. A manager can evaluate applications against the plan. Does this suggestion help us achieve our vision and strategy? Where does it fall given the priorities of our other projects? A well-prepared plan can create enthusiasm for IT, focus the technology effort on business imperatives as suggested above, and help manage and evaluate technology. The plan is a fundamental management tool for seeing that IT makes the maximum contribution to the organization. Table 24-4 is an example of the contents of one corporate plan for information technology.

We recommend that a representative group of managers work together to develop a plan for information technology and the organization. A plan developed by a CIO alone will probably not be acceptable to other managers. The CIO should act as a resource, consultant, and tutor for the planning committee. The idea is for technology not to be a separate plan, but to be integrated, and to some extent subsumed, in a corporate plan.

MANAGEMENT PROBLEM 24-2

Cookwell is a manufacturer of cooking utensils. Its products are sold in department and specialty stores throughout the world. The company has a large information services department and many applications in accounting, production, and sales. Historically, there have been a number of problems with IT at Cookwell. There have been five IS department managers in the past four years!

Systems seem to be late or are never implemented at all. Users in all departments are highly dissatisfied with technology services. Reports are always late, and there seems to be an inordinate number of errors. The IS staff generally blames users for all the problems.

Users, on the other hand, say the information services staff is the most arrogant group of people in the company. Whenever we ask them to do something, there is always some excuse why it cannot be done. Every new suggestion is rejected. If an application looks good, they come back with such an unrealistic cost estimate that no one will pay for it. We would be better off doing everything ourselves on PCs.

The president of the company has avoided these problems for as long as possible. However, things have become so serious that some action is required. Rather than fire the present manager of the department, who has been on the job for only four months, the president has decided to try a new strategy: He has hired a chief information officer. What should the new CIO do to solve IT problems at Cookwell?

Table 24-4
Contents of an Information Systems Plan

- Executive summary
- Goals—general and specific
- Assumptions
- Scenario—information processing environment
- Applications areas—status, cost, schedule, priorities
- Operations
- Maintenance and enhancements
- Organizational structure—pattern of computing
- Effect of plan on the organization—financial impact
- Implementation—risks, obstacles

Outsourcing Revisited

Outsourcing involves turning over responsibility for some part of a firm's technology effort to an external company. We discussed this option earlier in Part Four when we looked at the problem of selecting alternatives for processing. In addition to obtaining services like systems integration for developing a specific application, a firm can outsource all or part of most of its IT effort. For example, a large brokerage firm outsourced the operation

A Job and a Career

The information technology industry is helping to drive the American economy; technology stocks have been responsible for a steady, dramatic increase in the stock market. One expert estimated that technology is responsible for 5% of Gross Domestic Product in the U.S. Jobs in this area are growing rapidly as well. Manufacturing firms are busy downsizing while entrepreneurial companies are adding employees.

A good example is United HealthCare (UHC), a $2.5 billion Minnesota healthcare company. UHC does not employ physicians or own hospitals in its net. The company facilitates relationships among health care providers, insurers and patients; its objective is to achieve the highest possible care at the lowest cost. One officer described the firm as a "brokerage service" and a "technology company."

A major system interconnects almost 25,000 independent physicians and UHC facilities in North America. The company has won a patent for applying AI techniques to monitoring clinical databases. The company is in the throes of designing a new architecture for client-server computing with distributed Unix-based applications. In 1994 the company hired more than 100 new IS workers, and it plans to recruit more professionals in the future.

Other technology companies are experiencing similar growth; knowledge of IT can add a great deal to a resume when looking for a job!

of part of its communications function to a common carrier. The broker-age firm did not want to maintain the internal expertise to operate and continually update the configuration of the network.

Loh and Venkatraman (1992) have identified some of the factors which lead a firm to outsource:

- A firm that feels it is spending more on technology than it should (or more than the competition) may adopt outsourcing if it feels this option provides a lower-cost alternative than internal management. Even if the firm does not feel at a disadvantage compared to others, it may see outsourcing as a way to reduce IT-related costs in general. Several firms claim cost savings by turning their IT function over to an external firm. A study by Strassmann (Computerworld, August 21, 1995) suggests large outsourcing agreements are motivated by companies trying to return to profitability by cutting employment. (A company outsourcing all of its IT operations generally gets an immediate cash inflow when it sells equipment to the outsourcer, and the outsourcer usually hires a large percentage of the company's staff, reducing its salary expense.)

- A firm with a high-debt structure may not wish to invest in technology. It may view outsourcing as a way to lease technology instead of buying it.

- An organization may feel its IT function is not performing adequately. Outsourcing can be a way to arrange for a more professional and higher-performing IT operation in the company.

Turner and Kambil have added to this list (1993):

- An organization has decided to return to its core competencies. Managing IT is not one of these, so it outsources this task to another firm.

- The organization is interested in technology transfer from the expert outsourcing firm. It will learn from the outsourcer.

How can outsourcing accomplish the objectives above? The outsourcing firm must have a high level of expertise in technology. This firm should also be able to create economies of scale. For example, the telecommunications outsourcer can probably provide network services for a number of clients with a smaller staff than the sum of the networking staffs from all of the clients.

What are the arguments against outsourcing? The outsourcing firm may have a high-cost structure because of its need to employ highly skilled personnel. The need to have a contract with the outsourcing firm can lead to conflict and misunderstandings. Some companies are surprised at the cost of using an outsourcing firm to develop applications.

Probably the biggest deterrent to outsourcing is the question of control. If you regard technology as a competitive factor in business, you may be reluctant to turn control of it over to an outside firm. The brokerage firm described above examined the option of outsourcing all of its technology effort, but decided only one part of it was not sufficiently strategic to be outsourced.

Lacity and Hirschheim (1993) studied a number of firms that outsourced. Their criticism of outsourcing provides a cautionary note. Their study identified two myths of outsourcing.

Myth 1: Outsourcing vendors are strategic partners.

The outsourcing vendor cannot be a partner because the outsourcer's profit motive is not shared by the customer. The outsourcer makes more money if it is able to charge the customer higher fees. If the outsourcer can reduce service levels and collect the same fees, it also contributes to its profit margins. You might want to consider some kind of a cost reduction sharing arrangement with an outsourcer so that both the services firm and the client benefit from more efficient operations.

Myth 2: Outsourcing vendors are inherently more efficient than an internal IS department.

The outsourcer's argument here is that economies of scale help it to be more efficient. Today hardware costs do not favor huge installations. As we have seen, the cost performance ratio for smaller computers is better than for mainframes. It is possible the outsourcer can do some tasks more efficiently because it has done them before or because it can afford to share highly paid specialists among a number of clients.

An outsourcing agreement will probably extend for a number of years in order to justify the transition effort involved. All experts in this field suggest that developing a contract between the outsourcer and the client is crucial. Since an agreement may be for five or ten years, the contract must be highly flexible. Business conditions and technology are expected to change during the life of the agreement. General Dynamics, which has an outsourcing agreement with Computer Sciences Corporation, is reported to have eight contracts covering divisions that may each evolve in a different way (McFarlan and Nolan, 1995).

After entering a relationship with an outsourcer, the company still has to manage information technology! You will still need the equivalent of a CIO to manage the partnership and contract with the outsourcer. The client still must look at emerging technologies and plan for its technology architecture. Creative applications are most likely to come from users rather than the outsourcer, and there must be mechanisms for turning ideas into new applications of the technology. Outsourcing can be an excellent alternative for some companies, but you should not enter into an outsourcing arrangement with the idea you will no longer have to manage IT.

How Much to Invest in IT

Most firms are not in the business of developing technology. They have a product or service to offer. The technology helps them accomplish the mission of the organization. Managers frequently ask the question of how much they should invest in IT. A better question is how much benefit the organization can obtain from its investment in technology. The first question above looks at IT as a cost, the second as an investment.

However, you will undoubtedly be asked to justify an IT investment at some point in your career. We see that traditional discounted cash flow models do not work very well when applied to deciding whether to undertake a specific application. They are even less useful in determining how much to invest in technology in general. Industry averages are also suspect. The firm obtaining a distinct advantage from the technology is likely to be spending more than the industry average. The company wasting money on technology will also probably be spending more than the industry average!

If you are able to justify each new application, then the sum total of IT expenditures should be justified. What are the reasons for embarking on a new technology initiative?

- Using IT to design the organization
- Cost reduction or cost avoidance
- Increased revenue
- Competitive pressures or advantage
- Required by regulations
- Building an infrastructure

Restructuring the organization with IT changes the way you do business. It has the potential to create the most significant benefits in the list above, but forecasting those benefits in advance is extremely difficult. The second and third reasons above are the easiest to justify economically. It is difficult to demonstrate the gains from meeting the competition, and to be sure a new system will provide a competitive advantage. A system that is required to meet regulations or necessitated by the government will probably not be economically justified. Finally, an investment to build

The Weather As a Factor in Outsourcing

Burpee is a large mail-order and wholesale distributor of seeds and gardening products. As you might expect, its business is very seasonal. From January to March its customers prepare for spring; they typically have kept its IBM mainframe running to process a steady stream of orders and keep inventory under control. The rest of the year the computer runs on idle at about 20 percent of capacity because of light business.

To reduce the expense of keeping a computer and five operators available year-round, Burpee has entered an outsourcing agreement with Computer Sciences Corporation.

It is expected that the contract will cut the company's fixed processing costs in half over its five-year term. Burpee will continue to do applications development in-house and will also run its new local area network inventory management system.

The need for computing services that is highly seasonal may make outsourcing a viable alternative. Even with extensive LANs and a client-server architecture, firms are finding that maintaining the network is a nontrivial task. Outsourcing may also be attractive to some firms who do not have mainframe computing needs.

infrastructure is likely not to pay off until future applications take advantage of that new infrastructure.

It appears from this discussion the question of how much to invest in IT will continue to be raised. As with many other important managerial decisions, the ultimate answer is going to depend on good taste and sound judgment. Some days you will probably just have to act on faith and by seeing what other organizations have accomplished with their IT initiatives.

Bad Trips

In 1993 Greyhound was under a great deal of pressure to show progress to financial analysts. Senior executives had promised investors, lenders and securities analysts that Trips, a computerized reservations system for bus travel, would be ready for the 1993 summer travel season. The VP in charge of Trips tried to warn the company's chief financial officer that a gradual rollout was necessary given problems on a test run of the system in four cities in Texas. Management would not listen. In fact, the VP's report was destroyed and its mention purged from computer files.

In April, senior executives flew to Europe to promote a stock offering that was based on the promise of Trips. Greyhound rolled the system out that summer, and as the VP in charge predicted, it was a disaster.

In the old days, Greyhound allocated buses and drivers with data that was months old. It needed quick, reliable ridership data to determine how to set prices and how to allocate buses to routes. Margins were very thin and the company could not afford to send almost empty buses on trips. Unfortunately, a bus reservations system is more complicated than it sounds because of the number of possible stops. An airplane passenger flying from Baltimore to Los Angeles might make one stop, but the bus passenger on that route could make ten or more stops. A bus reservations system must account for many more segments than an airline system. Systems analysts estimated Trips would have to manage 1,800 vehicle stops a

day, about ten times those of an average airline. Because of heavy cost cutting, there was high turnover. Personnel using the system would probably have little experience with the company and only have a high school education.

Greyhound gave the 40 person Trips development group $6 million and a little over a year to develop a system. Contrast this to American's SABRE system which has been developed over thirty years by a large staff and probably represents an investment of over a billion dollars. An outside contractor developed the original software. Learning to use it took 40 hours of training for ticket clerks. The system did not include all Greyhound destinations, so clerks had to fall back to old log books at times. In tests, the new system took twice as long to generate a ticket as the old system.

The systems group wanted to redesign the software, but was pressured by management to press on. When the system had been installed at 50 bus terminals, it froze terminals unpredictably. At the same time, Greyhound decided to change its long-distance phone service provider and set up a toll-free number for reservations for the first time. The reservations center opened with 220 terminals connected to Trips. The combination of the bus terminals and 400 operators in Omaha taking reservations seriously degraded the performance of the central Trips computers in Dallas. Some days the system took 45 seconds to respond to a single keystroke and five minutes to print a ticket. Crashes occurred so often that many agents wrote tickets by hand. Passengers standing in line at bus terminals to get computer issued tickets often missed connections. Callers had to try up to a dozen times to get through to the toll-free reservations line. The slow system meant that operators had to spend 150 seconds on average on a call compared to 109 seconds before the system. By early September, Greyhound stopped using Trips west of the Mississippi River.

At the end of the summer, Greyhound announced a 12% decrease in ridership and that earnings would trail projections, causing its stock to plunge 24% in value in a single day. The VP in charge of Trips was relieved of this responsibility. A new vice president was assigned to Trips, and he was forced to resign in January of 1994. Executives now admit that by introducing the ill-fated reservations system at the busiest time of the year, they drove away passengers instead of attracting them.

The company failed to learn much from the summer of '93. In May of 1994 it offered riders the chance to go anywhere for $68 with a 3-day advanced purchase. Thousands of customers responded, and Trips went down. Buses and drivers were in short supply, and some bus terminals were so swamped that agents just stopped selling tickets. By the fall of 1994 the chief executive and CFO of Greyhound were forced to resign. A new executive from American Airlines is now in charge of Trips; it is working in 248 locations and beginning to provide planning data for the first time. Training time to use the system has been reduced from 40 to 16 hours, but even the new manager in charge of Trips reports trouble when he tries to use its cumbersome interface.

Trips is a sad tale of bad technology decisions, but first and foremost, bad management decisions made by people who did not understand the limits and problems of technology. More discouraging is the fact that these senior managers did not try to learn and did not listen to warnings from people in a position to know the risks.

A Summary of Issues in Managing IT

This book is about information technology and management. At this point we summarize some of the key management issues discussed in the text:

- The personal involvement of management in making decisions about technology is crucial, especially given the huge investments most companies have made and continue to make in information technology.

- You can use information technology to transform the organization. IT design variables let you develop entirely new structures like the T-Form organization.

- Information technology should be an integral part of a firm's corporate strategy. Managers and other users are the most likely source of strategic applications of the technology.

- Senior management needs a vision of how technology can be used in the firm.

- A corporate plan should include planning for IT.

- Management has the responsibility for designing and managing an IT architecture. It has to provide the basic infrastructure needed to take advantage of technology.

- There are a number of different structures for managing IT. Today the federal structure is probably the most popular in a large organization.
- Management is also responsible for developing new applications of technology. It needs to focus development resources where they are most needed.
- Systems development is one of the most creative activities in modern organizations. Managing development projects has been a continuing challenge for companies.
- Reengineering focuses attention on business processes instead of functions. It also contrasts radical redesign with incremental improvements in processes.
- Management must decide on the source of IT services, for example, there is the option of outsourcing to a consulting firm.
- Managers determine what level of support to provide users working with technology, and how much time users should spend developing applications themselves.
- Managers are in the business of change. No place is change more evident than in implementing new technology and using IT to redesign organizations.
- Information technology, while easy to use in some respects, is constantly growing more complex. There is a continuing need for IT professionals in the organization.

THE CHANGING WORLD OF INFORMATION

The percentage of IT expenditures controlled by the professional IS group has steadily dropped. A corporate IT group is likely to be responsible for "legacy" systems (older systems, often for mainframes), corporate-wide applications, and infrastructure technology, such as networks. More and more, the responsibility for IT management is shifting to users and line managers.

The challenge for senior management in this changing world is to exert the proper amount of influence and oversight of an increasingly complex technological environment. The hardware and software infrastructure is expanding rapidly as networks of servers and workstations grow (our business school has a network with more than a thousand nodes). It is difficult to keep track of, much less manage, all of the software and applications local units develop for their own benefit.

Senior management will continue to struggle with the balance between what appears to be critical for the organization and should be controlled centrally, and what is best left to local management. The trends that are likely to continue are the declining cost of hardware, the explosive growth of networking, the Internet, interorganizational communications, the development of more sophisticated software packages, and the desire of users to do more computing under their own control.

ACTION PLAN

It is very difficult to reduce suggestions for managing something as complex as information technology to a few, outline points. However, the following suggestions have proven helpful as guidelines for managing IT.

Use IT Design Variables to Structure the Organization

One of the most exciting attributes of modern technology is your ability to use it in designing innovative and highly effective organizations. You can use this technology to design components of an organization, or to structure an entirely new type of organization.

- IT design variables, in conjunction with conventional organization design variables, provide you with tremendous flexibility in designing an organization.
- The most likely outcome from using these variables will be a flat organization structure with decentralized decision making. The firm will use electronic communications and linking and electronic customer supplier relationships to form alliances with other firms and in general will resemble the T-Form organization described in Chapter 1.

Determine and Communicate Corporate Strategy

If you and others in the organization are to help the firm achieve its strategy, you must know what it is!

Develop a plan for how to use information technology. The plan should include:
- A list of opportunities for your business unit.
- A vision of how your unit should function and the role of IT in that vision.
- A survey of current business processes that are good candidates for major improvement through process reengineering.
- A catalog of areas for applying IT, including priorities.

Develop a long-range plan for the technological infrastructure.
- Plan for hardware/software architecture for your unit given the constraints of the corporation, that is, what technology already exists.
- Plan for the evolution of a network that forms the backbone of your technology.
- Invest in infrastructure.

- Investigate the use of standards to facilitate connection and inter-organizational systems.

Develop ongoing management strategies for IT.

- Support users in your unit and encourage them to work with the technology.
- Develop mechanisms for allocating resources to IT.
- Encourage innovation and reward it.

Manage systems development.

- See that design teams are formed for new projects.
- Participate in the design process.
- Be sure you understand what IT applications will do.
- Review and monitor development projects.

Be a user of technology.

- Use IT to improve your own productivity.
- Use technology to set an example for others.

Information technology is so pervasive in modern organizations, any manager will encounter it during his or her career. You will have the most success if you (1) look at IT as something to enable you and your colleagues to be more effective and (2) actively manage information technology.

CHAPTER SUMMARY

1. The future of the modern organization is inextricably intertwined with information technology. A successful general manager cannot afford to leave decisions about information systems to a group of IS professionals.

2. A political view of the IT organization suggests that the federal model is the most favored in today's medium to large organization.

3. The chief information officer serves as a liaison to link the professional information services staff with top levels of management.

4. Senior managers tend to fall into two groups: those who view IT as a cost and those who see it as an asset.

5. For either group, it is important for the CIO to find ways to add value to the corporation through the use of IT.

6. Outsourcing is an increasingly popular option for managing IT. It is important to negotiate an outsourcing contract carefully, and continue to manage IT with your outsourcer.

7. There are few guidelines on how much to invest in technology. This decision continues to be one of the most difficult for management to make.

8. A key message from the text is managers need to be knowledgeable about IT and involved in managing it in the organization.

9. The pervasive nature of the technology means managers at all levels in the organization, not just senior management, will use and make decisions about IT in the firm.

10. The role of management and IT is to bring change to the organization. Implementing change is one of a manager's most formidable challenges.

IMPLICATIONS FOR MANAGEMENT

The typical reader of this book will be planning a management rather than an IT career. However, before you dismiss our discussions as not relevant to your career plans, you should realize a number of CIOs actually are former users of technology rather than IT professionals. If you look at the qualifications and duties of the CIO, the reason becomes more obvious. The CEO wants a CIO who understands the business, someone who can figure out how to apply technology to achieve the goals of the company. At some point in your career, you could end up as a CIO. Patricia Barron was CIO of Xerox for a number of years. Her background was as a user, and she moved from CIO to president of one of Xerox's divisions. One of the things she did during her tenure as CIO was learn as much about technology as possible, which is good advice for all of us.

KEY WORDS

Anarchy
Chief information officer (CIO)
Federal model
Feudalism
Leadership

Monarchy
Networks
Outsourcing
Technocratic utopianism

RECOMMENDED READING

ComputerWorld, CEO/CFO Survey, 1995. (The results of a survey of top management about their companies' IT efforts.)

Davenport, T. H., R. Eccles, and L. Prusak. "Information Politics," *Sloan Management Review,* vol. 34, no. 1 (Fall 1992), pp. 53–65. (An insightful article on how many different organizations approach IT management.)

Earl, M., and D. Feeny. "Is Your CIO Adding Value?," *Sloan Management Review,* Spring 1994, pp. 11–20. (An excellent discussion of the challenges and actions for a CIO.)

Kambil, A., and J. Turner. "Outsourcing of Information Systems As a Strategy for Organizational Alignment and Transformation." Unpublished paper, Stern School, NYU, 1994. (A strategic look at outsourcing with a number of motivations for the practice.)

Lacity, M., and R. Hirschheim. "The Information Systems Outsourcing Bandwagon," *Sloan Management Review,* Fall 1993, pp. 73–86. (A somewhat contrary view of the move toward outsourcing.)

Loh, L., and N. Venkatraman. "Determinants of Information Technology Outsourcing: A Cross-Sectional Analysis," *JMIS,* vol. 9, no. 1 (Summer 1992), pp. 7–24. (An interesting study of outsourcing.)

DISCUSSION QUESTIONS

1. How do different CEOs view IT?
2. What is the role of the chief information officer?
3. Why do you think organizations have established the CIO position? What kind of individual should fill it?
4. Describe how at least one firm gained a competitive advantage with information systems.
5. How should corporate and IT planning be coordinated?
6. What is meant by the statement that a key challenge for management is the integration of information technology and the business?
7. Give an example how information systems can constrain the opportunities available to management.
8. What are the motivations for outsourcing?
9. What are the "myths" of outsourcing? Do you agree with them?
10. What are the options for structuring information processing in an organization?
11. How do managers react in a firm that views IT as a liability compared to a company where it is seen as an asset?
12. How should you manage an outsourcing relationship?
13. Why is a flexible contract important in outsourcing?
14. If you became the CEO of a firm, how would you evaluate its information technology effort?

15. Why should a manager insist on seeing different alternatives when a new system is being designed?

16. What kind of organization might want to follow a different political model of IT than the federal model?

17. Describe how a manager provides leadership with respect to information technology in the organization.

18. Discuss the problems with the different political models of IT in the organization presented in Table 24-1.

CHAPTER 24 PROJECT

THE CIO

Find an organization that is willing to let you interview the top information services manager in the firm. Develop a set of questions about what this individual does. In particular, ask him or her what the three most significant problems are for the top information services person in that company today. Based on the discussion in this text, include questions about the actions of top management and users' reactions to information technology. Prepare a written report of your findings and discuss whether you think the firm you visited would be typical with respect to systems.

CHAPTER 25

Societal Implications and Future Trends

● OBJECTIVES

1. Learning to manage information technology.

Systems often have unintended consequences. It has been speculated that during the 1987 stock market crash, a number of different trading strategies using computers interacted in unforeseen ways to drive down prices. Managers have to confront these problems and other policy issues, such as restrictions on the flow of data across national boundaries, the monitoring of workers, privacy, and education for technology. In addition, organizations are becoming more dependent on IT. You must manage technology successfully if the organization is to succeed.

2. Preparing to apply technology.

Designers face some of these same issues. For example, will a multinational firm be allowed to design an international system that collects data from a number of European companies and processes them in North America? As part of a design team, you have to consider whether your system is contrary to the policies and ethics of the organization. Does it compromise employee or customer privacy? Can it be abused?

3. Transforming the organization.

A manager has to ask what impact an application that transforms the organization might have. What will happen to the industry and the customer? Airline computer reservation systems transformed the industry, and the Department of Transportation issued elaborate rules regulating these systems to avoid unfair competition. What is an appropriate government and firm response to such applications which change the way an industry operates?

Information technology has an impact beyond any one organization. A user of systems may be affected directly as a member of an organization or indirectly as a citizen. Systems can transcend the boundaries of an organization. In this chapter, we discuss some of the social responsibilities associated with information systems. We also look at the future of the technology to understand better how to prepare for it today.

SOCIAL RESPONSIBILITIES

There are a number of issues for public policy concerning information technology. In this chapter, we consider some of the most important topics for an informed manager and citizen. Table 25-1 summarizes the issues according to the following framework:

- *Technology.* Issues that relate to the nature of the technology itself
- *Applications.* Problems that arise from applying technology
- *Impact.* Issues regarding the impact of technology on individuals, the organization, and society

Technology   **Complexity and Integrity**   Society in general is becoming more complex, as is information technology. As you look at the confluence of computers and communications technology, the increase in technological complexity is evident. What is the interaction between IT and societal complexity? Will it make things more complicated, or will IT help us cope with the growing complexity inherent in a postindustrial, information-based economy? The answer to both questions is probably yes. We may be able to trade off

Table 25-1
Social Issues

Issue	Concern
	TECHNOLOGY
Complexity and integrity	Are systems so complex that we cannot understand and manage them?
Reliability and failure	What are the risks if systems are not reliable; what if critical systems fail?
Piracy	What is the impact of piracy on the economy, trade, and international relations?
	APPLICATIONS
Securities markets	Has technology made securities markets more unstable? Has it negatively affected the small investor?
Monitoring	Should management use technology to monitor individual workers? What about workgroups?
Harassment	How can we prevent systems from harassing individuals?
Defense	Could "Cyberwar" disrupt the economy?
	IMPACT
Education	Is the U.S. educational system preparing students for the technology they will face as adults?
Technology gap	Are individuals who do not learn about technology at a significant disadvantage?
Employment	Does technology make it more difficult for the unskilled to get jobs? What is its impact on middle managers?
Privacy	Do we have a right to privacy? Does technology make it possible to violate that right?
Security	What harm can result when the security of systems is compromised?
International business	Can IT policies be used to inhibit the activities of firms trying to conduct business in foreign countries?

some organizational and societal complexity for information systems, but these systems in turn are likely to be complex in their own right.

The movement from batch processing to on-line systems and from PCs to client-server architectures and networking create greater complexity and dependence on machines. PCs bring power to the user's desktop, but at a cost of a more complicated environment. It takes considerable effort to learn a graphical user interface like Windows95 and to operate five or six applications packages. A networking environment is more complex than using a stand-alone computer. All of this complexity can result in problems with the technology: Software does not run right, there is downtime on the network, users encounter problems accessing data or programs on the **server**, and there can be printing difficulties. Because the environment is more complex, it can take longer to diagnose the problem and fix it compared with the days of simpler technology.

Reliability and Failure   We have discussed some of the problems of **control** and system reliability. Information technology is extremely complex. Although systems in the future are expected to feature more redundancy and lower failure rates, there is always the possibility of a system failing. The results of such a system failure range from inconvenience to catastrophe. There is serious public concern in seeing that systems are designed and installed with adequate considerations of reliability and backup. For critical systems, backup capabilities are crucial. For example, critical on-board systems in airliners have long featured redundancy, that is, several separate and independent hydraulic systems.

For the most part, the IS profession has not yet approached such levels of redundancy. Some systems have extensive hardware redundancy, but very few systems have software that is independently developed and executed on separate machines to provide reliability and backup. Obviously, such an approach is costly, but for certain kinds of systems envisioned in the future, it may become necessary.

More research is needed to conduct the cost/benefit analysis necessary for selecting the proper design for reliability. The computer profession in general does not have a well-developed procedure for analyzing the risks of various types of system failures. Without this assessment capability, it is difficult to determine the steps necessary to achieve acceptable levels of reliability for any given system. There are also many problems related to the prevention of system failure. In 1989, the SABRE airline reservation system failed for twelve hours, the longest period ever, creating a number of problems for travel agents and airline personnel.

Piracy   The technology industry in the U.S. is a strong engine for growth and jobs. Yet, this industry is threatened by piracy, primarily of software. Piracy is highly organized with factories and distribution channels. It is a violation of what is often referred to as **intellectual property** rights. The Asia/Pacific region is considered by most companies to be the largest center of piracy. Estimates of piracy in the People's Republic of China run as high as 98 percent! The score for Russia and Latin America is estimated to be 90 percent. An attorney for Microsoft estimated that the company is losing half its revenue worldwide to piracy. By his calculation, pirates are stealing another whole Microsoft. Given the U.S. dominance in software, piracy is a serious threat to the economy.

The violation of intellectual property rights is not confined to individuals selling pirated copies of software. Anytime you borrow a program a friend purchased with a licensing agreement and install it on your computer, you probably violated the licensing agreement. (There are many programs that are available without charge on the **Internet** and through various "shareware" bulletin boards.) Software companies offer a variety of licensing arrangements. Frequently universities are licensed to use software in a computing lab at a very low fee in order to introduce students to the programs. For the software vendor, the misappropriation of its intellectual property rights is a major problem.

Applications of IT   Electronic Securities Markets   On October 19 and 20, 1987, the stock market came close to what was later described as a "meltdown." There were a number of investigations of what happened during this collapse of the market. Two investment and trading strategies that are possible only because of computers were given a significant amount of blame for the problem.

Computers Fight Illiteracy

An experimental program at the Street Literacy Clinic in Harlem has been using computers to help illiterate people learn to read. Although a computer may intimidate someone, it is a very patient tutor for a person who cannot read. The computer will read something more than a hundred times without tiring.

Computers have not solved the country's literacy problem, but they do seem to help people who use them. A program in Santa Fe, New Mexico, provides remedial education for 250 people a year using a UNISYS system called ICON. The director said that he has seen students go from fifth-grade to twelfth-grade reading levels in a year.

These applications run on centralized systems and PC networks; most are multimedia and use touch screens, music, and pictures. They "speak" aloud the words they display.

At the Harlem clinic a student enters a booth and puts on earphones. When he or she touches the screen a letter appears. If the letter is an A, the student sees a red alarm box. The alarm rings and the computer says that the word *alarm* begins with the letter A; then it spells the word and writes it for the student. The developer of the system expected students to get tired after twenty minutes; some stay for two hours.

The extensive development required for these systems makes their costs high, from $5,000 to $10,000. The state of Ohio is buying the UNISYS system for more than $2.8 million to put in most of its prisons. The state figures it will pay for itself in a year.

It is hard to describe the joy that an adult experiences when he or she conquers illiteracy. It appears that technology can help in this process, and do so in a cost effective manner.

One strategy, called portfolio insurance, involves the sale of futures to offset a falling stock market. In addition, the insurer sells stock while the market is falling, thus contributing to a decline in the price of stock. Arbitrageurs look for differences between stock index futures prices and the prices of the underlying stocks. Investigations of the October 1987 crash suggest that this arbitrage, combined with portfolio insurance, drove the market down and was responsible for much of the volatility in the market following October 19.

These strategies require computers to perform calculations and alert the trader or to actually send trades to brokers. In addition, computerized trading systems at the New York Stock Exchange help the arbitrageur, who must simultaneously trade stocks and futures before a price change eliminates an arbitrage opportunity. The end result of investigations into the crash was a series of "circuit breakers." When different averages move by a certain amount, trading is halted for some period of time to allow the market to adjust.

There are concerns that technology contributed to a lack of stability in the market and it may discourage individual investors from investing.

Monitoring   Computer systems offer the opportunity to monitor worker performance closely. An insurance company can determine how long it takes a representative to serve a customer on the telephone. An airline can tell how long a reservations agent takes on each call and how many calls the worker handles in each shift. On the production line, errors are traced back to the individual making them. Control systems also track individual worker productivity. At least one company was sued by an employee for **monitoring** her e-mail messages.

Many individuals respond negatively to such monitoring. It is possible employees will refuse to work with or try to sabotage systems that closely monitor their work performance. One solution adopted by an automobile manufacturer formed workers into teams; the firm publicizes the performance of the entire team rather than that of individual workers. Team members discuss the team's performance and try to figure out how to do better. Coupled with a team bonus system, this approach to monitoring lets management keep track of production without a severely negative effect on individuals who resent having their performance measured by a computer system.

Harassment   Too many times, it appears we are harassed by computers. Systems are designed to automatically send second, third, and even further overdue notices when a customer has a legitimate complaint about a bill. Computers are connected to automatic dialing machines to harass consumers via the phone. Systems appear unresponsive to an individual's problems because of the need to process large volumes of information quickly. Some systems may be flexible but require cumbersome manual procedures to update records and keep them accurate. If a clerk makes an error or omission, the computer will continue sending letters to the customer. In other situations, employees learn to rely on systems and do not provide customer service when a system is unavailable. One bank installed an on-line inquiry system for tellers cashing checks. For backup, the tellers were provided with the same hard-copy microfilm used before installation of the on-line system. However, when the new computer system became unavailable because of a malfunction, many tellers refused to cash checks and told customers to come back when the computer was working.

Defense   Since so much of the economy of developed countries depends on technology, these nations are vulnerable to electronic warfare. In a recent, popular novel, a war with the United States begins when the aggressor country's banks make massive sales of Treasury bills through electronic markets, driving down the value of the dollar and impacting the U.S. stock market. A 1995 issue of *Time* had a cover story on "**Cyberwar**" in which the magazine interviewed officers at the Army Intelligence and Security Command who plan electronic offenses against enemies and defenses for the U.S.

As an example, a country might try to insert a computer virus in an enemy's telephone switching stations to cause a nationwide failure of communications. If you insert logic "bombs" in enemy communications networks, you can set them off to disrupt rail and air transportation as well. Other scenarios described various kinds of electronic mischief to disable an IT-intensive economy without firing a shot.

Gambling on the Net

Two companies are setting up casinos in Caribbean countries to get around U.S. laws that bar interstate gambling from home. From the comfort of home, you will be able to place bets using a credit card or money predeposited at the casino. One analyst estimated that gambling on the Internet could become a $10 billion a year enterprise.

A Canadian entrepreneur is opening the Internet Online Offshore Electronic Casino in the Turks and Caicos islands. Another computer expert is working on WagerNet, a sports betting service which will be located in Belize. WagerNet is to operate a bit like the Nasdaq, matching people who bet on a sports event. You will put a bet offer on the Net and see if anyone accepts the bet. There will be a 2.5% transactions fee, but that is much less than the 10% that often goes to a sports bookie.

Of course, there are problems. It is not clear that bettors will have confidence in electronic casinos—will the casino disappear into Cyberspace if you win too much? How can you be sure that the odds in the casino are not rigged against every better, with a much larger percentage to the house than in a regulated, physical casino? The other problem with gambling on the Net is U.S. regulators and Congress. Already disturbed by the prospect of offshore pornography becoming available easily in the U.S., various Congressmen are trying to regulate the Net. Do you think regulation is possible given the distributed nature of the Internet and the ability to access servers around the world?

The Impact of IT   Educating for Computing   There is a definite need to educate individuals for the following roles:

- *Users.* Probably the largest group we consider will be those who use technology—individuals in firms whose primary responsibilities are not in the IS field. These employees need to be able to use computers as a part of their work. The typical professional has some type of managerial workstation, a powerful PC connected to a network. The user will need to understand something about computers, networks, and different kinds of software. At the next level, the user needs to understand how to use this technology to improve his or her performance.

- *IS professionals.* These individuals will work with the technology. The category includes programmers, systems analysts, managers, and other staff members. Systems professionals must have an in-depth understanding of the technology and its applications. Some of these employees will develop hardware and software packages. Others will apply combinations of hardware, packages, and custom programs to the problems faced by organizations.

- *Interface personnel.* Between the IS professional and the user is an interface staff. These individuals have functional knowledge of how computers and software work but do not have a command of all the technical details. They need to be conversant with the kinds of problems faced by organizations and understand business and management.

- *Factory and office workers using computer equipment.* Factory jobs that used to require minimal education now require skilled workers. One factory has undergone dramatic changes over a ten-year period. A decade ago, the plant could operate with a largely unskilled and uneducated work force. Today, parts of the plant have been replaced by a "clean room" for production. Parts bins are tracked using computers and bar codes. In one room, a machine operator uses a touch screen on a computer-driven testing device to enter testing parameters.

Some of the best and highest paying factory jobs today are at semiconductor plants. At one of Intel's newest plants making Pentium and Pentium Pro processors, the minimum educational qualification for a job is an associate's degree from a two-year college. A factory worker with this background needs a far different educational experience than the steelworker or autoworker of twenty years ago.

Are primary and secondary schools preparing students for these types of jobs? Where will skilled employees come from in the future for clerical and factory jobs? Will business itself have to educate its workers? In a number of cities, companies are "adopting" local schools, especially in the inner city, in order to improve the quality of education. Businesses provide funding for special programs and encourage their employees to volunteer in the schools.

Our challenge is to provide education and on-the-job training for all these diverse needs. Without qualified individuals, progress in the application of information technology will be severely retarded.

The Technology Gap   There is a serious concern over whether computer and communications technology will accentuate the gulf that exists between the "haves" and the "have nots," among both individuals and societies. Will those who are able to acquire computer systems or knowledge of how to use them become the new elite? Will individuals who are not computer literate find themselves relegated to a second-class existence? It is unlikely such extremes will evolve, but it is likely significant segments of the population will become less able to deal with an economy that depends on information technology. (A low cost Internet Appliance would help here as it would make the technology more affordable for schools and the home.)

Employment   Labor leaders are extremely concerned about the possibility of wide-scale unemployment because of information technology. The computer and communications industries are two of the largest in the United States, and created hundreds of thousands of jobs. Naturally, the implementation of some information systems eliminated or modified jobs, though few statistics indicate the overall impact on employment.

It does appear the continued introduction of automation will reduce employment in manufacturing. The extent to which this effect will be offset by the creation of jobs assembling and servicing new manufacturing equipment is unknown. However, increased technology will certainly require a more highly skilled, better-educated work force.

There are also implications from the implementation of information systems on the pace of technological evolution, employment security, and

Talking Through a Mac

At the Toronto Pediatric Intensive Care Unit in the Hospital for Sick Children, many patients are unable to talk because they have tubes in their throats to facilitate breathing. For a child, being in intensive care is frightening enough; not being able to communicate just makes the experience that much more difficult.

Several doctors have used a Macintosh and the MacInTalk voice synthesizer to help children communicate. The Mac is suspended over the patient on a special stand at the foot of the bed. Children use a trackball and need only to be able to move one finger to operate the computer. The child selects messages with a pointer controlled by the trackball. If a child's hands are bandaged so he or she can't press the button on the trackball, the system plays the message under the pointer if it stays on it for a specified time interval. Quadriplegics can operate the computer by using a device that lets them move the pointer with head motions.

The system has eight screens with thirty messages each. Examples of topics for each screen include Pain, Position, Food and Drink, and TV and Games. Some screens have a stick figure so that the patient can point to parts of the body. The child can select a verb and point to a body part, for example, "please scratch my foot." There is a limited ability for the child to compose his or her own message as well, in addition to the more than six hundred messages already in the system.

the importance of retraining workers when jobs change. Have individual initiative and the interest of jobs been reduced or enhanced by computers?

Finally, there is speculation that firms' investments in technology are finally affecting middle management. With electronic communications, GDSSs, and groupware, individuals can communicate easily. There is no longer a need for a layer of middle management as a conduit for information between the next-lower and next-higher level in the organization. Many middle managers who lost jobs in the recession of the early 1990s are unable to find other work. There is no hard evidence IT is reducing these middle-management jobs, but many labor experts and economists suggest it is contributing to the reduction of middle-manager ranks. The T-Form organization uses IT design variables to create a flat structure with minimum overhead. It needs fewer employees than a traditional organization. The remaining employees will use IT as an integral part of their jobs.

Privacy   Certainly, one of the most widely debated topics relating to society is the issue of an individual's right to **privacy**. Foreign governments have placed restrictions on the international flow of information. Many bills and acts have been proposed to ensure the individual's privacy. At what point does the right to privacy conflict with other rights? Society certainly has the need and the right to have certain kinds of information that contributes to the general welfare. Demographic information and information on income levels are vitally important in establishing national policy. Information on wages and financial conditions, however, is considered to be extremely sensitive by most individuals.

Current thinking is that individuals should have the right to ascertain whether information held about them is correct and to enforce the correction of errors. There is less agreement on the penalties imposed for misuse of private information maintained in some type of data bank. Other questions arise as to whether individuals should have the right to know who requested information about them from a data bank. Some countries are very concerned about this trend. For example, Sweden enacted a comprehensive program to regulate the development of data banks.

Some legislators in the U.S. are concerned about the practice of state governments selling data. A number of states sell access to automobile registration data. Direct-mail marketing organizations use auto registration information to target mailings. In other instances, individuals obtain the license plate numbers of a group attending a meeting and use that information to harass the attendees.

A number of solutions have been proposed, and the federal government passed **legislation** affecting only federal agencies. There have been suggestions to extend the federal law to the private sector. As it stands now, the legislation requires a large amount of record keeping about the pattern of access to records containing any personal information. There are fears that the proposals for the private sector may prove extremely costly for organizations. One important issue, then, is what the balance should be between the individual's rights and the burdens and costs of protection and record keeping.

Security Closely related to problems of privacy is the issue of system security. There are many possible threats to the security and integrity of computer systems, particularly those with widespread accessibility by individuals external to the organization. Recently, there were a number of well-publicized penetrations of various computer systems, including a major cancer research hospital's on-line system. Researchers in the field are working on methods of encrypting data so they cannot be intercepted and decoded by an unfriendly user. Such concerns are very important, given the existence of highly sensitive data in on-line databases and the need for a secure payments system for electronic commerce.

The Growth of International Business One of the major changes in the global economy in the past decade is the growth of international business. The United States, Canada, and Mexico are reducing and eliminating most tariffs. Europe is working on creating one market to facilitate trade. Major corporations view themselves as worldwide global firms that happen to have a headquarters in a particular country. What are the implications of internationalization for information technology?

One major problem for the multinational is restrictions on the flow of data across borders. A related problem is the need for standardization, which may be antithetical to a management climate that stresses local control and initiative. Why might we need standards for information technology? Most headquarters operations collect financial data from various

MANAGEMENT PROBLEM 25-1

The president of the Cambridge Group, a 500-person consulting firm, came to the conclusion that the firm must use technology to reduce its overhead. She said, "We mark our consultants up five times what they earn, and it is getting very difficult to sustain the 15% a year increase we have had in overhead. Clients are beginning to use our competitors." Her plan is to adopt much of the technology described in this text for knowledge workers. In particular, she envisions a substantial number of consultants working out of their homes using notebook computers, fax, and cellular phones when on the road.

She also plans to implement Lotus Notes to act as a coordinating device among consultants, especially those working together on a project. The president hopes Notes will also form a kind of corporate intelligence of the skills and experience of the individuals in the firm.

She knows there will be a major impact on the work force from these changes. Consultants will have to adapt to new physical working conditions and to using a lot of technology that is foreign to many, especially the longer-term staff members. More troubling is the need to lay off about 20 secretarial and clerical staff members who will not be needed in a high-tech environment. "These people are generally not highly salaried and they have few options—I am very concerned about how to handle the layoffs."

What do you recommend to the President of the Boston Group? How should she approach her implementation problems?

subsidiaries. If there are no standards for reporting, the task at headquarters will be much more difficult.

Some countries try to support their domestic computer industries or are concerned about their balance of payments problems. They may make it difficult to import the kind of computers the multinational would like to use. It also may be difficult to expand processing capacity in such a country when the business grows.

Some Suggested Solutions

Education   The excitement over the Internet highlights the different opportunities available to students from homes with PCs compared to homes without. A $500 netsurfing computer that doubled as a TV set might help reduce this disparity.

Education about information systems should be a part of every high school curriculum, and certainly each college graduate should be exposed to information technology. Continuing-education programs on technology should also be encouraged for citizens who want more general knowledge, as opposed to those who want to enter the computer profession. Companies can do their part by providing general education and training in the effective use of information technology.

It is suggested by some that **multimedia** will revolutionize education. For this revolution to take place, schools will need to redesign and develop new curricula in which the capabilities of technology are exploited to provide new ways of learning. And of course the necessary funding for this will have to be found. If this revolution occurs, children will learn to work with the technology as a part of their entire educational experience.

Some companies are using computers to help illiterate workers function on the job. In one warehouse, forklift drivers who cannot read get instructions from "talking computers" they wear on their belts. At a Raytheon plant, inspectors looking at circuit boards through microscopes dictate reports into a voice-recognition computer instead of writing the report. This system makes it possible to employ workers for whom English is not the native language.

Technical Safeguards   Some problems involving **misuse of information** systems are technical in nature. We should attempt to make systems as secure as possible to avoid penetration by hackers. Thorough testing is needed to prevent programs from inadvertently disclosing sensitive data. There should be technical checks on procedures to prevent accidental entry by unauthorized individuals.

A more difficult challenge is to design a system to be secure from skilled agents or individuals attempting to commit **fraud** through the system. Protecting a system from malicious programs like viruses is also not easy. Protection may take the form of monitoring to keep track of users or introducing special encoding algorithms to maintain security.

Controls   Some of the controls discussed in the previous chapter can help prevent certain problems from occurring. Requiring several individuals to authorize changes in programming and databases and checking input carefully help maintain data integrity. Controls requiring all data to be processed help solve such problems as data not updated to reflect payments. Controls are important to the extent they ensure accurate processing and screen out requests in which access is aimed at fraud or mischief.

Legislation   Another solution to some of the social issues, particularly privacy and abuse of power, is legislation. In 1973, Sweden enacted a law regulating personal data maintained about individuals. The act established a data inspection board that grants permission to keep a data bank of personal information. Sensitive data, such as records of criminal convictions, can be maintained only by an agency charged by statute with the job of keeping these records. Once permission is granted, the data inspection board issues regulations to prevent undue encroachment on privacy. Responsibility for maintaining the correct data lies with the organization maintaining the data bank, not with the individual whose records are in the bank. Organizations whose key records are in error must make corrections demanded by the individual. Damages are specified for violations of these regulations.

   In 1974, a comprehensive Federal Privacy Act was passed in the U.S., requiring government agencies to keep elaborate records of the use of personal information. Records of inquiries by those whose records are kept must also be provided. To extend these requirements or a similar set to private-sector firms, some of the following topics are usually proposed in privacy legislation:

- Notifying of the subject about the existence of a record
- Responding to inquiries on the contents of data and the use of records
- Investigating complaints
- Obtaining consent for each use of the data
- Checking authorization for requests
- Keeping a log of all accesses
- Providing subjects' statements when disputed data are released
- Sending corrections and/or subjects' statements to past recipients of information
- Ensuring accurate compilation of records
- Providing additional data to give a fair picture
- Providing a secure system

Although many of these requirements would prevent abuses of data, the regulations are potentially expensive to implement.

System Design   Some of the preceding solutions will be implemented and will help solve some of the societal problems with information systems, but are they really sufficient? To a large extent, many social implications are determined in the process of designing a system. By asking appropriate questions during the design process, we can assess some of the potential problems with the impact of the system on society. For example, we can ask the following questions about each application:

- Is the application a potential threat to anyone's rights? What could go wrong? For example, do the files contain rumors, hearsay information, or unevaluated reports on individuals?
- Is there a built-in incentive against using the system? For example, does it police workers who contribute the data?
- Is it difficult for someone to use the system? That is, could an unauthorized individual fill out the forms, understand the input, enter data through a terminal, or do whatever is required?
- How many ways could someone find to defraud or penetrate the system?
- If someone wanted to misuse the data in the system, how could he or she evade the procedures that safeguard them? What could someone do to misuse the data?
- Is the system sufficiently reliable?

The design team should encourage independent attempts to penetrate the system along these lines to verify the completeness and viability of the design. A well-designed system is the best guarantee against harassment, abuse, privacy violations, and alienation.

Helping the Hospital

A 1995 study of two major Boston hospitals pointed out some serious problems with the operation of hospitals in the United States:

- Doctors sometime lack knowledge and information about a drug resulting in the wrong prescription or the wrong dosage.
- There is a lack of systems for checking the identity or dose of drugs, with a result that look-alike or sound-alike drugs lead to patients getting the wrong medicine.
- There is a lack of information about the patient leading to poor access to medical records or lab tests when the physician is prescribing drugs.
- There are errors in writing down drug orders so that sometimes it is necessary to copy or re-enter physician orders on a paper form, which can lead to further errors.

The authors concluded that "most preventable injuries are not due to just one system failure but result from breakdowns at several points in the system." The researchers also found that hospital information systems were outdated and that interdepartmental communications were unsatisfactory.

These findings suggest that at least these two hospitals would benefit from a reengineering effort. In what ways could information technology be used to solve the problems described above?

ETHICS AND INFORMATION TECHNOLOGY

There is a professional code of conduct for computer professionals developed by the Association for Computing Machinery, a society of individuals who teach and work in the field. This code applies only peripherally to users and managers who may work with technology, but who do not consider themselves professionals. Does IT create any new ethical dilemmas for management?

The discussion of social problems at the beginning of this chapter raise some of the ethical issues often associated with IT and management. Ethical considerations include concerns that:

- Data in the organization are used for their intended purpose and the intended purpose is legitimate.

- Monitoring of workers be undertaken with their consent and the data are used to help rather than punish the workers involved.

- Systems and services made available to individuals external to the firm behave as specified and cause no harm to others.

- Systems within the firm are not guilty of harassment.

- Appropriate privacy is maintained, for example, e-mail files are not read by individuals not involved in the exchange of messages.

- Appropriate software copyrights are observed and there is respect for intellectual property.

- Systems are secure and well controlled.

Ethical decisions arise frequently when dealing with information technology. Mason suggests how we can identify and approach a situation where ethical considerations arise. "The crucial point occurs when a moral agent—one that by definition has choices—decides to change the state of information or information technology in a human system. Changes in hardware, software, information content, information flow, knowledge-based jobs, and the rules and regulations affecting information are among the many things that agents do that affect others ... [W]e must use our moral imagination to guide our choices so that we can contribute positively toward making the kind of ethical world in which we want to live and want to bequeath to our future generations. How can we do this? ... [F]undamental is our conscience, aided by our understanding and expertise in information technology. If we have an inkling our behavior ... might in some way harm others, we probably should examine our decisions a little more carefully and from an ethical point-of-view" (Mason, 1995, p. 55).

Mason continues, "The facts of an ethical situation can be summarized by four factors. The first factor is to clearly identify the moral agent. Whose actions will bring about the technology-induced change? The next factor is the set of alternative courses-of-action available to the agent. These are the real world acts that will have an effect on the human system under consideration. Acts have consequences, hence the third factor: … delineation of the results that are expected to occur if each act is taken. Finally, it is essential to identify the stakeholders who will be affected by the consequences of the acts. … stakeholders have an interest in what the agent does" (Mason, 1995, p. 55).

It is easy to choose ethical behavior in a classroom setting when discussing a case study. It is much more difficult when working in an organization and facing budgetary constraints and pressure from peers, customers, top management, and stockholders. Kallman and Grillo (1993) suggest several informal guidelines for ethical behavior:

- *The family test.* Would you be comfortable telling your closest family members about your decision or action?

- *The investigative reporter test.* How would your actions look if reported in a newspaper or on a television news program?

- *The feeling test.* How does the decision feel to you? If you are uneasy about a decision or action but cannot understand why, your intuition is telling you it is not the right thing to do.

- *The empathy test.* How does this decision look if you put yourself in someone else's position? How would it look to another party affected by your actions?

Significant lapses in business ethics in the U.S. and around the world create a new awareness of the need for ethical behavior in highly interdependent societies and economies. The ethical issues surrounding technology

---

MANAGEMENT PROBLEM 25-2

Julia Reed is the vice president of sales for SV Semiconductors, a manufacturer of applications specific integrated circuits (ASICS). Customers design chips for special purposes like engine controls and SV produces the chips in volume. The company has a proprietary chip design program and manufacturing process. Customers use the chip design program, and it is one of the company's major selling points.

The company president, Ken Larson, heard from a customer that a sales representative was offering to provide company documents on the program and on SV's manufacturing process. He was very angry as the company had generous compensation and stock options for almost all employees. Larson viewed this incident as a case of extreme disloyalty and a threat to the firm. He demanded that Julia arrange to have the e-mail for all the sales force monitored, that is, she should obtain copies of all messages from computer files and read them to see if she can figure out who might be offering to give away company secrets.

Julia is very concerned about this request. It comes from the president, which makes it hard to turn down. On the other hand, she is troubled by the idea of invading every salesperson's privacy on a suspicion that one person may have done something wrong. She thought, "We don't even know for sure that an offer was made—what did the sales rep say and what did the customer think he heard?"

What advice would you give to Julia? What would you do in her place?

are probably easier than most and we hope your knowledge will help you make the right decisions.

THE FUTURE OF INFORMATION TECHNOLOGY

What are the likely future trends in IT that will affect managers and users of systems? The manager and the user should prepare to take advantage of opportunities provided by changes in information processing technology. It is unlikely any organization will remain untouched by this technology during the coming decade.

Hardware and Software

Today's trend is for organizations to move toward the client-server architecture. Users work with client computers connected to network servers. What other trends are likely to affect what we see in the future?

First, users have clearly voted for graphical user interfaces (GUIs). The graphical interface makes it possible to create more-complex software without a proportional increase in the complexity of the user interface. The popularity of the Macintosh, which has always featured a GUI, and

The Homebound and Cyberspace

Ilene Weinberg was becoming despondent as she lost her mobility to Parkinson's disease. In 1991 her son bought her a computer and enrolled her in SeniorNet, an on-line information service for the elderly. Though Mrs. Weinberg does not often leave her home, she spends several hours a day on her computer, chatting on-line with friends around the country, getting computer games from boyfriends, and even writing columns and essays.

Today's technology lets anyone who can blink an eye or move a toe control appliances at home. Using a large, visual keyboard, disabled people can move the cursor around a keyboard in a variety of ways, including a control rod manipulated by the user's chin. You click on different letters through some special means like puffing into a straw. A 40-year-old accountant in Pennsylvania who is confined to a wheelchair with muscular dystrophy uses the visual keyboard and manipulates a joystick with his lower lip. He can do accounting work and handle correspondence with his computer.

The accountant also uses an environmental-control unit (ECU) to operate a variety of home appliances. A user scans through a menu of objects including the telephone, lights, computer, etc., until he reaches the desired appliance. Through a switch like a toggle or a beam of light interrupted by blinking his eye, the user indicates that this is the appliance he wants to control. The ECU sends signals through a wall outlet to the regular household wiring. Each device under control is plugged into a control box that responds to the signals sent by the ECU.

the explosive sales of Windows95 for PCs ensures that a GUI is the interface of choice.

In hardware there is a great deal of interest in **parallel computers** featuring more than one central processing unit. There are a variety of parallel designs and strategies for building systems. Some designs feature a relatively small number of processors which may have their own memory or may share memory with other processors. Massively parallel computers have a large number of processors, possibly in the thousands, which are connected in a complex network typology.

Parallel computers were first designed to compete with supercomputers. Massively parallel systems have about 10 percent of the world's supercomputer market. Advocates of this type of design, however, are now targeting mainframes, a $40-billion business currently dominated by IBM. Intel, the manufacturer of the chip for the PC, has a division that sells a massively parallel computer made from Intel's own microprocessors.

A major bottleneck with parallel computing is software and writing programs. Almost all programs are sequential, and most programmers think sequentially. To exploit parallel computing we will need new languages, and programmers must adopt a different approach to writing software. There is much current research on making parallel machines easier to use. A Yale computer scientist developed a set of six extensions to a conventional language so these languages could operate in parallel. (This same computer scientist is developing a system called Piranah, which will assign parts of a problem to networked computers that are idle.)

Communications

Deregulation and competition are responsible for major changes in communications services. Common carriers are developing new products to encourage customers to use their facilities rather than design a custom network. Services like frame relay, ATM, and high-speed switched circuits are advertised as approaches to connecting LANs across a wide area. Companies have discovered the Internet which is clearly becoming the U.S. (and possibly the world) "Information Superhighway." Cable TV operators are becoming common carriers for voice and data and will provide Internet access as well.

Wireless technology is gaining increasing attention because of its flexibility, especially for workers who travel. The rapid growth of cellular and other wireless communications techniques led some experts to conclude the telephone and television industry are trading places. That is, originally, all television was broadcast and all phone calls were made through a physical connection. In the future, will most television come from a physical connection (cable) while phone calls are broadcast?

As one vendor likes to state, the network is the computer. We will have a workstation on our desks, and a network will determine where the data and programs we need reside. The network of a large number of computers will then provide us, its **clients**, with the data and programs needed to solve our problems.

Multimedia   Multimedia has generated a great deal of excitement. There are at least three broad uses for multimedia. The first of these is the most obvious: education. Multimedia offers the opportunity to promote interactive learning and bring a variety of visual images into the classroom. At this point in time, it is not clear if multimedia is more enjoyable for the student or if the student learns more from it. There have been anecdotal reports, but no large studies of the impact of multimedia on learning. It does appear that multimedia can help motivate students, which many educators consider a key to effective learning. Many reports of multimedia in education come from companies that use it for very task-oriented training for employees.

A second use of multimedia is for presenting information to employees and customers. Companies are experimenting with putting repair and user manuals on the Internet and/or on CD-ROM. Novell, a vendor of network software, maintains user manuals on the Internet for customers and employees to search. McDonnell Douglas is planning to put many of its manuals on the Internet. With a wireless connection, a mechanic working on a plane in New Delhi could access an up-to-date version of a jet's repair manual in St. Louis over the Internet.

The third area of interest in multimedia is entertainment. Microsoft is working to bring the Windows interface to home entertainment equipment. The motion picture and television industry are developing multimedia products for entertainment and for education. More than providing a new generation of video games, multimedia might be appealing enough to encourage further education in the home as opposed to formal classes.

Walt Disney Studies purchased Capital Cities/ABC, while Westinghouse bought the CBS television network, and Time-Warner acquired Turner Broadcasting. In general, content providers are purchasing communications firms. One objective for some players is to develop a 500-channel interactive television. We do not yet know all of the features such interactive TV might have, though we do know it will be controlled by a computer chip inside the TV or a control box. It might also be piped to your PC which will be equipped to show video. It is expected you could dial a specific show and move pieces of it about. You might be able to interact with the story line or even make decisions that would change the outcome! A sports fan might be able to choose camera angles at a sporting event. Of course, one important question is whether there is a market for these advanced services, especially, as one newspaper suggested, in a nation of people who have great difficulty recording a show on a VCR.

Virtual Reality   University laboratories are using technology to create other "realities" for a number of years. Now these efforts are showing possible commercial payoffs. **Virtual reality** is the use of technology to create an environment that is in some way removed from the real world. A user might put on a "data glove" with sensors that control a piece of equipment simulated on a computer. A game player puts on a helmet with tiny TV screens, and perceives that he or she is in another environment. The wearer controls parts of that environment with a data glove or joystick.

What are possible applications of this artificial reality? One graduate student at MIT noticed construction crane operators had to master a complex set of controls to operate a crane. This student used a data glove that allowed the operator to control a simulated crane using natural hand movements. Bechtel, a large construction firm, outfitted a pipe lifter with virtual-reality controls so an untrained operator can run the machine. This glove is also used by the Boston Red Sox to analyze how pitchers throw a baseball. It is expected the system will be useful in analyzing repetitive stress injuries. Engineers at Northrop Corporation are using a virtual reality system to redesign the F-18 fighter jet. The engineer wears a data glove and uses a type of mouse to move parts around in a simulated design and assembly application.

Another possibility is to use virtual reality to assist a physician. Researchers at the University of North Carolina at Chapel Hill created a simulated environment to allow a physician to see inside the body. This system employs a head-mounted display to superimpose ultrasonic images of a fetus onto a live video image of a pregnant woman's abdomen. The ultrasound image is placed over the video image on a liquid-crystal display (LCD) screen within the helmet to produce a window into the body. A physician can use this system to gain an accurate perspective of the position of, say, a probe inside the body.

A relatively new technology, virtual reality has a great deal of potential to make a dramatic change in the way certain tasks are accomplished.

CHAPTER SUMMARY

1. There is no question that information technology is becoming more complex, especially the combination of computer and communications technologies.

2. Society and its institutions are becoming more dependent on technology every day. The reliability of IT is a constant concern.

3. Software piracy is a threat to many companies, depriving them of revenue they need to continue to refine their products and remain in business.

4. Key applications of technology include the securities market, banking, and transportation.

5. Technology can be used to monitor workers, something most employees find unattractive.

6. There have been instances where individuals are harassed by systems.

7. The U.S. is increasingly concerned about electronic warfare in which an opponent tries to sabotage crucial computers and communications networks.

8. The successful use of IT requires an educated population, yet the quality of education in the U.S. seems to be in a general decline.

9. A dangerous technology gap may be developing between those who can afford and learn about IT and those who have no exposure to it.

10. Using IT to transform organizations is likely to lead to unemployment unless greater efficiency from technology is able to expand the economy to absorb displaced workers.

11. Technology, especially databases, can compromise privacy; there are various protection mechanisms suggested for individual privacy.

12. System security is a major concern, especially as computers become more interconnected through networks.

13. IT is an important facilitator of international business, yet countries sometimes raise barriers to the free use of technology within their borders.

14. It is important to consider the ethical implications of designing a system.

15. Current trends in technology suggest hardware will continue to evolve, putting more power in smaller packages on the desktop. Medium and large machines will be used for servers, and parallel processing will become more popular.

16. Communications networks will show higher speeds (greater bandwidth) and there will be increasing use of wireless communications.

17. Networking will continue to explode, especially the use of the Internet, and companies will have a myriad of electronic connections with customers and suppliers.

18. Multimedia, while expensive to develop, will expand for training and education. It will also be used to communicate with customers and employees, often via the Internet.

IMPLICATIONS FOR MANAGEMENT

The picture that emerges from our discussions about the future of information technology throughout the text suggests that IT, the organization, and the economy are inextricably intertwined. Organizations have been dependent on technology for many years to process basic transactions. Today, the technology is responsible for new organizational structures. Communications and workgroup technology create virtual organizations and electronic communities. Members of the organization are connected with each other through networks. These networks extend across multiple locations worldwide, allowing people to communicate easily, form unofficial, virtual departments and subunits, and coordinate their activities. A modern organization is connected electronically to customers and suppliers. Physical proximity no longer needs to be a constraint in defining workgroups and collegial relationships.

The challenge for you and for all managers is to understand the tremendous potential of information technology to change and improve the way organizations function. A powerful technology exists. The ability to effectively manage IT is the key to maximizing its value to organizations.

KEY WORDS

Clients	Misuse of information
Control	Monitoring
Cyberwar	Multimedia
Fraud	Parallel computers
Intellectual property	Privacy
Internet	Server
Legislation	Virtual reality

RECOMMENDED READING

IEEE Spectrum. (The January issues have an excellent annual forecast of technology.)

Kallman, E., and J. Grillo. *Ethical Decision Making and Information Technology.* New York: Mitchell/McGraw-Hill, 1993. (An interesting book on ethics with a number of cases to discuss.)

Communications of the ACM, vol. 38, no. 12 (December 1995). (An issue devoted to questions of ethics in information technology.)

DISCUSSION QUESTIONS

1. Why is the use of a system the responsibility of the systems design team and the organization?
2. Is there such thing as a right to privacy?
3. Does the presence of computer equipment make it easier to violate an individual's privacy?
4. Is fraud easier with a computer system than with its manual predecessor?
5. What would be your response to a proposal for a national data bank of information on citizens for purposes of social science research?

6. What are the ethical responsibilities of an IS professional?

7. It has been suggested that an electronic funds-transfer system could eliminate "float," that is, the use of money by a purchaser who has not yet been billed for goods or services. Would the elimination of float be desirable? How would an electronic funds-transfer system affect the public?

8. In your opinion, would it be possible for a group to utilize computers to rig a nationwide election?

9. Why do schools not teach more about information technology?

10. Do computers make it easier to violate an individual's right to privacy? What are the dangers of keeping centralized government records on each citizen? What are the advantages?

11. Do employers have a responsibility to retrain workers replaced by information technology?

12. Why is the public so badly informed about the capabilities of computer systems? Do you feel most problems seen by the public are caused by the computer, the procedures associated with the system, or the original systems design?

13. What can be done to reduce the possibility of a computer-based fraud that would cause the failure of a business?

14. How could IT be used to solve some of the pressing problems of society, such as reducing the amount of energy consumed?

15. What priorities should be used by underdeveloped countries in trying to develop IT capabilities?

16. What are the implications of continuing decreases in the cost of hardware?

17. How might a company use virtual reality?

18. What are the implications for technology education of the dramatically increasing home market for multimedia computers?

19. How is a highly technological society like the U.S. vulnerable to "electronic aggression"?

20. What kind of safeguards can a company or group of companies adopt to protect vital technology?

21. What does the statement mean, "the network is the computer"?

22. What is the appeal of parallel processing computers?

23. What advances in computer technology are needed to facilitate decision support systems and the development of unstructured applications?

24. Why do engineers constantly try to reduce the size of computer components?

25. What are the corporate applications of multimedia?

26. What is the relationship between the Internet and multimedia?

27. What advantages accrue from companies connecting to each other electronically?

28. What are the drawbacks of workplace monitoring? Why might management want to monitor worker productivity?

29.   What forms of resistance would you expect to see to monitoring programs?

30.   What are a manager's responsibilities for information technology?

CHAPTER 25 PROJECT

AN INFORMATION TECHNOLOGY DICHOTOMY

Some writers suggest that the United States risks falling into a system in which only a small elite with access to and an understanding of information technology will run the economy, while large numbers of undereducated and underemployed individuals perform menial jobs or subsist on welfare payments. Those who make this argument point to the poor quality of education and the lack of computer access in low-income areas. They also cite declining interest in mathematics and science, especially in poorer urban school districts.

Locate two or three essays by educators who discuss this problem, and critique them. Do you feel that the arguments have merit? Is the risk that is pointed out real? If so, what are the policy implications? What should government and private citizens do to prevent these dire predictions from coming true?

GLOSSARY

Access time   The time required to retrieve data from secondary storage and move them to primary memory.

Address   The location of a character or word in computer memory. Also the location of a track or record on a random-access device.

Agents   "Intelligent" software modules that perform some task for their human owner, like wandering through a network looking for a particular product for sale.

Algorithm   An effective procedure for accomplishing some task. A set of repetitive steps that when followed terminates in a solution.

Analog   Resembling something; analog voice communications represent voice as a continuous wave form.

ANSI   American National Standards Institute; develops industry standards for a number of technologies.

Application   The use of technology to accomplish a task, e.g., processing incoming orders.

Application program   A set of instructions that embody the logic of an application. It should be distinguished from a supervisory program, which controls the operations of the computer.

Architecture   An organizations hardware and software pattern, e.g., a client server architecture features servers with data and programs and remote clients usually with a graphical interface capable of accessing data and running programs to process it.

Applications package   A program or series of programs intended for use by more than one group of users.

Arithmetic registers   CPU registers that actually perform arithmetic operations on data.

Arithmetic/logic unit   The portion of the central processing unit that performs computations.

Artificial intelligence   A field of computer science that attempts to develop computer applications that exhibit human intelligence in a limited domain.

Artificial reality   The use of technology to create an electronic representation of reality in which the user can manipulate the environment.

ASCII   American Standard Code for Information Interchange; a 7-bit code used frequently for asynchronous (character-by-character) communications.

Assembler   A translator that accepts assembly language as input and produces machine language as output.

Assembly language   A language that closely resembles machine language, although mnemonics are substituted for numeric codes in instructions and addresses. Generally, one machine-language statement is produced for each assembly-language statement during the translation process.

Asynchronous operation   Any operation that occurs out of phase with other operations. For example, in certain CPUs, an instruction look-ahead feature, which fetches instructions before they are needed, operates asynchronously with regular instruction processing.

Asynchronous transfer mode (ATM)   A very high speed digital communications service that is likely to become standard for connecting different computer networks over medium to large distances.

Audio response   Vocal output produced by a special device that contains prerecorded syllables or synthesizes speech.

Audit trail   A means for tracing data on a source document to an output, such as a report, or for tracing an output to its source.

Background program   In a multiprogramming environment, a program that can be executed whenever the computer is not executing a program having higher priority. Contrast with foreground program.

Backup   Alternative procedures available for temporary or emergency use in case of system failure.

Bacterium   A program that infects a computer, replicates itself, and takes up as much time as possible.

Bandwidth   The range of frequencies for signaling; the difference between the highest and lowest frequencies available on a channel.

Bar coding   A series of bars that can be scanned and recognized by a machine; used to identify products and direct factory equipment.

Batch computer system   A system characterized by indeterminate turnaround time for output. Data and programs are collected into groups, or batches, and processed sequentially.

Baud   A measure of communications speed; the number of times the signal changes, which is roughly comparable to bits per second.

Benchmark   An existing "typical" program that is executed on a machine to evaluate machine performance.

Binary A number system using the base 2 and the digits 1 and 0.

Bit A binary digit, either 0 or 1; the smallest unit of information storage and transmission.

Bridge A device to connect two networks to each other.

Browser A program for accessing information on the World Wide Web.

Block mode Synchronous transmission in which characters are sent as a block with beginning and ending delimiters.

Buffer An area of memory used for temporary storage of data.

Bus A path used to carry signals, such as a connection between memory and the CPU in a microprocessor.

Byte Generally, an 8-bit grouping that represents one character or two digits and is operated on as a unit.

Cache A small, high-speed computer memory.

CASE (computer-aided software engineering) Hardware and software that helps to automate parts of the systems life cycle.

Case-based reasoning In Artificial Intelligence, programs that draw on a database of stored cases to locate problems similar to the one being faced by a user as a basis for recommending a solution.

Cellular The use of small cells or geographic areas for communications; signals are carried at low power so that the same frequency can be reused in each cell; computers "hand off" calls to new areas as a caller moves from one cell to another.

Cellular communications A type of communications in which low-power radio waves are transmitted to a stationary receiver. A computer "hands off" a conversation to an adjoining receiver as one of the communications devices moves toward it. An area is divided into many small cells so that a large number of connections are possible at one time using a minimum number of radio frequencies.

Central Processing Unit (CPU) The part of the computer that controls its operations; it contains the logic of the machine; for PCs the CPU is generally on a single chip or a small set of chips (Intel makes the 486 and Pentium chips which are CPUs).

Channel A computer component with logic capabilities that transfers input and output from main memory to secondary memory or peripherals, and vice versa.

Character Storing characters like the letter "a" as a code consisting of 7 or 8 bits; the common way most programs process data (like a word processor).

Character mode Transmission that is serial, one character at a time.

Check bit A word or a fixed-length group of characters to detect errors.

Check digit A number added to a key as a result of some calculation on the key. When data are entered, the computation is performed again and compared with the check digit to ensure correct entry.

Chip Small (6×6 mm) pieces of material, generally silicon, with various electronic components on the chip; the number of components can easily exceed one million.

CIO Chief Information Officer of a firm.

Circuit switching Communications in which a dedicated circuit is established between two devices as with a conventional telephone circuit.

CISC Complex instruction set computers; the original strategy for developing processors featuring microprogramming and a large variety of instructions.

Client The user's computer in a client-server system; contains local programs and storage.

Client-server architecture A computer architecture in which a number of computers in the PC to workstation class are clients of a larger computer which acts as a server; the server provides data and programs for the clients and in some cases does calculations for a client.

COBOL A popular business computing language used heavily on mainframe computers.

Cognitive style The orientation of an individual to approach decisions in a particular way, for example, from an analytic or heuristic view.

Compatibility The extent to which one can use programs, data, and/or devices of one computer system on another without modification.

Compiler A translator for high-level languages. Generally, several machine-language statements are generated for each high-level language statement.

Compression The use of an algorithm to reduce the amount of data that must be transmitted over communications lines.

Concentrator A device with some local storage that accepts data from several low-speed lines and transmits them over a single high-speed line to a computer installation.

Connectivity Related to having different computers and devices able to communicate with each other.

Control of computer systems Techniques to ensure the integrity and accuracy of computer processing.

Control unit (controller) A device that serves as an interface between channel commands and secondary-storage or peripheral devices.

Core storage A medium of computer storage; for most second- and third-generation computers, the term is used synonymously with "primary memory."

CRT (cathode-ray tube) A terminal resembling an ordinary television set that can display a large number of characters rapidly; many also have graphics capabilities.

Cycle time Either the time required to access information from primary storage and bring it to the CPU or the time required to fetch, decode, and execute an instruction within the CPU itself.

Data definition language The language used with a database management system to describe the relationships among data elements.

Data flow diagram (DFD) A graphical representation of an information system using a small set of symbols.

Data dictionary A component of a database management system that contains names of data elements and information about them.

Data structures The relationships among different fields of data on secondary storage.

Database A comprehensive, integrated collection of data organized to avoid duplication of data and permit easy retrieval of information.

Database administrator The individual in the organization with responsibility for the design and control of databases.

Database management system Software that organizes, catalogs, stores, retrieves, and maintains data in a database.

Debugging The task of finding and correcting mistakes in a program.

Decision support system A system designed to support decision makers, generally involving interactive computing and focused on one particular business problem.

Dedicated package A software package designed for a specific task, such as accounts receivable or payroll.

Demodulation The process of decoding the information from a modulated carrier wave; the reverse of modulation.

Digital Represented as a digit, usually a 0 or 1.

Direct access The ability to access data that is wanted without reading a large amount of irrelevant data; a disk is direct access while a tape is sequential.

Directory A dictionary or an algorithm for obtaining the address of logical records on a storage device.

Disk A random-access magnetic device used for secondary storage in computer systems.

Diskette A direct-access storage medium that is flexible; read/write heads of the drive actually touch the surface of the diskette.

Distributed processing The dispersion and use of computers among geographically separated locations; the computers are connected by a communications network.

Documentation Written descriptions of a system, usually with instructions on how to operate the system.

DOS The operating system used on many IBM personal computers.

Duplex Data transmission in both directions simultaneously using two separate paths.

EBCDIC Extended Binary Coded Decimal Interchange Code; an 8-bit code used by IBM to represent characters.

EDI Electronic Data (or Document) Interchange in which two organizations replace paper in transactions with electronic connections and transmission of data.

Electronic commerce The use of electronic networks as a market for buying and selling goods and services.

Electronic customer/supplier relationships The use of electronic connections like EDI to connect with customers and suppliers for processing transactions; these connections increase speed and reduce errors.

Electronic mail A system in which computer users have an electronic mailbox and send messages using terminals; communications occur at the convenience of the user without interruptions.

Electronic workflows The routing of work like an insurance application electronically within a company rather than in paper form.

Emulation Using a combination of hardware and software to make one computer device perform like another.

Encryption The coding of a data stream to prevent unauthorized access to the data.

End-user programming Users of information employ very high level languages and other tools to access information without having a computer professional develop a program for them.

Enhancement The process of making changes and improvements in operational programs.

Entity-relationship (ER) diagram A data model in which data structures are conceived of as entities which are connected by relationships.

Execute cycle (phase) The interpretation of an instruction and the execution of the operation it signifies, performed by the CPU.

Executive information system A system designed to support the special needs of top management.

Executive program The control program that schedules and manages the computer's resources.

Expert Systems An application of Artificial Intelligence in which a system captures the expertise of a human and makes it available to others.

Fault tolerant Computer systems that diagnose faults and reconfigure themselves; used for on-line applications.

Fetch cycle The retrieval of data or instructions from memory and moving of them to the CPU.

Fiber optic Thin strands of glass that carry data as a series of light pulses representing a 0 or 1.

Field A group of bit positions within an instruction. A subdivision of a record consisting of a group of characters.

Firmware An algorithm or process that is part way between software and hardware; e.g., taking a well understood program and encoding it on a chip to make it run faster.

Fixed point The representation of numbers as integers with no digits to the right of the decimal point.

Fixed-length record A record in which the length and position of each field is fixed for all processing.

Floating point The representation of a number as a quantity times a base raised to a power; for example, the number 472 as 4.72 times 10^2.

Floppy *See* Diskette.

Foreground program The highest-priority program in a multiprogramming environment.

Fourth-generation language A very high level language that produces a number of high-level language statements for every statement in the fourth-generation language.

Frame relay A high-speed packet switched communications service that can be used to link LANs in different locations.

Genetic algorithm An approach to problem solving that involves repeated cycles of selecting solutions, evaluating them, mutating the solution, and starting again.

Gopher A server on the Internet that provides character-oriented information in an easy-to-access manner.

Graphics Output involving figures, graphs, drawings, and/or animation.

Group DSSs Decision support systems designed to support a group of managers who have to make a decision.

Graphical User Interface (GUI) A computer interface characterized by graphics in addition to text; windowing interfaces are graphical.

Groupware The use of programs on a computer network to facilitate the sharing of information and communications between a group of people who have a common task in a shared environment.

Hardware The physical components of the computer system.

Heuristic programs Programs that are not guaranteed to arrive at an optimal or even an acceptable solution; nonalgorithmic coding.

High-level language A language closer to English than assembler language that, when translated, produces many machine-language instructions for each input statement.

Home page The first page of material an organization or individual presents on the World Wide Web.

Hypertext The use of references embedded (hidden) in text to allow a user to follow a topic through a document or different documents.

HTTP, HTML Hypertext transfer protocol: the protocol for transmitting HTML documents. Hypertext markup language is the language used to create hypertext documents for the World Wide Web.

Icon A small graphical representation of a program or command that is displayed on a user's computer screen; clicking on the icon with a mouse causes the program to execute or some action to be taken.

Identifiers The mnemonic symbols assigned to variables in a program.

Image Storing information more like a photograph than like coded characters; an image might be represented by a resolution of 300 dots per inch or 300 × 300 dots in a square inch; see character.

Index Some type of table to relate keys to addresses in a direct-access file.

Information Data that can be interpreted by an individual to provide meaning; a tangible or intangible entity that reduces uncertainty about a state or an event.

Information resources management (IRM) The active management of information as a corporate resource.

Information technology (IT) The combination of computers and communications including all types of computers from desktop workstations to supercomputers and all types of networks; also Fax machines, pagers, and communications modes like cable, satellite, and wireless.

Input/output Devices attached to computers which accept input, for example, a scanner, or produce output, e.g., a printer.

Inquiry system A system in which inquiries are processed, but updating is done in batch mode.

Inquiry-and-post system A system in which inquiries are made and data are entered and posted to a file for later updating.

Instruction location counter A register in the CPU that points to the next instruction to be fetched for execution.

Instruction register A CPU register that holds the instruction, decodes it, and then executes it.

Integer A number without decimal places, e.g., 32 is an integer.

Instruction set The repertoire of instructions available on a computer.

Integrated circuits The ability to put many electronic circuits on a silicon chip; made possible today's computers which consist of processor chips and memory chips.

Intelligent devices The addition of logic to a device or product, usually through the incorporation of an embedded chip.

Interface The boundary between two entities that interact.

Internet A network of networks; a world-wide network linking millions of users on their own networks. At first used for exchanging information among scientists and academics, more recently being used commercially. Suggested by some as the beginning of a national information superhighway.

Interorganizational system A system that connects organizations electronically.

Interpreter A hardware or software program that examines an instruction and executes it.

Interrupt A signal that causes the current program in the CPU to terminate execution. Depending on the nature of the interrupt, a different program may be loaded and executed.

ISDN (integrated services digital network) A network from common carriers that lets the subscriber send data and voice traffic over a digital network; the network provides a number of services to the user.

Iteration A single cycle of a repetitively executed series of steps.

JIT Just-in-time inventory in which parts arrive just before they are needed for assembly into a product.

Joint-applications development (JAD) An approach to systems design that stresses the use of a design team consisting of users and systems analysts.

Key The part of a record used for identification and reference, for example, an employee number.

Knowledge base Data and rules about the data form the knowledge base of expert systems.

Latency The time required for a mechanical storage device to begin transmitting data after a request. For a movable-head disk drive, the seek time to position the read/write heads plus the rotational delay time.

Legacy system Generally refers to an old mainframe application that has not been updated; typically it would be very costly to reprogram, and yet the system is probably outdated.

List A group of logically related items that are stored with pointers to the next item on the list. Also, a series of pointers running through a storage file.

Loader A program that places a translated computer program in primary memory before its execution.

Local area network (LAN) A collection of computers and other devices connected together in a local area such as one floor of a building or an entire building; increasingly LANs are being linked to form wide area networks.

Logic bomb A program that waits for a particular event such as a given date, and then does some damage to a system.

Logical record A collection or an association of fields on the basis of their relationships to each other.

Machine language Computer programming languages have to be translated into machine language, the actual machine the computer hardware is capable of executing.

Mainframe The original kind of computer; associated today with large computers using proprietary hardware and software and often having cost/performance ratios that are worse than smaller computers.

Maintenance The process of modifying operational programs to fix errors or add enhancements.

MAN (metropolitan area network) A network that connects LANs and other devices in campus of several buildings or in a city.

Managerial control decisions Decisions primarily involving personnel and financial control, concerned with ensuring that resources are applied to achieving the goals of the organization.

Megahertz A measure of transmission frequencies; megacycle or millions of cycles per second.

Microcomputer A small computer, often for a single user or a small number of simultaneous users. Developed from advances in chip fabrication such that only a few chips are needed to produce an entire computer.

Microprogramming Breaking down the machine language instructions of a computer into even finer steps which are used to create special, often complex, instructions.

Minicomputer Originally developed to compete with mainframes, offering fewer features and a better cost/perfomance ratio; increasingly today being called midrange computers.

Mnemonics Alphabetic symbols used in place of numeric codes to facilitate the recognition and use of computer instructions.

Model A tangible or intangible representation of some physical event, entity, or process.

Modem (*mo*dulate and *de*modulate)   A device that converts digital computer signals into analog form and modulates them for transmission. Demodulation is the reverse process that occurs at the receiving point.

Modular programming   The subdivision of a system and of programming requirements into small building blocks to reduce programming complexity and take advantage of common routines.

Modulation   The coding of a digital signal onto an analog one, for example, by changing the amplitude of the carrier signal to represent a 0 or a 1.

Monitor   The control program that schedules and manages the computer's resources.

MOSAIC   A very friendly program to access information on the Internet; it displays graphic images readily.

Multimedia   The use of more than one medium in presenting information, for example, the combination of graphics, video, and audio information.

Multiplexing   The combination of several low-speed signals onto a higher-speed line for communications.

Multiplexor   A device that combines signals received from a series of low-speed lines and transmits them over a high-speed line. No storage is provided, and signals must be demultiplexed on the receiving end.

Multiprocessing   A technique for executing two or more instruction sequences simultaneously in one computer system by the use of more than one processing unit.

Multiprogramming   The presence of more than one semiactive program in primary memory at the same time; by switching from program to program, the computer appears to be executing all concurrently.

MVS   The most popular IBM mainframe operating system, a system that controls the resources of the computer.

Network   A collection of communications devices and often computers connected together via communications lines and/or satellites.

Neural network   An artificial-intelligence approach in which software (or hardware) is constructed to simulate the way in which the human brain is thought to function; used for pattern recognition after the user trains the network.

Nonprocedural languages   Languages in which the user tells the computer what to do rather than exactly how to do the task. Statements are more declarative of what is to happen than specific about the procedure to produce the desired results.

Nonprogrammed decisions   Decisions that are unstructured and for which an algorithm for solution cannot be specified.

Normalization   A procedure for simplifying relational databases and reducing the chances for updating errors.

Object language   The output of a translator, usually machine language.

Object oriented   A systems development and programming philosophy that views system components as objects which programs manipulate; advocates claim that object-oriented programming will save development time, effort, and cost.

OCR (optical character recognition)   The machine recognition of certain type styles and/or printed and handwritten characters.

On-line transactions processing (OLTP)   Systems that process high volumes of on-line transactions such as credit card charge authorizations.

Off-line   Describes any operation that is not directly controlled by the CPU.

Office automation   The use of technology like word processing, electronic mail, and similar systems to improve the productivity of knowledge workers.

On-line system   A system that has the capability to provide direct communication between the computer and remote terminals; files are updated immediately as data are entered.

On-line updating   Pertaining to a system in which the data entered are used to update the files immediately.

Operating system   A supervisory program that controls the resources of the computer.

Operational control decisions   Day-to-day decisions concerned with the continuing operations of a company, such as inventory management.

Optical character recognition (OCR)   The scanning of a document and recognition of the text in the document.

Optical disk   A disk that holds a great deal of data which is "burned" on with a laser. Most of today's optical disks can be written once, and then read many times. Optical disks which one can write more than once are also available.

Optical storage   Storage devices using laser optical disks, characterized by extremely high densities of data.

Organization   A rational coordination of activities of a group of people for the purpose of achieving some goal.

Outsourcing   The practice of contracting out major portions of a business, for example, outsourcing the communications activities of a company.

Packet switching   A communications device breaks a message up into standard sized packets, each with an address; the packets are sent via the best available path through a network to their destination.

Paging   The segmentation of storage into small units that are moved automatically by hardware or software between primary and secondary storage to give the programmer a virtual memory that is larger than primary memory.

Parallel testing   The testing of a new system at the same time an existing system is in operation. The results from both systems are compared.

Parse   Separation of an input string of symbols into its basic components.

Peripherals   Input/output devices connected to a computer system.

Personal computers   The Apple Macintosh and IBM PC; desktop machines with commodity processor chips producing the most favorable cost/performance ratio of contemporary computers.

Personal digital assistant (PDA)   A small device that is designed to be portable and to help its user by storing and retrieving notes, addresses, phone numbers, and other information; can have communications capabilities.

Pipelined   A central processing unit that breaks instructions into pieces and works on each piece in sequence like an assembly line in a factory.

Physical record   One or more logical records read into or written from main storage as a unit.

Pointer   Data that indicate the location of a variable or record of interest.

Primary memory   The memory in which programs and data are stored and from which they are generally executed; main storage.

Problem program   A user-written program that uses only nonprivileged instructions. It should be distinguished from a supervisory, or control, program, which may have privileged instructions.

Problem-oriented   A language specifically designed for one particular type of problem, such as statistical computations.

Procedural language   A language designed to facilitate the coding of algorithms to solve a problem, for example, COBOL.

Program   A set of instructions that directs the computer to perform a specific series of operations.

Programmed decisions   Generally, decisions that can be made automatically by following certain rules and procedures.

Protection   Maintenance of the integrity of information in storage by preventing unauthorized changes.

Protocol   A set of rules or procedures for devices to communicate with each other.

Prototype   A model of a system or a version without all the final features desired used to provide early feedback to users.

Pure procedure   A program in which no part of the code modifies itself. Because a reentrant program is not modified during execution, it can be shared by many users.

Query language   A language used to provide access to data stored in a database or file.

Random access   The ability to retrieve records without serially searching a file.

Random-access memory (RAM)   Memory that can be read or written under program control.

Read-only memory (ROM)   Memory that cannot be written under program control; used to store microinstructions.

Reasonableness checks   General range checks on data to be sure that values are within reason.

Recognition   The process of converting scanned images which are represented by patterns of dots, into the character codes of the computer.

Record, logical   A collection of related data items.

Record, physical   One or more logical records combined to increase input/output speeds and to reduce space required for storage.

Redundant array of inexpensive disks (RAID)   A disk storage device consisting of many small disk drives such as those found on PC; various versions of RAID provide backup by writing data twice on different drives.

Reengineering   An approach to developing systems that focuses on major improvements rather than incremental changes; also known as business process redesign.

Reentrant program   Synonymous with pure procedure.

Registers   In general, storage locations capable of holding data. In particular, index registers that can be used to modify instruction addresses, or arithmetic registers that perform calculations.

Relational database   A database in which data are arranged in tables; columns in the table are fields in the database and rows are records.

Report program generator (RPG)   A class of languages used to prepare programs to print reports quickly from a set of files. Can also be used to program complete applications.

Response time   The time from submission of a request until the computer responds.

RISC (reduced instruction set computer)   A computer in which the CPU has a streamlined set of instructions for the operations most often executed. The computer is not microprogrammed and performs most operations in high-speed registers.

Rotational delay On rotating secondary-memory devices, the time required for a particular record to arrive under the read/write head.

Satellite communications The use of orbiting satellites to receive, amplify, and retransmit data to earth stations.

Scanner A computer input device that reads bar codes usually employing a laser of some type; also a device that reads printed text and in some cases, hand-printed characters.

Scanning The process of "reading" or converting a document for storage in a computer; similar to taking a picture of a document.

Secondary memory (storage) Random-access devices such as disks and drums; programs are not executed from secondary memory devices but must be loaded into primary memory.

Seek time For movable-arm disks, the time required for the reading mechanism to position itself over the track desired.

Semantics The meaning of a programming language statement or group of statements.

Semiconductor A small component having an electrical conductivity between the high conductivity of metals and the low conductivity of insulators.

Server The computer that provides data and some programs in a client server architecture.

Simplex Data transmission in one direction at a time.

Simulation The modeling of some process that often involves the use of a computer program and probability distributions.

Simulator A software program used to execute programs written for one machine on another.

Software Instructions that control the physical hardware of the computer system.

Source language The input language to a translation process.

SQL (structured query language) A language that is becoming a standard for retrieving data from databases.

Storage address register A register that holds the address of a memory location being referenced by the CPU or channel.

Storage buffer register A register that holds data to be moved to or from main memory.

Strategic-planning decisions Decisions of a long-term nature that deal with setting the strategy and objectives of the firm.

Structured design An approach to design that attempts to provide discipline for the designers and to clarify the design itself.

Structured programming A modular approach to program development that emphasizes stepwise refinement, simple control structures, and short one-entry-point/one-exit-point modules.

Superscalar The ability of a chip to process more than one instruction at a time.

Supercomputers Very large and fast computers designed for scientific computations.

Supervisor The control program that schedules and manages the computer's resources.

Synchronous Events that are coordinated and controlled.

Syntax The physical structure of a programming language or statement.

Systems programmer A programmer who works on the software associated with an operating or supervisory system.

TCP/IP The communications protocol used by the Internet.

Technological infrastructure The shared technology in a firm that is used by all employees as opposed to a system developed for an individual or small group; for example, communications networks.

Technological leveling The use of information technology to reduce the number of levels of management in an organization.

Technological matrixing The use of e-mail and groupware to create temporary work groups that cut across organizational boundaries.

Telecommunications The transmission of signals over a long distance, through either private or public carriers.

Terminal A device used to communicate with a central computer from a remote location, usually featuring a typewriter-like keyboard.

T-Form Organization An organization enabled by IT organization design variables; typically an organization with a flat structure, extensive electronic connections to suppliers and customers, virtual components, matrixed management and an advanced IT infrastructure.

Throughput The amount of processing done by a system in a given unit of time.

Time-sharing An on-line system that provides computer services (including computational capacity) to a number of users at geographically dispersed terminals.

Top-down design Planning of a system by looking first at the major function, then at its subfunctions, and so on, until the scope and details of the system are fully understood.

Trade-off The pros and cons of different alternatives; for example, one often is forced to trade cost savings for performance.

Transaction   A basic communication with a computer system, such as the receipt of cash from a customer.

Transactions processing systems   Basic systems that process routine transactions in an organization, such as the entry of customer orders.

Translator   A program that accepts a source language and produces an output, or target, language that differs in some respects from the source language.

Trojan horse   A program that attempts to disable security checks on a computer so that an unauthorized individual can penetrate the system.

Turnaround document   A computer-prepared document, usually a printed form, that is sent to a customer. When returned to the sender, the document frequently can be reentered into the computer without modification.

Turnaround time   The length of time elapsing between the submission of input and the receipt of output.

Turnkey system   A complete computer system with software installed for customer use.

Unbundling   The separation of prices for computer services and hardware.

Uncertainty   Lack of knowledge about a state or event.

Universal product code (UPC)   A bar-coded label found on many retail and grocery goods that uniquely identifies the product and its package size.

Unix   A popular operating system first used on minicomputers; it is available on a number of computers which makes programs running under Unix easier to move among machines.

Variable-length record   A record in which the number and/or length of fields may vary from those of other records accessed by the same program.

Very large scale integration (VLSI)   The production of computer chips with millions of components on each chip.

Virtual   Something that appears to exist, but does not exist in reality in the same way; for example, a group of workers looks like a physical department on an organization chart, but each member is actually in a different location and work is accomplished through electronic communications.

Virtual machine   The computer system as it appears to the user. The term was first used to refer to the extension of main memory to almost infinite capacity by the automatic use of secondary storage. The operating system automatically moves portions of a program that are too large for primary memory to and from secondary memory.

Virtual memory   Addressable space beyond physical memory that appears to the user as real; it is provided through a combination of hardware and software techniques.

Virtual organization   An organization that appears to an outsider to be complete, but is in fact composed of various components that do not necessarily belong to it, for example, its suppliers may actually have all of its raw materials inventory and deliver goods as needed.

Virtual reality   The use of technology to create a simulated world; often used in games, but also in industry and medicine. A flight simulator is an example of the use of virtual reality.

Virus   A program that infects an executable program on a computer and causes it to do some unplanned activity, often damaging the files or programs on the machine.

Wide area network (WAN)   A network that spans a large geographic area such as several sites in a city or a number of sites in a country.

Windows   A graphical user interface that runs on top of DOS on personal computers. Windows95 is the newest version and is a complete operating system in its own right. Windows NT is another similar operating system that is used often on servers and sometimes on desktops.

Wireless   Communications that does not require wires such as a conventional telephone; using radio frequencies for personal communications is an example of a wireless system.

Word   A combination of bits that forms a logical storage grouping. A word may be further subdivided into bytes, which can be addressed by instructions.

Workstation   A powerful computer generally assigned to one user; a desktop computer usually at least a Pentium processor or better or a Sun Workstation; the workstation should have windowing software.

World Wide Web (WWW)   A series of links among related topics among computers on the Internet; requests to follow a topic through different screens are handled automatically and user does not know that he or she is moving from one computer to another. Presentations are graphical rather than in text mode in most instances.

Worm   A program that wanders through a computer network looking for machines on which it can run; the program can quickly overload a network.

X.12   A standard for interchanging data among companies developed by the American National Standards Institute (ANSI).

BIBLIOGRAPHY

ACM Committee on Computers and Public Policy. "A Problem List of Issues Concerning Computers and Public Policy," *Communications of the ACM*, vol. 17, no. 9 (September 1974), pp. 495–503.

Alter, S. *Decision Support Systems: Current Practice and Continuing Challenges*. Reading, Mass.: Addison-Wesley, 1980.

"Amex Builds an Expert System to Assist Its Credit Analysts," *PC Week* (November 17, 1987).

Anthony, R. *Planning and Control Systems: A Framework for Analysis*. Boston: Harvard University, Graduate School of Business Administration, Division of Research, 1965.

Banker, R., R. Kauffman, and M. Mahmood. *Strategic Information Technology Management: Perspectives on Organizational Growth and Competitive Advantage*. Harrisburg, Pa.: Idea Group Publishing, 1993.

Barker, V., and D. O'Connor. "Expert Systems for Configuration at Digital: XCON and Beyond," *Communications of the ACM*, vol. 32, no. 3 (March 1989), pp. 298–318.

Bartlett, C., and S. Ghoshal. *Managing Across Borders*. Cambridge, Mass.: Harvard Business School Press, 1989.

Bell, W. J. et al. "Improving the Distribution of Industrial Gases with On-line Computerized Routing and Scheduling Optimizer," *Interfaces*, vol. 13, no. 6 (December 1983), pp. 4–23.

Benjamin, R. I., and J. Blunt. "Critical IT Issues: The Next Ten Years," *Sloan Management Review*, vol. 33, no. 4 (Summer 1992), pp. 7–19.

Bic, L., and A. Shaw. *The Logical Design of Operating Systems*. Englewood Cliffs, N.J.: Prentice-Hall, 1988.

Black, U. *Computer Networking*. Englewood Cliffs, N.J.: Prentice-Hall, 1989.

Bradley, S., J. Hausman, and R. Nolan. *Globalization, Technology, and Competition: The Fusion of Computers and Telecommunications in the 1990s*. Boston: Harvard Business School Press, 1993.

Carr, H. C. *Managing End-User Computing*. Englewood Cliffs, N.J.: Prentice-Hall, 1988.

Cash, J., W. McFarlan, J. McKenney, and L. Applegate. *Corporate Information Systems Management*, 3rd ed. Homewood, Ill.: Irwin, 1992.

Clemmons, E., and B. Weber. "Barclays de Zoete Wedd's TRADE: Evaluating the Competitive Impact of a Strategic Information System." Philadelphia: Wharton Working Paper 89-03-08, 1991.

Clemons, E. K. "MAC—A Venture in Shared ATM Networks," *JMIS*, vol. 7, no. 1 (Summer 1990), pp. 5–25.

Clemons, E. K., and M. Row. "Information Technology at Rosenbluth Travel," *JMIS*, vol. 8, no. 2 (Fall 1991), pp. 53–79.

Clifford, J., H. C. Lucas, Jr., and R. Srikanth. "Integrating Symbolic and Mathematical Models Through AESOP: A System for Stock Options Pricing," *Information Systems Research* (December 1992).

Copeland, D., and J. McKenney. "Airline Reservation Systems: Lessons from History," *MIS Quarterly*, vol. 12, no. 3 (September 1988), pp. 353–370.

Cureton, T. "An Eastern Approach to Global Networking," *Data Communications* (September 1992), pp. 119–121.

Davenport, T. *Process Innovation: Reengineering Work through Information Technology*. Boston: Harvard Business School Press, 1993.

Davenport, T. H., R. Eccles, and L. Prusak. "Information Politics," *Sloan Management Review*, vol. 34, no. 1 (Fall 1992), pp. 53–65.

Davis, G. B., and M. Olson. *Management Information Systems: Conceptual Foundations, Structure, and Development*, 2nd ed. New York: McGraw-Hill, 1985.

Deans, C., and J. Jurison. *Information Technology in a Global Business Environment*. Danvers, Mass.: Boyd & Fraser, 1996.

Deans, C., and M. Kane. *International Dimensions of Information Systems and Technology*. Boston: PWS-Kent, 1992.

Dearborn, O., and H. Simon. "Selective Perception: A Note on the Departmental Identification of Executives," *Sociometry*, vol. 21 (1958), pp. 140–144.

Dearden, J., and R. L. Nolan. "How to Control the Computer Resource," *Harvard Business Review* (November-December 1973), p. 68.

De Marco, T. *Structured Analysis and System Specification*. Englewood Cliffs, N.J.: Prentice-Hall, 1979.

Dos Santos, B. "Justifying Investments in New Information Technologies," *JMIS*, vol. 7, no. 4 (Spring 1991), pp. 71–90.

Emery, J. "Cost/Benefit Analysis of Information Systems," in *Systems Analysis Techniques*, J. D. Couger and R. W. Knapp (eds.). New York: Wiley, 1974.

Emery, J. C. *MIS: The Critical Strategic Resource*. New York: Oxford University Press, 1987.

Fichman, R., and C. Kemerer. "Adoption of Software Engineering Process Innovations: The Case of Object Orientation," *Sloan Management Review*, vol. 32, no. 2 (Winter 1993), pp. 7–22.

Galbraith, J., and E. Lawler. *Organizing for the Future*. San Francisco: Jossey-Bass, 1973.

Gane, C., and T. Sarson. *Structured Systems Analysis Tools and Techniques*. Englewood Cliffs, N.J.: Prentice-Hall, 1979.

Gorry, G. A., and M. S. Scott Morton. "A Framework for Management Information Systems," *Sloan Management Review*, vol. 13, no. 1 (1971), pp. 55–70.

Gurbaxani, V., and S. Whang. "The Impact of Information Systems on Organizations and Markets," *Communications of the ACM*, vol. 34, no. 1 (January 1991), pp. 59–73.

Hammer, M. "Reengineering Work: Don't Automate, Obliterate," *Harvard Business Review* (July-August 1990), pp. 104–112.

Hammer, M., and J. Champy. *Reengineering the Corporation*. New York: HarperCollins, 1993.

Hellerman, H. *Digital Computer System Principles*. New York: McGraw-Hill, 1967.

Hodges, D. "Microelectronic Memories," *Scientific American*, vol. 237, no. 3 (September 1977), pp. 130–145.

Ives, B., and S. Jarvenpaa. "The Global Network Organization of the Future: Information Management Opportunities and Challenges," *JMIS*, vol. 10, no. 4 (Spring 1994), pp. 25–57.

Ives, B., and G. Learmonth. "The Information System As a Competitive Weapon," *Communications of the ACM*, vol. 27, no. 12 (December 1984), pp. 1193–1201.

Ives, B., and S. Jarvenpaa. "Global Informational Technology: Some Lessons from Practice," *International Information Systems*, vol. 1, no. 3 (July 1992), pp. 1–15.

Jelassi, T., and O. Figon. "Competing Through EDI at Brun Passot: Achievements in France and Ambitions for the Single European Market," *MIS Quarterly*, vol. 18, no. 4 (December 1994), pp. 337–352.

Kallman, E., and J. Grillo. *Ethical Decision Making and Information Technology*. New York: Mitchell/McGraw-Hill, 1993.

Keen, P. *Shaping the Future*. Boston: Harvard Business School Press, 1991.

Kent, W. "A Simple Guide to Five Normal Forms in Relational Database Theory," *Communications of the ACM*, vol. 26, no. 2 (February 1983), pp. 120–125.

Korth, H., and A. Silberschatz. *Database System Concepts*. New York: McGraw-Hill, 1986.

Kraut, R. E. (ed.). *Technology and the Transformation of White-Collar Work*. Hillsdale, N.J.: Erlbaum, 1987.

Kraut, R., S. Dumais, and S. Koch. "Computerization, Productivity, and Quality of Work Life," *Communications of the ACM*, vol. 32, no. 2 (February 1989), pp. 220–238.

Kronke, D. *Database Processing*, 4th ed. New York: Macmillan, 1992.

Laudon, K., and J. Laudon. *Management Information Systems*, 2nd ed. New York: Macmillan, 1991.

Lawless, M., and L. Price. "An Agency Perspective on New Technology Champions," *Organization Science*, vol. 3, no. 3 (August 1992), pp. 342–355.

Leavitt, H. J., and T. L. Whisler. "Management in the 1980s," *Harvard Business Review* (November-December 1958), pp. 41–48.

Lientz, B. P., E. B. Swanson, and G. E. Tompkins. "Characteristics of Application Software Maintenance," *Communications of the ACM*, vol. 21, no. 6 (June 19, 1978), pp. 466–471.

Loh, L., and N. Venkatraman. "Determinants of Information Technology Outsourcing: A Cross-Sectional Analysis," *JMIS*, vol. 9, no. 1 (Summer 1992), pp. 7–24.

Lucas, H. C., Jr. *Implementation: The Key to Successful Information Systems*. New York: Columbia University Press, 1981.

_____. *The T-Form Organization: Using Information Technology to Design Organizations for the 21st Century*. San Francisco: Jossey-Bass, 1996.

_____. *Managing Information Services*. New York: Macmillan, 1989.

_____. *The Analysis, Design, and Implementation of Information Systems*, 4th ed. New York: McGraw-Hill, 1992.

_____. *Toward Creative Systems Design*. New York: Columbia University Press, 1974.

_____. *Why Information Systems Fail*. New York: Columbia University Press, 1975.

Lucas, H. C., Jr., and E. Walton. "Implementing Packaged Software," *MIS Quarterly*, vol. 12, no. 4 (December 1989), pp. 537–549.

Lucas, H. C., Jr., and J. R. Moore, Jr. "A Multiple-Criterion Scoring Approach to Information System Project Selection," *Infor*, vol. 14, no. 1 (February 1976), pp. 1–12.

Lucas, H. C., Jr., and J. Turner. "A Top Management Policy for Information Systems," *Sloan Management Review* (Spring 1982), pp. 26–36.

Lucas, H. C., Jr., and M. Olson. "The Impact of Technology on Organizational Flexibility," *Journal of Organizational Computing*, vol. 4, no. 2 (1994), pp. 155–176.

Lucas, H. C., Jr., and R. Schwartz (eds.). *The Challenge of Information Technology for the Securities Markets: Liquidity, Volatility and Global Trading.* Homewood, Ill.: Dow-Jones Irwin, 1989.

Lucas, H. C., Jr., M. Ginzberg, and R. Schultz. *Implementing Information Systems: Testing a Structural Model.* Norwood, N.J.: Ablex, 1991.

Luconi, F. L., T. Malone, and M. S. Scott Morton. "Expert Systems: The Next Challenge for Managers," *Sloan Management Review* (Summer 1986), pp. 3–14.

Malone, T., R. Benjamin, and J. Yates. "Electronic Markets and Electronic Hierarchies," *Communications of the ACM,* vol. 30, no. 6 (June 1987), pp. 484–497.

Martin, E. W., D. DeHayes, J. Hoffer, and W. Perkins. *Managing Information Technology: What Managers Need to Know.* New York: Macmillan, 1991.

Martin, J., and L. McClure. "Buying Software Off the Rack," *Harvard Business Review* (November-December 1983), pp. 32–60.

Mason, R. "Applying Ethics to Information Technology Issues," *Communications of the ACM,* vol. 38, no. 12 (December 1995), pp. 55–57.

Mason, R. E. A., and T. T. Carey. "Prototyping Interactive Information Systems," *Communications of the ACM,* vol. 26, no. 5 (May 1983), pp. 347–354.

Mason, R., and I. Mitroff. "A Program for Research in Management Information Systems," *Management Science,* vol. 19, no. 5 (January 1973), pp. 475–487.

McFarlan, W., and R. Nolan. "How to Manage an IT Outsourcing Alliance," *Sloan Management Review* (Winter 1995), pp. 9–23.

Mintzberg, H. *The Nature of Managerial Work.* New York: Harper & Row, 1973.

Mintzberg, H. *The Structuring of Organizations.* Englewood Cliffs, N.J.: Prentice-Hall, 1979.

Mukhopadhyay, T., S. Kekre, and S. Kalathur. "Business Value of Information Technology: A Study of Electronic Data Interchange," *MIS Quarterly,* vol. 19, no. 2 (June 1995), pp. 137–156.

Naumann, J., and M. Jenkins. "Prototyping: The New Paradigm for Systems Development," *MIS Quarterly,* vol. 6, no. 3 (September 1982), pp. 29–44.

Nelson, R. *End-User Computing: Concepts, Issues and Applications.* New York: Wiley, 1989.

Nielsen, J. *Hypertext and Hypermedia.* New York: Academic Press, 1990.

Nolan, R. "Managing Information Systems by Committee," *Harvard Business Review* (July-August 1982), pp. 72–79.

Panko, R. "Is Office Productivity Stagnant?" *MIS Quarterly,* vol. 15, no. 2 (June 1991), pp. 191–203.

Parsons, G. "Information Technology: A New Competitive Weapon," *Sloan Management Review* (Fall 1983), pp. 3–14.

Pounds, W. F. "The Process of Problem Finding," *The Industrial Management Review,* vol. 11, no. 1 (Fall 1969), pp. 1–20.

Quinn, J., J. Baruch, and P. Paquette. "Technology in Services," *Scientific American,* vol. 257, no. 6 (December 1987), pp. 50–58.

Rob, P., and C. Coronel. *Database Systems: Design, Implementation and Management.* Belmont, Calif.: Wadsworth, 1993.

Roche, E. *Managing Information Technology in Multinational Corporations.* New York: Macmillan, 1992.

Rockart, J. "The Line Takes the Leadership—IS Management in a Wired Society," SMR Forum, *Sloan Management Review,* vol. 29, no. 4 (Summer 1988), pp. 57–64.

Rockness, H., and R. Zmud. *Information Technology Management: Evolving Managerial Roles.* Morristown, N.J.: Financial Executives Research Foundation, 1989.

Ronen, B., M. Palley, and H. C. Lucas, Jr. "Spreadsheet Analysis and Design," *Communications of the ACM,* vol. 32, no. 1 (January 1989), pp. 84–93.

Row, S. *Business Telecommunications.* Chicago: SRA, 1988.

Scott Morton, M. S. *Management Decision Systems.* Boston: Harvard University, Graduate School of Business Administration, Division of Research, 1971.

Short, J., and N. Venkatraman. "Beyond Business Process Redesign: Redefining Baxter's Business Network," *Sloan Management Review* (Fall 1992).

Simon, H. *The Shape of Automation for Men and Management.* New York: Harper & Row, 1965.

Simons, R., and C. Bartlett. "Asea Brown Boveri." Boston: Harvard Business School Case, 1992.

Sinha, A. "Client-Server Computing," *Communications of the ACM,* vol. 35, no. 7 (July 1992), pp. 77–98.

Slade, S. "An Interpersonal Model of Goal-Based Decision Making." Ph.D. diss., Yale University, 1992.

Smith, B. C., J. Leimkuhler, and R. Darrow. "Yield Management at American Airlines," *Interfaces,* vol. 22, no. 1 (January-February 1992), pp. 8–31.

Sprague, R., and B. McNurlin. *Information Systems Management in Practice,* 3rd ed. Englewood Cliffs, N.J.: Prentice-Hall, 1993.

Sprague, R., and E. Carlson. *Building Effective Decision Support Systems.* Englewood Cliffs, N.J.: Prentice-Hall, 1982.

Stallings, W. "Local Networks," *Computing Surveys,* vol. 16, no. 1 (March 1984), pp. 3–42.

Stallings, W. *Business Data Communications.* New York: Macmillan, 1990.

Steinbart, P., and R. Nath. "Problems and Issues in the Management of International Data Communications Networks: The Experiences of American Companies," *MIS Quarterly,* vol. 16, no. 1 (March 1992), pp. 55–76.

Stohr, E., and B. Konsynski (eds.). *Information Systems and Decision Processes.* Los Alamitos, Calif.: IEEE Computer Society Press, 1992.

Strassman, P., P. Berger, E. B. Swanson, C. Kriebel, and R. Kauffman. *Measuring Business Value of Information Technologies.* Washington, D.C.: ITIC Press, 1988.

Straub, D. "The Effects of Culture on IT Diffusion: E-Mail and FAX in Japan and the U.S.," *ISR,* vol. 5, no. 1 (March 1994), pp. 23–47.

Swanson, E. B. *Information System Implementation.* Homewood, Ill.: Irwin, 1988.

Taylor, W. "The Logic of Global Business: An Interview with ABB's Percy Barnevik," *Harvard Business Review* (March-April 1991), pp. 91–105.

Turban, Efraim. *Decision Support and Expert Systems,* 4th ed. New York: Macmillan, 1995.

Walton, R. *Up and Running.* Boston: Harvard Business School Press, 1989.

Weber, R. *EDP Auditing: Conceptual Foundations and Practice,* 2nd ed. New York: McGraw-Hill, 1988.

Womack, J., D. Jones, and D. Roos. *The Machine That Changed the World: The Story of Lean Production.* New York: Harper Perennial, 1990.

Zahedi, F. *Intelligent Systems for Business: Expert Systems with Neural Networks.* Belmont, Calif.: Wadsworth, 1993.

SOURCES FOR APPLICATIONS BRIEFS

Page 392   "To Talk to a Computer," *New York Times*, June 16, 1995

Page 400   "Airport Objects," *Client/Server*, February 1995

Page 413   "Cutting the Home-Buying Cycle Time," *Computer World*, March 3, 1995

Page 470   "A Competitive Advantage Through Micromarketing," *Wall Street Journal*, May 31, 1995

Page 476   "Going Paperless," *Client/Server Computing*, December 1994

Page 505   "Where Have All the Middle Managers Gone?" *Wall Street Journal*, September 25, 1995

Page 521   "Tracking Signatures at FedEx," *Computer World*, June 19, 1995

Page 547   "PCs Can Help You Get a Job," *U.S. News and World Report*, October 26, 1992

Page 557   "Let's Go Sailing," *Sail*, September 1992

Page 562   "Another Way to Fill Perishable Airline Seats," *New York Times*, May 13, 1996

Page 568   "Looking at the Data," *Computer World*, June 19, 1992

Page 573   "Notes on the Net," Michael Zisman Lotus Notes Home Page, December 14, 1995

Page 574   "Notes Versus the Web," *Web Week*, September 1995

Page 577   "A New Videodisk," *New York Times*, September 16, 1995

Page 579   "A Dissenting Opinion on Multimedia," *New York Times*, December 23, 1992

Page 598   "An Expert Consultant for Your Doctor," Camdata Corporation, 1993

Page 606   "Neural Net After Credit Card Thieves," *Corporate Computing*, December 1992

Page 608   "Are the Markets Efficient?" *New York Times*, September 11, 1995

Page 620   "Taurus—The Project That Couldn't," Economic and Social Research Council Paper 33, March 1995 by W. Dutton, D. MacKenzie, S. Shapiro, and M. Peltu, London

Page 625   "Control in the Air," *New York Times*, August 20, 1995

Page 628   "Controlling Financial Risk," *New York Times*, September 27, 1995, *Computer World*, October 3, 1994

Page 629   "Robbing Citicorp," *Wall Street Journal*, September 12, 1995

Page 645   "A Job and a Career," *Computer World*, June 1995

Page 648   "The Weather As a Factor in Outsourcing," *Computer World*, October 12, 1992

Page 649   "Bad Trips," *Wall Street Journal*, October 20, 1994

Page 661   "Computers Fight Illiteracy," *Wall Street Journal*, May 10, 1995

Page 665   "Talking Through a Mac," *Computer World*, July 13, 1992

Page 670   "Helping the Hospital," *Wall Street Journal*, July 5, 1995

Page 673   "The Homebound and Cyberspace," *Wall Street Journal*, June 19, 1995

INDEX